Praise for *Arc

"A cracking good yarn of murder, mayh[...] model of literary nonfiction that holds the [...] novel. Stories that matter should be told [...]. This Boyle has done with uncommon success."
—*The Washington Post*

"Kevin Boyle's *Arc of Justice* is by far the most cogent and thorough account yet of the Sweet trial and its aftermath. . . . Boyle vividly recreates the energy and menace of Detroit in 1925."
—*The New York Times Book Review*

"*Arc of Justice* does justice both to its complex protagonists and the issues they embraced. Masterfully weaving crime reporting and social history, Boyle has produced a fine and moving work."
—*Los Angeles Times*

"*Arc of Justice* is one of the most engrossing books I have ever read. It is, at once, a poignant biography, a tour-de-force of historical detective work, a gripping courtroom drama, and a powerful reflection on race relations in America. Better than any historian to date, Kevin Boyle captures the tensions of the Jazz Age. . . . *Arc of Justice* is a masterpiece."
—Thomas J. Sugrue, professor of history, University of Pennsylvania, and author of the Bancroft Prize-winning *Origins of the Urban Crisis*

"Boyle has written a book that ought to become a standard text and might just become a classic of historical literature. . . . He is masterful at placing every nuance of the Sweet case within a larger context."
—*Houston Chronicle*

"What a powerful and beautiful book. Kevin Boyle has done a great service to history with *Arc of Justice*. With deep research and graceful prose, he has taken a single moment, the hot September day in 1925 when Ossian and Gladys Sweet moved into a bungalow on Garland Avenue in Detroit, and from that woven an amazing and unforgettable story of prejudice and justice at the dawn of America's racial awakening."
—David Maraniss, winner of the Pulitzer Prize and author of *They Marched into Sunlight* and *When Pride Still Mattered*

"A clear, precise snapshot of an incident that belongs in our collective memory . . . This is a tale worth listening to."
—Salon.com

"Writing with the immediacy of a journalist and the flair of a novelist, [Boyle has] produced a history that's at once an intense courtroom drama, a moving biography, and an engrossing look at race in America in the early 20th century."
—*The Christian Science Monitor*

"Kevin Boyle's vivid, deeply researched *Arc of Justice* is a powerful document that reads like a Greek tragedy in black and white. The lessons in liberty and law to be learned from it are color blind."

—David Levering Lewis, Pulitzer Prize-winning biographer of *W. E. B. Du Bois*

"[A] page-turning account . . . dynamic character sketches (especially of legendary defense attorney Clarence Darrow) make for riveting courtroom theater."
—*Entertainment Weekly*

"Boyle sketches concise, flavorful portraits of key players. Once the "great Defender" himself, Clarence Darrow, is brought in to argue for Sweet and his fellow defendants, the whole book seems to stand on its hind legs and gallop toward the case's thrilling denouement. *Arc of Justice* comes across like an old-style rural ballad, with its often rousing rhythms, its alternating keys of despair, humor and hope, and a melancholy coda."   —*Newsday*

"Told with exemplary care and intelligence, this narrative chronicles inflammatory times in black and white America and pays tribute to those heroes who struggled to get Old Jim Crow where he lived. The way history should be written."
—*Kirkus Reviews* (starred review)

"Boyle has brilliantly rescued from obscurity a fascinating chapter in American history. . . . This popular history grips right up to the stunning jaw-dropper of an ending."
—*Publishers Weekly* (starred review)

"By turns a crime story and a gripping courtroom drama, a family tale and a stirring account of resistance, an evocation of American dreams and a narration of American violence, Boyle's study takes us to the heart of interior lives and racist social processes at a key juncture in U.S. history."
—David Roediger, Babcock Professor of African American Studies and History, University of Illinois, author of *Colored White: Transcending the Racial Past*

"Careful and detailed . . . *Arc of Justice* is a necessary contribution to what seems like an insoluble moral dilemma: race in America."
—Paul Hendrickson, author of *Sons of Mississippi: A Story of Race and Its Legacy*

"A welcome book on an important case. The civil rights saga of Gladys and Ossian Sweet finally has the home it has long deserved."
—Philip Dray, author of *At the Hands of Persons Unknown: The Lynching of Black America*

Also by Kevin Boyle

The UAW and the Heyday of American Liberalism, 1945–1968

Muddy Boots and Ragged Aprons:
Images of Working-Class Detroit, 1900–1930 (coauthor)

Organized Labor and American Politics:
The Labor-Liberal Alliance, 1894–1994 (editor)

ARC OF JUSTICE

ARC OF JUSTICE

A SAGA OF RACE,

CIVIL RIGHTS, AND MURDER

IN THE JAZZ AGE

❖

KEVIN BOYLE

AN OWL BOOK

HENRY HOLT AND COMPANY   •   NEW YORK

Henry Holt and Company, LLC
Publishers since 1866
115 West 18th Street
New York, New York 10011

Henry Holt® is a registered trademark
of Henry Holt and Company, LLC.

Library of Congress Cataloging-in-Publication Data

Boyle, Kevin, 1960–
    Arc of justice : a saga of race, civil rights, and murder
in the Jazz Age / Kevin Boyle.—1st ed.
        p. cm.
    Includes bibliographical references (p.) and index.
    ISBN 0-8050-7933-5 (pbk.)
        1. Sweet, Ossian, 1895–1960—Trials, litigation, etc.
    2. Darrow, Clarence, 1857–1938. 3. Trials (Murder)—Michigan—Detroit.
    4. African Americans—Civil rights—Michigan—Detroit—History—
    20th century. 5. African Americans—Civil rights—History—
    20th century. 6. Detroit (Mich.)—Race relations. 7. United States—
    Race relations. I. Title.

KF224.S8B69 2004
345.73'02523'0977434—dc22   2004047352

Henry Holt books are available for special promotions and
premiums. For details contact: Director, Special Markets.

First Owl Books Edition 2005

Designed by Victoria Hartman

Printed in the United States of America

1 3 5 7 9 10 8 6 4 2

For Vicky, Abby, and Nan

with all my love

The arc of the moral universe is long,
But it bends toward justice.

—*Abolitionist Theodore Parker, c. 1850s*

That Justice is a blind goddess
Is a thing to which we blacks are wise.
Her bandage hides two festering sores
That once perhaps were eyes.

—*Langston Hughes, 1923*

CONTENTS

AUTHOR'S NOTE

Throughout the *Arc of Justice*, I refer to African Americans by the now antiquated terms "Negro" and "colored" as well as the still common "black." I do so for dramatic purposes: readers of early drafts told me that seeing "African American" in the text jarred them out of the story, so I substituted terms common in the 1920s. By that choice, I mean no disrespect to the subjects of the book or to present-day readers.

ARC OF JUSTICE

AMERICA: 1925

The migrants filled the train stations of the South every day in the summer of 1925, waiting on ramshackle wooden platforms of crossroads towns such as Opelousas, Louisiana, and Andalusia, Alabama, and in cantilevered caverns such as Atlanta's Union Station. When the northbound trains pulled in, hissing and steaming, the travelers picked up cardboard suitcases bought at five-and-dimes or battered trunks carried since freedom came. Summoning up their courage, they strode past the Pullman porters—race men like themselves—making their way down the platforms to the grimy Jim Crow cars, settling into their seats for long rides north.[1]

The landscapes rolling past the tense faces looked familiar: the seas of cotton fields that flowed from the Mississippi River to the Georgia coast; the tobacco plantations that ran from North Carolina to the outskirts of Washington, D.C.; the squalid lumber camps of East Texas; the blackened coal towns of Appalachia; and the rough mill villages of the Carolina Piedmont. Every place they passed bore the brand of segregation and the Jim Crow laws. Every station had its "whites" and "coloreds" signs hanging above separate waiting rooms. Every view had its hidden terrors.

Eight men had been lynched by white mobs in the first half of 1925, a quiet year by previous standards. Black newspapers like the *Chicago Defender* and the *Pittsburgh Courier* had given the atrocities front-page coverage. Porters had tucked the papers into their bags and carried them home to the South, to the barbershops and the roadhouses, the churches and the cafés. So the travelers had to wonder. Was that collection of sharecroppers' shacks slipping by as the train passed Greenwood, Mississippi, the place where a few months ago a posse murdered Hal Winters because he dared defend his daughter from the landlord's advances? Was that gnarled tree on the horizon just beyond Scarboro, Georgia, the site where a mob doused Robert Smith in gasoline and set him ablaze in March?[2]

Gradually, the world outside the filthy windows became less and less familiar. At some point, the cotton fields gave way to wheat and corn; the rolling hills of Appalachia sloped into the flatlands of the Midwest. Mining camps gave way to factory towns, where the trains slowed to crawls as they passed mammoth warehouses and crossed street after nameless street. When the trains pulled into stations here, the migrants saw no signs for whites or coloreds.

In the early days of the migration, during the Great War, travelers sometimes celebrated crossing into the North by breaking into song or prayer, but so many migrants had made the trip north now—almost a million southern-born blacks since 1917—that the joy was tempered. They knew now that northern whites were as capable of brutality and murder as southern men. Rampaging whites had killed twenty-three blacks during a week of rioting in Chicago in the bitter summer of 1919.[3]

Yet it was still hard to remain calm as the trains reached the outskirts of one of the great cities, where the industrial districts alone dwarfed anything the South could claim. Gary's vast steelworks, one of the wonders of the modern world, sprawled across the prairie south of Chicago. The streets of Trenton and Hoboken were warrens of tool shops and warehouses. On the banks of the listless Rouge River just outside Detroit, Henry Ford was building an automobile factory large enough to employ all of Nashville or Norfolk.

The migrants grew increasingly excited as the distant, hazy outlines of the downtown skylines appeared. Pillars of steel and glass gradually filled the cars' windows. Even the smallest skyscrapers—the twenty-one story Flatiron Building in lower Manhattan or the imposing Book-Cadillac Hotel in downtown Detroit—would have been landmarks almost anywhere in the South. Here they faded into the shadows of buildings that seemed to soar upward forever. Chicago's newly opened Wrigley Building stood majestically above the Loop, its brilliantly illuminated clock tower drawing all eyes, day or night. In New York, the

Woolworth Building's elegant terra-cotta façade reached almost eight hundred feet into the sky, higher than any other building in the world. Behind those structures rose the skeletons of the next generation of skyscrapers, sure to be even taller, even more stunning.[4]

•

The nation's cities sparkled in the summer of 1925. New York and Chicago, with more than two million residents each, were among the largest cities in the Western world, while Detroit, home to the fabulous new auto industry, was America's great boomtown, an industrial juggernaut of unprecedented power. Europe's cultural hegemony had died in the course of the Great War, its lifeblood drained away in the mud of Flanders's fields. Urban America filled the void, drowning out the ancien régime's death knell with the pounding of the jackhammer and the riotous joy of the jazz band.[5]

New York, Chicago, and Detroit coursed with cash in the mid-1920s. The war had made the United States the world's banker. The great American investment houses—J. P. Morgan, Goldman Sachs, Lehman Brothers—managed staggering sums, pouring international wealth into the soaring stock market and swelling corporate coffers. Manufacturers pushed their companies to new heights. Backed by the investment houses, many consolidated their operations. By the summer of 1925, the economy was awash in mergers, each larger and more spectacular than the last. Sprawling factories, marvels of machinery, poured out wonderful new products as merchants battled to build the grand stores befitting them. In 1924, Macy's completed additions that brought its floor space to two million square feet. The next spring, Detroit's leading retailer, J. L. Hudson, launched construction of a store twenty-one stories high, the world's tallest, and as lavish as anything Macy's or Marshall Field's could muster. The cities literally glowed with salesmanship, the new science of the 1920s. In the spring of 1925, a giant Moses towered over Times Square, advertising Cecil B. DeMille's epic *The Ten Commandments*. Every few minutes, a flash of electric light struck the tablets he held over his head.[6]

The cities' sparkle wasn't simply financial. It was also cultural. Massive immigration in the late nineteenth century had made the major urban centers strikingly polyglot places. By the turn of the century, the foreign-born and their children far outnumbered the native-born in almost every large city. The war slowed the mass migration from Europe, but it launched the Great Migration of Negroes from the

South. There were fifty-seven hundred blacks living in Detroit in 1910, ninety-one thousand in New York. Fifteen years later, Detroit had eighty-one thousand colored citizens, New York almost three hundred thousand.[7]

The flood of people—foreign-born and native-born, white and black—fit no single profile. Some of the newcomers were learned; others couldn't read or write. Some had spent their lives in cities; others had never been beyond the boundaries of their villages. A minority were professionals: businessmen and teachers, doctors and lawyers, priests, ministers, and rabbis. Most were working people who filled the factories, built the homes, scrubbed the floors, and nursed the babies of the well-to-do. These new residents brought more than brawn to the cities, though. They brought their religions, their politics, their institutions, and their art. They jammed the streets on the feast days of their village saints and they emptied them on the Day of Atonement. They talked of revolution in the cafés of Greenwich Village and of patronage politics in the saloons of working-class Chicago. They opened tiny storefront churches and substantial fraternal lodges. They rushed to the vaudeville theaters, where Jewish entertainers honed their craft, and to the ghetto dancehalls, where ragtime bands pushed the boundaries of American music. And they elbowed their way into the cities' public life. By the early 1900s, ethnic politicians filled city council seats and mayors' offices in city after city.

At first, native-born Americans were almost universally appalled by the world that the black and white migrants were building on the Lower East Side of New York or Chicago's Back of the Yards. In the early days of the twentieth century, though, a tiny number of sophisticates embraced immigrant working-class life as an antidote to the poisonous constraints of Victorian bourgeois culture. The first wave were artists enthralled by the color, the noise, the sheer vitality of the immigrant wards and determined to weave that life into an art that defined the modern and a politics that fostered liberation. In the 1920s, "slumming" became a mania, as urban elites sought out the exotic, the "real," wherever they could find it. They packed into the speakeasies that filled the cities after the imposition of Prohibition, where they could rub shoulders with Italian, Irish, or Jewish gangsters. They filled theaters to see ethnic entertainers such as Ragtime Jimmy Durante, late of Coney Island, or the anarchic Marx brothers. And in the most startling turn of them all, they discovered the Negroes living in their midst.[8]

In the early 1920s, sophisticates scrambled to grab a share of the black life that the southern migration was bringing into the cities. White producers mounted all-black musicals. White couples fumbled with the Charleston. And white patrons poured into Chicago's South Side jazz joints and Harlem's nightclubs. If they were lucky, they squeezed into the Vendome, where Louis Armstrong held the floor, or Edmond's Cellar, where Ethel Waters sang the blues. The frenzy was shot through with condescension. White slummers thought black life exciting because it was "primitive" and vital. Visiting the ghetto's haunts became the era's way to snub mainstream society, to be in the avant-garde. "Jazz, the blues, Negro spirituals, all stimulate me enormously," novelist Carl Van Vechten wrote H. L. Mencken in the summer of 1924. "Doubtless, I shall discard them too in time."[9]

◆

When the trains pulled into their terminals, the migrants jostled against one another as they began to gather up their belongings. Finally, they filed onto platforms already mobbed with passengers and porters. Many must have paused, unsure of what to do and where to go, then simply decided to follow the flow of people up the stairs to the stations' grand concourses. There they faced for the first time the grandeur of the city. Detroit's Michigan Central Station was a Beaux Arts masterpiece, a four-story colonnade dominated by a sequence of ornate arches and glittering chandeliers. The rotunda of the Illinois Central Station, built to awe visitors to Chicago's legendary World's Fair of 1893, was swathed in a marble wainscoting fourteen feet high. But nothing surpassed the great terminals of Gotham: Penn Station, with its main concourse sheathed in soaring steel and glass, and Grand Central Station, its great hall flooded with light from three monumental arched windows, its vaulted ceiling decorated by massive murals of the constellations. "You can identify the boys and girls [from the country] if you stand in Grand Central . . . and watch their behavior as they step from the train," *National Geographic* reported. "They hesitate a moment, oblivious to the crowds, looking upward, gripping their bags and bundles, hearing New York, sensing it."[10]

If they were lucky, the newcomers had friends or relatives waiting; they'd scour the crowds for familiar faces or hope to hear some voice calling their name, some voice they prayed they still might recognize. There would be the moments of reunion, hands outstretched in greeting, the sudden comforts of warm embraces. Others had no one to meet them. How terrifying it must have been to work through the waves of people alone, to step through the terminal's doors and onto the street without a guide. The Illinois Central stood at the southern end of Chicago's Grant Park, just outside the Loop. Detroit's station faced a large park ringed by hotels and boarding houses and beyond that, Michigan Avenue, the busiest thoroughfare on the city's west side. Penn Station fronted bustling Seventh Avenue, while Grand Central stood just twelve blocks away, facing elegant Park Avenue. All the streets pulsed with energy. Pedestrians, newsboys, shoeshine men, and redcaps crowded the sidewalks. Cabbies jockeyed for fares. Automobile horns blasted as drivers battled for places at the curb. Streetcars clanged by, jammed with riders. In the clamor, no one paid attention to a colored man or woman standing alone, wondering where to go and how to make his way in a new America.

◆

American cities didn't simply sparkle in the summer of 1925. They simmered with hatred, deeply divided as always. Native-born Americans had been denouncing foreigners since the first wave of immigrants—the ragged refugees of blighted Ireland—poured into the cities in the desperate days of the 1840s. Time and again in the late nineteenth and early twentieth centuries, urban whites proved themselves capable of savagery toward their black neighbors.[11] But no matter how deep their divisions, the cities never developed the formal systems of segregation perfected in the South. Then came the Jazz Age. And suddenly the very changes that made the cities glitter triggered a backlash so bitter that the nation's great metropolises skidded toward their own version of Jim Crow.

The backlash was fueled by a fear of moral decay. Many native-born whites were appalled by the cities' celebration of immigrant and black cultures, with its implicit condemnation of traditional standards and its unmistakable whiff of amalgamation. Political conflict and economic strain made the backlash even more incendiary. For the better part of a generation, native-born politicians had been trying to check ethnic influence in city governments. Their efforts were driven partly by self-interest, partly by their belief that politicians of immigrant stock simply weren't capable of providing disinterested public service. Calvin Coolidge, a dour Yankee from the tiny hamlet of Plymouth Notch, Vermont, had been propelled to national prominence in 1919, when as governor of Massachusetts he had broken a strike by the overwhelmingly Irish Catholic Boston police. Four years later, he became president of the United States. But his confrontation with the Boston cops still haunted him. "The unassimilated alien child menaces our children," he told the readers of *Good Housekeeping*, "as the alien industrial worker, who has destruction rather than production in mind, menaces our industry."[12] Politicians weren't alone in sounding the alarm. From his opulent estate just outside Detroit, Henry Ford raged against Jewish bankers and their Bolshevik allies, who were conspiring to destroy all that Anglo-Saxon businessmen had built, his fury tinged with longing for those halcyon days when immigrants and Negroes knew their place.

At least Ford had his millions to console him. Many native-born whites didn't have wealth or power to buffer them from the changes sweeping over the cities. They were solid citizens—schoolteachers and shopkeepers, office workers and factory foremen, tradesmen and housewives—and they'd worked hard to build a secure and respectable life for their families. Many resented the foreigners who intruded on their world. Now the cities were filling with Negroes as well, a race many native-born whites considered even more degraded than the wretched refuse of Europe's teeming shores. Everyone knew that Negroes were a breed apart, they said, charming in their simplicity but also frightening in their volatility, their carnality, their utter incapacity to learn the lessons of civilized society. It hadn't been so bad when only a few blacks lived in the cities. But now they were everywhere, walking the streets, riding the streetcars, looking for jobs and houses that put them alongside decent white people.

In the early 1920s, native-born whites braced themselves against the threats the city posed. Shopkeepers' associations mounted boycotts against foreign-born competitors. Church groups campaigned against lewd entertainment and demanded that Prohibition be enforced. Veterans' organizations tried to purge public schools of textbooks that didn't celebrate Anglo-Saxon culture with sufficient fervor. Foremen and tradesmen used their lodge halls to prevent immigrants and Negroes from gaining access to the better-paying factory jobs. And thousands of people poured into the newest and most exciting of the cities' many fraternal clubs, the Ku Klux Klan, which had been revived by D. W. Griffith's 1915 film, *Birth of a Nation*, a paean to the Reconstruction-era KKK. The founders of the new Klan were businessmen, pure and simple, who stood for "One Hundred Percent Americanism." They protected traditional morality: they defended the virtue of white

womanhood, assailed bootleggers and their besotted clients, celebrated sobriety and the triumph of a Protestant God. They made sure
that all those who threatened the nation—blacks, of course, but also
Catholics, Jews, and the foreign-born—were kept in their place. It was
a brilliant sales job. In the early 1920s, the Klan broke out of its southern base, racing through the small towns of the Midwest and West.
And it absolutely exploded in the big cities. By 1924, Detroit's Klan had
thirty-five thousand members, Chicago's fifty thousand. The money
rolled in, for memberships, robes, rulebooks. And the hatred spewed
out from the Klan rallies and marches, protests and political campaigns that spread across urban America.[13]

The anger seething up from the streets blended with the fears of the
well-heeled to create a fierce political movement. But the combination
wasn't stable. Powerful men like Coolidge and Ford weren't always
comfortable with the hoi polloi of white America; when fifty thousand
Klansmen in full regalia paraded past the White House in August
1925, Coolidge snubbed them.[14] But Anglo-Saxon politicians and businessmen also found plenty of common ground with their robed
brethren.

The nativists' campaign reached high tide in 1924. Anti-immigrant
groups had been demanding for years that Congress restrict entry into
the United States. The pressure became intense in the early 1920s.
Veterans groups lobbied their representatives, the Klan launched a
massive letter-writing campaign, businessmen endorsed restriction,
and nativist scientists and authors appeared before congressional
committees to explain the growing threat to the American racial stock.
Congress finally surrendered in the spring of 1924. The National Origins Act imposed such strict limits on the number of immigrants allowed into the country that, for all intents and purposes, it ended the
great era of immigration, now eight decades old. Ethnic spokesmen
pleaded with the president to veto the bill. But Coolidge remained
silent, as was his habit.[15]

The nativists followed up their triumph in Congress with a raw display of political power. It was a presidential election year in 1924.
When the Republicans met at their convention, a few delegates proposed that the GOP condemn Klan intolerance. But the Invisible Empire's influence was so strong that the proposal went down in flames.
The Democrats' convention, held at Madison Square Garden, took
an even more bitter turn. For some time, the governor of New York,
Al Smith, had been positioning himself to run for the presidency.

Smith was a first-rate politician. But he was also an Irish Catholic, the son of working-class parents, born in a third-floor walk-up on the Lower East Side, educated in the Fulton Street Fish Market and the smoke-filled rooms of Tammany Hall. The party's nativists were apoplectic at the thought of such a man in the White House. So they deadlocked the convention. Ballot after ballot, Smith's supporters and opponents battled over the nomination. At one point in the proceedings, William Jennings Bryan, the ancient populist turned champion of traditional values, stood up to address the convention. The Smith supporters in the gallery, New York's aspiring ethnics, showered him with catcalls. He raised his leonine head to them. "You," he shouted in the voice that had thrilled generations, "do not represent the future of our country." So it seemed. After 103 ballots, Smith—and his immigrant world—went down to defeat.[16]

The cities' white supremacists never had such signal victories. Their campaigns were more local, their initiatives more piecemeal. But they were in their own way even more sweeping than those of the nativists. No one outside the South suggested that the flow of blacks into the cities be prohibited. Bit by bit, however, urban whites carved a color line through the city. When the migration northward began during the war, blacks had been able to find a range of factory jobs. The opportunities shrank in the early 1920s, as many employers decided that all but the most menial and dangerous work should be reserved for whites. More and more white shopkeepers banned black customers from their stores and restaurants. And, most ominously, whites decided that blacks couldn't live wherever they wanted. They were to be hidden away in a handful of neighborhoods, walled into ghettos. Businessmen infused the real estate market with racist rules and regulations. White landlords wouldn't show black tenants apartments outside the ghetto. White real estate agents wouldn't show them houses in white neighborhoods. Bankers wouldn't offer them mortgages. Insurance agents wouldn't provide them with coverage. Developers wrote legal restrictions into their deeds, barring blacks from new housing tracts.

As the structures of segregation hardened, white homeowners became more and more determined to protect their neighborhoods' racial purity. Those whites who could afford to do so left the ghetto. Those who had no black neighbors organized to keep their areas lily-white. They formed legal organizations—protective associations, they called them—to write clauses into their deeds prohibiting the sale of their homes to blacks. They monitored real estate sales to make sure no one broke the color line. And if a black family somehow managed to breech the defenses, they could always drive them out, quietly if possible, violently if necessary.

The cities weren't segregated in one quick rush. White real estate agents, bankers, and homeowners had begun shaping Chicago's ghetto in the first decade of the twentieth century; white Detroiters didn't follow their example until the late 1910s and early 1920s. What's more, no one coordinated the businessmen's practices and the homeowners' actions. They spread by quiet agreement, sealed by a handshake in the boardroom, a directive from the home office, a conversation over coffee in the neighbor's kitchen. But the forces of the marketplace have a way of imposing discipline on disparate behaviors. By the summer of 1925, racial restrictions were assuming the power of convention across the urban North. As they did, the glittering cities of the Jazz Age were inexorably being divided in two.

◆

The migrants knew about the ghettos. Sometimes they just knew a name—Harlem, Chicago's Black Belt, Detroit's Black Bottom— sometimes even less: a direction from the train station, a stop on the streetcar line, an address committed to memory. So they set out for the subway line that ran uptown, the State Street el to South Side Chicago, or the Michigan Avenue streetcar to Detroit's east side, hoping that this was the correct place to go, that these trains were the last trains of a journey that seemed to be stretching on and on.

Racial etiquette heightened the tension. Southern whites expected blacks to be obsequious. Would northern whites expect the same? What would happen if they accidentally brushed against a white woman in the crush to board the subway train? Could they take the empty seat toward the front of the car, as they had been told they could? Or would it be better to sit in the back and avoid even the possibility of a confrontation? There was only a split second to make a decision that, if wrong, might have catastrophic consequences.

The ride across town must have seemed terribly long. The subway trains rumbled in and out of darkness; the streetcars clattered through the crowded streets. Finally, the migrants saw the stop they'd been waiting for, at 125th Street, on the rim of Harlem; at South State and 26th Street; on St. Antoine Street, in the heart of Black Bottom. As the trains rumbled away without them, the migrants turned toward the dazzling lights. The main thoroughfares were magical places. New-comers were amazed by the sweep of black-owned businesses: "restau-rants, barbershops, pool halls, cabarets, blind pigs, gamblin' joints camouflaged as 'Recreation Clubs,'" a migrant to Detroit remembered. They were awed by the street life, by the pushcart vendors hawking fresh fruits and vegetables; by the street-corner orators selling social-ism, separatism, or salvation; by the jazz and blues clubs pitching their performers to the locals and the slummers. "What a city! What a world!" thrilled poet Arna Bontemps upon his arrival in Harlem in 1924.[17]

But the migrants couldn't live in the stores and the nightclubs. No matter how entranced they might be, they eventually had to leave the gaudy brilliance of the business strips and head down the side streets in search of housing. There were a handful of attractive streets, like Harlem's 138th and 139th: Strivers' Row.[18] For the most part, though, the glamour of the main streets gave way to poverty. Knowing that the migrants had nowhere else to go, landlords had carved Harlem's brownstones and the workmen's cottages of Black Bottom and the Black Belt into tiny apartments, which they rented at exorbitant rates. The profits rarely found their way back into the buildings. Paint peeled from the clapboards. Broken windows remained unmended, leaky roofs unrepaired. As they took in the sights, many migrants sagged with disappointment, but they knew they had few alternatives. So they simply trudged on, looking for the address they'd been given, for a rooming house where they could spend the night, for a flat they could make their own, trying to find a home better than the one they'd left behind.

ONE

WHERE DEATH WAITS

The streets of Detroit shimmered with heat. Most years, autumn arrived the first week of September. Not in 1925. Two days past Labor Day and the sun blazed like July. Heat curled up from the asphalt, wrapped around telephone poles and streetlight stanchions, drifted past the unmarked doors of darkened speakeasies, seeped through windows thrown open to catch a breeze, and settled into the city's flats and houses where it lay, thick and oppressive, as afternoon edged into evening.[1]

Detroit had been an attractive place in the nineteenth century, a medium-size midwestern city made graceful by its founders' French design. Five broad boulevards radiated outward like the spokes of a wheel—one each running east, northeast, north, northwest, and west—from the compact downtown. Detroit's grand promenades, these boulevards were lined with the mansions of the well-to-do, mammoth stone churches, imposing businesses, and exclusive clubs. Between the boulevards lay Detroit's neighborhoods, row after row of modest single-family homes interspersed with empty lots, waiting for the development that boosters continually claimed was coming but never seemed to arrive.[2]

The auto boom changed everything. Plenty of cities had automakers in the early days, but Detroit had the young industry's geniuses, practical men seduced by the beauty of well-ordered mechanical systems and fascinated by the challenge of efficiency. German and French manufacturers had invented automobiles in the 1870s. It was Detroit's brilliance to reinvent them. In the early days of the twentieth century, the city's aspiring automakers had disassembled the European-made horseless carriages, studying every part, tinkering with the designs, searching for ways to make them work more smoothly and to manufacture them more cheaply. By 1914, when Henry Ford unveiled his restructured Highland Park plant north of downtown, the process was complete. Ford had created a factory as complex as the automobile itself, floor after floor full of machines intricately designed and artfully arranged to make and assemble auto parts faster than anyone thought possible. Three hundred thousand Model T's rolled out of the factory that year, inexpensive, elegantly simple, utterly dependable cars for ordinary folk like Ford himself.[3]

Ford's triumph triggered the industrial version of a gold rush. Other manufacturers grabbed great parcels of land for factories. The Dodge Brothers, John and Horace, started work on a complex large enough to rival Ford's on the northeast side; Walter Chrysler built a sprawling plant on the far reaches of the east side, near the Detroit River; Walter O. Briggs scattered a series of factories across the city. Aspiring entrepreneurs filled the side streets with tiny machine shops and parts plants that they hoped would earn them a cut of seemingly unending profits. The frenzy transformed Detroit itself into a great machine. By 1925, its grand boulevards were shadowed by stark factory walls and canopied by tangles of telephone lines and streetcar cables. Once fine buildings were now enveloped in a perpetual haze from dozens of coal-fired furnaces.[4]

More than a decade had passed since Henry Ford, desperate to keep his workers on the line, doubled their wages to an unprecedented five dollars a day. Word of Detroit's high-paying jobs had shot through Pennsylvania mining camps, British shipyards, Mississippi farmhouses, and peasant villages from Sonora to Abruzzi. Tens of thousands of working people poured into the city, lining up at the factory gates, looking for their share of the machinists' dream. Eleven years on, they were still coming. In 1900, when Ford was first organizing his company, Detroit had 285,000 people living within its city limits. By 1925, it had 1.25 million. Only New York, Chicago, and Philadelphia were bigger, and Detroit was rapidly closing the gap. "Detroit is Eldorado," wrote an awed magazine reporter. "It is staccato American. It is shockingly dynamic."[5]

And it was completely overwhelming. While the auto magnates retreated to the serenity of their sparkling new suburban estates, working people struggled to hold on to a sliver of space somewhere in Detroit's vast grid of smoke gray side streets. In the center city, where Negroes and the poorest immigrants lived, two, three, or more families shared tiny workmen's cottages built generations before. Single men jammed into desperately overcrowded rooming houses, sleeping in shifts so that landlords could double the fees they collected for the privilege of eight hours' rest on flea-infested mattresses. Beyond the inner ring, a mile or so from downtown, the nineteenth-century city gradually gave way to a sprawl of new neighborhoods. First came vast tracts of flats and jerry-rigged houses for those members of the working class lucky enough to find five-dollar-a-day jobs. Immigrants clustered on the east side of the city, the native-born on the west side, all of them paying premium prices for homes slapped up amid factories, warehouses, and railroad yards or along barren streetscapes. Workers' neighborhoods blended almost imperceptibly into areas dominated by craftsmen and clerks, Detroit's solid middle strata, who struggled mightily to afford the tiny touches that set them apart from the masses: a bit of distance from the factory gates, a patch of grass front and back. Finally, out near the suburbs' borders lay pockets of comfortable middle-class houses, miniature versions of the mock Tudors and colonial revivals favored by the upper crust, so beyond the means of most Detroiters it wasn't even worth the effort of dreaming about them.[6]

Garland Avenue sat squarely in the middle range, four miles east of downtown, halfway between the squalor of the inner city and the splendor of suburban Grosse Pointe. Despite its name, it wasn't an avenue at all. It was just a side street, two miles of pavement running straight north from Jefferson Avenue, Detroit's southeastern boulevard, to Gratiot Avenue, the northeastern boulevard.

In 1900, Garland was nothing more than a plan on a plat book, but developers had raced to fill it in. To squeeze out every bit of space, they cut the street into long blocks, broken by cross streets that could serve as business strips. Then they sliced each block into twenty or thirty thin lots 35 feet wide and 125 feet deep. A few plots were sold to families who wanted to build their own homes, the way working people always used to do. On the remaining lots, developers built utilitarian houses for the middling sort: long, narrow wood-frame, two-family flats, one apartment up, another down, each with its own entrance off a porch that ran the length of the front. Behind each house was a small yard, barely big enough for a garden, leading out to the alleyway; in front was a postage-stamp lawn running from the porch to the spindly elms planted at curbside. Only a few feet of open space separated one building from another, a space so small that, from the right angle, the houses seemed to fade one into another, much as one machine seemed to fade into another along an assembly line.[7]

The people who lived up and down the street didn't have the education, the credentials, or the polish of the lawyers, accountants, and college professors who lived in the city's outer reaches. But they had all the attributes necessary to keep themselves out of the inner city, and that's what mattered most. Of course, they were white, each and every one. The vast majority of them were American born, and the few foreigners living on the street came from respectable stock; they were Germans, Englishmen, Irishmen, and Scotsmen, not the Poles or Russians or Greeks who filled so much of the east side. Some of them were native Detroiters, and virtually all the rest had come to the city from other northern states, so they knew how to make their way in the big city: they understood how to work their way into the trades, how to use a membership in the Masons or the Odd Fellows to pry open employment-office doors, how to flash a bit of fast talk to sway a reluctant buyer.[8]

Such advantages helped the people of Garland find solid jobs, a blessing in a city that burned through workingmen, then tossed them aside. A minority of the men worked as salesmen, teachers, and shop clerks, the sort of jobs that didn't pay particularly well but kept the hands clean. A few more were craftsmen, the elite of the working class, trained in metal work or carpentry or machine repair and fiercely proud of the knowledge they carried under their cloth caps. Many more had clawed their way to the top rung of factory labor. They were foremen, inspectors, supervisors, men who spent their days in the noise and dirt of the shop floor making sure that others did the backbreaking, mind-numbing work required to keep shiny new cars flowing out of the factories.[9]

Most of the women worked at home. They rose early to make husbands and boarders breakfasts sufficient to steel them for a day of work, then bustled children off to school—the youngest to Julia Ward Howe Elementary, a brooding two-story brick building at the intersection of Garland and Charlevoix, three blocks north of Jefferson; the older ones to Foch Middle School and Southeastern High. Mornings and afternoons were spent shopping and sweeping and washing clothes streaked with machine oil and alley dirt. Their evenings were devoted to cooking and cleaning dishes while their husbands relaxed with the newspaper or puttered out in the garage.

No matter how many advantages the families along Garland Avenue enjoyed, though, it was always a struggle to hold on. Housing prices had spiraled upward so fearfully the only way a lot of folks could buy a flat or a house was to take on a crippling burden of debt. The massive weight of double mortgages or usurious land contracts threatened to crack family budgets. Men feared the unexpected assault on incomes that at their best barely covered monthly payments: the commission that failed to come through; the rebellious work crew that cost a foreman his job; the sudden recession that shuttered factories for a few weeks. And now they faced this terrible turn of events: Negroes were moving onto the street, breaking into white man's territory. News of their arrival meant so many things. A man felt his pride knotted and twisted. Parents feared for the safety of their daughters, who had to walk the same streets as colored men. And everyone knew that when the color line was breeched, housing values would collapse, spinning downward until Garland Avenue was swallowed into the ghetto and everything was lost.[10]

◆

Word that a colored family had bought the bungalow on the northwest corner of Garland and Charlevoix had first spread up and down the street in the early days of summer. The place was kitty-corner to the elementary school and directly across Garland from the Morning Star Market, the cramped neighborhood grocery where many of the women did their daily shopping. The rumors had caused a lot of consternation, much tough talk, and some serious threats. But most people were still surprised when, the day after Labor Day, policemen took up positions around the house.[11]

The Negroes had arrived in the morning, half a dozen of them. Since they didn't have much furniture, they'd finished the move in no time at all. But the police had stayed all day and into the night. They returned first thing the next morning. A couple of patrolmen wandered listlessly back and forth along the blistering sidewalk as school let out at 3:15. An even larger official presence was in position—eight officers stationed around the intersection—when the men came home from the factories a few hours later.[12]

Garland wasn't a friendly street. Neighbors might nod as they went to work, chat in line at the market. Kids might play together. But there were a few too many transients—a young couple renting out a flat, a single man boarding in a back bedroom—for folks to really feel connected to one another. Even longtime residents generally kept to themselves.

On the evening of September 9, 1925, though, neighbors couldn't wait to get outside. Partly, it was the soaring temperatures that drew them down to the street. But it was the pulsing energy, the surging excitement that really tugged at them. The Negroes were nowhere to be seen; there were no lights burning in the bungalow, no sign of movement anywhere on the property. But everyone knew they were in there. And everyone knew that the police were stationed out front because there might be trouble.[13]

So people finished up their suppers and, one by one, drifted out to Garland. It was close to seven when Ray and Kathleen Dove brought their baby daughter onto the porch of their flat, almost directly across from the colored family's house. Ray had spent the day in the Murray Body plant, up near the Ford factory, where he worked as a metal finisher. It was a sweaty, dangerous job, grinding down the imperfections in steel auto bodies, making them as smooth as customers expected them to be. As usual, Ray came home anxious for an evening of relaxation. Kathleen sat in the chair she brought outside and Ray leaned against the railing, watching the baby play at his feet. Their two boarders, George Strauser and Bill Arthur, soon joined them. Strauser kept himself occupied by writing a letter. Arthur, only three days in the neighborhood, was content to sit with his landlords and pass the time while the sun slowly set.[14]

As they chatted, the sidewalk in front of the Doves' house began to fill up with excited neighborhood children. Thirteen-year-old George Suppus dragged his little brother down the street as soon as they had finished their after-dinner chores. He met his best friend, Ulric Arthur, in front of the market. The three boys stood around for a while, watching the corner house, until a cop told them to move on. Then they wandered over to the Doves' front lawn, where no one seemed to care how long they loitered.[15]

Most adults wouldn't admit to sharing the kids' curiosity, so those anxious to be outside fished for excuses. Leon Breiner, a foreman at the Continental Motors plant, lived a dozen houses north of the Doves, in a frame cottage much more modest than the bungalow the Negroes had bought. He had good reason to stay at home: his wife, Leona, suffered from a heart condition and the heat left her drained and often cross. But Breiner grew restless sitting alongside her in the rockers they had on their small front porch, and he volunteered to pick up a few items from the Morning Star Market down at the corner. Puffing on his pipe, he headed down toward the police.[16]

Otto Lemhagen arrived at the corner shortly after seven to spend some time with his brother-in-law, Norton Schuknecht, a man of stature, an inspector in the Detroit Police Department, commander of the McClellan Avenue Station. This was all very impressive to Lemhagen, who in his career had risen all the way to investigator at the telephone company. Garland lay within Schuknecht's precinct, so Lemhagen knew his brother-in-law would be spending the evening out at the coloreds' house, making sure nothing untoward happened. Lemhagen sidled up to him while he stood kitty-corner from the bungalow, chatting with his lieutenant.

While the two men passed the time, Garland took on the feel of a carnival. Traffic was growing heavier, and there were knots of people in the school yard—maybe twenty, thirty people, or more—mostly women and children. Some sat on the lawn. A few tossed a baseball around on the gravel playground. More neighbors meandered up and down Garland or Charlevoix, sometimes alone, other times in small groups, although Schuknecht's patrolmen weren't allowing any of them onto the sidewalk directly in front of the Negroes' house. There was an air of good humor on the corner, an easy sociability that Garland Avenue rarely experienced. People talked about mundane matters: the weather, their summer vacations, the new school year. But Lemhagen also caught snatches of bitterness seething through the growing crowd. "Damn funny thing," he heard someone on the school yard say, "that the police wouldn't go in there and drag those niggers out."[17]

Eric Houghberg felt that same mix of bonhomie and anger as he made his way home from work a few minutes later. The twenty-two-year-old plumber—an angular young man, with ears too large for his long, thin face—rented a room in the upstairs flat next door to the Doves. He knew that the Negroes' presence riled people. Hadn't his landlady greeted him at the door yesterday afternoon with the taunt, "You got new neighbors over there. That's the nigger people. That's the people trying to move in over there." Houghberg wasn't the sort of man who went looking for trouble. But he couldn't resist the pull of the street, the chance to break his routine, to share the warm night air with people like himself. So he rushed upstairs to grab a bite to eat and to clean up: a quick wash, a shave, a new set of clothes. It was a bit of vanity, that's all. He wanted to wipe away the grime of the day, to look his best.[18] Who knew what might happen on a night like this?

◆

By 5:30, the late summer sun was already starting to sink toward the row of tightly packed houses. The light that had been filtering through the drawn curtains began to fade. But the gathering darkness did nothing to dissipate the heat that had built up over the course of the day. With the windows barely cracked open and the doors shut fast, the bungalow on the corner was enveloped in a suffocating stillness.

Dr. Ossian Sweet sat at the card table he'd set up in the dining room. He was a handsome man, short, dark, and powerfully built. A month short of thirty, he looked ten years older: his hairline was receding, his waistline was expanding, his face was taking on the roundness of middle age. Other men might have hated to see their youth slipping from them. Sweet cultivated the illusion of maturity. Where he came from, black men were permanently "boys," never worthy of white men's respect, never their equals. Dr. Sweet was no boy. He was a professional man, better educated, wealthier, more accomplished than most of the whites he encountered. He wanted others to know it the moment they saw him. So he favored tailored suits, well cut and subdued. He bought crisp white shirts and tasteful ties. He wore the round, tortoise-shell glasses popular with college men. He kept his mustache neatly trimmed, his hair stylishly short.[19]

Sweet attempted to project the casual confidence, the instinctual authority that set doctors apart from the ordinary run of men. It didn't come to him naturally. As a child, he had shared in the backbreaking work of his parents' Central Florida farm, tending the fields his father rented, hauling water from the stream so that his mother could do the laundry, caring for the ever-growing brood of brothers and sisters who filled every cranny of the tiny farmhouse his parents had built by hand. His mother and father had taught him what they could, immersing him in the religious traditions that had sustained the family through generations of struggle, making him want to succeed. Then, when he was thirteen years old, they had sent Ossian away, not because they wanted one less mouth to feed, though lifting that burden was a blessing, but because they loved him. Get away while you're young, they told him. Go north. Get an education.

And he did, though he left Florida with only as much as he could glean from six years in a one-room schoolhouse that shut down when harvest time came. It took him twelve more years to fulfill his parents' instructions, a dozen long, hard years of schooling to master the material that would make him an educated man and earn the pride that was expected of the race's best men, all the while working as a serving boy for white people—washing dirty dishes, waiting tables, carting luggage up hotel stairs—just to pay tuition and buy the books his professors required him to read. Ossian never excelled, but he got an education, as fine an education as almost any man in America, colored or white, could claim. By age twenty-five, he had earned his bachelor of science degree from Wilberforce University in Ohio and his medical degree from Washington, D.C.'s Howard University, the jewel in the crown of Negro colleges.

He'd come to Detroit in 1921 with virtually nothing, but in the four years since then he'd built a thriving practice down in Black Bottom, the city's largest ghetto; he'd earned the respect of his colleagues at Dunbar Memorial, the city's best colored hospital; he'd helped his brother Otis launch his professional career. Best of all, Ossian had found in his wife, Gladys, a young woman of grace, charm, and social standing, a wonderfully suitable doctor's wife. As a gift to them both—and a balm for their pain—Ossian had taken his bride on the sort of adventure one reads about in novels: a year-long stay in Vienna and Paris, where he completed postgraduate studies on the cutting edge of medical science.[20]

Yet, despite all those victories, Ossian remained, deep down, the frightened Florida farm boy trying to carry his family's expectations on his narrow shoulders. He didn't doubt his abilities; he knew he was a fine physician, better than most. But he often tried too hard to impress— to find just the right phrase, to strike just the right pose, to keep just the right distance—to reassure himself. Now, as the darkness slowly descended around him, his carefully constructed veneer crumbled away. He didn't feel sure of himself. He felt terribly, terribly afraid.[21]

This house was supposed to have been one more grand accomplishment. Ossian and Gladys had first seen the bungalow in late May 1925. She loved it from the start. A city girl, born in Pittsburgh, raised in a small but comfortable house in Detroit only a few miles north of Garland, Gladys knew quality when she saw it. She'd desperately wanted a home with a yard, where Iva, their fourteen-month-old daughter, could play. This house had much more to offer as well. The first-floor brick still had the sharply defined edges of new construction; the shingles above were newly painted. The front porch, shaded by the sloping roof, looked so cool and inviting, Gladys could imagine long evenings there, sitting on the swing, talking and reading.[22]

The interior was, if anything, even more attractive. The original owner, a Belgian-born contractor by the name of Decrudyt, had built it for his family, and he obviously had wanted the best. The first floor had the cool elegance of the arts and crafts style. Polished oak trim framed the long living room and the dining room behind it. Solid squared pillars stood on either side of the archway that divided the two rooms.

A built-in hutch—glass-fronted doors above, generous drawers below—dominated the dining room's far wall; on the opposite side of the room, small built-in bookcases, nestled into the base of the pillars, echoed the effect of compact craftsmanship that the hutch created. Gladys reveled in the small touches: the flower pattern on the decorative tiles surrounding the gas fireplace in the living room, the leaded-glass windows on the south side, the stylish chandelier hanging low in the dining room, the small alcove that extended from the same room. This would be the place to put the piano she envisioned them having, the place where she could re-create the music that had always filled her parents' home.[23]

Gladys had been thrilled by the spaciousness, so welcome after months of making do at her mother's house. Truth be told, she was pleased that her home had one more room than her mother's; she was moving up, ever so slightly, the way the next generation was supposed to do. Iva could have her own room. She and Ossian would take the front bedroom, overlooking Garland, for themselves. It was small, barely big enough for a bed and a dresser. But they'd get the morning sun streaming in through the three dormers and they'd avoid the late-night noise on Charlevoix, where the streetcar ran.[24]

Ossian also liked the house, maybe not for the stylish touches—though he was a stylish man—but for the message the house delivered. Most Negroes lived in Black Bottom on the eastern end of downtown Detroit. When he first came to the city, Ossian had lived there himself. But established physicians—doctors with solid practices and families to raise—almost always lived in better neighborhoods, and Ossian wanted nothing less for his young family. He deserved a home such as this, the newest, most impressive house on the block.[25]

But Ossian also saw the dangers he would be facing if they moved here. He had already seen what white men could do, and sometimes the memories grabbed hold of him. He could see himself as a small boy again, listening to the terrifying stories of colored men mutilated and murdered at the phosphate pits just outside his hometown. With terrifying clarity he could still see the mob of whites, hundreds and hundreds of them, gathered around that black boy, Fred Rochelle, the one who lived a few blocks from the Sweet family, who had been accused of raping a white girl. He could pick out individuals amid the throng, ordinary people from the white side of town—the jeweler, the livery owner, the butcher—their faces alight with anticipation as they waited for the moment when the torch met the pyre and the flames began to lick at Rochelle's battered body. Then the memories flashed to another time, another place, so far from Florida and yet so similar. Ossian could see the gangs of white soldiers and sailors roaming the streets of Washington, D.C., the summer after the war, looking for Negroes to maim and kill, marching up Seventh Street toward Howard University, toward the medical school, toward Ossian himself. He could see them coming for him.[26]

Ossian's status wouldn't protect him; he knew that. He read the atrocities that the race papers reported. He knew that social standing hadn't protected the four Johnson brothers—one a doctor like Ossian, another a dentist like Otis—riddled with bullets while sitting handcuffed in the backseat of a sheriff's automobile in the woods of Arkansas in 1919. It hadn't saved A. C. Jackson, the colored doctor shot down like a dog, his chest ripped open by a shotgun blast during the Tulsa riot in 1921. It hadn't saved the prosperous little town of Rosewood, Florida, a couple hours north of Ossian's hometown, when a rumor of rape triggered a white pogrom in January 1923. No one could say how many colored people died that day—a dozen, two dozen bodies had been dumped in unmarked graves—but Rosewood was gone, burned to the ground, its survivors scattered to the winds. No, Ossian's hard-won status wouldn't shield him at all, if the white people on Garland Avenue decided that they didn't want him as a neighbor.[27]

Still, it was hard to resist, to walk away, to just give up. Gladys had been so pleased with the bungalow, he didn't want to disappoint her or let her see just how terrified he was by the thought of moving in. Others encouraged him as well. His friend and colleague, Dr. Edward Carter, insisted that the purchase was a straightforward business proposition. Real estate was a good investment in a city like Detroit, he said, and a man of Ossian's age, health, and earning power shouldn't be afraid of debt. Ossian knew that he'd have to stretch to make the purchase. He had to pay far more than the neighborhood standard—the owner, Mrs. Smith, was asking $18,500—as whites always charged black home buyers a premium. But he could rent out two of the bedrooms: his brother, Otis, needed a place to stay, and there were plenty of other colored men who'd be happy to pay for a room in such a house. So he set his fears aside. On the fifth of June, he handed over $3,500 as a down payment.[28]

•

Detroit's race relations had been deteriorating ever since the Great War, when southern blacks had begun flooding into the city. But in the summer of 1925, white supremacy had flared to frightening new levels. The black newspaper, the *Detroit Independent*, reported repeated police assaults on Negroes. Fifty-five blacks had been shot by policemen in the first half of the year alone. A few of them had been executed—there was no other word for it—the way the Johnson brothers had been executed by Arkansas' lawmen. For more than a year, patrolman Proctor Pruitt had harbored a grudge against a colored man, Steve Tompkins. One August evening in 1925, Pruitt's commanding officer asked him to deliver a summons to the Tompkins' home in Black Bottom. Mrs. Tompkins politely invited the officer inside. Pruitt walked up to her husband, drew his service revolver, and fired a single shot into Tompkins's left temple. Pruitt had fired in self-defense, the police department claimed.[29]

Whether Pruitt was a member of the Ku Klux Klan no one knew. But there was no doubt that the police department was thick with Klansmen. The KKK had started recruiting in Detroit in 1921, and since then, their poison had seeped into almost every corner of the city. In private, Klan leaders claimed that there were more members in Detroit than any other place in the country. When ill health forced Detroit's mayor to resign in 1924, the KKK ran one of its own in the special election called to fill his seat. Only a rigged ballot count kept the Klansman from victory. The regular election was set for November 1925, and the Klan was determined not to be defeated again. All summer long, the Invisible Order organized, building its campaign, spreading its message. And one spectacular night in July 1925, it displayed its power. That evening, ten thousand white-robed knights gathered in a field on Detroit's west side, their rally brilliantly illuminated by the blinding light of a burning cross.[30]

Neighborhood violence, though, cut closest to the bone. Five times that summer, crowds of whites attacked blacks who had bought homes in all-white areas. One assault in particular haunted Ossian. Dr. Alexander Turner was one of the foremost colored doctors in Detroit, a widely respected figure who moved easily between the burgeoning black ghetto and the white world. The highly skilled chief of surgery at the colored hospital, Dunbar Memorial, Turner also held appointments at two major white hospitals, both of which barred most black doctors. But none of it meant a thing in June, when the doctor moved into a beautiful home on Spokane Avenue, in an all-white area of Detroit's west side. He had been inside only five hours when a white mob attacked, smashing windows, ripping the phone line, tearing tiles off the roof. Amid the terror, a small group of white men had arrived, claiming to be representatives from the office of Mayor Johnny Smith, an ally of the black community. When the doctor opened the door, thirty or forty members of the mob rushed in to ransack the place. Turner barely escaped, cowering on the floor of his Lincoln sedan as the chauffeur inched the car through the snarling, screaming hecklers. That night, shocked and humiliated, Turner signed the deed for the house over to the neighborhood improvement society that had whipped the crowd into its frenzy.[31]

•

Ossian had spent an anguished summer Sunday in a colleague's office, listening to Turner tell in minute detail the story of what had happened. Afterward, he couldn't keep the ugly scene from preying on his mind. So he sought out the assurances of friends and acquaintances, who invariably cited Turner's failures: the whites were nothing but bullies, Ossian's colleague Carter lectured him—they had meant to intimidate Turner, not kill him. The doctor should have confronted them; he could have made them back down. He had been a damn coward. Others insisted that, had they been in Turner's spot, they wouldn't have retreated. Relaxing in the Dunbar staff room one day, Ossian heard one of the hospital trustees swear: "I made up my mind what I would do if a mob comes to drive me out of my home. I have a revolver and a shotgun. I have a rifle. I'm not going to attack anyone that does not attack me, but the first individual that comes over to tear up my home, he'll pay with his life."[32]

Gladys also refused to be intimidated. She understood the risks, she said; she'd heard her cousins' terrifying stories of living through the Chicago riot of 1919, when rampaging whites had murdered twenty-three Negroes. But hearing stories wasn't the same as seeing the mob take control of the streets or hearing a colored boy's screams. Gladys was a northern girl; she hadn't lived with the daily humiliations of Jim Crow, and she'd never actually confronted the fury of white hatred. She had grown up in a white neighborhood, attended white schools, spent her evenings at the grand white theaters where her stepfather, a musician, performed. In fact, she was almost white herself. Her mother's father was a white man. And Gladys had such light, almost olive, skin she just might have been able to pass, had she been so inclined. There was simply no way she could understand the dangers that might await her on Garland, not the way Ossian understood them. But she wasn't going to be persuaded that the risks were too great. When they talked about the bungalow, Ossian could hear the steeliness creeping into Gladys's voice. You work in the ghetto, she told him, but we don't need to live there. We have a perfect right to live anywhere we please.[33]

Such brave talk stiffened Ossian's resolve. He couldn't stand the thought of his colleagues calling him a coward behind his back, and he desperately wanted to please Gladys, to give her all she wanted, all she deserved. He had to be strong, to prove to himself that he wasn't afraid of a handful of bitter memories and a summer of white hooliganism. "Well, we have decided we are not going to run," he said to an acquaintance in midsummer. "We're not going to look for any trouble, but we're going to be prepared to protect ourselves if trouble arises."[34]

Though Mrs. Smith had agreed to vacate the bungalow by the first of August, Ossian delayed taking possession until September 8, the day after Labor Day. The timing was important: with summer vacation over and school back in session, there was less of a chance his white neighbors would be out on the street when he and Gladys arrived. The Sweets would do their best to stay off the streets as well; better not to be seen too often. Even visiting the local stores would be dangerous, so Ossian had Gladys buy enough food to last a week. He asked his in-laws to keep the baby, Iva, for a while. It wouldn't do to have her underfoot, and he couldn't stand the thought of putting her in danger. No matter how hard he tried, though, Ossian knew he couldn't guarantee his family's safety. He had to be prepared for whites to attack; it was suicidal not to be ready for the worst. A friend asked the police department to provide the Sweets with protection during their first few days in the neighborhood. That was a comfort. But the police couldn't be trusted to put themselves between a Negro and a crowd of angry whites. If the mob should come, there was only one way to keep them at bay: Ossian would have to do it himself.[35]

He understood what it would mean to defend his home. Force was the only thing that a mob respected. Back in college, Ossian had been trained to handle a gun. He had a pistol, a .38 Smith and Wesson a patient had given him a few years back in lieu of payment.[36] But he had to be willing to use it, to point it into a crowd of whites and pull the trigger. If he wanted to save his home, Dr. Sweet had to be willing to kill. He knew that. It was just a fact.

What's more, he had to ask others to do the same. He couldn't possibly defend the house alone: while he was on the front porch, facing Garland, whites could be battering down the side door leading out to Charlevoix. Ossian's brother Otis immediately agreed to join him in the house the first few nights, as did his next younger brother, Henry, who by a stroke of luck was spending the summer in Detroit before heading back to college. Ossian's colleague Edward Carter also promised to be there, as did Ossian's friend and fellow Howard alumnus, lawyer Julian Perry; and an old school chum, William Davis, a battle-hardened veteran of the Great War who now worked as a federal narcotics officer. Henry also lined up another veteran, his cousin and college classmate, John Latting, who had been his roommate that summer. Ossian was gratified—and a bit thrilled—by the response. He wasn't the sort of man who built strong friendships. Yet in his time of need, he could draw around him six of the race's most promising young men, all of them pledged to face down the mob that the best of the older generation had fled in fear.[37]

◆

The Sweets' tiny caravan came rumbling down Garland Avenue shortly after ten o'clock in the morning on September 8, 1925. Ossian, Gladys, and Davis took the lead, sitting in the back seat of their Buick, trying to hide their nervousness, while their chauffeur, Joe Mack, drew up to the curb. Having a driver was a silly indulgence. The Sweets' Buick wasn't exactly a limousine, and family finances were tight enough without having to pay someone five dollars a day to do something that Ossian and Gladys were perfectly capable of doing for themselves. But Ossian loved the touch of ostentation Mack provided, the stares he drew from the sidewalks as the car glided by. Today, he was also glad to have another man around. Otis, Henry, Latting, and Norris Murray, a hired handyman, were right behind, riding in the moving truck.[38] As the day unfolded, the Sweets might need every hand they could get.

Garland was quiet when they arrived. A few housewives stood on the porches, their faces hardened, silently watching the Negroes clamber down from the trucks. But most of the neighborhood men had long since headed off to the factories, and the children, crisp and clean in their new clothes, had been bundled off to the first day of school. Still, Ossian hurried his friends to finish the move as quickly as they could. They hustled to unload the Sweets' few possessions—a bedroom set, a couple of mattresses, a few chairs, some trunks and bags—along with two special bundles: a makeshift package of gunnysack within which Ossian had hidden a shotgun, two rifles, and six pistols, and a bulging brown satchel weighed down by four hundred rounds of ammunition.[39]

The Sweets hadn't been in the bungalow an hour when someone rapped on the door. A police officer, an Inspector McPherson, was standing in the shade of the porch. He was short and stocky, the way a cop was supposed to look, with a shock of thick white hair and a scar running the length of his face. The department had received the doctor's request for protection, McPherson explained, and was pleased to comply. The inspector had four men on the job already, in fact, but he had ordered them to stay out of sight so they wouldn't draw a crowd. McPherson didn't expect any trouble, though; Ossian simply "had to be a gentleman and everything would be all right." Ossian could have taken offense; the last thing he needed was to be lectured on courtesy. But he was so desperate for any reassurance he simply shook the inspector's hand and thanked him for the help. He never mentioned the arsenal hidden in the linen closet in the upstairs hall.[40]

All day long, the Sweets kept waiting for trouble to start. Glancing out the front window, Gladys noticed women shuttling from house to house on the other side of Garland, staring hard at the bungalow as they went. As the children walked home from school at three o'clock, Ossian heard the fractured voices of teenage boys shouting "nigger," their friends' laughter ringing behind them. But the moments passed and the excitement of being in a new house pushed the Sweets' anxieties into the background. Joe Mack and the handyman, Murray, puttered around the house, cleaning floors, moving boxes and trunks. In midafternoon, Dr. Carter stopped by briefly, all good cheer, a set of china he had bought as a housewarming present cradled in his arms. Gladys's dear friend Edna Butler, maid of honor at her wedding two and half years earlier, and another friend, Serena Rochelle, arrived a short time later. Butler was a seamstress, Rochelle an interior decorator; Gladys happily pulled them into the living room, where they sat on the floor talking about curtains, furniture, and paint colors, losing themselves in the fun of planning Gladys's new home.[41]

Always the proper hostess, Gladys insisted that everyone—Butler and Rochelle, her two brothers-in-law, Davis, Latting, even Mack the chauffeur and Murray the handyman—stay for dinner. They ate earlier than was the Sweets' habit, so Butler, Rochelle, Mack, and Murray could leave for home before darkness fell. But somehow they lost track of time. When they finished supper around eight o'clock, the sun had set. The terror was about to begin.[42]

Everyone understood that danger skyrocketed as soon as darkness descended. The police knew it. As the sun set, the inspector had brought his men—a dozen or more—out of hiding and put them on the corner of Garland and Charlevoix, in plain view of the neighbors. Yet, at supper's end, Ossian looked out the living-room window and saw the crowd of white people gathered on Garland.[43] He couldn't tell how many were out there, but it was a huge number; he could see that. The cops weren't allowing anyone onto the sidewalk directly in front of the bungalow. So the whites—a hundred, maybe two hundred, men, women, and children, too—gathered in front of the houses across the street and in the school yard on the other side of the intersection. They were just milling about, that's all, standing and talking, sauntering slowly around. But that's the way it would start, Ossian knew, quietly and peacefully. That was always the way a nightmare began.[44]

Gladys's friends couldn't go out there now, nor could Mack and Murray. A Negro stepping out onto the porch, walking down the sidewalk past the police to the streetcar stop on Charlevoix—that would be the spark right there. There'd be a lynching, here, on Garland, under the amber glow of the streetlight. They'd have to stay, all of them, stay inside and pray.[45]

Ossian tried to calculate their chances. He had Otis and Henry, Davis and Latting; counting himself, that made five men prepared to open fire, should it come to that. Mack and Murray were trapped, too; they might lend a hand. But Ossian was also down two men. Julian Perry had never shown up. And Edward Carter hadn't returned, as he had said he would. Ossian needed them both. Now. But they didn't come. Half an hour slipped by, with Ossian and the others sitting in the darkness, waiting. Finally, the telephone rang, a sudden jangling noise that must have seemed like an explosion within the stillness of the house. It was Carter, wanting to know how the situation looked.

"Bad, very bad," Ossian said. Carter needed to come out right away. There was a moment of silence. "I could come out," Carter finally said. "But perhaps I would be better able to help on the outside."

Ossian couldn't believe what he was hearing. Carter had told him to buy this house. He'd assured him that he'd be safe, that if worse came to worst, he could face down the mob. Be brave, Carter had said. Coward. Coward. Coward. "If you can't come," Ossian snapped, "you can't do anything." Then he slammed down the receiver.[46]

They would have to do their best. Ossian brought the men upstairs—Mack and Murray, too—threw open the linen closet, and distributed the guns. Standing in the narrow hall, they settled on a plan. They'd establish a watch, sitting at the upstairs widow, lights out, weapons drawn, scanning the street below. That way, they'd be ready when the crowd turned on them.

Evening turned to night. Hour after hour they waited, watching the people come and go, staring at the men who passed in and out of the corner market, which never seemed to close. Some of them smoked to calm their nerves, stubbing out their cigars on the hardwood floors that Gladys had planned to cover with tasteful rugs. Once, just before midnight, a group of men darted out between the two houses on the other side of Garland and threw a few stones at the bungalow. Ossian and his friends stiffened, thinking the moment had come. But the stones bounced harmlessly off the roof, the whites faded into the darkness, and the stillness returned.[47]

Fatigue gradually set in. While others kept watch, Ossian rested for a while in the small bedroom on the north side of the house; Davis stretched out on a mattress they laid in the living room. But even then, they didn't let down their guard. Someone hid a handgun under a radiator in the living room, in case an intruder somehow managed to get through the defenses. The women catnapped on the lone bed during Gladys's first night in the bedroom she dreamed of sharing with her husband. No one really slept. Every noise from the street, every creaking floorboard, every unexpected sound in an unfamiliar house, made them jump. So scared she couldn't lie still, Gladys silently slipped out of bed around four o'clock and wandered through the silent house. She glanced out the window to the street below. Except for the policemen still standing on the corner, it was empty, the crowd gone at last.[48] The Sweets and their friends began September 9 exhausted but unscathed.

◆

It was a brilliantly sunny summer morning, without even a hint of autumn about it. After a hurried breakfast, Gladys's friends, Murray the handyman, Otis, and Davis left to start their days. Henry and Latting agreed to keep watch while Joe Mack took Ossian and Gladys on a round of errands. It was wonderful to be out, doing ordinary things, enjoying each other's company. At Lieberman's furniture store, the Sweets bought a dining-room set and several armchairs for the living room— all in mission oak, the perfect complement to the bungalow's arts and crafts style—and two bedroom sets for the boarders' rooms, for a grand total of twelve hundred dollars. From there, Mack drove them over to Gladys's parents so they could spend some time with Iva. Gladys stayed to do some shopping for the night's dinner, while Ossian headed down to his office in Black Bottom to put in an afternoon's work.[49]

As hard as he tried, though, Ossian couldn't stop thinking about the night ahead. Perry and Carter were lost to the cause. Otis and Davis were sure to return, but everyone was going to be so tired, he wasn't sure they could handle the pressure once more. Ossian was already feeling the panic creeping back, and he wasn't even home yet.[50]

He was still turning the situation over and over in his mind when the telephone call came. As part of his practice, Ossian conducted medical exams for the black-owned Liberty Life Insurance Company. When Ossian bought the bungalow, he had one of the company's agents, Hewitt Watson, write up a ten-thousand-dollar policy on the property. An error had been made—something to do with Ossian's birthday—and the home office in Chicago had sent the policy back. Watson was calling to see if he could stop by the doctor's office to make the necessary corrections.

Ossian barely knew the man. But he couldn't help himself. He poured out his troubles, pleading with Watson to come out to the house that evening and bring some friends with him. Maybe the insurance man was moved by Ossian's obvious distress. Maybe he thought of his own neighborhood, where he was the only colored man. Whatever his reasoning, Watson promised to help. They agreed to meet at three o'clock, after the insurance man had some time to talk to his colleagues.[51]

Right on time, Watson drove up to Ossian's office in his dilapidated Ford. With him were two fellow insurance agents, Leonard Morse and Charles Washington. Ossian had a nodding acquaintance with Washington, a fellow Howard alumnus with a wiry build and somnolent eyes. Morse was a stranger. Tall, broad shouldered, and handsome, dressed in a mismatched suit jacket and pants, he spoke in the salesmen's rapid-fire patter, his voice grating, his grammar hopelessly mangled. The trio had discussed Sweet's dilemma, Watson said, and they all agreed to join the defense that night. Ossian probably should have been concerned that three men he barely knew were volunteering to take up arms on his behalf. But in his desperation, the thought never crossed his mind.[52]

The doctor headed home around four o'clock, sitting silently in the Buick while Joe Mack wove his way eastward from St. Aubin to Garland. The traffic was heavy. Downtown businessmen were already beginning their commute to the far reaches of the city; factory workers were packed onto the streetcars, their faces darkened with the day's dirt, their shirts streaked with sweat. The streets that Ossian drove through bore an unmistakable sense of decay. Aged houses sat forlornly along the curbside, sagging in the sun, decrepit and poorly maintained.[53]

Mack had been driving twenty, maybe twenty-five minutes, before he swung the car onto Garland and headed up the long blocks to Charlevoix. Ossian could still hear the rumble of cars and the clang of the streetcar as the chauffeur approached the corner where the bungalow stood, but Garland was almost deserted. A handful of cars were parked along the curb. A few men and women were sitting on their porches; a few kids played listlessly on their lawns. As the Buick reached Charlevoix, Ossian noted the two police officers standing on the corner, just as they had been when he and Gladys had left that morning. Mack pulled the car around the corner, down the alley, and into the garage, away from the sun and the neighbors' view.[54]

Inside the bungalow, Ossian found Gladys standing by the sink, the makings of dinner spread on the counter around her. Something was wrong; Ossian could see it in her face. Before he even had a chance to ask, she blurted out that Edna Butler had just phoned. Riding the streetcar home that morning, Butler had overheard the conductor ask a white woman about the previous night's disturbance on Garland. "Some 'niggers' have moved in and we're going to get rid of them," the white woman had said. "They stayed there last night but they will be put out tonight."[55]

The information staggered Ossian.[56] He knew Garland was empty; he just seen it himself. But it didn't matter. The house had to be made secure. He had to protect his family from what he knew was possible.

Since the shades had been drawn all day, the house was almost completely in shadows. But the foyer was brightly lit and the front door wide open. When Ossian rushed to close it, he found Henry and John Latting sitting on the front-porch swing, smoking cigars, the newspaper spread in front of them. Henry had his own story to tell, just as terrifying as Gladys's had been. Earlier in the day, one of the patrolmen had come by with a warning. The neighborhood toughs had met in the corner market last night to plan their attack. "The crowd is coming back tonight double force," the policeman had said. "You better be on your guard." Henry, proud and determined, had refused to be intimidated. Just a while ago, in fact, he'd walked straight into the store himself to buy some cigars. Now he and Latting were just going to sit and read awhile.[57]

Ossian wouldn't stand for it. "Turn to your own business and don't bother" anyone, he told Henry and Latting. Don't "be walking out on the porch . . . so that people would think you're looking for trouble." They were to get out of sight immediately, go into the kitchen, and give Gladys a hand with dinner. Ossian followed them inside, then bolted the front door shut.[58]

His heart was pounding, his pulse racing. Five o'clock. He had a few hours of daylight left, a few hours before—

Ossian turned to Mack. Go down to Black Bottom and get Norris Murray, he said; tell him I'll pay him five dollars if he'll come out to the house tonight. It was a gamble to send the chauffeur away, to reduce their numbers by one. The mob might not wait for nightfall. But Ossian had to take the risk; he had to have more people alongside him. Mack slipped out the back door and was gone.[59]

Suddenly, he was alone. Ossian could hear Gladys and Henry chatting in the kitchen. But he was alone. He walked into the dining room, took a seat at the card table they were using for their meals, and waited.[60]

◆

In some ways, Henry was a better match for Gladys than Ossian. They were about the same age: she was just twenty-three, he twenty-one. And they both had a charm that Ossian simply could never claim. Although he sometimes imagined himself a gregarious man, others found him a bit too aloof, a trifle distant. He attempted to be open and friendly, but it seemed he could never remember people's names correctly. Some said he was formal; others used the word "arrogant." Ossian seemed to expect deference; he was quick to point out the shortcomings of others; he was prone to lecture even casual acquaintances. Dr. Sweet demanded people's respect but didn't easily win their love.[61]

Gladys certainly had some of Ossian's forcefulness. Deep down, she was stronger, tougher, and more confident than he was, but she was better able to blunt her sharp edges. Next to her husband, she seemed slight, a wisp of a woman, with a long, thin face that lit up when she smiled her toothy grin. She wasn't beautiful, at least in a conventional way, but her carefully honed social graces drew people to her. Gladys could chat with acquaintances about books and the theater; she knew how to entertain gracefully; although she was shy, she made friends easily. To all appearances, she was the dutiful wife, standing demurely behind her husband, following his lead. In private, though, she exercised a powerful influence over her family. Ossian considered her his prize, and he desperately wanted to please her. Gladys, in turn, expected to be her husband's confidante and partner. Not once had she considered staying away from the bungalow the first few nights; however great the risks, she would share them with Ossian.[62]

For his part, Henry worshipped Ossian. Nine years younger than his brother, he was only five when Ossian had left home, too young to truly remember sharing their parents' house, young enough to grow up hearing of his eldest brother's triumphs. As soon as he could, he set out to follow the path Ossian had set for him. At Wilberforce University, Ossian's alma mater, he began to train for the life of a professional man, having his hair cut like Ossian's, growing a mustache, even duplicating his brother's glasses. The resemblance was so great that the two could have been mistaken for twins, if Henry only had the fullness, the maturity that so clearly marked Ossian as his senior. But Henry still had the boyish playfulness of a little brother, the exuberance that led him to join every campus club he could, the naïveté that made him take a policeman's warning lightly.[63]

Ossian knew better. Sitting in the heat of the dining room, listening to the idle chatter and the clatter of pots, he knew that they were all in great danger. Tonight, the mob was going to have direction; someone was going to prod them into action, tell them what to do and when to do it. When that moment came, the patrolmen weren't going to be able to stop them, even if they had the courage to try. Only Ossian, his friends, and a trio of men he barely knew were going to prevent the destruction of his home, his life. The day was melting away, nightfall creeping closer. Time was running out. And Ossian was alone, as he felt he always had been.

Then relief arrived in a rush. The back door slammed and Mack walked in with Norris Murray. A short time later—around six o'clock— two of the insurance men, Washington and Watson, pulled into the garage. Leonard Morse wasn't with them; he hadn't been at the pickup spot, so they'd headed over without him. But a few minutes later, Morse surprised them all by sauntering into the house on his own. He'd been delayed by an appointment, he said. So he caught the streetcar out to Garland. It was almost too good to be true.[64] There was still an hour of sun left in the sky. The mob must not have taken over the streets if Morse could hop off the streetcar without any trouble. Only Otis and Davis were missing. But Otis wouldn't let his brother down; Ossian was absolutely sure of that. It was just like Little Doc to be late.

Ossian tried to be businesslike, walking the three insurance men through the house, showing them the upstairs closet where the guns were hidden and the various places established as defensive positions the night before. But he could see that they were jumpy. They needed some distraction, a bit of entertainment. Dinner wasn't ready, though the aroma of baked ham and sweet potatoes was filling the downstairs. So he suggested they play a few hands of whist while Gladys, Henry, and Latting finished cooking.

Morse, Mack, and Washington drew chairs up to the dining room table, while Watson stayed in the living room, trying to read a magazine by the slant of light the drawn shade allowed into the room. Everyone was on edge. Ossian kept getting up from the table and wandering around the house, checking to be sure that the doors were locked, walking to the upstairs closet where the guns were stored. After a while, Mack left the game, saying he wanted to take a bath upstairs before dinner. Murray sat in for a few hands, then he, too, headed up the stairs to check in on Mack, his only friend in the house. The clock inched toward eight.[65]

Suddenly, something slammed against the roof of the house. Henry dashed from the kitchen to the living room windows. "My God!" he shouted, "Look at the people!"[66]

Ossian rushed to the leaded-glass windows that overlooked Charlevoix. Everything looked just as it had the night before. The cops were out on the corner, keeping the sidewalk in front of the bungalow clear. And behind them, in front of the opposing houses and around the school yard, half masked in the dusk, were hundreds of white people, the same white people who'd been out on the street the previous evening. The same, Ossian knew, yet frighteningly different. Somewhere out there, standing among the women and children, lounging on the porches, lurking in the alleys, were the men who would incite the crowd to violence.[67]

All the colored men were up and moving now, though no one had any particular direction in mind. Ossian ran to the side door that led onto Charlevoix for one last check of the lock. He heard someone—in the confusion he couldn't say precisely who—saying, "Go around to the front. We're going to the back and raise some hell." He spun to the kitchen behind him, desperate to see if Gladys were safe. She was standing over a bowl of cake batter, the night's dessert; the ham sat in a pan on the stove top, ready for carving. Brushing past her, he tested the backdoor lock, then pounded up the stairs to the hallway and the guns.[68]

Henry, Latting, Mack, Murray, and the insurance men were all upstairs before him, ducking in and out of the bedrooms. Most of them had already grabbed weapons. Ossian opened the closet door but the hallway was so dim that the dark metal of the guns was indistinguishable in the shadows. Groping around on the upper shelf, he finally pulled out a pistol, then rummaged through the satchel for a fistful of ammunition. Only when he tried to pick out the appropriate shells did Ossian, a man so habitually in control of his emotions, realize how badly his hands were shaking.[69]

Hoping to camouflage his panic and quiet his unsteady nerves, he shoved the remaining bullets into his pocket and slipped into the front bedroom. Rather than resume the watch, he took a seat on the bed, slid off his shoes so as not to scuff the comforter, and lay down in the darkness, the pistol at his side. For the longest time, ten, fifteen, twenty minutes, he didn't move, the sound of his breathing slowly soothing him. Gladys silently entered the room—their room—and for a few moments the two of them talked, their voices hushed. But for the most part he was alone, inside himself. Occasionally, he stole a glance at the street below, peering between the drawn shade and the windowsill to see a considerable crowd of white people standing on the other side of Garland. In the stillness of the darkened room, they were just a distant hum of voices. Ossian could feel himself gradually regaining control.[70]

Then suddenly the window above him shattered. A rock thudded to the floor near the bed while shards of glass skittered across the room. Almost simultaneously, Ossian heard a voice from another room shout, "There's someone coming!"

A taxi had pulled up to the curb in front of the house. "That's your brother," someone else yelled.[71]

Ossian's first thought was of Gladys. The attack was starting; she was in danger. Rushing toward the stairs, he elbowed his way though the pandemonium in the hallway. The men were racing every which way, trying to take up the positions they'd staked out. He thought he saw Henry, Winchester in hand, heading for the front bedroom. There was a quick rush of fresh air: someone had opened the door at the back of the hall and gone out to the airing porch that overlooked the yard. Ossian thundered down the stairs. At the foot of the stairs, he found Gladys, who had been drawn there by the sound of breaking glass. Someone was pounding on the front door. Otis. The door was locked. Otis was trapped outside. Ossian raced through the living room, pulled open the French door that led into the vestibule, unbolted the front door, and threw it open.[72]

And there it was, the scene he'd dreaded all his life, the moment when he stood facing a sea of white faces made grotesque by unrea-soned, unrestrained hate—for his race, for his people, for him. Gar-land was a swirl of light and noise and motion, a blur of bodies moving this way and that, white shirts and summer dresses made stark by a background of darkened houses, the pale skin of the people eerie un-der the streetlights. Otis and William Davis were standing right in front of Ossian on the porch, terror-struck. The people on the other side of the street were screaming, "Here's niggers!" "There they go!" "Get them! Get them!" Stones were raining down from across the street, smashing into the lawn, crashing onto the painted wooden floor of the porch, and skittering under the swing where Henry and Latting had been sitting a few hours before.[73]

As soon as Otis and Davis stumbled inside, Ossian slammed the door behind them. Otis immediately ran to the phone, which sat in the alcove at the bottom of the stairs, so he could call a friend for help. Senseless with fear, Ossian stood alongside Gladys and Davis in the dining room as more rocks slammed off the roof and walls. "What shall I do?" he asked over and over again, "What shall I do?"

"Don't do anything," Davis replied. "Just take your time and give the police officers a chance." But as he spoke, Davis picked up a rifle that had been lying in the living room, and cradled it in his arms.[74]

A few minutes passed. Another second-story window shattered; the house was filled with the sound of splintering glass hitting the floor upstairs. Then came the deafening roar of gunshots from the bedrooms above, a moment's pause, and another volley, as fierce as the first. Ossian stood stunned, deafened by the report of the guns ringing off the bare walls, the acrid smell of gunpowder beginning to drift down the stairs.[75]

◆

Eric Houghberg was almost done shaving when the landlady's little boy burst in, breathless with excitement. "Eric, come on out," he said, "some guys throwing, small kids—throwing bricks and stones."

Stoning the coloreds' house; Houghberg had to see that. Before the boy could say another word, he bolted down the stairs and onto the porch of his flat, almost straight across from the bungalow. Some of the other renters were out there already: Mr. and Mrs. Dove and their baby; a few others he didn't know. Houghberg started down the steps to the lawn, where the crowd was thicker. Then the shooting started, a single ferocious blast from across the street.[76]

That was gunfire. The coloreds were firing into the street.

Up on the porch, Mrs. Dove was yelling hysterically, her husband scooping up his suddenly squalling baby and scrambling for the door. Some of the folks on the lawn were looking wildly about, as if they couldn't tell where the noise had come from; others were ducking low, falling to their knees, racing for cover. Houghberg didn't even flinch. He just kept going, down off the porch and into the crowd. Why he walked up to the man with the pipe—Breiner, the foreman who lived down the street—he couldn't say. Houghberg just wanted to find out what was happening, do a little commiserating, a touch of socializing. Without a thought, he pulled a cigarette out of his pocket.

Breiner said something about the Negroes shooting. "It is awful they should do that," that's what he said, barely enough to fill the silence before the colored men opened fire again, another vicious volley just like the first.[77]

Breiner screamed—a scream of shock and searing pain—as a bullet ripped into his lower back, clipped off the pelvic bone, and exploded out his belly. For a split second, Houghberg simply stared as Breiner bit down hard on his pipe, as if he were trying to suppress another cry, the way a man should. Then Houghberg felt the burn in his own leg, just above the knee; when he reached down to touch it, he felt blood soaking through his pants.[78]

His instincts told him to run. Houghberg stumbled back from the lawn, down the narrow passageway between his house and the one to the north toward the safety of the alley. But the pain was too great. Before he could reach the rear of the house, his legs buckled and he collapsed in a heap onto the dark, cooling cement.[79]

♦

Inspector Norton Schuknecht couldn't believe it. One second, he was chatting with his brother-in-law, Otto Lemhagen, and Lieutenant Schellenberger, standing on the corner in front of the schoolhouse shooting the breeze, not paying any attention at all to what was going on in front of the Negroes' house. The next thing he knew, guns were blazing from the upstairs windows. The shock of it almost took him off his feet.

Instantly, Schuknecht knew that this was big trouble. The department had a dozen patrolmen out here, but if the situation exploded—if the Negroes kept shooting, if the whites charged the house—twelve cops weren't going to be able to handle it. Someone was going to get hurt, one of his own men, maybe. Call for reserves, he yelled to the lieutenant. Then Schuknecht started across the intersection to the bungalow.

It was hard going. The inspector was a bear of a man—the brass buttons on his uniform pulled and strained across his stomach—and he lumbered more than ran. To make matters worse, he had to force his way through the melee in the intersection, people moving in every direction, pushing and shoving, shouting, cursing, calling for spouses or children. Pandemonium. That's what it was.

By the time he reached the doctor's front porch, Schuknecht was already out of breath. But his adrenalin was pumping and his temper was flaring. The house was pitch-dark. If the Negroes hadn't started shooting, it would have been easy enough to imagine that there was no one inside at all.

Schuknecht punched the doorbell.[80]

◆

Ossian was so distraught, so scared, so dazed, he didn't know what to do. He heard Davis screaming at him, "For Christ sake, tell them to cut that damn shooting out there," and he tried to do as he was told, shouting up the stairs, "Keep quiet up there!" When the doorbell rang, Ossian reacted as if a guest had arrived. He stepped to the door, Davis right behind him, and called out, "Who is it?"[81]

"The police," a voice replied. Ossian knew about Alexander Turner's mistake, opening his door to men who claimed to be city officials. Still, he didn't hesitate. A policeman, red faced with rage, stepped into the vestibule. He was an older man, considerably overweight and panting for air. "Jesus Christ," he demanded. "What in hell are you fellows shooting about?"

"Why, they're ruining my property," Ossian said, his first rational sentence since the shooting began.

"What have they done? I have been here right along. I haven't seen anyone throw anything and I haven't seen no disorder. I don't know why you men are shooting."

Ossian was stunned. Hadn't the officer seen? Where was Inspector McPherson? When he'd come by yesterday, he said he would protect the house. Couldn't he speak to McPherson?

"Doctor," the cop interrupted, "I was in charge last night and I am also in charge tonight. We have got men around your house, we got them in the alley, we got them on the side, and we got them on the front."

Ossian didn't argue. He didn't say that the police out front hadn't lifted a finger to protect his house and his family from the mob, that they'd been left to face the terror alone. "There will be no more shoot-ing," he promised. That was enough. Nodding his satisfaction, the po-liceman walked out of the house.[82]

◆

Leon Breiner lay at the foot of the steps leading up to the Doves' porch, a widening pool of blood seeping onto the brown lawn beneath him. A flashlight beam split through the shadows as a couple of cops pushed their way through the knot of people gathered around. More shouts came from down the passageway where Houghberg had collapsed: an-other man down.[83]

Already the crowd on Garland was changing. The terrified were clearing away, racing back to their homes, dashing down the alleys. As fast as they left, newcomers took their place, pulled out of their flats by the noise and excitement. If anything, the mob was growing larger, an-grier, more volatile. Not fifteen feet from where Breiner lay, twenty or thirty men stood facing the bungalow, some of them dancing with the jittery energy of prizefighters, trying to build up the courage to rush the doctor's house. All it would take was one of them to stride into the street, to breach the invisible barrier the police had created. Once that happened, they'd all start moving, not just the gang of twenty or thirty but all the thugs and hoods and closet Klansmen the crowd concealed.[84]

As soon as he stepped out of the house, Schuknecht could see that the situation was spiraling out of control. Still, it was a blow when one of his patrolmen sprinted up to him with the news: two men shot. One was wounded, hit in the leg. The other one, over there on the lawn, looked to be dead.

Sweet Jesus. The Negroes had murdered somebody. And they'd done it on his goddamn watch. The inspector quickly ran through his options. The Negroes were going to have to be brought downtown and booked; that was a sure thing. But he couldn't bring them out of the house now, not unless he wanted to see them ripped limb from limb. Better to keep the mob at bay until reinforcements arrived.

Schuknecht barked out a few commands. Set up a perimeter around the house. No one gets past. We'll take care of the coloreds when we can.[85]

It shouldn't have worked. So many people were pouring into the street that the intersection was almost impassable. The more the crowd pushed and jostled and jeered, the darker the mood became. Someone spotted three colored men trapped in traffic at Charlevoix and St. Clair

Avenue, a block east of the bungalow. "There goes some niggers now," came the cries. "Lynch them! Kill them!" A gang of white men surged toward the car, the quickest of them leaping onto the running board and swinging wildly at the trio inside. As the others closed in, the driver slammed his foot on the gas and swung into oncoming traffic, flinging his assailant to the pavement as he sped to safety. When a colored couple drove into the neighborhood a few minutes later, the mob moved more quickly, swarming over the car, smashing its windows, clawing off its cloth top, and pummeling the husband as he sat at the wheel. Only his wife's begging for mercy saved them.[86]

For all its fury, though, the mob stayed back from the bungalow. Once Schuknecht's men had established their ragged line around the Sweets' house, no one had the guts to test their resolve. The crowd kept growing larger, seeping farther and farther into the neighborhood. But the police perimeter held firm—a half-dozen cops standing along the sidewalk trying to keep their knees from shaking too badly, and they didn't break.[87]

Though it seemed much longer, no more than five minutes had passed when the reserve flyer eased its way through the mob with a truckload of reinforcements. While the patrolmen scrambled down from the flatbed, Schuknecht grabbed hold of their sergeant. Put together a squad and follow me, he said. We're going back in to get the Negroes.[88]

◆

Ossian must have known that something was wrong. He had to have heard the furor outside the house, the screams and shouts, the squeal of car tires, the wail of police sirens. But in the darkness of the living room, the terror was dissipating, the paralyzing fear of the previous few minutes loosening its grip. Davis had set down the rifle he'd been holding; Otis had given up trying to phone his friend and was standing beside his brother; someone was heading downstairs. Maybe Edward Carter had been right; maybe whites will back down when colored men show they won't be moved. When the doorbell rang again, Ossian stood by and let Gladys answer it.[89]

The cops burst in. No conversation. No accusations. They just shoved past Gladys and into the living room. One of them snapped on the lights—the first light in the house all day—and pulled up the shades. Ossian must have been momentarily blinded, stunned by the burst of brilliance and the flash of movement.

Gradually, the room came back into focus. There were cops everywhere, waving revolvers, shouting commands, demanding that Ossian, Gladys, Davis, and Otis move into the dining room, wanting to know how many other Negroes were in the house, searching around for the staircase, which was tucked away behind the dining room. So many voices, so much activity. No time to argue. Follow orders. Just do what the policemen say.[90]

Boots pounded overhead as the cops moved through the bedrooms rounding up the others. One by one they appeared: Washington and Mack first, then Henry and Latting, Watson, Morse, and Murray, followed by patrolmen carrying the cache of weapons Ossian had carefully assembled. With every new addition, the dining room grew tighter, smaller, more stifling. The cops patted them all down, searching for more guns. Then they wrenched Ossian's arm to one side, and he felt cold steel snap over his wrist. He was being handcuffed to Davis, the two men bound together like prisoners on the chain gangs that haunted the roads outside his hometown.[91]

The inspector was talking now, the fat one who'd come inside a few minutes before. Something about two white men shot. Killed. Murdered. All of them would have to go down to headquarters. It took Ossian a moment to realize what the inspector was saying. He was going to take them outside. Out to the mob.

In that instant, Ossian became a boy again. Not himself. That other boy, his hands bound, his head bowed, spending his last moments surrounded by his murderers, wailing, wailing, wailing, as the fire started to crackle.

He began to plead. Bring down the shades; we're on display for everyone to see. Don't take us out the front. They're waiting out there. The alley. Take us out that way. Please God, take us out the alley.[92]

Mack the chauffeur stepped forward. He'd spotted someone he knew standing in the living room, a rail-thin white man dressed in street clothes, his long, narrow face and blond hair blanched by the bright lights. He had to be a cop; every white man in the house was a cop. They talked in quick, hushed tones.[93]

When the conversation ended, the white man walked over to Ossian. He was a lieutenant with the Black Hand Squad, he said, working for Inspector McPherson. And he was here to see to the Negroes' safety. There was a kindness about him that Ossian couldn't have expected. The lieutenant drew the shades again and ordered Ossian's handcuffs removed; the doctor wasn't a threat, he said. Then he sent a patrolman outside to wait for the paddy wagon and send it around back. He'd take the men out first. Gladys would follow when the situation had cooled.[94]

It must have been the most terrifying step Ossian had ever taken, the first step out the back door into the yard. Otis, Henry, and the rest moved in a long single line, patrolmen on either side, the lieutenant in the lead. In the clear night air, the noise on the street was even more intense, more immediate, than it had been inside the bungalow. A wooden fence separated Ossian and the others from the crowd on Charlevoix, so no one knew they were there, moving silently across the grass that Gladys had hoped to turn into a garden. The plainclothesmen led them through the garage, where Ossian's Buick and the insurance men's old Ford were nestled, and into the alley.

Face-to-face with the mob.

The paddy wagon had been backed far enough into the alley so that its back doors were within a few feet of the Sweets' garage. That left the wagon's hood across the sidewalk along Charlevoix. Just to the front of that, all along the street, was a wall of frenzied whites, waiting for the moment when the coloreds appeared. A second passed before the mob realized that the suspects were within reach, a heartbeat before the charge began.[95]

The lieutenant knew exactly what he was doing. He had his gun raised above his head so that the front row of whites could see it, and he was moving straight toward the mob. If anyone makes a move to crash in, he shouted, I'll shoot to kill. The whites seemed to stop—straining to hear, waiting for someone else to act, too intimidated to move.[96]

That was all the time they needed. The patrolmen shoved Ossian and the others into the back of the wagon, slammed shut the metal doors, and slapped the side of the truck to get it moving. Ever so slowly the driver edged the vehicle forward, testing to see how far he could go before the mob stopped him, a few inches, a foot, closer to the cut in the curb and the crowd in the street. One person, then another and another, stepped back, parting to let him pass.[97] The paddy wagon pulled into the street, away from the bungalow and into the sweltering summer night.

TWO

AIN'T NO SLAVERY NO MORE

Ossian Sweet sat shoulder to shoulder and knee to knee with his brothers and the other men as the paddy wagon rumbled toward police headquarters. When the patrolmen had padlocked the door behind him, Ossian must have been relieved. Although the mob's screams pierced the wagon's steel walls, the crowd couldn't touch him, couldn't drag him down Garland Avenue to the school yard, couldn't lynch him from the streetlight that brightened the intersection in front of his new home. In the darkness of the wagon, he was safe.

Yet, as the tumult on Garland trailed away, Ossian's momentary confidence collapsed. It was so claustrophobic inside the steel cage that he could barely breathe. The others were straining, too, more than he was, since their hands were still cuffed behind them while his were free. Every time the paddy wagon lurched over a streetcar track or a sewer grate, they all heard the jingling of the bullets Ossian had jammed in his pockets, damning evidence of his intent to do bodily harm. That's what the cops at headquarters would be looking for: something they could use to build a case against Ossian and his compatriots, to turn them from the mob's intended victims into crazed colored men, criminals, murderers.[1] He would have to make them understand; that's all there was to it. When the police started to question him, he would have to give them a clear and cogent explanation as to why he'd moved into a neighborhood where he wasn't welcome, why he'd filled the house with guns, why he'd been prepared to use them.

But Ossian didn't have a coherent story to tell. He had the shards of his family's history: the legacy of a half-remembered moment when the world was full of promise; the dreams his mother had sustained during the bitter descent into segregation; the weight of his name, the meaning of which he barely knew. And he had his own memories, trailing backward from Garland Avenue to the Jim Crow South, backward to the dusty streets of his boyhood home, to the tidy kitchen of the house his father built, to the tiny school where the black children learned their lessons, to the riot of trees and tropical plants tumbling down the banks of the Peace River, to the smell of burning flesh wafting across the placid water, filling his imagination with the most grotesque of horrors.

•

Ossian knew his grandfather, Remus DeVaughn, as a wizened old man, bent and bowed, but when Remus was young, he had been at the center of a revolution. In those days, Remus and his brothers—George, Harrison, Hubbert, Edmond, Romulus, and Amos—were poor men, their hands thick with calluses from years of driving hoes into the red clay of other men's land. They had no homes of their own; their landlord supplied the rude log cabins where they raised their families. They had no education; when their children practiced their letters on their slates, their fathers couldn't help them.[2] But it wasn't the desperation of poverty that made the DeVaughns revolutionaries. It was hope.

The brothers had been born to bondage. In the early 1800s, most southern whites were subsistence farmers, tilling their own fields, growing their own food, making their own clothes. Their owner, Alexander Cromartie, was different. A slave owner's son born and raised on a prosperous plantation in the gently rolling hills of North Carolina, Alexander could have stayed home, waiting to inherit his share of his father's estate. But in the 1820s, young men like Alexander weren't settling for what their parents could give them. A man could better his fortune—if only he worked hard and took some chances—and Alexander wasn't afraid to take chances. Packing up his family, he headed to Leon County, Florida, just south of the Georgia border. Among his household goods was a black boy, Edmond DeVaughn, Ossian Sweet's great-grandfather and the father of Remus and his brothers.[3]

Since the last years of the eighteenth century, southern planters had been making themselves rich by selling cotton to the textile mills of industrial England. But these planters had already taken the best cotton land along the eastern seaboard. So ambitious young men like Alexander pushed deeper and deeper into the southern interior in search of new land to cultivate. They found the perfect conditions in the rich red loam that ran through southern Georgia, Alabama, and Mississippi and the northern reaches of Florida. Alexander grabbed his share, buying thirteen hundred acres of prime cotton land on the banks of Florida's Lake Iamonia in newly settled Leon County, fifteen miles north of the territorial capital of Tallahassee.[4]

It was a raw land, its red hills thick with forests, its roads rudimentary, its few settlements spartan. Tallahassee is "a grotesque place," sniffed the visiting Ralph Waldo Emerson, "rapidly settled by public officers, land speculators, and desperados." Small-time farmers here might work the fields themselves, but major planters needed slaves, as many as they could afford: there were twice as many slaves as whites in Leon County by 1840, three times as many by 1860. Keeping with the tradition of American slavery, bondmen had no rights, no legal or social standing. But Florida's lawmakers went further than other states: slaves couldn't leave their plantations, even for a walk, without the written permission of their owners. They couldn't trade goods among themselves or learn to read or gather for prayer meetings. If they committed crimes, their hands were burned by heated irons, their ears nailed to posts, their backs stripped raw by the lash.[5]

Badly outnumbered by their slaves, Leon County planters lived in fear of revolt. Sometimes violence burst to the surface. One evening, a planter dragged a slave into the yard for a flogging. Before the planter could begin, the slave grabbed an axe and split his master's skull. But the ferocity of the law undercut more organized rebellion. So slaves sought other ways out of bondage. Leon County planters were continually searching for escaped slaves who had fled to the swamps south of the cotton belt, where it was difficult for slave hunters to track them. Fugitives would find refuge in the scattered camps of the Seminoles. A few would strike out for the North, so very far away. Alexander's kinsman, Cornelius DeVane, followed him to Leon County in the early 1830s. Shortly after he arrived, a slave couple he owned, Loveless and Pink, stole his shotgun, gathered up their three children, the youngest just five months old, and headed into Georgia, there to begin the long, dangerous journey to the Ohio River and freedom.[6]

Alexander's young slave Edmond may well have dreamed about following their example. But nothing indicates that he ever acted on those hopes. Edmond passed into adulthood working the Cromarties' land, helping to strip the Florida hills of pine, to divide the acreage into fields the slaves filled with row after row of cotton, to make his master and his young wife a comfortable home appropriate to their station. By 1860, Alexander was one of the wealthier planters in Leon County, master of fifty-five slaves, a southern gentleman through and through.[7]

When he came of age, Edmond took a wife, a young slave woman named Gilla, and together they began to build a family. Between 1840 and 1852, the couple had seven sons, beginning with George in 1840 and ending with Amos in 1852. But the tiny, beautiful infants were never completely Edmond and Gilla's children. From the moment they entered the world, the boys became Alexander Cromartie's property, another asset on his ledger sheets, another measure of his success. And when they had children of their own, their bondage would be passed on once again, parent to child, generation to generation, forever and ever.[8]

Or so Cromartie and his fellow slave owners hoped. As the DeVaughn brothers passed through childhood, though, the institution of slavery was plunged into crisis. During the nation's first half century, America's political leaders did their best to keep the slavery question out of public debate. In the 1840s and 1850s, the issue exploded. Edmond and Gilla's fifth and sixth sons, twins Romulus and Remus, were six years old when southern slaveholders pushed Congress to open Kansas to slavery, an act that convinced antislavery forces to organize a new political party, the Republicans, as a counterweight to the slave power. The twins were eight years old when the advocates and opponents of slavery plunged Kansas into guerilla warfare, eleven when the United States Supreme Court affirmed the sanctity of slavery with the *Dred Scott* decision, twelve when the Republicans elected their candidate, Abraham Lincoln, president of the United States. The election became the breaking point. In the months leading up to Lincoln's inauguration, the southern states seceded from the Union and the nation descended into civil war.[9]

Alexander Cromartie dutifully sent his first-born son and namesake to fight for the planters' right to keep human beings in bondage. While young Alexander risked his life, his father did his best to maintain plantation life as it had always been. His rule lasted longer than did most planters'. As northern troops pushed farther and farther into the South, thousands of the enslaved fled their masters for the Union lines, there to claim freedom for themselves. Leon County was far from the main lines of battle so it wasn't until the Confederacy began to crumble in 1864 and early 1865 that the county's slave regime collapsed. Slaves started to talk back to their masters; some refused to work as ordered; many disappeared altogether, fleeing into the woods or slipping away quietly to meet the federal troops at last making their way toward the Florida state line.[10]

The Union Army finally took Tallahassee on May 10, 1865, a full month after Robert E. Lee's surrender at Appomattox courthouse. Word had passed through the plantations that when the slaves heard a gunshot, they were free. The shot came at midday, when they were in the fields. They dropped their plows and hoes where they stood, returned to their cabins to dress in their Sunday best, then joined the flood of black men, women, and children on the road to Tallahassee, hurrying, a participant said, "to go see the Yankees."[11]

◆

Edmond never saw slavery's end. He passed away in 1857, four years before the Civil War began. So Gilla brought her boys into adulthood on her own. When emancipation arrived that day in May, the DeVaughn brothers were young men in their teens and twenties, the perfect age to find their way in a new world of freedom. But freedom had no shape, no substance, in the spring of 1865. Negroes could work for wages but they had no jobs. They could learn to read and write but they had no schools. They could leave their former masters and strike out for themselves but they had no homes, no land of their own. They could plead for government assistance in their time of need. But they had no political power—no vote, no elected representatives—to assure that their voices would be heard.[12]

Across Leon County, former slaves tried to shape freedom for themselves. The vast majority of freedmen were farmers, and they knew they could provide for their families if only they had a few acres of their own. They dreamed of land, not row upon row of cotton, just enough to cultivate some crops. Freedmen also desperately wanted to school their children: free people needed to read and write if they were to manage their own affairs. But it was more than that. Everything their masters had denied them—schooling, family, property, freedom of movement—Negroes were now determined to claim for themselves, whatever the consequences. The mistress of a great Leon County plantation ordered a former house slave, her daughter's "dear black mammy," not to attend a political rally in Tallahassee, but the freedwoman said she would do as she pleased. The planter's wife was livid. "If you disobey me in this matter," she said, "you and your family must leave the place." By night-fall, the "dear black mammy" was gone.[13]

There is no knowing whether the DeVaughns likewise deserted the Cromartie plantation. It's possible that they stayed with their former master. Gilla might have had some distant memory of her North Carolina childhood, but any connection there had been severed long ago; Edmond was buried in Florida soil, and her boys knew no place other than Leon County. If they did leave the Cromarties, the DeVaughns didn't go far. Like most former slaves in the first days of freedom, they would have moved onto a neighboring plantation, close enough to the Cromarties to be familiar, far enough to be independent.[14]

For their part, the masters of Leon County were determined to make sure that the DeVaughns and their fellow freedmen went no further. A few months after Union troops occupied Tallahassee, the federal gov-ernment returned control of the state to the planters. Immediately, the former slaveholders passed a series of laws pushing blacks to the very edge of bondage. Freedmen were to sign year-long contracts to work the planters' fields; those who broke their agreements could be sold into service for a year's time; those convicted of even minor crimes against a planter's property—stealing his cotton or injuring his livestock—were to be whipped and pilloried. Once bound to the planters' land, Negroes were subject to the same casual cruelty their masters had always imposed.

But the planters overreached themselves. The federal government hadn't sacrificed the better part of a generation—360,000 soldiers dead—to assure the former slaveholders' continued domination over southern land and labor. Appalled by the planters' audacity, in 1866, the Republican Congress dissolved the southern state governments formed the previous year, put the entire region back under military control, and launched one of the most extraordinary experiments the nation had ever undertaken, its purposes masked by the bland name of Reconstruction.

The Republicans who controlled Washington pledged to remake the South root and branch. Congress would amend the Constitution to give freedmen all the rights that white Americans enjoyed, including the right to vote. What's more, Republicans would use the power of the federal government to give the South a glittering new economy, where every man, regardless of the color of his skin, could sell his labor in a free and open market. Congress would create opportunity by linking the South, devastated by four years of war, with the vibrant economy of the North. The federal government would encourage industry to build railroads so that southern farms and factories could ship their goods to the cities of the North. Congress would open public schools for southern children, white and black, and it would provide freedmen training in the rudiments of economic exchange—how to negotiate a labor contract, how to work for wages, how to sell crops for a profit— so they could compete for work on a free and fair footing.[15]

Knowing that planters would do all they could to resist such extraordinary changes, Congress dispatched thousands of federal agents across the South to implement Reconstruction programs. Most of these soldiers, teachers, and preachers were white, all aflame with the fire of the free-market gospel, but a precious few were colored. Many of the latter were men of the cloth, missionaries of the northern black churches. All the major black denominations sent ministers to the South in the late 1860s. But none of them was better suited to the Reconstruction project than the ministers of the African Methodist Episcopal (AME) Church.[16]

Methodists preached that even the most humble person could be reborn into God's grace, if only he or she rejected sin and embraced a life of holiness. Believers experienced rebirth in a moment of ecstasy triggered by the tumult of the vast camp meetings that preachers mounted. Once in the flock, the saved proved their virtue by following the strictest of moral codes. Methodists did not drink, swear, gamble, fornicate, or fight. They worked hard, paid their debts, dealt honestly with others. They taught their children to read, write, and do sums. Such discipline was the mark of grace. It was also the perfect match for the free market. "Religion must necessarily produce industry and frugality," Methodism's founder, John Wesley, proclaimed, "and these cannot but produce riches."[17]

In the early days, American Methodists spread the promise of deliverance through circuit riders who traveled the back roads, seeking converts among the poor and downtrodden, regardless of skin color. But like so many other institutions, the church foundered on the rock of racism. In the late 1700s and early 1800s, white congregants in a number of northern cities tried to segregate the free blacks in their midst. Rather than accept second-class salvation, Negroes walked out of the white churches and established their own denomination.[18]

AME preachers maintained the Methodist discipline, but they

enveloped it in a powerful racial consciousness. They would battle the evil of slavery, confront every manifestation of discrimination in the North, and prove to whites—by their thoughts and their deeds—that blacks deserved to be treated as equals. Indeed, they would do the whites one better: they would be more frugal, more hardworking, better educated than their white neighbors. By their accomplishments, they would force whites to acknowledge their equality. It was a heavy burden to bear. "If we are lazy and idle," explained the AME's founder, "the enemies of freedom plead it as a cause why we ought not to be free, and say we are better in a state of servitude."[19]

These AME circuit riders followed the Union troops into the South, determined to proclaim their message of racial uplift to the former slaves. Many freedmen were put off by the condescension and criticism the AME preachers leveled. They flocked instead to the Baptists, who were more willing to accept the freedmen as they were. But a significant minority joined the AME. The very sight of the ministers, forceful black men, brooking no opposition, demanding respect, must have been a draw, but the ministers' message—the wonder of God's word flowing into the promise of liberation—also riveted many to the church. Many more must have been attracted by the churchmen's temporal promises: the freedmen ought to buy land, the ministers preached; hard work and self-discipline would give them the means. Young people needed education if they were to seize the opportunities that would be opening up to them. The AME would build them schools.[20]

Elder Charles Pearce wound his way through the northern Florida cotton district in the spring of 1866. Bearded in the style of Lincoln, Pearce was a muscular man, physically and spiritually. Born and raised in freedom, almost twenty years an AME minister, Pearce was a lion of the church, a missionary zealot. Everywhere he went, he found the spirit of Jubilee drawing the freedmen to him and his church. Revivals burned long into the night: 116 new members in Tallahassee, 453 in neighboring Gadsden County, another 343 in Jefferson County. "It is only necessary for us to name the AME church to them, and they are willing to cast in their lot with us, and they are still coming by the score," Pearce wrote. "We are all looking forward to a glorious future." Religious fervor blended with political organizing. From the start, AME ministers were determined to carve out a role for themselves and their congregations in the Reconstruction government that would eventually replace military rule. Twenty-five hundred freedmen jammed a Leon County meeting ground in May 1867 to hear Pearce and other ministers denounce the evils of slavery and campaign for the Republican Party. Planters were stunned by the turnout, but the ministers were simply tapping into the political passions pulsing through black communities.[21]

The DeVaughn brothers were swept up in the AME's crusade. Gilla's oldest son, George, joined the ministry in 1867, at the age of twenty-seven, and was assigned to the Leon County mission; her third son, Hubbert, followed him a few years later. The family had no trouble adjusting to the discipline that racial uplift required. Gilla and her seven sons drew themselves into a tight circle, all settling together on Solomon Sill's plantation, just a few miles from the Cromarties. As sharecroppers, they tilled Sill's fields and earned a third of the crop they grew. It was a smart strategy: by living and working together, they maximized their earnings and set themselves on the road to buying land of their own. Undoubtedly, they sent their older children to the nearby AME schoolhouse, which was tied to George's mission, where two black teachers taught ninety-three children to read and write. When the federal government created a Freedman's Bank to encourage savings, the DeVaughns opened accounts. They couldn't have had much money to put on deposit. But a minister's family had to set an example, to show the faithful and the prodigal the virtues of hard work, thrift, and sobriety.[22]

It was never easy. The brothers were marrying and having children of their own now: Romulus and his wife, Lisa, had a daughter, Julia, in 1865; the next year, his twin had his first son, Robert; Hubbert had a daughter, Nancy, the year after that. Their growing families needed more food, more space, and more money. Every step was a struggle. In 1867, a drought withered the cotton in the fields, leaving black families so desperate that only the distribution of government rations staved off a winter of complete deprivation. The next growing season began well, but a midsummer plague of caterpillars destroyed much of the crop and left most blacks poorer than when the year began.[23]

Worse, the planters used their power to subvert the freedmen's efforts. Leon County landowners blocked government attempts to settle freedmen on federal land. And they refused to sell even small portions of their plantations to Negroes. Many planters ruthlessly exploited the colored families who rented small plots from them. A few used the slightest pretenses to expel their tenants from the land once the crop was close to harvest.[24]

The threat of violence was constant. Across the cotton belt, planters organized terrorist cells: the Regulators, the Whitecappers, the Ku Klux Klan. Operating under the protection of darkness, the Klan and their fellows targeted anyone who dared to challenge white domination. They forced teachers in colored schools to abandon their posts. They threatened, assaulted, and burned out those few freedmen who managed to acquire land of their own. Mostly, they waged war against the Republican state governments that set Reconstruction's rules. Vigilantes assassinated dozens of Republicans in the late 1860s and early 1870s, as many as seventy in the heavily black county just east of Leon, where the Klan ran rampant.[25]

Great as it was, the terror only pushed the AME's leaders toward an ever more vigorous defense of black rights. They made progress. In 1868, the Republican Party took control of Florida's state government, installing nineteen black state legislators, eight of them AME ministers or prominent laymen, Elder Pearce foremost among them. But the colored delegation was surrounded by a sordid collection of political opportunists more interested in bringing northern business interests into Florida—and fattening their wallets—than in breaking the power of white supremacy. Four years later, when the governor told Pearce that he was powerless to prevent further outrages against the freedmen, church leaders led a coup, overturning the Republican Party's established leaders and handing the 1872 gubernatorial nomination to an avowed reformer, Ossian Hart, to whom they delivered the black vote in the general election. "Elder C. H. Pearce saved this state to the Republican Party," a newspaperman wrote in the election's aftermath. "Florida is destined to become the negro's new Jerusalem."[26]

Hart wasn't quite that radical. Tall and broad shouldered, with a mane of white hair, he had the look of a planter, the unquestioning paternalism of someone to the manner born. He hadn't freed his own slaves until the last days of the Civil War, and he'd only grudgingly supported the freedmen's right to vote. Like his predecessors, Hart was primarily interested in tying the state to northern business; he wanted to see railroad lines brought into the peninsula, so he could link his friends, cattlemen who raised great herds on the open range of Central Florida, to the slaughterhouses of Chicago. But he understood who had put in him in the governor's mansion. And a gentleman always pays his debts.[27]

When antiblack violence broke out in Columbia County, east of Leon, Hart dispatched a contingent of black troops to the area to restore order. He rammed a civil rights law through the legislature, prohibiting discrimination in most public facilities. He named a Negro to head Florida's public school system and committed his administration to dramatically expanding state funding for education. And he appointed AME officials to dozens of minor political posts, from county superintendent to tax assessor.[28]

The DeVaughns got their due. In early 1873, Hart named Edmond and Gilla's third son, Hubbert, justice of the peace, Leon County's primary law enforcement official. The governor undoubtedly thought of the appointment as another political payoff, the price of victory. But the DeVaughns saw it as more than that, much more. When Hubbert claimed the position, he took the place of another promising young man, Alexander Cromartie, his former master's elder son.[29]

So the revolution had come. Eight years earlier, the DeVaughn brothers had been pieces of property. Now they were men who demanded respect: missionaries of the Word, spreading the gospel to their fellow freedmen; aspiring farmers, working to earn a share of the American dream. They were still poor, still landless, still struggling to be equal to whites in fact as well as in name. But they had come so very far, there was every reason to be hopeful. A few months after Hubbert took office, his younger brother Remus and his wife had their fourth child, Dora.[30] What must have run through Gilla's mind as she cradled her granddaughter in her leathery arms? This child wouldn't be like her babies, who had been born into a world now dead and gone. This child would have a future all her own.

•

Hope proved to be a very fragile thing. When Ossian Hart suddenly died in March 1874, his fourteen-month experiment in racial justice collapsed, and the Florida Republican Party slipped back into the hands of the opportunists whom the AME had overturned. The church bloc was broken.[31]

Democrats resumed their attack on "Negro rule." Landlords threatened black voters with eviction. The Klan renewed its terror against black officeholders. Intimidation and fraud peaked during the 1876 presidential and gubernatorial elections, Florida's first since Hart's death. When both the Republicans and Democrats claimed victory in the presidential election, the nation was thrown into a constitutional crisis. Only a Faustian bargain broke the deadlock. The Republican candidate, the ineffectual Rutherford B. Hayes, took the White House. Democrats took control of Florida's state government. Hayes promised them that there would be no more federal interference in their affairs. The Democrats, champions of white supremacy, could do as they wanted.[32]

Florida's Democrats had no intention of reversing the Republicans' economic policies. In fact, they pushed them harder than ever before. The Democratic legislature handed over huge sections of public land to northern railroad companies, which reciprocated by extending their lines south from the Georgia border all the way to the Florida Keys. Florida's economic might had always been centered on the panhandle, but when the tracks linked the peninsula to northern markets, the state's center shifted. Central Florida cattlemen expanded their herds, while farmers planted glorious citrus groves where wild grasses had always grown. Businessmen built lumber and turpentine camps to process the product of the forests they stripped bare. Land speculators platted towns where farmers could sell their goods and workers could spend their wages; shopkeepers and doctors and lawyers filled the new main streets with their stores and offices.[33]

This was the economic opportunity the Republicans had dreamed of bringing to the South. But the Democrats made sure that the New South would be for whites only and set about undoing the racial policies it had taken civil war to create. It took them until 1885 to assure the destruction of the Florida Republican Party and another decade to complete their oppression of the colored race. There were, after all, practical problems to overcome: the fourteenth and fifteenth amendments guaranteed Negroes their rights, and it was no simple matter to subvert the Constitution. The Democrats also had to overcome the limits of their imagination. They knew how to be cruel. But they had to create a social system premised on cruelty. That was a task that took some creativity.

Some steps were obvious. Black voters had made radical Republicanism possible. So they had to be stripped of the right to vote. As a start, the Democrats imposed a poll tax in 1887; voter registration plummeted by 50 percent the first year the tax was imposed. The Democrats followed that triumph by gradually tightening registration further. By 1895, when the last laws were put into place, it was almost impossible for a Negro to vote in the state of Florida.[34]

The next steps were more complicated. The vast majority of whites assumed blacks to be inferior. The trick was to make them act on those beliefs. Democrats began by defending the purity of the white race, not a straightforward matter in a society where interracial sex had a long history. But legislators, insisting that racial lines could be strictly drawn, imposed a stringent definition of who qualified as colored: a person was legally a Negro if just one of his great-grandparents had been black. Legislators also prohibited any further dilution of the white race. Blacks and whites couldn't have sexual relationships, couldn't marry, couldn't even spend a night in the same bedroom. With the groundwork laid, the Democrats gradually moved into the public sphere. Florida's whites had already barred blacks from some public places, such as theaters and hotels. But the segregation didn't have the force of law; it was custom, nothing more. The Democrats mandated the separation and extended it to the places where the New South was being created. Florida was one of the first southern states to require blacks to ride in separate railroad cars. And the legislature made it a crime to teach black and white children in the same classroom.[35]

As the Democrats made it more and more difficult to be black, whites became more and more determined to assert the power of their race. So they piled prohibition on prohibition. Blacks couldn't be buried in the same cemeteries as whites. They couldn't eat in the same restaurants. They couldn't ride in the front of city streetcars. They couldn't drink from the same drinking fountains. Whites also segregated their workplaces. Blacks could be servants and farm laborers, of course, and they could work in the turpentine and lumber camps, where most whites didn't want to go. But whites claimed the vast majority of jobs for themselves. They also demanded privileges that superiority conferred. They expected blacks to step off the sidewalk when a white person approached. They insisted that blacks keep their eyes downcast when they spoke to whites. They demanded that blacks call them "sir" or "ma'am," though they would never dream of reciprocating.[36] They felt free to level any insult, to inflict any injury, without fear of reprisal. Jim Crow taught the great mass of southern whites to see ordinary places and everyday interactions as sacred and to protect the sacred by embracing the profane.

◆

Remus DeVaughn's daughter, Dora, grew up as the great hopes of Reconstruction collapsed around her family. As soon as he became governor, Ossian Hart's successor removed her uncle Hubbert as justice of the peace. The family circle that the DeVaughns had drawn around themselves began to break. In 1876, the AME bishop ordered Hubbert to leave Leon County and take up a position at a mission to the south.

Maybe the bishop was trying to protect him; AME ministers had become a particular target of Klan violence. Remus's baby brother, Amos, just drifted away, and his other brother, Edmond, left to take a job teaching school in Jefferson County, a small triumph for the AME's promise of uplift. But for the most part, Jim Crow choked off the advancement the preachers had proclaimed. By Dora's seventh birthday, only her father, Remus, and his twin brother, Romulus, remained in Leon County. Romulus somehow sustained his family on the few dollars he earned as a whitewasher. Remus kept working the land, as he'd always done, but it was harder and harder to eke out a living.[37]

As black political power faded, white landlords were imposing harsher terms on their tenants than they had been able to do during Reconstruction. Each bale of cotton was bringing in less than before, and Remus didn't have a way to increase his production. Dora's older siblings, Robert, Eliza Jane, and Sally, were going to school, so Remus didn't have their help in the fields for much of the year. Dora was old enough to work around the house but too young to spend her days nursing the cotton crop. And she also needed to begin her education soon. Then there were the babies, Maggie and Remus, Jr., to feed and clothe.[38] Dora's father could have pulled the children out of school and sent them to the fields. But that would have meant turning his back on his faith in his abilities and in his church's teachings. It would have meant mortgaging his children's futures, just as he had surely mortgaged his own to land that wasn't and never would be his.

He finally gave up. Sometime in the 1880s, two decades after he'd been freed from bondage, Remus left Leon County and moved his family south, to the Central Florida boomtown of Orlando. Orlando had been nothing more than a frontier town when the Democrats had assumed control of the state. But when the Democrats convinced Florida Southern Railroad to connect it to the northbound lines in 1880, Orlando had become a bustling commercial center. Remus must have believed that there would be work at the railroad terminal, where the citrus farmers piled their oranges for shipment, or in the sawmills, where the pine trees being stripped from nearby forests were planed.[39] Maybe life would be easier there.

It wasn't. If anything, whites were more committed to enforcing Jim Crow in cities and towns than they were in the countryside. Remus did the best he could, settling his family in a small rented home in the black section of town. He tried to find steady work. But he never broke out of the narrow range of jobs to which whites relegated blacks, and after years of struggle, he was discarded. By 1900, he was unemployed; at fifty-two, he was probably too old to find steady work, certainly too old for the backbreaking labor most blacks performed. So he lived on the largesse of his youngest children, now grown to early adulthood. And they, in turn, scraped by on the little that whites were willing to offer them. Remus, Jr., worked as a teacher in Orlando's impoverished black school system; Maggie was a washerwoman.[40]

It would have been easy enough, under the circumstances, to abandon the AME's promises. It was painfully obvious that blacks couldn't raise themselves up in such a society, but for some reason Dora couldn't let go of the great expectations that had swirled around her birth. She had heard the message of uplift and improvement week after week at church, and she couldn't set it aside. A handsome young woman, powerfully built, she carried herself with a quiet dignity that would become her hallmark. But behind it lay a fierce determination to recapture the moment when her family's dreams had been on the verge of fulfillment. Dora wasn't driven by a sense of nostalgia; she didn't want to re-create the past. She wanted to revive its hopes and make them real.[41]

Dora DeVaughn couldn't have been more than sixteen or seventeen when she fell in love with Henry Sweet, an ordinary man, typical of the postwar generation. His family had never found the stability the DeVaughns had enjoyed until Jim Crow came. Henry's parents were enslaved in East Texas, the western reaches of the cotton kingdom. Sometime before the Civil War, they'd been moved to Tuscaloosa, Alabama, a desperate place to spend the war. Union forces slowly choked off the Alabama interior; by 1864, Tuscaloosa was suffering from severe food shortages, and even the most devout rebels dreamed of the day when the fighting would end. Family lore says that by then Henry's parents had escaped their master and fled to the Union lines. If the story is true, the couple had a ferocious desire for freedom. Federal and Confederate raiders waged bitter guerilla warfare all along Alabama's northern border during the last years of the war; the Sweets would have been walking into an area where there were no clear battle lines and no obvious sanctuaries. If they did find safety, they probably would have moved with the troops, perhaps even following them back to Tuscaloosa in the spring of 1865, when the slaves the Sweets had left behind finally won their freedom.[42]

Henry had been born in Alabama on December 16, 1865, a child of freedom. For the next quarter century, the Sweets simply faded from view, lost in the official record until the 1880s, by which time they had followed the railroad to Florida. Tall, thin, and rangy, Henry was the sort of young man who would never fill out, no matter how many years he spent working the fields. If Florida law hadn't maintained such a strict division of black and white, he would have been classified as a mulatto. His light brown skin, sharply drawn features, and wavy black hair put him as close to the American concept of white as black. Maybe Dora was drawn to his looks, maybe to his maturity; he was eight years her senior. Maybe she loved the fact that he shared her determination to make a mark. It was impossible to say where his desire came from. It may have been a reflection of his parents' flight to freedom, perhaps something else, now forgotten. But he had the businessman's drive, an entrepreneurial spirit, fueled by a strong sense of pride and tempered by a dedication to fair dealing.[43] Those were AME values, Dora's values. They were married in 1890 or 1891.

The first few years were very hard. Dora and Henry stayed in Orlando, scraping by and putting aside whatever money they could spare. They had their first child, Oscar, in March 1893. Dora became pregnant again in early 1895. She had another boy on October 30, 1895. They named him Ossian, a tribute to the memory of the Reconstruction governor who had made her uncle a government official, a reminder of what had been lost. Dora must have taken great pride in the name, which was surely hers to give. But the exhilaration of the moment didn't last. Eight days after Ossian's birth, Dora and Henry lost Oscar.[44] It's almost impossible to imagine the burden that the parents bore in those terrible November days, when they had to care for their newborn—so dependent, so insistent—while they buried their toddler.

Hope and despair, the birthright of the baby with the radical name.

•

At long last, land. In the summer of 1898, Henry fulfilled one of the DeVaughns' great dreams: he bought a plot of land. It wasn't much, just a housing lot in the tidy little town of Bartow, halfway between Orlando and Tampa. It was an ordinary town, a bit newer and more prosperous than most but just as dedicated to Jim Crow as any place in Florida. There was white Bartow, the solid respectable center of Polk County. And there was black Bartow, a cache of sun-baked homes separated from the center of town by the railroad tracks and the massive wall of segregation. The Sweets' lot naturally sat on the wrong side of the tracks. But Henry and Dora could afford it; the seller, a white man by the name of Milam, a northerner by birth, had fallen on hard times and was willing to let it go for $250. Henry put down a deposit, Dora packed up their belongings, and they headed the fifty miles west, to their new home.[45]

Bartow hadn't always been sharply divided. With only three hundred people in the entire county, Polk was still very much a wilderness in 1880. Bartow was a tiny trading post of seventy-seven souls, a ramshackle collection of stores barely rising above the dog fennel that flourished in the tropical sun. Blacks and whites didn't live in harmony: Democratic Party vigilantes had operated there in the 1860s, just as they had in Leon County. But the town was too small to segregate and too far out of the way for anyone to care. Then the railroad came.[46]

When Florida Southern extended its line from Orlando to Tampa in 1884, Polk County suddenly became an attractive destination. Aspiring farmers began buying up the land, filling the long empty fields with citrus trees and rows of vegetables. In 1889, prospectors discovered that the river basin of the Peace River, which cut through the heart of the county, was rich with phosphate, the basic ingredient in fertilizer. European investment houses rushed to grab up the tracts with the largest deposits. By the 1890s, the land southwest of Bartow had been slashed into open pits, and the countryside shook with the roar of mill machinery processing twenty thousand tons of phosphate each and every month.[47]

Prosperity made Bartow a substantial place. By the last years of the 1890s, there were close to three thousand people in town. The well-to-do built themselves imposing new homes—all peaks and porches—down Broadway, the elm-lined avenue that ran south toward the phosphate mines. Businessmen lined Main Street with groceries, drugstores, and specialty shops—the bicycle store, the millinery, the jeweler's, the telegraph office—all housed in handsome clapboard and brick buildings fronted by wooden sidewalks and glistening white streets paved with phosphate stone. The new courthouse sat at the corner of Main and Central, the new high school a few blocks to the south, both of them brick-and-mortar proclamations of Bartow's public prominence. There were many more black faces as well. They were drawn there by the ample work on the railroad, on the land, or in the mines. A man could make a living in Polk County; he might even hammer out a measure of the independence so many black folks wanted.[48]

But it just wouldn't do to have blacks mingling with whites, especially given Bartow's new importance. So, as the town fathers put in the sewer lines, the streetlights, and the telephone exchange, they split the town in half. The few blacks who had been able to vote in the 1870s and 1880s were barred by the poll tax; only whites voted by the 1890s, and they always elected Democrats. Blacks weren't welcome in the Orange Hotel, the opera house, or the Main Street stores. They couldn't attend the outdoor entertainments—the county fair in March, the occasional traveling shows—except on specially designated "colored days." They couldn't pray in the fine white churches. They couldn't bury their dead in the white cemetery. But all those prohibitions weren't sufficient. Just about the time the Sweets' wagon rumbled into town, Bartow officials pushed segregation to its logical conclusion. Blacks couldn't even live among whites. Those who owned land in the center of the town—including some of Bartow's founders—would have to sell their homes and move to the other side of the railroad tracks, to the subdivision Florida Southern had laid out ten years earlier, to the other Bartow.[49]

Forced to separate, the people of East Bartow built a thriving community for themselves, poorer than the white side of town, to be sure, but every bit as solid and respectable. Black businessmen opened general stores, barbershops, and restaurants along Wabash Avenue, which became the black downtown. Lawrence Brown, a part-time Bible salesman, built a small real estate empire selling home sites to black customers from the comfort of his handsome Queen Anne home on Second Avenue. East Bartow filled with social clubs and vibrant black churches: Mt. Gilboa Missionary Baptist on Laurel; Burkett Chapel on Third; St. James AME a block over, its grand bell tower rising above the neighborhood.[50]

The Sweets made themselves into pillars of the community. Their lot sat at the corner of Eighth and Bay streets, almost as far from white Bartow as could be. Henry set himself to work building a house, a single-story wood-frame home constructed from the local pine, bounded on two sides by covered porches that sheltered the inside from the noonday sun. Town officials didn't extend utilities into the black neighborhood, so the Sweets' home had no electricity, no running water, and no indoor plumbing. Henry added a barn for the mules he used to break the land he rented beyond the woods to the south. He built coops for the chickens Dora raised. He marked off a garden plot, where they grew the vegetables that filled the family table. And he began building a commercial farm, a farm that could make some money and set his family on its course.[51]

It was endless work. Henry would spend days behind the plow, preparing the fields for planting. Then there'd be the months of tending the cabbages, kale, rutabagas, and peas, hoping that rains would come when they were needed and that the sun wouldn't burn the plants before they could be harvested. He'd sell what he could in the neighborhood; he'd load the mule cart with produce and ride up and down the streets, calling out, "Cabbages," in a singsong voice that might bring the ladies out of their houses to take a look at what he had to offer. The bulk of his produce he'd haul the forty-five miles to Tampa, where the market was bigger and the prices better.[52]

Dora, meanwhile, did the constant round of chores the house required. There was the daily grind of floors to sweep, chickens to feed, meals to prepare, and pots to scrub. There were always clothes to mend and clean; on laundry day, she would have to haul up gallon after gallon of water from the small lake near her husband's fields. And more and more, there were babies to tend. Otis was born in 1899, Deloca, the first daughter, a year later. There were a few years without a newborn. But then Dora was almost continually pregnant. Henry was born in 1904, Parthenia in 1905, Nordica in 1907, Buck in 1908, Cynthia in 1909. Sherman, the tenth and last child, arrived in 1915.[53]

The farmhouse groaned under the weight of the family. But Henry and Dora fused the children into a unit, just as her father's generation had done back in Leon County. As soon as they were old enough, the children were expected to work. The younger ones could care for the animals: gathering the eggs, milking the cows, driving the few head of cattle up from the pasture to the barn each night. And Dora would send them into the woods to pick fruit for canning or to brighten a meal, though the rattlesnakes the children found there terrified them. Ossian and Otis gradually took over the plowing from their father. But Henry was too much of an entrepreneur to rest. As the boys freed him from the fields, he opened a lumberyard on his land as one more venture, one more way to bring the family a few precious dollars he could use to expand his operation.[54]

The Sweets thought of success in financial terms: Henry was too much of a businessman not to believe that hard work paid dividends. But money wasn't the only goal. Henry and Dora were honest, upright people. They wouldn't drink or smoke. They saved what money they could. They strived to live the solidly respectable life the church had taught them to cherish. Every Sunday, after services at St. James, the Sweets would put their round of chores aside. Dora would set the finest table: the china set she somehow pieced together, a freshly ironed tablecloth, a vase of newly cut flowers. The family would sit for a formal meal of the sort served in the grand homes on the other side of town. As they passed platters of food, the family would talk of the past and the future. Sometimes their grandfather would come over from Orlando to join them, and he'd tell tales of his childhood in slavery.[55]

Sometimes, Dora and Henry would lecture on responsibilities. Owning land was a wonderful thing, the great triumph of Henry's generation. But as the AME had taught them, land wasn't enough. The children had to have an education, they said, to take their schooling as far as it would go. For when they reached adulthood, they were duty bound—by their church, by the struggles of the generations that went before them—to be models of Christian virtue and race pride. And only education could give them the tools they needed.[56]

The children learned the lessons well. There wasn't a hint of rebellion; not one of them challenged the course their parents set for them. If all of the Sweet children were willing to take up their burdens, though, Ossian assumed the greatest weight. He was the oldest, after all, and he would have to blaze the trail for the rest. The others would depend on him, not simply as an example but also as the person who could give them the aid they'd need as they tried to fulfill Mama and Papa's exhortations. And he knew—how could he not know—that his parents were also counting on him, to prove them right and to make them proud.[57] He was their hope; their aspirations were his obligations.

But the Sweets' aspirations were inexorably consumed by Jim Crow. In the early 1890s, before the family arrived in town, black children had no school. The town fathers saw no need for it. "It seems to me that attempt at general education of the negroes is an injury rather than a benefit to the race," explained one of Bartow's leading lights. "It tends to pervert his intelligence to a dissatisfaction of his natural and moral condition in life." The pastor of St. James AME, however, refused to accept such an affront to his community. He tried to establish a church-run school, but his congregation simply didn't have enough money to keep the building open. Finally, the year before the Sweets arrived, St. James's elders struck a deal with the town. The church bought a lot in East Bartow and paid for the construction of a grade school, Union Academy, which it then deeded to town officials to operate.[58]

The devil was in the details. State law mandated that white and black schools be separate but equal. But white officials across the state starved black schools of funding. Bartow officials were no exception. Although there were almost as many black as white children in Bartow, the town gave Union Academy only half the appropriation they gave to the white grade schools and far less than they gave to the high school. In its earliest days, the academy could barely afford to keep its doors open: the Sweets' first full year in town, black children attended school an average of twenty-seven days. The situation had improved a bit by the time Ossian started school. The academy was open four months and there was more than one teacher. But the education was still rudimentary. The children learned to read and write, something many of their parents could not do. They were taught basic mathematics. They memorized a bit of history and some snatches of literature. But when the curriculum was completed at the end of eighth grade, the children had nowhere to go but the fields and the phosphate mines.[59]

White Bartow had a high school, of course, a wonderful new school, the pride of the community. Students entered the building through a broad veranda reminiscent of the finest antebellum plantation homes. Double windows six feet high flooded the classrooms with light. A large library filled one corner of the first floor, a laboratory another. An auditorium ran the entire length of the second floor. There was a thirty-foot-long stage at one end, complete with footlights and curtains, where the students could perform and lectures could be held. "With the completion of our new building," the principal told Bartow's newspaper, "we are as well provided with building accommodations as any town in the state. . . ." But Ossian and his siblings weren't allowed in the doors. It would have been illegal for the Sweet children to sit next to white boys and girls, and the good folks of Bartow always did their best to obey the law.[60]

Unless they chose not to. Antiblack terrorism hadn't ended when Reconstruction collapsed. Florida Democrats couldn't very well unleash violence during their election campaigns, then expect it to stop as soon as their victory was secure. Office holders were beholden to the thugs who beat black people into silence; sometimes the thugs and the office holders were one and the same. Violence wasn't just a political tool, though. It was a way of life under Jim Crow. Whites learned to have hair-trigger tempers. If a black person caused the slightest offense—anything at all would do—whites felt free to lash out. It was a right slaveholders once had claimed. Now any white person enjoyed the same privilege.[61]

When Ossian was a boy, the violence escalated to pathological proportions. There were reasons for the upsurge. Decades of sweeping economic change had stripped many southern whites of the security and independence they'd once enjoyed. In the 1890s, a stunning new political insurgency—the Populist movement—sought to rally embattled whites in an assault on the economic order the Democrats had built, even if that meant, as it did in some states, seeking out the support of colored men as well. Desperate to beat back the Populist threat, Democrats tried to redirect whites' anger away from their party and toward their erstwhile colored allies. It was a shockingly bitter campaign, playing on whites' deepest fears of moral decay, economic impotence, and sexual inadequacy. Blacks were poised to attack, speakers proclaimed, to steal honest white men's hard-won gains, to strip them of political power, to rape their women.

"I have three daughters," proclaimed the most fearsome of the demagogues, South Carolina's one-eyed governor, Ben Tillman, "but so help me God, I had rather find either one of them killed by a tiger or a bear and gather up her bones and bury them . . . than to have her crawl to me and tell me the horrid story that she had been robbed of the jewel of her maidenhood by a black fiend." Facing such an imminent threat, no decent white man could desert the party of white supremacy. It was a wholly irrational appeal, politics in its most degraded form, and it worked. As Populism crumbled, darkness descended on the South. Whites waited in fear and anticipation for outrages to begin. Even the rumor of an incident could drive whites into a frenzy of violence, an orgy of retaliation.[62]

Bartow's descent into barbarism began in the phosphate mines. Few white men would take the brutally hard work—breaking stones with pick and ax, sunup to sundown, six or seven days a week—so the mine owners hired large numbers of young, single black men desperate enough to work for a dollar a day. The companies packed the workers into squalid mining camps: rows of wooden shacks, sitting sullenly in the mud. But for all the rank exploitation they faced, the workers also built a world for themselves. It was a rough, often brutal world, built around the "lobbies"—the juke joints, blind tigers, and brothels—that ringed the camps. Come Saturday night, the streets pulsed with life. Miners sat on the porches, drinking and gambling. Prostitutes leaned in the doorways of the shanties, waiting for customers. The music poured out of the bars: "You don't know Polk County lak ah do," the bluesmen sang, "Anybody been dere, tell you de same thing, too."[63]

Whites were fascinated; the perverse alchemy of American race relations was changing the excluded into the alluring. At the same time, though, the allure simply heightened the terror whites felt. "It is said that the life of a decent white man who ventures into these lobbies is in his hands," a reporter warned in 1895. "The awful crimes of Negroes against whites that roused South Carolina . . . are increasing throughout South Florida, and it goes without saying that it is owing to the presence of large numbers of Negroes, lawless, unbridled, and drawing large cash wages, with every means at their disposal . . . for expending the same in riot and debauchery."[64]

White Bartow responded to the threat in the camps by sanctioning the most extreme forms of violence. In January 1899, a black laborer at the Land Pebble mine dared to argue with his foreman, who pulled out a pistol and shot the laborer dead. The foreman turned himself in to the Bartow sheriff. But the sheriff brushed the incident aside. Everyone knew what had happened, he said. The foreman should go back to work. Given such license, mob violence was almost inevitable. A black worker, Sam Smith, killed a white man during an altercation at the Kingsford phosphate mine in June 1900. He tried to flee but a posse tracked him down hiding in a black Masonic lodge not far from the mine. Sheriff's deputies began to bring him back to Bartow, but when a crowd waylaid them, the deputies quickly surrendered the suspect. The whites bound him to a post and riddled him with bullets.[65]

In May 1903, a white man was murdered at one of the blind tigers operating outside the camps. A mob marched on the bar, captured the owner and his two bodyguards, and hung them from the gnarled mulberry tree that curved over the train station nearest the mine, a short walk west of Bartow. Officials actually impaneled a grand jury to investigate the slaughter, but it dismissed the crime as justified. The blind tiger "was an abomination and a curse," the jurors said, "and repeated efforts had been made to have said curse removed, but to no avail." How could the murder of a white man at such a place not be avenged?[66]

East Bartow's respectable black folk tried to insulate themselves from the violence of the mining camps. They agreed with local whites that the camps were a terrible stain on the town. They joined in church campaigns to suppress drinking, gambling, and fornicating. They demanded reform.[67] But their efforts were in vain. Jim Crow didn't discriminate between "good" Negroes and "bad" Negroes; every black person was suspect, every community open to assault. No one was safe.

The violence broke on a glistening morning in May 1901. A white woman, Rena Taggert, the young wife of the town baker, was fishing off the Peace River bridge, less than a mile east of the Sweets' home, when someone dragged her into the thick brush lining the banks. A black man working a short way downriver heard her screams and rushed to town for help. A contingent of whites raced to the scene but Taggert was gone. It took them forty-five minutes to find her body, half buried in the mud of a nearby swamp. She had been raped and her throat had been cut.

In a fury, the whites interrogated the black man who had summoned them. He couldn't have seen much; he was a distance away, and the riverbanks were thick with foliage that time of year. But he said enough to convince his interrogators that Taggert had been murdered by Fred Rochelle, a light-skinned sixteen-year-old Negro, who roomed with his sister in East Bartow while working, like other members of his family, in the phosphate pits. With the interrogation complete, the whites marched en masse to the sister's home but Rochelle was gone, fled into the swampland south of town.

It was an incredibly dangerous moment. More and more whites were gathering as the news spread. And they had no suspect in hand, no one to punish for the outrage. East Bartow's political leaders—including several trustees of St. James AME—desperately tried to distance themselves from the crime. Frantically, they drafted a public declaration condemning Rochelle and proclaiming solidarity with the white mob forming in their streets. "We, the colored citizens of this community," they wrote, "must say that it is a shame and disgrace to our race to allow such brutish conduct [as Taggert's rape and murder] to occur. We should shoulder arms and march to the front and show to our white citizens that we do not uphold such conduct as this. Just to think that a white woman can't go out for air and exercise or fishing without being accosted by a brutish Negro." Colored families like the Sweets, meanwhile, must have been shuttering themselves inside their homes, barring their doors and windows, readying their rifles, waiting for the pogrom to begin.

Rochelle's flight may well have saved East Bartow from destruction. By midafternoon, the mine managers had sent their bloodhounds to town, and most of the able-bodied white men were organizing into posses to begin the manhunt. They spent the night and most of the following day scouring the countryside, vainly trying to pick up Rochelle's trail. Finally, late in the afternoon of the second day, three local black men found him hiding near the phosphate pits a few miles southwest of town. They turned him over to some passing whites, who marched him back to Bartow.

Three hundred townspeople gathered in front of the courthouse to see Rochelle's return. While the sheriff and his deputies stood by, the town's best men interrogated him. He confessed to every detail. The throng decided he should be returned to the scene of the crime. First, they brought him by the victim's house, where her stepfather asked that nothing be done until all of the posses were back from the hunt. Then they marched the victim through the empty streets of East Bartow to the bridge. The mob's leaders delayed until 7:00 P.M. White witnesses said that Rochelle showed no emotion during the ordeal, but the wait must have been agonizing, a sixteen-year-old standing before his executioners, the minutes ticking away, the fear rising and rising. Finally, Bartow's leading citizens placed the young man on a hogshead of flammable material and chained him to a tree. They stacked bone-dry wood around the base, poured gasoline on the pile, and invited the victim's husband to apply the flame. He touched a match to the kindling a few minutes after 8:00. The hogshead ignited into a fierce bonfire. Eight minutes later, Rochelle was dead, and the members of the mob began drifting back to their homes. "By midnight," the newspaper reported, "the town was as peaceful as ever."[68]

There would be other mobs. On Christmas Eve 1903, a group of whites tried to lynch a black man imprisoned in the Bartow jail, but the sheriff held them off. Two black prisoners were lynched in Bartow in 1906. And mob violence raced through Polk County in 1909. Two blacks were immolated in February when a suspicious fire burned down the jail in a nearby phosphate town. A few weeks later, whites in the town of Lakeland, just north of Bartow, dragged Jack Wade from police custody, hung him from a tree, and riddled his writhing body with bullets. In April, a Bartow mob lynched Charles Scarborough in a chilling reprise of the rape frenzy eight years earlier.[69]

As appalling as those events were, though, Ossian would always remember Fred Rochelle's death as the most terrifying moment of his young life. As an adult, he'd tell people that he had witnessed the entire scene, that he'd hidden in the bushes near the bridge and watched the burning. He'd recount it with frightening specificity: the smell of the kerosene, Rochelle's screams as he was engulfed in flames, the crowd's picking off pieces of charred flesh to take home as souvenirs. Maybe, just maybe, he did see it all. The bridge was a short walk from his home. He could have been outside—coming back from his father's fields—when the mob drove Rochelle through East Bartow. But he was only five years old in the summer of 1901. And it seems unlikely that Dora would have let him outside anytime that day. More likely, the horrific events imprinted themselves so deeply on Ossian's mind that he convinced himself that he had been there. Either way, the effect was the same. The image of the conflagration—the heart-pounding fear of it—had been seared into his memory.[70]

Dora and Henry already knew. Maybe they talked of it in the stillness of the night, after the children were asleep. Maybe they didn't talk about it at all. But they knew. Their families had struggled for two generations to get this far, to own land, to have a home no one could take from them. But it wasn't enough, not in this place, not at this time. They put off a decision as long as they could. But in the summer of 1909, they were forced to act. It was probably the coincidence of events. Ossian finished eighth grade that spring, just about the time the respectable people of Bartow left Charles Scarborough's broken body dangling from a rope.[71] How could Dora and Henry let their son stay with them? He'd have no hope of an education, no opportunity to make his way in the world, no chance of fulfilling the dreams their family had nurtured since they'd first tasted freedom almost forty years ago. And there was the possibility—almost too horrible to contemplate—that somehow he'd be caught in the terror that so often raced through their streets. It wasn't going to be easy. They'd stressed so much the ironclad bonds of family. Ossian had become a help in the fields, vitally important to a farm family with so many young children. And he was only thirteen, still a boy. But there was nothing else to do. They would have to send him away, to a place where he could pursue his education, to a place where he'd be safe.

The night before he was to depart, Ossian walked over to the parsonage of St. James AME. He was scared to leave Bartow, he said, without God's blessing. "So on the day of his leave," wrote his minister, Ossian "gave his heart to the Lord." Then he boarded the northbound train—and was gone.[72]

THREE

MIGRATION

Xenia was a placid little town, like hundreds of others scattered across the fertile farmland that rolled northward from the Ohio River. A string of shop fronts lined Main and Detroit streets, forming a town square around the county courthouse, its limestone façade shining in the sun. Xenia had touches of urban life—a few small factories, a handful of saloons, dark and mysterious, and a smattering of foreign-born workmen to fill them both—but the town moved with the rhythms of the countryside, gray winters giving way to early springs, blistering summers to muted autumns.[1] As he stepped down from the train at Xenia depot in the first week of September 1909, Ossian Sweet might have found it comforting to see a town that was, surprisingly, so much like the one he'd left behind. But he hadn't traveled a thousand miles in search of what was familiar. He had come to Xenia to take his place in a new world free of Jim Crow's oppression.

Ossian had been given strict orders about what to do. He was to arrive in daylight, not in darkness, but even if the weather were clear, he was not to leave the station on his own. Instead, he was to find the telephone exchange and ring the college office to request "a conveyance." Dad Harris, the venerable maintenance man, would bring his wagon around. Ossian and any other students could put their belongings—clothes, bedding, and Bibles—into the back and scramble aboard for the three-mile ride through the east side, where Xenia's Negroes lived. Out of town, they traveled down curving country roads past fields and farmhouses to a comfortable cluster of buildings set into a grove of maples and sycamores, the splendidly isolated campus of Wilberforce University, the first college in America dedicated to providing Negroes with the blessings of higher education. Here, Ossian would begin the slow, hard, thoroughly American process of transforming himself.[2]

◆

Dora and Henry Sweet were hardly the only southern blacks to send their son north in the bitter days of the new century. When politicians and businessmen extended rail lines into the smallest of southern hamlets in the years after Reconstruction, they had wanted simply to connect the region's fields and forests to the North's great factories. But the process also provided Negroes with a thousand escape routes. It was never easy to leave, to slip free of piles of debts, to shutter homes and abandon lands, to say good-bye to family and friends. But a hundred thousand colored people did just that between 1900 and 1915, many of them, like Ossian, very young and very scared.[3]

They were drawn by the promise of equal treatment. In the first few years after the Civil War, when the Republicans' commitment to racial change was still strong, most eastern and midwestern states had passed sweeping civil rights laws that prohibited segregation of public places and opened ballot boxes to colored men. What's more, white northerners didn't expect Negroes to kowtow the way they were forced to do in even the most enlightened portions of the South. "Ain't no Mistrus' an' Marster's up dere, say yes an' no up dere," an Alabama woman explained. "No gwin in de back door. White fo'ks an' 'Niggers' go in an' out de same door up dere."[4]

The dreams of the vast majority of colored migrants were also inextricably tied to hopes for steady work and reasonable pay. Even before the Civil War, the North had more than its share of factories and mills. In the late nineteenth century, the region had become the workshop of the world. From Minnesota's windswept Mesabi Iron Range to the backstreet shops of Baltimore, nine million working people transformed the nation's natural abundance into more goods than any other nation on earth. So insatiable was industrialists' demand for labor that it couldn't be met by the native-born whites who had once been the backbone of the American working class. To fill the gap, employers hired huge numbers of people who had never before set foot in a mine or factory. Most were immigrants, millions of whom were arriving each year. But employers weren't quite as open to colored men and women. A few factory owners placed Negroes in the full range of jobs they had to offer, but the son of small-town farmers like the Sweets could expect to fill one of the North's less desirable positions, feeding the blast furnaces of a Pittsburgh steel mill, hauling bricks at a Cleveland construction site, or cleaning offal from the killing floor of a Chicago stockyard.[5]

For Henry and Dora, that wasn't enough. They wanted their children to become men and women of distinction, models of the AME creed. And their oldest boy would show the way. To begin, he would need an advanced education, a college degree, which was an utterly audacious goal. Most Americans of modest means, white or colored, never attended high school, much less university. Southern blacks bore the double burden of poverty and unequal southern school systems; in 1900, half of the Negroes in Florida couldn't read or write. Even those who could stood little chance of further academic achievement. Of the ten million Negroes in America, fewer than two thousand were enrolled in college courses.[6]

Once the Sweets had set their sights on college for Ossian, Wilberforce was the obvious choice. There were better black schools—Atlanta University, Nashville's Fisk University, Lincoln University outside Philadelphia, Howard University, overlooking Washington, D.C.—where doctors, lawyers, teachers, and politicians sent their children. Graduates of those schools thought of Wilberforce as a backwater, provincial and pedestrian, and many of its students as earnest but utterly unsophisticated, well-meaning but not necessarily well educated. One of the century's great intellectuals and most important civil rights activists, W. E. B. Du Bois, spent a painfully long academic year teaching Greek, Latin, German, and history at the college in 1896 and 1897 before moving on to more prestigious postings. The first black man to receive a Ph.D. from Harvard, Du Bois cringed at the pupils who filled his Wilberforce courses. "A struggle with Antigone's struggles by wise and spectacled youths," he wrote acidly in his journal after one class, "all fading away into a dull headache and the bell for noon chapel."[7]

But the Sweets had no inkling of the carefully calibrated hierarchy of the academy. To them, Wilberforce offered extraordinary advantages. It was a northern school, far removed from the terrors of black Bartow. Those who weren't well prepared for the college's demands, such as thirteen-year-old Ossian, were enrolled in a four-year preparatory course before moving on to the university, where they would be given the skills necessary for a career in business or one of the professions. There was another draw as well: owned and operated by the AME, Wilberforce fostered the values that Dora and Henry prized. Such treasures didn't come cheaply; tuition ran $118 a year, far more than the Sweets could possibly pay. But Wilberforce had scholarships set aside for deserving students from the AME's Florida Conference. So at absolutely no cost, Ossian could receive a rigorous education at a college firmly rooted in his family's tradition. It seemed a godsend.[8]

It was a godsend built on desecrated ground. Tucked into the southwest corner of Ohio, a mere sixty miles from slave-owning Kentucky, the campus was originally the site of a grand resort hotel, Tawawa Springs, built for the pleasure of southern planters and the female slaves they claimed as their mistresses. When the resort went bankrupt in the 1830s, a few of the planters remade the property as a school for their mulatto children. But in the 1840s and 1850s, as abolitionism burned across Ohio, the slave masters' largesse came to be seen more and more as an affront to the state's good people. In the mid-1850s, Ohio's white Methodists bought Tawawa Springs, renamed it after the great British abolitionist Bishop William Wilberforce, and transformed it into a college for free blacks. Whites controlled Wilberforce until 1863, when they sold the school to the AME for the princely sum of $10,000. Half a decade earlier, a university run by and for Negroes would have been inconceivable. But in the year of the Emancipation Proclamation, everything seemed possible.[9]

In the sixty years before Ossian's arrival, Wilberforce's great expectations frayed. Chronic underfunding had taken its toll on the campus. There was a fine new library, a gift from Andrew Carnegie, but the older buildings—Shorter Hall, where the male students lived and classes were held; Arnett Hall, the women's dormitory; the small homes that housed faculty members—were starting to decay. Their shutters were going "a little awry," according to a doyen of white Xenia, "steps a little broken, foundations yellow with rain-splattered clay." The university maintained its own electric power plant but it only worked intermittently; most of the time, students worked by the flickering light of gas lamps. The equipment in the laboratories was woefully inadequate. There was simply no money for improvements. Wilberforce was $32,000 in debt in the autumn of 1909, and many of the university's accounts—including the scholarship fund Ossian was counting on to pay his way—were empty.[10]

When Ossian was informed that there would be no scholarship, he must have thought about putting his bags back on the wagon and catching the first train back to Bartow. He was a thirteen-year-old very far from home, and the lack of money would have given him the perfect excuse to head back to his family. But something kept Ossian from leaving. Maybe he didn't want to disappoint his parents. Maybe he felt an obligation to his younger brothers and sisters who were expected to follow his example. Maybe he could feel his own ambitions tugging, telling him that if he left Wilberforce he'd spend his life working his father's fields or breaking his body in the phosphate pits. Whatever his reasons, Ossian decided to stay. To help cover expenses, he took work stoking the college's furnaces and shoveling snow—hard, even humiliating, jobs on a campus where the distinction between scholar and tradesman was of great importance.[11] But Ossian accepted the work because he understood that a young Negro of humble birth would never have a better opportunity than that offered by this small, slightly run-down university. For what Wilberforce lacked in amenities, it more than provided in spirit.

◆

It was a spirit that faith bestowed, not a religious faith, though that was strong enough on Wilberforce's sylvan campus, but a faith in the mission of higher education. Du Bois had said it best: the Negro race, he famously argued in 1903, would move forward only on the strength of its "exceptional" men and women, the handful of scholars and scientists, professionals and poets who he claimed constituted the "Talented Tenth." The black colleges had to be the tenth's training grounds, he said, and to play that role, the schools had to be uncompromising in the education they offered, every bit as demanding as outstanding white colleges.[12]

Had Du Bois said the same thing during the heady days of Reconstruction, a healthy portion of northern whites would have agreed. The North had put great stock in black education in the ten years after Appomattox. Young Yankees had trooped south to help teach freedmen to read and cipher, and white congregations had spent precious sums to create Negro colleges such as Fisk and Howard. Gradually, though, the optimism of those days had faded. Northern whites had a hard time sustaining interest in the fate of freedmen with their own world shaken by economic depression, political corruption, and violent class conflict, all bitter by-products of the North's industrialization. In the 1870s and 1880s, the schoolteachers went home, donations dried up, and Negroes were left to the mercy of southern whites who insisted that colored people were incapable of anything but the most rudimentary learning.[13]

More cruelly still, many northern whites came to agree with the southerners. It wasn't as if northerners had suddenly discovered black inferiority: even the most ardent abolitionists had generally assumed themselves superior to the slaves they sought to free. But as memories of the Civil War grew dim and the humanitarian impulse of the abolitionist generation crumbled under the cudgel of Social Darwinism, white racial thinking ossified. The peoples of the world were set in a rigid hierarchy of development, academics explained, with Anglo-Saxons at its pinnacle, immigrant masses huddled in the middle range, and Negroes at bottom. Ministers, authors, judges, and politicians echoed the argument. "A perfectly stupid race can never rise to a very high plane," concluded Republican Theodore Roosevelt. "The Negro, for instance, has been kept down as much by lack of intellectual development as by anything else."[14]

A few powerful blacks, most notably Alabama's Booker T. Washington, seemed to endorse whites' low opinion of the Negro's potential. A consummate politician, Washington held up his manual training school, Tuskegee Institute, as a model for black education as Du Bois and his Talented Tenth fussed and fumed. But white philanthropists rewarded Washington, the aptly nicknamed Wizard, for his efforts, pouring millions of dollars into Tuskegee so that his students could learn skills deemed appropriate for Negroes, such as shoemaking and carpentry, in the most up-to-date workshops. The leaders of Wilberforce also understood the power of pandering to white prejudices. During one of its periodic fiscal crises, the college convinced the state of Ohio to provide the university with an annual subsidy in exchange for which Wilberforce established its own manual training school, modeled on Tuskegee. By Ossian's first year, the training school had more instructors than the college had faculty members. But the industrial arts students were still considered second-class citizens on campus. They performed the necessary labor—repairing buildings, laying sidewalks, fixing leaky pipes—while the college's men and women set the tone.[15] Wilberforce's new president, William Sanders Scarborough, was determined that it would always remain so.

Scarborough wasn't simply a devotee of the Talented Tenth ideal; he was its exemplar. Born a slave in 1850s Georgia, he was apprenticed to a shoemaker when freedom came. But in the finest AME tradition, Scarborough didn't want to settle for a trade when he could aim for the professions. After two years at recently opened Atlanta University, in the late 1860s, he moved on to Ohio's Oberlin College, a white institution as liberal in its politics as it was demanding in its academics. "I forgot I was a colored boy in the lack of prejudice and genial atmosphere that surrounded me," he remembered in later years, "and enjoyed such life and amusements with others as they presented themselves to me." He also enjoyed a sterling education, eventually earning both his bachelor's and master's degrees in the classics—training sufficient to launch him on a distinguished academic career. The author of a widely used textbook and a well-respected translation of Aristophanes, Scarborough was only the third black man elected to the American Philological Association and one of the finest scholars ever to serve on Wilberforce's faculty.[16]

Few Wilberforce students were going to match Scarborough's achievements, but the college would do everything in its power to give them the opportunity. Like its brother schools, Wilberforce provided its students with a traditional education, rooted in the liberal arts. Ossian spent his first year in the prep school studying Latin, history, mathematics, English, music, and drawing, a daunting program for a youngster from a one-room schoolhouse, made even harder by the demands that his campus jobs must have placed on him. Over the next two years, Ossian added a second language, most likely French, and an introductory science course. And in his final year as a prep student, he was exposed to philosophy and the social sciences. By then, Ossian was beginning to define his interests. When he started the college program in the autumn of 1913, he elected to pursue a degree in science. That meant four more years of chemistry, biology, Latin, and French, three more years of math, and a smattering of additional courses in philosophy, English, and social science. It wasn't a Harvard or Fisk education, to be sure. But it was more than enough to put Ossian into that precious tenth of the race.[17]

For all their emphasis on academics, however, President Scarborough and his fellow administrators didn't believe that higher education was confined to the classroom. The Talented Tenth would also lead the race using the strength of their characters. Wilberforce relied on the AME religious tradition to enforce a moral discipline bordering on monasticism. Ossian and his fellow students were required to attend a scripture service each morning at 8:10, a prayer meeting every

Monday evening, and two services on Sunday, morning and night. Students could have "association with the opposite sex" only when the president granted them written permission; men and women weren't even allowed to walk the same campus paths, lest they fraternize while taking their exercise. The use of profanity was prohibited, and anyone caught indulging in alcohol or tobacco was to be expelled. The only break in the regime came when the campus was swept up in one of its week-long revivals, moments of religious ecstasy that appalled more secular members of the Talented Tenth. During his brief tenure at Wilberforce, Du Bois felt himself driven to "mental imbecility" by the "wild screams, cries, groans and shouts" that shattered the sacred solitude of his rooms.[18]

While the college relied on the spirit of God to shape moral values, it counted on campus life to inculcate a sense of duty and responsibility. Wilberforce maintained the range of activities—the glee clubs, debating societies, and literary groups—typical of colleges across the nation. Students were free to pledge fraternities and sororities, where they could build the bonds of friendship they would need as they ventured into the business world. But for the young men, there was no more important campus institution than the cadet corps. In the 1880s, in one of the last gasps of Reconstruction-era policy making, the War Department had authorized Wilberforce to establish a military training program, the only black school in the country so honored. The United States Army assigned an exemplary string of officers to campus to direct the program. A few years before Ossian arrived, the corps was commanded by Lieutenant Charles Young, the third black to graduate from West Point and a military man of consummate skill and bravery. During Ossian's tenure, the post was held by Captain Benjamin Davis, who in time would become the nation's first black general. The commanders, in turn, built a program of exacting standards. Each morning at 7:25, Ossian joined his fellow cadets of Company A on the practice field for instruction in military drill, first aid, minor tactics, and small-arms fire. Cadets were encouraged to stay in uniform throughout the day, a corps of confident young black men sitting in Wilberforce's classrooms, dressed in the colors of their country.[19]

◆

Wilberforce rounded out its students' education with a heavy dose of racial politics. President Scarborough had never abandoned the radical Republicanism of the postwar years; any form of segregation was an insult to the race, he insisted, and a desecration of American principles. When white Ohioans began tearing down their own discriminatory practices after the war, Scarborough pushed them to go further. In the 1880s, he spearheaded a drive to outlaw the segregation of schools and to repeal state laws prohibiting intermarriage. And as Jim Crow hardened in the South, he fought to isolate the system within Dixie's benighted states. In one furious campaign, he prodded the state legislature to require railroads to remove "whites only" signs from their cars the moment they crossed into Ohio so that colored riders would know that they had passed out of the darkness and into the light.[20]

By the time Ossian arrived at Wilberforce, though, the light was starting to fade. It was galling enough to hear northern academics and politicians declare their belief in the innate inferiority of the colored race and to see white donations pouring into schools that reinforced Negroes' subordination. But it was absolutely appalling to see southern-style racism slither into everyday life above the Mason-Dixon Line. This hatred was spread in part through the power of ideas. While scientists and philosophers published learned studies measuring the chasm between Anglo-Saxons and Africans, an increasing number of ordinary northerners endorsed the racial slanders southern demagogues had perfected. Where whites had once talked bravely of racial justice, they now whispered of Negro workers stealing white men's jobs and colored rapists ravaging white women. And they cheered the demagogues themselves, who traveled the North lecturing on the True South's struggles to contain the black beast.[21]

Demographics turned harsh words into brutal actions. It had been easy enough for northerners to declare fealty to racial equality when more than 90 percent of the nation's colored population lived in the South. As the black migration accelerated, though, northern interest in segregation grew stronger. Many of those white workers lucky enough to belong to unions refused to extend solidarity to Negro workingmen, while a growing number of employers refused to hire colored people for anything but the most menial of jobs, unless they needed to break a strike, at which point Negro labor would do just fine. White homeowners were beginning to object to having colored families live nearby. And more and more white customers were demanding that blacks be excluded from restaurants, hotels, theaters, and other public venues. Neighborhoods and businesses weren't the only places where Negroes were increasingly unwelcome: at Scarborough's beloved Oberlin, there was talk of black and white students taking their Bible studies in separate classes. None of this segregation had the sanction of law—state civil rights statutes remained on the books—and it wasn't consistently applied: it was a patchwork of practices, differing from place to place and even street to street. But for colored people, the trend was frighteningly familiar.

Racism's rising tide inevitably reached Wilberforce. Half a century before, Xenia's whites had taken pride in the colored college just outside of town. Now they treated the campus community with derision, refusing to extend to the university any of the town's facilities or services, not even fire protection. They twittered at the parents who arrived in town each graduation day, amused at the very thought that colored families would try to dress well and carry themselves with elegance. No one came in for more disdain, though, than President Scarborough's wife of twenty-five years. Sarah Scarborough was a woman of high breeding and distinction. But on the rare occasions when she ventured into Xenia, she was shunned by the town's best people, not because she was black—they could have withstood that—but because she was white.

As painful as they were, insults and indignities were easier to endure than the most fearsome of southern imports, the race riot. Since before the Civil War, blacks and whites had shared the streets of Springfield, Ohio, a grim-faced factory town fifteen miles north of Wilberforce. Then, in 1886, the city's largest employers had used black strikebreakers to destroy Springfield's powerful all-white iron molders union, an action white workers never forgot and never forgave. One cold night in March 1904, tensions exploded: the violence began when a colored man, recently arrived from Kentucky, killed a white policeman down at the Levee, a dingy row of saloons and brothels hard along the railroad tracks. Enraged whites dragged the murderer from his cell and lynched him, then turned on the Levee itself, burning it to the ground. In the process, they destroyed the homes of the town's poorest Negroes as well. Colored people had just rebuilt when the mob struck again. Several minor confrontations in February 1906 triggered two days of terror, as whites rampaged through Springfield's colored quarter, beating those who dared to be on the streets and burning out those who hid indoors. "The North has reached the point where it is ready to echo almost anything the South chooses to assert," Scarborough raged in the aftermath of the second pogrom. "It thinks the early education of the Negro a mistake, the ballot a blunder, the Negro a fiend. . . . It has become hypnotized by the assiduous efforts of . . . men who have succeeded in muzzling the press, muzzling the pulpit, muzzling the platform—muzzling the mouths of nearly all those who in the past saw any good in the Negro people."[22]

Scarborough understood that outrage wasn't sufficient; if black America were to retain the rights it had struggled so mightily to attain, the Talented Tenth had to organize against the racist juggernaut. He became a charter member of the Du Bois–led Niagara Movement, founded in 1905 to counter the appeasement of the Washingtonians and to mount a vigorous defense of racial equality. The movement rang with the same militancy that the AME ministers had spread through Leon County back when Ossian's grandfather was a young man. "We claim for ourselves every single right of freeborn Americans, political, civil, and social," Du Bois proclaimed during the movement's second conclave, held at the abolitionist Gethsemane of Harpers Ferry, Virginia, "and until we get those rights we will never cease to protest and to assail the ears of America." Brave words, but they were hard to pair with vigorous action. Crippled by lack of funds and torn by infighting, the Niagara Movement limped along for several years, until another night of bloodshed galvanized a new round of activism.[23]

◆

The paroxysm of violence that convulsed Springfield, Illinois, on August 14, 1908, was induced by the familiar toxic blend of economic conflict and racial hatred. That most explosive of events, a rumor of rape, led the white citizens of Illinois' capital on a rampage against their black neighbors. National Guardsmen restored order the following dawn, but by then six Negroes had been shot dead, two more had been lynched, and two thousand driven from town. Northerners had come to expect such atrocities in the South. But there was something truly shocking about the violence in Illinois. Springfield wasn't just another place on the map, after all. It was the home and final resting place of Abraham Lincoln.[24]

The symbolism of the Springfield pogrom was so stark that progressive whites couldn't help but take notice. The southern race war was moving north, the indefatigable reformer William English Walling wrote in New York's influential newspaper, the *Independent*, and it cannot be stopped until "a powerful body of citizens" revived "the spirit of the abolitionists." Du Bois, Scarborough, and their colleagues in the Niagara Movement had been saying precisely the same thing for several years. But whites such as Walling brought resources and connections that the Talented Tenth couldn't match. Throughout the balance of 1908, a gradually expanding group of New York liberals began discussing ways of fulfilling Walling's charge. In the early months of 1909, they announced plans for a new organization of "fair-minded whites and intelligent blacks" who together would fight for the rights of Negroes across the land.[25]

If Scarborough was put off by the white progressives' sudden discovery of racial hatred, he didn't show it. When he received his invitation to attend the inaugural meeting of the new civil rights organization, to be held in Manhattan on the last day of May 1909, only a few months prior to Ossian Sweet's arrival on the Wilberforce campus, he was pleased to accept. The overwhelming majority of attendees were white, men and women of sure social standing and enormous goodwill, drawn to the black cause for a host of deeply personal reasons. They were the progeny of the abolitionist generation, led by Oswald Garrison Villard, millionaire grandson of the great William Lloyd Garrison, who saw in the new racial terrors the destruction of his ancestor's lifework. Walling brought along a number of his fellow reformers, many of them, like the young social worker Mary White Ovington, drawn from the ghetto settlement houses that had become the seedbeds of social justice in industrial America. They were joined by a solid contingent of Jewish liberals, who understood the profound dangers of injecting racial supremacy into the body politic. For their part, the black participants were drawn heavily from the Niagara Movement. Du Bois was in attendance, of course, as were William Monroe Trotter, the fiery Boston publisher; antilynching crusader Ida B. Wells; esteemed Mary Church Terrell; and, sitting in silent fury, Scarborough, the slave-born philologist. It would take another few months to settle on a permanent name for the new organization. But in the course of one long day, the National Association for the Advancement of Colored People was born.[26]

Ossian entered Wilberforce three months after the NAACP's founding meeting. Over the next eight years, he would be repeatedly exposed to the association's principles of uncompromising opposition to segregation, North and South, and unremitting struggle to secure equality before the law. He sat in his assigned seat in the chapel as a steady stream of speakers—academics, ministers, and politicians—lectured on the state of race relations. On special occasions, he shared the campus with some of Scarborough's best-known associates in the fight for justice: Terrell's National Association of Colored Women came to campus for its annual meeting in the spring of 1914, and that summer, Du Bois, by then editor of the NAACP's monthly magazine, the *Crisis*, spent several weeks at the college teaching economics. Ossian attended the monthly "rhetoricals," where students debated the issues of the day. And within the cozy confines of the Carnegie Library, he could find the best of Talented Tenth thought. Du Bois's brilliant book *The Souls of Black Folk* sat on the shelves, as did his newly published biography of John Brown, the abolitionist who sought justice through the barrel of a gun.[27]

•

Ossian couldn't help but be affected by it all. He was little more than a child when he first stepped off the train at the Xenia depot. He had never met a black man or woman as accomplished as the professors who taught his classes or the soldiers who directed him in drills. And no one back in Bartow dared to speak so forcefully, so publicly, of justice and rights as did President Scarborough and his distinguished friends. It must have been very exciting to move into this new world.

Ossian didn't find it easy to adjust. The work he performed on campus put him in the margins between the prized college students and the second-rank industrial arts students; one year, in fact, university officials inadvertently listed him as enrolled in the shoe department, a simple clerical error, no doubt, but also a stinging reminder that Ossian wasn't a substantial figure on campus. He worked hard at his studies, but others were better prepared and more capable. He joined a few clubs, pledged a fraternity, Kappa Alpha Psi, and did his duty as a member of the cadet corps. But he wasn't the sort of person who attracted his fellow students' attention or won their admiration. Others were elected president of their clubs or named company commanders; Ossian remained one of the crowd, a reliable member of the fraternity, a dependable private in the cadet corps, but never a star.[28]

Only once did he make his mark, and it wasn't a proud moment. One spring day in 1914, Ossian was spotted in Xenia with two of his fellow cadets from Company A. None of the three had been given permission to go to town, a serious enough infraction. Worse, one of Ossian's companions was drunk. The faculty disciplinary committee charged all three with having gone to Xenia "to partake of the whiskey," an offense punishable by expulsion. Ossian was devastated. "I will admit I was in bad company," he wrote the committee in desperation. "I will admit that I left the campus without . . . permission. And again I will admit that I did not go to town for the purpose of buying intox- icating drinks and I firmly say, I am a 'total abstainer.' After having been part of this institution for three years and having to face this worthy body under no circumstances. And then to be brought to you for such an offense is indeed very grievous unto me, as I am wholly in- nocent as far as the intoxicants are concerned. I humbly beg that you reconsider my case."[29]

Ossian's pleading worked: although one of his friends was expelled, the faculty committee let him off with a public reprimand. But the in- cident and Ossian's response reveal that, despite his five years on cam- pus, he remained an insecure young man, determined to please his superiors, to say just the right thing, even if it meant turning on his friends.[30]

Money concerns added to his insecurity. Rather than head back to Bartow when the 1909–10 school year ended, Ossian decided to spend the summer working in the North. His younger brothers Otis and Henry were old enough to help their parents bring in the crops, while he could use three months' work to add to his meager savings. There were plenty of places for Ossian to go. It was only a dozen miles from Wilberforce to Dayton, which was filled with factories, and thirty miles to bustling Cincinnati. But Henry and Dora's son had too sharp an eye for money to settle for the sort of job he could find in a second-tier city. Instead, he chose to spend his summer in big, booming Detroit, where bosses were begging for workers. Three months' work there could earn Ossian more than he'd make almost anywhere else.[31]

It didn't work out quite that well. Detroit was the first big city Ossian had ever lived in, and he must have enjoyed the excitement of walking in the shadows of towering downtown buildings and sharing side- walks with polished businessmen. But he had a lot to learn about mak- ing a living in the big city. A man working in one of Detroit's brand-new auto factories might be paid as much as $2.50 a day; that much was true. But those jobs weren't going to fourteen-year-old colored boys. Though practices differed from plant to plant, the best positions gen- erally went to native-born whites: craftsmen, farm boys, and former miners who knew how to tinker with machines and didn't need a trans- lator to follow the boss's orders. For the huge middle range of jobs that didn't require any special skill—increasingly Detroit's specialty—most of the big employers hired the foreign-born. For a few years, the Board of Commerce went so far as to pay a hiring agent to work the great hall of Ellis Island, recruiting workers for Detroit's factories before they even cleared customs. Once in a while, a Negro managed to slip his way in alongside a foreigner—Henry Ford in particular liked to hire a colored man now and again—and there were a small number of black professionals and businessmen. But most members of the city's small colored community ended up doing service work: unloading the Great Lake steamers that drew up to the Detroit docks, waiting tables, shining shoes, doing white folks' laundry, or minding their children.[32]

Ossian couldn't do any better. He spent his first two summers in the city, 1910 and 1911, washing dishes and selling sodas to the throngs of pleasure seekers who crowded onto Bob-Lo Island, a whirligig of amusements and sideshows a few miles downriver from Detroit. His wages began at a dollar a day, not much more than he would have earned working the fields for a white farmer back home, then gradually rose to dollar and a half. In the summer of 1912, he took a job as a bellhop at the Hotel Norton, a small downtown establishment catering to out-of-town salesmen and other small-time operators; the next year, he moved on to the Fairfax Hotel a few blocks away. Finally, in 1914, he began a four-summer run as a waiter, working on the excursion boats that ran between Detroit and Cleveland.

Each job was an improvement, with better working conditions and slightly higher wages and tips. Though many of his coworkers were older, stretching meager wages to keep their families fed, Ossian also found friends much like himself, driven young men such as Caribbean-born Vollington Bristol, head bellhop at the Fairfax Hotel, who had come north filled with dreams of doing great things. Northern cities had their edges, Bristol told Ossian the summer they worked together. But they were still the only places in America for colored men who wanted to better themselves. Down south whites feared blacks with ambition, and a Negro who tried to get ahead had to spend most of his time watching his back. In a city like Detroit, Bristol insisted, white folks respected ambition, and a Negro who worked hard, saved his money, and had a head for business was going to be rewarded. Bristol already had his plans plotted out; one day, he was going to open his own funeral parlor, as respectable and profitable an undertaking as anyone could imagine. Ossian could do just as well if he put his mind to it. This was the sort of talk Ossian took to, but it didn't quite square with his day-to-day experiences. Lugging someone's bags down a hotel corridor or carting away the remains of a roast beef dinner, it was hard to think of oneself as a member of the Talented Tenth.[33]

More than anything else, it was the financial struggle that shaped Ossian. A decade later, that was what he remembered of his college days: not the classes he took, not the friendships he made or the speakers he heard, not the halcyon days he spent walking on the leaf-strewn campus, but his constant battle to make ends meet. There was an edge of bitterness, an unspoken resentment, in his memories. But deprivation also gave shape to his ambitions.[34]

From childhood, he'd been taught the virtues of entrepreneurship and the pleasures it could buy: he'd seen how his father had squeezed every penny he could out of his land and how his mother had taken such pride setting the Sunday table with fine china of the sort East Bartow's Negroes weren't supposed to have. But, at some point in his Wilberforce years, Ossian decided that he wanted more than a solid living and a few creature comforts. He made it his goal, he told a reporter years later, "to rise in his profession and to amass a substantial fortune."[35] A Du Bois or a Scarborough might look on those ambitions as unworthy of the Negro elite, since they were driven by the pursuit of Mammon rather than the advancement of the race. But to a struggling student shoveling snow off the walkways so that his classmates wouldn't ruin their boots, such goals were noble enough.

By the time he entered the college program, Ossian had selected his path to success: he had decided to become a doctor. Of all the professions open to him, he couldn't have made a more extraordinary choice. Not so long before, it had been perfectly reasonable for someone of Ossian's social standing to consider a career in medicine: there were any number of barely trained practitioners prescribing nostrums from inconspicuous offices and backroom clinics. But times had changed. Stricter standards and tighter regulation had driven marginal doctors out of business; by the 1910s, medicine had become the preserve of the highly educated and the well-to-do. The more exclusive the profession became, the more status it accrued. Americans might still joke about quacks and con artists, but in the end no one commanded more respect than a doctor. Therein lay its attraction for Ossian. A life in medicine would give Ossian the status he dreamed of—and the money he craved: a doctor could easily take home fifteen hundred dollars a year, an almost unimaginable amount to a young man whose father probably earned a fifth of that figure. If Ossian should rise in the profession, as he intended to do, his income could go even higher: the director of

Washington's foremost black hospital earned a staggering four thousand dollars a year. But it wasn't the money alone that mattered. A high income would give him the outward signs of success: the dapper clothes he never had the chance to wear, the fashionable home so different from the farmhouse his father had built. But to be called doctor—Doctor Ossian H. Sweet—that would be the greatest mark of respect he could imagine.[36]

It was also wildly unrealistic. There were fewer than twenty-five hundred Negro doctors in the United States, and the profession's new standards threatened to cut the number further. Few black men had the luxury of devoting four years of their lives to the classes and clinical work the profession now required. To make matters worse, most of the nation's medical schools had stopped admitting colored candidates at all, one more sign of the racism spreading through the North, and the handful that would consider allowing a Negro within their halls enrolled one or two such students a year. Black colleges didn't fill the void. There were only two black medical schools in operation—one at Howard University in Washington, D.C., the other at Meharry Medical College in Nashville—and neither admitted more than forty or fifty new students at any one time. Most of the available slots went to the best graduates of Lincoln, Howard, or Fisk, not to average students from schools like Wilberforce.[37]

Just as Ossian was completing his undergraduate education, though, world events shook black America to its core. For two and a half years, the United States had watched in mounting horror as the European powers slaughtered their peoples in what was coming to be known as the Great War. Finally, in the winter and spring of 1917, Woodrow Wilson could stand no more. On April 2, 1917—just two months before Ossian's graduation—the president asked Congress for a declaration of war against Germany. The United States fought not for territorial gain, Wilson said in his achingly eloquent address to the nation, but "for democracy, for the right of those who submit to authority to have a voice in their own Governments, . . . for a universal dominion of rights by . . . a concert of free peoples."[38]

For the Talented Tenth, it was a siren call. The NAACP's white president, Joel Spingarn, scion of a wealthy Jewish family and a lauded literary scholar at Columbia University, secured the army's permission to establish a training camp for black officers in faraway Des Moines, Iowa. In the pages of the NAACP's magazine, the *Crisis*, W. E. B. Du Bois pleaded for volunteers. The leaders of the race would fight for democratic principles abroad, he argued. And by their blood sacrifice, they would force white America to recognize the rights of black people at home.[39]

War fever raced across Wilberforce. There was talk that the former commander of cadets, now Lieutenant Colonel Charles Young, living just outside the campus, would be given command of black troops and perhaps even be elevated to general. The current corps commander, Ben Davis, had already been called to active duty. His cadets rushed to join him. In the spring of 1917, thirty of the ninety-three students in the college passed the qualifying exam and headed to Des Moines to join the fight for democracy. Ossian wasn't among them. He had dutifully taken the army's test, but his eyesight was so poor that he was placed in Class 5, disqualified for service.[40]

It was a very lucky break. As the army drained away college men, the competition for the few slots in medical schools became much less keen. Sometime that spring, Ossian received word that he had been accepted into Howard University's College of Medicine. It must have been a triumphant moment, a vindication of his parents' faith and his effort, as well as a huge stride toward the fulfillment of his ambitions. Another summer waiting tables in Detroit, then, come September, as many of his classmates were heading into the charnel house of Europe, Ossian would move on to the nation's capital, itself awash in war.

◆

The lights of official Washington burned late every night in September 1917. Not since the Civil War had the United States undertaken such a thoroughgoing mobilization. There was a massive army to raise, train, and ship to the trenches of France: the military was expecting some four million young men to serve, the vast majority of them draftees. There were thousands of factories to be converted to the production of military material. Great sprawling complexes like the Ford Motor Company's Highland Park plant in Detroit had to be made part of the American war machine, as did tiny sweatshops hidden down alleyways and in tenement garrets from New York to Seattle. And there was a polyglot nation to be rallied. Government spokesmen fanned out across the country to explain to farmers and factory workers that America was fighting to preserve freedom and democracy, while government agents rooted out those who dared to dissent. Socialists and pacifists were censored and even imprisoned when they questioned the wisdom of war. German-Americans, Irish-Americans, and other immigrant groups were harassed because they didn't live up to the new government standard of "100 percent Americanism."[41]

Washington's drive for unity halted at the color line. Southern-born Wilson had already done a great deal to advance segregation during his first four years in office, having extended Jim Crow into Washington's offices, cafeterias, and lavatories and purging thousands of Negro civil servants from government payrolls. Now he dashed the Talented Tenth's hopes that they might win civil rights by serving their country. There was never any question that the army would be segregated, but no one was prepared for the flagrant insults the military leveled. The young men training in Des Moines were told that when they went to war they would all serve in a single division commanded by whites; not one of them would be commissioned at field rank. The very best black officers were simply shunted aside. When a white Mississippian wrote to his senator to object to serving under Charles Young's command, the War Department conveniently classified Wilberforce's finest officer as medically unfit to serve, even after the lieutenant colonel proved his stamina by riding horseback from Xenia to the nation's capital.[42]

Wartime changes, moreover, raised racial tensions to frightening new heights. In the spring and summer of 1917, the steady stream of colored people out of the South suddenly became a torrent. It was a classic economic migration. With the Atlantic Ocean turned into a battlefield and the nations of Europe feeding an entire generation of young men into the slaughter, immigration to the United States was all but cut off. The American military draft, meanwhile, drained factories of workers at precisely the time industrialists were desperately trying to fill the flood of military orders. Facing a labor shortage of unprecedented proportions, employers sent word south that long-standing racial barriers were being torn down for the duration. The news had an electric effect on sharecroppers, day laborers, and domestics desperate to escape grinding poverty and decades of unrelenting brutality. Almost half a million southern blacks left the South for industrial centers like Detroit, Chicago, and New York in 1917 alone, an exodus so great that southern whites feared the economy of their region might well collapse from want of workers.[43]

Instead, the North lurched ever closer to southern-style violence. The first sickening incident came in East St. Louis, Illinois, in July 1917. Blacks had been migrating to the grimy town alongside the Mississippi

River for the better part of a decade, but the influx had suddenly shot upward in late 1916 and early 1917. Democratic Party politicians, including President Wilson himself, declared that the black migration was a Republican plot designed to flood Illinois with GOP voters. White workers, meanwhile, became convinced that black newcomers were about to steal their jobs. When the city's employers crushed a series of strikes—a replay of the dynamic that had underlay the Springfield pogrom a few years earlier—union members blamed the defeat on blacks who they said crossed their picket lines. East St. Louis teetered on the edge of violence throughout the early summer.

On July 1, 1917, it toppled over the precipice. For days, rumors of an impending white attack had swirled through the black neighborhood. Late on the first, jittery blacks mistakenly opened fire on a police car, killing two plainclothesmen. In retaliation, white mobs rampaged through the black part of town in an explosion of violence that made the Springfield riots seem like minor affairs. Whites killed at least forty Negroes and perhaps many more; some victims were hurriedly buried in unmarked graves, while others were dumped into the creeks that fed the Mississippi. Hundreds were injured, thousands made homeless as the mob burned block after block to the ground. The Talented Tenth pleaded with the president to condemn the outrage, but Wilson refused to say a word. So the NAACP responded with a stony silence of its own. In New York City's burgeoning black enclave of Harlem, the association's recently hired field secretary, poet, composer, journalist, lawyer, politician, and diplomat James Weldon Johnson, organized a massive protest parade, ten thousand Negroes—women and children in white, men in black—marching down Fifth Avenue without a sound except for the tramp of boots and the tattoo of muffled drums. At the head of the column waved the Stars and Stripes and a banner reading "Blood Is On Your Hands."[44]

•

The ruins of East St. Louis's ghetto were still smoldering when Ossian arrived in Washington, D.C., in time for the 1917–18 school year. Most likely, he had read Du Bois's searing editorial on the summer's barbarism. "Russia has abolished the ghetto—shall we restore it?" Du Bois had roared in the just-published September issue of the *Crisis*. "India is overthrowing caste—shall we upbuild it? No land that loves to lynch 'niggers' can lead the hosts of Almighty God." Ossian must have noticed how Washington itself was swollen with migrants:

southern-born job seekers, of course, but also bureaucrats and soldiers drawn to the capital by the wartime emergency. Perhaps he realized that the crush of people was stretching city resources and straining tempers. It wouldn't have taken him long to hear word of Jim Crow's mounting popularity in the capital. Even as the Supreme Court was striking down Louisville, Kentucky's ordinance requiring the segregation of its neighborhoods—the NAACP's first great legal victory—southern Democrats were calling on Congress to impose similar laws on the district. But when Ossian arrived at the wrought-iron gates of Howard University, it was almost possible to forget just how dire the state of race relations was becoming.[45]

Like Wilberforce, Howard had been born in the great rush of hope that emancipation had engendered. But there the similarity ended. Created by an act of Congress in 1867 and supported by federal appropriations, Howard didn't struggle to pay its bills or sustain its ideals. The graceful campus, an eclectic mix of Victorian display and classical understatement, sat upon a hill in northwest Washington. To the south and west lay a struggling neighborhood of row houses backed by the capital's infamous alleys, where Negro servants and laborers lived in crushing poverty. But Howard preferred to look to the elegant houses northeast of campus, home to many of America's most elite Negroes—the "Black 400"—highly accomplished, extraordinarily cultured, and invariably light-skinned men and women such as Robert and Mary Church Terrell; the brothers Grimke, who headed the NAACP's Washington branch; and the Langston family, which would produce the finest poet of the Harlem Renaissance. At its best, Howard's faculty was just as accomplished. Kelly Miller, dean of the Liberal Arts College, spent his career trying to build the discipline of black studies; his young colleague, professor of philosophy Alain Locke, the first Negro to win a Rhodes scholarship, acted as midwife to a new generation of black artists and aesthetes; at the law school, James Cobb, a former assistant U.S. attorney, helped to set the groundwork for a legal assault on segregation north and south.[46]

The medical school was the jewel in Howard's crown. When the school opened its doors in 1868, medical education in the United States was very much a haphazard affair. Determined to raise the quality of care—and the status of its members—in 1910, the American Medical Association imposed strict new standards on medical schools. Students had to have at least a highschool diploma before they could be accepted into medical school, the AMA ruled. They were to have four years of training, at least part of which was to be clinical work in a teaching hospital. And when their education was complete, they had to pass comprehensive examinations before they would be licensed to practice.[47]

There had been seven black medical schools in operation when the AMA set its standards; five of them couldn't possibly comply with the new rules and were forced to close, while the sixth—Meharry—barely survived. Howard thrived. It easily met the AMA's benchmarks for admission, since most of its incoming students held college degrees. It maintained an exhaustive and exhausting course of study. In their first two years, students took classes in anatomy, histology, physiology, pharmacology, pathology, bacteriology, therapeutics, diagnosis, and preventative medicine. Then they moved on to a two-year round of clinical experience, much of it completed at Freedmen's Hospital, right next door to the medical school's imposing four-story building. Founded a few years before Howard, Freedmen's had been little more than a barracks where Washington's indigent could go for emergency care. But in 1908, the federal government spent six hundred thousand dollars to build a new three hundred-bed facility, as well-appointed as almost any city hospital of its day. Freedmen's still treated the poor, but it also gave Howard's medical students exposure to a full range of specialties, from surgery to ophthalmology. The AMA was very impressed. "The future of Howard is assured," the association announced when it issued its standards. "Indeed the new Freedmen's Hospital is an asset the like of which is in this country extremely rare."[48]

Ossian also must have been impressed—and a bit intimidated. Coming from Bartow, he had thought Wilberforce was such a grand place; it must have been something of a shock to see how much more imposing Howard looked, how much more professionally its laboratories were equipped, how much more cocksure its students seemed to be. His entering class was small, twenty-two in all. Almost half of them were northerners, and more than a few were coming from first-rate schools where the Negro elite sent their sons: a number were Howard men, one was a graduate of Northwestern University, outside of Chicago, and another had received his degree from Williams College, the elite school tucked away in Massachusetts's Berkshire Hills. Wilberforce had trained Ossian well enough—he had his Latin, his chemistry, and his biology—but he was surrounded by better students, by and large, more comfortable with the rigors of the first year: the long days in the classroom trying desperately to master the flood of information presented by Professors Bartsch, Just, Lamb, and Mitchell, each more distinguished and more demanding than the last; the hours spent dissecting cadavers under the meticulous instruction of angular Doctor West, peeling back the skin, exploring the musculature, and probing the organs of the black corpses the District of Columbia provided from among those too destitute to afford burial.[49]

Ossian's finances made the work all the harder. In its early days, Howard's medical school had expected its students to hold down jobs; all of its classes were held in the evening so the students could work during the day. But in its determination to meet the AMA's benchmarks, Howard had reversed its policy. University officials made it quite clear that medical students should come with funds sufficient to cover the three hundred dollars in tuition and fees; the curriculum was too demanding, they said, to permit students to have jobs during the school year. But Ossian simply had to be employed. The money he had saved from his work in Detroit wasn't enough, not with rent at a local rooming house adding to the bills. So he took a part-time job serving at social events. Ossian would spend evenings waiting on guests at local soirees, pocket a dollar or so, then head back to his room for a long night pouring over massive textbooks, memorizing conditions and prescriptions, so that he could perform for his professors the following morning.[50]

He was no more a standout at Howard than he had been at Wilberforce. Some of his classmates were less capable, to be sure; a few were asked to leave at the end of the first year, their performance was so poor. But Ossian didn't do well enough to attract particular attention. When it came to choosing class officers, others were selected; when the professors identified the most promising students, others were mentioned. It was a familiar enough position for Ossian, a repetition of his undergraduate experience. If he had felt the sting of marginality at Wilberforce, though, at Howard, he experienced the thrill of soaring status. No matter what his academic standing, a graduate of Howard's medical school was never average. He was a professional of the highest order, a young man who deserved and demanded respect.[51] As he learned the intricacies of the human body, therefore, a Howard man also had to learn how to carry himself with towering confidence. He couldn't simply be a doctor. He had to act like one.

A few of Ossian's colleagues were naturals. Even in their first year, they had the proper air about them: the brow knitted in concentration, a pipe clenched between the teeth. Ossian must have found it harder to adopt the physician's proper pose; he'd been taught to do as he was told, to keep his eyes downcast when his superiors talked to him, to answer them with all the politeness and deference he could muster. Bit by bit, Howard transformed him. Ossian was made to dress as a doctor should, pressed shirts and tasteful ties peaking out from beneath crisp white lab coats. In the lecture hall and the laboratory, he was taught to answer questions with all the authority he could manage, as if he harbored no doubts about his abilities. When he moved on to Freedmen's, he learned the proper way for a doctor to act around the infirm. He was to be understanding but not overly sympathetic, friendly but never a friend, a bit distant, a bit detached. That was the demeanor his patients would expect and his colleagues would demand.[52]

For a poor boy determined to make good, it was hard to keep such lessons in perspective. Once acquired, professional detachment slid easily into haughtiness, self-assurance into arrogance. Ossian grew more forceful, more brusque, more judgmental. Even those closest to him no longer measured up. His younger brother Otis devotedly followed Ossian's example, completing his degree at Florida State College, a third-rate Negro college, then advancing to dental school at Meharry. Ossian openly criticized the shortcomings of the schools, so obviously inferior to Howard.[53] Others might well bristle. But they had to understand that Ossian wasn't the country boy he had once been. He had become learned, highly skilled, poised to achieve great things.

Dreams of greatness inevitably collided with the bitter reality of racism. Ossian was used to the sting of segregation. He had never even been inside most of Bartow's public buildings; he'd ridden back and forth from Xenia in Jim Crow railroad cars; he'd worked in hotels where Negroes weren't welcome as guests. His parents had taught him, in their own quiet way, not to accept the humiliations that such discrimination imposed. Time and again, he had heard the same message from President Scarborough and his NAACP colleagues. But only now, in the middle of his medical-school years, did Ossian squarely face the enormous injustice of white supremacy.

It was partly the way that discrimination struck at the professional pride that he was so eagerly embracing. Ossian had no doubt that he was going to be a more talented doctor than most graduates of white medical schools. But almost no white hospital in the country would welcome him as an intern. The AMA wouldn't permit him to be a member. Virtually no white patients would have him as their physician. So for all his training, all his hours of study, all his skills, chances were good that he would have to build a practice among people too poor to pay his fees, that he'd have to serve as an attending physician in an ill-equipped and underfunded black hospital, and when one of his patients needed the sort of care that only a superior facility could provide, Ossian would have to turn over the case to a white doctor who was his inferior in everything but the color of his skin.[54]

Ossian wasn't shaken solely by his confrontation with the medical profession's discriminatory practices, as galling as they were. Halfway through his time at Howard, he also had to face the terror buried deeply inside him. In the summer of 1919, the racial tensions that the Great War had triggered exploded in an unprecedented surge of violence. This time, the bloodshed didn't occur in some distant place like Springfield or East St. Louis. It swept through the streets of Washington itself, from Pennsylvania Avenue all the way to Howard's gates. As it did, all the newfound confidence faded away in a blinding fog of fear.

◆

Ossian was in military dress, drilling alongside his fellow students, on the day the Great War ended. At the beginning of the 1918 school year, Howard had required its medical students to enlist in the Student Army Training Corps, established on campuses across the nation to prepare college men for active duty. There was very little risk of them actually seeing combat. The United States had its massive army built by the summer of 1918, and more than three hundred thousand Americans were already in France, preparing for battle. In August, British, French, and American troops launched their first combined offensive, and the German lines buckled. Three months of bloody fighting followed. Then, on November 11, 1918, Germany sued for peace and the guns fell silent.[55]

Victory in Europe didn't restore harmony at home. Instead, it seemed to feed division. The government's wartime crackdown on dissent fostered a blinding hatred of anyone thought to threaten the American way of life. In the months after the war, workers worried about the security of their jobs mounted a massive wave of strikes. Determined to defeat their workers and destroy their unions, employers condemned the strikers as communists, intent on bringing the recent Soviet revolution to American soil. As the fear mounted, the Wilson administration launched a fevered campaign against left-wing politicians and activists, the nation's first Red Scare. Radicals were swept up in government dragnets, held without trial, and in many cases deported. The government's panic, in turn, stoked the furnace of Anglo-Saxon supremacy. Long a power in American politics, nativists argued that the only way to prevent further subversion was to cut off the flow of foreigners into the United States. Anti-Semites and anti-Catholics rushed to support immigration restriction. "When the Bolshevists in Russia are overthrown there will be a great massacre of Jews," one prominent American coolly explained, "and I suppose we will get the overflow unless we can stop it."[56]

Racial hatred was even more vicious. For its part, the Talented Tenth greeted the peace with a surge of militancy. "We are returning from war!" Du Bois wrote in the *Crisis*. "This is the fatherland for which we fought! But it is *our* fatherland. . . . The faults of *our* country are *our* faults. Under similar circumstances, we would fight again. But by the God of Heaven, we are cowards and jackasses if now that the war is over, we do not marshal every ounce of our brain and brawn to fight a sterner, longer, more unbending battle against the forces of hell in our own land." But the forces of hell proved very strong. The South had its share of outrages. A score of Negroes were lynched in the first half of 1919, including one veteran hung for wearing his uniform in public. There were two major antiblack pogroms, one in Charleston, South Carolina, in May, another in Longview, Texas, in June. When news of the latter incident reached New York City, the NAACP's white executive secretary, John Shillady, hurried to Austin to demand an investigation. His second day in town, a gang of whites assaulted him. A pacifist, Shillady didn't fight back and was beaten senseless. His body recovered. But his spirit never did. He resigned from the NAACP within the year.[57]

The violence reached Washington, D.C., in mid-July 1919. Like so many cities, the capital had been stretched to the breaking point. The city's three black areas—the section around Howard in the northwest, a neighborhood to the southwest, and Foggy Bottom close to downtown—were overflowing with southern migrants, who continued to pour into the city even though the promise of wartime jobs had ended. Washington had another influx as well: thousands of white soldiers were billeted on the outskirts of town, waiting to be mustered out of service. Boredom was itself a hazardous thing. A series of sexual assaults, all attributed to black men, heightened the danger, as it had in Bartow all those years ago. When word reached the military camps that a soldier's wife had been raped, the conflagration began.[58]

Saturday night, July 19, a hundred soldiers, sailors, and marines marched on the colored neighborhood to the southwest and attacked blacks unlucky enough to be on the streets. The violence spread on Sunday, as more soldiers and sailors joined the mobs roving the city in search of victims. Brutality swirled around the seats of power: several black men were pummeled in full view of the White House, where President Wilson, exhausted from his efforts on behalf of world peace, lay ill in bed. Anarchy peaked the third day. The *Washington Post* opened the morning with a call to arms: "Every available service man stationed in or near Washington or on leave here" was to gather at Pennsylvania and Seventh avenues at nine that evening, the newspaper reported, for a "'clean-up' that will cause the events of the last two evenings to pale into insignificance." By nightfall, more than a thousand white men crowded the downtown area. Military authorities tried to pen them in with a hastily assembled corps of four hundred cavalrymen. But the mob surged through the lines and fanned out toward the Negro sections.[59]

Foggy Bottom was quickly overrun and the southwest neighborhood again imperiled. But in northwest Washington the mob met massive resistance. All day long, the area's Negroes had been preparing to defend themselves. Residents bought up any gun that was for sale, and when the stock ran out, they grabbed free weapons that had been rushed in from Baltimore. Many families barricaded themselves inside their homes to await the mob's attack, while groups of men organized themselves into neighborhood defense units. Whites arrived as darkness descended. Down the side streets, gunfire blazed from upstairs windows; passing automobiles were riddled with bullets and members of the white mob scattered for cover. Main thoroughfares became battlegrounds. The intersection of Seventh Avenue and T Street, a few blocks south of Howard, saw the most fearsome fighting. Blacks and whites engaged in hand-to-hand combat throughout the night. Dozens were seriously injured, including two policemen, and one black man was shot to death. Only exhaustion and the approaching dawn ended the bloodshed.[60]

Violence finally ended on the fourth day. From his sickbed, Wilson ordered two thousand federal troops into the capital to secure the streets. And a furious rainstorm drove both whites and blacks indoors. Negro spokesmen insisted, however, that neither federal action nor a fortuitous turn in the weather had quelled the attack. James Weldon Johnson, soon to be named Shillady's successor as NAACP executive secretary, arrived in the city just as the soldiers were taking up positions. "The Negroes saved themselves and saved Washington by their determination not to run, but to fight," he concluded after two days of consultation and investigation, "fight in defense of their lives and their homes. If the white mob had gone on unchecked—and it was only the determined effort of black men that checked it—Washington would have been another and worse East St. Louis."[61]

There's no sign that Ossian joined in the defense that Johnson celebrated, though he undoubtedly had more training with firearms than most of those who stood their ground on Seventh Avenue. He couldn't have helped but hear the screams of the combatants, the report of the guns, and the wails of the injured during the long night's battle. He was then living at the Chi Delta Mu fraternity house at Third Avenue and T Street, four blocks from the intersection where black Washington made its stand. But he didn't venture out.[62]

Perhaps he was paralyzed by fear. Sometime in the first few days of the riot, Ossian had been walking down the street when a gang of whites descended on a passing streetcar, pulled a black passenger down to the sidewalk, and beat him mercilessly. It is easy enough to imagine the terror of the scene: the sickening sound of fists and boots slamming against bone, the victim curling his body into the fetal position to avoid the blows, the stream of blood filling the cracks in the cement. After two years of medical school, Ossian would have known the details of the damage the thugs had inflicted, the way a skull cracked, the ways internal organs hemorrhaged. But it would have been the memories that the attack evoked—those terrible childhood memories—that would have been most frightening. It was a visceral emotion, a wrenching deep down in the gut. He could bury his past under years of education. He could live hundreds of miles from his parents' home, in the heart of a great city. But no matter what he achieved or where he went, he was never safe from the mindless fury of the mob.[63]

As it happened, the summer's savagery was just beginning. Less than a week after peace was restored in the nation's capital, whites on Chicago's South Side stoned to death a black boy who mistakenly had gone swimming at a beach whites considered their own. Rumors of imminent black retaliation sparked yet another assault, this one much worse than either East St. Louis or Washington. In the course of five days, twenty-three Negroes and fifteen whites were murdered, five hundred were injured, and millions of dollars in property was destroyed. Fears of sexual violence, that most potent of provocations, triggered smaller riots in Knoxville, Tennessee, in August, and Omaha, Nebraska, in September. And in October 1919, whites in eastern Arkansas slaughtered a hundred or more black sharecroppers they feared were going to form a union. With such a staggering series of offenses to occupy the public mind, most Americans soon forgot about the Washington riot. But for Ossian, the violence on the streets of the capital had reopened the wound cut in Bartow years before. The wound was sure to close; he was young and resilient. Yet there was always the chance of another rupture, should the terror come again.[64]

♦

The most fearsome violence abated late in 1920. Northern riots came to a sudden halt, the worst fears subsided, and the national mood began to swing toward an optimism that in a few years' time would create the Jazz Age. But the forces the war unleashed were never really contained. The Red Scare of 1919 shattered the union movement and destroyed radical political organizations. Those victories didn't satisfy the nativists, who continued to assail the immigrants in their midst. If anything, the intellectual attack on the foreign-born grew even more shrill as the 1920s got under way. "Our country, originally settled by the Nordics, was toward the close of the nineteenth century invaded by hordes of immigrant Alpines and Mediterraneans, not to mention Asiatic elements like Levantines and Jews," Boston lawyer Lothrop Stoddard wrote in one of 1920's most widely read books, *The Rising Tide of Color Against White World Supremacy*. "As a result, the Nordic native American has been crowded out with amazing rapidity by the swarming, prolific aliens, and after two short generations he has in many of our urban areas become almost extinct." Bitter rhetoric blended seamlessly with political action. In the course of 1920, the Ku Klux Klan, reborn in Georgia five years earlier, began its race into the North by adding anti-Semitism, anti-Catholicism, and xenophobia to its traditional appeal to white supremacy. In the wells of Congress, meanwhile, the nation's representatives pushed relentlessly toward closing the country to further immigration, a fundamental reversal of the policy that had made the nation's industrialization possible.[65]

Race relations in the cities of the North likewise remained tense. The informal segregation of public places continued to metastasize. "As a colored woman," Mary Church Terrell reported from Washington, D.C., "I may walk from the Capitol to the White House ravenously hungry and supplied with money to purchase a meal without finding a single restaurant in which I would be permitted to take a morsel of food if it were patronized by white people, unless I were willing to sit behind a screen. And in some places I wouldn't be allowed to do even that." Farther north, segregation wasn't yet so advanced. But the situation continued to be dangerously unstable. On Chicago's bloody racial frontier, whites bombed eight separate properties bought by Negroes in the first three months of 1920. Ongoing guerilla warfare wasn't enough, though, to stem the flow of migrants out of the south; it was better to risk a sudden outburst on the streets of a major city than to face perpetual poverty and oppression in the cotton fields of Alabama or Mississippi.[66]

◆

Ossian also felt the fever fade and his hopes revive. He spent most of his last two years in medical school, 1920 and 1921, sharpening his skills at Freedmen's Hospital. It wasn't quite the glowing place the AMA had thought it to be. The hospital's appropriations had been cut during the war, so the administration couldn't afford to maintain the building properly: when Ossian began his clinical work, paint and plaster were peeling in two of the three wards, floor tiles were cracked, and even in the main operating room there were broken windows. Freedmen's nevertheless provided an excellent experience for senior medical students. Since its founding, the hospital had never turned away patients simply because they couldn't afford to pay for care. Washington's poor therefore flocked to Freedmen's; most of the patients the hospital accepted were on charity, their fees paid by the federal government at the princely sum of two dollars a day. As the poor arrived, they brought with them a staggering array of conditions and diseases. So Ossian saw the routine cases—expectant mothers, injured workmen—and the cases he never would have seen had he been working in a hospital treating more prosperous patients: children suffering from malnutrition, men whose untreated wounds had turned gangrenous, families devastated by diphtheria or typhoid.[67] By the end of his two years in the wards, Ossian had the kind of experience most medical students would have envied.

Ossian received his medical degree in the spring of 1921. At twenty-five years of age, he still had a young man's face. His rich brown skin was smooth and clean, his eyes bright and alert; the furrows and crow's-feet that came with age and worry had yet to appear. His high hairline hinted that one day soon he would go bald but the process had yet to begin. He had his mother's tight dark hair, which he kept carefully trimmed. He had taken to wearing round horn-rimmed glasses, his version of the academic look that was de rigeur on campus. And he had learned to effect an appearance that made him seem not simply serious but stern. He arched his eyebrows, set his lips, and glowered, a pose meant to impress a professor, intimidate a patient, and just perhaps, to convince himself that he had become a member of the most esteemed profession possible.[68]

He wanted more. Every year, Freedmen's Hospital offered eleven year-long internships to recent medical-school graduates. No post was more coveted. Internships weren't yet a required part of American medical education, though for white doctors they were becoming much more common. For colored doctors, unwelcome in most white hospitals, internships were a mark of distinction; those who undertook additional study were considered the crème de la crème of the profession, its rising stars. So winning an extra year's study at Freedmen's was a particularly great honor. For Ossian, it would be the first marker that he was in fact on his way to becoming a physician of the first rank.[69]

Ostensibly, the internships were awarded purely on merit: applicants took a competitive exam in May and those with the highest scores were appointed the following month. Behind the scenes, however, candidates used whatever influence they could to secure a spot. One of Ossian's classmates had a United States senator write on his behalf; another applicant had an important local politician intervene. In such a competition, Ossian never stood a chance. Somehow he managed to secure an extra two months' work at Freedmen's, an abbreviated internship. But the year-long posts went to others. It must have been terribly disappointing to receive his rejection, an unmistakable indication that despite all his labors he had yet to work his way into the elite of the race.[70]

Ossian didn't have the time to brood over his defeat, though. The completion of his brief internship would bring to a close his student years; come September 1921, a new class would arrive at Howard, fresh faces from Fisk and Lincoln, and his classmates would move on, leaving the capital for careers across the nation. Without an additional year at Freedmen's to occupy him, Ossian, too, would have to set out on his own. He could have gone back to Bartow, back to the embrace of his family. It would have been a victorious return, twelve years in the making. How his parents would have beamed with pride as their neighbors clucked over the fine young man their son had become; how the community would have rejoiced to finally have a colored doctor who could deliver their babies, treat their children, and help the elderly gently pass; how whites on the other side of town would have bridled at the impressive home he could have built on Second Avenue, facing the railroad tracks so all the Crackers could see its splendor. Or Ossian could have moved to a small town in the North, a place like Xenia perhaps, where he could have set up a general practice, bought one of the best houses in the black part of town, and settled into a quiet life, the beloved county doctor growing gray among a generation of townspeople he'd nurtured into adulthood. There were appeals in pursuing such paths. But Ossian still held to the pledge he'd made himself at Wilberforce—to rise in his profession and make his fortune—and he wasn't about to surrender it for a career of comfortable obscurity. To be the sort of man he wanted to be, he needed a bigger stage.

Perhaps he'd always thought of returning to Detroit when his training was complete. But Ossian claimed, later in life, that it was the summer he'd spent at the Fairfax Hotel in 1913 that brought him back. The wonderful promise the head bellhop had dangled before him—Detroit rewarded the ambitious—that was the draw. Of course, it would be hard to start a practice in a city where he had no relatives to support him, where most of his acquaintances were servants of one sort or another, where life moved at the relentless pace of the assembly line rather than to the rhythm of the seasons. But ambition—since the day he'd stepped off the train at Xenia station and scrambled aboard Dad Harris's cart, he'd been driven by ambition. It was the gift his family had given him and the burden it had placed on him. It was the lesson he'd learned best at Wilberforce and Howard; not languages or biology or anatomy or even racial militancy but dogged determination. That's what drew him down to Washington's Union Station in the late summer of 1921 for one more move, one last migration, one more train ride to a new beginning in the Motor City.

FOUR

UPLIFT ME, PRIDE

When Ossian Sweet arrived in Detroit late in the summer of 1921, he had two hundred dollars in his pocket, his diplomas packed away in his bags, and a few tenuous connections left over from his days working as a bellhop and waiter. Beyond that, the new doctor had nothing: no home, no office for a practice, no real friends, no family to give him a start.[1] He was on his own.

The first time Ossian had seen Detroit, in the summer of 1910, it was already a brawny manufacturing center elbowing its way into the front ranks of urban America. Eleven years later, the city had arrived as an industrial colossus, a modernist metropolis of steel, smoke, and sinewy assembly lines. Auto factories that a few years before had been hailed as engineering marvels were already being dwarfed by new facilities. Just behind the train station on the west side, Wall Street's latest conglomerate, General Motors, was putting up a brand-new factory for the production of its luxury line of Cadillacs; on the narrow streets of the east side, the Dodge Brothers were feverishly expanding their elegant Albert Kahn–designed plant, already one of the nation's largest. For sheer audacity, though, none could outdo Ford. The incredible Highland Park plant was only a decade old, but along the banks of the placid Rouge River, just west of Detroit, the company was building a complex five times the size that would eventually cover over a thousand acres and employ almost a hundred thousand workers.[2]

Such dramatic economic expansion fueled massive migration: more than a million people now lived in Detroit, twice as many as in 1910. No matter how furiously officials tried to annex more land, they couldn't make room for all the people. In the city center, where empty lots had once sat waiting for development, neighborhoods had become so crowded they were beginning to resemble Manhattan's Lower East Side or Chicago's infamous Back of the Yards. "A city which is built around a productive process . . . is really a kind of hell," wrote a young Detroit minister, Reinhold Niebuhr. "Thousands in this town are really living in torment while the rest of us eat, drink, and make merry. What a civilization!"[3]

The tenor of the streets was rough and sometimes shocking. In the boom's early days, the automakers thought they could create a model industrial city, full of hard-working, patriotic, efficient workmen, and for a few heady years, they seemed to have their way. In 1914, when Ford raised wages to five dollars a day, he sent a team of one hundred inspectors out to his workers' homes to assure that they were living according to the highest standards of decency and frugality. Those who didn't measure up had their wages cut in half. The following year, Detroit's largest firms launched a citywide Americanization campaign, designed to teach immigrant workers the English language and the manufacturers' definition of citizenship: "Each one in his sphere keeping busy, doing honest work, and contributing to the sum total of wealth for the support of the nation." To break the power of the ethnic political bosses, the automakers and their allies remade city government, putting power in the hands of upright Anglo-Saxon businessmen. The first mayor elected under the new charter, in 1918, was Henry Ford's bookkeeper. And to clear the city of workingmen's saloons, city fathers pushed through a prohibition law two years before the nation went dry.[4]

But by 1921, dry, decent Detroit, with its fine new government and its strict moral laws, had split wide open. There wasn't a time of day or night when liquor wasn't flowing somewhere: the swells patronized speakeasies on Grand Boulevard, and those looking for an edgier experience went down to the black and tans along Hastings Street, where jazz bands played, drinks were first-rate, and slumming was all the rage. But there were thousands of other places in the city, joints the slummers didn't even know existed: blind pigs offering teacups of fine whiskey smuggled in from Canada and Mason jars full of white lightning made in basement stills; tenderloin jukes jumping with the piano blues of Speckled Red, Big Maceo Merriweather, and Tupelo

Slim; back-room dives hidden in the rear of cigar stores and sweet shops; and dingy apartments where locals sat at beat-up tables downing shots and home-brewed beer. And breaking Prohibition was only the beginning. Drugs, gambling, prostitution were sweeping the city— if a person had a vice, Detroit had a venue for it.[5]

Detroit's newfound license extended to brutality. Bootleggers, numbers runners, drug dealers, pimps, and assorted mobsters waged war for their share of the city's illicit trades, but viciousness wasn't limited to hoodlums. Businessmen's faith in their ability to remake the city was crumbling, and in its place was rising an increasingly bitter and repressive politics. Once again, Henry Ford led the way. Determined to explain moral decline, he latched onto *The Protocols of the Elders of Zion*, purportedly the Jewish blueprint for undermining Christian civilization, but in truth a rambling, nearly incoherent forgery created by czarist agents at the turn of the century to justify Russians burning shtetls and pillaging synagogues. By the summer of 1921, the automaker had already mass-produced some half million copies.[6]

Ford's extremism fed fires of xenophobia smoldering among the city's Anglo-Saxon minority, blending anti-Semitism with anti-Catholicism, nativism, and a deepening racism. Detroit's cops, themselves overwhelmingly native-born whites, were almost as likely to rough up foreign-born and colored suspects as they were to arrest them. In the poorer districts, more than a few innocent citizens felt the whack of a billy club in the course of a year. Down on the factory floor, meanwhile, Ford and his fellow manufacturers turned a blind eye to the dictatorial regimes of their foremen, who forced out ever-increasing production by threatening their men hour after hour, day after day. Worst of all, there was no saying when the pressures of life in a boomtown—too much drink, too much work, too much worry about making ends meet— would trigger an outburst: the back of a hand across a spouse's face, the flash of a fist in a packed barroom, the flame of a pistol shot in the midst of a neighborhood dispute. In 1920 alone, ninety-four people had been murdered in Detroit, many of them gangsters slain on back streets or dumped into the Detroit River, others just ordinary folks, victims of the city's growing penchant for solving problems with brutish force. "That's a hard-boiled burg all right. . . . Lots of tough muggs in Detroit, lots of whorehouses and tough joints," remembered one migrant who fled for home the first chance he got. "It was too goddamn hard working for Ford. That assembly line stuff is a sonofabitch, I'm telling you. That's nothing but slavery."[7]

Ossian Sweet could have been excused for taking his time to adjust. Instead, he moved into the heart of the city, renting a room on Clinton Street, half a mile east of downtown. It was a dingy place, squeezed in alongside Walter Green's trucking depot in a block of well-worn houses on the edge of the toughest, most desperately overcrowded neighborhood Detroit contained. But that was exactly where Ossian wanted to be. For inside this area were forty thousand Negroes, an entire generation of southern migrants jammed into a four-square-mile section of squalor, the very people the newly minted doctor hoped would make him his fortune.[8]

•

Ossian was no stranger here. Most of his summers in the city, he'd lived just a few blocks east of Clinton Street, in one of the many boarding houses that dotted the area everyone called Black Bottom. Well-to-do colored families lived scattered around the city, but most of Detroit's poorer Negroes—the laborers, waiters, shoeshine boys, and domestics—lived nearby. At the time of Ossian's first visits, it was still a tiny community: in 1910, there were only fifty-seven hundred colored people living there, not that many more than in Bartow and its surrounding countryside. And despite its name, Black Bottom wasn't really a colored area. Most of its residents were immigrants, not Negroes. A few were Germans, half-forgotten old men and women left behind when their prospering sons and daughters moved into other, more comfortable parts of the east side years earlier. More came with the huge wave of foreigners from eastern Europe and the countries of the Mediterranean rim, the kind of people America's Anglo-Saxons were convinced lay somewhere between black and white. In the center of Black Bottom, along Hastings and St. Antoine streets, Negroes lived alongside recently arrived Russian Jews, refugees from the czar's pogroms. On the neighborhood's fringes, blacks shared streets with Italians, Greeks, and Syrians, refugees from grinding poverty.[9]

Only in Ossian's final two years in Detroit, the cataclysmic summers of 1916 and 1917, had the neighborhood begun to change, the transformation beginning with the same dynamic that altered so many parts of the North—the cutting off of European immigration, the coming of war, industrialists' desperate need to find new workers to fill factories humming with military orders. But true to form, Detroit made the process more intense, more furious than anywhere else. News of high-paying jobs up in the Motor City shot through every portion of

the South, carried from town to town, farm to farm, by labor re-
cruiters, colored newspapers, word of mouth, and even the blues. "I'm
goin' to get me a job, up there in Mr. Ford's place," they sang in roadhouses deep in the delta and across the Black Belt, "Stop these eatless
days from staring me in the face. When I start makin' money, she don't
need to come around, 'Cause I don't need her now, Lord, I'm Detroit
bound."[10]

So they were, by the trainloads. Some thirty thousand colored people
came to Detroit during the Great War, thousands more in its immediate
aftermath. The vast majority were working people, sharecroppers,
lumber-camp hands, and maids. But they were looking for exactly the
same thing that had drawn Ossian to Detroit: the promise of opportunity, the chance for something better. "I was reading the paper," remembered one migrant, "and it say where the plumbers were making twelve
dollars a day and the brick layers and plasterers, too. . . . Well, that's
more I ever made in a regular job during off season down in Georgia.
Down there when the crop was in and it was wintertime pay over two
dollars a day. So I just know I could make big money in Detroit."[11]

Most migrants didn't find those fabulous tradesmen's wages. By
southern standards, though, typical Detroit pay rates were nothing
short of spectacular: assembly-line workers earned up to six dollars a
day during the war years, some of the highest industrial wages anywhere in America. No wonder Detroit's black population shot up at
such an extraordinary rate: between 1910 and 1920, Detroit's black
population had increased by 600 percent. No other colored community above the Mason-Dixon Line, not even Harlem, had grown so
fast.[12]

The results were drearily predictable. Like so many other parts of
the North, Detroit's race relations had been decaying since the turn of
the century. The Great Migration dramatically accelerated the decline.
There was no serious attempt to repeal the state's long-standing civil
rights statutes, which outlawed discrimination in public places, prohibited segregated schools, and even sanctioned interracial marriage.
But in practice, white Detroiters grew more and more insistent on
keeping Negroes in their proper place. Segregation came in fits and
starts, imposed by random acts of cruelty. The owner of an auto-parts
plant set up separate toilets for his white and colored workers. The
management of a tire factory strung a thick iron chain across the cafe-
teria so that white men could eat their sandwiches without fear of
amalgamation. A white high school teacher required colored students

to sit apart from their Caucasian classmates. Government officials rejected appeals to put more than a handful of Negroes on city payrolls, no matter how menial the jobs. Whites bludgeoned a colored man because he sat in the wrong seat at a baseball game in a neighborhood park.[13]

Segregation spread into the job market, too. To be sure, the Great War opened auto-factory jobs to Negroes, but colored workers faced a bewildering array of discriminatory practices. A few automakers, Henry Ford foremost among them, sometimes hired Negroes for the full range of production positions, though almost never for the skilled work that native-born whites had always controlled. The precious few colored men who were placed on the assembly line faced repeated harassment. From the minute he punched in to the minute he punched out nine hours later, an assembler worked at breakneck speed, doing one simple job—putting a side panel into place or screwing on a bolt—over and over again. He'd feel his muscles screaming at him to stop, to just sit down and rest. But the foreman was always behind him, yelling at him to keep going, to get the production out. Not a word of respect, just "nigger do this" and "nigger do that," barked over the relentlessly throbbing machinery. When the foreman wasn't riding him, his fellow workers often were. Colored men had to guard against their workmates sabotaging their machines, breaking their tools, even taking a swing at them when they weren't looking. Most manufacturers didn't allow such conflicts to develop. Instead, they restricted colored men to specific jobs, mostly those so dangerous or so miserable only the most desperate migrants were willing to take them.

At the Dodge Brothers factory, Negroes spent their days in the toxic cloud of the spray rooms, applying the black paint that made the roadsters shine. At Cadillac Motors, they were slotted into the wet-sanding department. And in plant after plant, even Ford's, they were disproportionately assigned to the foundries, feeding iron into the face of furnaces so large they dwarfed the mighty monsters of Birmingham, Alabama's steel plants, drawing out buckets of molten metal and pouring the contents into the castings from which parts were made, hoping and praying that this time there'd be no accident, because foundry workers didn't recover from accidents.[14]

At least a man could get a factory job. Auto manufacturers wouldn't so much as think of hiring a colored woman. So a young lady coming out of the South had to take whatever work she could get. If the color of her skin wasn't too dark, she might land a job in a second-rate store or downtown hotel. More likely, she went into domestic service. Wages were a lot higher than in the South; working in one of the big houses in suburban Grosse Pointe, a woman could bring home thirteen, maybe fourteen dollars a week. But the work was as demanding as anything a factory hand endured. A maid had to be up before the sun so she could have "her" family's breakfast on the table before they came downstairs to begin their day. By the time she headed home on the streetcar, hollow eyed from exhaustion, the sun was long gone and the streets passing by were draped in darkness.[15]

Most likely, she went home to Black Bottom. Detroit wasn't like Bartow or other southern towns, where officials tried to mandate where Negroes could live. In Detroit, the neighborhood color line was drawn in the same jagged way that segregation was imposed everywhere else in the city, through a host of individual actions arbitrarily imposed. Many migrants, like Ossian, headed to Black Bottom of their own accord, knowing that was the place where they'd make connections and find friends. Other newcomers were steered into the neighborhood the moment they got off the train, pointed in the right direction by the women who staffed the Visitors Aid desk or the Black Bottom landlords who prowled the station's cavernous hall looking for potential renters.

But it was mounting discrimination in the real estate market that increasingly sealed Negroes into Black Bottom. Since the early 1910s, white real estate agents and landlords in Chicago and New York had refused to so much as show Negroes homes in white neighborhoods, saying that the presence of colored people depressed property values. In the course of the Great War, those practices spread to Detroit. Not every real estate agent or landlord signed on: if colored folks were willing to pay a premium for a piece of property in a white part of town, some real estate men were happy to oblige them. But to defy the new racial conventions took more courage—or more avarice—than many real estate agents and landlords had. So discriminatory practices passed from office to office, property to property, and racial hatred gradually turned into common business practice, the way things were done.[16]

Where the market failed to keep colored people contained, white homeowners sometimes threatened to do the job themselves. Detroit never experienced the racial conflagrations that exploded in Chicago in 1919, but there were certainly brushfires during the war years. Well-to-do whites tried to buy out a black doctor who moved into their neighborhood. A contingent of property owners threatened another colored man with expulsion unless he and his family abandoned their newly rented apartment.[17] Then there was the trouble on Harper Avenue, just north of Black Bottom. It began when a white landlord couldn't resist the thought of raising the rents in his four-family flat to the usurious level colored people paid. In August 1917, he offered one of the apartments to a group of Negro workingmen and their families. The new tenants weren't in the flat more than an hour when a mob of two hundred whites gathered in the street.

Speaking for the crowd behind them, two former aldermen informed the colored men that they wouldn't be allowed to stay the night. The Negroes appealed to a policeman they spotted walking by, who told them it would be "best to leave and not to have any trouble." Before the migrants could figure out what to do, the mob surged past them, gathered up their clothes and furniture, carried all of it off to the four trucks they had waiting, and drove the goods back to Black Bottom, where they dumped them in the street. "Before we'll stand for these niggers staying here," one of the whites said as he dragged the Negroes' belongings down the stairs, "we'll turn this house upside down." Strange thing was, a colored family lived just two doors down from the flat. They'd been there for years, and no one seemed to mind until the segregationist fever raced through the neighborhood.[18]

Thus did the rough walls of segregation begin to rise around Black Bottom as Ossian settled into Clinton Street at the end of summer 1921. Wealthier blacks still lived in different sections of Detroit, many of them in otherwise completely white neighborhoods, some in tiny black enclaves miles from the inner city. And there were still plenty of foreigners on the streets of Black Bottom. When Ossian took a walk down his block, more than half the neighbors he passed were immigrants: Joseph Saprenza, right next door; the Catalanos, a few houses up; Frank Gidzie, Sam Monecatto, and Alex Schuwalow, living together closer to the corner of St. Aubin Avenue, where the business strip lay. But if Ossian kept walking east to the blocks just beyond St. Aubin, from the edge of Black Bottom to its center, the concentration of colored people became dramatically more intense, street after street filled with southern migrants who, because they were black, had no choice but make their new home in Detroit's emerging ghetto.[19]

◆

Black Bottom buckled under the weight of thirty-five thousand colored newcomers. Like many of Detroit's older neighborhoods, the area was a long, narrow strip running several miles north from the Detroit River. Downtown, full of glittering new skyscrapers, movie palaces, and swanky hotels, served as the neighborhood's western border. The area's central section ended seven blocks to the east, at the Grand Trunk Railroad lines that ran just behind St. Aubin, though the population pressure was so great that more and more Negroes were moving to the streets on the other side of the tracks, where Ossian was living.[20]

Black Bottom's worst section was down by the river, where beat-up boardinghouses catered to sailors trying to find some action and winos willing to sleep in a roach-infested room rather than spend the night huddled in a warehouse doorway. Conditions slowly improved as one moved toward the white neighborhoods that formed Black Bottom's northern boundary. The flophouses became fewer and farther between, replaced by blocks of dilapidated wood-frame homes, each of them no more than a couple of feet from the one next door, without so much as a touch of greenery front or back. The only open space came from the alleyways that ran along the back of the houses, where little girls jumped double Dutch amid the piles of refuse that hid the nests of rats.

As depressing as it was to walk Black Bottom's streets and back ways, it was worse to climb up a set of broken steps, push open a door, and begin the search for a place to sleep. A migrant from the Mississippi delta was used to making do; sharecropper shacks didn't come with amenities. But Black Bottom pushed the limits of endurance. Landlords knew there were far more Negroes looking for places than the neighborhood had to offer. So they ratcheted up rents as high as they would go.

To get a couple of dingy rooms barely big enough to house a family would cost a man and wife fifty or sixty dollars a month. And groups of rooms were hard to come by. Many landlords wanted to squeeze in tenants until they were stacked like cordwood. A sign reading "Room for Let," pasted up on a house window might well mean that there was nothing more than a bed available—a tangle of threadbare sheets and blankets resting on a soiled mattress, the head and foot pushed up against other beds, ten, twelve in a room that at one time had been the parlor of the house. Day or night, there'd be men trying to rest, still dressed in their sweat-stained overalls, blankets pulled up around them to block out the talk and the chill of the room.[21]

With demand so high, landlords didn't see the need to make repairs. There were houses in the central section of Black Bottom where the water cascaded through the ceiling every time it rained; houses where the walls were so sodden the tenants had to pull their beds into the center of the room so they wouldn't spend the night drenched to the skin; houses where the plaster on the walls had crumbled so that the wind whistled through the exposed laths; houses without glass in the window frames all winter long. Bathtubs turned black from overuse. Toilets stopped up and overflowed. Kitchen sink spigots that spewed rust red water. And in half the houses of Black Bottom, there was no running water at all. To fill a cooking pot, a tenant had to prime the backyard pump. To relieve himself, he had to endure the outhouse, fending off the swarm of flies in the summertime, the cutting cold in the winter, and the stomach-churning stench any time of year.[22]

Some migrants had to settle for even worse. For a fee, the owners of the pool halls on Hastings Street allowed men to bed down on top of the tables. Down on Mullet Street, where Ossian had roomed in 1917, two men paid twenty-five dollars a month to sleep in a sagging shed hammered together in the backyard of a rooming house. A couple and their baby lived in a single windowless room off a barbershop; the outhouse was so close to the well that both mother and child were poisoned by the drinking water. A family from Tennessee—husband, wife, and a gaggle of children—crowded into a tarpaper shanty, which they lit with kerosene lamps, insulated with scrap paper, and heated with the embers from the kitchen stove. The family dreamed of owning the place one day, if only they could come up with the fourteen hundred dollars the owner was asking for it.[23]

Official neglect reinforced Black Bottom's burdens. City Hall spent Detroiters' tax dollars putting sewer lines and proper lighting into the new housing developments being built out near the suburbs, while many Black Bottom folks lugged pails of pump water through dimly lit yards. The neighborhood's working people had to rely on inadequate streetcar lines to carry them to their jobs; maids with plum positions in Grosse Pointe could count on almost an hour's ride to work, while men lucky enough to get jobs at Ford's new River Rouge plant figured on twice that long squeezed onto overcrowded trolleys.[24]

Detroit policemen treated Black Bottom's colored residents with absolute contempt; it was common practice for patrolmen to stop black men at random and subject them to searches, often at gunpoint, and those taken into custody sometimes spent days in jail just waiting to be charged with a crime. At the same time, the police department did nothing to check Black Bottom's illicit trade. On weekend evenings, when pay packets were full, white men crowded the streets of Detroit's most notorious vice district, which overlapped with Black Bottom's eastern edge. The most entrepreneurial brothels had their prostitutes stand in the front windows, trying to lure the johns inside. But those in the know—white or colored—found the best deals in Black Bottom's numerous buffet flats, where pimps and madams provided customers with a full range of services: liquor, dope, cards, dice, sex, the buffet flats had it all, even a bit of the blues. "There's a lady in our neighborhood who runs a buffet flat," the incomparable Bessie Smith sang of a Detroit dive she knew well, "And when she gives a party she knows just where she's at." The cops knew, too, but they didn't care, unless they saw a colored man walking in the company of a white woman. Then they ran him in.[25]

Of all the problems that afflicted the neighborhood, none was greater than disease. Contagion was a constant threat, partly because everyone lived in close quarters, partly because no one was vaccinated: a migrant carried smallpox up from the South a few years before Ossian arrived and in short order Black Bottom faced an epidemic. Syphilis, the plague of the vice district, also was widespread. But dramatic illnesses weren't the real threat. Straightforward diseases—those that afflicted the poor, that flourished in dirt and fetid air—those were the ones that devastated Black Bottom. Pneumonia was twice as likely to kill a Negro as it was a white person, tuberculosis three times as likely. Parents buried children lost to afflictions as simple as diarrhea and enteritis, malnutrition and exposure. In 1919, 595 colored babies were born in the city; 89 of them were dead by 1920.[26]

Rudimentary care would have saved some of them. But Black Bottom didn't get even that. Visiting a doctor was a luxury for a working person when there was rent to pay and food to buy. In any case, there were only twenty-seven colored doctors in the entire city in 1921, one for every fifteen hundred Negroes. A truly desperate person might drag himself to one of Detroit's white hospitals, far outside Black Bottom. But chances were, he'd get no more than a quick once-over in the outpatient clinic, since most white institutions wouldn't admit Negroes, no matter how sick they were, unless they could pay their own way, and not many migrants could do that.[27]

The city welfare office was willing to pick up the tab for particularly poor Negroes, but only a few white hospitals were willing to provide them with beds, and even then, they restricted colored patients to segregated wards and prohibited their physicians from seeing them; it wouldn't do to have a colored doctor darkening the hospitals' pristine white halls. So in 1919, only 3 percent of Detroit's ill Negroes went to hospitals for treatment, while the rest tried their best to get by. They bought up the patent medicines that drugstores kept on their shelves. They brewed home remedies from recipes they'd carried up from the South. They relied on midwives to deliver their babies and, in some case, root doctors and faith healers to cool fevers and quiet tremors. But mostly, they suffered.[28]

With his sharp businessman's eyes, Ossian knew that the desperation that stalked Black Bottom would give him the opportunity he wanted. He wasn't in an ideal position to open a practice. The few months he spent preparing for the state medical exam slowly ate away at his small savings, so that by the time he received his license in November 1921—the only colored man to qualify that year—he couldn't afford rent on an office of his own. But around the corner from his house, along St. Aubin Avenue, was a small pharmacy, the Palace Drug Company, owned and operated by Cyrus Dozier, a southern-born colored man just about Ossian's age. Maybe it was affinity, maybe economic necessity, but Dozier was open to a deal. Ossian agreed to invest one hundred dollars in the pharmacy, in exchange for which he received office space in the back. Palace Drugs was an ordinary storefront, long, dark, and narrow, sharing a wall with Sam Delisli's dance studio next door. But the location was first-rate, an easy walk from anywhere in Black Bottom, and the customers who came in to pick up a cold remedy or a stick of candy were sure to spread the word about the handsome new doctor looking for patients. All in all, Ossian had gotten himself off to a very good start.[29]

Years later, he still recalled his first case. Lucius and Elizabeth Riley were fairly typical Black Bottom folks—he worked as a barber, while she kept house for her husband and two boarders in a cramped flat just around the corner from Palace Drugs—and the problem that brought them to Ossian was a typical Black Bottom malady. Mrs. Riley's jaw had grown stiff, and the couple suspected that she had contracted tetanus. The disease was terribly simple to acquire—the bacteria thrives in dirt and passes into the body through the smallest of punctures—but the consequences were fearsome: the infection races through the nervous system, triggering spasms so severe that the victim's malfunctioning body literally chokes her to death. A careful examination convinced Ossian that there was no infection: Mrs. Riley had simply dislocated her jaw. The relieved couple gave him five dollars to reset the bone. And they started to spread the word that the young man in Palace Drugs knew what he was doing.[30]

Through the balance of 1921, Ossian's practice grew at a steady pace. Most of the work was routine. Parents arrived with sick children in their arms; factory workers came looking for treatment of blistering burns they'd received in the foundries; men and women sat at his desk and mumbled about the excruciating pain of venereal diseases. Once in a while, something unusual came his way. Patching up a patient battered in a Christmas Eve brawl—another victim of Detroit's mean streets—brought in fifty dollars, a staggering sum for a few hours' work. In celebration, Ossian treated himself to a fine holiday dinner, then banked the balance.[31] Most of the time, though, his patients couldn't afford to pay more than a dollar or two for treatment, and sometimes Ossian had to settle for nothing more than a thank-you and a vague promise that the cash would be on its way as soon as payday came.

Still, the fees added up. On a reasonably busy day, Ossian could make twice as much as Black Bottom's best-paid factory workers and far more than he had ever earned toting suitcases at the Fairfax Hotel and waiting tables on the D & C Lines. As cash came in, he squirreled it away. It was his nature to be disciplined about money matters, like his parents before him, to think of the future rather to indulge in the immediate gratification that Detroit provided in abundance. There would be time for extravagances later. But in the early going, it was more important to set his practice on a firm foundation, to build a reputation for dependability and prudence. So through the gray winter of 1922, Ossian worked as hard as he could treating the physical burdens that poverty imposed on his patients, letting his reputation spread through Black Bottom, his office grow busier, his bank account fatten. And in his precious spare moments, he began to look beyond the poor people who filled his days to the professional class he'd spent the previous twelve years preparing to join.

◆

Ossian knew any number of people like him, ambitious young entrepreneurs who saw in the flood of southern peasants the chance to make their fortunes. He spent most days at Palace Drugs in the company of Arkansas-born Cyrus Dozier; occasionally he ran into his old friend from the Fairfax Hotel, Vollington Bristol, now proud owner of a funeral parlor on Division Street; walking along St. Aubin, he passed

A. G. Wright's real estate office and Harry Nuttall's drugstore. Ossian had no trouble easing his way into that world. Black Bottom's businessmen were ebony Babbitts, spending their days wheeling and dealing, their evenings slapping backs and trading jokes in a dizzying array of social clubs and service organizations. Ossian did his share of joining, taking membership in the Benevolent and Protective Order of Elks, in the Free and Accepted Masons' Hiram Lodge No. 1, and in Kappa Alpha Psi's graduate chapter, where he rose to the exalted position of Polemarch. He couldn't have been all that comfortable with the mandatory conviviality of the lodge hall—not exactly his style—but a businessman had to have connections. In much the same spirit, Ossian joined a church, Ebenezer AME, which prided itself on being one of the more progressive congregations in Black Bottom. It must have been an obvious thing to do; no son of Dora and Henry Sweet was going to put aside his religion. But the step had its practical side, too. Church folks expected to see their doctor sitting in a pew on Sunday morning, and if they didn't, they'd be quick to take their business elsewhere.[32]

All his effort paid dividends. It was probably through one of the lodges that Ossian was named a medical examiner for Liberty Life Insurance, an appointment that assured him a steady stream of patients he might not otherwise have acquired. He even made a few friends, no easy matter for a man of Ossian's studied reserve. He came to enjoy the company of Julian Perry, a fellow Howard man struggling to set up a legal practice in Black Bottom. Slight, quiet, and serious like Ossian, Perry made an amiable companion for the occasional evening out. When he needed advice, though, Ossian increasingly turned to his fellow Elk, Mason, and fraternity brother, Dr. Edward Carter, whose office was several blocks north of Ossian's on St. Aubin.[33]

Though Carter was ten years Ossian's senior, there was a real affinity between the two. A shared profession drew them together, but it was more than that. Both of them were sons of humble southern families who had worked their way through school—Carter was the first black doctor to graduate from the University of Iowa's College of Medicine—an experience that gave them a fierce determination that Perry never really had. Like every other Black Bottom businessman, Perry wanted to do well for himself. Carter encouraged Ossian's desire to go further, to work his way beyond the lodge hall and into the upper reaches of black society.[34]

There must have been times in 1922 when Ossian wondered whether such a leap was possible. The elite of colored Detroit wasn't as rarified a circle as Washington's fabled Black 400—no one in Detroit had roots that deep in the American aristocracy—but it was imposing enough. Most members of the black upper class were northerners by birth, a healthy portion of them Canadian-born progeny of fugitive slave families that had prospered in the safety of Ontario's flat farmlands. With their families' money to support them, they had attended the best colleges. Some of them went to Howard, naturally, but many others graduated from white schools: abolitionist Oberlin, the University of Michigan, Columbia, even Harvard. Most of them preferred the quiet elegance of St. Matthew's Episcopal Church to the intensity of the Baptists and the AME. Though they sometimes held leadership posts in the Masons or the Odd Fellows, they rarely went to meetings. And they certainly weren't shopkeepers. The men were invariably doctors, lawyers, and ministers. The women devoted themselves to the social clubs that were the backbone of black philanthropy.

And though they often worked in Black Bottom—even the most skilled colored professionals had a hard time securing white clients—they almost never lived there. A few, such as Dr. Cleague and Dr. Young, owned handsome homes in the small black area nestled among the solidly middle class, native-born white neighborhoods of Detroit's west side. Most of the colored elite, though, settled in otherwise exclusively white parts of the city. Dr. Charles Green, so light skinned he could have passed for white, lived on a gracious side street north of Black Bottom, not far from the grand homes of Boston Boulevard, where Henry Ford had lived when his first Model Ts were rolling out of his factories. Rev. Robert Bradby, the enormously powerful pastor of Second Baptist Church, had a house in a comfortable east-side neighborhood miles from his church, while regal Dr. Albert Johnson, son of one physician and brother to another, lived even farther east, well on the way to Grosse Pointe, a world away from Ossian's room on Clinton Street.[35]

But Sweet and Carter had one entrée into the charmed circle that wasn't open to most of Black Bottom's aspiring entrepreneurs. When the Great Migration reached floodtide in the spring of 1918, eleven of Detroit's foremost colored doctors decided that the city simply had to have a hospital that accepted black patients without discrimination. The city government certainly wasn't going to provide it. So the physicians took it upon themselves to build an appropriate facility. Rather than look for a building in Black Bottom, they bought a rambling old house on Frederick Street, three blocks beyond the ghetto's northern boundary.

The physicians gave their new hospital an appropriately grand name, Dunbar Memorial. It was much harder to make it into a grand institution; Dunbar survived on donations from white charities and the continual effort of its founders. It wasn't enough: the hospital was so small it could admit only twenty-seven patients at a time and so underfunded it could maintain only a single ill-equipped operating room. Still, the doctors took enormous pride in their achievement. They had given the colored people of Detroit their own hospital, a place where they could be treated with care and dignity. They'd hired an entirely black staff of nurses. And they had given themselves a place where they could practice their craft without suffering insults and exclusion, a place of their own.[36]

It was about two miles from Palace Drugs to Dunbar Memorial, just far enough to be inconvenient. But Ossian made the trip as often as time would allow, climbing into the rattletrap of a Model T he bought in the spring of 1922 and bumping through the streets. After years of working at Freedmen's Hospital, he must have found Dunbar's facilities disappointing and the medicine practiced there utterly routine; if a colored doctor encountered a genuinely difficult case, he'd invariably swallow his pride and send the patients off to a white hospital. But the hospital's social opportunities were sterling. Undoubtedly, the contacts Ossian made were casual: standing on Dunbar's broad stone steps, perhaps, chatting with the chief of surgery, Alexander Turner, while the good doctor's chauffeur kept the sedan idling at curbside; trading stories of Howard University with Dr. Ames, the last colored man to serve in the state legislature; asking H. Peyton Johnson, Tufts Medical Class of '96, for his opinion on a puzzling case.[37] It was through such moments—so ephemeral as to seem almost meaningless—that a young man of no pedigree brought himself to the attention of the elite and taught himself their ways.

There is no way to recover all the pieces of information Ossian must have gathered as he listened to his senior colleagues: the name of a tailor who knew how to give a suit coat the right cut, perhaps the merits of one school, one neighborhood, or one church over another; the way the midwesterners' nasal twang altered the pronunciation of a medical term Ossian had learned to say with his deep southern drawl. But there is no doubt that once he made his way into Dunbar's cramped wards, Ossian was again enveloped in the fervid politics of the Talented Tenth, as he had been at Wilberforce years earlier.

◆

Times had certainly changed. By the early 1920s, the Bookerite movement that had so enraged Scarborough and his associates in the first decade of the century had been thoroughly routed, and Booker T. Washington himself was gone from the scene, killed by an unspecified disease—syphilis, some whispered—in the closing days of 1915. The tectonic shifts brought on by the Great War, meanwhile, opened new fissures within colored America. NAACP liberals found themselves under attack from a new generation of radicals, while integrationists such as W. E. B. Du Bois turned on the black nationalists who were surging to the flamboyant standard of Jamaican-born Marcus Garvey.[38] However deep their difference, though, civil rights activists shared a sense that the war had fundamentally altered the terms of combat in the battle for racial justice.

While Du Bois pledged that Negroes would return from Europe ready to fight for equal rights, socialists A. Philip Randolph and Chandler Owen preached the power of armed resistance. "We are . . . urging Negroes and other oppressed groups confronted with lynching and mob violence to act upon the recognized and accepted law of self-defense," the pair wrote during the bloody summer of 1919. "Always regard your own life as more important than the life of the person about to take yours, and if a choice has to be made between the sacrifice of your life and the loss of the lyncher's life, choose to preserve your own and to destroy that of the lynching mob." Garvey's fellow Jamaican Claude McKay captured the same sentiment in a verse that swept through black communities like a sudden summer storm. "If we must die, let it not be like hogs / Hunted and penned in an inglorious spot. . . . Like men we'll face the murderous, cowardly pack / Pressed to the wall, dying, but fighting back!" The black press personalized the new militancy with a telling name. "The NEW NEGRO . . . does not fear the face of day," proclaimed the *Kansas City Call*. "The time for cringing is over."[39]

The crosscurrents of civil rights cut through Detroit, as they did most major urban centers. The Motor City had a handful of black radicals struggling mightily to organize the proletariat. And for a few seasons, Garvey made deep inroads among Black Bottom's working people, some five thousand of whom joined his United Negro Improvement

Association in the early 1920s.[40] The medical men of Dunbar, however, had no truck with such newfangled movements. They were steadfastly devoted to the ideals Du Bois had articulated almost a generation earlier, committed to the principle of integration through agitation and convinced that they, colored Detroit's leading lights, were obligated to take the lead.

The effort was shot through with condescension, the dark side of racial uplift. Most of Detroit's elite were convinced that the city's race relations had declined partly because whites were appalled by the bad manners migrants had brought with them from the rural South. "Why is segregation increasing?" sniffed the head of the Detroit Urban League, a graduate of Tufts and Harvard. "Chiefly on account of the loud, noisy, almost nude women in 'Mother Hubbards' standing around on the public thoroughfares. . . . There are dirty white people of course, but white people are the judges and colored people are being judged."[41] It must have been comforting to think that the Talented Tenth might break down the growing wall of segregation by scrubbing clean the face of the ghetto. Dunbar's physicians were certainly willing to give it a try.

The Detroit Urban League, which had Dr. Green and Dr. Johnson on its board, sent its members into Black Bottom to hand out pamphlets instructing the poor on how to carry themselves with the necessary decorum. "Don't crowd inside of a street car filled with people in your dirty, greasy overalls," the leaflet helpfully suggested. "Wear a coat over your clothes when you are going back and forth from the foundry." Under the direction of Dr. Turner's wife, the colored YWCA on St. Aubin Avenue brought working girls off the streets and into sewing circles. For their part, Dunbar's senior staff organized its own Health Week, during which the hospital's doctors traveled across Black Bottom denouncing folk practices carried up from the South and urging those crowded into rooming houses and dilapidated flats to keep their homes neat and clean. The doctors found it an edifying experience. "It has been found," they reported, "that in a great many homes in Detroit that rats enjoy as much care and comfort in the house as do some of the members of the family."[42]

As they preached to the poor, the elite struggled to maintain the militancy that the New Negro was supposed to embody. In the 1910s, Detroit's black professionals had built one of the more vibrant NAACP branches in the country. The branch's guiding force was Father Robert Bagnall, pastor of St. Matthew's Episcopal, the colored elite's church of choice. In typical NAACP fashion, Bagnall and his Talented Tenth associates used the full force of law to batter away at the discriminatory practices spreading across the city. The branch filed dozens of legal suits against businesses that refused to serve colored customers. When trains leaving the Michigan Central Terminal for points south required Negro passengers to ride in separate cars, Bagnall demanded that the railroad companies rescind the practice. With the branch's backing, lawyer Charles Mahoney, a Republican of some influence in Detroit politics, forced the nearby town of Ypsilanti to abandon the school segregation it had practiced for half a century. And in a singular act of solidarity, Bagnall's branch waged a long campaign on behalf of a luckless Georgia farmhand, Thomas Ray, who in June 1920 had murdered his abusive landlord.

After the fatal shooting, Ray had fled north toward Canada, but before he could cross the border, the Detroit police had taken him into custody. The branch's attorney, W. Hayes McKinney, quickly launched a series of legal maneuvers to block Ray's extradition to Georgia; should he be sent back, McKinney argued, he'd surely be lynched. The case generated enormous passion in the black community: when a rumor passed through Black Bottom that a white mob was going to seize Ray during a court appearance, a phalanx of Negroes threw a protective cordon around the courthouse. The branch finally sealed the victory in June 1921, a full year after the shooting, when Michigan's governor declared the homicide justifiable.[43]

By then, though, the branch had also suffered a crushing loss. Perhaps it was the surging militancy of the New Negro, perhaps just a matter of timing, but in June 1920, the white progressives who ran the NAACP's Executive Board finally decided to place the association's day-to-day operations in the hands of a colored man, James Weldon Johnson. As soon as the appointment was made, the new secretary set out to build a black staff. Du Bois was already an institution unto himself in the offices of the *Crisis*. But Johnson added three more men. For the position of assistant secretary, he hired Walter White, a twenty-seven-year-old blond-haired, blue-eyed bantam with a genius for self-promotion. William Pickens, a longtime NAACP activist, signed on as field organizer. And Robert Bagnall agreed to serve as national director of branches. Bagnall resigned his pulpit at St. Matthew's in January 1921 to take up his post at the NAACP's New York headquarters.[44]

The Detroit branch couldn't function without him. Bagnall's successor, attorney McKinney, launched a few initiatives of his own, including a half-hearted attack on police harassment of interracial couples, but the branch quickly became engulfed by infighting so vicious it all but ceased to function. McKinney eventually resigned, turning the organization over to a businessman who wouldn't even answer his mail, much less confront segregation's steady advance. From Manhattan, Bagnall raged at the destruction of his handiwork, but at such a distance, he couldn't pull the branch back together.[45]

By the time Ossian integrated himself into Dunbar in 1922, the coordinated civil rights campaigns of the 1910s had devolved into a series of ad hoc actions, sporadic protests hastily conceived by friends and colleagues in response to the latest affront to the race. A handful of doctors, tired of having women in the throes of labor turned away from Detroit's best maternity hospital because they were colored, tried to have the facility's public funding cut. When rumors of a Negro crime wave pushed police repression in Black Bottom to frightening new heights, the Talented Tenth threw together a committee to plead with city hall to hire more colored officers. A prominent Negro attorney, caught up in the force's crackdown, was dragged out of his car and searched at gunpoint by a snarling cop. The lawyer sued the officer for fifty thousand dollars in damages. Such forays were brave enough—it was riskier to confront discrimination without the protection an organization provided—but against the consolidating forces of white supremacy, they had a quixotic air about them, the colored elite imitating, in their way, Claude McKay's tragic hero, fighting back against an enemy that in the end was destined to win.[46]

It wasn't a role that came naturally to Ossian. Though he bridled at the discrimination spreading across the city, he'd never participated in any sort of challenge to white supremacy. Under his colleagues' influence, though, he took an increasing interest in racial affairs. He never got around to joining the NAACP, perhaps because the Detroit branch was moribund, but he took out subscriptions to all the black publications favored by the Talented Tenth: Du Bois's *Crisis,* Randolph and Owen's *Messenger,* the *Chicago Defender* and the *Pittsburgh Courier,* two of the nation's largest and most influential black newspapers. Poring over the pages of those papers, he came to fancy himself a student of the nation's racial problems, a specialty he'd never claimed at Wilberforce or Howard. He was even drawn into a few of Dunbar's initiatives. During Health Week in 1922, he walked over to Macedonia Baptist Church to deliver the doctors' prepared lecture on cleanliness and proper garbage removal. It didn't take much effort on Ossian's part, since the church was only a block away from Palace Drugs. But Ossian took one step more. He actually joined one of the small protests that his senior colleagues mounted.[47]

One day, Charles Green approached Ossian with an invitation, a precious thing to a young man striving to be noticed. A local college group planned to host a testimonial dinner in honor of the city's greatest sports hero, the Detroit Tigers' brilliant outfielder, Ty Cobb. The best hitter the game had ever seen, Cobb was a baseball genius and, in Ernest Hemingway's delicate phrase, "an absolute shit": a bully, a thug, and, thanks to a childhood spent in backcountry Georgia, a racist of frightening ferocity. The venom of lynch law surged through his veins; even the slightest violation of the color line was an insult to his honor and a cause for violence. When a Negro worker yelled at him to stay off the tar he had just laid on a Detroit street, Cobb assaulted the man. When a colored groundskeeper tried to shake his hand, Cobb knocked him to the ground and kicked him in the head, then tried to choke the man's wife. When a colored elevator operator mistakenly took him to the wrong floor of a Cleveland hotel, Cobb slapped him; the hotel's black security guard intervened, and Cobb responded by pulling a knife and slashing him in the face.[48]

What a delicious thought, to have Cobb sitting on the dais watching in horror as a squad of black men strode into the auditorium to join the festivities. So Green bought a table's worth of tickets. Then he asked Ossian and eight other colored men to join him for the evening's entertainment. It is easy to imagine that Ossian hesitated to accept; this would be his first involvement in any protest, and the dinner was going to be a very public affair. To refuse Green's invitation, though, was to risk being thought a coward, unworthy of a place among the city's Talented Tenth. In the end, the risks were small. Though the white crowd stirred as the group made their entrance, no one tried to stop Ossian and the others from taking their seats, not even Cobb, who for once managed to keep his temper.[49]

Ossian relished the moment enough to remember the details several years later. Undoubtedly, he reveled in the sense of solidarity that the ten men felt that evening, the slap on the back from a senior colleague when the dinner was done, the raucous laughter in the staff room when the tale was retold, the slightly more vigorous nod the next time he passed Green in the wards, the way that just a little bit of courage opened up the charmed circle of Detroit's elite, if only for an evening. But he also must have realized just how small a protest it had been. Going through the race papers stacked up in his Black Bottom rooms, Ossian couldn't miss all the brave talk about the New Negro, the exhortations to self-sacrifice on behalf of the race, the glorification of confrontation, a politics for young men who knew no fear. No matter how enjoyable the experience had been, spoiling the color scheme at Cobb's testimonial certainly didn't measure up to such great expectations.

But Ossian did know fear. In his nightly reading, Ossian inevitably focused on the most recent installments in the nation's long history of racial horrors. There was the unusual litany of lynchings, fifty-one in 1922, including three black men murdered on the same day in a small Texas town. It was the larger cruelties that most often caught his attention, though. He brooded over Tulsa's epic 1921 pogrom, still a raw wound the following year. More than a hundred colored people had died in two days of white rioting, all of it brought on by a Negro teenager accidentally brushing up against a white girl in a downtown elevator. But Ossian fixed on a single death, which Walter White had movingly chronicled for the *Nation*. Dr. A. C. Jackson was one of Tulsa's most promising young men, a skilled surgeon who, White carefully noted, had done advanced study at the Mayo Clinic. On the first day of the riot, Jackson exhausted himself treating the wounded, and when darkness finally came, he hid in the basement of his substantial home, which by some miracle the rioters had yet to set ablaze. Early in the morning of the second day, Jackson smelled whiffs of smoke from the fires that were beginning to consume his block. Facing immolation, he came out of his hiding place to surrender to the vigilantes filling his street. "Here I am," the doctor yelled out, his arms upraised. "Take me." But one of the mob, a teenager out for a night of fun, lowered his rifle and pumped two bullets into Jackson's chest. Then another white boy stepped over the doctor as he writhed in pain on the sidewalk and shot him again.[50]

A year and a half later, Ossian's attention was riveted by another southern riot. On New Year's Day 1923, news of a rape shot through the hamlet of Sumner, Florida. Enraged whites marched on the nearby colored town of Rosewood, though they had no proof that the rapist was hiding there. Like the black men of Washington, D.C., in 1919, Rosewood's Negroes tried to defend themselves from the assault, but they were overrun. At least seventeen of Rosewood's residents were murdered that day, and the rest were driven into the countryside while the mob burned the town to the ground. The story cut into Ossian partly because the attack took place just seventy miles north of Bartow.[51] But there was more to it than that. In Tulsa and Rosewood, Ossian could see the reflection of the fires that had burned above the banks of the Peace River and along the streets of Washington, D.C., and in those flickering flames—searing light dancing off the deepest blackness—he knew that the terror that balled up inside him at the thought of truly confronting white supremacy was entirely justified.

◆

Maybe it was the color of her high yellow skin, maybe the way the lights above the dance floor brought out the hints of auburn in her hair. It could have been her self-assurance, the deeply ingrained confidence he never quite secured, or her gracious manner or her warm toothy smile that drew him to her. Whatever the reason, when Ossian met Gladys Mitchell one evening in 1922, he felt an immediate attraction.[52]

It's hard to believe that Ossian hadn't been in love before. If he'd had other infatuations, though, there hadn't been much opportunity to act on them. Wilberforce maintained such high walls between its male and female students it would have taken tremendous effort to scale them. Though Howard's co-eds were some of the race's most accomplished young women, Ossian spent his days in the medical school's almost exclusively male world and his nights either hunched over textbooks or working to pay his bills. In any case, the timing was never right. Ossian had degrees to earn, a practice to establish, a career to build. There hadn't been room for a wife. By 1922, though, he'd made such great strides that whatever reservations he had felt melted away.

The moment wasn't completely free of calculation. With all the diversions and entertainments Black Bottom had to offer, from smoldering nightclubs and red-hot dance halls, Ossian went looking for companionship at one of the most respectable venues in all of black Detroit, a formal dance at the St. Aubin Avenue's colored YWCA, a favorite charity of Dunbar's doctors and their wives. Gladys was precisely the kind of young woman he would have expected to find there. A slender, almost frail twenty-year-old with a long, thin face and weak chin, almond skin, deep brown eyes, and luxuriously long hair that flowed to her waist when she uncoiled it, Gladys carried herself with the charming reserve and sure grace that the middle class bestowed on its daughters.[53]

They were gifts she almost didn't receive. Gladys's mother, Rosella, was only seventeen, a native of Washington, D.C., living in Pittsburgh, when she gave birth to her only daughter; if Gladys's father was a presence in the early days, he apparently didn't remain so, though it's not clear what happened to him. In a city as rough-hewn and unforgiving as Pittsburgh, it would have been simple for a teenage mother without a husband's income to slip into the miasma of poverty. But Rosella had the great fortune to meet and marry Benjamin Mitchell, a musician by trade, just barely out of his teens himself. When Gladys was seven, the family moved to Detroit, where her stepfather built a successful career playing for pit orchestras in downtown theaters while teaching piano on the side.[54]

Rosella and Benjamin handed their only daughter every advantage they could. They joined St. Matthew's, Bagnall's prestigious church, where Gladys was surrounded by the colored elite that Ossian scrambled to join. They moved to the northeast side of the city, settling into a pleasant two-story house on Cairney Street, directly across from The Nativity of Our Lord Catholic Church, a massive edifice built to serve the immigrants who filled the surrounding streets. There was one other colored family on the Mitchells' block, a doctor and his wife; otherwise, the neighborhood was completely white, not wealthy certainly, but solidly working class, a safe, stable area full of hardworking families.[55]

Comfort didn't come cheaply—Rosella had to take in boarders to meet the mortgage—but the extra work was worth it. Gladys was able to go to the local grade school, where she was the only black child in her class, and to Northeastern High, where the education was far better than it would have been in the colored part of town. The Mitchells trained Gladys in the social graces that a young lady should have when she ventured into the world: the soft handshake, the ready smile, the ability to carry a casual conversation without so much as a trace of effort. And they gave her a home filled with books and music; études and nocturnes drifted through the parlor, a world away from the rough sounds of the roadhouses and the buffet flats.[56]

A secure childhood made Gladys a strikingly poised young woman. Unlike Ossian, she felt no need to impress acquaintances by overpowering them. Instead, she drew them in with her impeccable manners, so carefully cultivated as to be almost invisible. Having extended courtesy, she expected courtesy in return, even when dealing with whites. Gladys certainly wasn't naive enough to think that race didn't matter. Sitting in her family's pew at St. Matthew's, she heard Bagnall continually condemn the discrimination that marred Detroit. And white violence had brushed by her family; some of her cousins had been trapped in the Chicago Riot of 1919 and one of them, a policeman, had almost been murdered by a mob. But racism hadn't scarred her the way it had Ossian. She was comfortable in the presence of whites, was, in fact, a quarter Caucasian herself. The auburn in her hair was an inheritance from her grandfather, a Scotsman transplanted to Virginia. So when whites didn't treat her as the equal she knew herself to be, she assumed a steeliness—so hard-edged it cut to the quick—that Ossian, for all his bitter memories, couldn't manage.[57]

Comfort also made Gladys less focused than her husband. Ossian had marched through his schooling with the single-mindedness ambition creates. Gladys drifted. After high school, she enrolled at Detroit City College but she was not a serious student, moving from teachers' education to nursing without settling on any course.[58] It wasn't a matter of intellect but rather of expectation: Gladys didn't need education's imprimatur the way Ossian did. On the contrary, she must have understood that any time she spent in front of the classroom or in the hospital ward was likely to be temporary. Her parents had trained her to follow the middle-class path, to be a wife and mother; they assumed that managing a household would be her life's work, not teaching schoolchildren or caring for the sick.

There were other differences as well. Ossian was almost seven years older than Gladys and much more experienced: he had been on his own for a dozen years, whereas she had never lived outside her parents' home. Within the Mitchells' world, though, Gladys had the advantage; for all of his mother's attempts to bring an air of refinement to the Sweets' home, Ossian was still too much of a country boy to be completely at ease amid the flowered divans and fine lace doilies of a formal sitting room. For Ossian, such contrasts must have only added to the attraction. When this charming young woman slipped her hand into his, he knew he had found the sort of mate a young doctor of such obvious promise ought to have. After a few months of dating, Ossian summoned up the courage to propose. The wedding was a small but gracious affair, held at St. Matthew's—her church, not his—five days before Christmas 1922. Ossian's friend Julian Perry stood by his side while Gladys made her way up the aisle on the arm of her stepfather. Father Bagnall's replacement, Everard Daniels, read the vows. Then the best man and Gladys's maid of honor, her friend Serena Rochelle, handed the couple the wedding bands they were to place onto their spouse's finger, a permanent sign of devotion, a moment of triumph for both bride and groom. Though she probably didn't know it, it's very likely that Gladys was pregnant.[59]

There was never any possibility of Ossian taking his bride to live in Black Bottom. Naturally, Gladys had spent plenty of time in the neighborhood; St. Matthew's was in the heart of the district, and the Y where she'd met Ossian was on its eastern edge, close to Palace Drugs. But a middle-class northern girl couldn't be expected to live among the migrants and the foreigners, to shop in the same stores as foundry workers and maids, to share the sidewalks with bootleggers and numbers runners. And with Gladys's light skin, it was only a matter of time before a beat cop pulled the couple over, slapped Ossian up against a wall, and demanded to know why he was keeping company with a white woman. So, instead of settling into the Clinton Street apartment or even searching for something better nearby, Ossian packed up his rooms and moved with his bride into her parents' house.[60] For the first time in his life, he was going to live among white people.

◆

They didn't plan to stay with the Mitchells for long. Sometime during their brief courtship Ossian told Gladys that he intended in the near future to spend a year in Europe studying the latest medical advances. Perhaps he dangled the idea as an extended honeymoon: pleasing Gladys is one of the few explanations for why the usually practical young doctor wanted to shut down a practice that was just beginning to thrive. Maybe, since being rejected for an internship at Freedmen's Hospital, he'd been hoping to obtain postgraduate training that was better than anything Washington could provide. The notion of studying in Europe, rather than looking for a domestic program, may well have come from listening to his colleagues at Dunbar; Alexander Turner's wife had spent six years studying music in Leipzig, a fact sure to impress someone the first dozen times she said it. Perhaps the idea reflected a touch of sibling rivalry. When Ossian's brother Otis completed his dental training at Tennessee's Meharry Medical School in 1922, he went on to an advanced course in the treatment of pyorrhea at Canada's McGill University; studying in Europe would certainly outdo that achievement. Surely it was important to Ossian that there Negroes were actually treated with respect, dignity, and even, at times, a touch of honor. "For what am I thankful for this night?" W. E. B. Du Bois wrote from France in the April 1919 issue of the *Crisis*. "For nothing but the most commonplace of commonplaces: a table of gentlewomen and gentlemen—soft-spoken, sweet-tempered, full of human sympathy, who made me, a stranger, one of them." It wouldn't be easy to pay for such pleasures; no matter how much money Ossian had managed to put away in his first year of practice, his bank balance couldn't have been high enough to pay for a transatlantic voyage and a year's living expenses. But a few months living rent-free would help to top off his accounts and make such an extraordinary adventure possible.[61]

Gladys's pregnancy must have complicated matters. By springtime, she was showing, by early summer well along. Surely she would have had some reservations about leaving the country shortly after giving birth. But Ossian seems to have forged ahead, plotting out a course so grandiose it would have taken a great deal of advance planning. The couple would spend their first few months at the University of Vienna, where he could attend lectures by surgeon Anton von Eiselsberg. Once the fall semester was complete, he, Gladys, and the baby would spend a few weeks touring the Mediterranean, then settle in Paris for the winter and spring, when Marie Curie would be teaching at the Sorbonne.[62]

Ossian couldn't have chosen more impressive names. Baron von Eiselsberg had helped to create the field of neurosurgery: he'd been the first doctor in the world to resect tumors of the spinal cord and the brain, accomplishments widely considered two of the most amazing medical feats of the age. For her part, Curie was an international icon: the meticulous scientist who first isolated radium; the brilliant theorist whose work on radiology promised to transform medical practice; twice winner of the Nobel Prize. During her triumphant tour of the United States in May 1921, about the time Ossian was applying for a Freedmen's internship, a New York magazine had hailed Curie with only slight exaggeration as "the greatest woman in the world." Word of Ossian's agenda would have left Dunbar's doctors—and anyone else even slightly acquainted with the scientific world—in open-mouthed awe.[63]

As it turned out, the Sweets didn't have a newborn to take with them. On July 17, 1923, Gladys went into premature labor. It's impossible to say precisely how far the pregnancy had advanced. If Gladys had become pregnant on her wedding night, her baby boy was born two days short of thirty weeks, old enough to have opened his eyes but too young to breathe without a struggle. Chances are he was a few weeks older, since he managed to survive three days. Ossian and Gladys's firstborn died at three o'clock in the afternoon of July 20 and the next day was buried in Roseland Park Cemetery, in an all-white suburb north of Detroit. Having expected the worst, his parents hadn't given him a name.[64]

The Mitchells' house must have been wrapped in mourning. Even if the pregnancy hadn't been well-timed, the Sweets surely had indulged themselves in the excitement of anticipating parenthood. With the death of his boy, moreover, Ossian had to have heard the echo of his parents' experience losing their first son as a toddler years ago. Under the circumstances, the European trip probably took on added meaning. Traveling abroad would have offered a chance to get some distance from Detroit, to begin to forget, to put the tragedy behind them. Exactly one month after the baby's birth, Ossian and Gladys completed their passport applications. The itinerary was already set, passage booked. All that remained was packing trunks and leaving home.[65]

The Sweets set sail for Europe aboard the S.S. *Carmania* on October 6, 1923. It must have been a bit frightening watching New York harbor fade into the distance. Neither Gladys nor Ossian had ever been outside the United States, except perhaps for a day trip across the Detroit River to Ontario, hardly an experience in world travel. But the couple also must have been exhilarated by it all. It had been fourteen years since Ossian boarded the train out of Bartow, a terrified child sitting alone in a filthy car reserved for colored people. A decade and a half later, he and his wife were standing on the glistening deck of an ocean liner, the chill wind whipping their faces, heading toward the sort of experience most Americans, white or black, could only dream of having. The first fine surprise came when the couple went below deck to find that their stateroom lay between two cabins occupied by whites. On the Cunard Line, there was no Jim Crow.[66]

The trip from New York harbor to Vienna took Ossian and Gladys through a world still shuddering from the horrors of the Great War. The *Carmania*'s first port of call was in Queenstown, Ireland, a nation engulfed in civil war, the final fratricidal act of the revolution begun in high drama during Easter week 1916. The Sweets disembarked in Liverpool, where years of deprivation had given way to waves of working-class protest and a leftward swing in public life. Once on the Continent, the couple passed through land made desolate by the most merciless combat the world had ever seen. Paris's glittering streets were haunted by the maimed, blinded, shell-shocked veterans of the trenches and by the too-young widows of those who didn't return. Vienna, capital of the fledgling republic of Austria, had lost three hundred thousand of its inhabitants during the war, but still the city confronted a severe shortage of decent housing that the new socialist government was desperately trying to fill. It must have been so strange, so shocking, to see a new Europe struggling to be born.[67]

Settling into a daily routine created challenges that at times had to have seemed more than daunting. Whenever they walked into a shop or encountered a neighbor, Gladys and Ossian had to rely on the less-than-polished German and French they had learned in school. Though Vienna and Paris weren't expensive cities by the standards of boom-town Detroit, the Sweets still had to make do without an income, so they undoubtedly counted every schilling and franc. But the greatest test was personal. Shortly after arriving in Vienna, Gladys discovered she was pregnant again. The realization must have opened up all sorts of fears. Should something go wrong this time, Gladys wouldn't have family and friends to comfort and console her, and should the baby die, it would have to be buried in foreign soil. Even if all went well, if she carried to term, the child would be born toward the end May 1924, before the Sorbonne's term ended, so she would have to deliver in Paris, itself an intimidating prospect.[68] It was comforting to have a doctor for a husband, of course, but there must have been times when Gladys longed to have her mother hold her hand.

For Ossian, though, the year was magical. Attending lectures didn't put him at the center of the academic world; the truly innovative work was being done not in university amphitheaters but at the Eiselsberg Clinic and the Curie Institute, where doctoral students toiled away under their supervisors' intimate direction. Still, Ossian could pick up information on the latest medical innovations, as long as he could follow complex technical presentations in languages that weren't second nature to him. The knowledge Ossian acquired wasn't going to be transferred back home easily. No matter how well he understood the details of Eiselsberg's neurosurgeries, it was inconceivable that he would replicate the procedures in Dunbar's rudimentary operating room. And while Curie lectured on radium therapy's curative powers—her presentations delivered to the throng of students in her elegant Polish-accented French—Ossian knew that patients in Black Bottom weren't about to gain access to expensive experimental treatments, not when something as simple as an X-ray was hard to come by. But Ossian wasn't really looking for practical training. He wanted the imposing credentials that studying with Eiselsberg and Curie bestowed, credentials most American physicians only dreamed of having. In that regard, the trip was enormously successful. Though Ossian didn't earn a degree during his year abroad, the Sweets would always think of his European education as his greatest accomplishment, a point of unending pride.[69]

Ossian also reveled in the lack of racial discrimination. European nations had their deep, disturbing prejudices: cosmopolitan Vienna sustained an anti-Semitic current strong enough to have swept along its most infamous prewar resident, Adolf Hitler, while republican France showed no interest in the liberty of its colonial subjects in Africa and Indochina. On the side streets and boulevards of the two capitals, though, dark skin simply didn't bear the stigma that it did in the United States. Along Franz Josef's magnificent Ringstrasse, a colored couple was something of a rarity, worth a second glance but hardly a cause for concern. The world war had brought many more blacks to Paris, most of them Africans serving in the French military but a sizable number of them American soldiers, members of the black battalions raised in the spring of 1917. The French were fully aware of Jim Crow—the U.S. military made sure of that—but they insisted that it would not be imported. Colored Americans were free to go into any public establishment, to live wherever they wished, to socialize with whites, even to keep company with members of the opposite sex. Some Parisians went beyond openness to admiration. Immediately after the war, black culture became all the rage in the quarters of the avant-garde. Intellectuals embraced the "primitivism" of African art, literature, and dance, while the city's sophisticates fell head over heels for American jazz. The combination of equality and fraternity made Paris into a mecca for Negro artists. When the Sweets arrived in early 1924, the greatest migration was still a year or so away. But there was already a small thriving community of black Americans in Montmartre, the bohemian neighborhood that lay in the shadow of Sacré Coeur. At night, young Parisians crowded into its nightclubs and filled its black-owned restaurants, where haute cuisine gave way to downhome cooking.[70]

Ossian and Gladys were no more interested in the Montmartre scene than they were in the nightlife of Black Bottom. Most likely, they settled in the Latin Quarter, where Ossian could walk to the university and Madame Curie's lectures. However far they were from the smoky clubs, though, they shared in the freedom that drew jazzmen and poets to the City of Lights. For the first time in his life, Ossian experienced what it was like not to be branded an inferior. Small pleasures must have been so invigorating: to walk into a café off the Boul'Mich without having to wonder whether he would be turned away; to be called "monsieur" by a shopkeeper; to have a white man surrender his seat on the streetcar to Gladys, now uncomfortably large with their baby; to have a white woman smile at him as he held open a door to let her pass. Simple courtesies that in the United States he would never have received: that's what Ossian remembered from his springtime in Paris.[71]

Only one incident marred the Sweets' time abroad. As Gladys's due date drew closer, Ossian set out to make arrangements for a hospital stay; better to have her surrounded by professionals in case of emergency. The obvious choice was the American Hospital in the nearby suburb of Neuilly-Sur-Seine, an excellent private institution founded by well-to-do expatriates to care for Americans living in the city. Knowing that the hospital depended on donations to pay its operating expenses, Ossian contributed three hundred francs—not a major sum but generous enough for a couple of a tight budget—on the assumption that administrators would reciprocate by assuring Gladys a bed. He was wrong. Shortly before his wife's delivery date, Ossian was informed that the hospital couldn't accept Gladys. The white Americans who made up the vast majority of patients, he was told, wouldn't be comfortable with the idea of sharing a ward with a colored woman.[72]

Luckily, Gladys didn't need any special medical care this time. On May 29, 1924, she gave birth to a healthy baby girl, the first daughter of freedom's third generation. The Sweets gave her a suitably Gallic name, Marguerite, though they soon took to calling her Iva. Even as he rejoiced in the safe arrival of their child, however, Ossian couldn't bring himself to forgive the hospital's insult. Here was the truly cutting pain of Jim Crow. With its casual rejection, handed down simply as a matter of course, the American hospital had imperiled the health, and perhaps the life, of his wife and child, and there was nothing he could do but endure the affront. Timing made it all the worse. By late May, the Sorbonne's academic year was drawing to a close; Ossian and Glady had already booked passage aboard the S.S. *Paris*, sailing out of Le Havre on June 21. During the Sweets' last precious weeks in Paris, while Gladys fussed over the baby, Ossian had time to dwell on the hospital's callous reminder of the world awaiting his family when they went back home.[73]

FIVE

WHITE HOUSES

Through most of June 1925, the rumor passed up and down Garland Avenue. It was handed off in casual conversations, tossed across kitchen tables, turned over on front porches, where people liked to gather when the weather turned warm. The bungalow on the corner had been sold, neighbors told each other, and a colored man had bought it. Right off, people had been concerned, but they knew better than to believe every bit of gossip that came their way. The couple who owned the bungalow kept to themselves mostly—folks didn't even know their names—and no one dared to ask them whether the story was true. So there was no panic until Sunday, July 12, when the posters were nailed to the lampposts.[1]

The posters' tone was temperate enough, as such things went: there was none of the wild ranting of the Klan broadsides plastered around town, no skull-and-crossbones warnings crudely copied out. This message read as if a real estate agent had written it. "Do you want to maintain the existing good health conditions and environment for your little children?" the flyer asked. "Do you want to see your neighborhood kept up to its present high standards?" Those who shared those goals were invited to organize "in self-defense" at what the Waterworks Park Improvement Association was calling a mass meeting. It was to be held at the schoolhouse on Tuesday evening, two nights after the signs went up. No one had ever heard of the Waterworks Park Improvement Association, but the message was clear enough. Standing on the sidewalk, staring at the poster hanging limply on the rough wood, people knew the Negroes were coming.[2]

There was no stopping the panic then. In the privacy of their flats, husbands and wives talked nervously of fragile family budgets, mortgages years from being repaid, and the specter of plummeting property values. Children heard the fear in their parents' hushed voices and spun out the horrors that the Negroes would bring to their homes, terrifying and thrilling themselves with thoughts of assault and pillage. Out on the streets, there was rage at the audacity of the coloreds, moving where they didn't belong, buying the best goddamned house on the block.[3]

Seven hundred people turned out on Tuesday night, July 14, for the meeting at the elementary school, far more than organizers had expected. Despite its size, it was a polite, orderly crowd: foremen washed and groomed after a day's work; salesmen and clerks in their crisp white shirts; young mothers; teenage boys with arms crossed and faces set, all gathered on the schoolhouse lawn. The chairman of the Waterworks Park Improvement Association, a local man named Harold McGlynn who lived a dozen doors up from the bungalow in question, said a few words about the need for neighbors to band together. Then he turned the meeting over to the keynote speaker, and the attitude of the evening changed.[4]

He was a stranger, an outsider, and the moment he began talking everyone knew he was a hard case. He had come to tonight's meeting, he said, as a representative of the Tireman Avenue Improvement Association, and that alone riveted folks' attention. For weeks, the violence in and around Tireman had been front-page news: three times in the past month Negroes had tried to move into that neighborhood, and three times whites had driven them out. So heated had the conflict been that the mayor publicly appealed for calm, saying that Detroit was heading down the same bloody path as East St. Louis, Chicago, and Washington, D.C. But the speaker on that summer evening hadn't come to Garland to preach the peace the mayor hoped for. He shouted so that even those on the far reaches of the crowd could hear him say how vital the fight was that lay ahead. Tireman's homeowners didn't want coloreds in their neighborhood: Negroes were a pestilence, a plague. The Tireman Avenue Improvement Association had done its duty. Now Garland should do the same. Use legal means if possible, force if necessary. But put the niggers out. Put them out.[5]

The assembly cheered. Not just a few rabble-rousers, not just the

Klansmen, but all of them, although some standing amid the crush were ashamed afterward. Before the speaker could even finish his address, the entire crowd, seven hundred decent, hard-working, sober citizens cheered harder than they had the entire evening, their applause rolling across the schoolyard, rumbling through the clear summer night, and echoing off the bungalow on the opposite corner not a hundred feet away.[6]

•

"If I had known how bitter that neighborhood was going to be," Ossian said later, "I wouldn't have taken that house as a gift." It was the sort of thing he had to say then, when his life depended on striking just the right tone. But it wasn't true. To be sure, Ossian and Gladys didn't have an intimate knowledge of the surrounding area. But in the summer of 1925, there was no missing the hatred seething through the streets of Detroit. And there was no reason to think that Garland Avenue was immune from its contagion.[7]

The Sweets had returned to the States on June 28, 1924 and within a day or two were back at the Mitchells' cozy house on Cairney Street. It was a triumphant homecoming, with a baby to show off and, when Gladys needed a rest, to hand off to doting grandparents. Ossian had his sparkling new credentials: no new degrees to add to his name, but his stories of Baron von Eiselsberg and Madame Curie were more than enough to impress anyone who cared to listen. And the Sweets undoubtedly had their tales of travel—the wonderful details of the exotic sights they'd seen, the strange foods they'd eaten, the tourists' misunderstandings and mistakes that seemed so funny in the retelling. Gladys seemed to have acquired an air of sophistication in her year abroad, acquaintances remarked, and Ossian seemed to stand just a bit taller, if such a thing were possible.[8]

In many ways, 1924 was a pivotal year for Ossian, a moment of passage from one age to another. It wasn't simply that his twenties were coming to a close—he turned twenty-nine on the thirtieth of October— or that he now had the responsibility of fatherhood. It was more a matter of expectations. With his reputation secure and his credentials now dramatically enhanced, the time had come to move beyond the strict frugality of his early days in Detroit. He could demand a new status. Rather than driving his old Model T, which was hopelessly out of fashion, he bought a brand-new Buick touring car, an automobile to match the fine machines his senior colleagues parked outside Dunbar

Memorial. There wasn't any question that, after his time away, he'd rebuild his practice in Black Bottom. But instead of moving back to Palace Drugs, he rented space a few blocks north of the pharmacy. It was just a storefront, right next door to a funeral home, hardly a reassuring sight for sick folk making their way into his waiting room, but for the first time in his career, Ossian had an office of his own, an indulgence perhaps, but also a sure sign of upward mobility.[9]

The year saw another shift as well, more subtle but even more profound. Ever so slowly, Ossian was beginning to replace his parents as the center of the Sweet family. Dora and Henry had nurtured the change each time they'd regaled their younger children with stories of Ossian's successes. Now the older ones were beginning to follow the path Ossian had made for them. In the summer of 1923, Dora and Henry's second boy, Otis, arrived in Detroit to begin his career as a dentist. A few months later, their third son, Henry, left his parents' farm for Wilberforce, the first step in his march to be just like the elder brother he barely knew.

Living apart for the past fourteen years, Ossian and Otis weren't close friends. Their personalities widened the gap between them. They shared the businessman's touch: within a few months of coming to Detroit, Otis was running a promising practice ("Dr. O. O. Sweet, Painless Dentist") not far from Palace Drugs, in an office he shared with the president of the Detroit branch of Marcus Garvey's Universal Negro Improvement Association. Unlike his brother, though, Otis didn't combine dedication to his profession with a relentless drive to excel. A friendly, engaging man with a guileless, boyish face, he loved to take in the baseball games at Mack Park, where the Negro League played; to go dancing on colored nights at the glittering Graystone Ballroom; to while away the hours at the Nacrima Club or one of the other lodges he rushed to join. Ossian cringed at Otis's lack of sophistication, and he was not one to hold his tongue when he saw something to criticize. An acquaintance once remarked that Otis wasn't as articulate as his older brother. "The difference," Ossian bitingly replied, "is the difference between a Negro who has been educated in the North and one who has been educated in the South." Had they not been brothers, Ossian wouldn't have chosen Otis as a friend.[10]

For their part, Ossian and Henry were almost complete strangers. Four years old when his brother first went north, Henry had grown up seeing Ossian only a few times a year. But the distance between them only intensified Henry's determination to match his brother's accomplishments. Temperamentally, Henry was more like Otis. Genial and gregarious, he'd made more friends in one year at Wilberforce than Ossian had in eight. Young women enjoyed his gentle teasing, and campus groups appreciated his earnestness and reliability: in addition to his membership in Ossian's old fraternity, Kappa Alpha Psi, Henry played on the football team, performed with the choral club, managed the military corps' band, and kept the books for Wilberforce's YMCA. But in other respects, he was Ossian's double. When Ossian traveled down to Xenia one Saturday in 1924 to watch Henry play football, he found a younger, more solidly built version of himself, almost every detail an imitation. In academics, too, Henry was following his brother's example, pursuing a bachelor of science in anticipation of graduate school, hopefully at Howard, and a life in the professions.[11]

If Ossian's recollections can be trusted, he and Henry also shared an interest in racial affairs. But while Ossian stood on the fringes of New Negro activism, Henry was more than likely drawn into the thick of it. A few weeks after Wilberforce's 1924 school year opened, night riders began to terrorize a local sharecropper, William Martin, shooting into his house and setting his hayrick on fire. The first few nights, Martin faced the attacks alone. Then Wilberforce's cadet commander decided to intervene. One evening, a contingent of college men, rifles in hand, marched across the harvested fields and with military precision established a defensive perimeter around the sharecropper's house. The night riders didn't dare challenge them; from that point on, William Martin slept in peace. Whether Henry was among those who stood guard isn't clear, though a popular, eager young man active in the college military program seems a likely candidate for frontline duty on behalf of the race. In any case, he must have been caught up in the militancy that burned across campus that month, and it's hard to believe he didn't share his enthusiasm with his brother in the course of their weekend together. Ossian was impressed enough to invite Henry to come live with him in Detroit the following summer, by which time, Ossian must have assumed, he'd have a new home base for the generation of Sweets that was starting to circle around him.[12]

The timing didn't quite work out. Detroit's manic boom had become even more intense by late 1924 than it had been before Ossian and Gladys went to Europe: the population had soared to a million and a quarter, far more than the city's already strained housing stock could absorb, and home prices were skyrocketing, up 67 percent from the year before. To make matters worse, the Sweets would have to buy above the market rate, since colored families were always expected to pay a premium for property. With all the other expenses Ossian was incurring, it took more time than expected to put aside a decent down payment. Through the winter of 1924–25, Ossian, Gladys, and baby Iva stayed with the Mitchells while they saved what they could. Only in the spring did they begin to scour the city for a house of their own. They couldn't have picked a more volatile moment.[13]

•

It had begun with the smallest of tremors, the first rumble in what would become an earthquake so great it would reconfigure the American political landscape. When the Anglo-Saxon elite took control of city government in 1918, they made it a priority to restructure Detroit's criminal court, long known as Recorders Court, which they considered hopelessly soft on crime. To toughen it up, they increased the number of judges from five to seven, put control of case assignment in the hands of a presiding judge, then made sure that hard-nosed conservatives won election to four of the seven seats on the bench, enough to assure them a permanent hold on the presiding judgeship and thus on all the court's activities. In short order, the conservatives launched a massive crackdown on petty crimes and the poor people who committed them, a judicial complement to the police brutality rampant in the foreign-born and colored districts of the city.[14]

When the judges came up for reelection in the spring of 1923, the lower classes struck back. In February, just two months after Ossian and Gladys's wedding, Frank Murphy, a thirty-two-year-old Detroit lawyer and Democratic Party activist, announced that he was joining the court's three progressive judges in a campaign bloc expressly designed to take control of Recorders Court away from the conservatives. The campaign had its cynical side: one of Murphy's key supporters, Irish-born criminal attorney Tom Chawke, specialized in keeping mobsters out of prison, and another, *Detroit Times* editor Red Mulcahy, another Irish American, saw in his candidacy a way to boost circulation and take a swipe at the paper's conservative competition. But it was also a genuinely liberal crusade, backed by reform-minded clubwomen, liberal ministers, and trade unionists determined to reverse justice's decline into repression.[15]

In Murphy, the campaign found its ideal spokesman. Handsome in an Irish American sort of way, with a long, sharp, serious face made dramatic by thick eyebrows and a shock of deep red hair, Murphy was charming, devout, well educated, and ambitious to a fault. Although he enjoyed being seen in Detroit's toniest clubs and cabarets, Murphy had never so much as touched a drop of liquor, an abstemiousness he learned watching his father's descent into alcoholism. He dated a string of starlets and society girls, but those closest to him knew he'd never marry; he reserved his deepest passions for his career, which he was convinced would take him to the White House, and for his mother, Mary, to whom he wrote ardent, painfully Oedipal love letters. Mary Murphy had given her beloved son a Catholicism so fervent—a faith of pilgrimages, prayer cards, and the sweet smell of incense floating above a golden sanctuary—some of his contemporaries thought him literally suited to the priesthood. But Frank was sure that he had been called to public service. He also knew precisely how to tap into the deep resentment the court had created among foreign-born and colored voters. Detroit's legal system favored "political grafters, exploiters of the poor, and profiteers," he proclaimed as he crisscrossed Detroit's working-class wards, while "the friendless and the penniless have less than an equal chance of justice." As word of his attacks spread, the crowds swelled. "I have gone among the humble of Detroit," he told a throng of five thousand at one rally, "and it is their great desire to free this city from the shackles of judicial tyranny." If elected, he shouted above the cheers, "I will try to have a temple of justice, not a butcher shop."[16]

The business elite and its political allies shot back with the full force of moral righteousness and fearmongering. The conservatives' newspaper, the powerful blue-blood *Detroit News*, gleefully quoted a well-known madam saying she was for Murphy and his running mates "heart and soul," then for good measure added a dose of anti-Semitism, tracking down two aged political fixers, Abe Ascher and Abe Ackerman, so that they could be put on record in support of the liberals. As the election approached, the *Detroit News* and its reactionary rival, the *Detroit Free Press*, played the race card, running simultaneous exposés purporting to show that "underworld characters" were "herding" twenty thousand Black Bottom Negroes into the registrar's office so that they'd be eligible to vote for Murphy. "Do we want to discourage crime in Detroit?" the *Detroit News* asked on its front page. "Or shall we adopt the theory that every stranger to a bathtub, clean collar, and upright life, who has committed a crime, is a victim of modern society and should be treated very tenderly? They are voting heavily in the tenderloin districts—Can you do less as a citizen?"[17]

For the most part, Detroit's Talented Tenth reacted to the campaign with an understandable confusion. Here was a new kind of politics, centered around an ethnic Democrat, the product of a party that had long championed white supremacy, appealing to the masses, black and white, with promises of equal rights before the law while the most respectable people in the city raged against him. Black Bottom's ordinary folks understood. On election day, April 2, 1923, Detroit split right down its ethnic, racial, and economic fault lines. The conservative judges carried the heavily white, native-born, more middle-class west side. But Murphy and his running mates swept through the east-side wards crowded with colored and foreign-born working people, piling up such huge margins that they crushed the conservatives in the overall vote. "We have met the enemy and we are theirs," a dejected member of the city's elite wrote a few days later, as Detroit faced "an entirely new deal in the court." He couldn't have picked a more prescient phrase, for Murphy had pieced together the coalition that in another nine years would make Franklin Roosevelt president of the United States.[18]

◆

If the spring of 1923 belonged to Murphy and his supporters, the Ku Klux Klan controlled the summer. The first Klan organizer had come to Detroit in 1921, just as the organization was trying to push its base into the urban North. He spent the next year spreading the carefully crafted message of moral renewal, 100 percent Americanism, anti-unionism, anti-Catholicism, anti-Semitism, and racism: a more overt, cruder version of the politics that the *Detroit News* had vainly employed against Murphy. So great was the reception, the Klan could barely keep up with the flow of recruits. By 1923, there were twenty-two thousand Klansmen in Detroit, and the Invisible Order was ready to go public. Throughout that summer, the KKK held nighttime rallies on the far west side, complete with cross burnings so spectacular and speeches so incendiary they drew upward of eight thousand. Klan newsboys took to selling the organization's newspaper, the *Fiery Cross*, on street corners. And on Christmas Eve 1923, Klansmen marked the season by burning a six-foot-tall cross in front of city hall, then cheering a hooded Santa Claus, come to entertain the kids.[19]

Perhaps the Klan would have remained happy torching lumber and rallying the faithful had it not been for a peculiar turn in city government. In early 1924, Detroit's businessman mayor announced that he was too ill to complete the second half of his two-year term, and a special election was called for November 1924 to select a replacement. When a local politician, John Smith, emerged as the front-runner, the fissures that had split the city during Murphy's campaign cracked wide open again. It wasn't just that Smith was sure to appeal to the same alliance of Negroes and foreigners that had put Murphy on the bench. Johnny Smith was actually *from* the east side's working class, a genuine product of the streets. And that made him anathema to the militant Anglo-Saxons who spent their nights draped in Klan sheets.[20]

The youngest of seven children raised by his widowed Polish Catholic mother, Smith had gone to work at age five, hawking newspapers on downtown streets mornings and evenings, setting pins in a bowling alley at night. With only a fourth-grade education, he had no hope of entering the professions. Instead, he became a soldier—a wounded veteran of America's imperial adventures in Cuba and the Philippines—a steamfitter, a trade-union activist, and, bit by bit, a politician of considerable reputation. Smith had the manner of an old-fashioned political boss who seemed happiest when puffing on a good cigar in the backroom of a corner saloon. When it came to public policy, though, he was a fierce progressive. Murphy could talk about helping the humble people of Detroit; Smith had done it, battling for strict enforcement of Michigan's child labor and tenement improvement laws. Murphy could talk about checking police aggression; Smith had actually confronted the cops, in one famous episode literally facing down a squad sent to break up a strike in a Detroit-area chemical plant, an intervention that cost him a broken nose that forever after made him look like a second-rate boxer. As mayor, he promised more confrontations. He'd put an end to arrests for drunkenness, he said, unless the suspect was dangerous; he'd stop illegal raids on neighborhood speakeasies; and, most controversially, he'd see to it that the police department hired more colored officers.[21]

A Catholic, a labor sympathizer, and a wet who promised to put Negroes in uniform and give them guns: to a Klansman, there was no more horrifying combination. For the previous three years, the Klan had been storming through northern politics, winning control of state governments in Indiana, Colorado, and Oregon. As Smith's candidacy gained momentum, the Kluxers decided they had to take charge of Detroit as well. Their campaign was painfully amateurish. As their candidate, they chose a complete unknown, lawyer Charles Bowles, whose only qualification for office was a successful term as president of the

Masonic Order's youth league. As if their man wasn't weak enough already, the KKK then failed to get his name on the November ballot and had to hope he could be elected as a write-in candidate. But none of that really mattered. The Klan's forte wasn't polished politics; it was thuggery and intimidation. At times Bowles's campaign seemed more suited to Mussolini's Rome than to the fourth-largest city in the United States. At one point, the KKK torched a cross on the front lawn of Smith's west-side home. When an anti-Klan group tried to stage a rally at a downtown arena late in the campaign, six thousand Klansmen massed in front of the venue, chanting "Bowles! Bowles! Bowles!" and intimidating anyone who tried to enter. The weekend before the election, the Klan mounted an even more frightening display. That Saturday night, upwards of fifty thousand gathered under a flaming cross in the western suburb of Dearborn—Henry Ford's hometown—to hear last-minute exhortations and the usual round of condemnations. Klan pickets kept nonmembers away, so no outsider knew precisely what was said. But the message was clear enough. The KKK was preparing for power.[22]

Johnny Smith, however, didn't mind going toe to toe with the Invisible Empire; in fact, the Klan's crusade strengthened his appeal. The KKK's slurs won Smith the allegiance of the Talented Tenth, who closed ranks behind him in a way they hadn't with Murphy the year before. What's more, it solidified the mayor's support among both the middle-class progressives who had long anchored reform and the most ambitious of Detroit's up-and-coming ethnics—some of them now-seasoned politicians such as Frank Murphy and his tough-minded backers, Tom Chawke and Red Mulcahy, others political newcomers, like the brilliant young pastor of the west side's Bethel Evangelical Church, Reinhold Niebuhr. The son of German immigrants whose intellectual gifts had carried him from tiny Lincoln, Illinois, through Yale Divinity School, Niebuhr saw in the Klan's militant Anglo-Saxonism a repudiation of the assimilation he worked so hard to achieve and the Social Gospel he was determined to preach. Supporting Smith wasn't a perfect fit for a man of Niebuhr's sobriety: "It seems to me rather unfortunate that we must depend upon 'publicans' for our social conscience to so great a degree," he wrote in his diary, but it was better than draping city hall in the white robes of the Klan.[23]

Best of all, Smith traded on the fears the KKK engendered to energize his political base. While the Kluxers lit up the western sky, he worked his old east-side neighborhood, visiting as many synagogues,

Catholic parishes, and black churches as would have him. Klansmen "have robbed Catholic churches and attempted to burn them," he told a crowd at St. Stanislaus, one of the sacred sites of Polish Detroit. "They have tortured and slain Negroes and Jews." The tactic worked to perfection. With Mulcahey's *Detroit Times* trumpeting every charge and the mayor's ethnic and black backers working the streets on his behalf, Smith swept the immigrant and colored wards by margins even greater than Murphy had managed: 99 percent of Black Bottom went his way. But the west side's Anglo-Saxons did even better for Bowles. A record 325,000 people cast ballots in the 1924 mayoral election, and when the polls finally closed, the Klan candidate had a majority of seven thousand votes.[24]

Or he would have, had Smith been the sort of politician who suffered defeat gracefully. But he was too much of a street fighter not to take one last punch. A review of the ballots showed that Bowles's backers weren't always sure how to spell their man's name: by official count, voters tried 120 variations. Most of the mistakes were minor—a missing letter, the wrong middle initial—but Smith's cronies on the Detroit election commission threw out every vote that wasn't precisely right, seventeen thousand in all, more than enough to strip Bowles of his victory and make a former pin setter and pipe fitter mayor of Detroit.[25]

No one was under the illusion that the war was over. Because he was only serving out his successor's term, Smith had to stand for reelection in a year's time, November 1925. And the KKK was dead-set on having its revenge. At the end of 1924, the Klan's national leadership dispatched to Detroit one of its more effective political operatives, Ira Stout, an owlish former boy scout and fundamentalist preacher, who was to prepare the groundwork for the fall campaign.[26] Michigan's frigid gray winter wasn't prime time for political organizing. But with the coming of spring—just as Ossian and Gladys were beginning to hunt for a house—the Klan headed into its marching season, when crosses could be burned and the emotions of a hundred thousand nativist voters could be set aflame. And in Detroit, there was no better way to fuel savage anger than to raise the specter of the Negro masses pouring across the color line into white man's land.

◆

Gladys insisted that, as far as she was concerned, they could live in either a colored neighborhood or a white one. But the chances of finding a suitable house in a black area were slim. There were several small Negro enclaves on Detroit's west side, one of which was home to several of Ossian's colleagues. If the Sweets had settled in that area, though, Ossian would have had a terrible commute to his office, while Gladys would have been very far from her parents. On the east side, the only colored neighborhood was Black Bottom, where life was increasingly intolerable. In the first few months of 1925, cops working the Black Bottom beat had shot a dozen or more colored people, several of them fatally. In one of the most egregious cases, a patrolman opened fire on a truck that failed to obey his order to stop. One of the bullets shattered the jaw of the truck's passenger, a twenty-five-year-old expectant mother. She died seven days later, having given birth to her baby. An investigation found the patrolman completely justified in his actions, and he was returned to duty. No, Ossian couldn't possibly take his family back to Black Bottom.[27]

Neither was it a simple matter to move beyond its boundaries. Ossian's senior colleagues had moved into white neighborhoods before discrimination had started to course through the housing market. Even in the early 1920s, Detroit's growing wall of segregation still had its gaps. But in 1923 and 1924, as Ossian and Gladys enjoyed the freedom of Vienna and Paris, developers, real estate agents, and bankers sealed the wall shut, so that now a Negro family looking to live outside the ghetto faced an almost impossible task.

For the developers who were furiously building housing tracts on the edge of the city and in the suburbs, the job was simple, a matter of a few words inserted onto all the development's deeds. For years, builders had placed restrictions on properties when they first went on sale, in order to give an area a certain character; it was common practice to say that a house couldn't be changed into a business, say, or be subdivided into apartments. In Chicago and other cities, developers regularly added racial restrictions as well: property owners could not sell their homes to colored buyers or, at times, to Jews. But that wasn't common practice in Detroit until the early 1920s, when suddenly developers blanketed the new houses on the city's outskirts with restrictive covenants, a practice they turned into a selling point. "We have carefully restricted this section to include only the kind of people you would be glad to have next door," one of the biggest firms proudly proclaimed as it unveiled its newest development on the far west side. "Here you can feel free to make friends with your neighbors."[28]

In established neighborhoods, too, the Sweets would immediately run up against a whole new series of prohibitions. Ever since the Great War, many white real estate agents had refused to show colored families properties outside Black Bottom. But it wasn't until 1924 that the real estate agents' trade association absolutely barred its members from selling houses in white neighborhoods to Negro customers and imposed sanctions on those who dared to break the rules. At almost exactly the same time, housing appraisers made it official practice to downgrade the value of any neighborhood that had even a single black resident, a requirement that immediately transformed even the most well-to-do colored homebuyers into credit risks, since the moment a purchase was complete the property wasn't worth as much as it had been. And because blacks drove down property values, there wasn't a bank in Detroit willing to give Negroes a mortgage.[29]

Ossian and Gladys ran into the restrictions right away. Three times, they found promising houses on the east side, and three times, they were turned away as soon as they made inquiries. One can imagine how much the rejections hurt; Ossian with his fine education and studied air of authority, Gladys with her lifetime living among whites, staring into the impassive face of a real estate agent while he shook his head and told them nothing was available. Friends urged them to stop searching on their own and hire a white agent to buy a house for them. Ossian wouldn't hear of it; he had no intention of skulking into a neighborhood, as if he didn't belong there. Instead, the Sweets found the tiniest of cracks in the wall that real estate agents and bankers had built, and they squeezed their way through.[30]

The break came in a completely unexpected way. One day in May, Lucius Riley stopped into Ossian's office with a bit of news. Riley had been a devoted patient of Ossian's ever since the day he'd brought his wife into Palace Drugs fearing she had lockjaw. Now Riley extended his own professional courtesy. He knew of a fine house just about to go on the market, he told Ossian, a nine-year-old bungalow, well built and well maintained, in a white neighborhood a few miles east of Black Bottom. The house sat on a corner lot, so it had a bit more land than most, and it was right across from an elementary school. Best of all, Riley was absolutely sure that the owners would be willing to sell to a colored family.[31]

When the Sweets first went out to the house on Garland Avenue in late May 1925, they had to be a bit disappointed in the neighborhood. It was a workingman's area, by and large, certainly not poor but not imposing either, filled with modest houses and two-family flats. But the location was just about ideal. Ossian would have an easy twenty-minute drive to his office on St. Aubin, while Gladys would be about fifteen minutes south of Cairney Street. The intersection in front of the house was busy. Though Garland Avenue was a quiet residential street, the cross street, Charlevoix Avenue, was a major thoroughfare, complete with a streetcar line. As long as they were newcomers and their presence might stir resentment, though, the Sweets had no intention of spending much time in the front of the house. They could get all the fresh air they needed in the backyard, which was safely hidden by a high wooden fence.[32] All in all, the bungalow was a very attractive home.

For their part, the owners were more than pleased to find the Sweets. By all appearances, Ed and Marie Smith were a completely conventional white couple, hardly the sort one would expect to shatter the neighborhood's color line. But the Smiths weren't exactly what they appeared to be. Mrs. Smith was indeed Caucasian. But her husband was a light-skinned colored man who had spent most of his adult life passing for white. The deception had given him the ability to build a successful business selling real estate in areas no black real estate agent could operate, while his brother, who was just as light skinned, had risen to the rank of sergeant in the Detroit Police Department.[33]

They saw the Sweets as a couple of easy marks. Had the Smiths sold to whites, the bungalow probably would have gone for $12,000 or $13,000, the standard for the neighborhood. But Ossian and Gladys had nowhere else to go, so the Smiths upped their asking price to $18,500. To make sure the Sweets couldn't walk away, they offered to finance the purchase themselves. Ossian and Gladys would put down 20 percent of the asking price and pay the balance directly to the Smiths in 120 monthly installments of $150 each. Of course, there were a few catches. The Smiths would keep the title to the house until the final payment was made, so Ossian and Gladys wouldn't actually own the bungalow until 1935. In the intervening ten years, they would pay the Smiths an extraordinary 18 percent interest on the balance they owed, so far above bank rates as to be almost criminal. Then again, there was no way the Sweets were going to get a bank loan. They had to take what they could get.[34]

That's exactly what they did. On June 7, 1925, Ossian and Gladys handed over their down payment of $3,500 and signed the purchase agreement. The Smiths needed a few months to move out, but come August 1, the Sweets would have their home.[35]

Yet Ossian's fears persisted. When the papers were signed and the real estate agents were packing up their briefcases, Ossian took Marie Smith aside for a quick word. Was the neighborhood safe for colored people, he asked her? Would he have to worry about the Klan?

Oh no, she said, there weren't any Klansmen in the area. Garland was a nice quiet street. The Sweets would be very happy there.[36]

◆

The rumor started right away. Someone saw Ossian and Gladys sitting on the front porch swing during one of their visits to the bungalow. "It just isn't right," said Ray Dove, the factory worker who lived in the upstairs flat directly across from the bungalow, and he didn't need to say any more. Some of the men must have feared for the safety of their wives and children, knowing that the black beast was moving into their midst. George and Alvina Hamming, just two doors north of the corner, had two teenage daughters, fifteen-year-old Ruth and Grace, the thirteen-year-old; a couple of doors beyond them lived nine-year-old Margaret Rudge, and on the opposite side of the street were Leon and Leona Breiner's girls, fourteen-year-old Evelyn and twelve-year-old June. Surely it crossed the parents' minds that their daughters soon would be sharing the street with brooding Negro men and sitting in classrooms next to colored boys whose passions knew no restraint. At least some people also felt in the rumor a blow to their pride. Having Negroes in the neighborhood would ruin standards, Harry Monet insisted, dragging whites down to the coloreds' level, degrading everything people up and down the block had worked so hard to achieve.[37]

But it was the marketplace that really induced panic along Garland Avenue. Once the Negroes arrived, real estate agents would start steering white customers elsewhere, banks would downgrade home values, some of the neighbors would try to sell as quickly as they could, and the downward spiral would begin, housing prices tumbling, family budgets crumbling, disaster looming. It was a process shot through with irony, whites suddenly being victimized by the very practices that were supposed to protect them from Negro invasion. The thought was simply terrifying.

It hadn't always been like this, a family's fate hinging on the value of its house. Just a generation earlier, working-class Americans had considered owning a home the ultimate form of security, a bulwark against the vagaries of life, not an investment to be protected. Instead of taking out mortgages, they saved every penny they could until they could buy a house free and clear, or they'd do what Ossian's parents had done: pay for a lot, then put up the house themselves. That's how the cottages of Black Bottom had been built in the nineteenth century, home by home, until the neighborhood was full. It wasn't always easy. Though land was cheap enough—two hundred dollars would buy a lot in turn-of-the-twentieth-century Detroit—and houses could be constructed for a thousand dollars or less, many parents sacrificed their children's future, sending them off to work as newsies or maids, so that they could put together the cash they needed. But once a purchase was completed, a family forever after had a roof over its head, and come what may—an economic depression, an accident at the plant, a sudden illness, a tragic death—nothing could take it away.[38]

But boomtown Detroit had no place for security. The fields that became Garland Avenue had been bought up at the turn of the twentieth century by one of the city's large real estate developers, the Bewick Company. When the developer carved the fields into narrow lots, he wrote into each deed that no house built on a plot would be worth less than two thousand dollars, a figure expressly set to shut out workers who planned to build their homes the old-fashioned way. Instead, the Bewick Company and a handful of contractors put up most of the houses along Garland, slapping the flats together in a rush in the first half of the 1910s, then setting prices high enough that no one could get by without a mortgage. The piano tuner and his wife, John and Della Getke, had to borrow two thousand dollars to buy their home next door to the bungalow in February 1915. A few years of frenzied growth later, that seemed a steal. When the Smiths bought the bungalow on the corner in July 1923, they had to go five thousand dollars in debt to make the purchase possible.[39]

That's where the trouble began. By working-class standards, the people who lived on Garland were to be envied and just a little feared. They were the carpenters, streamfitters, and electricians who roamed the factories as if they owned them, skilled men standing proudly above the mass of common laborers. They were the salesmen in the cheap suits who breezed through the plants, sample cases in hand, on the way to having a chat with the manager up in the front office. Mostly, they were the foremen who spent the day stalking the assembly lines, breathing down the workers' necks, cursing and threatening and cajoling to make sure that the chassis kept moving inexorably toward the factory doors. Fourteen foremen lived within a block of the bungalow, an imposing concentration of hard-nosed men making their living in an unforgiving job. There was no doubt that they had risen in the ranks because they weren't immigrants or Negroes, because they came from Ohio or New York or small-town Michigan instead of Alabama or Galacia or Lodz, because they wore a Masonic pin on their lapels when they went to see the boss who did the hiring, and the bonds of brotherhood extended to the factory floor. Still, it hadn't been easy climbing into the upper reaches of blue-collar life. Before he landed his job at Continental Motors, before he moved to Michigan and met Leona, before he was even old enough to vote or serve in the army, a teenage Leon Breiner had done the most brutal work of all, mining coal far beneath the hard earth of Carbon County, Pennsylvania. After that, a man had to feel that he'd earned whatever safety and comfort a foreman's wages could bring.[40]

But solid wages weren't enough, not when a mortgage dangled around a man's neck like a noose waiting to be pulled tight. It was bad enough that families had to borrow more than their incomes could bear simply to get into Detroit's raging market. The pressure was compounded by the crippling terms financial institutions had to offer. The major downtown banks, rock-ribbed conservatives that they were, wouldn't allow their customers to borrow more than 50 percent of a house's value, and they required that loans be repaid in the briefest of periods, often within three to five years. With housing prices so high, most families couldn't possibly put down 50 percent of a purchase, so they had to take out second and even third mortgages just to piece together a down payment. Because banks refused to make such deals, borrowers were forced to turn to mortgage companies and local moneylenders, who gouged their desperate customers with usurious interest rates. Even if homeowners did manage to make their multiple payments, loan periods were so short that they were constantly refinancing. By the summer of 1925, ten years after they bought the tiny house next to the bungalow, the Getkes had already taken out three mortgages and were in negotiations for a fourth, a thousand dollars larger than the original.[41] It was a terrible burden to place on the money a man could make tuning pianos.

And it couldn't withstand the shock that the coming of the Negroes would bring. It was easy enough to spin out the economic consequences of Garland's color line giving way. When property values started falling, lenders wouldn't refinance, and loans would come due. Some families would try to pull themselves out of the morass by trying to sell their houses, but that would only trigger a price war, pushing values down even faster and making it that much harder to earn enough on a sale to pay off the mortgage holders or to start over in a city where houses in decent neighborhoods were so expensive. Others would stay put, hoping they could scrape together enough money to pay off the mortgage when the loans came due and refinancing fell through. But if they failed, the cost would be extraordinarily high. There'd be a few months of grace before the bank or mortgage company came calling. But sooner or later, they'd show up on the doorstep demanding their due, their workmen standing behind them, itching to begin piling the furniture at the curb for all the neighbors to see. When that happened, a good-paying job as a foreman or a craftsman wouldn't mean a damn thing.

As worried as they were, though, no one on Garland Avenue did anything at first. They didn't know what to do. The neighborhood didn't fit neatly into Detroit's polarized political communities: it was too full of the native-born to share in the sense of oppression that united the east side's foreign-born and colored populations, too far from the west side to participate in the politics of rage that fueled the Ku Klux Klan. Nor was it a street that lent itself to organizing. Some neighbors were tied together by personal connections—Ray Dove and Leon Breiner belonged to the same Masonic Lodge; Albert Suppus's son played with the Arthur boy—but otherwise people tended to keep to themselves. The neighborhood didn't give folks a chance to develop deep friendships: work was too demanding to leave much time for socializing; renters came and went; and even the most long-term resident had only been there a decade. Much of Detroit was like that; "A city of strangers," a journalist called it. On Garland Avenue, that description was just about right.[42]

Then the west side exploded.

◆

The clashes came as a shock, they flared so quickly and in such an unexpected place. For years, several thousand Negroes had been living in a small triangle of streets wedged between two of the near west side's largest thoroughfares, West Grand Boulevard and Tireman Avenue. Compared to Black Bottom, the west-side enclave was prosperous and stable, and the whites who surrounded it had never seen it as threatening. Though the neighborhood's borders were clear enough, they had also been somewhat porous. Dunbar Memorial's head of surgery, Dr. Alexander Turner, had been living in a nearby white area for the previous fifteen years, caring for Caucasian patients, without so much as a complaint. But in the summer of 1925, the whites who encircled the enclave suddenly became passionately, violently committed to preventing Negroes from crossing the color line.[43]

The first incident occurred in the spring of 1925, just as Ossian and Gladys were about to begin their search for a home. On March 7, two young colored couples, Aldeine and Fleta Mathies and their friends, the Burtons, all recent migrants from Georgia, rented a flat just one street west of the black neighborhood's traditional boundary. Almost immediately, the families received a series of frightening letters from the local KKK, demanding that they surrender their lease. When they didn't respond, the neighbors came calling. Twice in the first week of April, mobs gathered in front of the flat, and twice the men of the house faced them down, standing on the porch with rifles in their hands. But it was twenty-two-year-old Mrs. Mathies who eventually pulled the trigger.

Monday night, April 13, she and Mrs. Burton settled themselves in the side bedroom, the safest part of the house, since it didn't face the street or the alley but rather the home next door, where a policeman and his wife lived. The two women had just nodded off when a rock shattered the windowpane. Without a moment's hesitation, Fleta Mathies grabbed the pistol lying on her bedside table and fired two shots through the gaping hole of shattered glass, hitting the frame of the window directly opposite. The police rushed to the scene. But instead of restoring order, they took Mathies into custody, charging her with careless use of a firearm. When the patrolmen brought her in, the Mathies' next-door neighbor was waiting for her. "If I had been home," he told her, "your husband would have been going down to the undertakers after a coffin for you instead of coming down to the police station to get you. You people have got more privileges than you're entitled to. You want to spoil our street." Another cop took a cat-o'-nine-tails off a shelf and dangled it in front of her. "You see this," he said. "If you were a man, I'd give you a sound thrashing."[44]

Still, the families refused to be intimidated. To defend his wife, Aldeine Mathies hired two colored lawyers, W. Hayes McKinney, the former president of Detroit's NAACP branch, and criminal attorney Cecil Rowlette. When the case went to court in May, McKinney and Rowlette convinced the judge that Fleta Mathies had fired in defense of her home and therefore had committed no crime. Afterward, young

Mrs. Mathies was as defiant as ever. "I'm not afraid and will not move until I am positive that I have made it possible for some other colored person to live here after I'm gone," she told the Negro press. "The race needs people who are not afraid to die to defend their pride."[45] With that, the threats and intimidation stopped, and for the better part of three months, the area was as calm as it had ever been. Then Dr. Alexander Turner grew tired of the traffic noise on his street and decided to move his family to a new home a mile away.

As was his habit, Turner bought the very best he could afford, an impressive two-story brick home on Spokane Avenue, eight blocks north of Tireman Avenue. Had it not been for the Mathies' troubles, the doctor wouldn't have given a second thought to moving onto an all-white street. Certainly his situation was different: the Mathies had barely crossed out of the black neighborhood whereas he was moving a considerable distance from it; they were newcomers, whereas he was an established member of the community. Still, it was better to be cautious. Shortly before Turner moved, a small group of his colleagues met with Mrs. Mathies's lawyer, Cecil Rowlette, to ask whether they could join the doctor in his house on the first night so that he might have some protection. Absolutely not, Rowlette said. A man had the right to defend his own home. But it would be a serious mistake to have others defend it for him.[46]

So the Turners moved to their new home on their own. They took possession on the morning of June 23. Within a few hours, a mob of two hundred, most of them women and children, had gathered out front. First, they stoned the colored painters Turner had hired to touch up the trim, then they started smashing windows. The escalating violence brought the police, who arrested one fifteen-year-old boy as he stood on the sidewalk, rock in hand. But the cops did nothing to stanch the flow of people into the street. By dusk, the mob had swelled to more than a thousand, far more than the forty policemen on the scene could possibly control. The doctor and his wife were cowering inside, every escape route hopelessly blocked, when they heard a rap on the door and the voices of several white men calling to them, saying that they had been sent by Mayor Smith to provide the couple with the protection they needed. In his desperation, Turner opened the door.

Dozens of people surged past the doctor into his house. While the police stood by, the mob trampled through the downstairs rooms, wrenching open closet doors, pulling up rugs, grabbing furniture and unpacked boxes full of precious belongings to cart outside. The ringleaders took hold of Turner. They were representatives of the Tireman Avenue Improvement Association, they said, and they wanted the deed of the house signed over to them. It was an utterly audacious demand, robbery in the midst of pillage, and under normal circumstances, Turner, a man of supreme self-confidence, never would have given in to it. But there was no saying what would happen next: whether the mob would destroy everything he owned; whether they'd turn on him and his wife; whether he'd ever escape this accursed neighborhood alive. More people were trying to push their way inside every minute, and those outside cheered as the first pieces of furniture were dumped into the street. Turner choked out his agreement.

Satisfied that the problem was solved, the police agreed to escort the doctor and the men from the improvement association back to Turner's office, where they could complete the property transfer. The Turners managed to make it safely into the back seat of their sedan. But the sight of the chauffeur firing up the engine enraged the mob again. A barrage of stones and bricks hit the car, smashing the windows. A piece of flying glass struck Turner above the eye, gashing his forehead. Blood trickling down his face, he pulled himself and his wife down to the floor of the car and ordered the chauffeur to get through the crowd as quickly as he could. Somehow they managed to move forward, slowly, then with real speed. Within a few minutes, they were free of Spokane Avenue. The Turners raced to his office, where they summoned lawyer Rowlette and signed away the house they had lived in for less than a day.[47]

Precisely two weeks later, the Tireman Avenue Improvement Association struck again. This time, they made their target one of Ossian's oldest friends in Detroit, Vollington Bristol. The Bristols had long owned a house on American Avenue, ten blocks east of Turner's place on Spokane Avenue. They had never lived in the home—it was simply too far from their funeral parlor in Black Bottom—but instead had rented it out to a secession of white tenants. But the tenants had been nothing but trouble: rents went unpaid; apartments had been damaged. Figuring that whites were defying them because they were black, the Bristols decided in the spring of 1925 to rent to colored families. Several times, they found suitable tenants, but as soon as they moved in, the newcomers received notes so threatening that they moved out again. Finally, on July 4, Vollington Bristol reached his breaking point.

He arrived at the property that day with four families in tow. A delegation of twenty-five white neighbors met him there. This was his last warning, they said. He was not to rent to coloreds anymore, and if he tried again, he'd regret it. All right, Bristol replied, he wouldn't rent to Negroes. He'd live there himself.

Unlike the Turners, Bristol asked for police protection before he moved in, and the day he arrived, July 6, two cops were on duty in front of the house. As he was taking his belongings into the building, Bristol's next-door neighbor came by to ask if he really intended to go through with his threat. When Bristol said he was, the man turned on his heels, growling, "You will hear from us later." Nothing happened the first night. But the next evening, July 7, all hell broke loose.

The police had a small contingent of five patrolmen and an inspector surrounding the house when the mob began to form. Initially, the crowd kept its distance, not daring to test the police line. Then, a woman who lived across the street from Bristol's house mounted her porch and launched into a harangue. "If you call yourselves men and are afraid to move these niggers out," she screamed, "we women will move them, you cowards!" That was it. Almost instantaneously the mob began stoning the house. Someone approached the police to ask if they would step aside for five minutes; it wouldn't take any longer to drive the coloreds away. When the inspector refused to move his men, the mob stoned them, too. Fearing that at any moment they would be overrun—perhaps killed—by the hundreds of people in front of them, the cops fired a volley of warning shots into the air. Members of the mob returned fire, rifles blazing from so many directions it was impossible to tell where in the crowd the gunmen were standing.

The patrolmen could have been mowed down right there, but by pure luck no one was hit. They could have broken ranks and run, but for some reason they held their ground long enough for reinforcements from precincts around the city—two hundred or more—to arrive. Such a massive show of force tipped the balance. The cops waded into the mob, pushing those they could all the way back onto Tireman, arresting those who resisted. In all, nineteen white men were jailed that evening, and the police seized thirty-five guns, two knives, and hundreds of rounds of ammunition. But it took several more hours to realize just how dangerous the situation had become. Around midnight, patrolmen stopped eight colored men making their way through the neighborhood and found that they, too, were armed. When word of the melee had spread into the black neighborhood, the men had decided that they would provide Bristol with the defense he needed. Had the mob still been in the street, American Avenue might have run red with the mingled blood of blacks and whites.[48]

Blood did flow finally, but not on American Avenue. The police were still providing round-the-clock protection to Vollington Bristol when the violence shifted several blocks northeast to 9428 Stoepel Avenue. John Fletcher, a waiter, bought the house on July 1 and, with extraordinarily bad timing, moved his wife, children, and two boarders into the home a week later, on July 9, two days after the chaos in front of Bristol's house. The family had just seated themselves at the dinner table on the tenth when they heard a commotion outside. Across the street, a woman was going door to door, urging her neighbors to come get "the niggers." Fletcher hurriedly called the police. But to his amazement, instead of driving the whites off the street, the seven cops who showed up stood and chatted with them.

The mood remained light enough until the sun began to set. In front of the house next door sat a ton of coal, a recent delivery from the coal dealer. Around eight, the mob started raiding the pile, throwing chunks at the Fletchers' place. In short order, every window was broken, a mirror cracked, and two prized pieces of furniture destroyed. The sudden assault brought another forty policemen to the scene, but by then, the mob had worked itself into such a fury it wasn't going to be stopped. Through the shattered windows, Fletcher could hear the shouts from the street: "Lynch him! Lynch him!" Trapped inside the house, the walls around them cracked and blackened by the lumps of coal now scattered at their feet, the four adults could barely contain their panic. Fletcher picked up a rifle he had brought with him, went to the upstairs window, and opened fire on the mob below. Fifteen-year-old Leonard Paul collapsed on the pavement, two gaping holes in his hip.

Instantly, the mob's exuberance drained away, the joy of destruction, the promise of an evening's brutal excitement, replaced by wild-eyed fear. While the teenager lay writhing on the ground, most of his neighbors fled, racing to the safety of the surrounding streets. The cops took advantage of the opening to get Fletcher safely down to the local precinct. The next day, Saturday, July 11, he made bail, returned to Stoepel Avenue and, under heavy police guard, moved his battered belongings onto a truck and out of the neighborhood. "I couldn't live in the house anyway, because all the windows and screens were smashed and the paint on the outside was all marred up," he explained, adding, as if an afterthought, "I was afraid of my life."[49]

That night, calm finally returned to the area around Tireman Avenue. The Turners were gone; the Fletchers were gone. Only Vollington

Bristol remained, and he barely dared to go outside, so intense was the hatred on his block; already his mailbox was jammed with death threats, and the one time he'd tried to leave his home, a passing car had swerved onto the sidewalk and tried to run him down. It had been a terrible three weeks, the worst in Detroit since the Great Migration began. But the members of the Tireman Avenue Improvement Association were proud of the work they'd done. The neighborhood had been saved from a Negro invasion, property values preserved, the walls of segregation shored up, the streets cleansed with only a little blood. The stain that the wounded boy left on Stoepel Avenue would fade eventually, but the color line would remain inviolate.

◆

From the moment they heard of the attack on the Turners, Ossian and Gladys watched events on the west side with a sickening sense of dread. The assaults would have been frightening enough had they happened to complete strangers. But to think of friends and associates being mobbed—less than a month before the Sweets themselves were scheduled to move—was utterly terrifying. Had he been willing to try, Ossian probably could have gotten out of the deal he'd made for the bungalow, trading his down payment for his family's safety and his own peace of mind. To back down, though, would be to admit that he wasn't willing to live up to the principles that had been preached to him ever since Wilberforce, that he had no claim to a place among the Talented Tenth. It would have been a very public humiliation. Gladys and Otis would have seen it, of course, as would Henry, who had recently arrived in Detroit for the summer and was rooming at the Mitchells'.[50]

What's more, Ossian would have had to face his Dunbar colleagues at the worst possible time. After two years of inactivity, the local branch of the NAACP was finally being revived. In March, the national officers had taken it upon themselves to appoint a new branch president, Rev. Robert Bradby, the extremely powerful pastor of Second Baptist. Bradby, in turn, had named several Dunbar men, including Ossian's friend Edward Carter, to the executive board. Aflame with the NAACP spirit, they were anxious to push against the color line, not surrender to it.[51]

In fact, Carter had almost dragged Ossian into the middle of the melee at Turner's house. The night of the assault, the two men were out with several of their colleagues. Carter tried to convince the group to drive over to Turners', just to be sure that all was well. In the end, they decided against it, and the four physicians had drifted to their homes, having enjoyed an evening of bravado. Ossian must have felt his stomach clench as he read the newspaper's bare-boned account of the incident the following morning. And he couldn't help but cringe when, over the next few weeks, Turner was vilified. "The dirty coward got down on [the] floor of his car and made his chauffeur drive thru the mob," one man said, repeating a refrain heard across Black Bottom. "He knew when he moved in he was going to have trouble and he should have gone prepared to stay or die." No doubt they'd say the same thing about Ossian, if he decided to give up the house on Garland.[52]

It wasn't until Fletcher was driven out, though, that events truly closed in on the Sweets. That weekend, Detroit shuddered with talk of segregation and the implicit threat of violence. On Friday night, the Ku Klux Klan opened its bid to channel white anger. While a group of Klansmen burned a cross in an empty lot not far from Bristol's besieged home, their fellow Kluxers posted huge placards around the neighborhood inviting "every free-minded citizen of Detroit" to a mass rally the next evening. The event turned into a frightening show of force, ten thousand white-robed knights and assorted hangers-on gathering before a blazing cross to hear Klan leaders denounce the Negro invasion and demand legislation barring blacks from moving beyond the ghetto.[53]

Sunday morning's newspapers carried Johnny Smith's carefully crafted reply. The mayor began with a warning. "The condition which faces Detroit is one which faced Washington, East St. Louis, Chicago, and other large cities," he wrote. "The result in those cities was one which Detroit must avoid, if possible. A single fatal riot would injure this city beyond repair." Then he tried in as circumspect a way as possible to turn the west troubles against his opponents. He blamed the violence on "malign influences which are willing to go even to the limits of bloodshed to gain their ends." He called the cops to task for letting the mobs take control of the streets. "The police department can have but one duty in connection with all such incidents," he said. "That is, to use its utmost endeavors to prevent the destruction of life and property. . . . The law recognizes no distinction in color or race." Had he stopped there, Johnny Smith would have placed himself squarely in defense of equal rights and integration. But he didn't. Instead, he urged black "leaders of thought" to back down, to accept the color line as it stood for the sake of peace and order. In the furies of the street, the mayor had found the limits of his electoral coalition.[54]

Dunbar's doctors and their associates in the Talented Tenth barely had time to read the mayor's statement before they gathered that afternoon in Herbert Sims's Black Bottom office to discuss the crisis. Ossian listened intently as Alexander Turner described the desecration of his home and justified his surrender to the mob's demands. There was no missing the defeat in his voice. He and his wife planned to take a trip, Turner said, to get out of town for a few months. They were trying to put behind them the memories of that night on Spokane Avenue, no doubt, but also to escape the sniping that the doctor couldn't help but overhear.

In the midst of the conversation, the telephone rang. Marie Smith was on the line—undoubtedly Gladys had given her the phone number—and she had to speak to Dr. Sweet right away. Posters had just gone up around Garland, she told him; the neighbors were organizing. Ossian must have returned to his colleagues shaken. But they bolstered him up, the room bristling with a militancy made all the stronger by Turner's presence. Attorney Cecil Rowlette expounding on a man's absolute right to protect his home just as his client, young Mrs. Mathies had done, while Edward Carter and Julian Perry boldly promised to be by their friend's side come moving day. If any doubts drifted through Ossian's mind—if he thought back to the days of the Washington riot, when he stayed off the street while others took up arms; if he saw himself walking from Carter's car into the safety of his mother-in-law's house the night of the attack on Turner—he didn't express them. It was so much easier, so much more satisfying to be enveloped in his colleagues' unquestioned confidence, to become, in that moment, the man that Turner had failed to be.[55]

◆

It's not clear who on Garland Avenue first thought of mimicking the Tireman Association. The idea probably started with someone hunched over the morning newspaper, the *Detroit Free Press,* reading the story of the Turners' expulsion. From there, it must have spread the way the rumors of the Sweets' arrival had spread, through casual talk out on the street. Harry Monet, a tire-factory worker who lived half a block north of the bungalow, volunteered his garage for the first meeting. It must have been stultifying, two dozen people crowded into a one-car garage on a hot summer night. But the group did its job, officially forming the

Waterworks Park Improvement Association, named after a majestic public park at the foot of Garland Avenue, a few long blocks away. As chairman, they selected one of Monet's neighbors, Harold McGlynn, a thirty-six-year-old husband and father who worked as an inspector in a nearby auto plant.[56] Perhaps McGlynn got the nod because the association had been his brainchild. But it wasn't completely his to run. From the start, the organization bore the unmistakable imprint of a more seasoned hand in the real estate game.

Most likely, the driving force behind the Waterworks Park Improvement Association was the man elected secretary the night of the first meeting, a thirty-five-year-old real estate agent by the name of James Conley. Like Monet and McGlynn, Conley lived within a block of the bungalow, in a modest home he shared with his wife, Lillian, their two children, Margaret and Eddie, and his maiden aunt, Alice. But Conley had a second stake in the neighborhood that set him apart from the others. He and a partner ran a real estate office on the corner of Charlevoix and St. Clair avenues, not a minute's walk from the Smiths' house. So word that the Negroes had bought the bungalow was doubly devastating: once the sale was final, his property values would tumble and his client base would dry up. More than anyone else on Garland, Conley needed to keep the coloreds out.[57]

Conley also brought an expertise to the task that his neighbors simply didn't have. Within a week or two, the association had adopted and printed up a constitution and bylaws filled with real estate agent boilerplate: members would "render constructive civil and social service," would "assist to maintain a clean and healthy condition in our streets and alleys," would "cooperate with the police department, that the rule of 'law and order' shall be maintained." More important, he began to direct its energies into the proper channels. Members agreed to undertake a campaign to blanket the neighborhood in restrictive covenants, something they undoubtedly wouldn't have thought of without a real estate agent to guide them. In the meantime, the association's leaders would try to convince the owners of the bungalow to call off the sale. Someone suggested that they begin both efforts with a rally at Howe Elementary, an event that could spread news of the association's existence and send a message of the neighborhood's resolve. Conley likely used his connections to make it a spectacular event. Like the Waterworks group, the Tireman Avenue Association was run by a real estate agent whom Conley undoubtedly knew. A friendly phone call and the rally had its featured speaker.[58]

There couldn't have been much doubt about what he would say. The invitation must have gone out just about the time the mob attacked Vollington Bristol's house, and the posters were nailed to Garland's lampposts the same day the mayor's message was printed in the newspaper. But Conley, McGlynn, and the others had no intention of heeding Johnny Smith's call for calm. They wanted neighbors to feel the power of numbers. And they needed the couple in the bungalow to hear the frenzied cheers of the mob, to see what the future would hold if they dared to go through with the sale. To keep Garland Avenue safe from invasion, the Waterworks Park Improvement Association had to be willing to dance with the devil.

In the end, the rally was a stunning success. The skies threatened rain Tuesday night, July 14. But the crowd began arriving early, hundreds of people streaming into the elementary school with the proud abolitionist name. Leon Breiner was there, as were Ray Dove, the Getkes, and so many other neighbors that the school auditorium couldn't hold them all. Rather than turn anyone away, the association moved the rally out to the school-yard lawn, in full view of the Smiths' house. From a makeshift platform, the speaker delivered his incendiary speech. The crowd roared. And the rally organizers stood by and listened to the message ring out. When the Negroes came to Garland Avenue, there was going to be trouble.[59]

◆

The undercover cops sprinkled through the crowd that night took no notes and when they were done, they prepared no report. They simply sat down with their commanding officer, Inspector Norton Schuknecht, and told him everything they'd seen and heard. The inspector didn't need any more than that. He'd spent his lifetime on the east side of Detroit, growing up on St. Aubin back when it was a German neighborhood instead of a district full of Negroes and Italians; walking the beat as a rookie back at the turn of the century; settling with his wife, Emma, in their house off Gratiot Avenue, two miles due north of the school yard; visiting his sister Matilda and her husband, Otto Lemhagen, in their house a block away from the bungalow where the colored man was supposed to be moving; running the precinct that covered all the territory in between. Those streets were his streets, the people in the school yard his people. He knew them better than any of his men ever would.[60]

Schuknecht also knew the ins and outs of the force. The police department had 2,660 cops on the payroll, most of them just as likely to have ended up working in a factory as to be wearing the blue. If Norton hadn't gone into the force, he might have followed the same path. Once his brother Alfred took charge of their father's bookbinding business, Norton's other brothers had settled into working-class jobs: Walter was a trucker, Elmer, a foreman living less than a mile from the Garland house. Norton had done better for himself. Being a beat cop didn't pay well, but Schuknecht had moved slowly and steadily up through the ranks until, six years before, he was named a precinct commander, a desk job suitable for a fifty-five-year-old man with a stomach that stretched over his belt, an extra chin or two to strain his collar, and half a year until he could take a pension. Other cops were flashier, filling their records with commendations for bravery that Schuknecht never came close to winning. But having the city treasurer for a brother-in-law had helped his career no end, as had the gaudy Masonic ring Schuknecht squeezed onto his pudgy finger. Police departments were all the same: a little pull and the right pedigree went a long way. In New York, Chicago, or Boston, a man couldn't rise in the ranks unless he had an Irish name, a lifetime membership in the Hibernians, and a monsignor's imprimatur. To make it in Detroit's force, a cop had to have ties to the white, native-born Protestants who had always run the city.[61]

Now Schuknecht was in a hell of a spot. Ever since the mayor's statement criticizing the force for its handling of the west-side violence, the brass down at police headquarters had been making it clear that they wouldn't tolerate any more incidents. Not that they cared for Johnny Smith; most men in the department, from the top officers down to the traffic cops, couldn't stand the way the mayor had made them a target in the previous campaign while playing up to the Negroes and the foreigners. But the patrolmen's complicity in the mobbing of the coloreds was an embarrassment, even on a force where discipline was perpetually paper-thin, and the mayor was right to say that the city was spinning toward a repetition of Chicago and Washington. To make matters even worse, there were rumblings of revolt in the ranks; word had it that a lieutenant in the Vinewood Station had resigned rather than "protect niggers." So the higher-ups had to assert themselves, to prove that they had control of the situation and to make sure that, the next time there was trouble, Johnny Smith couldn't pin it all on them.[62]

Personally, he felt for the people of Garland Avenue. He had a teenage daughter at home and he had a mortgage to repay, too. He also felt for the men under his command, who would hate being assigned to protect that colored family while they moved into the bungalow. Some of his officers were Klansmen; no one could say for sure how many men on the force had joined the Invisible Empire, but the number was high. But it wasn't just the Klan's influence that made his cops angry. They had signed on to defend these neighborhoods, to keep them clear of trouble and free of crime, not to stand down people just like themselves so a Negro could live in a place where he didn't belong.[63] Come moving day, it would be easy enough to drive the coloreds out. All Schuknecht would have to do was wait for the mob to form, then tell his men to stand back. It would be over within a matter of minutes. People in the neighborhood would love him for it, and every precinct in the city would hail him as a hero. But the brass would have his head.

•

In the weeks after his Sunday afternoon meeting, Ossian grew into the role his silence had won him. His fears remained as strong as ever, a primal pull away from the terror he knew he was walking into. But to see how friends and family admired him was nothing short of intoxicating. He loved the feeling that came when, in the course of an ordinary conversation, he told the head of Dunbar's board of directors that he wasn't going to run, and it was thrilling to see how Vollington Bristol looked at him with respect the day the two met in a bank lobby, and Ossian said he, too, was willing to face the mob.[64]

It was the reaction on Cairney Street that really mattered, though. When Ossian told Gladys that he wanted to see the sale through, she no doubt set her jaw and said she would join him in the bungalow the first night it was theirs to own, and when Gladys made up her mind, no one in the world was going to dissuade her. Henry pledged to be by his brother's side, whatever might happen; Otis, too, promised his support. Even Gladys's mother approved of his decision, though it would put her daughter at grave risk. One day she took her son-in-law aside and put a pistol in his hand, telling him that he should be ready to use it.[65]

There were times when his courage began to crack, but friends were always there to pull him back. The worst moment came when Marie Smith called to report that she was receiving anonymous phone calls: someone said that her house was going to be dynamited; another said that they planned "to kill the nigger." Putting down the receiver, Ossian's commitment collapsed, shattered by confirmation of a lifetime's nightmares. Edward Carter calmed him down. Whoever was saying such things was simply trying to intimidate her into revoking the contract, he insisted. The people who lived around the bungalow weren't the type to commit violence. It was tough talk, nothing more, and Ossian shouldn't be afraid of it.[66] It was the weakest of assurances, based on nothing but instinct, and Ossian must have known it. But he wanted to believe it was true.

Mostly, though, Ossian was swept up in the fervor of the moment. Throughout the balance of July and August, the question of neighborhood segregation remained white-hot. When members of the Detroit real estate board gathered in a west-side library to discuss ways of restricting Negroes to Black Bottom, several dozen colored men stormed the meeting, demanding to be heard; the terrified real estate agents summoned the police, who shoved the black men outside and locked the doors.[67]

From his pulpit, the associate pastor of Second Baptist urged those black homeowners threatened by mobs to seek legal redress; one of the city's leading papers shot back that the minister "prefers a race riot to the surrender of a single legal right by a few Negroes." That exchange, in turn, brought a sharp reply from one of the most powerful voices in black America. The NAACP's national officers had been keeping tabs on the Detroit situation ever since the *Pittsburgh Courier* reported the west-side violence in late July.

The first week of August, James Weldon Johnson fired off an open letter reprinted around the country. "In Detroit," he wrote, "Negroes have been driven from their homes by mobs, those who refused to go having defended themselves in the absence of adequate police protection. We now have the spectacle of white . . . newspapers taking sides with the mob and warning Negroes that if they cleave to their citizenship rights they are inviting a 'race riot.' . . . It is a frightful commentary upon American civilization that any editor should dare to threaten any group of citizens with riot because they will not 'surrender a single legal right.'" Privately, the NAACP took an even tougher stand. "Whenever the price of our rights is made to be a riot or death in another form," field secretary William Pickens wrote the new branch president, Robert Bradby, "we would prefer to pay the price rather than give up the rights of men." Detroit's Talented Tenth didn't need the exhortations, Bradby replied; branch meetings, which a few months before had been all but deserted, were now drawing four or five hundred people.[68]

Ossian wasn't among them. Not once that summer did he present himself to the branch as a symbol of resistance, nor did he ask for its help, though Carter and other members of his circle must have informed him of the NAACP's commitment to make a fight of it. But in the end, Ossian confronted the terrors awaiting him on Garland the way he'd tackled so many other challenges in his life, hefting other people's expectations and marching relentlessly forward. He worked methodically all through the balance of July and into August, trying to anticipate the most volatile moments, to compensate for his vulnerabilities, to prepare for the worst. Gladys bought extra food, enough for a week's siege, and stored it away, while he carefully assembled the cache of weapons they'd need and sought out a few more men to join the Sweets, Perry, and Carter in defending the house the first few dangerous nights. Full of enthusiasm, Henry talked a college friend and fraternity brother, John Latting, into signing on, while Otis recruited one of his numerous friends, an army veteran and federal narcotics agent by the name of William Davis, dangling the offer of a room in the bungalow as compensation. Ossian, meanwhile, hired a young Black Bottom man, Joe Mack, to serve as his chauffeur, an idea he undoubtedly took from Turner, and he made arrangements for another hired man, Norris Murray, to help around the new house. Mack and Murray weren't explicitly asked whether they were willing to take up arms, but neither did Ossian tell them of the dangers that would be facing them on moving day. So, by default, they, too, joined the defense. By mid-August, the contingent was complete: eight young men, Ossian and Gladys, a makeshift Talented Ten.[69]

The final few weeks were given to last-minute details. When they met in the bank, Vollington Bristol urged Ossian to inform the police of his plans. Ossian was skeptical, so Otis, who seemed to know all the ins and outs of Black Bottom, took it upon himself to contact Detective Inspector Robert "Bert" McPherson, head of the department's flamboyant Black Hand Squad, the office in charge of policing Italian mobsters and Negroes of every description. McPherson promised to give the Sweets the protection they needed. Ossian, meanwhile, thought through defensive tactics—guns in the upstairs windows where the sightlines were better, a couple of men out on the rear porch to protect the flank—the way he'd learned to do on Wilberforce's parade grounds.[70] Then, when everything was in place, he waited for summer to end and the confrontation to come.

•

But the summer didn't end. The heat of July carried through the dog days of August and into the first week of September. City hall all but shut down as Johnny Smith rested in anticipation of the autumn's bruising campaign, when Detroit would again be up for grabs. The Klan kept its crosses burning, and by the first week of September, they'd gathered the signatures they needed to put their man, Charles Bowles, back on the ballot in November's mayoral election. So sure was kleagle Ira Stout of the Klan's eventual success, he announced plans to put a brilliant neon sign atop the Invisible Empire's downtown headquarters, so that white, native-born Detroit could see the letters "KKK" blinking bloodred in the night and know where the city's center of power was soon to be. At the McClellan Station, Norton Schuknecht kept his eye out for trouble, waiting for word that the Negroes were about to move.[71]

And on Garland Avenue, the neighborhood's meager lawns turned from green to brown and the weeds that had poked up through the cracks in the sidewalk withered and died. Immediately after the Improvement Association's school-yard rally in mid-July, there'd been a flurry of activity. A thousand people signed membership cards and handed over their dollar dues. Encouraged by the flood of support, Conley and McGlynn appointed block captains to go door to door getting neighbors to add restrictive covenants to their deeds. But the campaign ran up against the reality of life along Garland. The Doves, right across the street from the bungalow, would have been happy to restrict the sale of their flat to whites, but they were renters: the owner lived miles away, far beyond the Improvement Association's reach. More troubling was the response of most of those who did own their homes. Time and again, the block captains were told that families wouldn't dare sign away their right to sell to Negroes without the assurance that everyone else in the neighborhood would do the same. The logic was unassailable. Just a few exceptions, a few people doing like that woman in the bungalow did and selling out to Negroes, and everyone else would be trapped, prohibited from accepting an offer from coloreds and stuck with a house whites wouldn't buy. It was all well and good to talk about banding together. But in the end, a man had to look out for himself and his family. After weeks of work, the Waterworks Park Improvement Association managed to convince 150 people to restrict their deeds.[72]

Intimidation also failed miserably. While the memory of the rally was still fresh, a three-man committee called on Marie Smith to see if she were willing to renege on her deal with the Negro and sell the bungalow to the association instead. She certainly was, she replied, as long as they were willing to pay her new asking price of thirty thousand dollars, a figure so ludicrously high they had no choice but to walk away. When the threatening phone calls began, Smith lost some of her moxie. One threat left her so rattled she blurted out that she hadn't sold her house to a Negro after all; she'd sold it to a Jew, and the Jew sold it to the colored man. Instead of giving in to the pressure, though, in early August, Smith packed up her belongings and fled—gone to California, some said—leaving the house dark and empty. That was about the time silence descended on Garland. The association called no more meetings; the block captains, defeated by their neighbors' self-interest, abandoned their rounds; and news of the Negroes dried up. There was still plenty of talk out on the porches and the street, bad feelings made worse by the incessant heat, but no one knew for sure when or if the coloreds were going to arrive.[73]

♦

Norton Schuknecht also spent the balance of the summer waiting for word of the Sweets' intentions. Twice in the weeks after the July rally, he sent men out to ask the bungalow's owner when the Negroes were going to move in, but she insisted that she didn't know anything. It never occurred to him to track down the coloreds themselves, though it wouldn't have been hard to do. Then again, the Negroes hadn't come looking for him, either. When they put in their request for police protection, they went to Bert McPherson, the inspector in charge of the Black Hand Squad. That decision alone was enough to make Schuknecht livid. McPherson was a high flyer—fourteen meritorious mentions in his first eight years on the force, a full inspector at forty-three—but he was too undependable for Schuknecht's taste. It wasn't clear how long McPherson had news of the Negroes' plans, but he didn't pass it to Schuknecht until the evening of September 7, just twelve hours before the coloreds showed up on Garland Avenue. Schuknecht was so angry he didn't even ask the Black Hand boys for assistance, though they knew a thing or two about dealing with Negroes.[74]

Instead, he scrambled to put together a plan he hoped would keep the peace. The Sweets would have around-the-clock protection, he decided: four cops at the bungalow in the morning, eight in the afternoon, ten or more by nightfall. To make sure that everything was done right, Schuknecht would personally direct operations on the street. In case of emergency, he arranged to have two hundred men held in reserve at the precinct house during the first few nights the Negroes were in their new neighborhood.

Almost immediately things went wrong. Late on the night of the seventh, as Schuknecht was making his final arrangements, two patrolmen spotted a Negro chasing a white man down one of the west side's major thoroughfares. When they tried to intervene, the Negro pulled a gun and opened fire, killing one of the cops and wounding the other. By the time Schuknecht's men gathered for roll call the next morning, word of the murder must have spread across the police department, and emotions were undoubtedly running high. He tried to be tough. Those officers assigned to the doctor's house should avoid using excessive force, he said; simply keep the crowds from congregating. But, he insisted, "we're there to preserve peace and order, and that man, Doctor Sweet, can live there, if we have to take every man in the department to protect his home."[75] In private, though, Norton Schuknecht must have known that in a department thick with Klansmen, this wasn't a day to count on his men to do their duty.

◆

Tuesday, September 8, began with the small shivers of excitement that the break of seasons brings. Most men and a few women were up and off to work early that morning, anxious to punch in on time after the long holiday weekend. Mothers and the few fathers who stayed behind wrestled wriggling children into brand-new dresses and sharply creased shirts and marched them down the street to the first day of school. By midmorning the bustle had eased and Garland had settled into a blessed quiet. Those who worked at home such as Kathleen Dove, with the baby to care for, were in the midst of their morning chores when the Sweets' touring car passed slowly down the block and pulled up to the curb just short of Charlevoix.[76]

Most of the day, the neighbors kept watch surreptitiously, peering out from behind blinds or glancing over to the bungalow, anxious to see every move the coloreds made. They watched as a gang of Negroes drew in behind the sedan with a truckload of trunks and suitcases, a few packages of gunnysack, and a couple of pieces of furniture. They saw the cops arrive—that was a surprise—two patrolmen idling on the corner, another officer walking right up to the front door and standing in the shadow of the porch talking to one of the colored men for a minute or two. In the course of the afternoon, some of the movers left and other Negroes showed up, jauntily striding up the steps and disappearing into the house.[77]

It wasn't until late afternoon that the neighbors began to move outdoors. The kids came first, drawn to the corner by the sight of policemen and the frightening, thrilling news that at long last the Negroes were on their block. But the cops had no trouble shooing the youngsters away, and by suppertime, the street was largely clear. Once meals were finished and dishes cleared, though, the crowd began to gather. There were a lot more cops on the street by then, a dozen or so, a few on each of the four corners of the intersection where the bungalow stood, several more in the alleyway behind.[78]

Nothing happened. No one from the Waterworks Park Improvement Association—not Conley the real estate agent or McGlynn the autoworker or Monet the rubber worker—went among the men exhorting them to challenge the police line. No neighborhood woman mounted the Doves' front porch and dared the men to attack. No one picked up a stone and lobbed it across the street. No one did anything to pull the crowd together, to transform the curious into the murderous, to make a mob. The sun set, the streetlights blinked on, and still the neighbors stood on the street until the hour grew so late that they started to think of the following day's work and, one by one, drifted home to bed.

◆

The next day, September 9, Garland was again rife with rumors, the way it had been back in June. The Negroes were to be put out, people told each other. There'd been a meeting in the corner market where the attack had been plotted; some of the men from Tireman Avenue were on their way over to lead the assault; tonight was the night. There was a lot of angry talk that day, so much that the cops stationed at the corner heard it, the motorman on the Charlevoix Avenue streetcar heard it, residents on nearby streets heard it, and the Sweets heard it, too.[79]

By eight, the crowd was as thick as it had been the night before, maybe thicker. As the streets grew clogged, the police officer in charge—the obese fellow over near the school yard—huddled with a couple of his men, who then closed Garland to traffic a block north and south of the bungalow. Without the occasional car rumbling past, the street grew empty, only a few feet of asphalt still hot from the day's sun separating the patrolmen in front of the Negroes' house from the people gathered on the lawns and porches on the opposite side. The Getkes came out onto their porch to sit for a while. Across from them, neighbors filled the Doves' front yard from the sapling planted next to the curb all the way up to the porch where Ray Dove stood leaning against the railing, his wife and their roomers behind him. Eric Houghberg strode past, slipping into his flat so that he could grab a quick supper and get back out onto the street. Leon Breiner sauntered down to the corner store, then, as he headed back home, stopped by the Doves' to chat and smoke his pipe. Bored with the view from the corner, thirteen-year-old Ulric Arthur and his friend George Suppus squeezed through the men and women gathered on the Doves' lawn and planted themselves on the porch steps, where their view of the bungalow was just about perfect.[80]

No sign of the corner-market conspirators or the men from Tireman Avenue. Darkness coming, cover of night. Maybe then. Maybe never. Rumors. Bitter words filling a summer evening. Put the niggers out. Dancing with the devil.

They came from opposite directions, the taxi rattling past the police checkpoint down Garland toward the corner and the gang of teenagers—six or seven local boys, neighborhood kids—spilling out from the half lot between the Doves' flat and the grocery store next door. But it was as if their movements were choreographed. The first stones flew as the cab came to a stop, rocks and chunks of coal grabbed from the alleyway arching gracefully over the policemen's heads and thudding onto the bungalow's sloping roof. A dormer window shattered, though in the sudden noise and confusion the sound of breaking glass was hard to hear. As the cab door swung open the cries went up, "Here's niggers!" "There they go!" More stones—aiming at the porch, at the other windows, at the two coloreds racing for the bungalow's steps. The front door suddenly opened and another Negro appeared. For a fraction of a second, he stood stock-still in the doorway, staring beyond the coloreds running toward him to the people on the Doves' front lawn. Then he was gone, faded back into the darkness of the house.[81]

The stones kept coming a minute more, maybe two. Then the bungalow's upstairs windows slid open and the guns blazed, brilliant flashes of light illuminating the blackening sky.

SIX

THE LETTER OF YOUR LAW

The paddy wagon pulled up in front of the police department's downtown headquarters, its back door creaked open, and a patrolman signaled for the ten men to climb down. Enough time since the shooting had passed for the force's high command to confirm the worst: the Negroes' fusillade had struck two white men. Eric Houghberg, rushed to Receiving Hospital bleeding profusely from a bullet wound in the thigh, was expected to survive, but Leon Breiner had been killed by what appeared to be a single bullet in the back.

As news of the murder spread, Garland Avenue was teetering on the edge of a riot. An hour after the shooting, there were five thousand people thronging the intersection in front of the bungalow, a crowd greater than anything the west side had seen that summer, and though its members still seemed leaderless and unsure of themselves, the risk of a rampage was dangerously high. Desperate to impose order, Norton Schuknecht rushed the entire force he'd put on reserve, two hundred men, into the neighborhood, their authority bolstered by a new weapon, the department's own whippet tank.

As Ossian and the others uncurled themselves from the wagon's benches and gingerly stepped down to the street, they had only the most basic sense of what was happening. Someone in the mob had been killed and they were in deep, deep trouble.[1]

Police headquarters loomed above them. Opened just two years earlier, it was a monumental building, with the force and grandeur to disquiet a powerless man. Its architect, Albert Kahn, had made his reputation designing Detroit's auto factories, spare utilitarian structures of glass and concrete, but for this commission, he had drawn on classical forms. To report to duty, the city's men in blue passed through a vaulted entranceway flanked on either side by four soaring arched windows. Above them rose eight four-story-tall faux Doric columns ostensibly supporting a final floor of crisp, clean lines: seventeen Tuscan columns capped by a frieze decorated with bas reliefs. The building was nothing less than a civic temple, an evocation in stone and sculpture of the Western tradition's highest ideals.[2]

But it was nothing more than a façade, as inside the police headquarters, corruption was rampant, and every Negro in the city knew that justice received here would be tempered at best, lethal at worst. Colored people raised in Alabama, Mississippi, or Florida hardly expected justice to be blind, but still they despised the blinding prejudice that seemed to consume Detroit's cops. Colored men were two and a half times more likely to be arrested than whites, colored women almost seven times as likely as their Caucasian counterparts. Once they were in custody, Negroes routinely were held for days without being formally charged and often were denied access to lawyers— sometimes suspects were moved from precinct to precinct so they couldn't be found, then were threatened and even beaten until they confessed. And those were the colored people lucky enough to have been spared cops' summary justice.[3]

So when Ossian and the others followed Lieutenant Blondy Hayes of the Black Hand Squad into the police headquarters, they were under no illusions. Hayes had been incredibly kind in the terrifying moments after the shooting, taking off Ossian's handcuffs, calming his fears, and arranging for the back-alley exit from Garland. His willingness to confront the mob in the alleyway behind the bungalow may well have saved the Negroes' lives. But when the colored men were delivered to the officers who were going to take on their case, they had to be prepared for accusations to be leveled and intimidation to begin. They could assume no degree of sympathy; they couldn't risk an errant word. And they had to fear, as the lieutenant led them up flight after flight of stairs until they reached the fourth-floor offices of the homicide squad, whether they would ever be free again.[4]

It was about ten o'clock when Hayes settled Ossian and the other nine men into a long, narrow anteroom in the Detective's Bureau.

Gladys arrived a short time later, escorted by a patrolman from the reserve unit. All of them must have felt ragged and worn, drained by the stifling heat of the room—at the end of a summer's day, the air had to have hung heavy and still—the lateness of the hour, and the surreal sense of watching a nightmare unfold. Somehow Davis, the narcotics agent, managed to fall asleep, the skill of a military man who'd learned in the course of combat how to grab rest whenever he could have it. The others sat hollow eyed around the room's large table or against the wall, waiting for something to happen.[5]

As soon as the opportunity presented itself, Ossian and one of the insurance men, Hewitt Watson, asked for the chance to call their lawyers. Although he was surely still angry at his friend's failure to show up at the bungalow the previous night, Ossian phoned Julian Perry, while Watson talked to Charles Mahoney, one of the most able black attorneys in the city. Precisely what the lawyers said isn't known, but most likely they urged the prisoners not to give the police any incriminating information. Not that the eleven needed that advice. In the time they spent together in the anteroom, Ossian and the others agreed on a makeshift defense they would share when the police starting asking questions. As they whispered out their alibis, though, they had to have wondered whether the story they assembled would hold through eleven separate interrogations, or whether one of them—too tired to think, too scared to keep the details straight, too anxious to save himself—would say something that condemned the rest. When no one was watching, Ossian squeezed his hand around the bullets he still had in his pocket and silently slipped them into the cuspidor that sat on the floor next to his chair.[6]

There was still no sign of the lawyers when, at 10:45 P.M., two hours after the shooting, Hayes asked Ossian to follow him into the interrogation room. In a panic, Ossian got to his feet, and this strange and terrifying night entered its next dangerous phase.

•

As he walked into the tiny room, Ossian must have expected intimidation, perhaps even the threat of violence. Instead, he found the makings of a formal legal procedure. In front of him sat Assistant Prosecuting Attorney Ted Kennedy, dispatched by his boss, Wayne County Prosecutor Robert Toms, to personally conduct the interrogations in an effort to make sure the record wasn't contaminated by the force's usual abuses.[7]

Kennedy began gently enough, introducing Ossian to the stenographer and to the two officers, Blondy Hayes and Lieutenant William Johnson of the Homicide Squad, who sat around the table with him, then inquiring about the details of the doctor's move. As he tried to answer, Ossian grew agitated, talking too fast, stumbling over words. And when the prosecutor moved onto dangerous ground, Sweet offered painfully clumsy denials, so transparent they defied belief. Kennedy asked him whether Garland Avenue was a white neighborhood. Ossian said he didn't know.

"Well, I mean, before you bought it, you investigated, of course," Kennedy replied in genuine surprise.

"No," insisted Ossian, "the house was for sale; and I simply asked her would she sell it."

His other answers were no more believable. He hadn't asked the other men to help him defend his home, he said; they were just visitors, boarders, there on business. They weren't huddled inside waiting for attack; he had invited them all to dinner and they were waiting for the ham to finish cooking. They had only started shooting once the rocks started hitting the house and the windows were smashed. He couldn't say who fired when. "I was so excited," he explained, "I wasn't normal then; I don't know what was there." But they had been provoked; he knew that. They'd had to shoot or the mob would have destroyed the house.

Kennedy took it slowly at first, letting the doctor put together his version of events, not probing too much. But the closer it got to midnight, the more aggressively the prosecutor pushed. Why had Ossian filled the house with guns? Sweet backtracked ever so slightly, saying he had heard "rumors" that the whites were going to drive him off and he wanted to protect himself. How did the men know where to find the guns once the attack began? He had showed them the weapons in the upstairs closet. When did Ossian buy the guns? "Oh, when the trouble started around here, sometime ago," Ossian answered. "About a month ago."

Kennedy knew he was close to getting the answer he wanted. One more step and Ossian would admit that he had planned his defense, had conspired with the other Negroes. "Now, doctor," he said, "isn't it a fact, you moved up in the neighborhood, knowing it was a white neighborhood; if you went up there, there was going to be trouble?"

"No."

That had been too direct. Kennedy tried again. "You say that certain

things developed, after the place [was] bought, which led you to believe there was going to be trouble after you moved in?"

"Yes."

"When you moved in, you had the arsenal up there with you. . . .
You took them up there, knowing you were going to have trouble,
didn't you?"

Ossian tried to hedge. "No," he said, "I didn't know [I was] going to
have trouble." But Kennedy wouldn't let him slip away that easily.
"You had a pretty good reason to believe it," he asked, "didn't you?"

"Yes."

"Why did you move in there, then?"

"Because I bought the house," Ossian said, "and it was my house,
and I felt I had a right to live in it."

Principle. After an hour of evasion, Ossian fell back on the fundamental point of the entire affair. The house was his, and he wasn't going to be driven from it. At midnight, Kennedy sent him back to the
anteroom and started working his way through the others one by one.[8]

The differences between them were dramatic. Insurance man Charles
Washington had the salesman's touch, shaking hands all around when
he walked into the interrogation room, while his colleague Leonard
Morse was so desperate to please he came across as obsequious. "Have
I threatened you in any way?" Kennedy asked as the interrogation
came to a close. "No," Morse replied. "I believe you too much of a gentleman for that, Mr. Kennedy." William Davis was much more guarded,
his answers brief, his words carefully chosen, his participation in the
Sweets' defense edited down to a minimum; not once did he mention
that he'd spent the night of September 8 trapped inside the bungalow,
waiting for an assault that didn't come. Small John Latting, Henry's
college friend, was so terrified he had trouble putting words together.
And poor Joe Mack, the chauffeur, had to stop in the middle of his interview so he could gather himself. He had been sick for quite some
time—heart trouble—and the pressure was too much to bear.[9]

When Kennedy moved them through the evening's events, though,
almost all of the suspects told the same story Ossian had offered. No
one had gone out to Garland to help the doctor protect his house.
Mack was doing his job, and handyman Norris Murray had come by
hoping to get paid for the work he'd put in the previous day. Davis and
Latting were to look at rooms they were hoping to rent. And the three
insurance agents agreed that they were there to correct a mistake on
the doctor's policy. Once they had assembled inside the bungalow,

there'd been no talk of a mob attack, no discussion of tactics, no distribution of the guns hidden upstairs. Washington and Morse described a casual evening of cards and conversation. "Why I didn't do anything but sit down and went to talking," Morse said, "principally joking." Murray said he set to work in the basement, getting the boiler heated up so Mrs. Sweet could finish cooking the dinner. Joe Mack went up to the bathroom to "take a bath and a crap."[10]

As quickly as the suspects assembled their alibis, Kennedy tore them down. Sometimes, he played one witness off another. Did you hear any water running into the bathtub in the hour before the shooting, he asked Latting, or notice anyone go into the basement to start the boiler? No, the young man said, bewildered by the questions. Other times, Kennedy confronted the suspect directly. Was it necessary for three insurance men to deliver news about a mistaken policy, he asked Watson. Do you always devote so much time to your clients, he said to Washington. You couldn't have spent the whole evening lighting a boiler, he pressed Murray. What else did you do?[11] Once or twice, the prosecutor came tantalizingly close to breaking the weakest of the group. "When did you start to talk about the trouble out there, that might arise there," Kennedy asked Joe Mack. "You started to talk about that, didn't you?"

Mack tried to stall. "Sir?"

"You started to talk among yourselves, about some trouble you might have?"

"Yes," the chauffeur replied. "They says they might run us away from out here tonight."

"They might what?"

"The white people says, going to run us away from here tonight."

"Was the doctor talking about that, too?" Kennedy said. "What I mean is, when you were playing cards with these men in the room there, weren't you talking about this trouble you might be having tonight?"

But there was something in the question—the doctor's name, perhaps, or the hint of excitement in Kennedy's voice—that reminded Mack of what he was supposed to say. "No, I didn't hear," he said, suddenly adamant. "There wasn't nobody saying anything about no trouble; wasn't paying no attention."[12]

If the suspects had trouble keeping all the pieces of their story together, though, on the two most pivotal points there was complete agreement. In the moments before the shooting, the bungalow was under intense assault. "Stones. [They] started throwing stones," Latting insisted. "Bricks and so forth being throwed against the house and bricks comed through the window," agreed Morse. "I wasn't in the room but I heard the breaking of the glass." Davis, the narcotics agent, heard the glass shattering as well. "Bricks or rocks or something, some kind of missiles, hitting the house . . . from all sides," he said. "Then there came a big crash upstairs, a window going through, something like that." And when the guns went off, none of the suspects were anywhere near the upstairs windows. Mack was still in the bathroom, Murray in the basement. Latting was cowering in the upstairs hallway, away from the shards of glass flying across the bedrooms. Morse stayed downstairs, hiding in the alcove right behind the front vestibule. Davis was standing in the living room. Otis Sweet was at the phone near the back staircase. Washington kept moving from room to room. And Watson couldn't recall where he was. "I'm sure I don't know," he told Kennedy. "You know, [there was] quite a lot of excitement." Ten guns, two hundred rounds of ammunition, fifteen or twenty shots fired, and no one pulled a trigger.[13]

So through five hours of interrogation, the feeble story arranged in the anteroom held together—but for two moments when caution gave way to defiance.

Gladys Sweet was tougher than Ossian and the other men, a lot tougher. She wasn't intimidated the way Kennedy must have expected her to be, the way her husband had been. She didn't have excuses to offer or an unlikely story to tell. On the contrary, she seemed proud of what she and her husband had done, that they'd taken a stand. And she resented being questioned, as if there were no reason to investigate the night's events, as if it were painfully obvious what had occurred, as if the Negroes had a right to shoot into a crowd of white people.

Kennedy asked her whether she knew she was moving into a white neighborhood. "Certainly did," she replied.

"You knew and expected if you went out there, there was going to be trouble?"

"Possibly, yes," Gladys said. "They informed us they was going to be trouble."

"Why did you go up there?" Kennedy asked.

"I think it is my perfect right to move where I please," she said.

"You brought all those guns up there, didn't you?"

"Well, yes."

"And talked about using them, too, if necessary?"

"If necessary."

But she'd go no farther. For the better part of an hour, Kennedy tried to get her to re-create the evening, to describe the conversations her husband had with the other men, to retrace their movements immediately before the shooting, something, anything, that he could use to show that the men planned the shooting. Gladys couldn't recall a single moment, not a word spoken, not a step taken. Kennedy tried to shake her. He showed her the guns. He brought a couple of extra cops into the room, to make her feel small and vulnerable. But Gladys still stonewalled. Finally, Kennedy couldn't contain his frustration. "Do you want this attitude throughout the entire statement," he snapped. "You don't remember anything, is that right?"

"I don't remember what I don't remember," she fired back. "You can't make me."

"No. Is it because you don't want to remember?"

"It is because I don't remember."

He didn't need this, not from this little colored woman barely out of her teens. "Will you remember tomorrow morning?" he asked.

"No, I won't."

"Will you remember a week from now?"

"No."

It was useless. She wasn't lying, at least not in the way that the others had lied. They had tried to fool Kennedy by misdirection and obfuscation of the most obvious sort. She was defying the prosecutor, taunting him by withholding the information they both knew she had. He wouldn't break her, no matter how much of the night he wasted. Kennedy sent her back to be with her husband.[14]

Henry Sweet's answers were even more startling—and much more dangerous. A few minutes into his interrogation, Kennedy asked him what happened when the stones began hitting the house. For some reason, Henry didn't follow the script. He went upstairs, he said, picked up his rifle, walked into the front bedroom, knelt at the window, and scanned the mob standing across the street.

It took Kennedy a second to realize where Henry was going with his story. The prosecutor started to ask about the rifle. Which gun was it? Could Henry identify it? But that wasn't the line to follow. Not yet. Kennedy had the weapons, all piled up outside the interrogation room, waiting to be tagged as evidence. What he didn't have was the suspects' actions, the key to establishing their intentions, the foundation for the prosecution's case. What did you do then, once you were at the window, he asked.

"I didn't do anything until the stones began coming in on me," Henry replied.

"Then what happened?"

"I tried to protect myself."

"What did you do?"

"I fired the rifle," Henry said.

"Where did you fire it?"

"The first time in the air."

"Then what did you do?"

"I fired again in the crowd." He hadn't aimed at anyone in particular. He'd tried to fire a foot or two above the mob, to "frighten them so they would leave us alone."

He said it without a hint of braggadocio or remorse. Henry was just setting out the facts, putting himself on record. He was also giving up his best alibi, his surest hope of avoiding conviction. Kennedy had the sudden hope that he would hand over the others as well. Was anyone else in the room with you, he asked. There were two or three men kneeling alongside him, admitted Henry. Perfect. Kennedy pushed as hard as he had all evening. Who were they? Which window was the doctor at? Had the others fired into the street as well? But Henry wouldn't take the next step. He couldn't say. The room was dark; he couldn't make out their faces. There had been too much confusion; Henry couldn't recall who was doing what.

That was ludicrous. The others must have been standing a foot or two away from you, Kennedy said. You had to have seen them or at least heard their guns going off. But Henry was adamant. He would implicate himself, but he wouldn't implicate anyone else. So Kennedy tried a different tack. When did the group plan the defense? They must have talked over what each man would do if trouble started. "Never to my knowledge," Henry said. They all intended to shoot the moment they picked up the guns, didn't they? "Not necessarily," Henry replied. There wasn't a mob, was there? Henry saw the policemen on the street, didn't he? He knew the police had the situation under control. He didn't need to fire into the crowd.

Henry stiffened. "Before I made the first shot," he said, "the stones pouring down like rain."

Kennedy wouldn't let up. "Did any of them hit you? How close they come to you?"

"Very close."

"If you stayed out of the front room," Kennedy said, "you wouldn't have been hit, would you?"

"Probably I would have been dead by now," Henry answered, "if I hadn't gone out there."[15]

He'd pulled it back to self-defense. Henry had been moving right toward a confession. Then he had pulled it back to self-defense.

It was almost three thirty in the morning when Kennedy finished the interrogations, packed up his notes and transcripts, and headed home to prepare the report for his boss's desk first thing in the morning. When the young man was gone, the cops clasped manacles onto the eleven Negroes and led them outside into the stillness of the deep city night, across the street to the decrepit Wayne County Jail. Gladys, again separated from the others, was taken to the women's ward. Ossian was escorted into one of the men's cellblocks, his brothers and the seven others into a different section of the jail.[16] It must have been almost dawn by the time all the cell doors were finally slammed shut.

◆

News of the Sweets' arrest rocketed through Detroit's Talented Tenth. Ossian's panicked call to Julian Perry got the word out. As soon as Sweet was off the line, Perry phoned his fellow lawyer, Cecil Rowlette, to ask for help. Having represented both Fleta Mathies and Alexander Turner, Rowlette had an intimate understanding of the legal and political issues the Sweets would be facing. He also had the temperament any defense counselor was going to need. Perry, a short, slight, light-skinned young man five years out of Howard University's law school, embodied the physical attributes and educational achievements the colored elite most prized, but he had no real fighting instinct. Brawny, dark-skinned Rowlette made up for what his colleague lacked. The youngest of eleven children born to former slaves outside Richmond, Virginia, he was weaned on stories of oppression; when she was just twelve, his mother used to tell him, she was sold three times in one day. Like Ossian, Rowlette pulled himself into the Talented Tenth by taking advantage of the opportunities black colleges provided, graduating from Virginia Union University in 1908 and Howard Law four years later. In his ten years of practice in Detroit, he'd established himself as a first-rate criminal lawyer—tough-minded, relentless, extraordinarily confident in his abilities, and a bit of showman. As soon as Perry explained what had happened on Garland, Rowlette signed on to the case. They agreed to meet at police headquarters right away.[17]

Hewitt Watson's call to attorney Charles Mahoney, meanwhile, went instead to William Osby, a Negro engineer who lived across the street from Mahoney in an otherwise white neighborhood not far from Tireman Avenue. Mahoney, it turned out, didn't have a phone, so Osby took his evening calls. The arrangement put the Sweets' news into the heart of the Talented Tenth. Head of the Dunbar Board of Trustees, a member of the executive board of Detroit's fledgling NAACP branch, and a founder of the Detroit Urban League, Osby was a powerhouse in black Detroit. Mahoney was every bit his equal. The son of a businessman, Mahoney had grown up the only colored child in a small Michigan town. When he reached college age, his parents sent him to Fisk University, one of the finest black colleges in the country. He received his law degree from the University of Michigan in 1911 and immediately set up a successful practice in Detroit, taking civil rights cases for the NAACP on the side. His work in breaking the segregation of nearby Ypsilanti's school district won him widespread attention, even from white politicians: he already had three years on the city's planning commission behind him, and Mayor Smith had made him one of his closer advisers, a prelude, many thought, to Mahoney seeking office himself. The moment he heard what had happened, Mahoney also headed downtown, while Osby started contacting his NAACP colleagues across the city.[18]

Most likely, Perry, Rowlette, and Mahoney ran into one another at police headquarters that night; they certainly ran into the same stone wall. In 1925, criminal suspects had no legal right to have their attorneys present during questioning, and Detroit's cops weren't in the practice of erring on the side of leniency toward Negroes. It was an indication of Mahoney's stature that he managed to get all the way up to the Homicide Squad offices before being booted out the door, but Lieutenant Johnson came out of the interrogation room to personally send the lawyer packing. "Get the hell out of here," he growled. So the attorneys headed home that night without so much as a glimpse of their clients.[19]

But they knew that the battle was just beginning. As always, the cops had brute force on their side, but the Talented Tenth had the weight of politics, or so they thought. Colored voters had helped to give progressive judges control of the criminal court in 1923 and had put Smith in the mayor's office the following year. It was time to call in some debts. By Thursday morning, September 10, Perry, Rowlette, and Mahoney had agreed to create a joint defense team. Their first order of business was to gain access to their clients; every hour that passed heightened the risk that one of the suspects would say something incriminating, and in any case, the prisoners deserved to know that someone was working on their behalf. The key step was to secure a writ of habeas corpus, forcing the prosecutor either to surrender the suspects or file charges. Already the bench's progressives were incensed about the department's abuse of procedural rights: just a few weeks before, the criminal court's leading liberal, Frank Murphy, had released thirty-six accused gamblers because the cops had held them a day and half before any charges were lodged. By the time the lawyers' plea reached the bench, Ossian and the others would be closing in on twenty-four hours. As long as Mahoney, Rowlette, and Perry put their case before one of the four liberal judges, there was no way the court was going to turn them down.[20]

By itself, the writ wouldn't release the eleven suspects. In fact, it would probably do nothing more than force the prosecutor to present charges against them. But the lawyers were convinced that the court wouldn't let the charges stand. When Fleta Mathies had taken a potshot at her neighbor on Northfield Street, Rowlette had argued that she had acted in self-defense, and the judge had agreed, quashing the warrants before the young woman ever faced a jury. The court had also thrown out charges against John Fletcher, the last victim of the Tireman mobs, and he had actually shot a white boy. Again, the pivotal step was to get the case put before one of the progressives. As luck would have it, Murphy was the presiding judge for the month, in charge of assigning all cases. It would take some time and a lot of effort, but Rowlette was sure the eleven could be freed.[21]

In the meantime, Osby had pulled the NAACP branch into the action. The branch's former president and current legal counsel, W. Hayes McKinney, put his considerable political weight to the task of prying open the Sweets' jail cells. What's more, the branch president, Rev. Robert Bradby, pledged to open his church, Black Bottom's Second Baptist, for a mass rally in support of the Sweets after Sunday morning services. Three months before he stood for reelection, Johnny Smith would have no choice but to pay attention. And if he did, the course of the battle would shift and the forces of reaction would suddenly be on the run.[22]

Instead, the Talented Tenth was blindsided.

◆

The intersection of Garland and Charlevoix was still in chaos when the reporter from the *Detroit Free Press* arrived an hour or so after the shooting. So he avoided the corner and headed to the victim's modest home farther up the block, where a stunned Leona Breiner and her girls kept a death watch. Then he met with the leaders of the Waterworks Park Improvement Association, gathered in an emergency meeting at Joseph Rudge's house, seven doors north of the Sweets'. Only around midnight did he venture down to the bungalow, hoping to have a few minutes with the cops' commanding officer.[23]

By then Norton Schuknecht must have been utterly exhausted. As soon as McPherson's man, Blondy Hayes, led the Negroes to the paddy wagon, Schuknecht had turned his attention back to the massive mob gathered around the bungalow. There had to have been four thousand, maybe five thousand people on the street, he guessed, though in the pandemonium of the moment, it was impossible to get an accurate estimate. It took no more than a few minutes for the two hundred patrolmen he had put on reserve to pour into the neighborhood—truck after truck of heavily armed cops ready for riot duty. Immediately, Schuknecht reinforced the hastily arranged cordon he'd put around the coloreds' house, and when the department's tank rumbled down the street, he ordered it to protect his men's vulnerable flank along Charlevoix. For a while, he had to have wondered whether the line would hold; several times, gangs of men tried to push their way through to the bungalow, but the cops drew their billies, and the sickening sound of wood whacking against skull bone drove even the most fearless back down the block. Gradually, Schuknecht could feel the balance tipping his way. Passions spent, most folks drifted home as midnight closed in, until only a few hundred troublemakers remained, too angry or too stupid to know that the battle was over, too gutless to risk taking on cops they no longer outnumbered twenty to one.[24]

It was about that time that the reporter showed up on the bungalow's rock-strewn porch. Schuknecht could have begged off, citing all the work he still had to complete—the reports to file, the evidence to catalogue—before he could go home to bed. But it seems he wanted to talk, to make clear who was responsible for putting that white man into the morgue. So he invited the reporter inside for a tour of the house and a few words of explanation. He'd been on the street himself right before the shooting, Schuknecht said, and he knew the truth: there hadn't been any mob threatening the Negroes, no one surrounding the house, no one throwing stones. Garland Avenue was perfectly peaceful when the coloreds opened fire.[25]

By sunup the next morning, September 10, the spectacular story lay on stoops and newsstands across Detroit. "Shots poured without warning and seemingly without provocation last night at 8:30 . . . from the upstairs windows at 2905 Garland Avenue, into which Dr. and Mrs. Ossian H. Sweet, a Negro couple, had moved Tuesday, cost one man his life [and] put another in the hospital with a bullet in his leg," the front-page story began under a blaring headline. "A police inspector, a lieutenant, and a patrolman had been standing within 35 feet of the house which was lighted only in the upper window. They had been talking over the potential trouble that might result from Sweet's moving into the white neighborhood. A rain of bullets ended the conversation. As if the triggers of a dozen guns were being pulled simultaneously, the firing started. It stopped with the same suddenness that it began. While the police ran up the steps and hammered at the door, the gathering throng counted the casualties."

From there the story moved into the poignant details of a senseless death. In the course of the summer, the Waterworks Park Improvement Association had tried to talk the previous owner out of selling to Negroes, but she wouldn't cooperate. The Sweets themselves seemed to have come to Garland looking for trouble: they brought almost no furniture into their new home—not even enough chairs for all the Negroes who gathered inside—but they made sure the house was stocked with guns and ammunition. Leon Breiner posed no threat; he was simply strolling down the street when a bullet from the bungalow hit him in the head. All evening long, the victim's wife and daughters waited for Breiner to return from his walk. "Both girls heard rumors that their father had been hurt but did not suspect that he was killed," the story ran. "From time to time, as anxiety swept over them, they cried out, 'Daddy, daddy, where's my daddy?' When at last she learned that her husband wouldn't be coming home, his widow collapsed and by press time had yet to be revived."[26] Altogether, it was a damning story, sure to inflame passions all over the city.

The afternoon papers, the *Detroit News* and the *Detroit Times*, followed the *Detroit Free Press* onto the newsstands a few hours later. Normally, the papers were fierce competitors. For the better part of a century the *Detroit Free Press* and the *Detroit News* had split the Detroit market, the former claiming the workingman's penny with a host of homey touches and a dependable racism, the latter serving as the august voice of the business class, champion of Prohibition, good government, and Anglo-Saxon virtue. In 1921, William Randolph Hearst had taken control of the city's third paper, the long moribund *Detroit*

Times, transforming it from a staid sheet almost no one read into a champion of the working class, which it entertained with lurid stories of romance gone wrong and murder most foul. With the city's readership suddenly split three ways, the newspapers tried desperately to distinguish themselves, disagreeing on almost every issue, endorsing opposing candidates for elective office, spinning the same stories in dramatically different directions. But when it came to describing the tragic events on Garland Avenue, the three newspapers reached a remarkable unanimity.[27]

Like the *Detroit Free Press*, the *Detroit Times* took its lead directly from Schuknecht. "The outbreak occurred," the paper reported, "at a time when police, already guarding the house around which a hostile but orderly crowd had gathered, were congratulating themselves on having the situation well in hand. Without the slightest warning, and without any overt act from the outside, police said, a volley of shots burst from the upper window." The *Detroit Times* repeated some of the *Detroit Free Press*'s damning details: the lack of furniture in the Sweets' house; the abundance of weapons. And it added yet another fact even more condemning of the coloreds. According to assistant prosecutor Ted Kennedy, one of the Negroes, Henry Sweet, had confessed to shooting into the street.[28]

The *Detroit News* could have taken a very different tack. One of its reporters, Philip Adler, was heading home from a dinner party on the evening of the ninth, driving along Charlevoix Avenue a few blocks east of Garland, when he was stopped by a police roadblock. Curious, he parked on Goethe, the cross street north of Charlevoix, left his wife and baby in the car, grabbed his notebook, and walked past the barricade into the mob. When he asked a woman what was happening, she said, "A nigger family has moved into the neighborhood and they're going to put them out." Adler mingled with the mob momentarily, until things turned ugly. He saw stones hitting the house, the shots exploding from the upstairs window, and the police rushing the bungalow. Scared for his family, he ran back to his car and got them safely home. Then he headed to the newsroom.[29]

His editors, though, weren't interested in what he had seen. Perhaps they feared readers' response to an article describing rocks hitting the Negroes' house "like rain" just before the shooting; maybe they feared the political implications of a report that shifted the blame for Breiner's death from black to white. Whatever their reason, the editors tossed Adler's story into the wastebasket and went instead with a thoroughly professional account contradicting everything their own reporter had observed. "The shooting was not provoked," the *Detroit News* explained, again citing Shucknecht. "A small crowd was in front of the house, on both sides of the street, but no threats were made and no missiles were thrown. Suddenly an attic window was thrown up and a rifle was fired. A score or more shots followed in quick succession." By the afternoon shift change at the auto plants, the three papers had half a million copies flooding the city, each and every one of them turning the Sweets into killers.[30]

◆

By all accounts, Wayne County Prosecutor Robert Toms was a decent man. He came from the solid midwestern stock that in the years before the Civil War had championed abolitionism; Toms's grandfather had been a founding member of the Republican Party in the 1850s, when Abraham Lincoln was still an unknown backwoods lawyer. Unlike many other big-city prosecutors, Toms didn't measure his office's performance by the number of convictions secured. He didn't want to prosecute a case, he claimed, unless he deserved to win. And he absolutely dreaded the thought of sending an innocent man to prison. Better to let ninety-nine criminals go free, he told the press in a surge of sanctimoniousness, than to condemn one man for a crime he didn't commit.[31]

Yet as soon as he finished reading the previous night's interrogation transcripts, Inspector Schuknecht's brief report to his superiors, and Thursday morning's papers, Toms knew he had to bring those eleven Negroes to trial. It wasn't a matter of principle, at least not obviously so. It was politics. At thirty-eight years old, Toms had years of public life ahead of him, dozens of election campaigns to wage, and a spate of offices to win. There was no saying how far he might go. He had the standard good looks—the forceful square jaw, the deep blue eyes— voters loved. He held degrees from the best midwestern schools, the University of Chicago and the University of Michigan, and belonged to the right church and clubs: he was a Methodist and a Mason, an Odd Fellow and a Son of the American Revolution. Years ago, a politician with such a pedigree could have been magnanimous with Negroes. But these were bitter times. When the press ran stories that he was a member of the Klan, Toms vigorously denied them. With the KKK whipping racial tensions to a fevered pitch, though, Toms would squander every one of his advantages if he failed to prosecute the Sweets and their accomplices.[32]

But the interrogation transcript showed Toms the obvious weakness in his case. Time and again, the suspects said that the house was, in fact, under attack when the fatal shot was fired. Even Henry Sweet, who virtually confessed to the crime, was adamant that he was acting in self-defense. By saying that, the Negroes were handing their lawyers one of the most firmly established principles of common law. Hundreds of years of precedent granted a man an absolute right to defend himself and his property—even by deadly force—as long as he had reasonable cause to believe he was in imminent danger. The assessment didn't even have to be correct; according to the law, self-defense was all a matter of perception, not reality. To justify their actions, the Negroes simply had to say that they *believed* they were about to be attacked by a mob.

Toms would have only one effective reply. The Negroes had no reason to be afraid, he would have to say, because there was no mob in front of the doctor's house and therefore there was no threat. But that was the rub. Laymen might think of a mob as a howling mass of humanity waving torches and pitchforks. According to the State of Michigan, however, a mob existed when twelve or more armed people or thirty unarmed people assembled to intimidate or inflict harm. To make matters even more difficult, the legal definition of "harm" set an extremely low threshold: as soon as those thirty unarmed men and women caused twenty-five dollars in damage to a piece of property, they were breaking the law.[33]

According to the *Detroit Free Press*, there had been several hundred people out on Garland the night before, precisely the same number the Negroes cited during their interrogation. The suspects also told Kennedy that the rocks the mob had thrown shattered a window, and Schuknecht's report confirmed that one of the panes upstairs had been broken. Given these facts, Toms was going to have a very difficult time arguing that the Sweets hadn't faced a situation well beyond the legal requirements justifying self-defense.

Of course, Toms wasn't naive enough to believe that jurors decided cases according to fine points of law. When they went to trial, the Sweets would face an all-white jury—Toms would see to that—and the prosecutor didn't deserve his salary if he couldn't convince twelve Caucasians to convict eleven Negroes who invaded a white neighborhood armed to the teeth. There was every chance, though, that the case wouldn't get that far. At the preliminary hearing, the Negroes' lawyers would move to have the indictments quashed. When they did, the judges weren't going to overlook the legal technicalities, particularly if Toms ended up with one of the liberals hearing the motion. There were no two ways about it. To move his case all the way to trial, the prosecutor had to find some way to bring his argument within the letter of the law.

So before Toms had his office prepare indictments, he sent Assistant Prosecutor Kennedy out on more rounds of interviews. Kennedy had to have known that he was looking for any information his boss could use to downplay the threat the Negroes faced from the street, anything at all that would cast doubt on the whites' intent to do harm. But even he seemed surprised by what he heard when he went down to Garland that afternoon.

◆

The Sweets' bungalow was quiet when Ted Kennedy, the stenographer, and Lieutenant Billy Johnson from Homicide arrived in the early afternoon of September 10. Norton Schuknecht had cordoned off the house while detectives photographed the scene, gathered the empty shell casings strewn upstairs, and scoured the closets and cabinets for whatever shards of evidence remained. Kennedy couldn't help but notice that the police hadn't catalogued the dozen stones littering the front porch and its overhanging roof.[34]

Schuknecht was waiting for him inside, his brother-in-law, Otto Lemhagen, still by his side. Kennedy began by reviewing the details the inspector had put in his report. Schuknecht confirmed them all. He was standing at the intersection when the shooting occurred, just as he told the newspaper reporters. The Negroes weren't being threatened; his men were in charge of the situation, and the firing began "without any warning. It was such a surprise to us," he said. "It rather took us off our feet." Then Kennedy asked the first critical question. "Did you observe any people standing in front of the house, directly across from the Sweets?" Schuknecht said he did.

"How many would you say there were?"

"I would say twelve or fifteen people across the street there."

It was the precision that was startling. Twelve or fifteen was a figure perfectly pitched to keep the crowd below the legal definition of a mob. Schuknecht had never before claimed that the gathering on Garland was so small, not when he talked to the press, not when he filed his incident report at police headquarters.[35] It was too unlikely a number to be coincidence; the inspector must have read the statute books and learned the law.

Kennedy gently probed the soft spots in Schuknecht's story, using an approach that was certainly softer than the one he had taken with the Sweets the night before. "It appeared there were a few missiles on top of the roof of the porch there, seven or eight," he pointed out. "Did you see those thrown?"

"Right after the shooting," Schuknecht said, "when I got across the street and ran to the front door, there were several missiles thrown then, because I know one or two struck the porch."

"After the shooting?" Kennedy asked.

"After the shooting, yes."

It was too good to be true. No crowd, no stones thrown until the Negroes opened fire, the physical evidence of the assault accounted for: it was the perfect testimony. Kennedy tested one more area. The papers were reporting several hundred people in the streets around Garland in the hours after the shooting. Did the inspector see a crowd gather after the shooting?

Absolutely, Schuknecht said. The moment the Negroes opened fire, he rushed into the bungalow. He wasn't inside for more than a minute or two. When he came out, a crowd "was closing up into the house." But Schuknecht's men held them off.

Here was a potential problem. If there were only a dozen people in front of the bungalow before the shooting, how could several hundred people be there seconds later? "How many would you say were out in front or across the street there," Kennedy said, "when you came out on the porch?"

"Oh, there may have been twenty-five," Schuknecht replied, "twenty-five, thirty people across the street then, when I got out there."

Twenty-five or thirty: just the right number again. Even after the shooting, after the Negroes killed Breiner, the whites had stayed within the law.[36]

Kennedy turned to Schuknecht's brother-in-law for confirmation. Everything the inspector had said was absolutely true, said Lemhagen. But his brother-in-law left out one telling observation. He had tagged along with the policemen when they entered the bungalow to arrest the coloreds. He took a good long look at Gladys, standing in the kitchen. Then she did the oddest thing. "She just laughed. I looked at her and [she] laughed, and I thought to myself: hard boiled." A perfect little detail, the sort of thing a jury was sure to remember when it came time to convict.[37]

As soon as Kennedy was finished with Shucknecht and Lemhagen, he crossed Garland to the flat opposite the bungalow, where Ray and

Kathleen Dove, their boarders, and the Sweets' next-door neighbors, the Getkes, were waiting for him. Homicide detectives would interview most of the people on Garland, but Kennedy needed to take these statements himself.[38] The Getkes had spent the evening sitting on their porch, not twenty feet from the Sweets' front door; if the Negroes' house had been stoned, they would know it. And the entire Dove household was an arm's length from Breiner when he'd been hit. They'd watched him die.

The interviews started on a promising note. The neighborhood was absolutely calm, not a bit of trouble, Ray Dove said in the soft, slightly southern drawl of his native Indiana. When Kennedy asked him whether there was a crowd in front of his house, though, Dove didn't give the right answer. "Oh yes," he replied, "quite a crowd." His wife, Kathleen, agreed. "There was more than fifty, I would say."[39]

Kennedy couldn't have been surprised by the Doves' estimate, which seemed more realistic than Shuknecht's. But at this point, the prosecution didn't need the truth seeping into the record. So Kennedy let the question drop; no point in being precise if the facts were going to undermine the state's case. When he interviewed the Doves' boarders and the Getkes, Kennedy didn't ask them how many people were on the street when the shooting began. Instead, he concentrated on whether the crowd, whatever its size, was threatening the Negroes.[40] But even that line of questioning spun off in the wrong direction.

"Did you see anything strike the Sweets' house," Kennedy asked John Getke, as he had asked the others.

"Different times seems as though we heard something," Getke said, "but yet we couldn't tell what place it was."

This was potentially damaging, an eyewitness account of stones hitting the house. Kennedy tried to find out how much the piano tuner had seen. He tried to exaggerate the attack to see if the man would back down. "Did you hear any great tumbling of rocks, stones, anything like that, on the house? Did you hear any crashing of glass?"

Getke seemed to realize that he'd said the wrong thing. "Absolutely no," he answered, there was nothing like that. It was just that—well—he had heard something right before the coloreds started shooting. "While we were sitting on the porch, my wife asked me what was that noise? I says, 'I don't know what—I can't hear it.' She says, probably throwing a pebble, you might call it; in fact, much lighter than a pebble. I scarcely heard it myself. Then two or three others [were thrown] and I heard them, and there was a volley [from the Sweets' house] immediately after that."[41]

That was better—not perfect but encouraging. The neighbors clearly knew what they were supposed to say, even if they didn't have the details down the way Schuknecht did. With a little bit of luck and maybe a few words to the wise, they could be counted on to testify that the Negroes had faced no threats, no stones, no mob. That's all the prosecutor's office would need to push the case through the preliminary hearing. And when that hurdle was cleared, the way would be clear for Toms to put the Sweets' fate before a jury of their Caucasian peers.

◆

Day or night, the Wayne County Jail rattled with noise. By Detroit standards, it was an ancient building, a four-story rattrap built thirty years earlier, now utterly inadequate to house the hundreds of suspects who passed through the city's overburdened legal system. The jail had a few individual cells, primarily in solitary, a dank dungeon hidden away in the basement, but most prisoners were placed in the upstairs cell blocks—long, cramped holding pens that housed a dozen or more suspects each. The guards set the cell blocks rules. But behind the bars, the prisoners were on their own. Many whiled away the days lying in a stupor on the tiny metal cots. But there was always someone up and about: drug addicts screaming through withdrawal pains or alcoholics suffering the d.t's; young people too scared to settle down; the guy who had been waiting months for a hearing and simply couldn't stand to be caged anymore; the woman who'd been through it all before and enjoyed needling the newcomers.[42]

It wasn't the clamor that bothered Ossian, Gladys, and the others, though. It was the silence. All Wednesday night and through the day Thursday, the eleven had waited for some word from their lawyers, from friends, from anyone who would be willing to fight for them. But they had heard nothing but silence, the burden of which grew heavier and heavier as the hours passed. Gladys, for all her bravado, felt it most. Alone in the women's block, sharing a cell with hardened criminals— one of her cell mates was awaiting trial for murder, or so she said, another for bootlegging—separated from her husband and toddler, Iva, Gladys was so sick with worry she couldn't even manage to eat, though her stomach was raw with hunger.

Ossian also felt the isolation crushing him. Put in a separate cell block from the others, he sat surrounded by pimps, thieves, and thugs, tortured by the thought of Gladys and his brothers, whom he had pledged to help and protect, whom he had failed. At least Henry and Otis had each other. By a stroke of luck, the guards had put them in the same cell, along with Davis, the narcotics agent. So they had the comfort, small as it was, of sharing the silence as it dragged through the meager lunch and into Thursday afternoon.[43] Almost a day gone by since the shooting and not so much as a hint of what was to come.

William Davis was the first to break under the pressure. He'd been true to the others during the interrogation the night before, sticking to the story the ten terrified men had thrown together in rushed whispers. But the more Davis thought, the more he must have realized how much he had to lose. He was a federal officer, whom his superiors considered a credit to the department; he earned a good paycheck; he had a government pension to look forward to. This threatened it all. He hadn't done a thing out at Sweet's house, hadn't been there more than a few minutes before the gunfire started. He had to extricate himself. He had to talk to the prosecutor again, before it was too late.

Ted Kennedy brought Davis back to the Detectives' Bureau in the middle of the afternoon Thursday, shortly after he completed the interviews on Garland. Davis opened the session with an apology. During the previous evening's interrogation, he said, he had forgotten to mention that he had been at the bungalow the evening before the shooting; in fact, he'd spent the night with Sweet and his wife, protecting the house, as had Otis and Henry, their cousin Latting, the chauffeur, and the handyman. If Kennedy hadn't been so tired himself, he might have leapt at the new information, additional evidence of conspiracy. Instead, the interrogation slogged along, Kennedy repeating his standard questions, half listening to the responses. Finally, he asked whether Ossian had given Davis any instruction on defending the house. Davis let his guard slip away. "Here's what he told me," he said. "That he was going out there; he wasn't looking for any trouble. But he was prepared to look after himself if he didn't get protection."

Kennedy suddenly revived. "Well, didn't you ask him what he meant by that, or how he was going to protect himself?"

"No, I didn't ask him other than to say to him, what do you mean? Just like that. He says—oh, he says: The boys will take care of things."

"Didn't you ask him how they are going to take care of things? Or did he tell you he had plenty guns and ammunition there to take of things with?"

"He says he had sufficient arms to look after things."

Kennedy could see it now, Davis's determination to be helpful. He fumbled for the right words, he was so anxious for more. "Was there anything—do you know—did any of these men tell you who fired the shots upstairs?"

"Now, you mean," Davis began, stopped, started again. "I will tell you when I did hear that? Was afterwards, after we were, after we were taken down to police headquarters."

"What did you hear?"

"I heard, it sounded like the voice of the insurance man, the bald-headed man, light one."

Kennedy had to get this right. "What's his name," he prompted. "Leonard C. Morse, was he the man with the gray suit, and kind of bald?"

"Yes," Davis replied. "I heard him make the remark that Henry—Henry Sweet, that is, the doctor's brother . . . I heard him say he was on the back pumping the rifle, something like that now; he spoke of Sweet being on the back [porch]."

"Did you hear anything more?"

"Well," Davis replied, "I heard Joe, Joe Mack. . . . Joe says, 'I shot that damn pistol three times, and then it hung up on me, and the police officer was shooting back at me.'"

"Is that what Joe Mack said?"

"That is what Joe Mack said."

It was done. Kennedy asked if Davis had heard anyone else talking about the incident, but he had no more information to share. So the assistant prosecutor brought the interview to a close and sent him back to the jail.[44] It wasn't going to be easy for Davis, sitting with the others in their cells, pretending to be one of them, waiting for the silence to break. He knew better than to tell them what he had done; they'd never forgive him. But it was better to deceive his fellow suspects than to have the previous night's lies come crashing down around him in a court of law. The authorities would have to treat him fairly now that he had told the truth, now that he had given them Sweet and Morse and Mack. He had betrayed them; there was no other way to look at it. But a Negro couldn't expect to be handed justice as a matter of right. One way or another, he had to pay for it. And it never came cheaply.

•

For Julian Perry, Cecil Rowlette, and Charles Mahoney, the first hint of trouble came on Thursday afternoon, September 10, when they presented their petition for a writ of habeas corpus to Judge John Faust. A dedicated member of the court's liberal majority, Faust should have been happy to approve the petition. Instead, he turned it down flat. A mad scramble secured the writ from a sympathetic circuit court judge, but that only led to the next round of shocks. As expected, the prosecutor's office responded to the defense lawyer's move by presenting its warrants to the criminal court's presiding judge, Frank Murphy. Toms sent his assistant, Lester Moll, to make the presentation. "The evidence shows no act of violence or provocation on the part of the victims or any other persons," he told Murphy. "The prisoners were found in a room filled with deadly weapons. As we are unable to say who fired the fatal shots we must charge them all with the same crime." Ossian, Gladys, and the nine others "did make an assault, with intent, [against] Erik Hougberg [sic] . . . feloniously, wickedly and of their malice aforethought, to kill and murder," and "feloniously, willfully, and of their malice aforethought did kill and murder one Leon C. Breiner." The pivotal phrase was imbedded in the text: "malice aforethought." The black lawyers had expected their clients to face serious charges, perhaps even manslaughter. But the prosecutor was going for the maximum, assault with intent to commit murder and murder in the first degree. If convicted, all eleven suspects would spend the rest of their lives in prison.[45]

By all rights, Murphy should have been skeptical of such a scattershot approach to the most serious of crimes, submitted to his court at precisely the same time the three dailies were declaring the accused guilty in twenty-four-point type. In the two years since his election, he'd proved to be every bit the liberal he'd claimed to be on the stump. So devoted to saving souls that the officers of the court called him "Father Murphy" behind his back, he had limitless patience for the procession of drunks, prostitutes, gamblers, drug addicts, and petty thieves whom he saw as victims of an unjust social system. "I want mercy," he wrote his brother in the cloyingly pious style to which he was given. "I don't believe in [punishment] much and I do a great deal in mercy." Like Judge Faust before him, though, Murphy showed absolutely no sympathy toward the suspects. He simply took the warrants under advisement and ordered the lawyers to return the following day.[46]

That night the city seethed. After a month of inaction, the Waterworks Park Improvement Association called a mass meeting for Thursday night, September 10, at the Amity Lodge Hall a few blocks west of Garland. A thousand people showed up, filling every inch of the auditorium and spilling out into the street. Real estate agent James Conley ominously shared the podium with two avowed Klansmen, one of them a former kleagle running for a seat on the Detroit City Council, the other a spokesman for the KKK's campaign to segregate the city's public schools, a sure way, said the latter, to keep Negroes in their place. Later that night, the Klan held its own rally, an open-air affair filled with the fiery rhetoric and ringing endorsements of Charles Bowles's mayoral campaign that had marred the summer. In one important respect, though, the meeting was dramatically different than the dozens of others the Klan had staged in previous months. This time, the Invisible Empire didn't gather in its west-side stronghold. Instead, it met in Waterworks Park itself, just three blocks south of the Sweets' bungalow, in the center of Mayor Johnny Smith's east side. The message couldn't have been clearer. In the murder of Leon Breiner, the Klan believed it had found the wedge it needed to crack open the coalition of black and white that had denied it the mayor's office the previous November.[47]

Facing such fearsome anger, the courage of Detroit's progressive bloc seemed to buckle, as Perry, Rowlette, and Mahoney learned when they filed back into the courtroom Friday morning. Without a word of explanation or apology, Murphy handed down the warrants, now affixed with his florid signature, and ordered a hearing Saturday in Judge Faust's chambers on the defense lawyers' hurried request that their clients be released on bail.[48]

◆

There was only one bright spot in the entire proceedings. Now that the charges were set, the attorneys finally had a firm legal right to meet with their clients. It took until Saturday afternoon—almost three days past the shooting—to arrange a jailhouse conference. Perry, Rowlette, Mahoney, and their NAACP associate, W. Hayes McKinney, brought the defendants the only positive news of the day. After a furious round of organizing, McKinney grandly announced, the Detroit NAACP was committed to underwriting the entire defense, no matter the cost.[49]

Fund-raising was to begin with the Sunday rally at Second Baptist, which everyone expected to be wildly successful. Ossian wept at the thought of his Talented Tenth colleagues rallying to his side. Even at such a crucial moment, though, he couldn't completely let down the guard he'd built around himself. When the lawyers had him make a formal statement explaining what had happened in the bungalow, Ossian repeated the unlikely story he had told Prosecutor Kennedy the night of the interrogations. All of the defendants had been there by coincidence, he insisted; there had been no planned defense, no principled stand. The attorneys dutifully wrote it all down but they couldn't have believed a word of it.[50]

Nor could they have hoped that such a painfully weak alibi could withstand an opposition that was growing stronger hour by hour. Saturday morning, Judge Faust rejected the defense's request for bail, the third time in three days the court's liberal bloc had failed to come to the Negroes' aid. Even Gladys, who everyone agreed had never so much as picked up a gun, was to be held indefinitely. Worse, Detroit was rife with the sort of shadowy rumors that every Negro knew proceeded pogroms. Colored men were on the march, whites whispered to each other all through the weekend. A Negro had murdered a white man just up the street from Garland Avenue, they were saying; another colored man shot a Caucasian through the chest; a gang of Negroes assaulted three whites, putting them in the hospital with fractured skulls. The attacks were unprovoked; no one was robbed; it had to be the beginning of a race war. "The situation is very tense in Detroit," McKinney wrote that evening as the stories swirled around him.[51]

Then came the last brutal blow of the week. Ever since the shooting, Mayor Smith had kept his peace: not one word of condemnation for the cops who had failed to protect the Sweets from attack; not one reply to the blast of biased newspaper reporters; not one response to the Klan's bold incursion into his territory. It almost seemed as if street-fighting Johnny, pin boy turned progressive, had been frightened into silence.

Finally, on Saturday night, September 12, Smith issued an open letter to the police commissioner, his first comment on the crisis that was threatening to split the city. Sunday morning's newspapers carried the full explosive text. "The outrage" on Garland, the mayor said, was not a singular event but rather a culminating point in the KKK's campaign to establish "a dictatorship" in Detroit. All summer long, the Invisible Empire had been trying to "induce Negroes to go into districts populated entirely by persons who would . . . resent such an invasion," hoping that as blacks broke through the color line, Detroit would be consumed by racial violence so severe the city government would topple, a white supremacists' beer-hall putsch. Of course, Negroes had a legal right to live wherever they wished. But, insisted Smith, "it does not always do for any man to demand to its fullest the right which the law gives him. Sometimes by doing so he works irremediable harm to himself and his fellows." In fact, segregation was a social good and those who dared to challenge it an enemy to their people and their city. "I deprecate the moving by colored persons into districts in which their presence would cause disturbance," Smith concluded. "I shall go further. I believe that any colored person who endangers life and property, simply to gratify his personal pride, is an enemy of his race as well as an incitant of riot and murder. These men who have permitted themselves to be the tools of the Ku Klux Klan in its effort to fan the flames of racial hatred into murderous fire have hurt the cause of their race in a degree that cannot be measured. I feel that it lies with the real leaders of the colored race in Detroit to dissipate this murderous pride."[52]

The Talented Tenth was still seething at the mayor's broadside when they gathered at Second Baptist for the NAACP's three o'clock rally. The mammoth church was filled to capacity, the pews jammed not only with Ossian's colleagues from the professional and business classes but also with ordinary Black Bottom folks, who felt the burden of neighborhood segregation every time they paid the rent on a decrepit apartment or felt the wind whistle through a broken windowpane the landlord refused to replace. Even as they surveyed the crowd in front of them, though, Bradby, McKinney, Edward Carter, and the other branch leaders had to have felt the city closing in on them. The Klan was in the ascendancy; the Negroes' white allies on the bench had deserted them; the mayor they had helped to elect had endorsed injustice and declared the pursuit of civil rights a threat to peace and liberal democracy. No longer was this simply a question of whether the Sweets were justified in firing into the mob on Garland Avenue. Now the Talented Tenth was locked in combat against segregation itself, battling to preserve some shred of the promise that brought almost a million people out of the South in the previous ten years, to show that the North was different, to prove that there were places in America where Jim Crow would not be allowed to rule. This had become a fight over fundamentals.

SEVEN

FREEDMEN, SONS OF GOD,
AMERICANS

James Weldon Johnson saw the potential right away. Each
year the NAACP's Manhattan headquarters received so many reports
of racial incidents that even some of the most tragic stories were simply set aside, new additions to black America's ever-expanding
archives of unanswered injustices. But the paragraph-long wire-ser-
vice article tucked into the back pages of *New York World* on Friday
morning, September 11, was different. As soon as he finished reading
about the Sweets' arrest, Johnson knew he was on to something big.[1]

It wasn't that the arrest of eleven Negroes was more outrageous
than the other news. Both Philadelphia and Gary, Indiana, had opened
the new school year by segregating colored children; a New York
City theater was launching a run of D. W. Griffith's incendiary 1915 film,
Birth of a Nation; and the city council of Norfolk, Virginia, had passed
an ordinance prohibiting Negroes from living in "white communities"
unless a majority of Caucasians gave their express approval. But the
timing of the Detroit story was exquisite. And James Weldon Johnson
wasn't the sort of person who let a promising moment pass him by.[2]

"He was a tall graceful man, always immaculately attired, calm and
uneffusive," said his friend and associate Arthur Spingarn. "The first
impression on strangers was one of extraordinary urbanity and poise.
In fact it has been said that when he first came in contact with white
men of position he was at ease several minutes before they were." Johnson saw no reason for it to be otherwise. "I will not allow one prejudiced

person or one million or one hundred million to blight my life," he explained. "I will not let prejudice or any of its attendant humiliations and injustices bear me down to spiritual defeat. My inner life is mine, and I will defend and maintain its integrity against the forces of hell."[3]

Such supreme self-confidence had its source in a Florida childhood far removed from the brutalities of Bartow. Johnson's father was a freeborn Virginian, a headwaiter at an exclusive Jacksonville hotel. His mother, a West Indian—daughter of a Bahamian politician of some note—held the distinction of being the first colored woman hired by a Florida public school. From birth, James defied racial convention: while his mother recovered from a difficult delivery, his father hired a neighbor to serve as his son's nursemaid. "In the land of black mammies," he often said, "I had a white one." As boys, James and his brother, Rosamond, were wrapped in a cocoon of middle-class gentility: Johnson's earliest memories were of the serenity of the family parlor, with the Bible opened on a marble tabletop, the piano standing majestically in a shaded corner, and his mother sitting by the fireplace, reading *David Copperfield* to her sons.[4]

When he was old enough, Johnson's parents sent him to Atlanta University's preparatory school and then to the university itself, a tiny bastion of New England Congregationalism on a hill rising above the quintessential New South city, "a spot fresh and beautiful," Johnson recalled, "a rest for the eyes from what surrounded it, a green island in a dull, red sea." Yet venturing out inevitably brought him face-to-face with Jim Crow. He was seventeen years old in the spring of 1888, taking the train home from his freshman year in Atlanta, when he had his first real encounter with white supremacy. As always, he rode in the first-class car. This time the white passengers objected. At first there were murmurs against him, then "the remarks in the car became . . . open and loud. Threats began to reach our ears." There was talk of a mob waiting at the next station, armed with guns and rope. Terrified, Johnson abandoned the car. But by then, it was too late to teach Johnson his proper place. Upon graduation, he returned to Jacksonville to begin what would be a lifetime of breakthroughs. By the turn of the century, he had established the first Negro daily newspaper in the United States, had become the first colored lawyer admitted to the Florida bar, and had founded the first black public high school in the state, which he served as principal. In his spare time, he wrote poetry, composed an opera with his brother, a classically trained musician, and dreamed of a life in the arts. When his opera received encouraging reviews, he decided to put aside the academic life. In 1902, he packed his bags and headed to New York, one more aspiring songwriter starry-eyed with thoughts of finding success along the Great White Way.[5]

In typical Johnson fashion, he surpassed all expectations. Within a few years, he and his collaborators, brother, J. Rosamond, and friend Bob Cole, had a string of hits to their credit, wonderful Tin Pan Alley confections that filled their bank accounts and made them international stars. Still, he wanted more. Even as his songs swept Broadway, Johnson proclaimed his fealty to the high arts, both as a hallmark of civilization and as a weapon in the struggle for equal rights. "No people that has produced great literature and art has ever been looked upon by the world as distinctly inferior," he insisted. "And nothing will do more to . . . raise his status than a demonstration of intellectual parity by the Negro through the production of literature and art." It was an extremely roseate vision, to imagine that a finely crafted poem or well-told tale might help to break down white supremacy, but Johnson committed himself to pursuit of the ideal. His stirring "Lift Every Voice and Sing" became the "Negro national anthem," sung by hosts of children too young to understand its subtle blend of mourning, celebration, and ongoing struggle. His 1912 novel, *The Autobiography of an Ex-Colored Man*, exposed the bitter ambiguity of the color line whites took to be inviolate. The *New York Times* published his celebratory 1913 poem marking the fiftieth anniversary of the Emancipation Proclamation—"Far, far the way we have trod/From heathen kraal and jungle den/To freedmen, freedmen, sons of God/Americans and citizens"—while Du Bois's *Crisis* printed his searing 1916 verse giving voice to the lynch mob: "Stop! To each man no more than one man's share/You take that bone, and you this tooth; the chain/Let us divide its links; this skull, of course/In fair division, to the leader comes."[6]

What would have been a brilliant career for most men was for Johnson a springboard to even more success. Theodore Roosevelt so enjoyed a ditty Johnson wrote for the 1904 presidential campaign he appointed the composer to the consular service. He spent seven years living abroad, first in Venezuela, then in Nicaragua. Reserved, quietly charming, and preternaturally politic, he proved to be a gifted diplomat. When Woodrow Wilson took control of the White House in 1913, he had Johnson fired. Three years later, after a spell of editorial work and a stint as a speechwriter for the Republican Party, he joined the NAACP's staff, beginning as an organizer and moving up in 1920 to executive secretary, the first black man to be given responsibility for the association's day-to-day operations. It was a superb appointment. With his finely honed diplomatic skills, Johnson captivated the whites who dominated the association's board of directors and soothed the NAACP's notoriously contentious staff; even the imperious Du Bois was willing to listen to his advice. He also filled the association's New York headquarters with vigorous recruits, most notably peripatetic Walter White as assistant director, and devoted himself to building up the NAACP's membership, so that by the mid-1920s the association had branches in more than three hundred towns and cities, many of them south of the Mason-Dixon Line, where before the Great War the association had hardly made a ripple. And he infused NAACP activism with an extraordinary dramatic flair, beginning with his masterpiece, the 1917 Silent Parade down Fifth Avenue, a peerless example of protest as performance art, and reaching full flower in the literary renaissance of 1920s Harlem, when Johnson helped to make art into a performance of protest.[7]

Now the *New York World* had placed the précis for another piece of racial theater in Johnson's hands. With nothing more than a hundred-word story to go on, it was impossible to say whether Ossian Sweet's was the case Johnson was looking for, but it seemed extremely promising, with a perfect protagonist; a sharp, clear, and compelling conflict; and a final act miraculously undecided. So Johnson fired off a telegram to the officers of the Detroit branch asking for details.[8]

The first reply from Detroit was guarded, as if local officials were wary to have outside interference. "Will get full details from Dr. Sweet today which will be given in letter," W. Hayes McKinney wired early Saturday, before the full force of events came crashing down on him. "Branch handling matter." Johnson responded with his customary cool, graciously offering "all cooperation possible," then waiting for circumstances to break his way. It didn't take long. He and a few friends were spending their Sunday morning on a New Jersey golf course when the clubhouse man rushed across the greens with word of a long-distance phone call "We would like to have Mr. White leave for Detroit if possible tonight," Johnson jotted down as he listened to McKinney's frantic plea for help. "Very urgent." He didn't record his answer. But within an hour or two, Johnson was back home in his 135th Street brownstone, ready to launch the NAACP's next great campaign.[9]

◆

For Johnson, the increasing segregation of the cities was a personal affront. In the two decades since he left steaming Jacksonville, he'd come to think of himself as a "cosmopolite," happiest when he was caught up in cultural Manhattan's dizzying swirl, perfectly content in a darkened theater or an elegant uptown cabaret. He had long since settled in Harlem, which he adored for both its vitality—its "movement, color, gayety, singing, dancing, boisterous laughter and loud talk"— and its passionate respectability. "Harlem is indeed the great Mecca for the sight-seer, the pleasure-seeker, the curious, the adventurous, the enterprising, the ambitious, and the talented of the whole Negro world," he wrote. "It is a city within a city, the greatest Negro city in the world." And New York, he concluded, was the greatest city for Negroes. "New York guarantees its Negro citizens the fundamental rights of American citizenship and protects them in the exercise of those rights," he proclaimed. "In return the Negro loves New York and is proud of it, and contributes in his way to its greatness."[10]

But Johnson simply couldn't ignore the precipitous decline in northern race relations. The Klan's stunning success above the Mason-Dixon Line was devastating to the NAACP's officers. New York remained largely immune from the KKK's contagion, a fact Walter White attributed to the city's polyglot peoples. "Its Jewish, Italian, German, French Greek, Czecho-Slovakian, Irish, Hungarian quarters with their teeming thousands and hundreds of thousands form so great a percentage of the city's population," he argued, "'white, Gentile, Protestant' Nordics have but little opportunity to develop their prejudices as they do, for example, in Mississippi or the District of Columbia." Yet there was also no denying that whites were carving the color line deeper and deeper into the urban landscape. The NAACP was painfully aware that blacks weren't welcome in many restaurants, clubs, and theaters in northern cities. But it was the relentless segregation of neighborhoods that was most frightful. "Lynching has been the peculiar institution of the south," declared a colored newspaper in an editorial circulated through NAACP headquarters. "Forceful residential segregation has taken root and is spreading so fast till if it's not soon checked it will become the peculiar institution of the North."[11]

Not even Johnson's beloved New York could avoid that particular curse, as he explained in a scintillating 1925 analysis. Colored families first moved to the area around 134th Street and Lenox Avenue, in the heart of Harlem, in the early 1900s, he said. In response, nearby whites unleashed the real estate market's arsenal of discriminatory practices, creating neighborhood improvement associations, trying to impose restrictive covenants, convincing banks not to extend Negroes mortgages.

The efforts failed. Using their own capital, a handful of black businessmen, among them Johnson's brother-in-law, bought up a few un-
derpriced apartment blocks, which they opened to colored tenants.
Once their defenses were breeched, whites "became panic-stricken
and began fleeing as from a plague. . . . House after house and block
after block were deserted. It was a great demonstration of human beings running amuck." And a textbook example of the power of the
marketplace. By the mid-1910s, property values had plummeted, thousands of whites had departed for other sections of the city, and Harlem
had been transformed into New York's colored quarter, a ghetto gilded
by the presence of men like Johnson, who lived in one of his brother-
in-law's properties, but a ghetto nonetheless.[12]

The NAACP struck its first blow against residential segregation in
1917, Johnson's first full year in the association's employ. During the
course of the 1910s, a number of southern cities passed ordinances
barring blacks citizens from living anywhere but in carefully pro-
scribed colored neighborhoods. In response, the NAACP decided to
mount a Supreme Court challenge, taking as its target Louisville,
Kentucky's segregation law. The case was presented by Beacon Hill's
august Moorfield Storey, head of the NAACP board of directors, former president of the American Bar Association, and, in an era long
past, personal secretary to one of the greatest abolitionists of them all,
Massachusetts's fiery senator Charles Sumner. Even a court ill disposed
to equal rights couldn't withstand the force of Storey's argument, or
perhaps the justices were just offended by the thought of a city government limiting the ability of landowners to sell their property to
whomever they pleased. Either way, the Supreme Court struck down
Louisville's ordinance, and by extension, all other such laws, handing
the NAACP the first of what would become a half century of landmark
constitutional victories.[13]

Although the pressure to segregate northern cities was beginning to
grow, no city government tried to follow Louisville's example and segregate by statute. But the dramatic surge in discriminatory market
mechanisms in every major urban center threatened to have the same
effect. So, in 1923, the NAACP went back to court, this time to test the
right of individual homeowners to prohibit the sale of their property to
Negroes. Howard University law school professor James Cobb found
the perfect test case when Helen Curtis, wife of a colored surgeon
and professor at Howard's medical school, bought a home just off
Washington, D.C.'s Dupont Circle, not knowing that a few years

before, the seller, a Caucasian woman, and thirty of her neighbors agreed to keep their block lily-white by adding restrictive covenants to their deeds. When the white neighbors secured an injunction against the transaction, the colored couple turned to the NAACP's Washington branch for help. Cobb, chairman of the branch's legal committee, carried the fight to Johnson, arguing that it was "the most important case of its kind ever handled by the Association." Johnson pledged the NAACP's support.[14]

A disciple of Booker T. Washington who had worked his way up from tiny Arcadia, Louisiana, to a post as Howard University's professor of negotiable instruments, Cobb directed the case's first test before the District of Columbia Court of Appeals. He argued, reasonably enough, that by using restrictive covenants, white property owners were contravening the principles established in the Louisville ruling and therefore were in clear violation of public policy. The stakes were enormous, warned Storey from his home in Back Bay. Should the association's appeal fail, similar cases pending in Baltimore, St. Louis, Los Angeles, St. Paul, and Detroit would be lost, and the NAACP's chances of stemming the segregationist tide would be dealt a devastating, perhaps mortal, blow. What's more, southerners would take the association's defeat as a signal that they could have the Louisville decision itself reversed; already New Orleans had passed a segregation ordinance designed to get the ruling back before the Supreme Court. Come that day, Storey concluded, "Heaven help us all!" It arrived all too quickly. In June 1924, the D.C. court ruled against Cobb and his clients, saying it couldn't compel white people to sell to Negroes. The Howard professor immediately appealed to the Supreme Court. And the NAACP promptly handed the case to a stellar legal team led by Storey and his eminent associate, the great constitutional lawyer and longtime Jewish activist Louis Marshall, relegating Cobb to a supporting role for the final confrontation in a battle he had made possible.[15]

By the time it agreed to hear the case, the high court's docket for the upcoming year was full, so the NAACP wouldn't have the opportunity to present its argument until the autumn of 1925, at the earliest. In the meantime, James Weldon Johnson prepared to make the fight into a nationwide crusade. Of course he wanted publicity, but he also needed the money. The association's most recent Supreme Court case—a defense of six Arkansas sharecroppers convicted of murder without so much as a vestige of due process—had cost fifteen thousand dollars, enough to push the association to the brink of insolvency.

Even with Marshall and Storey working pro bono, the Washington case and a second challenge, this one against Texas's exclusion of black voters from its state Democratic Party primaries, would eat up ten thousand dollars, twice what the NAACP had in its bank accounts. To see the fight through, Johnson simply had to get the association an infusion of cash, and that meant convincing black Americans that the cause was important enough to be worth donating five, ten, or twenty dollars that many of them couldn't afford to spare.[16]

There was more to it than money, though. If New York City had been saved from the most rabid forms of racism simply by the overwhelming presence of ethnic Americans, as Walter White believed, then an explicit coalition of such peoples might have the power to beat back the white supremacists' advance through the rest of the urban North. Du Bois had raised the possibility in 1922, the first year the Klan's crosses burned under city lights. "The Anglo-Saxon cult" sought nothing less than "the disfranchisement of Negro, Jew, Irishman, Italian, Hungarian, Asiatic, and South Sea Islander—the world rule of Nordic white by brute force," he said, and it had to be countered by its opposite, an alliance of Negroes "and disadvantaged groups like the Irish and the Jews and between the working classes everywhere. . . . And in that battle the triumph of Democracy for the darker races, for the segregated groups, and for the disadvantaged classes is written in the everlasting stars."[17]

The logic of the alliance was unassailable, as politicians such as Frank Murphy and Johnny Smith understood when they went trolling for votes in the immigrant and colored quarters. But blacks and the ethnic masses were also divided by decades of fierce competition for a share of industrialism's dregs, a tortured history of mutual distrust, and the poison of the American racial ideal, which made the swarthiest of immigrants desperate to prove himself a white man. For all his optimism, even Du Bois had to admit that the workers of the world showed little inclination to unite across the color line. Negro laborers "are not part of the white proletariat," he wrote elsewhere. "We are the victims of its physical oppression, social ostracism, economic exclusion and personal hatreds." And he bridled against the United States' "'new' white people"—"Irish and German, Russian Jew, Slav and 'dago'" who are trained "to [the] despising of 'niggers' from the day of their landing."[18]

With its fight against restrictive covenants, though, the NAACP believed it had a way to show its erstwhile allies that in the era of the

KKK they were not assured of being on the safe side of the color line. Already the NAACP had reports of builders barring Jews from new housing developments. And there was every reason to believe that Anglo-Saxons would soon extend such prohibitions to Catholics and immigrants as well. Every opportunity they had, association officials hammered the message home. Agreements that denied blacks access to the homes of their choice were "the entering wedge of the Ku Klux Klan program of elimination," insisted Louis Marshall, who had seen firsthand the expansiveness of white supremacy in 1915, when a southern mob lynched his client, Leo Frank, for the crime of being a Jew. Johnson also emphasized the point. "Of course it's not the Negro alone who is concerned in this fight," he said. "There is no minority group in this country that will be unaffected. If it is possible to segregate Negroes, then why not Catholics and Jews, or Italians or Irish?"[19]

But for all the association's efforts, the NAACP's campaign didn't catch on. The white press paid no attention whatsoever, and in the first half of 1925, Johnson's fund-raising stuttered, then stalled. It was a problem of dramatics, Johnson concluded. "Colored people of America are not awake to the danger which threatens them," he complained. "So long as the mob is not at their door ordering them to move into another neighborhood, threatening them with death if they do not give up their home and sell their house, they seem to think the danger a distant one." So all through the summer of 1925, he scoured the nation's newspapers for an incident he could make into a rallying point. He looked into the case of Lola Turner, driven from her new house in Los Angeles by a white mob. He asked for details on a string of bombings against black homeowners in Kansas City. He had his Legal Committee meet with Samuel Browne, a colored postman who refused to abandon his Staten Island home despite repeated death threats. And he paid particular attention to the month-long violence on Detroit's west side that July, when Alexander Turner, Vollington Bristol, and the Fletcher family came under attack. Perhaps it was the intensity of the troubles that piqued his interest, or perhaps it was the fund-raising possibilities he saw in Detroit's huge black community. By the end of July 1925, Johnson had decided to intervene. Not only did he send a blistering open letter to newspapers across the country condemning the violence, but he also told the branch officers that come autumn the entire NAACP high command would travel to the Motor City for a series of "great meetings." Johnson intended to kick off the campaign personally as soon as the summer was over. Then he headed off to a much-needed vacation in western Massachusetts's bucolic Berkshire Hills.[20]

While he was relaxing in the shade of the Berkshire pines, he struck upon a marvelous solution to the association's money problems. In 1922, twenty-three-year-old Charles Garland had inherited a million dollars from his father, a highly successful Wall Street broker. But young Garland didn't want the money, pointing out quite rightly that he hadn't earned a penny of it. At first, he thought about simply refusing his inheritance. But the timely intervention of a couple of cash-starved radicals, muckraking journalist Upton Sinclair, and Roger Baldwin, chairman of the newly formed American Civil Liberties Union, pushed him in another direction. With Baldwin's help, Garland established a philanthropic organization, the American Fund for Public Service, which he put under the guidance of a board full of prominent civil libertarians, trade unionists, and one civil rights activist, James Weldon Johnson. Over the next few years, Johnson managed to secure the NAACP several thousand dollars in grants. Now he decided to ask for much more. He sketched out a proposal to create an NAACP Legal Defense Fund of fifty thousand dollars, more than enough to cover both the Washington and Texas cases. Garland might contribute half that amount, he believed, if black America could raise the other half.[21]

As a member of the American Fund's board, Johnson couldn't submit the proposal himself. So as soon as he returned to Manhattan after Labor Day, he wrote to Moorfield Storey asking if he would approach the board on the NAACP's behalf. But even in the excitement of the moment, Johnson had to admit that, given his dismal experience with the residential segregation crusade, he couldn't guarantee the twenty-five thousand dollars in matching funds that the proposal required. "I face the actual fact that it will not be possible to raise any such amount," Johnson admitted, "unless [association members] have a tremendous incentive that they can pass over to the people whom they solicit."[22]

Then the Sweet-case clipping passed across his desk. And Johnson knew he had exactly the story he had been looking for.

◆

Detroit was the last place Walter White wanted to be. While his boss was taking his August holidays in the Berkshires, White had hammered away at his second novel, *Flight*, the highly anticipated follow-up to his widely praised inaugural effort, *The Fire in the Flint*. Once the new manuscript was in the hands of his good friends, Alfred and Blanche Knopf, White had resumed the rounds of parties that occupied his nights. To launch the Labor Day weekend, he and his wife, Gladys, had filled their apartment at 90 Edgecombe Avenue, which peeked over Harlem's glorious Strivers Row, with a glittering array of literary lights. It had been a riotous time, Sinclair and Grace Lewis and a bevy of friends sharing drink, music, and gossip almost until dawn. White was the most indefatigable of men. But even he couldn't keep up such a furious pace without his body claiming some of the attention denied it. So he was battling a cold—and planning the following weekend's soirees—when James Weldon Johnson called on Sunday afternoon, September 13, to tell him that he was to be aboard *The Wolverine* out of Grand Central Station as soon as possible Monday.[23]

As much as he disliked the idea, White knew the assignment was a perfect fit. When Johnson recruited him for the NAACP staff in 1918, White had been a twenty-four-year-old Atlanta insurance salesman, but Johnson was drawn by his boundless energy and peerless background. The son of a postman and a schoolteacher, White was raised in a home very much like Johnson's, where good manners, strict rules, and educational excellence were prized above all else. In the years since Johnson came calling, White had made himself into the association's indispensable man, a public relations genius particularly skilled at communicating the terror of racial violence to white audiences. It was a talent built partly on the electricity he brought to any task, partly on his unquestionable courage, and partly on a family inheritance that set him apart from most of black America. To look at White was to see a man of decidedly Anglo-Saxon features, a Caucasian through and through. "I am a Negro," he once wrote. "My skin is white, my eyes are blue, my hair is blond. The traits of my race are nowhere visible upon me."[24]

Had he wished to, White easily could have spent his life passing. But one terrifying evening in September 1906 foreclosed that possibility forever. Jim Crow's fervor was at its height that autumn, and Atlanta was shot through with rumors of the Black Beast hunting down white women. Thirteen-year-old Walter and his father were downtown on the afternoon of the twenty-second when the tensions exploded and whites took control of the streets. They rushed back to their home on the edge of the black neighborhood. Hidden inside, the Whites could hear the mob moving toward them, could see the flickering light of their torches in the distance, could hear their shouts ripping through the night: "That's where the nigger mail carrier lives! Let's burn it down! It's too nice for a nigger to live in!" Walter's father took him into the parlor, handed him a rifle, and positioned him at a window. "Son," he remembered his father saying, "don't shoot until the first man puts his foot on the lawn and then—don't you miss." Walter never had to pull the trigger. As the mob come upon the house, friends of his father's who had barricaded themselves into a nearby home opened fire, driving the whites back into the darkness. But the moment had changed Walter forever.

"I was gripped by the knowledge of my identity," he said, "and in the depths of my soul I was vaguely aware that I was glad of it. I was sick with loathing for the hatred which had flared before me that night and had come so close to making me a killer; but I was glad that I was not one of those who hated; I was glad that I was not one of those made sick and murderous by pride. I was glad I was not one of those whose story is in the history of the world, a record of bloodshed, rapine, and pillage. I was glad my mind and spirit were part of the races that . . . had still before them the opportunity to write a record of virtue as a memorandum to Armageddon."[25]

Still, like many Negroes, White couldn't quite set aside the standard American equation of light skin and virtue. One night in the 1920s, he sat down for a heartfelt talk with Joel Spingarn, a former Columbia professor of literature who had devoted much of his life to the NAACP's causes. Spingarn recounted the conversation a few days later in a private letter to his wife. "I asked him frankly if he thought men of unmixed Negro blood capable of the highest achievement and character," Spingarn said. "At first he hedged. . . . But finally he admitted that he had virtually never met a pure Negro whom he really could trust, that he didn't believe it was in them, that they *were* inferior, infinitely inferior now, whatever they might possibly become in the future. So there's the conflict—nine-tenths white loathing the one-tenth black, one-tenth black hating the nine-tenths white. The passionate pro-Negro loyalty is a conflict, a whirlpool, and a mask." Over the years, White's opponents would level the same charges publicly. "In the first place, Walter White is white," Du Bois would say about his colleague during one of their many bitter feuds. "He has more white companions and friends than colored. He goes where he will . . . and naturally meets no Color Line, for the simple and sufficient reason he isn't 'colored.'"[26] At the start of his career, though, White's ability to move freely in a Caucasian world was his, and the NAACP's, greatest asset.

When Dr. Ossian Sweet bought a house in an all-white section of Detroit in the summer of 1925, he knew his move might trigger white violence. "Well, we have decided we are not going to run," he told a colleague a few weeks before taking possession of his new home. "We're not going to look for any trouble, but we're going to be prepared to protect ourselves if trouble arises." (Walter P. Reuther Library, Wayne State University)

In May 1901, a white mob lynched a black teenager steps away from the Peace River Bridge in Bartow, Florida. The incident scarred young Ossian Sweet, who forever after remembered hiding in the bushes, a terrified five-year-old watching the mob set its victim ablaze. (Florida State Archives)

So that their son might escape the brutality of Jim Crow, Ossian Sweet's parents sent him north. At Ohio's Wilberforce University (above), he was immersed in the politics of Black America's Talented Tenth. Howard University's medical school vaulted Sweet, fifth from right (below), into the highest rank of professionals. (Ohio Historical Society / Moorland-Spingarn Center, Howard University)

"Detroit is El Dorado," said a Jazz-Age visitor to the city. "It is staccato American. It is shockingly dynamic." Inside Detroit's burgeoning black ghetto, though, living conditions were desperate, poverty pervasive. (Wolff Family Photograph Collection, Bentley Library, University of Michigan / Walter P. Reuther Library, Wayne State University)

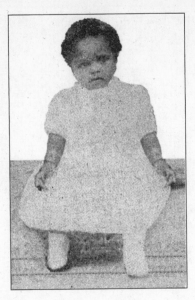

Having lived among whites all her life, Gladys Sweet (upper left) saw no reason why she and Ossian should be forced to buy a home in the ghetto simply because they were black. The bungalow at 2905 Garland Avenue (bottom) had the stylish touches she loved, and she looked forward to her daughter, Iva (upper right), growing up in a safe, secure neighborhood. (Walter P. Reuther Library, Wayne State University / Walter P. Reuther Library, Wayne State University / *The Chicago Defender*)

A bullet fired from the bungalow on the evening of September 9, 1925, killed Leon Breiner (upper left), a former coal miner who lived half a block north of the Sweets' house. (*The Chicago Defender*)

As soon as news of the Sweets' arrest crossed his desk, NAACP secretary James Weldon Johnson (upper right) knew he had found a case he could turn into a national crusade. (Carl Van Vechten Photograph Collection, Library of Congress)

Ten of the eleven defendants (below), all charged with Breiner's murder. Top row (from left to right): Otis Sweet, John Latting, Norris Murray, Joe Mack, Charles Washington. Bottom row (from left to right): Ossian Sweet, Henry Sweet, Hewitt Watson, William Davis, Leonard Morse. Not pictured: Gladys Sweet. (*The Chicago Defender*)

Walter White (upper left), Johnson's indefatigable assistant secretary, spent months shaping the Sweets' story as if it were one of his Harlem Renaissance novels. (Library of Congress)

When he first met trial judge Frank Murphy (upper right), White was amazed by Murphy's determination to give the defendants a fair trail. "It is so seldom that those of us who are trying to secure even-handed justice for Negro citizens encounter one like yourself," he wrote the judge, "you may well imagine our joy when that experience does come." (Walter P. Reuther Library, Wayne State University)

Park Avenue lawyer Arthur Garfield Hays so enjoyed fighting alongside Clarence Darrow in the previous summer's "Monkey Trial" in Dayton, Tennessee, he volunteered to join Darrow in defending the Sweets and their friends in November 1925. (Seeley G. Mudd Library, Princeton University)

When the case went back to trial in May 1926, the principled Hays was replaced by Thomas Chawke (second from right), a criminal lawyer best known for his association with Detroit's many mobsters. Chawke stands alongside Henry Sweet (far left), Ossian Sweet's friend Julian Perry, and Darrow. (Walter P. Reuther Library, Wayne State University)

Before settling on the twelve men who would decide Henry Sweet's fate, defense attorneys demanded that potential jurors reveal whether or not they were prejudiced against blacks. (*Detroit News*)

"I've heard about lawyers making a judge cry," said an attorney who witnessed Clarence Darrow's closing plea in the Sweet case, "but Darrow was the first man I ever saw do it." (Walter P. Reuther Library, Wayne State University)

White wasn't on the NAACP's staff two weeks when he was dispatched to Tennessee to investigate a horrific lynching. Johnson had done such work before, but White's Nordic face gave him access to information his boss couldn't have secured. Posing as a traveling salesman for an Atlanta hair-straightening company, White spent a few days chatting up Caucasians, who were more than glad to tell him all about the recent excitement. His searing exposé of the victim's crimes—among other things, he'd returned from a stint living in Detroit unwilling to bow to Jim Crow—was so original and immediate it won the association widespread attention in the popular press and set White on a path that would make him famous.[27]

Over the next few years, he exposed lynch mobs across the South, walked the streets of riot-torn South Chicago, uncovered the perfidy behind the 1919 pogrom in Phillips County, Arkansas, exposed electoral violence in 1920 Florida, and revealed the gruesome details of the infamous 1921 race riot in Tulsa, where he went so far as to join a white posse patrolling the burned-out black section of town. It was extremely dangerous work. As he was gathering information in the tiny town of Helena, Arkansas, in 1919, a colored man took him aside to say that whites had discovered his identity. Walter raced to the nearby depot and leapt onto the first train heading north. The conductor couldn't understand why he was in such a rush to get out of town. "But you're leaving, mister, just when the fun is going to start," the man said. "There's a damn yellow nigger down here passing for white and the boys are going to get him." "What will they do with him?" White asked, all innocence. "When they get through with him," said the conductor, "he won't pass for white no more!"[28]

Such daring made for marvelous copy, a traditional trickster tale dressed up for the Jazz Age. Northern newspapers, black and white, regularly recounted White's exploits, and leading liberal journals such as the *Nation* and the *New Republic* published his firsthand accounts of racial terrors, told in clean, clear prose made all the more chilling by their crispness.

Although James Weldon Johnson reveled in the publicity that White's reporting provided the NAACP, he wanted more for the young man he increasingly considered his protégé. He tried unsuccessfully to temper White's frenetic enthusiasm with a touch of diplomacy, gently tutoring him on the power of a quiet word and a well-placed compliment. He introduced him to the highest level of politics, bringing White with him to Capitol Hill while he lobbied for an ill-fated antilynching bill, and even sending him to Paris as one of the NAACP representatives to the 1921 Pan-African Congress. More than anything else, he drew White into the world of the arts, the new frontier of civil rights advocacy. As with everything else he did, White responded to Johnson's instruction with gusto. In a city rapidly filling with young people of extraordinary talent, Walter made himself one of the great promoters of the Harlem Renaissance—and its first star.[29]

Just as he had ingratiated himself into southern lynch mobs, so did White charm his way into the inner circle of Manhattan's cultural avant-garde. The moment was ideal. From the cutting-edge publishing houses clustered near the NAACP's Fifth Avenue headquarters to the jazz clubs of Harlem, from Greenwich Village salons through Broadway all the way to Provincetown, white artists were scrambling to claim a share of the vibrant black culture they saw as an antidote to the banalities of white society. "What American literature decidedly needs at the moment is color, music, gusto, the free expression of gay or desperate moods," gushed editor and critic Carl Van Doren. "If the Negroes are not in a position to contribute these items, I do not know what Americans are." Ziegfeld girl Gilda Gray put it more succinctly in a 1922 show tune: "You must black up to be the latest rage."[30]

Walter White wasn't given much to blacking up. But he was more than willing to exploit the avant-garde's sudden interest in the race. Johnson provided some of the necessary introductions, and Walter's conviviality did the rest. By the mid-1920s, White knew just about everybody worth knowing. Sinclair Lewis, H. L. Mencken, and Carl Van Vechten—three of the most acerbic critics of middle America—were particular friends. But at one time or another, George Gershwin, Dorothy Parker, Eugene O'Neill, Heywood Broun, Rebecca West, George Jean Nathan, Horace Liveright, Andre Siegfried, Nancy Cunard, and a host of others partook of White's hospitality. All he asked in return was that the cultural elite lend a hand to the remarkable collection of colored artists he had helped to assemble. Langston Hughes, Countee Cullen, Claude McKay, Paul Robeson, short-story writer and graduate of Howard University College of Medicine Rudolph Fisher, tenor Roland Hayes, and baritone Jules Bledsoe all made valuable contacts via White, who relentlessly trumpeted their skills and shopped their manuscripts. He also didn't hesitate to inform them when they didn't measure up to his rigid standards of racial uplift. After her debut at New York's Town Hall, the sublime Marian Anderson received word that while White very much enjoyed her operatic performance he thought her willingness to sing popular songs during the encore was in "bad taste."[31]

In 1922, H. L. Mencken suggested that White try his hand at a novel. It took the better part of a year for Walter to carve out the necessary time, but after twelve feverish days and nights of writing in the summer of 1923, he had a draft. On the strength of Mencken's endorsement, Knopf snatched up *The Fire in the Flint*, which it published in September 1924. It was, as Somerset Maugham said, "a terrible book, but a very powerful one, and it gives one a tragic feeling of truth." In breathlessly melodramatic style, White told the story of young Dr. Kenneth Harper, a Negro graduate of an unnamed northern medical school and a Great War veteran, who returns to his Georgia hometown to open a clinic. At first, Harper is determined to avoid racial politics. But the hostility of local whites, who hate his family's success, and the tutelage of Jane Philips, the beautiful, accomplished young woman with whom he falls in love, gradually break down his reserve. "It's men with your brains and education that have got to take the leadership," she tells him in a moment of transformation. "That's just the reason they try to make it hard for men like you—they know if you ever get going, their treating the Negro as they have has got to stop!" In the novel's climactic closing scene, Harper becomes the exemplar of the heroic New Negro, facing a murderous, cowardly pack, pressed to the wall, dying, but fighting back.[32]

The novel's publication was one of the signal events of the Harlem Renaissance's breakthrough year. Sinclair Lewis called it one of the two most important books of the autumn—E. M. Forster's *A Passage to India* was the other—while Heywood Broun gave it a glowing review in *New York World*, Freda Kirchwey did the same in the *Tribune*, and Konrad Bercovici gushed in the *Nation* that the novel was nothing less than "the voice of the new Negro"; there was even talk of Eugene O'Neill mounting a stage adaptation, with Paul Robeson playing the lead. Alfred Knopf made sure to send copies to the most rabidly racist southern newspapers so that the predictable cries of outrage could fuel sales. But it was Du Bois who, as usual, got it just right, hailing the book in the *Crisis* as "a stirring story and a strong bit of propaganda against the white Klansman and the black pussyfoot," the ideal combination of form and function, in the editor's utilitarian vision of racial art.[33]

◆

Detroit's Talented Tenth wasn't expecting the whirlwind that pulled into the Michigan Central Depot at 8:15 Tuesday morning, September 15.

The NAACP branch officers had asked Johnson to send White their way hoping he'd do a bit of his legendary investigating, perhaps even slipping by the police cordon that was preventing the black lawyers from scouring the Sweets' bungalow for any evidence that would help their clients.[34] Instead, they were swept up in White's frenetic stage management.

White planned to be on the train back to New York on Friday, so as not to miss the weekend's parties. That left him four days to get the Sweet case into the proper shape, more than enough time for a man who could write a best seller in less than two weeks. A round of conferences with branch officials on Tuesday gave him all the information he needed to craft the scenario of the Sweet case that the NAACP would need to attract attention and support. In his telling, the characters bore a remarkable resemblance to those in *The Fire in the Flint*: Ossian was a "very highly respected" doctor just a few weeks back from a year's study in Vienna, White reported to Johnson, while Gladys "is from one of Detroit's oldest and most respected colored families." When it came to scripting the next part of the drama, though, the performance threatened to unravel.[35]

Trouble started in the segregated dining room of downtown Detroit's most elegant hotel, where White had arranged a late breakfast with Ira Jayne, the only NAACP executive board member living in Detroit. A forty-three-year-old circuit court judge, Jayne was, in a colleague's words, "an incorrigible public servant," a former schoolteacher and social worker who relentlessly championed the rights of the poor and the powerless. Like his fellow NAACP board members, he was anxious to combat the spread of residential segregation, so he was pleased to hear that the NAACP wanted to make the Sweets the centerpiece of its crusade.[36]

But Jayne wanted White to understand that the case wasn't lining up the way the association wanted to. Since the shooting, the city had cracked straight down the color line, and the chasm was widening by the day. The mayor and the Ku Klux Klan were locked in a venomous exchange of race-baiting: when the Sunday papers printed Johnny Smith's broadside linking the Sweets and the Klan, the Invisible Empire immediately issued a bitter response—stuffed into mailboxes across white Detroit that very afternoon—charging that the mayor himself had triggered "the negro agitation" with his promises to the coloreds of equal treatment in city affairs. The east side's white neighborhoods, meanwhile, still teetered on the edge of violence. All weekend long, the police had battled rumors of rampant colored criminality. And on Monday, the day Leona Breiner buried her husband, the police department had held hundreds of officers in reserve, fearing that the sight of the deceased's Masonic brothers bearing his casket down Garland Avenue might trigger renewed rioting, perhaps even the long-feared pogrom. Under such dire circumstances, there was simply no way for the association to save the Sweets from a sure conviction—as long as Negroes were doing the talking. Hire the most prestigious white attorney the NAACP's money could buy, Jayne insisted, and hope that his presence might win back the city's progressives and ease the blood lust coursing through the working-class wards.[37]

White must have seen Jayne's proposal as no more controversial than handing the Washington case to Marshall and Storey or passing a brilliant piece of Harlem art to Knopf or Mencken. But that afternoon when he informed the Sweets' three colored attorneys that they were to be demoted, he met a firestorm of resistance. The defense couldn't be derailed now, the lawyers insisted, not with their clients facing a preliminary hearing the very next day. Cecil Rowlette heatedly argued that there was no need to change course; legal precedent was clearly on their side, and in time, the court would dismiss the charges. The attorneys even raised the specter most likely to terrify the NAACP's national office. The black community was fully aroused, they said, money was pouring in—the branch already had eleven hundred dollars in a defense fund, seven hundred dollars alone from the Sunday afternoon rally at Second Baptist—and donors would expect to see black men leading the fight. White, they pointed out, had been in Detroit less than half a day; he couldn't possibly understand the situation.

White tried to counter with Johnson's diplomatic touch. The decision "cast no reflection" on the lawyers' legal skill, he said, "but [the Sweet case] was bigger than Detroit or Michigan . . . for it was the dramatic climax of the nation-wide fight to enforce residential segregation." What's more, politics demanded a change. "As even the best white sentiment of Detroit was against Sweet," he said, drawing on the ammunition Judge Jayne had given him, "the retention of an eminent white lawyer would serve to win over this alienated opinion, alienated because many white people believe the killing was unwarranted." But the attorneys wouldn't hear a word of it. Should the association hire a white man ahead of them, Rowlette and Mahoney pledged to tender their resignations, a move sure to cause so much controversy that the NAACP's campaign would be thrown into complete disarray. In the end, White had no choice but to back down, promising to postpone any decision until after the next day's hearing.[38]

In private, though, he was livid. Sitting in the quiet of his hotel room early Wednesday morning, he ripped off a blistering letter to Johnson, filtering the fight through a scrim of quick assumptions and unspoken prejudices. All three attorneys were shysters, he said, out for a cut of the defense fund. Mahoney, with his soft voice and northern ways, seemed able enough. But Julian Perry was dismissed with a wave of the hand: the young man had "no personality and commands no respect as far as I can see either as a man or as an attorney."

For Rowlette, White pulled out the knife. He "is a blustering, noisy, pompous individual, with a very inflated opinion of his own ability," he wrote. "You may judge his ability as a lawyer from the fact that yesterday, when I pointed out to him that in the trial of this case as in most criminal cases, the issue was of fact and not so much of law. He flatly contradicted me and declared that this case was wholly a matter of law."[39] White didn't seem to know that a few months earlier Rowlette had saved Fleta Mathies from prison simply by invoking her fundamental right of self-defense. Nor did he notice that he'd saved his worst invective for the rough-edged, dark-skinned son of a slave, the one attorney farthest from the face White was determined to put on the NAACP's crusade.

◆

Tensions were so high as the preliminary hearing got under way Wednesday afternoon that the police commissioner sprinkled a whole squad of undercover cops among the spectators jammed into Judge John Faust's courtroom. He needn't have worried. Though five hundred Negroes showed up to support the Sweets, there were no demonstrations or confrontations, just a peaceful assembly gathered in silent witness to the promise of justice. It was White's first chance to see the defendants, Ossian dapper in a tasteful suit and sober gray and red tie, sitting at the head of two long rows along one wall, Gladys hidden away at the far end of the second row, next to Hewitt Watson, the insurance man.[40]

But it was Assistant Prosecutor Lester Moll's masterful manipulation of the proceedings that truly caught White's attention. Technically, the prosecutor's job was to establish that he had a strong-enough case to take to trial. But Moll neatly sidestepped the state's central assertion of whether Ossian and the others conspired to shoot into the crowd, which he had no way of proving. Instead, he zeroed in on the technical question of whether the Negroes had cause to open fire, assuming that once he'd established the peacefulness of Garland Avenue, the judge would make the critical connection on his own. If the coloreds were in no danger, they must have moved into the neighborhood looking for a confrontation: conspiracy by implication, conviction by assumption.[41]

Within the first few minutes, Norton Schuknecht was in the witness box, recounting his painstaking preparations to keep the Sweets safe, the complete calm on Garland Avenue, and his shock at the shooting. Ray Dove followed with a perfectly matched testimony. A few days earlier, he'd told prosecutors that the night of the shooting there was "quite a crowd" directly across the street from the Sweets' bungalow; now he recalled seeing only "a few" people in his yard, certainly no more than ten or fifteen, a figure precisely set to be just below the legal definition of a mob.[42] When Ossian's next-door neighbor John Getke took the stand Thursday morning, his memory had also taken a turn for the better. The day after the shooting, he recalled hearing stones hit the Sweets' house right before the Negroes opened fire. Prosecutor Moll asked him to revisit the moment. "Was there anything happened in the ten or fifteen minutes in which you were on your porch that would attract your attention to that house? Was there anything to call your attention to the Sweets' house?"

"No, sir," Getke replied. "Not particularly."

Moll asked again, as if to underscore the point. "Was there anything at all before the shooting . . . that would attract your attention to the Sweets' house, that would cause you to notice it particularly as you sat on your porch?"

Getke answered more emphatically. "No, sir, absolutely nothing."

A third time Moll asked. "It was quiet around the house?" Absolutely quiet, Getke said.

"You saw nothing thrown?"

"No, sir."[43]

For its part, the defense was prohibited by the hearing's rules from presenting evidence of its own. So Perry, Rowlette, and Mahoney faced the extraordinarily difficult task of using hostile witnesses to break the state's case. While Schuknecht was on the stand, Rowlette slammed away at the logical inconsistency of pursuing murder charges without having any sense of who the murderer was. Do you know of your own knowledge whether Doctor Ossian Sweet fired the shot that killed Leon Breiner, Rowlette asked. "I don't," the inspector admitted.

"Do you know whether Doctor Otis Sweet fired those shots?"
Rowlette asked. Schuknecht started to say that one of Ossian's brothers had confessed to shooting into the crowd, but the lawyer cut him
off. "I am not asking you about that. Stand up, Doctor Otis Sweet. Do
you know whether this man fired those shots there or not?" Shucknecht
had to say that he didn't. Down the line Rowlette went. "Morse, stand
up. Do you know whether this man fired those shots?" "Latting, stand
up. Do you know whether this man fired those shots?" Ten times he
asked—only Henry wasn't ordered to stand—and ten times Schuknecht
had to say that he wasn't sure. "Do you know of your own knowledge
whether any of those people fired those shots or had anything to do
with firing those shots or not?" Rowlette persisted.

"All I know," Schuknecht replied weakly, "[is] those shots came out
of the house."

Rowlette also focused on the pivotal question of crowd size. His first
approach was too strong. How many people were in front of the flat
where Breiner was shot, he asked Schuknecht. Ten or twelve, the inspector said. "Wasn't there more than twenty there?" Rowlette fired
back. "Isn't it a fact, inspector, that there were two hundred people there
at 8:25 on the evening of September 9?" But the figure was too high and
Schuknecht shrugged it off with an emphatic "absolutely not."[44]

By the time Ray Dove took the stand for his cross-examination
Thursday morning, Rowlette had honed his technique. "You said yesterday there were fifteen people in front of that place, didn't you?" he
began, inching the previous day's estimate to its upper limit. When
Dove agreed, Rowlette started jabbing. Who were these people? Could
you name them? Surely you can recall fifteen names? Were they all
neighbors? Don't you know your neighbors? Was there anyone in the
vacant lot between the flat and the corner grocery store? How many?
Gradually, Dove began to raise his estimate. Maybe there were fifteen
people on his lawn and a few more in the lot next door. Seeing his
opening, Rowlette pounced. "There must have been thirty-five or forty
people there, weren't there?" It was a perfectly chosen number, just
enough beyond the legal definition of a mob to slip by a layman.
But Dove knew better than to concede the point. "No, sir, there wasn't
that many," he said.

"How many would you say?"

"Maybe fifteen to twenty."

There was no missing Rowlette's disappointment. "Altogether?" he
tried again.

"Yes, sir, altogether."[45]

But if Dove could withstand Rowlette's badgering, Getke was no match for Mahoney's stern authority. As soon as Moll finished quizzing the piano tuner, Mahoney unfolded his lanky body from the defense table and approached the witness box. He opened with a gentle question. "Where did you say you lived, right next door?"

"Next door, yes," Getke said.

Suddenly, Mahoney took the offensive. "You understand you are under oath in this matter?"

"Yes, sir."

"And you understand, too, you could be punished for perjury in a case of this kind?"

Only Moll's immediate objection and a rebuke from the bench drew Mahoney back. But the attack had its desired affect. When the attorney pressed Getke to repeat his testimony that all had been quiet before the shooting, the witness wasn't quite as confident as he had been. "And you want to testify there were no stones thrown on the night of the ninth," he asked. "I do," Getke ventured. "You do," Mahoney repeated with a trace of exasperation—or was it disgust—in his voice.

Getke folded. "I will recall that," he said. "I want to testify that there was or wasn't, because I don't know whether there was or not."

"That's better," Mahoney replied.[46]

It was an impressive performance under terribly unfavorable circumstances. By the time the hearing ended Thursday afternoon, September 17, Judge Faust must have realized that prosecutor Moll hadn't explicitly tied any of the defendants to Breiner's murder, and it would have taken a profound act of will not to see that the prosecution had coached its witnesses. But in the end, neither White nor Rowlette had understood the true dynamic in the courtroom; the case didn't pivot on the facts or on the law. It was all about politics. In the superheated atmosphere that Breiner's death had created, even a judge as progressive as Faust didn't dare side with the Sweets. Friday morning, he ruled that the prosecution's case was strong enough to advance to trial. Then he passed it on to the court's presiding judge, Frank Murphy, for assignment.[47]

The decision wasn't two hours old when White swept into Rowlette's Black Bottom office for one last meeting before heading back to Manhattan. Since his confrontation with the three colored lawyers on Tuesday afternoon, Walter had shelved every other activity— even his investigations fell by the wayside—so he could focus on remaking the defense team to his satisfaction. He'd prepared a legal agreement for the eleven defendants to sign, ceding "ultimate choice of attorneys" to the NAACP. He'd lined up the branch officers behind him. And with the help of Judge Jayne, he'd drawn up a list of prestigious replacements, topped by the longtime president of the Detroit Bar Association. All that stood in his way were the lawyers themselves, and surely their opposition would have weakened now that they had given the case their best effort and been utterly defeated.[48]

Sure enough, Faust's ruling had robbed Rowlette of his earlier confidence; perhaps it would be best to add a white lawyer, he agreed, so that the Talented Tenth wouldn't take complete blame for the conviction that now seemed almost inevitable. But even with the sting of his loss still smarting, he refused to bow out of the case. As Perry scribbled notes on the back of an envelope, Rowlette laid out his terms for changing the defense team. He and his cocounsels would select the white attorney, who was to receive five thousand dollars for his services. The three colored lawyers would split another five thousand dollars between them. And the only acceptable addition would be Thomas Chawke, the most skilled criminal lawyer in Detroit.

White was stunned. He had planned to offer the colored lawyers no more than five hundred dollars for their services; to demand anything more was nothing short of blackmail. The association certainly wasn't going to give a no-name "rough and tumble artist" like Rowlette dictatorial control over its case. Worst of all, White couldn't countenance having Chawke fronting the defense. By all accounts, he was a "corking lawyer"; even Jayne had told White that. But Chawke's specialty was keeping the guilty out of jail—rumor had it that a coalition of mobsters had pooled their cash to keep him on retainer—and that wasn't the image the NAACP planned to put before the public. This was meant to be a drama of injustice fairly fought and soundly defeated, not a sordid tale of legal manipulation. Jamming Perry's envelope into his pocket, White turned on his heels and headed for the door.[49]

On the train ride home, White's fury began to fade, replaced by his natural enthusiasm. Sometime in that long evening, as the sun set and the landscape of farms and factories faded into the darkness, he tried out a few tentative lines of publicity for use in one of the dispatches he intended to send the following day, when he was safely back in Manhattan's glowing embrace. "Doctor Sweet and the others are martyrs to the cause of freedom for the Negro," he wrote, his rhetoric rising to the cause. "The eyes of America are on Detroit." But even as he eased himself back into the joy of literary creation, White couldn't stop himself from thinking about one pugnacious lawyer—and a story that was not yet what he wanted it to be.[50]

◆

James Weldon Johnson wasn't concerned. As soon as he had White's confirmation that Dr. and Mrs. Sweet were the symbols he was looking for, he set the NAACP's crusade in motion. And like any first-rate publicist, he wasn't about to be knocked off message by a few messy details.

News of the Sweets' arrest was already spreading, thanks to the Associated Negro Press, the Chicago-based wire service that provided copy to the hundreds of weekly newspapers published across colored America. The ANP's Detroit correspondent cobbled together his first report largely from the white newspapers' accounts of the shooting, though he gave the story the militant twist that was the service's trademark. "A bitter legal battle with far reaching significance is about to be fought here as a result of the fatal wounding of one white man and the wounding of another in a segregation clash in this city on Wednesday night," the story opened, "a thing that had long been calculated the inevitable outcome of the wave of prejudice that has been sweeping the country. . . ." Colored editors snatched it up, plastering the report on front pages from Dallas to Boston, St. Louis to Baltimore. Even the biggest papers, less dependent on the wire service for their news than were the smaller sheets, gave the story prominent play. The mammoth *Chicago Defender*, with a circulation stretching from the Windy City's sprawling South Side ghetto all the way to the Mississippi delta, made the tragedy its lead story for the week of September 19, the account accompanied by a bitter editorial demanding to know "what's wrong in Detroit?"[51]

Johnson, however, had to make sure that the story was spun in just the right way. For a campaign created on the run—its strategy and publicity shaped in the snatches of time the association's frenzied schedule permitted—it was very effectively fashioned. Beginning with the press release announcing that the NAACP "will throw its entire power to the defense of Dr. O. H. Sweet," sent out the day the defendants lost the preliminary hearing, Johnson never failed to link the Sweet case and the Washington supreme court challenge, companion pieces in a seamless struggle against residential segregation. At first, he also tried to tie in the other incidents he'd learned of in the course of the summer, in hopes of bringing the campaign home to as many Negroes as possible. As the Sweets' story gained traction, though, the focus sharpened. In early September, Johnson had arranged for a Sunday rally at Harlem's Abyssinian Baptist Church on behalf of the Staten Island postman whose home had come under repeated attack a few months earlier. By the time the rally was held at the end of the month, the postman's plight was pushed to the periphery, as Johnson regaled the audience with details of the battle for Detroit. Once he was back in New York, White fed to the black press the Sweets' own stirring jailhouse declarations, which miraculously matched the themes the association wanted to highlight. "For a good cause and for the dignity of my people," Ossian was quoted as saying in late September, "I am willing to stay indefinitely in the cell and be punished. I feel sure by the demonstration made by my people that they have confidence in me as a law-abiding citizen. I denounce the theory of Ku Kluxism and uphold the theory of manhood with a wife and tiny baby to protect." Tough as nails on the night of the shooting, Gladys became in White's hands a black Madonna, her arms aching for the child she could not hold. "Though I suffer and am torn loose from my fourteen-month-old baby," she said, "I feel it is my duty to the womanhood of the race. If I am freed I shall return and live at my home on Garland Avenue."[52]

The manipulation of pride and pathos slipped smoothly into appeals for financial support. The directors of the Garland Fund weren't scheduled to meet until the last week of October, so there was plenty of time to put the final touches on the association's proposal for a permanent Legal Defense Fund. In the meantime, Johnson tried to embarrass Negroes into giving. "Do you want to be a segregated race?" he demanded to know in one press release. "Do you want the Jim Crow system extended to the residential streets of northern cities? Or will you fight residential Jim Crow through the courts and before the tribunal of public opinion? The answer rests with colored Americans. The NAACP stands ready to carry out their mandate. It is already embarked upon this immense struggle with shamefully inadequate funds."[53]

Johnson hoped that the excitement of mass meetings also might get the money flowing. Each Sunday in September and the first weeks of October, colored Detroiters trooped to a different Black Bottom church to hear the Talented Tenth plead for contributions to the defense fund they had established for the Sweets, while Johnson and White arranged for companion rallies not only in Harlem but in New Jersey and Washington, D.C., as well, each event to be headlined by one of the NAACP's stars. Johnson even considered White's extravagant proposal that the association send a letter of solicitation to each of the nation's seven hundred thousand colored homeowners, a suggestion that no doubt sent the NAACP's miniscule secretarial staff to the want ads in search of alternative employment.[54]

Money didn't pour in. Even in Detroit, donations didn't keep pace with expenses, so the local defense fund ended September with a lower balance than the NAACP branch had after its first rally. Still, Johnson had to be pleased with the way the association's message was taking hold. By early October, the black press was beginning to fall into line. "The heroic defense of their homes exhibited by those brave and fearless Detroiters . . . makes every Negro in this country their debtor," insisted the editors of Philadelphia's race paper. "And so it ought to be left to that splendid organization, the National Association for the Advancement of Colored People, to undertake their defense. . . . Every Negro in the United States should pay the debt we owe them. We helped with our lives to pay Germany for the horrors of the Belgian invasion. Should we do less in the face of what our own citizens inflicted upon our own flesh and blood in Detroit?"[55]

Selling the Sweets' story to white audiences was a tougher proposition, as there was no sign that the NAACP's publicity blitz was reaching beyond colored America to the ethnic masses whose support the association dreamed of having. To make matters worse, Johnson picked up indications that white liberal opinion was starting to break in exactly the wrong direction. White's reports of the progressives' full-scale retreat in Detroit were worrisome enough, but at least they could be discounted as political maneuvers, cynical but understandable. Other opinions were harder to dismiss. In late September, the editor of the journal *Christian Work*, one of the leading voices of the Social Gospel, sent Johnson his most recent editorial. In light of the tragedy in Detroit, the editor argued, "neither the whites nor the Negroes seem to get any advantage from living next to each other. . . . In Anglo-Saxon lands, at least, the social mixture of white and black leads to unhappiness." Johnson was quite taken aback. It was bad enough to think that liberal Christians could see the separation of God's children as a social good. But he couldn't have missed the stinging irony of this particular publication decrying the integration of urban neighborhoods. *Christian Work*, after all, had its editorial offices directly across the street from NAACP headquarters.[56]

The association countered, as usual, by turning to powerful friends for support. The editor of the *Nation*, NAACP cofounder Oswald Garrison Villard, was pleased to accept White's long piece on the case,

written in a rush the week White returned from Detroit. Though it
lacked the immediacy of White's earlier reports from the darkest re-
gions of Jim Crow, the article hit all its marks. White opened not with
the violence on Garland Avenue but with the NAACP's defeat of city ordinances requiring neighborhood segregation and the subsequent rise
of restrictive covenants, both of which he claimed were pieces of "a
nation-wide effort on the part of certain groups backed by the Ku Klux
Klan" to lock Negroes into ghettos. The attack on the Sweets wasn't
simply an outgrowth of that campaign but "its dramatic high point,"
the tragic culmination of a Klan conspiracy, a lineage of hatred so pure
it was sure to appeal to the *Nation*'s invariably progressive readers, "the
better class of white citizens" that White insisted were already joining
with Negroes to defend the Sweets.[57] But James Weldon Johnson knew
his job too well to imagine that one strategically placed article was anything more than a good start. To take the cause across the color line, he
had to draw out all the dramatic potential he'd seen in the tiny clipping
that had first caught his attention, to make whites feel the injustice that
Negroes felt, to make them care. For all his skill, Johnson hadn't found
a way to push the campaign to that level. Then the situation in Detroit
reached a crisis point, and everything suddenly fell into place.

◆

As soon as he was back at his desk Monday morning, September 21,
White had renewed his offensive against the colored lawyers. The safety
of distance gave his efforts a harder edge. He sent Judge Jayne a detailed
account of Cecil Rowlette's demands and a plea for help "in checking
the rapacity of these lawyers." His closest ally in the Detroit branch,
meanwhile, received strict orders to ratchet up the pressure. "I do not
think it would be a bad idea for you to hint gently that . . . if necessary
we will make public all of the various things these lawyers have said and
done which will end them for all time in the eyes of the colored people,"
he said. "They have got to know that we are doing the employing in the
case and we are going to pay the bill and it's not for them to dictate to us
what we shall do." By week's end, he had the response he wanted. Julian
Perry, who had been all but silent throughout White's time in Detroit,
stopped by Jayne's chambers to say that he, too, wanted a "first-class
white attorney" to take over the defense. He would insist that his cocounsels follow his lead. What's more, he would personally offer the job
to the NAACP's first choice, the former Bar Association president. "The
situation is simmering along nicely," Jayne reported Friday.[58]

He couldn't have been more wrong.

All week long, word of White's pressure on the defense team had been spreading through colored Detroit. Friday night the backlash hit, striking at the true heart of the NAACP's campaign. That evening, Reverend Joseph Gomez, pastor of powerful Bethel AME, told a packed meeting at the colored YMCA that he was launching his own Sweet Defense Fund, explicitly intended to be "a local organization, uncontrolled by outside politics." Gomez himself was probably doing a bit of ministerial maneuvering, setting himself up against Second Baptist's control of the NAACP branch, perhaps even exacting a bit of revenge for Bradby imperiously shutting Gomez out of the branch's executive board earlier in the year. Whatever his motivation, Gomez tapped into a deep well of resentment at the association's high-handedness. By meeting's end, some of the most important organizations in the black community—including Gladys's home church, St. Matthew's Episcopal—had joined Gomez's campaign, and plans were under way for a competing series of Sunday rallies that were sure to drain money away from the NAACP.[59]

That news, in turn, gave Cecil Rowlette all the leverage he needed to derail White's offensive. In the course of a bitterly fought conference with the branch officers Saturday afternoon, Rowlette tossed aside his earlier concessions to White and instead demanded the right to take the case to the next stage the following weekend, when the defendants would be arraigned before Judge Murphy and the defense would have its last opportunity to have the charges dropped. To make sure that the branch was listening, he resurrected his promise to resign if he didn't get his way, a threat that suddenly seemed much more dangerous than it had the week before.

So the NAACP's local officers threw themselves into full retreat. Not only did they promise Rowlette control of the case through the arraignment, but at the next day's church rally, they also passed a resolution promising "that the matter of defense attorneys be left entirely to the persons imprisoned and the present defense attorneys, and that there would be no interference by the association in this regard."[60] Those concessions, though, simply triggered another sharp reaction, this time from the defendants themselves.

◆

In the course of September, life inside the Wayne County Jail grew more comfortable for Ossian, Gladys, and the others. The prominence of the case made it impossible for jail officers to maintain the isolation they had imposed on the Sweets the first few days after their arrest, and by midmonth, the defendants were seeing a steady stream of visitors. The NAACP's Detroit branch, meanwhile, took to providing the eleven with catered meals, sure to be better than prison fare, and to covering some of their more pressing debts, including the $150 a month the Sweets owed on the bungalow's land contract. Still, it must have been terribly difficult for the defendants to endure weeks of imprisonment—suffering the continual taunts of the guards and the perpetual company of their fellow prisoners, trying to remain optimistic even as their attorneys' maneuvers failed again and again, fighting back the terrifying thought that they might never be freed. As the month came to a close, one of the Sweet brothers suddenly decided that it was time to fight back.[61]

It's impossible to say what caused the outburst, but there's no doubt that it was an emotionally wrenching time. For on the last weekend of September, the Sweets received the most important visitor of them all: their father.[62]

Three months shy of sixty, the elder Henry Sweet must have begun showing the signs of age. To his boys, though, he was still a commanding figure—the stern man who had taught them the virtues of hard work and respectability—and they hated the thought of him coming all the way from Bartow to see his sons behind bars, charged with the most serious of crimes. When the guards brought Henry Sweet into the detention pen to talk to his second son, Otis tried to apologize. No explanations, no rationalizations, no appeals to principles that he wanted his father to understand. He simply said he was sorry for the embarrassment he and his brothers had brought to the family.

But Henry Sweet, himself a son of runaway slaves, wasn't angry; he was proud. "You have nothing to be embarrassed about," he said to Otis. "You know who runs? Only rabbits run."[63]

Maybe those words—that blessing—had no affect on the events of the next few days; maybe the cause lay solely in the Detroit branch's decision to abrogate responsibility for finalizing the selection of defense attorneys. But on Tuesday, September 29—at most two or three days after his father's visit—Otis Sweet took his only public stand during the entire Sweet affair.

Along with two of the insurance men, Charles Washington and Leonard Morse, and the narcotics agent William Davis—whose attempts to incriminate his fellows remained unknown to his cell mates—Otis drafted a pair of long letters to the NAACP Detroit branch and the association's national office. Gone were the equivocations the defendants had employed on the night of their interrogations, replaced by a fierce determination to stand up for the cause they now represented. "We feel," they wrote, "that this is a case in which more is involved than the liberties of the eleven persons concerned; it is a case that boldly challenges the liberties, the hopes, and the aspirations of fifteen million colored Americans. If the prosecution should win, in that very act, they erect over the head of every Negro not only in this city but in every community in this country a very formidable threat of residential proscription whose consequences none of us can now predict. He would be forced to face the future with only the feeblest hope as to the positive maintenance of his inalienable right under the Constitution to live without molestation and persecution wherever he may. We feel that the prosecution realizes this and will spare no cunning in the prosecution of their dastardly program."[64]

Given the stakes, Otis and his three associates insisted, the NAACP must assume complete control of the case immediately, rejecting Rowlette's machinations and putting in his place "the best legal talent available." The four defendants admitted that the rest of the accused didn't necessarily agree with their demand for a complete change in the defense team—"the other seven concerned . . . have been just a bit more gullible than we," emboldened Otis wrote in an uncharacteristic rebuke to his brothers—but "we feel this is no time to permit the sordid efforts of narrow self-seekers [such as Rowlette] . . . to place in jeopardy an issue of such vital moment to the race." Then, just to be sure that their message received the attention it deserved, they had Morse's wife send an urgent telegram to the NAACP's office, care of Du Bois, whom they assumed ran the association. "We the undersigned prisoners in the Sweet Case want to know if the Legal Department of the NAACP [is] in complete charge of the defense," the telegram read. "If not, please do same at once."[65]

◆

The moment the messenger boy dropped the telegram off Thursday afternoon, Walter White flew into action. If the colored attorneys couldn't be threatened into following the NAACP's script, perhaps they might be awed into compliance. After a flurry of phone calls and a hastily arranged Saturday morning meeting, White convinced the chair of the association's Legal Committee, influential Arthur Spingarn, to come with him to Detroit the following weekend to lay out the NAACP's bedrock demands. Spingarn prepared the brief they would carry. "[The] color line should be put aside in this case," he wrote, "and . . . the very best lawyer we can afford to retain with the highest professional and personal standing should be secured at the earliest possible time." Then came the hammer blow: "In the event that this very definite opinion of the National Legal Committee is not adopted by the defense, it is recommended that the NAACP decline to accept full responsibility for the ultimate outcome of the case."[66]

Even as he and Spingarn finalized arrangements, though, White knew that the color line wasn't about to break. While Rowlette and Mahoney prepared for the arraignment, Perry had quietly visited the prominent attorneys on the NAACP's list, asking if they might be interested in taking on the case, and one after another, they turned him down. All of them had reasonable excuses: they weren't taking new clients; their schedules were full; they weren't sufficiently skilled in criminal law. But there was no doubting the real reason they wouldn't sign on. The Klan's flame was burning brighter than ever as September came to a close. The four glistening new printing presses in the basement of KKK headquarters were spewing out reams of campaign literature; Klansmen were going door-to-door soliciting votes; there was to be another giant KKK rally on the west side the same day that the Negroes were to be arraigned, Saturday, October 3. Three days after that, Detroit was scheduled to hold its primary election, when the field of candidates would be set for the November general election, and there was every reason to believe that those men who had the Invisible Empire's backing would do very well indeed. Under the circumstances, any white man interested in having a future would be a fool to stand up for the Sweets and their friends. Only Thomas Chawke was willing to take on the challenge, for the gold-plated price of seventy-five hundred dollars, far more than the association's suddenly beleaguered defense fund could bear.[67]

Perhaps White's irrepressible optimism prevented him from admitting the truth even to himself. But there would be no white lawyers. The fate of the Sweets and of the NAACP's fledgling crusade rested in the ebony hands of Cecil Rowlette and his two colored colleagues.

The next few days played out with dreadful predictability. Having staked his hopes on the power of the law, Rowlette arrived at the arraignment on Saturday, October 3, armed with a briefcase full of precedents. Because the witnesses at the preliminary hearing had refused to concede that there had been a mob in front of the bungalow, Rowlette was forced to back off from the argument for self-defense that had proved so successful in the Fleta Mathies case. Still, his nine-page motion to quash was a fine piece of work, striking first at the same soft spots he'd attacked in the preliminary hearing, then citing almost a dozen state Supreme Court rulings to show that those weak-nesses made the charges unsustainable. He tacked on a particular plea for Gladys, arguing that according to common law, a wife was not to be implicated in her husband's crimes simply because she shared his household. As quickly as that point was entered into the record, he swung back to general principles. Without an identifiable murderer and compelling evidence of conspiracy—without showing malice aforethought—the prosecution had no grounds for bringing forward a charge of murder. To preserve the dignity of the judicial system, the Sweets and their friends had to go free.[68]

Judge Murphy paid Rowlette the compliment of taking his motion under advisement for the balance of the weekend. No doubt he ago-nized over the brief; he was too fine a student of the legal process not to see the strength of the argument the defense was making and too sensitive a soul not to be bothered by the possibility of Ossian, Gladys, and the others spending the balance of their lives behind bars. But he also understood the play of city politics, the coursing of emotion on the street. So the balance of justice tipped as it had time and again since the night of the shooting.

On Monday, Murphy announced that he was willing to grant Gladys bail of ten thousand dollars, a balm, perhaps, to a troubled conscience. But Rowlette's motion was denied. Court would convene two weeks hence to begin hearing *The People v. Sweet*. The following day, Tuesday, October 6, the Ku Klux Klan swept the city primary, rolling up imposing majorities for its candidates in district after district, from the west side's Anglo-Saxon strongholds to the rows of working-class flats on the east, where the Invisible Empire was thought to be anathema. Whites of every description, it seemed, were consolidating behind the Klan and its program of racial purity. One more month, one last election, and Detroit would become the Invisi-ble Empire's latest prize, the world's most modern metropolis turned into the Great White City.[69]

◆

If it hadn't been for the trouble with the lawyers, the letter from Chicago probably wouldn't have made such an impression. Had he not slipped his business card into the envelope, no one at NAACP headquarters would have known that N. K. McGill served as general counsel for the *Chicago Defender*. Nor would they have been so intrigued by his extraordinary offer. "I am interested in the procedure in the case of Dr. Sweet in Detroit and I would thank you to let me know if I can assist your efforts in that case," McGill said. "I have free access to such minds as Mr. Darrow's and other great lawyers here and it may be that we could use their knowledge and experience without actually paying the regular fee that they charge in such cases."[70]

As it was, the letter sat in Walter White's in-box all day October 5 as he occupied himself with more pressing matters. It wasn't until the next day, while Klansmen were filling polling places across Detroit, that he found time to reply, and even then he was more concerned with getting the NAACP's campaign bigger play in the *Chicago Defender* than in tapping McGill's legal connections. Not until the day after that, October 7— four weeks since the shooting, twelve days to trial—did someone in the office pull the name off the page.

Clarence Darrow was for a quarter century the most brilliant defense attorney in the country, counsel for Debs and Haywood, Leopold and Loeb, and a Tennessee schoolteacher named Scopes; perhaps he could be convinced not simply to offer his advice but his services. If the idea wasn't Johnson's—if it came instead from White or Du Bois or another member of the staff—he saw its potential right away, just as he had seen the potential in the Sweets' story from a few paragraphs of newsprint. It would be such a marvelously theatrical turn, classic in its form, riveting in its imagery: Clarence Darrow lumbering to the defense table in a Detroit courtroom, the NAACP's faltering racial drama saved by a deus ex machina resplendent in red suspenders and a rumpled suit.

EIGHT

THE PRODIGAL SON

James Weldon Johnson's invitation to Clarence Darrow's Chicago office rang with the staccato rhythm that Western Union imposed: two sentences summarized the specifics of the Sweets' arrest, then Johnson broadened his appeal. "Case is dramatic high point of nationwide issue of segregation in which National Association for Advancement of Colored People has case now pending in United States Supreme Court. *Stop.* This issue constitutes a supreme test of the constitutional guarantees of American Negro citizens. *Stop.* Defense requires ablest attorney of national prestige that we can possibly secure who would be willing to undertake such a case. *Stop.* Please wire us collect if you would consider favorably request that you assume charge of the case. *Stop.*" The next morning, October 8, Johnson received a reply. Darrow wasn't at home, reported his secretary. He was in Manhattan, visiting his friend and fellow attorney, Arthur Garfield Hays. Within a few hours, Johnson had put his sterling connections to use and had an invitation to meet with Darrow that very day.[1]

The NAACP secretary arrived at Hays's Greenwich Village home with Walter White, Arthur Spingarn, and Spingarn's law partner, Charles Studin, in tow. They were ushered into the guest room, where they found Darrow propped up in bed, fully clothed but still looking exceedingly comfortable. Despite his advancing age, he retained the broad-shouldered, barrel-chested body of the workman he'd never been. His face, though, had grown old, his dappled skin sagging from his high cheekbones, the furrows around his mouth and eyes deeply etched. A forelock of unruly hair, gray and thin, fell over his forehead. As the celebrated attorney's gray-green eyes locked on his visitors and his brow knitted in concentration, though, there was no doubt that his mind remained as agile as it had ever been.[2]

As head of the NAACP's National Legal Committee, Spingarn took the lead in laying out the details of the case, a presentation he handled with expertise. A decade later, Darrow would recall how Spingarn's words had stirred the idealism of his youth, when the great abolitionists had graced his father's humble Ohio home. "I made the usual excuses that I was tired, and growing old, and was not physically or mentally fit," he recounted. "I knew that I would go when I was making the excuses. I have always been interested in the colored people. I had lived in America because I wanted to. . . . The ancestors of the negroes came here because they were captured in Africa and brought to America in slave ships, and had been obliged to toil for three hundred years without reward. When they were finally freed from slavery they were lynched in court and out of court, and driven into mean, squalid outskirts and shanties because they were black, or had a drop of negro blood in their bodies somewhere. I realized that defending negroes, even in the north, was no boy's job, although boys were usually given the responsibility."[3]

The others in the room that evening remembered the conversation differently. When Spingarn was finished talking, Darrow offered him the subdued sympathy for which he had become famous. "Yes, I know full well the difficulties faced by your race," he said.

"I'm sorry, Mr. Darrow," replied Spingarn, whose naturally swarthy skin had grown even darker after a summer in the sun at his Dutchess County estate, "but I'm not a Negro."

Embarrassed, Darrow turned to Studin, whose face was the same shade as Spingarn's. "Well, you understand what I mean," he said.

"I am not colored either," Studin answered.

Finally, Darrow took a look at Walter White. "I wouldn't make the same mistake with you," he said.

"I am a Negro," White replied.

Darrow broke into a smile. "That settles it," he said. "I'll take the case."[4]

◆

The response was vintage Darrow, a rage for justice combined with an adoration of irony, the absolute and the ambiguous fused together and presented to the world as dark-edged humor. His critics thought him nothing more than a cynic. "He is never happy except at a funeral," a prominent social reformer complained, "and not then unless . . . the deceased had committed suicide." To see Darrow in such a light, though, was to assume that he believed everything he said. Poet Edgar Lee Masters, who knew and despised Darrow, understood his complexity. "This is Darrow," he wrote three years before the Sweets' arrest, "Inadequately scrawled, with his young, old heart / . . . And his artist sense that drives him to shape his life / To something harmonious, even against the schemes of God."[5]

The harmony Darrow sought was built on the discordant notes of metropolitan modernism. Like the self-styled bohemians who filled turn-of-the-century Greenwich Village, Darrow wanted to shatter what he saw as the smug self-satisfaction—he'd say self-delusion—of mainstream America and to build in its place a society free, open, and savagely honest. Darrow's route to cultural revolution was typical, if somewhat circuitous, his rebellion nurtured by a childhood spent on the radical fringe of the small-town Midwest and given shape by a young man's encounter with the full force of urban life.[6]

Born on the eve of the Civil War, he came of age in the northeast Ohio hamlet of Kinsman, where his father served as furniture maker, undertaker, and, in Darrow's words, "village infidel." An agnostic in a town filled with pious Presbyterians and Methodists, a Democrat in an area dominated by Republicans, a workingman who preferred to spend his days reading his well-worn volumes of Voltaire, Paine, and Jefferson than practicing his craft, the elder Darrow relished the role of free-thinking outsider. At first, Clarence seemed determined not to follow in his father's footsteps. After an abbreviated college career and a year at the University of Michigan Law School, he established a conventional small-town practice in Kinsman, married a conventional small-town girl, and settled into what seemed to be an utterly conventional small-town life. But the pull of ambition and ideas was too strong to resist. In 1887, at age thirty, he abruptly drew up stakes, moving his family, which now included a son, and his practice to the place his hometown newspaper called "the wickedest city in the United States."[7]

Late-nineteenth-century Chicago had its share of sin, doled out in dingy working-class saloons and first-class sporting clubs, steaming Turkish baths and smoke-filled gambling dens. Mostly, though, Chicago had the throbbing energy of a great industrial center, where the natural bounty of the West met the manufacturing might of the East and

the two were transferred in a massive tangle of railroad lines. Just sixteen years removed from the cataclysmic Great Fire, Chicago had become "the heart of the nation," as Frank Norris said, "brutal in its
ambition, arrogant in the new-found knowledge of its giant strength,
prodigal of its wealth, infinite in its desires." It was teeming with people,
a million in 1890, almost 80 percent of them immigrants or their progeny. It roiled with class conflict, the byproduct of industrialists' relentless drive for profit. And it absolutely seethed with ideas. Social
Darwinism, populism, progressivism, socialism: Darrow raced through
them all, an intellectual drunkard on a decade-long binge. Eventually,
he found his place not in any of the city's political circles but rather in
the slightly seedy salons of the artistic avant-garde, where the icono-
clasm of his father's generation was being updated for the Machine
Age. It proved a perfect fit.[8]

Of course the avant-garde were themselves highly political, but
theirs was a cultural rather than electoral politics, a battle for the soul
rather than the ballot box. They took as their enemy bourgeois respectability, which they saw as the polite face of oppression. Through
their art, they sought to strip away the middle class's illusion of decency and to expose the "real" America, at once more bleak and, in the
raw simplicity of its immigrant working class, more beautiful. At the
same time, they tried to turn themselves into respectability's shocking
antithesis, doggedly determined to flaunt convention in their work,
their dress, their living arrangements, and their relationships—to subvert the established order by emancipating themselves. There was a
good deal of artifice to it all: small-town transplants, late of Davenport
and Terre Haute, sitting on well-worn Persian rugs in Jackson Park
studios, drawing tea from samovars and talking of free love, free
speech, and the impending revolution. But Darrow adored it. In 1897,
the year he turned forty, he began the first of a series of seductions, di-
vorced his wife, moved into a cooperative apartment building tucked
in among the immigrant slums of Chicago's west side, and created his
own bohemian salon filled with writers, painters, and assorted hangers-
on. "A more interesting group of peculiar people could not be brought
together," a rattled visitor reported after a night in Darrow's digs.
"Their points of agreement are first, weariness with life as lived by normal society and a desire to live a strained abnirmal [sic] life. . . . Both
male and female members of the club smoked and used profane language as they discussed politics and political leaders; lauded extreme
socialism and anarchy, and cheered anarchists."[9]

For a while, Darrow thought of abandoning the law to become a writer. He even published two novels: *Farmington*, a scalding portrayal of his boyhood hometown disguised as a rural idyll; and *An Eye for an Eye*, a pitch-black portrait of life in Chicago's working-class wards. But his facility with the written word couldn't match his brilliant artistry in the courtroom. He'd burst onto the national scene during one of the worst of Chicago's periodic outbreaks of class conflict, the epic 1894 Pullman strike, when he'd taken up the cause of Eugene Debs, the dynamic president of the American Railway Union. Debs hadn't started the strike—the men and women who made Pullman railroad cars did that—but he had escalated the confrontation dramatically by convincing the members of his union to boycott work on any train that contained a Pullman car. As the nation's rail system all but ground to a halt, the federal court issued an injunction ordering the railway men back to work. When they refused, Debs was charged with contempt of court. Darrow took his case all the way to the United States Supreme Court, which ruled against him. Debs was dispatched to a federal penitentiary to serve out a six-month sentence. And Darrow was transformed into the Great Defender, champion of the embattled working class.[10]

For close to twenty years, Darrow fought for labor's cause. There were the predictable confrontations with capitalist power, fighting for the Amalgamated Woodworkers Union, threatened with conspiracy because they dared to call a strike; for Chicago's switchboard workers, facing imprisonment unless they abandoned their walkout; for the United Mine Workers, desperate to improve their abysmal working conditions. Then there were the truly spectacular cases, which bathed Darrow in the national spotlight. He devoted most of 1906 to defending one-eyed Big Bill Haywood, the excruciatingly romantic, indisputably radical leader of the Western Federation of Miners, who stood accused of murdering Idaho's bitterly antiunion former governor. Five years later, in a case that almost destroyed his career, he waged a fierce battle to save a pair of Irish-American ironworkers, John and James McNamara, from the hangman's noose. The McNamara brothers had dynamited the *Los Angeles Times* building, prosecutors claimed, killing twenty and injuring hundreds. Champions of labor knew it was a frame-up, perhaps orchestrated by the *Times'* owner himself, the bitterly antiunion Harrison Gray Otis. "When the weak and friendless masses clamor for the sweat of his very soul in their behalf," gushed one of his lovers, "Clarence Darrow will appear again and yet again, with flaming sword."[11]

As much as he was moved by the plight of the masses, though,

Darrow was truly driven by the attention that controversial cases won him. Once he embraced the avant-garde, he lost all faith in the legal system—"society is organized injustice," he insisted—and grew bored with the intricacies of legal procedure. But he continued to practice law because in the glare of a high-profile case he found the perfect opportunity to attack the status quo and proclaim the modernist creed. "This meant more than the quibbling with lawyers and juries, to get or keep money for a client so that I could take part of what I won or saved for him," he said in his old age. "I was dealing with life, with its hopes and fears, its aspirations and despairs. With me it was going to the foundation of motive and conduct and adjustments for human beings, instead of blindly talking of hatred and vengeance, and that subtle, indefinable quality that men call 'justice' and of which nothing is really known."[12]

Darrow never presented himself as a sophisticate. In personal appearance, he remained very much a country lawyer, his clothes slightly disheveled and with each year increasingly old-fashioned, his shoulders slumped, his voice tinged with a soft drawl that listeners found endearing. When he rose from the defense table, though, trials were transformed into great social dramas. Prosecution witnesses were turned into symbols of society's stupidity and corruption, defendants into victims of its cruelty, avarice, and ignorance. His closing statements became legendary: no carefully constructed argument, no review of precedent, just cascades of images, emotions, cheap sentiments, and complex ideas, jabs of sarcasm, hints of philosophy, and snatches of poetry, presented in shouts and whispers and sometimes in tears. For eleven hours, he held the Haywood jury spellbound, pleading, preaching, and cajoling, until the trial had become a test of capitalism itself, "that accursed system upon which the favored live and grow fat" while "the poor, the weak, and the suffering of the world stretch out their hands in mute appeal." It was all so convincing, so moving, so tragic, the twelve Idaho farmers who finally trooped into the jury room couldn't bring themselves to convict the anarchist miner sitting by Darrow's side.[13]

Over the decades, Darrow's passions shifted and changed. Six years after his divorce, Darrow married again, taking as his wife Ruby Hamerstrom, a journalist twelve years his junior. Although Clarence maintained his artistic friends and occasional lovers, Ruby shut down his west-side salon, eventually enveloping Clarence in an opulent cocoon of an apartment near the University of Chicago campus. For all his talk of liberation, he happily accepted his new wife's perpetual attention to his needs and comforts. Lincoln Steffens once asked him how his marriage was faring. "Fine," he replied, "because Ruby and me, we both love Darrow." His love affair with the labor movement, in contrast, came to a bitter end during the 1911 McNamara case. Hired to clear the movement's bloodied reputation, Darrow instead pled his clients guilty in exchange for the state's promise not to put them to death. It was a reasonable trade, given that the McNamara brothers had actually committed mass murder. But union leaders were convinced that Darrow had betrayed them, a sentiment made all the stronger when the Great Defender himself was brought up on charges of bribing a juror shortly before the plea bargain was completed. Darrow managed to keep himself out of jail. But his days as the hero of the working class were over.[14]

No matter how much his life twisted and turned, though, Darrow's dedication to modernism didn't waver. With the collapse of his labor advocacy, in fact, the scope of his attacks on the existing order widened. He spent more and more time on the lecture circuit, enthralling audiences with his marvelously sharp assaults on religion, Prohibition, criminal justice, capital punishment, and the very meaning of life. Inside the courtroom, he took up a new string of cases and causes, each more spectacular than the one before. As the fever of "One Hundred Percent Americanism" burned through the nation in the aftermath of the Great War, Darrow defended Italian-born anarchists, Irish-born socialists, and Russian-born communists thrown into jail for preaching revolution on street-corner soapboxes and in radical papers almost nobody read. Their ideas might not stand the test of time, he said, but the nation dare not deny "the right of men to think; to speak boldly and unafraid; the right to be master of their souls; the right to live free and to die free," for "there is no other cause so worthwhile." In 1924, in the wildly publicized case of child killers Nathan Leopold and Richard Loeb, Darrow abandoned his defense of unlimited freedom to argue that his clients were compelled to kill by their damaged psyches, traditional notions of crime, sin, and personal responsibility swept away by the dark art of modern psychoanalysis.[15]

Then came the most brilliant performance of them all. For a man who had participated in so many capital cases, the stakes in the Scopes "Monkey Trial" were ludicrously small. But the case was so furiously spun, so expertly promoted, it became the "trial of the century." In early 1925, the Tennessee state legislature prohibited the teaching

of evolution in public schools, lest students come to question the unerr-
ing truth of holy scripture. Appalled by what it took to be an assault on
academic freedom, Roger Baldwin's American Civil Liberties Union announced that it would defend any Tennessee schoolteacher willing to
test the new law. Hoping for a windfall of publicity for their tiny town,
the good folks of Dayton, Tennessee, promptly offered up their high
school science teacher, twenty-four-year-old John T. Scopes. At first, it
was assumed that Scopes's defense would be led by the ACLU's favorite
attorney, forty-three-year-old Arthur Garfield Hays. The son of a German Jewish businessman, Hays made himself rich practicing corporate
law. He kept himself happy by lending his considerable legal talent to
the defense of civil liberties. Hays's list of pro bono clients read like a
who's who of the dispossessed: imprisoned unionists, silenced radicals, and two poor immigrants named Nicola Sacco and Bartolomeo
Vanzetti, living out their days on death row.

As Hays and the ACLU's directors began preparing for their careful
constitutional challenge, though, the Scopes case slipped out of their
hands. First, three-time presidential candidate William Jennings Bryan,
once the champion of populist politics, now the defender of fundamentalism, announced that he would join the prosecution. Then Darrow elbowed his way onto the defense team. Suddenly, everyone forgot about
the core issue of academic freedom. Down in Dayton, Tennessee, in July
1925—just as the streets of Detroit's west side exploded into racial violence—the Old Time Religion went on trial.[16]

Some ACLU officials were appalled at the change of emphasis.
Hays embraced it, reveling in the dark-hued idealism he and Darrow
shared and in the frenzy of attention the Great Defender inevitably
attracted. More than two hundred reporters trailed the pair into the
Bible Belt, Hays to take care of the trial's legal issues, Darrow to
provide the drama. As newsreel cameras captured the excitement,
Chicago's WGN broadcast back to the big city every word uttered in
the sweltering courtroom. Darrow gave them all a brilliant show. In
his two-hour opening, he pillaged the Temple: "We are marching backward to the glorious age of the sixteenth century," he proclaimed,
"when bigots lighted fagots to burn the men who dared to bring any
intelligence and enlightenment and culture to the human mind."[17]

His masterstroke came on the seventh day, when he asked Bryan
himself to take the stand as an expert on the Good Word. For two interminable hours, Darrow battered away at Bryan's simple faith, daring him to defend the Bible as literally true, laughing at him when he

tried, humiliating him when he faltered. At one point, Bryan grew so flustered, he blurted out, "I do not think about things I don't think about." Darrow shot back, "Do you think about things you do think about?" "Well, sometimes," Bryan meekly replied. When the judge finally put a stop to the assault, Bryan stepped down from the witness stand a broken man.[18]

Darrow's dismantling of fundamentalism didn't help Scopes, who was convicted in a mere nine minutes' deliberation and fined one hundred dollars. But Darrow returned north more famous than he'd ever been before, his mailbox bulging with accolades, invitations, and condemnations, his reputation as modernism's ageless warrior burnished to a blinding sheen. "When [Darrow] confronted Bryan at last, the whole combat came to its climax," wrote Walter White's friend and literary mentor, H. L. Mencken, the enfant terrible of the next generation's smart set. "On the one side was bigotry, hatred, superstition, every sort of blackness that the human mind is capable of. On the other side was sense. And sense achieved a great victory." Now that he had reached the pinnacle of his extraordinary career, Darrow talked of retirement, although he knew he didn't mean it. "I had practiced almost fifty years," he recalled, and for a long time wanted to stop. "But it's not easy to follow one's inclinations." In his heart, he knew there'd be another trial, another cause, another engagement in the battle for the American mind.[19]

Then, just three months after the Monkey Trial ended, the NAACP came calling.

As Darrow listened to Spingarn tell of the Sweets' dilemma, he recalled the radical abolitionists who had tramped through his father's door when Clarence was a boy: William Lloyd Garrison, Wendell Phillips, Charles Sumner, Frederick Douglass, and, most of all, John Brown, who in 1859 had gathered his ragtag troops just fifteen miles from the Darrows' home in Kinsman before marching on to fulfill his destiny at Harpers Ferry. The elder Darrow wasn't himself a participant in the abolitionist crusade. Although the Underground Railroad ran through that area around Kinsman, there's no record of the Darrow family ever secreting escaped slaves to freedom. But Clarence's father loved to hear the abolitionists talk, and to repeat their sweet words to his son; many Sunday evenings, the town agnostic gathered his family around the dinner table and read sermons to them from the most progressive Protestant ministers, such as abolitionist Theodore Parker, with his glorious promise of a universe arching toward justice.

Clarence feigned indifference, but the lectures marked him deeply. The abolitionists were, he wrote, "poor, sensitive, prophetic souls, feeling the suffering of the world and taking its sorrows on their burdened backs," as honest a self-portrait as Darrow would ever put into print. He often mourned the abolitionists' passing, even when it wasn't entirely appropriate to do so. "Whilst a black man was lynched in the shadow of the monument built to the memory of Abraham Lincoln and in the town where he lived and was laid to rest . . . where were the Garrisons?" he roared from the stage of the NAACP's second annual conference in 1910, as the Liberator's grandson, association cofounder Oswald Garrison Villard, sat in red-faced fury. "The Garrisons were preaching in rich pulpits and pointing their aristocrats to an aristocratic heaven. . . . And the voice of humanity and justice was still. What has happened in fifty years?" Until the Sweet case came his way, though, Darrow had never truly stood against the segregationist tide that had swept away so much of the abolitionists' work. Now, in his advancing age, it was time to be about his father's business.[20]

But there was also calculation in the decision to accept the NAACP's offer. When his host, Arthur Garfield Hays, announced that he also was willing to join the defense—"freedom of residence" was at stake, he thought—Darrow leapt at the opportunity to re-create the publicity juggernaut that had been built in Dayton, Tennessee. Better still, Darrow loved the idea of turning the juggernaut against the most sacred of American creeds, more beloved even than the Good Word that he had battered the previous summer. With the Sweet case, Darrow would have his chance to make Americans confront the sheer stupidity of white supremacy.[21] So he smiled at the splendid confusion of hues he saw in the earnest faces gathered around him. And he pledged to go to Detroit.

◆

Had they given it much thought, James Weldon Johnson and Walter White would have recognized the risks of bringing Darrow into their employ. For all his courtroom skills, he hadn't amassed an enviable record in high-profile cases: Debs, the McNamara boys, Leopold and Loeb, all had gone to prison, and even Scopes, whose crime was so miniscule it didn't merit jail time, had paid his fine and handed the school board his resignation, his teaching career ended forever. Darrow hardly bore sole responsibility for the defeats—it was a miracle that some of his clients hadn't ended their days dangling from the gallows—but there was no doubt that he cared more for the fight itself than for victory. And when the heat of battle grew intense, Darrow often indulged in the sort of provocations that the association's habitually respectable leaders considered anathema. Not only had he insulted Villard at the NAACP's 1910 convention, he'd horrified a number of the association's members by urging Negroes to fight for "social equality," including the right to marry white folks, and arguing that miscegenation offered the best solution to the nation's race problem. Colored men had been lynched for saying less.[22]

But Johnson and White weren't worried about how Darrow's penchant for the outrageous might be received in the dangerously enflamed streets of white Detroit. It was the publicity that mattered to them, the phosphorescence of celebrity, which illuminated the black cause so brilliantly that white America couldn't help but take notice. Spending evenings with Mencken, Lewis, Knopf, or Van Vechten meant enduring the occasional idiocy—sharp tongues loosened by liquor and the thrill of being uptown after dark—but discomfort was a small price to pay for the benefits the Harlem Renaissance bestowed on the fight for civil rights. So, too, was it worth risking a bit of Darrow's bombast for the opportunity to cast this particular story, and the crusade it was meant to dramatize, in the dazzling light generated by his incomparable star power.

It took another week to settle the details. There was, as always, the matter of money. Because of the principles involved, the lawyers were willing to reduce their usual fees to rock-bottom prices: Darrow would take the case for five thousand dollars and expenses—a tenth of his typical fee to defend those charged with murder—while Hays would work for a token three thousand dollars and expenses. But even such marginal costs were too much for the NAACP's depleted defense fund. So Johnson couldn't guarantee payment until he convinced his executive board, full of flinty New Englanders, that retaining the services of the nation's most famous attorney was worth the investment.[23]

While Johnson waited for the board's approval, Walter White set out to solve the tangle of problems that had led him to Darrow in the first place. A day after the meeting in Hays's guestroom, he and Arthur Spingarn headed to Detroit on the overnight train for the consultations they'd scheduled with the Sweets' three lawyers. When they'd planned the trip a few days earlier, White and Spingarn had expected a weekend of acrimony, the two of them pressuring the colored lawyers to surrender the case to an unknown white attorney, Julian Perry, Cecil Rowlette, and Charles Mahoney resisting, both sides growing even more frustrated and angry. But the promise of Darrow's and Hays's intervention had restored White's enthusiasm. Although he now had the leverage he needed to force the Negroes out of the case, he no longer cared to do so.

Darrow had made it clear that he wouldn't take the case unless he were welcomed by the local attorneys, and in any case, the defense now had its white face, and the presence of a few black men in the background would do no harm. So White swept into Detroit on Saturday morning, October 10, determined to settle the conflict as quickly and amicably as possible. A few broad hints of Darrow's coming and a suddenly replenished well of goodwill worked wonders. By noontime Sunday, White and Spingarn had promised to keep all three attorneys on the case at a fairly generous fee of fifteen hundred dollars each, to be paid not by the national office—White wasn't in that agreeable a mood—but by the Detroit NAACP branch. In exchange, Perry, Rowlette, and Mahoney agreed to surrender control of the defense to an officially unnamed white counsel whom White coyly referred to as "one of the most prominent lawyers in the United States."[24]

Putting to rest the problem with the attorneys, in turn, promised to resolve the conflict over fund-raising that had exploded a few weeks earlier, when a considerable portion of the city's Negro leadership, angry at White's insistence that the association control the case, had created its own Sweet Defense Fund in competition with the local branch's effort. Now that Perry, Rowlette, and Mahoney were to stay on the defense, the main point of friction was removed. But to be on the safe side, White launched a diplomatic offensive that would have made James Weldon Johnson proud. Though his schedule was filled to bursting, he took the time to meet with the rival fund's director, Reverend Joseph Gomez of Bethel AME, and "by the use of a little judicious flattery," he reported a few days later, tried to convince him that the association desperately needed his help—and the two thousand dollars Gomez had already collected. "To nullify any feeling that we outsiders are interfering and contributing only advice," he and Spingarn made a dramatic appearance at the Detroit branch's regular Sunday afternoon rally, Black Bottom's Macedonia Baptist ringing with cheers as the pair grandly presented Bradby with a five-hundred-dollar contribution from the national office to the branch's coffers, a considerable down payment on the colored lawyers' fees. By the time White boarded a train for a Chicago rendezvous with Darrow Tuesday afternoon,

Detroit's Talented Tenth was awash in warm feelings for the association's selfless efforts on their behalf, a month's worth of conflict seemingly forgiven and forgotten.[25]

Finally, on Thursday, October 15, James Weldon Johnson sent word to the nation's newspapers that Darrow and Hays had been retained. Except for the fact that the trial was set to open the following Monday, the timing was perfect. The NAACP's legal campaign against residential segregation was about to reach its climax: though the clerk of the Supreme Court had not yet given the association's legal team a firm date for oral arguments on the Washington, D.C., restrictive covenant case, everyone assumed the session would be held sometime in November. In preparation for that day, Louis Marshall had put the finishing touches on the association's brief; copies lay in stacks around NAACP headquarters, waiting for the press to take notice. What's more, the meeting of the Garland Fund's board of directors was only two weeks away. Johnson had his application for seed money to create a permanent Legal Defense Fund nearly ready for Moorfield Storey's approval and submission.[26] Now all he needed was the rush of publicity that would make the progressives on the board take notice of the association's battle to beat back the segregationist tide.

There was no press conference to announce Darrow's joining the defense team, just a page-long announcement crafted with the skill of a veteran publicist who knew the importance of framing a breaking story. First came a quick recounting of the shooting, justified as an act of self-defense, followed by an explicit linking of the violence on steaming Garland Avenue with the fight about to be waged in the Supreme Court's velvet-draped chamber. Finally, Johnson made his pitch to the masses he'd been trying to rally to the cause for the better part of a year. To colored men and women, he offered the same warning he'd been issuing since the association first took up the Sweets' case in September: "If in Detroit the Negro is not upheld in the right to defend his home . . . then no decent Negro home anywhere in the United States will be safe." To white progressives, he appealed to principle, to ethnics, he presented self-interest, the two arguments blended together in the message he'd been honing ever since the KKK's brand of Anglo-Saxon supremacy had spread across the urban North. "This practice of segregation must be faced in a common sense way," he argued. "The practice is absurd and un-American. If you begin by segregating members of one race, you may easily come to the point where segregation is made into a matter of creed as well as race. . . . Of course America is not going to stand for it. It would undermine the very foundation of American citizenship."[27]

The result was electric. After a month of maddening silence, the Sweets' story suddenly raced across the color line, virtually all the major dailies down the east coast urban corridor giving the story prominent play while the wire services flashed the association's announcement to smaller papers nationwide. Understandably, most of the press focused on Darrow taking up the defense of Negroes, race substituted for religion in the autumn version of the summer's Tennessee extravaganza. But in a few cases, slices of James Weldon Johnson's message came through as well. Having recounted the NAACP's version of the shooting in graphic detail, Darrow's hometown newspaper, the *Chicago Daily News,* dismissed the prosecutor's presentation of the same events as "peculiar," while the Pulitzer family's prized possession, *New York World,* called on the Detroit courts to immediately dismiss the case. "Unless there have been flagrant misrepresentations in the press reports of the incident this is a clear case of self-defense, and the Negroes had a right to protect their own lives by firing on those who sought to kill them," insisted the *World's* editors. "The law in America is presumably broad enough to cover the Negro as well as the white man."[28]

In Detroit, Walter White punctuated the news by leading Darrow into a perfectly staged surprise appearance at the downtown courthouse to ask for a two-week delay in opening the trial. Filing the motion for a continuance was a routine matter—any of the colored lawyers could have done the job without a fuss—but when word of Darrow's presence shot through the hallways, lawyers, judges, clerks, and secretaries dashed up to Judge Murphy's fifth-floor courtroom to catch a glimpse of the nation's most famous attorney in action. An impromptu press conference followed, with a hastily assembled pack of reporters clamoring for a good quote for the early editions, photographers' flashes exploding around them, passersby stopping to point and stare. Darrow stood casually amid the chaos, surprisingly dapper in a dark pin-stripe suit and stylish pale tie, spinning the case into his personal crusade against racial intolerance. That afternoon, the story was splashed across the front pages, filling the space the Klan's mayoral candidate had hoped would be devoted to his first major appearance since the Invisible Order's sweep of the city primary ten days earlier. But a long-winded speech on the need for economy and Christian morality in city government simply couldn't compare to news that, on

Frank Murphy's order, the next trial of the century was to open in the Motor City on October 30.[29]

◆

The news seeped into the Wayne County Jail the way a crisp autumn morning of incarceration began, a wan shaft of sun breaking through the darkness, gradually spreading into a pool of brilliant light dancing off the filthy gray of the cellblock walls.

The first few days of October had been particularly cruel. Cecil Rowlette had given the eleven defendants some hope that at the October 3 hearing Judge Murphy would grant his carefully argued motion to dismiss the charges. So when the proceedings ended like the ones before, with Murphy denying the motion and the defendants marching back to their jail cells, the defeat seemed particularly crushing. Amid the depression of the next days, the conflicts between the defendants flared again, most of the group desperately clinging to their faith in their lawyers' ability, the three insurance men and Davis, the federal agent, again complaining that Rowlette, Perry, and Mahoney were incompetent, their failures "almost criminal." So deep was their anger that the four sent off yet another telegram to the NAACP's New York office, all but demanding new representation, the absence of the others' signatures a silent condemnation of their foolishness.[30]

Almost as soon as the telegram was dispatched, however, the situation began to improve. On Tuesday evening, October 6, Gladys was released on bail, her ten-thousand-dollar bond secured by friends of her parents. For Ossian, the news must have come as a great relief. At last she could have a taste of the comforts he desperately wanted for himself: a decent night's sleep, a measure of privacy, a few moments of peace, the chance to cuddle with their daughter. Three days later, Ossian received an enigmatic telegram from Walter White, saying that the association was "conducting negotiations with one of the most eminent criminal lawyers in [the] country." A week passed without any elaboration. Then, on October 15, Bradby arrived at the jail with word that Clarence Darrow would be taking control of the defense. The news seemed so unlikely that the defendants didn't quite believe it at first. Late the next morning, though, the guards escorted the ten men out of their cells and down to the visitors' room, where they found Darrow waiting for them, Walter White beaming by his side.[31]

Darrow remembered the moment in his memoirs. "On my way

home from New York," he wrote, "I stopped in Detroit to find out what I could about the case. I found my clients all in jail, excepting one, the wife of one of the defendants, who had been admitted to bail; the rest were men and boys." That wasn't quite the way it happened. Darrow came from Chicago, not New York; before he arrived in the jailhouse, he had already spent the better part of a day with White, poring over the case's details; and from that discussion, he knew all of the defendants still imprisoned were men, not boys.[32]

"Did the defendants shoot into that mob?" Darrow had asked White in the course of their conversation. White hesitated, fearing the Great Defender might be put off if he thought his clients responsible for a white man's death. "I am not sure—" he mumbled. Annoyed, Darrow cut in. "Don't try to hedge. I know you weren't there. But do you believe the defendants fired?" White reluctantly admitted that in his opinion they had. Good, growled Darrow. "If they had not the courage to shoot back in defense of their own lives, I wouldn't think they were worth defending."[33]

"I have seldom seen such joy in the faces of any persons as appeared on those of the defendants when I introduced Mr. Darrow to them," White recalled a few days later. For the longest time, Darrow sat with Ossian and the others, listening to them recount the evening on Garland Avenue, gently pressing them to admit to the shooting rather than cling to the unlikely stories they had concocted the night of the police interrogation, quietly reassuring them that the case could be won even if they had fired into the crowd, bridging the chasm between the famous white lawyer and ten desperately afraid colored men with his remarkable gift for empathy. As he strained to hear Darrow's words, spoken so softly they seemed a whisper, Otis Sweet felt the numbness that had afflicted him—the sickening sense of inevitable defeat—begin to fade. "He talked to you and tried to [see] just how you felt," Sweet remembered years later, "then he'd fill in to show you there wasn't nothing to be afraid of."[34]

A month of perpetual fear wasn't dissipated that easily. But the defendants couldn't help but be caught up in the excitement triggered by Darrow's presence. Otis and most of the others felt it in the cell block. "The whole atmosphere of the jail changed" in the days after Darrow's appearance, he recalled. "Even the turnkeys spoke to you. . . . That's when you built up a little hope. Then they started to bet in jail between an acquittal and a conviction. Before it had been ten to one for conviction."[35] For Ossian and Gladys, the flicker of hope quickly flamed into something more. It took a few days for the Negro press, dominated by weeklies, to pick up the news of Darrow's hiring. When the story finally broke, Ossian—the cowering boy in the bulrushes, the medical student hiding in his rooms as gunfire filled the streets of the capital, the ambitious doctor determined to secure his place among the Talented Tenth—suddenly found himself not simply one of eleven defendants but a national symbol of New Negro militancy, while his charming young wife was swept into the marvels of celebrity.

Not even James Weldon Johnson and Walter White had anticipated just how vigorously colored newspapers would support the Sweets once Darrow had drawn their attention to the cause. From the South came uncharacteristically forthright calls for equal justice, editors emboldened by the fact that they were writing about a northern outrage. "As goes Dr. Sweet," Houston's black weekly shouted, "so goes the American Negro! Selah!" "The case affects every Negro in America, whether he lives in Detroit, Chicago, Jacksonville, or Bartow," echoed the *Florida Sentinel*. "If a group of people can band themselves together and exclude a Negro from one particular section in any American [city] they can bind together and keep a Negro out of every section." For the colored paper in Little Rock, Arkansas, an hour's train ride from the ruins of black Tulsa, the cause was even broader. "Dr. Sweet and . . . his friends have set an example worthy to be followed by all true American citizens," the paper read. "The question is deeper and farther reaching than . . . whether Negroes shall be secure in their inalienable rights but a question as to whether American citizenship shall be robbed and pillaged of their most sacred heritage, a heritage vouchsafed in the constitution; the question whether prejudice and hatred shall rule our nation or whether a pure democracy shall prevail. . . ."[36]

The more influential big-city sheets were just as enthralled with Ossian's courageous stand. "If it is true that Dr. Sweet fired into the crowd of whites to keep them from rushing his home . . . then he was certainly within his rights, and should be supported by every law-abiding citizen in Detroit," wrote the *Chicago Defender*'s fearsome publisher, Robert Abbott, in an editorial Ossian was almost sure to have read. "White people in Detroit, as well as other cities, may as well know now as later that our Race will no longer run from our homes because they object to us. They may as well learn, also, that we will live where we can afford to live if we have to keep an armed guard posted continuously. If the police cannot protect us from mob violence, then we must be prepared to protect ourselves."[37]

Washington, D.C.'s colored paper seconded the *Chicago Defender's* militant righteousness. "We have learned through the years since slavery passed to fight our enemies with their own weapons. If physical violence is offered we kill in self-defense." The *Amsterdam News*, Harlem's hometown newspaper, likewise rang with pride in Ossian's actions. "Possibly the most important court case the Negro has ever figured in all the history of the United States is [about to be] heard out in Detroit Michigan," proclaimed the paper with a touch of hyperbole. "Thank God Dr. Sweet moved in! Thank God that his noble wife moved in with him! And thank God nine of his relatives and friends came in with him! . . . This is the spirit of unity the Negro must more and more evidence if he is to survive. He must face death if he is to live! He must be willing to die fighting when he is right! When police authorities fail to protect him and his family; when courts of law desert him; when his own government fails to take a stand in his behalf, he faces death anyway, and might just as well die fighting!"[38]

Publicity begot money. Johnson waited for the initial rush of news to abate before announcing that the NAACP's accounts were empty and donations were desperately needed to pay even the reduced fees of Darrow and Hays. Almost instantly, the cash came pouring in. The Detroit defense fund, which had been slowly dwindling since the Sweets' arrest, shot upward. The first Sunday mass meeting after Johnson announced Darrow's hiring brought in two hundred dollars, a very solid showing; the second—held amid the crush of stories in the Negro press—netted three times as much. "It's a pity I had not laid out ten days for Detroit," the NAACP's field secretary, William Pickens, reported back to New York after a furious weekend of fund-raising. "We just have things HOT now." The heat spread to other cities as well. NAACP branches in Chicago, New York, Philadelphia, Cleveland, Toledo, and Washington, D.C., organized rallies on the Sweets' behalf, as did the students of Howard University, who packed the campus's spiritual center, Rankin Chapel, in a stirring demonstration of support for one of their own. Wilberforce could claim three of the defendants, two of them current students, but there wasn't quite as much money in Xenia's glens as there was on Howard's hill. When the faculty passed the hat, the most generous donation—five dollars—came from the commander of the campus cadet corps, on whose parade ground the Sweets had learned the skills of self-defense.[39]

Now that she was free, Gladys became the defendants' public face. Rather than move back to her parents' house, she rented a flat four long blocks away from her mother, on another completely white street a little more than a mile northwest of the deserted bungalow. It was a small but comfortable place, well-appointed with the furniture that was supposed to have gone into her family's new home. But in the weeks before the trial, Gladys was too busy to spend much time there. Her days were filled with requests from Darrow and Hays, filtered through Walter White, for information to track down and witnesses to secure, and with appearances at NAACP meetings, Sunday rallies, and, for one poignant evening, a benefit at the Arcadia Ballroom, where she sat with the other defendants' wives watching couples twirl around the dance floor as she and Ossian had done the night they met. She found all the attention thrilling. "I consider it quite an honor and of no little importance to be noticed by a person as busy and so much in demand as yourself," she wrote White with just a touch of flirtation the last week of October. "If things keep on I shall soon believe myself to be quite a personage."[40]

The outpouring of support turned Ossian's head, too. Gladys packed her visits to the jail with news of the latest rallies, and no doubt she handed over the most recent issues of the *Chicago Defender*, the *Courier*, and the other Negro publications to which the couple subscribed so that her husband could see the tributes being lavished upon him. How extraordinary it must have been for Ossian to read the great Du Bois's searing treatment of his case in the November *Crisis*, which arrived in the mail at the tail end of October, to have the very man who coined the term "Talented Tenth" hold him up as a model for the young men of the race to emulate, in explicit contrast to Alexander Turner, whose decision to flee from the rabble the editor bitterly recounted. "Which [example] would you follow," Du Bois asked his forty thousand devoted readers, "if you were 'free,' black and 21?"[41]

To be the object of such praise was so heady an experience it was easy for Ossian to let slip the memory of his own hesitations and prevarications. He couldn't forget the paralyzing terror he'd felt the night of the shooting: the uncontrollable shaking of his hands as he tried to load the pistol he never fired; the sight of the mob as he opened the door to let Otis and Davis inside; the moment the guns went off above him and the very walls seemed to shudder. But he began to see the road he had followed to Garland Avenue as much straighter, his steps more purposeful, than they had actually been. Over time, Ossian would find just the right words. He had dared to move into the bungalow, he would say again and again, "only because my group had been chased all over town and there didn't seem to be anyone left to take the lead in the great fight to secure a decent place in which to live." The reluctant hero standing for principle when all others had failed: it was a worthy image for a man who so desperately wanted to make his life exemplary and a comforting thought when the light of day faded and Ossian was forced to contemplate the weeks ahead, when his future would depend on Clarence Darrow's ability to tell a story as inspiring as the one Ossian had come to believe.[42]

•

"It is a thrilling situation," a buoyant Walter White wrote one of his many friends a week before the trial was to open. "We have got a very hard fight on our hands. [But] with Mr. Darrow as our chief counsel, we have got a fighting chance to win out." Obviously, the Great Defender was the key. White loved being in his company, listening to the old man talk of philosophy and politics, gossiping about their mutual friends among the literati, watching him map out the defense in his mind, adding the occasional suggestion, for which Darrow seemed genuinely grateful. White also adored the swirl of excitement Darrow brought in his wake. Walter's schedule was crowded with speaking engagements at rallies and forums devoted to the Sweets, while his mailbox overflowed with congratulatory messages: bringing Darrow into the case was "a great stroke," wrote James Cobb, himself immersed in the upcoming Supreme Court challenge; it was "a masterstroke," said another lawyer who'd fought his share of race cases; even the young poet Langston Hughes, hidden away in a Montmartre garret, sent a note saying that Darrow's hiring "is certainly fine."[43]

But it wasn't Darrow's presence alone that gave White hope that the case might be won. There were also surprising signs of movement in Detroit, where the white progressives seemed at last to be shaking off their month-long stupor. White picked up the first hints of change during the weekend he spent settling the NAACP's conflict with the colored lawyers, when he squeezed in an hour or so to chat with Frank Murphy about the trial. White didn't know much about the man before the meeting, but what his informants had told him wasn't particularly encouraging. Word was that Murphy had maneuvered the Sweet case into his courtroom because he hoped his unbiased handling of the trial would solidify his support among colored voters, whom he had to have on his side when he ran for mayor in two years' time. But then Murphy had rejected Cecil Rowlette's motion to dismiss the charges against the Sweets, a bitter disappointment, and now a lot of colored men—and not a few whites as well—doubted whether Murphy would have "the grit to stand boldly" against the prosecution's framed-up case.[44]

As soon as White settled into the judge's rooms, though, he was bathed in Murphy's self-conscious compassion. He didn't record the judge's precise words. But White was struck by his seemingly deep sympathy for Negroes ("I like them," he told a girlfriend, "because they are so out of luck and get the worst of each deal"), his commitment to maintaining a color-blind courtroom, and his obvious relish in taking on a case that would put his principles to the test. "The question of how to secure a fair trial for the eleven colored defendants is constantly on my mind," Murphy said to his sister a few weeks later. "Above all I want them to know that they are in a court where the true ideal of justice is constantly sought. A white judge, white lawyers and twelve white jurymen are sitting in judgment of eleven who are colored black. This alone is enough to make us fervent in our effort to do justice. I want the defendants to know that true justice does not recognize color." No doubt White heard much the same speech, Murphy's matinee-idol face soft with emotion, his blue eyes glistening. The performance was so impressive that as soon as he arrived in Chicago, where he was to spend the day with Darrow, White rushed off to Marshall Field's and bought a thumbed-through copy of *The Fire in the Flint*. The book arrived in Murphy's mailbox a few days later. "It was a very real pleasure to meet you, and a most pleasant surprise to find one with such lofty ideals," read the inscription. "It is so seldom that those of us who are trying to secure even-handed justice for Negro citizens encounter one like yourself you may well imagine our joy when that experience does come."[45] Obviously, White was indulging in his incomparable gift for flattery. But the note also expressed a genuine sense of awe—and not a little relief. In a city full of Klansmen, White had found St. Francis.

Murphy's almost ethereal sense of fairness was complemented by a suddenly surging, uncompromisingly aggressive campaign to crush the Ku Klux Klan's drive for control of city hall. Once the enormity of the KKK's sweep of the October 6 primary sank in, Mayor Johnny Smith shunted aside his race baiting of early September—the hints of a colored-Klan conspiracy, the promises to keep Detroit's white neighborhoods racially pure—and again embraced the muscular street politics that had been his hallmark.

Day after day, he worked to ignite the passions of his electoral base in the ethnic neighborhoods of the east side, rubbing his voice raw with speeches at the Holy Name Society, the Weinman Settlement House, and St. Margaret Mary's Hall; swapping war stories with the grizzled men gathered at the VFW post; pumping hundreds of calloused hands as the afternoon shift trooped through the gates of the Dodge Brothers' mammoth factory. Everywhere he went Smith hammered at Klan intolerance, his square jaw firmly set, his fist slamming into his open palm in his signature style. The city's foreign-born, its Catholics, its Jews—they were all victims of the Invisible Order's attacks, he insisted. He, too, felt the sting. "I was born in this country," he told a banquet hall full of Lithuanian businessmen on the day Darrow's hiring was made public. "My father fought in the Civil War. I myself fought in the Spanish War and the Philippine Insurrection. I have done nothing but work hard all my life. . . . Yet they say I am not an American." He wouldn't let such a slander stand. Neither should they. "Those who have made America great are the men and women of all races who have mingled in this country," he proclaimed from the dais. "I venture to say there is not a person at this table who does not better understand and more truly follow the concepts of America than any of these self-styled '100 percent Americans' who goes around with a hood over his head."[46]

Smith worked Black Bottom the same way, slashing away at the Klan's campaign, using its expansive hatreds to build a bond between himself and his audiences, whose sufferings he shared and whose dignity he was determined to defend. Though he arrived an hour late for a Sunday rally sponsored by a host of Negro organizations, including the NAACP branch, he had the crowd on his side within moments of beginning his remarks.

"Mr. Chairman," he said, "I was going to say 'my fellow countrymen,' but there is a question about my being a countryman of yours. They say I'm a foreigner, despite the fact that I was born in the city of Detroit and twice raised my right hand and swore to bear honestly and faithfully the arms of my country. But they tell me I'm a foreigner so I will have to say 'ladies and gentlemen,' I guess." As laughter rippled across the room, Smith drew his audience in. "I come to you as a candidate for mayor, not of any secret organization, but as a candidate of all the people, without regard to race, religion, or creed. . . . I feel as mayor of the city of Detroit—and it is my wish as an American citizen—that we could understand these foolish yokels who pay ten dollars apiece to hate you and me, and we could do more by trying to understand them than by abusing them and . . . preaching hate. I have not any malice in my heart for any of them; I feel sorry for them."[47]

Smith did feel malice toward Klansmen, though, deep personal malice—and as he talked his audiences felt it, too. The crowds that came to the mayor's east-side rallies hadn't necessarily experienced the Klan's chauvinism firsthand. But many of them understood what such hatred could mean. Some of them had felt it in other forms and other places. They'd seen the cossacks riding to the synagogue's steps, heard the tattoo of the Orangemen's drums coming down the road, or felt the pulse-pounding terror of the night riders' arrival at their door. For others, it was a bitter memory passed from previous generations. It was the smug landlord in Calabria, Connemara, Macedonia, or Louisiana who put out his tenants after years of faithful service. It was the petty official in some half-remembered village who said a Russian Jew couldn't own property, an Irish Catholic couldn't vote, a Negro couldn't walk the roads without a white man's permission. It was the boss at the Ukranian iron mill, the Belfast shipyard, or the North Carolina textile mill scowling at a grandfather, then a young man desperate for work, and saying, "We don't hire your kind here."

Then there were all the insults and injuries that Detroit imposed: the way a Polish-born autoworker could give Ford thirty years' labor and still never make foreman because that job was reserved for real Americans; the way a colored man had to painstakingly plot a day's outing with his sweetheart so as to avoid all those places where he wouldn't be welcome; the way a child's face looked when he had been taunted with one of the ubiquitous school-yard epithets—kike, dago, wop, mick, hunky, nigger—and knew in the very sounds of the words that he was hated. The humiliation, frustration, and fury of such moments: that was what Johnny Smith wanted his audiences to feel when he mocked the Klan.[48]

Once the mayor made the Klan his target, the city's progressive bloc rallied round him, as they had the year before. Liberal lawyers, judges, businessmen, clubwomen, and leaders of the city's fragile trade unions, all of them took to the attack, their charges invariably reprinted by the proudly partisan *Detroit Times* and normally reactionary *Detroit Free Press*, which had swung its support behind Smith. A vote for Bowles was a vote for prejudice, insisted wealthy Harriet McGraw, the doyenne of Detroit's progressive reformers, as she launched a "Women for Smith" club from the ballroom of a fine downtown hotel. If the Klan won the mayor's office, a prominent attorney said at another rally, Detroit would become "a leper colony in the eyes of the rest of the nation." From his pulpit, the minister of prestigious First Presbyterian slammed the

Klan's racism: "The blond Nordic," he proclaimed, "has no barter from the Almighty to dominate the rest of humanity."[49]

Of all the Protestant voices, though, none spoke with more authority than thirty-three-year-old Reinhold Niebuhr, whose eloquent addresses on social issues over the past few years had won him widespread attention among the city's progressive bloc. "We fair-minded Protestants cannot deny that it was Protestantism that gave birth to the Ku Klux Klan, one of the worst specific social phenomenon which the religious pride and prejudice of peoples has ever developed," he preached in a Sunday sermon that so impressed the editors of the *Detroit Free Press* they put it on the front page. "I do not deny that all religions are periodically corrupted by bigotry. But I hit Protestant bigotry the hardest at this time because it happens to be our sin and there is no use repenting for other people's sins. . . . We are admonished by Scripture to judge men by their fruits, not by their roots; and their fruits are their character, their deeds and accomplishments."[50]

Smith's opponent, Charles Bowles, tried desperately to escape the pummeling, claiming over and over that he wasn't a Klansman, that the candidates should be debating Detroit's rampant vice and criminality rather than the KKK, that Smith was heightening the fears of foreigners and Negroes to obscure his failings in office. But Bowles had drawn around himself a circle of supporters who weren't about to be silenced by their papist opponent and his progressive allies. When Bowles wasn't at the podium, his rallies shook with condemnations of the immigrant "rabble with their thumb-worn creeds," with warnings of black-robed priests engaged in papal plots to destroy American liberty, and with dark threats to "pure womanhood."[51]

Just beneath the surface lurked the danger of violence. From the sanctuary of her husband's church, a minister's wife proclaimed that any woman who voted against the Klan candidate should be "tarred and feathered." From his downtown headquarters, kleagle Ira Stout warned the newspapers to send over only Protestant reporters, since the safety of Catholics and Jews could not be assured. And when the workingmen of the Kelsey Wheel plant declined to spend their lunch break listening to one of the Klan's candidates for city council harangue them, the man pulled a pistol from his jacket and demanded that attention be paid. Such talk simply played into the hands of Smith's supporters.[52]

Bowles is undoubtedly a decent man, said the editors of the *Detroit Free Press*. "Nevertheless, about him have joined all the elements of intolerance, the haters of Catholicism, the haters of the Negro, the haters of cosmopolitanism, hundreds of sincere people who believe in the Christianity exemplified by Bryan. . . ." There was the central conflict of the campaign just as Darrow might have framed it: crabbed champions of indefensible traditions battling the heterogeneous masses of modern America; the prejudices of the old order pitted against a new vision of openness and justice.[53]

But justice had its limits. Twice during the campaign, Johnny Smith came face-to-face with those most responsible for the summer's violence: on October 16, he met with a large group of real estate men in the office of James Conley, the driving force behind the Waterworks Park Improvement Association, and four days after that, he made a foray to the city's west side—"into the very heart of the district that is reputed to be the stronghold of his Ku Klux Klan opponent," the *Detroit Times* breathlessly reported—where a mass meeting of the Tireman Avenue Improvement Association was waiting to hear him speak. It would have been easy enough to confront both those groups—surely their votes were already lost—to lecture them on rights and justice and respect for the law. But Smith didn't so much as mention the racial tensions roiling the city's neighborhoods.[54]

Nor did he find another, less volatile venue in which to make a principled stand. Not once in the many appearances that the newspapers reported did Smith defend the right of colored families to live wherever they pleased, as he had done during the July disturbances; not once did he criticize banks, insurance companies, builders, and real estate agents for hemming Negroes into Black Bottom, nor did he condemn mobs for assaulting those few who managed to break through its boundaries; not once did he talk about the Sweets, although the story was white-hot as the mayoral campaign came to a climax. It was a politic silence, given white Detroit's hostility to Negroes crossing the neighborhood color line, a simple act of omission—and an unrepentant sin of commission in the ongoing construction of a segregated city.

◆

Clarence Darrow saw it all unfold in front of him.

Frank Murphy had given him just two weeks to prepare for trial, two weeks to gather whatever evidence he could and to make of it a solid defense. Most attorneys would have been overwhelmed by the thought of it. But Darrow simply sat in his office, watching the information pile up around him, waiting for inspiration to strike.

News of Detroit's maelstrom arrived in fragments. From his lone jail-house visit, he had his clients' own version of the fatal night on Garland Avenue. Perry, Rowlette, and Mahoney also provided Darrow with the evidence they'd accumulated of the summer's violence: clippings from the *Detroit Independent* detailing the mob attack on the Mathies' home; a statement by Vollington Bristol recounting the assaults he endured; newspaper stories of the Turners' expulsion and Johnny Smith's subsequent plea for peace, all of which he filed away. During his stop in Detroit, he took the time to visit a few old friends—a venerable anarchist who once dominated Detroit's left, a judge made sympathetic in a long-ago encounter—who brought him up to speed on the mayor's furious battle to swing the ethnic masses against the Klan, while the Chicago papers provided him periodic updates on Detroit's mayoral campaign.[55] He didn't need much more. Having spent half a career defending desperate workingmen and three decades slipping in and out of Chicago's electoral cockpit, he knew better than most men how fiercely the flames of ethnic, racial, and class politics could burn once the fuse was lit.

Arthur Garfield Hays and Walter Nelson, a white Detroit attorney who was added to the defense team on Darrow's suggestion, balanced impressionistic political reporting with a cache of precise legal analyses. Although he liked to strike the same cynical pose toward his profession that Darrow had perfected, Hays was by all accounts a marvelous lawyer, a brilliant logician—as a young man he'd tutored a teenage Walter Lippmann on the fine art of debating—who was much more likely to exploit precedent and procedure than to dismiss them, in Darrow's fashion, as garroting the pursuit of justice. His talent showed in the crisp, concise material he prepared for Darrow's perusal. Many of the memos dealt with strategic issues: whether the defense would be better demanding separate trials for each of the eleven defendants, as the law allowed; how to prevent the prosecution from blurring the charges of murder and conspiracy, a tactic that had hamstrung the defense during the preliminary hearing. Most importantly, Hays and Nelson took up the painstaking work of fashioning the defense's basic brief.[56]

Using Cecil Rowlette's well-crafted motion to dismiss as a reference point, they continued to home in on the critical point of whether the people who had filled Garland the night of the shooting constituted a mob. But they stripped away the colored lawyers' concern for who fired the fatal shot, which Rowlette had seen as the weakest point in the prosecutor's case, and instead focused on whether the defendants had cause to shoot into the crowd. Rowlette's motion provided the defense with the precedent that Prosecuting Attorney Robert Toms had feared they would find: in the 1860 case of *Pond v. The People of Michigan*, the state supreme court ruled that a man threatened by mob assault had the right to defend his life and property, even if his perception of the mob's intentions proved to be incorrect. Rowlette had buried the ruling among a dozen citations; Hays and Nelson turned it into the centerpiece of the defense team's new brief, incontrovertible proof that the law was on their side.[57]

Walter White, meanwhile, handed Darrow reams of information on the perilous state of American race relations. At Hays's request, White gathered together a primer on mob violence that included James Weldon Johnson's summary of the 1919 Washington riot, a wrenching expose by the NAACP field secretary of an Arkansas field hand's immolation in 1921, White's compelling account of the Tulsa horror, and the association's careful tally of the previous year's lynchings. It was powerful material, but almost all of it dealt with southern atrocities, and none of it touched on the crusade against residential segregation that had brought the NAACP into the Sweet case in the first place. To be sure that Darrow understood that the battle of Detroit was but one part of that crusade, White also sent on copies of Louis Marshall's brief against restrictive covenants and Du Bois's long article in the November *Crisis*, two brilliantly intense analyses of the very institutional arrangements that Johnny Smith so assiduously avoided mentioning.[58]

A constitutional scholar of the first rank, Marshall built his case on a careful balancing of public policy and legal precedent. Having time and again committed itself to the principle of equality before the law, he argued, the nation cannot condone private agreements that brand one segment of its citizenry as inferior, nor can it endorse—or worse yet advance—economic arrangements that, once put into practice, would eventually balkanize the nation. For his part, Du Bois combined the rigor of the sociologist he had once been with the outrage of the propagandist he had become. In slashing strokes, he exposed the deadly interplay between prejudice and the "organized real estate interests" that controlled the modern urban housing market. White men wail that Negroes depress property values, Du Bois wrote, but it was "an ancient and bearded lie" manipulated by profit-hungry real estate agents, bankers, and builders to codify racial exclusion and by so doing to create the fetid ghettos that even "decent, quiet, educated" colored families cannot escape. And when, "by bribery, politics and brute force," a few brave

Negroes manage to break through the barriers erected against them, they had to face white homeowners transformed into murderous mobs by the fears that these interests induced. "Dear God! Must we not live?" he roared so that heaven and Harlem both would hear. "And when a whole city full of white folk led and helped by banks, Chambers of Commerce, mortgage companies and 'realtors' are combing the earth for every bit of residential property for whites, where in the name of God are we to live and live decently if not by these same whites?"[59]

A more disciplined mind might have moved methodically through such a jumble of material, fitting facts into the law's rigid rules, organizing ideas and arguments into logical sequences, building an ironclad case. That wasn't Darrow's way. He didn't see the need for painstaking preparation, not when he had at his command forty years' worth of words and images that he was sure could hold a courtroom transfixed, not when he knew that there was always a way to make a jury want nothing more than to set his clients free, not when he intended to transform the trial into yet another engagement in his life-long battle against the established order. It was enough to have a feel for the case and its context, and to rely on wit, manipulation, and his incomparable persuasive powers to do the rest. A fellow lawyer, anxious to see how Darrow constructed "the steelwork" of another murder case, once asked to see the file the Great Defender had assembled to lead him through the trial. Clarence showed him "four or five little half line notes on a yellow pad, which he then proceeded to throw down and leave behind him on the desk when the court said, 'Very well, you may proceed now, Mr. Darrow.'" The Sweets deserved no less of his attention, and received no more.[60]

By Friday morning, October 30, Clarence Darrow was ready to go to court.

◆

Walter White had taken the overnight train to Detroit so often in the past two months that the trips had started to blend together. But this time, the journey had a special edge. It must have been difficult to say good-bye to his wife and baby daughter knowing that he might not see them again for a month or more, to watch out the train window as Manhattan gradually faded into the dusk, and to awaken the next morning to the sight of smog-shrouded Detroit drawing into view, its skyline particularly bleak in the weak light of dawn. The burdens of the assignment were eased, though, by the thought that within an hour of his arrival he'd be sitting at the press table of Frank Murphy's courtroom watching Darrow open the drama that he and James Weldon Johnson had helped to create, and that whatever happened over the next few weeks, the NAACP's triumph was all but assured.[61]

The news had come shortly before White left headquarters to catch his train. After careful consideration, the board of directors of the Garland Fund had voted to support James Weldon Johnson's proposal to create a permanent Legal Defense Fund. The decision wasn't surprising. Johnson's position on the board assured the proposal a full hearing, while the hiring of Darrow and Hays, both close friends of board chairman Roger Baldwin and champions of the causes other Garland Fund members held dear, made approval all but automatic. Still, the announcement was extraordinarily exciting.

The NAACP was to receive five thousand dollars of Charles Garland's fortune immediately—enough to cover Darrow's entire fee—to be followed by an additional fifteen thousand dollars as soon as the association raised twice that sum on its own. A few months earlier, Johnson would have despaired at the thought of having to secure thirty thousand dollars in donations. But now that the Sweet case was riveting black America, even such a demanding goal seemed well within reach. Naturally, the fund-raising would require a great deal of organizing. But there was every reason to believe that by the time the jury rendered its verdict and White finally headed home to Harlem, the NAACP would have an astounding fifty thousand dollars endowment, "the munitions of war," as Johnson put it in his first blast of publicity, "for such a fight in behalf of justice for the Negro as has not been fought since the Civil War."[62]

When White walked into the downtown courthouse sometime after nine o'clock, the corridors were already packed with people—two hundred or more, the vast majority of them Negroes, a boisterous mob crowded outside the courtroom's closed doors, jostling for position so that when the specially posted guards opened the way, they were ready to make a mad dash for seats. Gradually, White pushed his way to the front, flashed the press pass Murphy had provided him, and with a nod to the policemen slipped inside.[63]

It was a compact space, much smaller than the cavernous courtroom from which the Scopes trial had been broadcast to the world, but it had a simple elegance unusual in a city that valued speed of production over quality of workmanship. Its floor was a slick marble, as was the six-foot-high wainscoting that ran along all the walls. Above the white wainscoting, the plaster was painted a tasteful gray, its dark hue softened by the light that streamed in through three large windows. White passed by the six or so rows of chairs reserved for spectators—all of them sure to be filled as soon as the guards allowed the crowd in the corridor to stream in—pulled back the low gate in the railing that ran the fifty-foot length of the chamber, and stepped into the courtroom's overcrowded well. Directly in front of him stood the judge's towering mahogany bench, beside it the witness box, and in front a long, narrow table where the clerk of the court and the stenographer would sit. To White's left, along the far wall, was the bench reserved for the defendants and to his right the still-empty jury box. Somehow the court had managed to fit in two more substantial tables as well, one to be shared by the prosecution and the defense, the other set aside for the press. White squeezed in among the other reporters and within a matter of minutes was working his charm, chatting happily about the editors he knew back in Manhattan, all of whom he was sure would love to read the novels his fellow newsmen had tucked away in the bottom drawers of their desks, awaiting discovery of their genius.[64]

Prosecuting attorney Robert Toms, tall, handsome, and dignified, arrived first, accompanied by his assistant, Ted Kennedy, and together they took possession of the half of the lawyer's table nearest the jury box. Then the quiet of the courtroom was broken by a burst of cheers in the hallway. Again the doors creaked open and in ambled Darrow, seemingly oblivious to the applause that had greeted him, more an old man come to do another day's work than the acclaimed champion of the poor, the dispossessed, the weak, and the erring. A few minutes later, the clerk called the court to order, Frank Murphy took the bench, and *The People v. Sweet, et al.* was called to the bar of justice.[65]

Most of that first day struck White and his fellow reporters as terribly tedious. In his determination to be scrupulously fair, Murphy had summoned a particularly large panel of one hundred and twenty potential jurors. Almost half of those called failed to show up. But that still left sixty-five men and women for the opposing lawyers to sift through in search of the perfect twelve. Prosecutor Toms began the process. All morning and well into the afternoon, he stood before the jury box, methodically quizzing each of the dozen men and women picked at random from among the sixty-five, while Darrow sat silently at the far end of the lawyer's table, one arm slung over the back of his chair, his head hunched between his broad shoulders, his eyes fixed on the middle distance. Toms tinkered with the panel, excusing four men for cause, questioning their replacements as he had the others in his unfailingly professional manner. It was close to three o'clock when he declared the jurors in the box acceptable to the prosecution and turned the twelve over to the defense for examination.[66]

Darrow slowly got to his feet, jammed his hands into his pockets, and sauntered over to the front rail of the jury box. When he began to speak, his voice was so soft that the reporters on the other side of the room strained to hear him. His questions were equally intimate. He wanted to know the jurors' birthplaces, nationalities, professions, and political affiliations. He asked them whether they owned their homes, what they thought of Negroes moving into their neighborhoods, and whether a man had a right to defend his property from mob attack. It was almost always done in a casual way, as if Darrow and the juror he was questioning were two strangers standing in a corner bar making conversation. There were moments, though, when the tone would change. Frank Buell's answers seemed ordinary enough: born and bred in the United States, just like his parents before him, he was in his sixty-fourth year; over the course of his life he'd held a number of jobs—the best of them working as a clerk in a factory—but now that he was getting older, he was scraping by on a night watchman's wages and living under his son-in-law's roof. Darrow heard something, though— a phrase, a word, perhaps just an inflection—that he didn't like. "Are you a member of any secret societies which you do not care to discuss here?" he suddenly said, and everyone in the courtroom knew he was asking about the Ku Klux Klan. Buell admitted that he was.[67]

You may step down, Darrow snarled, and in that unexpectedly sharp command rang the righteousness of Garrison, Douglass, Brown, and their abolitionist brethren.

The first great battle in James Weldon Johnson's newly proclaimed war against racial injustice had begun.

NINE

PREJUDICE

All of Friday afternoon and Saturday morning, October 30 and 31, Clarence Darrow interrogated the jurors that the prosecution had passed. Slowly, the faces in the jury box changed. A second juror was dismissed because he held membership in the Ku Klux Klan, two others because they made their living as real estate agents. When a colored man was called, Darrow sent him off without a single question, saying that the prosecutor was sure to discharge him. A white woman was asked to step down when she revealed that she had recently served on a jury that had convicted a defendant of manslaughter. A second woman said that if Negroes moved into her neighborhood she would fear for her property values; she, too, was dismissed. As the overcrowded courtroom grew restive, a few colored spectators took to heckling the whites eliminated; prospective jurors complained that they were being intimidated; Frank Murphy, bristling, issued a sharp rebuke to the spectators from the bench. Still, Darrow kept up his exhaustive examination, lingering over each juror as if the entire proceedings depended on the answers he received. "Two days of the trial have already passed," Walter White told James Weldon Johnson on Saturday night, "most of the regular panel . . . is exhausted—and additional panel of 65 has been called—and thus far there are only two of the twelve jurors in the box who are at all satisfactory."[1]

Darrow wasn't concerned. In virtually every U.S. criminal court, lawyers were given two ways to remove a potential juror. If the venireman, as he was called, made it clear he couldn't be objective, either the prosecution or the defense could ask the court to dismiss him "for cause." Or an attorney could exercise a peremptory challenge, which allowed dismissal for no reason whatsoever. Most of the time, courts imposed strict limits on both. A hostile judge—and Darrow had met more than his share of those—could refuse a lawyer's request to dismiss for cause. And the law typically restricted the number of peremptory challenges at an attorney's disposal: when Darrow defended Big Bill Haywood, he had just ten such challenges. A defense attorney had to press each juror hard in hopes that, as the pressure mounted, the venireman would expose any biases: Darrow worked over the jurors in the Haywood trial, Big Bill said, as if he were "killing snakes." Peremptory challenges, meanwhile, were hoarded, to be used only for those jurors an attorney didn't trust but couldn't crack.[2]

This time, the circumstances were much more favorable. From Walter White's reports, Darrow understood that Frank Murphy was determined to give the defense every advantage he could, so challenging a juror for cause carried virtually no risk of judicial veto. Better still, under Michigan law, an attorney defending a client charged with murder received a generous thirty peremptory challenges. Since Darrow had not one but eleven clients, he went into jury selection with an extraordinary three hundred and thirty challenges, enough to reject three entire jury pools single-handedly. Securing that tremendous advantage was one of the key reasons he and Arthur Garfield Hays had decided against demanding separate trials for each of the defendants. Now the defense had the power to shape the perfect jury.[3]

Darrow knew what he wanted. A national magazine once asked him how to pick just the right juror. "Let us assume we are representing one of 'the underdogs'" in society, he replied. In that case, never accept a wealthy man: "He will convict, unless the defendant is accused of violating the anti-trust law, selling worthless stocks or bonds, or something of that kind. Next to the Board of Trade, for him, the penitentiary is the most important of all public buildings." A prohibitionist was just as poor a choice. "He is too solemn and holy and dyspeptic. He knows your client would not have been indicted unless he were a drinking man, and anyone who drinks is guilty of something, probably worse than what he is charged with, although it is not set out in the indictment." All women should be dismissed, since they have only recently been allowed to serve on juries "and take their new privilege seriously." Avoid any Presbyterian—"He believes in John Calvin and eternal punishment; get rid of him in the fewest possible words before he contaminates the others"—and reject all Baptists, as "they too are apt to think that the real home of all outsiders is Sheol." If a defense attorney must choose a religious man, pick a Catholic, since "he loves music and art; he must be emotional and will want to help you." An Englishman is acceptable: "He comes from a long tradition of individual rights and is not afraid to stand alone; in fact, he is never sure he is right unless the great majority is against him." So, too, a German, though he "is not so keen about individual rights except where they concern his own way of life. . . . Still he wants to do what is right, and he is not afraid." And then there were the Irish, Darrow's ideal jurors. "An Irishman is called into the box for examination. There is no reason for asking about his religion. He is Irish; that is enough. We may not agree with his religion, but it matters not, his feelings go deeper than any religion. You should be aware that he is emotional, kindly and sympathetic. If he is chosen a juror, his imagination will place him in the dock; he is trying himself. You would be guilty of malpractice if you got rid of him, except for the strongest of reasons."[4]

That was Darrow the court jester, standing the social order on its head, laughing all the while. The humor must have struck younger sophisticates as a tad old-fashioned: florid Catholics, freethinking Germans, and misty-eyed Irishman may have seemed the shocking antithesis of polite society in the small towns of nineteenth-century Ohio, but the avant-garde had long since passed that honor to the Bohemians, Italians, Russians, Poles, and Negroes who filled the modern city's poorest quarters. If Darrow's cultural criticism wasn't quite up-to-date, his understanding of social conflict remained as sharp as the day he set aside his regular practice to defend the saintly Eugene V. Debs. Across America, there were millions who knew that the powerful and the pious looked down on them because they'd been born in the wrong country, they worshipped in the wrong church, they belonged to the wrong class, or their skin was too dark a shade. Those who recognized these bitter realities were just the sort of people Darrow wanted to fill a jury box, because when he put society's bigotry and brutality on trial, those were the citizens whom, he believed, would take his side.[5]

And in the trial's brief weekend recess, it became clear to Darrow that Detroit was full of the people he wanted to find.

◆

Johnny Smith's voice was reduced to a rasp as he headed into the final few days of the mayoral campaign. With the election scheduled for Tuesday, November 3, he maintained a feverish pace, barnstorming through the east side, his entourage enveloped in ever-larger crowds wherever he appeared. Hundreds gathered at St. Hedwig's Church, in Black Bottom's Masonic hall, and at the Moose Temple. Fifteen hundred greeted him at the Elks headquarters, two thousand at the Dom Polski Hall, and a reported six thousand at the downtown Detroit armory, just three blocks from Hastings Street. Yet however weak his voice, however much fatigue his face revealed, when Johnny Smith started to speak, he pulled them all to their feet—the workingmen, the ethnics, the Negroes, and the middle-class reformers—with his uncompromising attacks on the enemy they shared. "Kill forever this unholy, un-American thing—the Ku Klux Klan," he told the throng at Dom Polski. "Go to the polls. See to it that your wives and sisters and brothers, your friends and your neighbors go to the polls. You have a sacred duty to perform. It is not to elect John Smith mayor. That is of little importance. Your duty is to serve notice for all time upon the forces of intolerance and bigotry that they have no place in an American community. . . . Keep Detroit an American city!"[6]

For those who didn't find their way into Smith's rallies—two thousand were turned away from the armory because there wasn't an inch of space in which to put them—the mayor's supporters spread his message through a furious last-minute assault on the Invisible Empire. Both the *Detroit Times* and the *Detroit Free Press* reached their overwhelmingly working class readerships with front-page editorials so fierce they seemed almost incendiary. "When a Catholic or a Jew or a Negro of the A.E.F. went slogging in the mud beneath the Flanders stars to hellish death beyond," sneered the editor of the *Detroit Free Press* in an open letter to the Klan's campaign manager, Ira Stout, "some people called it Americanism, but you and I, Ira, refused to be misled. We had small sympathy for those women back home who cried over the O'Reillys, the Cohens and the Bert Williamses in the roll of casualties. Americanism, we know, is a special monopoly of native-born white Protestants."[7]

A phalanx of religious leaders rallied the faithful. Once again, Reinhold Niebuhr led the attack. "The tragedy of today is that so many Protestants are being corrupted by prejudice instead of using their influence to dispel intolerance," he declared in a perfectly timed Sunday evening address. "Prejudice has supplanted the American ideal of brotherhood and good will. The bestial attitude of our jungle ancestry flames up anew." At Temple Beth El, the oldest and most prestigious synagogue in the city, Rabbi Leo Franklin pleaded with Detroit Jewry to stand up for "the American ideal of freedom and equality and the rights of men which you wish to hand down unsullied and unstained to your children." And imperious Bishop Michael Gallagher, the son of an Irish-born boilermaker, fairly shook with fury as he condemned the Klan's attempt "to make Detroit the 'Atlanta' of the north, in preparation to undo the work of Grant, Sherman and Lincoln, who preserved . . . the unity of the nation and the equality of all citizens—black or white, Jew or Gentile, native or foreign born."[8]

Black Bottom, meanwhile, was flooded with copies of the Saturday, October 31, issue of the *Chicago Defender*, which proclaimed that twelve million Negroes were waiting for their brothers and sisters in Detroit to "deal the death blow to the Ku Klux Klan." Colored men and women hardly needed the encouragement. When Smith's opponent, Charles Bowles, tried to deliver a long-planned address at a hall on Sherman Street, not far from Otis Sweet's empty office, he was all but driven from the stage. By Monday night, emotions were running so high the police department was readying its riot squad, should Election Day descend into violence.[9]

There was no violence, though, just a massive outpouring of voters, a quarter million of them, filling polling places from the moment they opened Tuesday at 7:00 A.M.—slightly too late for those who worked the auto factories' morning shifts—until they closed at eight o'clock that evening. The Klan vote slipped somewhat on the west side, while Johnny Smith swept through the east side with extraordinary force. In the heart of Black Bottom, Smith won 2,048 votes, Bowles just 94, while the precinct around Clinton Street, Ossian's first home on the ghetto's edge, gave Smith 447 votes to Bowles's 43. The near east side immigrant wards went for Smith by margins of two or three to one. And even in the Garland Avenue area—bloody Garland—Smith beat Bowles by 68 votes. By midnight, word was leaking out of city hall. Smith had been reelected by a 31,000 vote margin.[10]

Only then did trouble flare. Some thirty Klansmen were gathered on the sidewalk outside the Invisible Empire's headquarters north of downtown when a motorcade of three hundred Smith supporters rumbled into view. In panic, the Kluxers fled inside, where they huddled together awaiting assault. A few rocks were thrown, some windows smashed. Then one courageous Klansmen, J. S. White, strode out the front door cradling a rifle and threatening to shoot into the crowd. A squad of policeman arrived before he had the chance to open fire, and with a quick, efficient show of force, order was restored. The next day's newspapers buried the incident beneath an avalanche of election news. But perhaps Fleta Mathies, Vollington Bristol, or the Sweet brothers noticed it—and smiled.[11]

Clarence Darrow must have smiled, too, in his silent way. He never commented on the election—not to the pack of reporters who followed his every move in the courtroom, not in the numerous lectures he gave while he was in Detroit, not in the memoir he wrote a decade later. But he had to have read at least some of the weekend's papers, which put the initial accounts of the trial right alongside detailed reports of the campaign's final furious days. On Saturday, he heard the assurances of his lunchtime companion, one of the city's most generous Jewish philanthropists, who said that the bitterness that had gripped Detroit throughout the long summer had in the last few weeks begun to give way.[12] And he was confident that the time was right to pick a jury.

When Darrow returned to court Monday morning, Arthur Garfield Hays finally at his side, his mood was positively buoyant. To squash the heckling of the previous session, White had stacked the gallery with members of the Talented Tenth, including two of the most powerful pastors in Black Bottom, Joseph Gomez and Everard Daniels. As it turned out, the spectators had few opportunities to give the jurors a hard time. Though he still had 307 of his peremptory challenges remaining, Darrow and Hays dismissed only eight veniremen that day, six of them for cause, before declaring that they were satisfied. Prosecutor Toms spent the balance of Monday undoing most of the defense's handiwork, clearing out nine jurors with his peremptory challenges and another fifteen for cause. Even that didn't seem to bother Darrow, who seemed more intent on winning over the courtroom with his gentleness than in crushing whatever snakes may have been lurking in the jury box. "[He] is the most amazing figure I've ever seen," Walter White wrote, one master manipulator admiring the work of another. "He's got the . . . judge, clerk, [and] attendants all with him. Most of the jurors are eager—too eager in view of the strength of the Klan here—to serve, and he every so often makes some droll remark that sets the entire court to laughing and instantly all tension is relieved." By the close of court Monday, the jury was still completely in flux, but Darrow headed off to dinner confident that after Tuesday's election he would have no trouble settling on twelve men and women to his liking.[13]

Robert Toms opened Wednesday as he had finished Monday, moving veniremen in and out of the box in search of the perfect combination. Three potential jurors he dismissed for cause and four others, the only women on the panel, he eliminated with his peremptory challenges, so that by the time he was done, shortly after lunch, half the jurors who had begun the day in the box had been replaced. Although they had the ability to reject all of Tom's choices, Darrow and Hays asked just one to step down: a clerk at Studebaker who defiantly admitted to being a member of the Klan, the third member of the Invisible Order that the defense had ferreted out of the jury pool. A substitute was selected. Then Darrow signaled to the bench that he would ask no more questions. The jury was set.[14]

The panel wasn't as cohesive as it might have been had Darrow taken more time with the selection process. All the jurors were white, as everyone in the courtroom knew they would be. But beyond that obvious similarity, the differences among them seemed great. A handful spoke with immigrants' accents—a Scot's burr, a German's throaty rumble—though most had the flat twangs of native midwesterners. Seven were Catholic, the others, presumably, from various Protestant denominations or of no faith at all. Many of them were family men with children at home, though John Welke, at seventy-three, was well beyond that stage of life, while twenty-one year old John Moralle, who still lived with his parents, was yet to enter it. They came from all across the city, from the relentlessly grim factory district on the southwest side, not far from where Henry Ford was building his monumental Rouge Plant, to within walking distance of the bungalow on Garland Avenue, and one man, Harold Anderson, lived so close to Spokane Avenue that he would have heard the mob's cheers the night they drove out Alexander Turner. Some were homeowners, others renters, and several boarded with relatives.

Even in his haste, though, Darrow hadn't neglected what he considered the basics. The jury had the class bias he hoped to see. John Welke and William Whalen had retired, and poor John Zang couldn't seem to keep a job. All the others were working men: six were factory hands, one a housepainter, another an electrician, yet another a streetcar conductor. Though most of the twelve were native-born, every one of them was related to immigrants. Zang's parents had come to the United States from Alsace-Lorraine, his wife's people from Ireland. William Irvine's parents were Scots—dreaded Presbyterians, most likely—John Geis's wife was French Canadian, and Charles Naas's in-laws Bohemian, born and raised in Prague. There was no saying whether any of the jurors had voted for Johnny Smith. But they were the sort of people who had packed the mayor's rallies, cheering as he condemned intolerance, jeering the Klan. One day after Smith's victory, Darrow had twelve of them in the jury box.[15]

As the clerk of the court prepared to administer the jurors their oath, the Great Defender leaned over the press table on the opposite side of the room. "The case is won or lost now," he said sotto voce. "The rest is window dressing."[16]

◆

When the proceedings resumed at half past nine on Thursday, November 5, the courtroom had been transformed into a tableau of American justice. On a simple bench along one wall sat the eleven defendants, Ossian and Gladys side by side on the far end, exchanging occasional whispers but otherwise watching events with grim-faced concentration. Against the opposite wall sat twelve of their peers—in name if not in fact—arranged in two neat rows of chairs set behind a low railing. Between the two groups in the well of the courtroom stood the representative of the people, the accuser facing the accused as the finest of Anglo-Saxon traditions required, a handsome young white man come to say why eleven Negroes should spend the rest of their lives in prison paying for their crimes.[17]

The thought of squaring off against Clarence Darrow would have terrified many prosecutors, but Robert Toms refused to be intimidated. At the preliminary hearing, his office had presented just enough testimony to assure that the case would move forward. Now he wanted to overwhelm the court with witnesses willing to say that there had been no hint of violence on Garland until the Negroes started to strafe the street with gunfire. Twenty policemen were scheduled to appear for the prosecution—a parade of blue sure to impress the jury—as were forty-one of the Sweets' Garland Avenue neighbors. It wasn't a random sample of neighbors, either. To finalize the list, Toms had worked hand in hand with the officers of the Waterworks Park Improvement Association, who knew far better than he did which of the people who lived along Garland's row of houses could be trusted to say just the right thing. The association's officers themselves—James Conley, Charles Garrett, and Harold McGlynn—were kept off the witness list, so as to protect the prosecution from the secrets they might reveal under Darrow's withering cross-examination.[18]

Toms also prepared himself. Like almost everyone else in the country, he had followed the Scopes trial the previous July, and he knew that if he pushed his case too hard, Darrow would turn on him the way he'd turned on William Jennings Bryan, making him into the foil for whatever countercase the defense intended to make. So Toms decided that there would be in his performance no imitation of brilliant William Borah, Darrow's opponent in the Haywood trial, who could make the courtroom shake with his thunder, nor of the late lamented Bryan, filling Dayton, Tennessee, with bombast and bluster. Instead, Toms intended to move calmly through his witness list, piling fact upon fact, impression upon impression, a thoroughly professional, incessantly polite young man preparing to debate a point of law rather than a crusading prosecutor bringing eleven murderers to justice. "I began a studied course of humility," he said years later. "I was almost obsequious at times, and I showed [Darrow] the utmost deference." All the better to throw the old man off his stride.[19]

So when Arthur Garfield Hays demanded that the prosecution not be allowed to call its first witness until it presented to the court a bill of particulars—a maneuver designed to constrict the state by forcing it to define precisely the charges it intended to prove—Toms replied with a presentation so bloodless the jurors' eyes must have glazed over: "The theory of the people in this case," he told them, as if they were a panel of particularly strict professors of law, "is that the defendants premeditatedly and with malice aforethought banded themselves together and armed themselves with a common understanding and agreement that one or more of them would shoot to kill. . . . Further, the deceased came to his death by a bullet fired by one of the defendants, aided and abetted by all the others, in pursuance of their common understanding as set forth above." And when Darrow, slouched nonchalantly in a chair he'd pulled alongside the jury box, interrupted his examination of the first few witnesses with a string of offhand comments, Toms let the remarks pass him by while he concentrated on putting the preliminary pieces of evidence into place. A neighbor who had identified the victim's body at the morgue testified that it was indeed Leon Breiner, and the county coroner explained how the bullet that had killed him had ripped through the body from back to front, a passage he illustrated by tracing a line across the torso of the assistant prosecutor, Lester Moll.[20]

Then, shortly before noon the first day, Toms turned to the core of his case. He called Norton Schuknecht to the stand.

In his sharp dress uniform, brass buttons gleaming, gold-braided hat neatly positioned on his lap, the inspector cut a surprisingly impressive figure. Toms knew better than to expect an equally impressive performance once Schuknecht started talking. For most of the first morning, he led the inspector through the events of September 9, and with Schuknecht's terse answers, he laid the foundation upon which the state would rest its argument for conviction. Yes, his men had the situation under control that evening. No, there was no crowd on the street, "nothing more than the ordinary person walking by." Yes, there had been a few people standing on the lawn directly across from the Sweets: "I daresay there were ten or twelve," but they were "simply standing there and talking, as far as I know, I didn't see them do anything." No, those folks hadn't been throwing rocks or yelling or threatening the bungalow in any other way before the Negroes opened fire. Yes, immediately after the shooting he had gone into the pitch-black house, where his men found an arsenal of rifles and pistols but very little else, just "a few chairs and a very small table," a couple of mattresses, and "a roast of some kind standing on the oven." It was an ominous image—eleven heavily armed Negroes hidden away in an all but empty house, waiting for the opportunity to commit evil acts—and Toms let it linger as he turned from Schuknecht and stepped back toward the lawyer's table, the prosecution's most difficult task successfully completed.[21]

◆

Over the next week, Toms built on his first day's work. From his parade of policemen, the prosecutor gathered a host of damning details that rounded out Schuknecht's account. Ranking officers told of the protective cocoon that surrounded the Sweets as soon as they arrived on Garland Avenue. Within an hour of Ossian and Gladys moving into the bungalow on September 8, detective inspector Bert McPherson said, he was at their front door, telling the couple "that any time of the day or night that [they] seen anything that looked suspicious to call me."[22]

From that point on, Sergeant Clayton Williams explained, the Negroes were under continual guard, provided by himself and four other patrolmen during the day and by Inspector Schuknecht each evening. And Deputy Superintendent James Sprott, second in command in a force of twenty-six hundred, described how he had personally reviewed the protective measures just an hour before the incident and found them wholly satisfactory. The men in Schuknecht's squad recalled the shooting itself. The inspector's right-hand man, Lieutenant Paul Schellenberger, saw the gunfire blaze from the bungalow's front windows; Sergeant Joseph Neighbauer heard the bullets whistle over his head as he raced across Charlevoix Avenue to call for reserves, and patrolmen Frank Lee Gill, posted in the alleyway behind the bungalow, watched two black men burst onto the second-story airing porch at the back of the house and squeeze off eight or ten shots into the street; Gill returned fire but the colored men slipped back inside unscathed.[23]

The officers who followed Schuknecht into the bungalow after the shooting told of the sparsely furnished rooms—that image again—and of the guns they found hastily hidden under mattresses and inside dresser drawers. When the patrolmen finished testifying, Toms had them come down from the witness stand to identify the weapons he'd piled up on the lawyers' table as those they'd brought out of the Sweets' home on the night Breiner died.[24]

The most dramatic testimony, though, came not from those who swarmed into the Sweets' home after the shooting but from one of the officers who stayed out on the street. Sergeant William Grohm arrived on Garland with the reserves that Schuknecht's men had summoned. No sooner had he and his fellow officers hopped down from the truck than he heard someone screaming that a man had been shot. Grohm rushed over to the Doves' front yard, where he found Leon Breiner sprawled on the porch steps, his shirt drenched in blood. "Did you see anything in the hands of the deceased?" asked Toms. "Not in his hands," Grohm answered, "not in his hands, no."

Toms led the witness to the place he wanted him to go. "Did you see anything in his mouth?" he said. "Yes, sir," replied the officer. "He had a pipe." The memory seemed so poignant—a glimpse of an ordinary life destroyed in a burst of inexplicable violence—that the moment she heard it, the widow Breiner, sitting beside her teenage daughter in the front row of the gallery, caught her breath and fainted dead away.[25]

When he turned from the cops to the Sweets' neighbors, Toms abandoned the compilation of specifics for a kaleidoscopic re-creation of the moments surrounding Breiner's death. Around the bungalow he moved, from in front of the school yard opposite the house, where seventeen-year-old Dwight Hubbard was waiting for the truck that would take him to the night shift at the Hudson Motor Car Company; to the intersection of Charlevoix and Garland, where Otto Lemhagen stood chatting with Norton Schuknecht; over to the corner market, where Edward Wettlaufer had gone to buy a loaf of bread, a bottle of milk, and a couple of bananas; to the steps of the house next door to the Sweets, where John and Della Getke were relaxing after their supper; back across the street to the Doves' front porch, where Ray Dove played with his baby, thirteen-year-olds George Suppus and Ulric Arthur were settled to watch for any excitement, and Eric Houghberg strode into a hail of gunfire; and north up Garland, where Bruce Stout was strolling on the way to visit his girl. No matter who was in the stand, Toms's questions remained the same. Was there any sort of crowd on the street before the shooting started? If a small group did gather, did the policemen move them along? Was there any threat to the peace—epithets shouted, rocks thrown, windows shattered in the doctor's house? From your angle, did you see or hear gunshots coming from the bungalow? Did you see the victim fall or hear him cry in pain?[26]

There were times when the witnesses stumbled. John Getke's recollection of events had been shaky enough when he'd spoken to Toms's assistant the day after Breiner's death. Under the pressure of the courtroom, his memory seemed to fail completely. Even the simplest facts escaped him—whether he'd been home for dinner on September 9, what time he heard the gunfire, whether he and his wife stayed inside all night after the shooting—and on crucial details, such as how many shots he heard fired from the bungalow, he refused to even venture a guess until Toms snapped, "Well, can you remember anything you sa[id], felt or heard," at which point Getke stopped talking altogether.[27]

Several others said too much. While you were waiting for your ride to work, Toms asked Dwight Hubbard, "what did you see happen?" "Well, there were a great number of people and the officers..." Hubbard began. Then he caught himself. "I won't say a great number— there were a large—" Again he stopped. "There were a few people there," he said, more sure of himself on the third try, "and the officers were keeping them moving; suddenly there was a volley of shots."[28]

Edward Wettlaufer started his testimony much more strongly. A poolhall proprietor who lived around the block from the Sweets, Wettlaufer described coming out of the corner grocery and turning up Garland toward the knot of people gathered on a nearby lawn. He was twenty feet from the Doves' porch, he said, when he heard the roar of the guns and saw Leon Breiner crumple to the ground. Toms was moving smoothly toward the last of his standard questions, quizzing Wettlaufer about conditions prior to the shooting, when things went wrong. "Did you hear any sound of broken glass?" he asked. "Yes," the man admitted, "I heard; I heard something sounded like glass breaking." Quickly, Toms tried to repair the damage. "Where did the noise come from," he pressed, "which direction?" "Well, I don't know just where it came from," Wettlaufer said, backtracking furiously. "I know it sounded like broken glass; it might have been the house and it might not." Toms ventured another question. "Was the glass broken before or after the shooting?" Wettlaufer hesitated. "Well," he finally said, "it was before."[29]

But such missteps were few and far between. It was often painful to watch the people of Garland struggling to keep their composure on the stand. Some were so scared they could barely get their stories out. Others tripped over their own tongues. Still others mangled words beyond all recognition: it took Toms several tries to understand that when his witnesses said they lived near "Gothee," they were talking about Goethe Street, one block north of the bungalow.[30]

For all their rough edges, though, the state's witnesses gave Toms precisely what he wanted. In the minutes before the shooting, there had been a group of five or ten people gathered around the Doves' house, swore witness after witness, while a few other folks meandered around the neighborhood or stood in the school yard. But there was no mob, and there hadn't been a hint of trouble—"everything was in peace and quiet," said Edward Belcher—until the Negroes started shooting.[31]

Some saw flames flashing from the upstairs windows; others heard the report of the guns; one or two swore they noticed the gunmen themselves in the shadows. Almost all agreed that there were fifteen or twenty shots, a brief pause, and then another, less intense blast of gunfire. It was the second volley that brought down Breiner, said those who hadn't run for cover after the first fusillade. "My God, I'm shot!" Eric Houghberg heard him say. But everyone else thought he just hollered, his hands clutching his chest, before he toppled onto the porch steps. By the time the cops came running over, pushing back the bystanders and pointing their flashlights into the victim's face, the man looked to be dead.[32] That's what they remembered, almost forty people repeating the same story, the same sequence of events, the same tragic climax, until the consistency of the telling became almost mind-numbing and the prosecution's case started to seem ironclad.

But for Hays and Darrow.

•

They worked in an exquisite choreography. On legal questions, Darrow invariably deferred to Hays, who time and again used his intimate knowledge of precedent and finely honed debater's skills to knock Toms off stride. When the prosecutor asked a police detective to say whether the weapons found in the bungalow had been fired any time close to September 9, Hays objected; too imprecise, he said. When Toms tried to supplement Ray Dove's testimony with photographs of the bullet-pocked front porch, Hays objected; the material was prejudicial, he insisted. And the moment Leona Breiner fainted, he leapt to his feet, arguing that such a tawdry attempt to play on the jury's sympathies was grounds for a mistrial.

Judge Murphy almost always sustained Hays's objections—even the defense must have been surprised when he agreed that photos of the crime scene weren't admissible—though he stopped short of declaring a mistrial over an incident that eight of the twelve jurors hadn't so much as noticed. But Hays wasn't counting victories. He was breaking the momentum of Toms's questioning, shattering the jurors' concentration on the witness stand, and reminding everyone that he was the foremost legal authority in the room. "He never asked the court," recalled Otis Sweet, who along with the other defendants took to celebrating whenever Hays won another challenge. "He demanded the court and brought up law to prove that he had a right to demand it. He'd give citations on every [point] . . . sometimes for as long as fifteen minutes in cases similar, from Florida to California. In fact, in my opinion he was a little too smart for the court."[33]

Once Toms turned his witnesses over to the defense for cross-examination, Hays slipped into the background and Darrow stepped forward. It was the sort of challenge he loved, taking on the prosecution's witnesses and finding a way to turn them into spokesmen for the defense. "The trying of a case in court calls for an acute intelligence, the capacity for instantaneous thought and for deciding what to do in the twinkling of an eye," he explained in his memoirs. "Most of the men in the [jury] panel have some sense, plenty of charity and understanding, and often have made mistakes themselves; in short, they generally are human and, after all, if a jury wants to save the client they can find a good reason why they should, and will. The problem is to bring about a situation where court and jury want a lawyer's client to win."[34]

Like Toms, Darrow adopted a professional appearance that surprised those who had come to know him through the Scopes extravaganza, but his demeanor remained as casual as it had always been. "The 'galluses' which featured in his appearances in the hot court house of Dayton are not on view," wrote a reporter that first week of the trial, "but their place is taken by the armholes of his vest, the place of repose for his thumbs when things are proceeding more or less normally." Some witnesses he dismissed with a question or two. There was no point in keeping Eric Houghberg on the stand a moment longer than necessary, for instance, so Darrow asked him whether the bullet that passed through his leg had ever been found, and when he had the answer he wanted—no, it hadn't—he sent the young man on his way.[35]

When Darrow saw an opportunity to deal the prosecution a blow, though, his homey manner gave way. Once on the offensive, noted the reporter, "his left arm hangs limp by his gangling figure while his right is thrust directly out from the shoulder, his index finger moving convulsively as he punctuates his questions," his soft voice suddenly replaced by a rattle of piercing questions.[36]

He began late in the morning of the first day, when Toms finished spinning out Norton Schuknecht's story and Murphy nodded for the defense to begin its interrogation. Darrow must have been tempted to go for the jugular, to bring down the prosecution's case with a slashing attack on its first significant witness. But this case required a more subtle touch. For close to four hours, Darrow kept Schuknecht on the stand, until the defender himself, too tired to continue, asked for a recess shortly before five o'clock. In the course of the long afternoon's questioning, he gradually transformed the inspector from the authority figure he had been under Toms's handling into the sort of sullenly indifferent cop at least some of the jurors would have recognized from their own dealings with the Detroit police.

In the month before Sweet moved into the house, Darrow asked, did you ever contact him to tell him he would have protection? When you heard that the people on Garland had formed the Waterworks Park Improvement Association, did you try to uncover the organization's intentions? On the nights of September 8 and 9, did you ask any of the bystanders on the street why they were there? When you had the traffic on Garland diverted shortly before the shooting, did you stop any of the motorists to ask what brought them into the neighborhood on a supposedly quiet Wednesday night? Did you so much as overhear any conversation on the street? Did you notice a taxicab with two Negroes pulling up to the house a few moments before the shooting began? Did you react in any way? No, no, no, Schuknecht answered again and again, always no, until, as the *Chicago Defender* reported, "Darrow gave a toss of his head and a shrug of his shoulders as if to ask, 'What did you do?'"[37]

There were moments, moreover, when Darrow forced Schuknecht to give the jury a glimpse of something worse than incompetence. As the day was winding down and exhaustion setting in, Darrow asked the inspector to describe again his search of the bungalow on the night of the shooting. Reinforcing the most powerful image of the morning's testimony seemed to be a tactical error, until Darrow brought Schuknecht back to the bungalow's front bedroom. Besides a bed and a few chairs, he asked, did you find anything else in the room? Schuknecht hesitated for a moment before replying, "I found a small stone." If Darrow was surprised by the concession, he didn't show it. "Did you find any broken glass?" he asked. Yes, the inspector admitted, there were shards scattered about the room. "Why didn't you mention finding broken glass on the floor?" demanded Darrow more sharply. "Why didn't you ask me?" Schucknecht fired back, his response so aggressive it made the omission seem all the more suspect. Darrow could have answered with a burst of righteous anger, but he chose a cooler approach. Would the fact that the glass was inside the house, he asked, "lead a policeman to the idea that [the stone] was thrown from outside?" "We found the stone on the inside, and I believe it was thrown from the outside," said Schuknecht. "I do not doubt that at all." Back at the lawyers' table, Toms slumped in his seat. "You cannot ask for anything better than that, can you?" he muttered loud enough for those in the well of the court to hear.[38]

But Darrow was just getting started. All that first week, he tried different angles of attack. There were the personal questions, quick and cutting. I suppose you didn't want Dr. Sweet as your neighbor, he said to Ray Dove. "I cannot say I am prejudiced against anyone," Dove answered. "Well, I am not talking about that," said Darrow. "You didn't want him in your neighborhood, did you—any colored man." Dove ventured another evasion—"I don't own property there myself," he said—but Darrow wouldn't let him slip away. "Is there any trouble about your answering that question," he demanded, so that Dove felt he had to give a proper response. "I don't believe in mixing people that way," he replied, "colored and white." "Well now," Darrow said, "with that preface you can answer it, can't you? You didn't want him there?" "No," Dove admitted at last.[39]

Then there were the questions intended to shatter the silences the prosecution's story imposed. Are you a member of the Waterworks Park Improvement Association, Darrow asked witness after witness, hoping that the question would open to the jury the series of threats that had terrorized his clients in the months before they moved to Garland Avenue. No, said Russell Burns, who lived a block north of the bungalow, though his sister, who owned the house, belonged. No, said real estate agent Raymond Alf, without mentioning that his business partner was the association's leading figure. Yes, said Della Getke, while she furiously chewed a wad of gum; both she and her husband, silent John, had signed up. But as soon as she had made that admission she was struck with the same amnesia that had afflicted her husband when he testified. "Did anyone stop by to talk about the organization before you joined," Darrow asked. "I don't remember," she replied. When did you join? "I can't remember." Where were you when you joined? "I couldn't say." Did you attend any meetings? "Not that I know of." His frustration rising, Darrow tried a different approach. "Do you know what the group was for," he asked. "Sure," Mrs. Getke answered. "Improvement."[40]

It was harder still for Darrow to crack the witnesses' accounts of the fatal night. No matter how long he kept the policemen on the stand, he couldn't shake their testimony the way he'd rattled Schuknecht. In fact, their stories seemed to harden under pressure: every time he asked an officer how many people were on the street before the shooting, the number seemed to shrink. There had been "eight or ten" at the Doves' place, said Sergeant Neighbauer, and another "eight or ten" on the school-yard lawn. There wasn't anyone at all in the school-yard, said patrolman Walter Doran, though there were "seven or eight" people out along Charlevoix. Doran's partner, Ernest Stanke, saw six people on Charlevoix; officer Roy Schaldenbrand saw only three or four; and Deputy Superintendent Sprott didn't notice anyone anywhere in the neighborhood. "No one standing north of Charlevoix on Garland?" Darrow asked. "No sir." "Nobody standing around the schoolhouse corner?" "No sir." "And nobody on the south side of Charlevoix?" "I didn't see anybody," Sprott insisted. "Well, you looked to see, didn't you?" sneered Darrow, but Sprott remained adamant. "I didn't see anyone," he repeated, as if Darrow hadn't heard him the first time. But Darrow was already moving the interrogation in a different direction. If Garland was deserted, he demanded, why did you order your men to close the street to traffic a half an hour before the shooting occurred? "Precaution," Sprott laconically replied.[41]

Most of the witnesses from Garland Avenue were just as stiff-necked. Like Ray Dove, Harry Monet, Otto Eberhardt, Florence Ware, Abbie Davis, and Eban Draper all admitted to Darrow that they didn't want coloreds in their neighborhood. But even under the Great Defender's most relentless cross-examination, they wouldn't concede that anything more than idle curiosity brought them onto the street the night of the shooting, or that while they were there they saw even a hint of danger for the Negroes barricaded inside the bungalow. Finally, Darrow's patience snapped. "You understand these eleven people are on trial, charged with murder, don't you?" he thundered at Draper, whose house was opposite the Howe School. "Are you reluctant to tell what you really know, where a life sentence is in danger?" Toms's assistant, Lester Moll, shouted out an objection but Darrow ignored him. "Are you reluctant to tell us what you know, fully and frankly," he said again. "Are you reluctant to tell it?" "What do you mean?" Draper stammered. "Well, I don't think I could explain the word," Darrow fired back. "You know the meaning of the word, don't you?" "No," said Draper, and Darrow threw up his hands in exasperation, started to say something to Murphy, thought better of it, then silently turned his back on the witness.[42]

There were other witnesses, though, who couldn't stand up to Darrow's assault, and when they fell, the prosecution's carefully constructed case threatened to tumble with them. Dwight Hubbard had already tripped over Toms's question about the size of the crowd on Garland when Darrow walked slowly up to the young man to begin his cross-examination. "When you first started to answer the question," Darrow began, "you started to say you saw a great crowd there, didn't you?" "Yes, sir," Hubbard responded. "Then you modified to say a large crowd, didn't you?" "Yes, sir." "Then you said a few people after that?" "Yes, sir." "Do you know how you happened to change your mind and whittle it down so fast?" "No, sir," said Hubbard. "You have been talked to a great deal about it, haven't you?" "No, sir." "Any [police] officers talk with you about it?" Darrow asked as he gazed distractedly out the window. "Just Lieutenant Johnson" (the detective in charge of the investigation), said Hubbard, "if you consider him an officer." "Well, I suppose he does," Darrow said, "and I haven't any reason to think otherwise. . . . How many times did he talk with you about it?" "Once." "And you kind of forgot you were to say a few people, didn't you, when you started in?" Toms tried to object—"Just a minute," he shouted, "that is an innuendo. . . ."—but Murphy overruled him. Darrow repeated the question: "When you started to answer [Toms's] question, you forgot to say a few people, instead of a great many?" "Yes, sir," said Hubbard, and the courtroom burst into laughter.[43]

No one laughed when Alf Andrews broke. The forty-four-year-old foreman undoubtedly found his way onto the witness list because the officers of the Waterworks Park Improvement Association knew he was dependable: he and his wife, Mabel, owned the home next door to the association's president, Harold McGlynn, and it's hard to imagine that the two men hadn't stood at the backyard fence some warm summer night in 1925 discussing how much they hated the thought of Negroes living down the block from them; when the association's membership cards were passed up and down the street that July, he'd signed his name and handed over the dollar it cost to join. But Andrews, tough enough to make his living whipping factory hands into shape, wasn't tough enough to withstand Darrow's most vigorous cross-examination. Almost all afternoon Thursday, November 12, Darrow pushed and pushed, until Andrews revealed the secrets the prosecution had hoped to keep hidden from the jury. He did indeed belong to the Waterworks Park Improvement Association, he said; he'd been at the association's mid-July rally at Howe Elementary; and the crowd that night had been huge—six hundred people was his guess—an entire neighborhood came out, as Andrews himself had come out, to demand that Garland remain lily-white.[44]

When thirteen-year-olds George Suppus and Ulric Arthur were on the stand, Darrow took a softer approach. The defender's looming presence so scared the boys that he took a few steps back from them, moving almost to the lawyers' table, then with the utmost gentleness, he walked them through the evening of the shooting: finishing dinner, walking down to the corner to see the policemen, settling onto the Doves' steps. Gradually, the boys relaxed—it was so hard to resist the old man's charm—and as they did, the truth came tumbling out. Everybody on the porch was talking about the colored family, George and Ulric agreed; that's how they passed the time as darkness fell.

Then a taxi pulled up in front of the bungalow and let off two colored men, who dashed into the house. "Did you see anyone throw any stones," Darrow asked Ulric. "Well," he answered, "there was four or five kids between the houses, they were throwing stones." "Where were they throwing them?" "They were throwing them at the house where the colored people moved in," Ulric said. "Did you hear the stones hit the house?" "Yes, sir." Do you know whether any of them broke any glass?" "I heard glass break," said the boy. "I guess it was the stones." "And the shooting occurred right after it, didn't it," Darrow said. "Well . . ." Ulric began before Darrow cut him off with a commanding, "What?" "Yes, sir," the boy meekly replied.[45]

There it was, a simple, honest account shining through a thousand lies. And all Darrow could do was hope that the twelve men sitting in the jury box would take hold of it like the precious thing it was.

◆

All through the first stages of the trial, Walter White pushed himself as hard as he had ever done before. From the moment James Weldon Johnson had heard that the Garland Fund was willing to help the NAACP create its longed-for Legal Defense Fund, he had set his staff to work full-time on the fund-raising circuit. So White spent the first two weeks of November scrambling from courtroom to train station, city to city, rally to rally across the Midwest, constantly talking of the trial and the principles for which it was being fought. The outpouring of support was nothing short of phenomenal. White's swing through the old abolitionist stronghold of northern Ohio—one bleary night in Cleveland, the next in Toledo—earned the fledgling Defense Fund almost seventeen hundred dollars in donations. After a quick stop back in Detroit to see Darrow complete jury selection, White was off again, this time to Chicago, where more than nine hundred NAACP stalwarts jammed a mass meeting to protest the Sweets' incarceration and the recent bombing of a South Side Chicago church, the latest in a string of terrorist attacks against Negroes stretching back almost eight years. From there, he raced to Minneapolis and St. Paul for a whirlwind of appearances that brought in another five hundred dollars. "Eighteen speeches since last Sunday!" he boasted to Johnson as he prepared to board the train back to Detroit to watch Darrow and Hays conduct their cross-examinations.[46]

The pace in Detroit was even more frenetic. Up at seven o'clock each morning, by half past nine White was at the courtroom, joining the stream of lawyers, politicians, and reformers who had angled the special passes they needed to sidestep the line of ordinary people—working stiffs with lunch pails in hand, church folks in their Sunday best, the young woman with a ukulele under her arm—who waited hours to catch a glimpse of the proceedings. "To get a seat without danger of personal injury," wrote one of the dozen reporters who crowded alongside White at the press table, "one almost has to be a friend of somebody who is 'somebody' in the court." Ruby Darrow attended every day, sitting close to the defense team so that she could keep a hawk's eye on her husband. Arthur Garfield Hays also brought his new wife, Aline, and Frank Murphy invited the young socialite he was then dating, who arrived chastely chaperoned by her mother, as the judge preferred her to be. All day long, White watched the quietly furious battle between Toms and Darrow, straining to hear the witnesses over the buzz of conversation from the overflowing gallery, adding to the cacophony by continually offering his fellow newsmen editorial suggestions that, more often than not, found their way into the next day's papers.[47]

When the workday was done, White joined Darrow and his oversized entourage as they headed out for long nights of talk, drink, and, when Ruby wasn't looking, a few flirtations. Almost every evening, it seemed, Darrow was on a stage somewhere in the city, preaching the modernist creed. At prestigious Orchestra Hall, he lectured on evolution; to the Detroit Federation of Labor, he talked of crime and punishment; at the swanky Penguin Club, he spoke on birth control; and at the colored YMCA, in the heart of Black Bottom, he addressed the problem of race. He never restricted himself to a single topic, though. Once he had his audience's attention, he roamed across the social questions of the day, slashing away at fundamentalists and self-styled patriots—"one hundred percent Americanism is a slogan for selling prunes," he told one gathering—eugenicists and white supremacists, capitalists, socialists, anarchists, anyone who fooled himself into believing he was wiser, better, more decent than the common run of humanity.[48]

Darrow "made everyone writhe as he pictured the injustices and immoralities of our present industrial system," Reinhold Niebuhr wrote after attending one lecture. "The tremendous effect of his powerful address was partially offset by the bitterness with which he spoke . . . [but] I suppose it is difficult to escape bitterness when you have the eyes to see and the heart to feel what others are too blind and too callous to notice." For his part, Darrow did what he could to keep from becoming too depressed. When he was finished speaking at an event, two or three hours after taking the stage, it was back to his hotel room for cocktails and conversation, Hays reciting verse, the Great Defender holding forth, their entourage of friends and hangers-on sitting entranced, too content or too tired to be bothered to call it a night.[49]

There were times when seeing Darrow in action must have made White wince. At the Penguin Club, the defender spotted a young woman, Josephine Gomon—a married mother of five, as it turned out—who had been in the courtroom several times during the first weeks of testimony. Gomon was a political activist in her own right, an associate of Harriet McGraw, Detroit's foremost progressive, and through McGraw, a friend and ally of Frank Murphy and Johnny Smith. All that mattered to Darrow, though, was that Gomon had a pretty face. The first chance he got, he sidled up to her, slid his hand around her arm, and guided her into the lobby. "Do you mind if I walk to the streetcar with you," he asked. "I'd be delighted," she replied, "but I'm driving." "Then you'll drive me home," he said, smoothly moving her out the door. As they headed toward the car, the seduction began. "Come up to my room," he told her. "I'm expecting a couple of interesting fellows and we'll read poetry." As soon as the invitation was extended, though, Harriet McGraw swooped down upon them, saying that she, too, could use a ride home. Darrow smiled and let his hand slip away. "You seem to be well protected," he whispered with obvious disappointment, an old reprobate suddenly condemned to spend another night in the company of his wife.[50]

His performance at the colored Y was even more embarrassing. As the session opened, it looked to be a triumph. Fifteen hundred people filled the cavernous auditorium; Detroit's Talented Tenth lined the dais; the press was there to record whatever Darrow had to say. But the guest of honor was in a particularly pessimistic mood—a particularly honest mood, he would have said—and his presentation quickly veered off in all the wrong directions. Had it not been for slavery, he lectured the crowd, "you might still be savages in Africa, and at that you might be better off there. But I still think civilization is worth the price we pay for it; what the white man paid in his upward struggle, what you are paying today." But Negroes shouldn't expect too much. Hope was an illusion, after all, conflict a constant. "If the race problem is solved, there will come along new maladjustments," he insisted. "Always the man on the ground has feared the newcomer, because he didn't understand him. If a white man went to the Congo he would be hated and misunderstood. That is your lot here. You have a long, hard road to travel, an arduous foe to fight, and that foe is prejudiced, a fact we have always had with us."

At last, he turned to the Sweets themselves, and for the briefest of moments, he seemed to get back on the message the NAACP wanted him to deliver. "I shall not discuss the case now being tried," he said, "but it is certain that a district built to house five thousand Negroes will prove a bit too small to accommodate the eighty thousand now in Detroit. Obviously they have to live somewhere." Then came the qualification: "And yet if they move into white neighborhoods they depreciate property values. That's true—and . . . I don't know what can be done about it." It was more than a qualification, really. It was a capitulation to the forces that were most responsible for segregating the great cities of the North and, worse yet, a confession that even the most sympathetic of white Americans couldn't imagine a nation truly defined by justice.[51]

Still, the Great Defender's star power was such that when the collection plates were passed through the crowd they came back filled. That day, $378.65 was taken in, 1 percent of the total the NAACP had to raise to create its Defense Fund paid in a pile of coins and crumpled bills that a lot of folks in the audience probably couldn't afford to surrender. So if White grimaced at Darrow's remarks, he didn't say anything.[52] He simply gathered up the donations and headed on to the next rally, the next speech, the next wearying train trip, knowing that the association was one step closer to the day when it would be able to fight its legal battles the way it saw fit rather than relying on those who, for all their goodwill, didn't understand just how much was at stake.

•

By all rights, Walter White should have skipped the morning session in court on Saturday, November 14, and spent the time catching up on his sleep. Thursday night's Penguin Club meeting had kept him out later than expected; Friday night he hadn't gotten to bed until four in the morning; and he had to be on a train by half past one Saturday afternoon so as not to miss his scheduled appearance at a rally of colored physicians in Chicago that evening. Despite what must have been crushing exhaustion, though, White was in his place at the press table when court convened at nine o'clock, waiting for the moment when

Robert Toms rested his case and the trial moved to its most challenging phase.[53]

White was sure that Darrow's cross-examination had shattered the
state's improbable version of events: "Every witness for the past three
days put on by the prosecution has helped the defense," he reported to
NAACP headquarters the previous evening. "Contradictions so glaring
as to be unmistakable have abounded and numerous of those testifying have been so obviously lying. . . ."[54] Now the truly hard work began. Over the next few days, the defense would have to replace the
prosecution's splintered story with another tale, so well told, so compelling that it would convince twelve white men that they should not—
could not—convict eleven Negroes of murdering a man very much like
the jurors themselves.

There were so many ways the defense's case could be constructed.
Darrow and Hays might have turned the courtroom into a classroom,
as they'd tried to do in Dayton the previous summer, filling the witness
stand with experts on the race problem—Du Bois, perhaps, or the brilliant sociologist Charles Johnson, author of the epic 1922 study *The
Negro in Chicago*—who could speak with authority on how the pressures of a segregated housing market pitted white homeowners against
black house hunters and, through that conflict, fostered in whites a
murderous rage. They could have overwhelmed the court with the
most imposing of character witnesses—the doctors of Dunbar Hospital, the businessmen who ran the Liberty Life Insurance Company,
professors from Wilberforce and Howard, the vicar of Gladys's church,
St. Matthew's Episcopal—who together might have convinced the jurors that the defendants were incapable of conspiring to commit a
heinous crime.

The cocounsels also thought seriously of trying to misdirect the
jury, arguing that the fatal shot came not from inside the bungalow
but from the alleyway, where patrolman Frank Lee Gill, a white south-
erner just five months on the force, had tried to shoot at the black men
he saw on the back porch but instead had fired wildly into the night.[55]
But each approach had its weakness: too bloodless, too indirect, too
far-fetched. And all of them ran the same terrible risk. Perhaps Darrow
had misjudged the jurors, made the wrong choices, acted too quickly
and too impulsively in putting them on the panel. Perhaps those
twelve men couldn't set aside the prejudices they carried with them
into the jury box. Perhaps they'd vote to convict no matter what.

To be safe, Darrow and Hays agreed that they would begin their case not with the grand opening statements of which they were capable but with a motion to the court to dismiss all charges against their clients. Only if the motion failed would the defense place before the jury the story it wished to tell, the pieces of which Hays was still assembling Thursday night.

White wasn't entirely pleased with the strategy. "There will be great advantage for us in putting in our testimony and finishing the job of education which gives the trial its greatest ultimate value," he complained to Johnson, and in "getting a verdict of acquittal by a jury which will influence public opinion infinitely more than a dismissal of the case by the judge." But Hays and Darrow were adamant. Of course, prolonging the courtroom battle would make for more dramatic political theater. But a conviction would be catastrophic, both for the defendants and for the cause for which the NAACP was fighting. Better to let the trial end with a whimper than with a crushing defeat. "So," said White with a resigned shrug, "we won't refuse a dismissal if Murphy should see fit to do it."[56]

Half of Saturday's session was finished before Toms's last witness completed his testimony and Hays rose to make his motion. Murphy immediately ordered the jury removed from the courtroom, then invited the defense to argue the motion's merits. For the balance of the day, the Sweets' counsel held the courtroom in their hands. For his part, Hays tripped the legal trap he had set on the first day of testimony, when he'd demanded that the prosecution present a bill of particulars. That document clearly stated that the state's case rested on a charge of conspiracy, he pointed out, yet, in nine days of testimony, the prosecution hadn't presented the court a single shred of evidence establishing that the defendants had joined together to plan Leon Breiner's murder. What's more, all the evidence they had presented—the large number of people inside the bungalow, the lack of furniture, the collection of guns—was not only circumstantial "but consistent with a lawful purpose." So, by the standards it had set for itself, the state had no case at all. Hays leavened the relentless logic of his argument with flattery so perfectly suited to Murphy's self-perception as to be utterly shameless. "I am aware of the responsibility and courage required of the court, especially in view of the prejudice of the community against the defendants," he said, "but the defense has the greatest confidence not only in your honor's learning and knowledge but also in your honor's courage." And just in case that appeal wasn't enough, he turned to a classic bit of courtroom razzle-dazzle. As the court sat hushed, trying to follow the tight twists of Hays's presentation, a baby suddenly burst into tears. Murphy asked the bailiff to have the infant taken out into the hall, but Hays objected. "That is the Sweet baby," he said with a flourish. "We had her brought in here as an illustration. Had she been in that house that night, she might well have been arrested and tried and the evidence here would condemn her to the same extent it does the defendants." Two decades later, Hays still relished baby Iva's exquisite timing. "What inspired that child to break out at that special moment, I don't know," he wrote in the 1940s. "The mother[-in-law] of Doctor Sweet had the baby in charge but I am certain that my instructions were merely to bring the child into the courtroom."[57]

When Hays was done, Darrow took over. He, too, hit at the logical gaps in the state's case. "It is very evident," he said, "[that] one bullet killed Mr. Breiner. It could have been fired by only one man and from only one gun. Suppose excitement should occur in this courtroom and someone was shot. Would everyone be charged with murder?" Mostly, though, he unleashed the righteous anger that had been building ever since Norton Schuknecht took the stand on the trial's first day. "It has been evident that the state's witnesses have purposely and consistently misstated the facts in this case," he insisted. "There was a meeting of five hundred or more persons of a society pledged to keep Negroes out of the district. A house had been bought by a Negro in a district that hitherto had been given over to the Noble Nordics. I know what racial and religious prejudices are. There was an organization in the neighborhood long before this family moved into their home. The police had escorted them into their home on the day of the moving. On September 8 people gathered around the home. [The Sweets] were besieged. On the ninth they were penned in. The crowds began to gather. That number grew larger. I am not maligning the police but I want to say here that they misstated the facts in this case. It was night. Out in the streets people moved. The worst and best we can say is that they had white faces."[58]

"I have never in my life heard such magnificent presentations," gushed White that evening, his reservations washed away in a wave of ebullience. "Hays the logician, relentless, keen, incontrovertible; Darrow the great humanist, pleading with fervor for decency and justice and tolerance, breathing into the law romance and beauty and drama. The jury was excluded during the motions but I am sure that had they heard Darrow they would have voted at once for an acquittal though they had heard none of our evidence."[59]

The weekend's optimism spiked even higher when the proceedings resumed on Monday. For the first time since the trial began, Toms came into court ready to make the defense a concession: the state was willing, he quietly informed Darrow and Hays, to drop all charges against Gladys Sweet. Although Gladys wouldn't even consider the possibility—she wanted no special favors, she said—the very fact that Toms had made the offer told the defense that the prosecutor's confidence was starting to crack. That impression had to have hardened during the morning session, as Toms struggled through his argument against the defense motion, his chain of thought repeatedly broken by Murphy's searching questions. By the time Toms stumbled to a finish, Walter White must have believed that victory was a hair's breadth away.[60]

It wasn't. Murphy never explained his decision to rule against the defense. Some thought it was a political move; Father Frank was planning to run for mayor himself one day soon, they said, and he didn't want to be known in white neighborhoods as the judge who freed the Sweets. Others claimed he'd been thinking of the Negroes: a verdict of not guilty would be much stronger coming from a jury rather than from the bench, that's what they said. Still others thought he'd made a principled stand. The prosecution hadn't proved conspiracy; that much was true. But neither had the defense proved the necessity of the Negroes firing thirty some shots into Garland Avenue. So Murphy listened politely to the lawyers' arguments, gave the question a few minutes' consideration, then set the defense's motion aside. The bailiff brought the jurors back to the courtroom, and Murphy signaled to Darrow that he was to begin making a case for the innocence of his clients. The defender deferred to Hays, who again stepped forward from the defense table, the defeat already shrugged off, and started to tell his tale.[61]

◆

Ossian was alone once more. Gladys was at his side, Henry and Otis a few feet down the defendants' bench, supporters and associates scattered in among the strangers who filled the gallery. Yet Ossian was alone, the thirteen-year-old on the train to Wilberforce, the medical student picking his way through the bloodied summer streets of Washington, D.C., the promising doctor sitting in the gloom of his new dining room, trying to beat back the fear welling inside him so that he might act like the man he thought he ought to be.

The story Hays told the jury was Ossian's story. His presentation had the requisite flights of oratory: an opening citation of William Pitt the Elder, authoritative and uncompromising, championing the ancient Anglo-Saxon right of self-defense; a closing recitation of the Harlem Renaissance's most gentle protest poem, Joseph Cotter's elegiac "And What Shall You Say?" But the balance of Hays's opening statement belonged to Sweet. Hays told Ossian to stand "so the jury can look you over"—an unfortunate choice of words, with their echoes of the slave market—and while the jurors stared at the handsome young man on the opposite side of the courtroom, the attorney talked of the doctor's rise from poverty, his years of hard work, his marvelous academic achievements, his loving marriage. He took the jury through the summer of 1925—through the terrors that confronted Bristol and Turner and Fletcher—and from there, he moved to Garland Avenue, into the bungalow on the night of the shooting, as Ossian thought not only of the mob on the street but of "lynchings . . . in various parts of the country, of negroes taken from policemen said to be guarding them and burned at the stake by slow fire, even of women mistreated by mobs . . . of East St. Louis and Tulsa and Chicago and Washington and Arkansas, where the lives of negroes have been wantonly taken." It was as if there were no other defendants, no other lives hanging on the jurors' decision, just this solitary man shouldering the brutal burdens of Black America.[62]

For the next two days, Ossian sat in silence as the defense used a dozen witnesses to flesh out Hays's account. John Fletcher and Vollington Bristol both took the stand to describe the attacks on their homes. Ossian's associate, Edward Carter, spoke of Sweet's agonizing decision to go through with his move after he learned of the west-side violence, and of the threats he received as word of his coming spread along Garland Avenue. Gladys's friends Serena Rochelle and Edna Butler told of the night they spent trapped inside the bungalow on September 8, so scared of the crowd gathered outside that they didn't dare go home. And in a riveting round of testimony, the defense led the jurors out onto the street on the night of the murder, out into the mob that the prosecution said didn't exist. Philip Adler, the white *Detroit News* reporter who happened on the troubles a few minutes before the shooting, said that at the intersection in front of the Sweet house the crowd was so thick—"between four hundred and five hundred people," he estimated—he had to elbow his way through it.

The number was confirmed by Bruce and Mary Spaulding, a handsome young black couple who were driving down Charlevoix shortly before the shooting; when they first saw the crowd milling around Garland, Mary Spaulding said, they assumed there must have been some sort of terrible accident. A young colored man, James Smith, and his uncle Alonzo recalled how they were out for an evening drive when, moments after the shooting, they ran into the police roadblock. They tried to turn around but before they knew it, a "considerable mob" was racing toward them, screaming racial epithets and throwing stones. Though the windshield was shattered, the Smiths managed to escape unscathed. Charles Shauffner wasn't so lucky. He, too, drove into the neighborhood by accident, he told the court, and when a mob swarmed his car, he was so panicked he stalled the engine. Somebody hit him in the head with a brick—he pointed to the scar above his left eye—but amid the blood and blinding pain, he somehow managed to get the car moving again. How many people were in the mob, asked Hays. "It seemed to me like five thousand," Shauffner said.[63]

Then, on Wednesday afternoon, November 18, Ossian heard Arthur Garfield Hays call his name. He rose from the defendants' bench, leaving Gladys and the others behind him, and walked the few paces to the witness stand, where the bailiff was waiting for him, Bible in hand.

Ossian didn't have to testify. No one could have objected to his refusing, so great was the responsibility: if he said the wrong word, put the wrong inflection in his voice, sat in a way that struck the jurors as too casual or too confident, grew rattled under cross-examination, succumbed to a single flash of anger, whatever sympathy Darrow and Hays had won for the defendants could be lost, the entire defense destroyed. But Ossian didn't refuse. Undoubtedly he agreed out of pride—the intoxicating sense that in the past few weeks he had become the representative of his race and the champion of its rights—and, as always, out of obligation. He would do what his lawyers wanted him to do, what his wife and brothers and friends needed him to do, what his colleagues surely expected him to do. He had no choice, really, but to take the stand.

Most of the examination was devoted to retelling the tale Hays had sketched out in his opening statement. In his precise and methodical way, the attorney walked Ossian through his life story from Bartow to Howard, Detroit to Paris, and back again. When that work was done, Hays asked the doctor to recall, one by one, the racial incidents that scarred him most. "Without hesitating for word or phrase," said a reporter, Ossian began to recite his litany of horrors: Fred Rochelle burning at the stake, the nameless colored man pummeled during the

Washington riot, the stories he'd heard of the Chicago pogrom. Toms tried to object to the line of questioning—certainly all this information was of no relevance to the case, he said—but Darrow, who had remained silent the entire afternoon, immediately countered with a response adapted from his defense of Leopold and Loeb. "This is the question of the psychology of the race," he argued, "of how everything known to a race affects its actions. What we learn as children we remember—it gets fastened to the mind. . . . Because this defendant's actions were predicated on the psychology of the past I ask that this testimony be admitted."

Murphy granted him the point, and the litany resumed: Ossian described the mob murder of Alexander Jackson in Tulsa and the Johnson brothers in the Arkansas countryside, the assault on Rosewood, Florida, and, finally, with Hays's prompting, of his reaction when he learned of the attacks on the west side the previous July. Though the information wasn't new, the presentation was absolutely gripping. Looking about him, Walter White thought the courtroom had been made "breathless" by Sweet's terrible accounting. A reporter from one of the Detroit dailies agreed. Sweet's intimate description "of morbid details," he said, "held the jury and spectators silent and immovable." Ever so slowly, Hays took Ossian back to Garland Avenue on the night of September 9. "Then began one of the most remarkable direct examinations to be found in all the records of criminal cases," wrote another reporter, young David Lilienthal, come to cover the trial for the *Nation*, "a vivid picture of the fear-ridden mind of a black man, terrified by a hostile crowd of whites outside his home."

"When did you first observe anything outside?" Hays asked.

"We were playing cards," Sweet said. "It was about eight o'clock when something hit the roof of the house."

"What happened after that?"

"Somebody went to the window and I heard them remark, 'People, the people!'"

"And then?"

"I ran out to the kitchen where my wife was. There were several lights burning. I turned them out and opened the door. I heard someone yell, 'Go and raise hell in front; I am going back.' I was frightened and after getting a gun ran upstairs. Stones kept hitting the house intermittently. I threw myself on the bed and lay there a short while—perhaps fifteen or twenty minutes—when a stone came through the window. Part of the glass hit me."

"What happened next?"

"Pandemonium—I guess that's the best way of describing it—broke loose. Everyone was running from room to room. There was a general uproar. Somebody yelled, 'There's someone coming.' They said, 'That's your brother.' A car had pulled up to the curb. My brother and Mr. Davis got out. The mob yelled, 'Here's niggers! Get them! Get them!' As they rushed in, the mob surged forward, fifteen or twenty feet—"

Ossian faltered—a second, no longer—and his hand slipped over his eyes. Darkness, like the darkness that had enveloped him as he lay in the bedroom that evening, soothing and terrifying. His body shuddered slightly, just enough for the men of the press to notice. Then his hand fell away and he glanced over to Gladys, tried to smile, and started to speak again.

"It looked like a human sea. Stones kept coming faster. I was downstairs. Another window was smashed. Then one shot—then eight or ten from upstairs. Then it was over."

"What was your state of mind at the time of the shooting," asked Hays softly.

"When I opened the door and saw the mob," Ossian said, "I realized I was facing the same mob that had hounded my people through its entire history. In my mind I was pretty confident of what I was up against, with my back against the wall. I was filled with a peculiar fear, the fear of one who knows the history of my race."[64]

Ossian Sweet, standing alone.

◆

It was done. The final four days of testimony had their dramatic moments: Ossian fending off Robert Toms's uncharacteristically aggressive cross-examination, his answers delivered with a dignity so fierce it was inspiring; Hays fighting with every legal weapon available to prevent the prosecutor from introducing into evidence Henry Sweet's admission on the night of the shooting that he had indeed fired into the crowd, only to suffer a rare defeat; the defense countering by calling Lieutenant William Johnson as a witness, then battering him with questions about the interrogation that night, which was intended, Hays implied, to force the defendants into confessing to a crime they didn't commit; Walter White making a surprise appearance on the stand to describe his extensive research into mob violence, a threat so pervasive, he explained, every Negro lived in terror of it. All of that testimony, though, was denouement. The moment Ossian opened the bungalow door for the jurors and let them see the Garland Avenue crowd through his eyes, Clarence Darrow had everything he needed to bring the trial to its conclusion.[65]

The final witness stepped down on Monday, November 23—the start of Thanksgiving week—but some last-minute legal wrangling prevented closing statements from beginning until the following morning. Although Detroit's most powerful radio station, WJR, intended to broadcast the proceedings so that the entire city and much of the Midwest could hear Darrow's plea to the jury, the crowds arrived at the courthouse even earlier than usual, knowing that the chance to watch the Great Defender at his finest would make the competition for seats particularly intense. As soon as the doors swung open, the crowd surged in, spectators pushing and shoving past one another; fistfights broke out, and a few of those who came to watch justice unfold instead found themselves spending the day in jail. Hundreds never even got inside. So they stood in the packed corridor for hours on end, determined to catch a fraction of the day's orations.[66]

The morning's session belonged to the prosecution. For two and a half hours, Toms's assistant, Lester Moll, led the jury through the facts of the case, "building a gigantic structure of reason," according to one of the numerous newsmen there that day, interspersed with "short sarcastic darts" at his esteemed rivals. "The defense has advanced a fear complex theory," he sneered. "It's poppycock; it's bunk. What a situation—a premeditated murder. If that's a fear complex . . . then give me something else."[67]

The defense took its turn after lunch. Arthur Garfield Hays led off with a slashing, sometimes rambling attack on the state's argument, complemented by the recitation of yet another Harlem Renaissance poem—a piece by Countee Cullen this time—and a final, soaring appeal to principle. "Gentlemen of the jury, the opportunity doesn't come often in life to do a great act," he said. "The writing of the Emancipation Proclamation for a nation is given to few. And yet you men here have an opportunity to write a charter of freedom, not for eleven men but for a race, for an oppressed race; you have an opportunity to write that charter of freedom by your verdict . . . and if you do that, gentlemen of the jury, you will do more to end all of the outrages than all the race commissions appointed by all the mayors of all the cities, of all the states, of these United States."[68] It was Hays's weakest performance of the trial, too highbrow for a jury full of workmen—one can only wonder what juryman John Zang thought of Cullen's poetry—and too convoluted to be convincing. But everyone knew that it was nothing more than a prelude. At three o'clock sharp, Darrow sidled up to the rail in front of the jury box. Instantly, the normally clamorous courtroom fell into a deep silence, so that the only sound came from the defender's gentle, weary voice. "If the court please and gentlemen of the jury," he began, "I wish it was not my turn, that I didn't feel it was my duty to talk to you in this case. It is not an easy matter to talk about a case of this sort, and I am afraid it won't be an easy matter to listen but you can't help it any more than I can."[69]

With that, Darrow was off and running. He spoke until half past six that evening, spent another night on the town, and when court resumed the next morning at nine o'clock, he started up again, sweeping the courtroom with a great torrent of softly spoken words. There were almost no histrionics; Darrow "just chatted with [the jurors]," Toms said later, drawing them and the audience gathered around them into his confidence, challenging them as he'd challenged so many before them to abandon the self-deceptions that gave them comfort and to face the world as it truly was.[70]

First, he talked of "the everlasting problems of race and color and creed that have always worked their evil in human institutions." He talked of prejudices "that have been taught to us and that began coming to us almost with our mother's milk, and they stick almost as the color of the skin sticks." He talked of the evils that prejudice produces, the way "it will take good, kindly, human men and women and make them fiends [who] throw reason to the wind and throw justice to the wind and throw mercy to the wind." And he admitted, the way only a man of Darrow's confidence could admit, that the jurors surely were prejudiced themselves, as was he, though he liked to think otherwise. "I would guess that some of you—maybe most of you—believe that colored people should have one neighborhood and white people the other," he said. "If you ask me what I think about it, I would say I don't know. That is an idea—I have an idea that that is not the right way, but I can very well understand that many very rational and considerate white people believe it; I can very well understand it." As he spoke, wrote David Lilienthal, "the old man with the unalterably sad face and the great stooped shoulders seemed no mere lawyer pleading for hire. He seemed, instead, a patriarch out of another age, counseling his children, sorrowing because of their cruelty and hatred, yet too wise in the ways of men to condemn them for it."

When Darrow turned to the weeks of testimony, though, his sorrow became tinged with gall. He understood, he said, that the seventy people who testified for the state were "in the ordinary affairs of life honest and decent. . . . But in this case man and woman and child alike have come into this court and under oath have deliberately lied to send eleven people to the penitentiary for life . . . and there is not an officer who has testified in this case that is not partially guilty of this murder and who to shield himself has not perjured himself on account of the character of this case." No one was fooled, though, because there wasn't a person in the courtroom, "whether he be a policeman, a neighbor, a prosecutor, a juror, a mere spectator, that does not know what happened" on Garland Avenue that terrible night.

Then with the seasoned lawyer's dexterity, Darrow smoothly slid the tragedy into the political conflict that had roiled Detroit for the past year, transforming the people of Garland from ordinary folks into proxies for the Klansmen that the men of the jury—all of them members of the city's sprawling working class, all of them connected in some fashion to the immigrant masses—were likely to despise. "Up and down the street were the lines of these Noble Nordics"—that phrase again, so perfectly chosen—"father and mother and child, a lodger, a boarder, a tenant, and friends coming from far and near, lined up on their front porches and cast a glassy eye over toward the Sweet house and waited to see what happened. . . . They were gathered together just the same as the Roman Coliseum used to be filled with a great throng of people with their eyes cast to the door where the lions would come out; they were gathered together just as in the old days a mob would assemble to see an outdoor hanging and waiting for the victim with their eyes set on the gallows. . . . And they were gathered together to awe and to intimidate the poor black family which had bought the corner house and who had a right to buy it under every law of the land. That is why they were there." And they'd done it all—the conspiracy, the mobbing, the perjury—"in behalf of what they think is their noble Nordic race."

And that, said Darrow, was the story's bitter irony. For the testimony proved that the ignoble Nordics of Garland Avenue were determined to purge from their neighborhood—"not especially a high-toned neighborhood at that, nothing swell about it"—people who were clearly their betters. "We have presented witnesses that are as intelligent, as attractive, as good-looking as any white man or woman," he insisted, "and who are as far above the bunch which testified against these men as the heavens are above the earth and you know it and they know it." Think of Gladys's friends Edna Butler and Serena Rochelle, he commanded the jurors, "bright, intelligent, cultured, truthful, modest" young women, so much more impressive than the white women who testified for the state. Think of Walter White, "the peer of any man in this courtroom." Think of the defendants sitting across from the jury box, "half of them are at least college graduates or attending college. . . . They would compare almighty favorably with anybody who lives around the corner of Garland and Charlevoix."

Think, most of all, he continued, of brilliant Dr. Sweet, seeing in the mob the history of his race, "loaded like sardines in a box in the middecks of steamers and brought forcibly from their African homes, half of them dying in the voyage. He knew they were sold like chattels as slaves and were compelled to work without pay; he knew that families were separated when it paid the master to sell them; he knew that even after he had got liberty under the Constitution and the law he knew that . . . in every state of the Union telegraph poles had been decorated by the bodies of Negroes dangling to ropes on account of race hatred and nothing else." He had the jurors with him now, moving through Sweet's terrors, back to Bartow, up to Garland, into the face of hatred. "He knew they had been tied to stakes in free America and a fire built around living human beings until they roasted to death; he knew they had been driven from their homes in the north and in great cities and here in Detroit, and he was there not only to defend himself and his house and his friends but to stand for the integrity and the independence of the abused race to which he belonged . . . a hero who fought a brave fight against fearful odds, a fight for the right, for justice, for freedom, and his name will live and be honored when most of us are forgotten." Judging by men and women such as these, Darrow archly asked, wouldn't any reasonable person conclude that it was not the Nordic but the Negro who belonged to the superior race?

The question was meant to be shocking, both in its audacity and in the sudden realization that it had to be answered in the affirmative. Darrow had taken on the Sweet case for just this moment of terrible honesty, when, with a twist of the evidence and a flash of eloquence, he made the courtroom see that white supremacy was an illusion, a poisonous, ruinous fantasy, just as it was an illusion to believe that capitalism was just, that men were responsible for the evil that they did, and that there was a God in Heaven.

As soon as the illusion was shattered, he presented the court with the harrowing, beautiful truth. "I know," he told the jurors, "that back of me and back of you is an infinite ancestry stretching a way back at least five hundred thousand years, and we are made up of everything on the face of the earth, of all kinds and colors and degrees of civilization, and out of that come we. Who are we, any of us, to be boastful above our fellows?" A world made one by miscegenation: to say such a thing in 1925 America was an act of startling insight and singular courage. But that was Darrow's genius, drawing a new understanding and a new humility out of the violence that Americans inflicted on one another.

Then something—caution, calculation, the limits of his own imagination—drew Darrow back. He could have pressed the logic of his argument, demanding, in the spirit of the abolitionists, that the jurors see segregation as illusion's folly, a social system built upon a bold-faced lie. As he drove toward his closing, though, idealism gave way to the same tired realism he'd demonstrated at the colored YMCA the week before. "Ask yourself this question, gentlemen," he said, "if you could settle [the race problem] as you wanted to, not this case but this infinitely troublesome problem that is back of it, how would you do it? How would you do it? If I were asked the question as to how I would do it, I could not answer it. I know that trouble and sorrow are incident to human life. . . . I know that many of our deepest problems are worked out in the secret travail of body and of mind. I know that nature takes time, infinite time, and the adjustment of races, the adjustment of religions, and the understandings of human beings by each other is the question of infinite time. I see no way that we can help it."[71]

Darrow was all but shouting now, his voice ringing out "like a brass gong," according to David Lilienthal, "his eyes . . . hard and grim, every muscle of his huge body tense and strained." But his message was soothingly soft. He wouldn't demand that the walls of segregation be brought down, that whites welcome blacks into their neighborhoods, or that they acknowledge Negroes as the brothers they were. Like Johnny Smith before him, he asked for nothing more than tolerance. "I ask you gentlemen in behalf of my clients," he boomed. "I ask you more than everything else, I ask you in behalf of justice, often maligned and down-trodden, hard to protect and hard to maintain, I ask you in behalf of yourselves, in behalf of our race, to see that no harm comes to them. I ask you gentlemen in the name of the future, the future which will one day solve these sore problems, and the future which is theirs as well as ours, I ask you in the name of the future to do justice in this case."[72]

Lilienthal understood what Darrow had done. "He seemed to be pleading more that the white man might be just than that the black be free," the young man said, "more for the spirit of the master than the body of the slave." But the rest of the courtroom was simply swept away by the power of a presentation so brilliantly concluded. "I've heard about lawyers making a judge cry," one of the colored attorneys, Charles Mahoney, recalled of the moment the plea was finished, "but Darrow was the first man I ever saw do it." "It was wonderful, eloquent, logical," wrote the young woman from the Penguin Club, Josephine Gomon, in attendance at Darrow's request. "People wept and [the] jurors were moved." The Great Defender himself wiped a tear from his eye, quickly scanned the courtroom to find if his beloved Ruby was in attendance, then seeing that the coast was clear, slipped over to where Gomon was seated and asked if she might be interested in joining him for a very private lunch.[73]

•

By the time Darrow had finished his plea midway through Wednesday morning, Frank Murphy could see the court's Thanksgiving break looming before him. So he pushed the trial to a speedy conclusion. Robert Toms cooperated by keeping his address to the jury mercifully short: an hour spent reviewing the facts one more time, another hour trying to counter Darrow's closing with a series of sarcastic jabs. "How little attention is paid to poor Breiner," he said at one point. "Poor Breiner? Breiner? Oh yes, yes. Breiner. Why yes, oh yes, he is the man who was killed. I had forgotten about him. We have gone to Orlando, we have gone to Tulsa, we have gone to Washington, we have gone to Vienna, we have gone to Paris. . . . And we have left poor Breiner dead here in Detroit."[74]

Murphy took another hour to read to the jurors legal instructions so learned and precise—at one point he provided them the Latin derivation of the word "homicide"—it's hard to imagine that they followed half of what he told them. As soon as the judge's instructions were complete, at 3:20 P.M., the bailiff escorted the jurors into a small room directly off the court. The door was locked from the outside. And the waiting began.[75]

At first Gladys, Ossian, and the other defendants were positively buoyant, chatting and laughing among themselves as if the verdict were a foregone conclusion. Their defenders also seemed hopeful of an early victory. Rather than head back to his hotel, Darrow lingered at the lawyers' table, while Arthur Garfield Hays and Walter White made plans to be aboard the seven o'clock train back to Manhattan, so as to be home in plenty of time for Thanksgiving dinner. As the afternoon slipped away without so much as a sound from the jury room, though, optimism began to fade. Darrow, Hays, and their wives drifted off to dinner; White's train left without him. Shortly after ten o'clock, someone from inside the jury room rapped on the door, and suddenly the courtroom, still crowded despite the hour, was transfixed.[76]

But the jurors didn't have a verdict to deliver; they simply needed to clarify a few points. Could they convict some of the defendants and not others? Could the murder be justified if Dr. Sweet thought he was in danger, even if his perception proved to be wrong? Murphy reread the appropriate portions of his complicated instructions—yes, the jury could convict one or more of the accused, as they saw fit; yes, perceptions could be taken into consideration—and sent the jurors back to their deliberations. This time there wasn't silence. For the rest of the evening, those dogged enough to stay in the courtroom could hear the jurymen shouting at one another, though no one could quite make out their words. And when, at 2:10 A.M., Murphy finally sent the jurors off to the courthouse's sixth-floor dormitory for what remained of the night, the dozen men trudged out of the jury room looking angry and utterly bedraggled.[77]

Although it was a holiday, the crowds filled the courthouse again Thursday morning. With Murphy closeted in his chambers rather than on the bench, spectators spilled all over the courtroom, some perching on the rail that divided the gallery from the well, others dozing in the jury box, still others loitering about the witness stand. Ossian and the other male defendants remained in jail, where they were to be treated to the county's traditional turkey dinner, but Gladys kept vigil, continually pacing the length of the courtroom in a vain attempt to relieve the tension. Darrow and Hays sat glumly at the lawyers' table, playing cards, while White forced down a Thanksgiving meal of "two sandwiches and a bottle of skimmed milk so thin it was blue instead of white," his thoughts no doubt on the fine celebration he could be hosting in the comfort of 90 Edgecombe Place. As the day dragged on, cigarette smoke grew so thick that the bailiffs had to throw open the windows, though the day was cold and raw. A newsboy arrived with a bundle of papers, which in short order were strewn about the floor, rustling underfoot as the restless stood up to stretch their legs or wander into the corridor. Otherwise, the room was remarkably quiet, as everyone strained to pick up some scrap of the conversation going on behind the bolted door of the jury room.[78]

What they heard wasn't encouraging. The jury resumed deliberations at half past nine, and almost immediately the shouting began again, accompanied this time by the crash of furniture being tossed about the tiny room. The jurors seemed to settle down after that, but as noon approached, there was another outburst. "Damn it," one of the twelve yelled so loudly his voice rang throughout the courtroom, "I am a reasonable man, I tell you!" Obviously, the other eleven didn't agree. All afternoon, the arguments continued, occasionally punctuated by the hammering of fists upon tables and the shoving of chairs against walls. At six o'clock, Murphy, making his one concession to the day, sent the jurors off to a downtown hotel for a fine Thanksgiving dinner, which they ate in sullen silence. As soon as the meal was done, the bailiffs brought them back to the jury room for another interminable evening in one another's company.[79]

Darrow and Hays, meanwhile, took their holiday dinners as honored guests of the colored YMCA, a nice diversion on an otherwise dismal day. Considerably brightened, the pair returned to the court ready for a night's entertainment. Murphy's clerk, already awash in the spirits of the day, happily agreed to unlock an adjoining courtroom so that the defender might have a private space for entertaining; someone purloined a few bottles of scotch; and Darrow and a handful of his closest friends—including the ubiquitous Josephine Gomon, miraculously free of her husband and five young children—passed the evening in conversations made exciting by a deepening alcoholic haze. ("Something was said about newspapers and prohibition," Gomon recorded in her diary. "I don't recall [what] but my retort was that it made me so damn mad. Mr. Darrow reached over and took both my hands. 'We are affinities. To think I should ever hear such an opinion from a woman.'") The party was still going strong at 11:10 P.M., when word came that Murphy was bringing the jury out.[80]

The judge had to clear the crowd from in front of the bench so that there was room for the jurors to gather before him. "Are you unable to reach agreement?" he asked the foreman, thirty-eight-year-old Charles Naas.

"We can't agree," answered Naas, visibly shaking.

"Do you think you will be able to reach an agreement at any time?" Murphy pressed.

"No," the foreman admitted.

Murphy paused for a moment to consider his options. Then he spoke. "My duty is plain. This trial has been running almost a month at great expense to city and defendants, and it is absolutely necessary that I keep you here some time more. You may go to bed and resume deliberations at 9:30."[81]

At Murphy's decision, almost everyone in the courtroom sagged with weariness. But the frustration of the moment struck Gladys particularly hard. From the first, she had been the most iron willed of all the defendants, always defiant, always confident in the justice of the cause. Now she buried her face in her mother's shoulder and wept.[82]

◆

The jurors slogged back into deliberations as ordered the next morning, but they had nothing left to discuss. At lunchtime Thursday, foreman Naas had polled the others. All agreed that eight of the defendants should be acquitted. But they split on the guilt of the remaining three: Ossian, Henry, and, for some inexplicable reason, insurance salesman Leonard Morse. Five of the jurors thought that Morse and the Sweet brothers should be acquitted as well. But seven other jurors wanted them convicted of murder in the second degree, not quite the crime Toms was after but serious enough to merit its perpetrators fifteen years imprisonment. For the balance of the day, each group had tried to sway the other to its position, but no one had budged. A second night of tossing and turning on the courthouse's cots did nothing to soften opinions. Once they had been locked inside the jury room for the third day, Naas polled the men again. The votes remained the same.[83]

Murphy kept them sequestered from 9:30 Friday morning to 1:30 that afternoon, long enough to break a deadlock if it were to be broken. Then, forty-six hours after he'd put the case in their hands, he had the twelve brought back to the bench. Was there the slightest chance of the jurors rendering a verdict, he asked twice, and each time Naas gave the same weary reply. No, there wasn't. So Murphy surrendered to the inevitable. With great regret, he dismissed the jurymen from their duty and declared *The People v. Sweet* a mistrial.

Immediately, Darrow and Toms were on their feet, clamoring for the court's attention, ready to renew the battle that after four ferociously fought weeks no one had won.[84]

TEN

JUDGMENT DAY

Clarence Darrow and Arthur Garfield Hays stayed in Detroit just long enough to ask that their clients be released on bail, to inform Frank Murphy that when the case was resumed they wanted separate trials for each of the defendants, and to talk to the press one last time. Then they were gone, Clarence and Ruby back to the amiable confusion of their Chicago apartment, Hays and his young wife, Aline, off to Manhattan in the company of Walter White, who couldn't wait to end his month-long exile from the East Coast.[1]

The jury had been out too long for the mistrial to come as a surprise, but the lack of acquittal still stung. Unlike many other battles they had waged over the years, everything had gone just right this time. The judge had been remarkably sympathetic; the accused had held themselves with dignity and grace while the prosecutions' witnesses had repeatedly stumbled; on the stand Ossian Sweet had been nothing short of magnificent; and in his closing, Darrow had brought the case together as brilliantly as any advocate could. Yet all of that wasn't enough to convince twelve white men that the defendants deserved to go free. "I have had a strenuous time of it at Detroit in the biggest legal battle we have ever handled," a disgusted White wrote a friend during his first weekend home. "After thirty days of trial the jury still could not agree . . . necessitating a new trial though the State's case fell down completely and the defense proved beyond the shadow of any reasonable doubt that if a member of the mob who was killed was shot by one of the eleven defendants, there was ample provocation." The jurors' "stubbornness is going to cost us about $25,000 more," he told another friend. "Thus six thousand years of civilization reaches its finest flower!"[2]

A few days free of the courtroom's all-consuming combat helped restore perspective. Obviously, the Sweets' defenders had wanted an acquittal, but no one had gone into the case simply to win it. This had been a show trial, a piece of political theater, and as such, it had been spectacularly successful. The fight had riveted black America. Mention anywhere in the country that you are from Detroit, wrote a newspaperman the first week of December, "and immediately Negroes . . . inquire, 'How about the Sweet case?'" The mainstream white press had proved much tougher to crack. After an initial flurry of interest in Darrow's latest battle, the major East Coast newspapers had become transfixed by the story of wealthy New Yorker Kip Rhinelander, who married the daughter of a cab driver, then sued for divorce when he discovered that his new bride was a Negro. One spectacular race trial was as much as the white press could handle, it seemed, and sex sold better than murder, so the Sweets' story had faded from many of the most important papers, much to Walter White's annoyance.

Still, the drama in Detroit had breached the color line in a few strategic places. David Lilienthal's marvelously evocative account of the Sweets' trial in the *Nation* brought the story into the headiest circles of white progressivism, though, like Darrow, Lilienthal seemed more concerned with exposing the power of prejudice than exploring the forces dividing urban neighborhoods along the color line. And White's shameless stroking of Detroit's reporters had almost completely reversed the way their papers portrayed the Sweets. There were still a few bitter voices. "Noble Nordic Darrow . . . exhibited in numerous ways the most degenerate form of race prejudice," snarled Henry Ford's weekly newspaper, *The Dearborn Independent*, "prejudice against the race that bore him. Negroes don't respect white men who fawn upon Negroes." But such sentiments were all but drowned out by a chorus of praise for the defendants: by the trial's close, even the *Detroit Free Press*, the most blatantly racist of the dailies, was writing glowing stories of Ossian's courage. Such a remarkable turnaround seemed to be softening white opinion across white Detroit. "From the comments that have come to me since the Sweet trial, I am satisfied that a great deal of good was accomplished," an unnamed "prominent Detroit attorney," most likely Judge Ira Jayne, wrote James Weldon Johnson a week or so after the mistrial was declared. "One man who used to live in the neighborhood of Garland and Charlevoix told me that he believed that the people of that locality have a new understanding of the right of the colored people to buy property and live in it." Weighing the evidence, Arthur Garfield Hays began to wonder whether the mistrial had been a defeat after all. "From the public point of view, both as concerns negroes and whites," he mused in a private note at the end of December, "a disagreement was perhaps better than would have been a verdict either way."[3]

Walter White wasn't willing to go that far. It pained him to hand out the raft of payments that the first trial required—a total of $12,400—when he knew that the same bills would have to be paid numerous times as Darrow fought through the eleven separate trials he'd demanded. And it took all of White's congenial conviviality to nurture the personal relationships that the NAACP would need when the defendants returned to court. White targeted Hays for particular attention that December: there was a tasteful get-together one night at White's apartment on Edgecombe Place, another evening at the theater to see *Hamlet* performed in modern dress, and a somewhat more raucous night touring Harlem's hotspots. Frank Murphy, meanwhile, received a series of letters so chummy that in his replies the judge began referring to White as "uncle" and "Walt old dear." White's friends from the press table also were informed that the résumés and draft novels they had entrusted to White's care were being passed around Manhattan's best publishing houses. Even Robert Toms got a generous thank-you note for his kindnesses during the trial, pointedly accompanied by an NAACP pamphlet on the horrors of lynching and an autographed copy of *Fire in the Flint*.[4]

For all the duties it imposed, though, the mistrial also bestowed one great benefit on the NAACP. A month of rallies and appeals on behalf of the Sweets had brought the association tantalizingly close to completing its long-sought Legal Defense Fund. As always, the association's well-heeled allies had come through: reformer Florence Kelley wrote the campaign a two-hundred-dollar check; Joel Spingarn gave five hundred dollars; and longtime benefactor Julius Rosenwald, newly named chairman of Sears, Roebuck and Company, contributed two thousand dollars. But it was the passionate interest of ordinary black folk that made the difference. They'd done what they could, dropping fifty cents into a collection plate, stuffing a dollar into an envelope and mailing it to Manhattan, cajoling lodge brothers or sorority sisters to raise fifty or a hundred bucks, tiny sums that, put together, amounted to a stunning twenty-three thousand dollars. Just another seven thousand dollars to raise and the NAACP would receive the fifteen-thousand-dollar match-

ing grant pledged by the Garland Fund. Maybe the euphoria of a courtroom victory would have brought in the balance. Or it might have
stopped the campaign dead in its tracks, as the case faded off the front
pages and out of the public mind. Now the Sweets' story was sure to
stay bitterly, wonderfully alive at least until the new year.[5]

Through all of December, the association's officers raced to push the
campaign to its triumphal conclusion. James Weldon Johnson tried to
use his peerless connections to wheedle a few more substantial donations, while W. E. B. Du Bois imperiously commanded Negroes to pay
the balance as the price of racial pride. "No listless foolishness, no carp-
ing criticism," he barked in the *Crisis*, "but to work! Pay! Sacrifice! Be
men and women! Be free!" Walter White, meanwhile, cast the campaign
in the glow of Renaissance Harlem. Some gentle persuasion convinced
Charles Boni, publisher of Alain Locke, Jessie Fauset, and Jean Toomer,
to host a Park Avenue fund-raiser. The company of *Mooching Along*, the
newest revue from the team that gave America the Charleston, donated
the entire box-office receipts of a special midnight performance. *New
York World* accepted White's long piece on the trial, while H. L. Mencken,
Blanche Knopf, and Sinclair Lewis received chatty notes informing
them of the latest battle against the Nordic Neanderthals and discreetly
inquiring whether they might be interested in seeing something on the
Sweets put into print. And for the campaign's crescendo, White brought
the heroes of Detroit home to Harlem with him.[6]

Darrow came in mid-December 1925. His social schedule was too
full to fit in Walter White's offer of an evening's entertainment. But the
NAACP made sure that Darrow was suitably feted during the afternoon rally at Salem Methodist Episcopal, the Harlem church pastored
by Countee Cullen's adoptive father. With J. Rosamond Johnson leading them, the crowd of three thousand joined together on "Lift Every
Voice and Sing." Tenor Taylor Gordon, fresh from his highly praised
performance at Town Hall, performed a few spirituals. Donations were
presented from black fraternal organizations, church groups, women's
clubs, and the colored schoolchildren of Yonkers, Manhattan, and
Staten Island. Then James Weldon Johnson introduced the Great
Defender—"a champion of causes that need a champion"—and the audience leapt to its feet, cheering wildly as the old man made his way to
the pulpit. For the next hour, he flayed his favorite targets, the church
rocking with applause as he condemned prejudice, religion ("You're
too blooming pious," he told the crowd as the ministers sitting him behind him squirmed) and his new bête noir, the "Noble Nordics" of

Garland Avenue. When the day was done, the Legal Defense Fund was $5,057 closer to completion.[7]

Three weeks later, White put the newest NAACP stars on the New York stage. On January 3, 1926, Ossian and Gladys made their Harlem debut.

◆

At first, Gladys was livid with White for deserting Detroit without seeing to it that her husband was released from jail. Frank Murphy had been more than willing to grant the request from Darrow and Hays that their clients be granted bail, but he'd set the bar very high: five thousand dollars for each of the seven defendants that the jurors had wanted to free, ten thousand dollars for Ossian, Henry, and Leonard Morse, over whom the jurors had disagreed. As it turned out, Gladys didn't need White's help; while some of the defendants, such as chauffeur Joe Mack and handyman Norris Murray, had a terrible time securing the necessary funds, Sweet had much of Detroit's Talented Tenth clamoring for the honor of posting his bond.[8]

Ossian came home on December 3, eighty-two days after the gates of the Wayne County Jail doors first shut behind him. Hays desperately wanted him to move directly into the bungalow on Garland, but he was too weary to face the anger still seething through the streets around the house. With the trial completed, the Waterworks Park Improvement Association had resumed meetings. Already there had been one ugly incident: just the week before Ossian's release, someone had tossed gasoline-soaked rags into the bungalow's garage and tried to set them ablaze. Had the police guard not been in place, the structure, and perhaps the house as well, would have burned to the ground. To make matters even worse, Inspector Norton Schuknecht sent word that as soon as Sweet was released, he would withdraw the guard, since the doctor could protect the property himself. So, instead of claiming his house, Ossian moved into the flat Gladys had rented among the foreigners on Belvidere Avenue, a mile northwest of Garland. The new neighborhood wasn't prepossessing, the apartment a small, unattractive flat in a nondescript building the Sweets shared with a white waiter and his unemployed roommate. However much the surroundings disappointed him, though, it must have been a relief for Ossian to finally stand in the tiny sitting room that Gladys had filled with a few of their favorite things, holding his beaming wife and squealing daughter in a luxuriously long embrace, knowing how close they'd come to being separated forever.[9]

Decades later, Otis Sweet claimed that his older brother and the other defendants had taken the mistrial philosophically; "we kind of expected something like that," he said. Perhaps. But any sense of resignation Ossian may have felt disappeared as the first reviews of the trial came in. The December issues of the *Crisis*, the *Nation*, and Harlem's militant *Messenger* all praised Ossian's unparalleled courage, while the Negro weeklies—almost universally incensed at the jury's inability to reach a verdict—proclaimed him the latest in a noble line of heroes and martyrs. To the *Arizona Times*, he was an exemplar of the New Negro ideal: "The Sweet case has positively proved to the world at large," the paper said, "that the American Negro will fight and stand up for his rights as a citizen until every ounce of blood is spilled from his veins." Having witnessed Ossian's performance on the witness stand, the editor of the *Cleveland Call* stretched for a greater point of comparison. "The newspapers commented on Doctor Sweet's poise, evident refinement, lucidness and fearlessness in his quick and accurate replies," he wrote. "One was proud of Sweet, yet there was a pathos, a scene like . . . one other scene two thousand years ago when One Who Opened Not His Mouth was being baited." People clamored to see Sweet in the flesh. Just three days after his homecoming, the Detroit NAACP branch made him the keynote speaker at its regular Sunday rally. Although it was a bitterly cold afternoon, a huge crowd filled every inch of Black Bottom's Ebenezer AME to hear the famous doctor. Shortly thereafter, Ossian's college fraternity invited him to address its annual conference in New York City. James Weldon Johnson all but ordered him to decline. The association's leaders had big plans for the good doctor. And they weren't about to be trumped by the men of Kappa Alpha Psi.[10]

Walter White timed Ossian and Gladys's visit to New York to coincide with the NAACP's annual business meeting, which was always capped by a mass rally in Harlem. It proved to be an intoxicating experience. Advertisements in New York's leading black newspaper, the *Amsterdam News*, announced their arrival in the city. Ossian was invited to sit in on the business meeting, and listen to such towering figures as James Weldon Johnson, W. E. B. Du Bois, and Arthur Spingarn discuss the state of the antisegregation campaign that the Sweets had made a success. When he and Gladys walked into the sanctuary of Lenox Avenue's Mount Olivet Baptist Church for the public rally, the crowd of fifteen hundred Harlemites broke into sustained applause. Elegant Mary White Ovington, the most devoted of the association's white members, introduced the couple. The church choir sang "America" while ushers passed through the aisles gathering donations. Arthur Garfield Hays, appearing uptown at White's personal request, capped the event by turning the day's major address into a soaring tribute to his client. "I presume no man has ever had a greater opportunity to do more for his race or for mankind than Doctor Sweet," Hays said, "and never in his life will he ever have a greater opportunity to do a bigger thing than to lead the fight against segregation. . . . It would be a glorious thing for a people whose ancestors only a few generations ago were slaves, if they could lead the fight for emancipation from ignorance, bigotry, prejudice, such as exists today. . . ." For Ossian, sitting proudly beside his wife, facing the throng come to cheer him, Hays's address must have been an extraordinary confirmation that his greatest hopes had come true. By his bravery, Dr. Sweet had become a leader of his race.[11]

Ossian's sense of himself soared with all the acclaim. When the Harlem rally was finished, Walter White dispatched the Sweets on a six-day tour of NAACP branches. The association wanted the couple simply to appear at each venue, say a few words of thanks, and stand by quietly while the association's director of branches, Gladys's former pastor Robert Bagnall, appealed for contributions. But whenever Ossian saw the people waiting for him—twenty-five hundred in Philadelphia; twelve hundred in Pittsburgh, despite a blizzard; two thousand in Cleveland, with hundreds more turned away for lack of space; five hundred at a badly managed affair in Chicago's cavernous Eighth Regiment Armory—he began to hold forth like the luminary everyone said he was. "Each day he got more egotistic," Bagnall grumbled as the trip wound down. "He draws crowds—but—!!" It was a fair complaint. Although he claimed to be no orator, Ossian "thundered" at his audiences, according to the *Chicago Defender*, trying to impress them with a mix of exaggeration, self-righteousness, and more than a touch of arrogance. "I have had the good fortune to have traveled in Europe and in many parts of Africa," he proclaimed at the tour's last stop. "Even in the jungles where the so-called barbarians and semi-civilized people live, a man's home is his castle. It was then that the thought came to me that the least we who claim to be civilized and more progressive can do is to uphold this principle at the cost of our very lives. I am thoroughly convinced that we have the best people everywhere with me in this fight, as I believe no man who thinks highly of himself and his own household can in any way disregard my stand by saying that there was another way out."[12]

In private, too, Ossian's usual assertiveness descended into a persistent abrasiveness. "I averted no fewer than four scenes," reported

Bagnall, "[and] abated five quarrels between the Sweets. . . ." The couple's clashes may have been rooted in family matters: both Gladys and one-and-a-half-year-old Iva were wracked by coughs that winter—the family was convinced that Gladys had caught a bug during her weeks confined in an overcrowded cell block, then passed it on to Iva—and there could have been some conflict over the decision to be separated from the toddler for almost two weeks. But Bagnall thought he saw "hero complexes" at play. Since November, Gladys had been the defendants' spokesman, appearing at dozens of rallies, smiling shyly as attention was lavished on her, impressing everyone with her poise and charm; now she was cast back into the shadows—Ossian's "girl-wife," the *Chicago Defender* called her—while her husband stood in the spotlight, telling tales about himself that she knew weren't always true. It's easy to imagine Gladys taking her husband aside for a few words, his bristling at her challenge to his authority, tempers flaring, voices rising, and the two of them saying things that would have seemed unimaginable a month before, when Ossian was satisfied to cradle his wife in his arms. "When I saw them off this morning it was a relief beyond description," Bagnall wrote to the NAACP's headquarters on the day he sent the Sweets home to Detroit. "Tell Walter—never again!"[13]

Bagnall had nothing to fear; the tour was such a smashing success there was no need to consider an encore. When news of Ossian and Gladys's arrest first passed across his desk back in September, James Weldon Johnson was dreaming of the day when the NAACP might have a fifty-thousand-dollar Legal Defense Fund at its disposal. Thanks to the Sweets' compelling story, the fund stood at a remarkable seventy-six thousand, an endowment large enough to carry the association not only through its pending cases but into battles so distant they had yet to be imagined.[14]

•

The first test came with the perfect timing that James Weldon Johnson so loved. All though November, as the dispatches from Detroit piled up on his desk, Johnson waited for word that the United States Supreme Court had placed on its docket the NAACP's case testing the constitutionality of restrictive covenants. Nothing would have been finer than to have the two cases culminate at precisely the same moment, but it wasn't to be: the Sweet trial was two weeks past when the clerk of the court finally set a date for oral arguments. Nevertheless, the timing was superb. If the justices accepted the association's argument that homeowners be prohibited from placing restrictive covenants on their properties, the Court would strip from the marketplace one of the seg-regationists' most potent weapons. The association's lawyers were to present their case to the justices on January 8, the same day that Ossian and Gladys appeared before an overflow crowd in snowbound Pittsburgh. Thus did Johnson and his fellow officers mark the creation of the Legal Defense Fund by bringing before the nation's highest tri-bunal the case that might just halt Jim Crow's grim march through the streets of urban America.[15]

Swaddled in tradition and decorum, the Supreme Court didn't per-mit the sort of theatrics that had made the Sweet trial such a gripping story. But with the stakes infinitely higher, the court's cramped cham-ber crackled with intensity. At precisely two o'clock, the chief justice, former president William Howard Taft, settled his great weight into the center seat at the justice's ornate bench and signaled for the attorneys to begin their presentations. Although the NAACP had a considerable con-tingent on hand—James Cobb, the Howard professor of law who had seen the challenge through the lower courts; Arthur Spingarn, the head of the association's legal committee; several former United States attor-neys—only the two most senior and august members of the group ad-dressed the court. Eighty-year-old Moorfield Storey struggled through a brief introduction, his once formidable skills blunted by age and illness. Then he surrendered the podium to his colleague, Louis Marshall, who carried the NAACP's case for the balance of the afternoon.[16]

At sixty-nine, Marshall was himself slowing down, and some in the courtroom thought his performance lacked vigor. But he was at his best when tracing for the justices the frightful logic of segregation in the nation's most heterogenous places: first blacks would be banished to the ghetto, he said, repeating the NAACP standard warning, to be followed by Catholics, Jews, indeed anyone the majority considered undesirable. And when that day came, "that which has been most no-ble and exalted and humane in American life will have been shattered. Great as are the mental and spiritual sufferings of those against whom the shafts of prejudice and intolerance are aimed, the lasting injury is, however, inflicted upon a civilization of a country which connives at a covenant such as that which has been enforced by the decrees here sought to be reviewed." It was a judicial jeremiad delivered with the grand old lion's customary eloquence, certainly enough to offset Storey's fumbled opening.[17]

As he turned to the legal basis for the association's case, though,

Marshall lost his edge. His argument was, by necessity, complex. The most obvious position would have been to say that restrictive covenants violated the equal protection clauses of the fifth and fourteenth amendments. But because the covenants were private agreements rather than government mandates, they fell outside the amendments' purview.

So Marshall had to approach the question of constitutionality through a flanking attack. Individuals may be free to add discriminatory provisions to their deeds, he argued, but judges should be prohibited from enforcing those provisions, since to do so would be to give government sanction to neighborhood segregation, something that the Louisville case said was unconstitutional. "The legislature may not segregate," he said. "The governing body of a city or village may not do so. Can a court, acting as a branch of government, by its mandate bring about segregation without running foul of the [Louisville] decision? . . . I think not."

The justices clearly weren't convinced. Marshall was peppered with questions from the bench, most of them concerning not his legal argument but whether the Court had the right to decide the case at all. Perhaps because he'd entertained those doubts himself, Marshall seemed to be thrown off stride; his answers were so hesitant and unsure, said Cobb with a twist of the knife, "that we who knew the case were greatly alarmed." When Taft gaveled the session to a close at four o'clock, it almost seemed a relief.[18]

"I do not feel very much gratified by what occurred," Moorfield Storey confided to James Weldon Johnson. "Mr. Marshall spoke for about three-quarters of an hour and I hope made an impression on the court. The feeling however among our friends seemed rather to be that we had not succeeded in persuading the court, and I am afraid they will find some way of dodging the question on the ground that the court has no jurisdiction in the case." But in the end, he remained hopeful, unable to put aside his faith in the justices' willingness to see the righteousness of the cause. "In the [Louisville] segregation case I was given to understand we should probably lose the case, but the result was favorable and it may be again," he told Johnson. "We can only wait and hope," a fragile coda for a campaign that would decide the future of the millions of Negroes who had come to call the nation's cities their home.[19]

◆

The Sweets also waited that winter. Ossian and Gladys came home from their January tour expecting to head back to court within a few weeks. But there were delays. First, Robert Toms begged off, citing his commitment to prosecute another major case. Then there wasn't space on the court's calendar. When open dates finally were found, Frank Murphy canceled them; his father had fallen ill and he needed to be by his side. January, February, and early March drifted past, deep winter giving way to a tentative spring, and still the defendants' fate hung precariously before them.[20]

The anxiety of those long, dreary months should have been unrelenting. For Ossian, though, the power of celebrity transformed them into a peculiarly promising time. With his storefront office on St. Aubin Avenue continually packed with people wanting his care, there was more work than he could possibly handle—and more money coming into his accounts than ever before. So dramatic was the increase he considered expanding his business. There was talk that Garafalo's Pharmacy, a substantial corner shop on one of the busier streets on the eastern edge of Black Bottom, might be for sale; with its fine location and established reputation, the store would give Ossian the firm foundation upon which he could build his fortune. Money also gave him the opportunity to enjoy the sweet taste of avenging a wrong, albeit indirectly. Although there was still the bungalow's mortgage to pay, he moved his family out of the dismal flat Gladys had found them and into a bright, airy, third-floor apartment in an immaculately maintained sixteen-unit building due north of Black Bottom. Probably he chose the place because it was an easy stroll to Dunbar Memorial. But more than geography went into his choice of homes. The building wasn't exclusive, any more than Garland Avenue had been, but when Ossian and Gladys made their way up the narrow staircase with their boxes of books and satchels of clothes, all the other tenants they passed were white.[21]

His success led to whispers against him—Sweet was getting too big for himself, some said—but Ossian paid no mind. When a man rose above the average, he had to expect petty jealousy from those he left behind. He moved in different circles now: when Walter White came to town, lawyers and judges trooped to his hotel room to pay their respects, but when White needed to see Ossian, he came down to the doctor's office. Where it mattered most, moreover—inside the Sweet family circle—Ossian reigned supreme. Tensions remained, of course. Baby Iva's winter illness seemed so impervious to treatment her parents must have known that something was seriously wrong. And it's impossible to believe that Gladys set aside the fierce resolve that was central to her personality. But at the appropriate moments, she knew to defer to her husband's authority. One early spring Sunday, an out-of-town reporter, a friend of Darrow's, accepted an invitation to dinner at the Sweets' new apartment. Family and friends had gathered—brother Henry, cousin John Latting, lawyer Julian Perry— all but Ossian, who was occupied with pressing business. So when the meal began, Gladys sat at the head of the table she'd draped in linen, chatting amiably with her guests. The moment the doctor walked in, though, she surrendered the seat to him, and for the rest of the evening sat in silence at the table's far end while he described his triumphal tour on behalf of the NAACP, dropped the names of famous people he'd met, and expounded on the problems of the race, the undisputed head of the family exercising a hero's prerogatives.[22]

There must have been moments during the months of waiting when Ossian's confidence threatened to break. Friends and associates certainly gave him reasons to worry. Through Julian Perry, he learned of the colored lawyers' angry analysis of the first trial. Darrow and Hays were brilliant, they admitted, but because they had refused to share even a sliver of the spotlight, the defense never had a local face; all the jurors saw were high-priced outsiders talking about principles that didn't have much meaning on the grimy streets of Detroit.

More distressing was the continual criticism of Darrow's decision to seek separate trials for each of the defendants. Almost everyone in Detroit's Talented Tenth said the same thing: as long as the eleven were kept together, the prosecutor would have to confront the conspiracy charge that had tied him into knots during the first trial. Once they were split apart, that pivotal protection would evaporate, leaving the most vulnerable of the defendants dangerously exposed to a jury's whims. And that, said one colleague, "would be suicidal to the cause."[23]

If Ossian shared those fears, he refused to express them. Maybe he thought it his responsibility to maintain a courageous face; perhaps he couldn't admit even to himself that a future that suddenly seemed so bright might come to a bitter, brutal end. But he didn't protest when Walter White renewed his efforts to purge the colored lawyers from the defense team, saying they were an unnecessary expense. Nor did he flinch—publicly, at least—when he learned that, contrary to all expectations, he wasn't going to be the first defendant brought back to trial. In early February, Robert Toms announced that he would bypass Ossian in favor of prosecuting the one man who on the night of Leon Breiner's death had admitted to shooting into the street: Henry Sweet, the doctor's little brother. The news had to cut deep. Henry was Ossian's charge, after all; his parents had entrusted him with the duty of leading the young man to a better, safer life. And instead, he'd led Henry into the face of a mob, only to leave him alone in the defendant's chair and, if his associates in the Talented Tenth were correct, dangerously vulnerable to conviction. Yet Ossian remained unfailingly optimistic. "When I get out from under the criminal [charges]"—that's the way he put it when people asked him about his future; not "if" or "whether" but "when," as though he were simply waiting for an acquittal that was sure to come.[24]

He even reacted with equanimity when, on March 22, Walter White arrived at the office to say that Henry's trial date was set at last. Jury selection would begin on April 1. There was one more thing, added White. Now that the trial was a week and a half away, the defense team had fallen apart.

◆

Clarence Darrow didn't devote much time to the Sweet case during the prolonged delay of the second trial. After his Harlem appearance, he headed off to Colorado to spend Christmas—"the hollow-days," he called them—with his grandchildren, after which he occupied himself with his normal round of public appearances, lambasting all his favorite targets for the entertainment and edification of the great unwashed. On the few occasions that the Sweets came to his attention, he was every bit as confident as Ossian that the next round of prosecutions would end in complete victory for the defense. He said it in early December, when Arthur Garfield Hays and Walter White were still licking the wounds that the mistrial had inflicted. And he repeated it in February, when White dutifully reported the Talented Tenth's fears about holding separate trials. "There is practically no chance of convict[ing] Henry Sweet," he reassured the NAACP, "and . . . despite pressure that might be brought on the prosecutor by the Ku Klux Klan, Mr. Toms would not try more than one or two [of the defendants, once] the first tried was acquitted."[25]

Darrow never explained what made him so uncharacteristically optimistic. No doubt he was buoyed by Detroit's political situation, which in the run-up to the second trial seemed to be breaking just the right way. On January 1, 1926, Johnny Smith recited the oath of office that made him mayor for two more years. Almost immediately, it became clear that bluenoses no longer set the rules. From city hall came orders that beat cops were to stop rousting workingmen just because they'd imbibed too much at the corner speakeasies. There was to be more money for neighborhood parks and additional construction to ease overcrowding in city schools. And to address Detroit's festering racial problems, the mayor appointed a blue-ribbon commission, to be headed by one of his most loyal supporters in the previous campaign, Reinhold Neibuhr. It was understood that the appointment was a political payoff. But for Niebuhr, it was also a marvelous opportunity to study race relations in a systematic way. So he packed the committee's board with Sweet supporters—the bishop of the Detroit-area AME was named vice-chair, Ossian's friend Edward Carter secretary—then turned the commission's real work over to a specially arranged team of social scientists, who were to investigate every aspect of black life in Detroit and to propose specific policies the mayor might pursue.

The recently fearsome Ku Klux Klan, meanwhile, plunged into freefall. After its humiliation in the mayoral campaign, the KKK's national office—itself scarred by a sex scandal so vicious polite society couldn't discuss the details—ousted Detroit's kleagle, Ira Stout, amid accusations of incompetence and embezzlement. Rather than go quietly, Stout fought back. Account books disappeared; warrants were issued; ever more venomous charges and countercharges were exchanged, each bitter turn splashed across the front pages of the city's newspapers until even the most devoted Klansmen must have wondered what had become of the brave-hearted men who had promised to purify America. "Bob [Toms] is a nice fellow and I can't for the life of me see why he is connected with that bunch of hoodlums," Walter White's friend on the *Detroit Times* wrote him as the sorry story spun out. "Besides he should know that the Klan is a dead flower in this community populated by Ethiopians, Jews and followers of the Roman Catholic church."[26]

Darrow also seemed convinced that he could exploit the situation in Detroit more effectively than he had in the first trial. Not that the defense had done a poor job the last time round. But mistakes had been made, and with a second trial, he had the opportunity—rare even in his long career—to correct them. That was the reason he had asked for separate trials. Others thought he was simply trying to intimidate the prosecution into dropping the charges against some of the defendants. In fact, Darrow was righting what he saw as a fundamental error. By allowing all eleven defendants to be tried together, he had given the jurors the freedom to divide their votes in any number of ways; little wonder deliberations had dragged on for days without producing anything close to consensus. Better to present a jury with a single defendant and a simple choice: send him to prison or let him go free.[27]

There were to be other changes, too. But all that winter, the Great Defender kept his confidence—until a Jazz Age gem of a story forced him to reveal a bit of the hand he was planning to play.

Through the first weeks of March, the national press had been salivating over the salacious tale of Vera, Countess Cathcart, come to New York for the debut of her first play, only to be denied entry into the United States because, once upon a time, she had a very public affair with the Earl of Craven and thus was guilty of the unpardonable crime of "moral turpitude." Every day, the front pages were filled with the countess's tragic plight, trapped on Ellis Island while her high-priced Park Avenue attorney, Arthur Garfield Hays, gallantly fought for her release. Had Vera's incarceration occurred just a few weeks earlier, Hays might have managed to settle the case in time to return to Darrow's side by April 1. As it was, he had to pick between two great causes. On March 13, Hays summoned Walter White and James Weldon Johnson to his brownstone to offer his regrets. He desperately wanted to come back to Detroit but, well, he couldn't bring himself to abandon the countess in her moment of need.[28]

White waited until a March 21 strategy session in Detroit to give Darrow the bad news. The Great Defender must have seen it coming, since he had already settled on a replacement. If he couldn't have Hays as his cocounsel, he wanted Thomas Chawke.[29]

White almost choked on the idea. He had investigated Chawke back in September, when the NAACP was desperate to find any white lawyer willing to take the Sweets' case, and the reports hadn't been good. It wasn't a question of skill—by all accounts Chawke was the best criminal lawyer in Detroit—but of appearances. Chawke tried to strike the sophisticated pose that Hays held as a matter of course, draping his six-foot frame in a two-hundred-dollar suit, the crease in his pant leg so sharp it could draw blood, the French cuffs of his silk shirt perfectly positioned below the sleeve of his jacket. But there was no masking the truth. At thirty-eight, Chawke remained rooted in the parochial world of working-class Detroit: an Irish-born immigrant who still lived with his widowed mother and spinster sister in the east-side neighborhood that had been his home since childhood; a devout Catholic with a brother in the priesthood; a backroom politico admired for his ability to make or break careers; and worst of all, a trusted associate of the boys who kept the booze flooding across the border and the blood flowing in the streets of Detroit.

Rumor had it that the big-time mobsters—the locals with ties to

Johnny Torio and Scarface Capone—loved Chawke's bruising courtroom style: his intimate knowledge of the law's tricks and turns; his relentless attacks on hostile witnesses, whom he sometimes subjected to
questioning so intense they'd say just about anything to escape him;
the outsized oratory he used to manipulate jurors into acquitting even
those obviously guilty of the crimes lodged against them—and a few
more besides. For his part, Chawke saw such work as nothing more
than business. His clients put up a considerable amount of cash to
keep him on retainer. And he provided the services they needed, no
questions asked, no excuses necessary. Not the sort of man Walter
White imagined representing the NAACP in the climactic battle of its
fight for justice in the urban North.[30]

An afternoon conference hardly eased White's concerns. Chawke listened politely as White described the NAACP's mission, his presentation
sprinkled with the names of the distinguished attorneys who had battled for the association's causes. Then the lawyer laid out his terms. He
was willing to take the case, he said crisply, but it had to be handled correctly. Each potential juror would be investigated beforehand so that
when jury selection began, the defense would know precisely whom to
choose. If there were new evidence to be had, he wanted it. He wouldn't
be Darrow's lackey; the two men would share equal time before the
court. And he expected to be paid properly. Darrow might be willing to
settle for five thousand dollars, but Chawke would expect half again as
much. Should that prove to be too high a figure, the NAACP could look
elsewhere. White was aghast. "I found [Chawke] . . . obviously a shrewd
lawyer with a pleasant personality but with none of the idealism of
Darrow or Hays," he reported to NAACP headquarters. "So far as I can
judge he has no prejudice against Negroes but he is going into this case
as a business proposition and because, as he phrased it, it is a case that
can be won." Darrow had made it clear that he had to have a cocounsel,
however, and the association had nowhere else to turn. After a few days
of dickering, the deal was struck. A week to trial and the NAACP had
placed the fate of Henry Sweet in the hands of the Detroit mob's favorite
front man. Darrow couldn't have been more pleased.[31]

·

As it happened, the trial didn't begin on April 1 but almost three weeks
later, on Monday morning, April 19, 1926. Although it was an unusu-
ally cold day for early spring, with temperatures hovering in the low
thirties, the streets outside the courthouse seemed, said one observer,

to be in "half holiday." For days, the Detroit newspapers had been announcing the trial's renewal, stoking the anticipation of another dramatic Darrow performance. But it was the morning's surprising announcement that gave the day a particular edge. According to the *Detroit Free Press*, Robert Toms had decided to stake his entire prosecution on the outcome of the case, just as Darrow had predicted he would. If the jurors convicted Henry Sweet of murder, Toms would try the remaining ten defendants, each in his turn. Should Henry be acquitted, the charges against all the others would be dropped.

Inside the sun-streaked courtroom, the tension was palpable. Henry Sweet sat silently at the lawyers' table, stiff and serious in a dark suit, Thomas Chawke by his side, Darrow lounging in a chair off to the side. Ossian, Gladys, and their eight compatriots squeezed into the visitors' gallery, relegated to being spectators in a trial that would decide the course of their lives. Around them gathered hundreds of their supporters, the "the same tense [black] faces," Darrow later said, "watch[ing] every move in what to them represented a part of the tragedy of the whole race." Walter White was noticeably absent—he'd begged off a return visit, saying he was too busy preparing for the NAACP's upcoming convention—but Josephine Gomon was back in her seat, waiting for the Great Defender to stop by, and Ruby Darrow in hers, prepared to pounce the moment her husband made his move.

Frank Murphy had lost his father the week before—one of the reasons the proceedings had been delayed yet again—and he took the bench in a subdued, somber mood. Robert Toms matched him with an opening performance so predictable it became tedious. Although the state's entire case now rested on this one prosecution, Toms intended to call precisely the same witnesses as in the first trial and to make precisely the same argument: there had been no mob on Garland Avenue the night of September 9; the Negroes had been perfectly safe inside their home; the shooting of Leon Breiner was premeditated, an act not of self-defense but of murder in the first degree. Then Toms began the soporific process of jury selection, laboriously sifting through the pool of a hundred prospective jurors, most of them the sort of stolid white workingmen who in the first trial had proved impervious to persuasion, carefully doling out a few of the ten peremptory challenges he had to command. By the time he had assembled a preliminary panel— again all white and male—the once animated crowd had slipped into a late afternoon stupor.[32]

When Toms turned the panel over to the defense for review, Darrow didn't even bother to get out of his chair. Instead, he stretched out his legs, slipped his hands into his pockets, and casually began quizzing each of the jurors the prosecution had put in place. Most of the questions were the same as those he'd asked in the first trial, questions about the jurors' families, their birthplaces, their religion, their political beliefs, though he added a new set of inquiries, too, delivered in the same offhand way. "Well you've heard of this case, I suppose?" a reporter recorded him as asking, "Read about it? Talked about it? Formed an opinion? Got it yet? Ever had any association with any colored people? Understand, Doctor Sweet's a colored man—bought a house in a neighborhood where there were no colored people. Well, that's the background. My client is a colored man. . . . Now you wouldn't want not to be fair. You just tell me yourself whether any views you have or surroundings you have would handicap my client or the state." When Chawke took his turn, the questioning was considerably sharper, a cross-examination rather than a conversation, but the focus was precisely the same. Background. Experience. Prejudice; again and again, prejudice.[33]

Gradually, the prosecution realized what was happening. However consistent his style, this wasn't the Darrow of the previous trial, searching for appropriate jurors by instinct and assumption; this was a disciplined defense transforming jury selection into a prolonged opening statement, repeatedly presenting its central argument for all the jurors to hear, winnowing out those least likely to listen.

On Tuesday morning, the assistant prosecutor, Lester Moll, tried to break the momentum. One of Toms's choices had just admitted to Darrow that he wouldn't want Negroes moving into his neighborhood, and the defense had asked Murphy to dismiss the man for cause. Moll suddenly broke in. "This is not a trial of race prejudice," he objected. "We are not trying to determine whether or not a colored man has the right to move into a white neighborhood. . . . The state is trying Henry Sweet for murder. His guilt or innocence on that charge is the only issue." But it was a pointless appeal. As soon as he heard Darrow's sharply honest reply—"I think we're trying the race question and nothing else"—Murphy endorsed it. There was no room for prejudice in the jury box, he ruled; the defense could proceed as it saw fit.[34]

With that, Darrow and Chawke assumed control of the selection process. For the rest of the week, they methodically moved through 4 jury pools, 198 people in all, searching for the 12 men most likely to sympathize with the defense's cause. Sometimes it was enough to hear a hint of personal identification. George Small was a young Catholic of the professional class—a man much like Chawke—who, when asked about his contact with colored people, spoke affectionately of his family's maid. Eighty-five-year-old Charles Thorne had put in half a century working for the Detroit and Cleveland Navigation Company, the same steamship line that had employed Ossian as summer help when he was a student at Wilberforce, while twenty-three-year-old Edward Bernie was just starting his career as a druggist; perhaps he would see something of himself in a defendant so close in age and ambition.

At other times, the defense was attracted to a juror's self-description. With eleven years' service in the navy, much of it abroad, Ralph Fuelling considered himself a man of the world, comfortable in the company of people from varied backgrounds Then there was ancient Louis Sutton, night watchman at Detroit's Catholic seminary. The old man hadn't heard a word about the previous trial—his reading tended toward church history and poultry science, not newspapers—but he knew he could be objective, he said, because "all my life I have tried to love my neighbor as myself." Not until noon Saturday did they settle on their final man, a middle-aged factory worker who had long lived alongside Negroes on the ragged edge of Black Bottom and couldn't quite see why one colored man had caused such a fuss on Garland. At Judge Murphy's order, the bailiff led the dozen jurors up to the courthouse's sixth-floor dormitory to be sequestered until 9:30 Monday morning, when the prosecution was to begin making its case against Henry Sweet.[35]

Toms intended it to be the day he took back the jury. For his opening statement, he planned to combine the circumstantial evidence upon which the previous prosecution had been built—the bungalow's lack of furniture, Gladys's stockpiling of food, Ossian's gathering of ten men inside the house on the night of the shooting—with Henry's damning admission to the assistant prosecutor that he'd aimed his rifle toward the street and squeezed off at least two shots. Toms hoped that with the young man's mumbled words eight months earlier—"I fired the rifle . . . the first time in the air," then "again in the crowd"—the rickety framework of the state's case would seem much more firm and reliable.

If he followed his pattern from the first trial, Darrow would then defer his opening statement, preferring to wait until the state closed its case and the defense was ready to begin presenting its evidence. So Toms would be free to move straight to his first witnesses, Inspector Schuknecht and his lieutenant, Paul Schellenberger, who'd finish the day with detailed descriptions of quiet, pacific Garland in the moments before the Negroes started shooting. Words alone wouldn't do, though. Before the jury was brought into the courtroom Monday morning, Toms stacked onto the lawyer's table the entire cache of weapons the police had found in the Sweets' house the night Breiner died so that when the jurors glanced at Henry Sweet, sitting directly behind his lawyers, they'd see the murder weapon, too, defendant and rifle reunited in a single indelible image.[36]

But again the defense moved in an unexpected direction. When Toms finished his opening statement, Murphy invited the defense to offer its response. Rather than demurring, Darrow rose from his seat, and, leaning on the jury box rail, told the jurors that the prosecutor was right: most likely a bullet from one of the guns now spread on the table killed Leon Breiner, and it was entirely possible that Henry Sweet pulled the trigger. But that tragic fact didn't make the young man into a killer, for he had been driven to his desperate act by the real villains of the story: the "average people"—"not any more than average," he added, "[As] you'll see"—who were now waiting to testify on the prosecution's behalf.[37]

Then the assault really began.

◆

There were times when it was painful to watch. Every day for a week and a half, Toms would carefully lead his witnesses through their testimony, ordinary folks unaccustomed to public appearances nervously recounting for the packed courtroom the events of September 9 precisely as the prosecutor needed them told. Then Darrow or Chawke would start the cross-examination, alternating the task between them. Except when children took the stand, there would be no gentle buildup, no attempt to beguile witnesses into saying something damaging, the way the defense had sometimes done during the first trial. The questions would come hard and fast, as they'd come for William Jennings Bryan in the stifling heat of Dayton, Darrow's typically gentle voice dripping with sarcasm, Chawke's deep bass raised in anger, the two men daring Toms's witnesses to hold their ground, pressing them to crack.[38]

Of course, they wanted to squeeze from the witnesses the critical admission that would bring the prosecution's version of events tumbling down—on the night of the murder, Garland was in the grip of a mob; the air was thick with threats; the bungalow was being pelted with stones—and they tried hard to get it. In the first trial, Darrow had allowed some of the state's witnesses to slip by with only perfunctory cross-examinations. Now, almost every witness was subjected to an intense

interrogation, every detail pressed and probed, any equivocation a cause
for attack. His hands clasped behind his back, his body leaning slightly
toward the witness like a hawk looking for prey, Chawke asked Lieutenant Schellenberger whether he saw "an unusual number of automobiles" on Garland in the hour before the shooting. "I should say not," the
young officer replied. Then why did you stop traffic on Garland but not
on the streets immediately east and west of it, Chawke said.

Schellenberger hadn't seen that question coming and he tried an
evasion. "I think the streets are wider and can accommodate more
cars." Chawke pounced. How wide is the street to the east? How wide is
the street to the west? Schellenberger said he didn't know. Then why
did you stop the cars on Garland, Chawke demanded, the questions
fired so rapidly now there was barely time for a reply. Were there
strangers in the autos pouring into Garland, people who didn't belong
in the neighborhood? Who were they? Why were they there? Thoroughly flustered, Schellenberger fumbled out an answer. "It appeared
to me that people were getting curious, more so than anything else, and
there was an unusual amount of traffic." That was what Chawke
had been looking for. "Then there *was* an unusual amount of traffic [on
Garland]," he said, "wasn't there?" Schellenberger gave Toms a desperate look, then said in as firm a voice as he could manage, "There was."[39]

Most of the witnesses proved tougher than Schellenberger. If a man
or woman's lies couldn't be exposed, though, the liar could. In the trial's
first fierce confrontation, Darrow took on Norton Schuknecht, "the veteran attorney fac[ing] a veteran police officer," as one reporter put it.
The inspector struck a nonchalant pose, one arm draped over the witness chair, his hand dangling limply, his Masonic ring glinted toward
the gallery. For an hour or more they battled, Darrow digging into every
detail of the inspector's two nights on Garland. How many people were
on the street on September 8? September 9? What did you hear them
saying? How heavy was the traffic? Did you see the taxi bringing Otis
Sweet to the bungalow? Did you see rocks thrown? Glass broken?

Doggedly, Schuknecht stuck to the story he'd been telling since
September—no crowds, no violence, no cause—but that simply gave
Darrow the opportunity to press the witness all the harder. If the Sweets
were in no danger, he asked, why did you have a dozen men around the
house and a reserve squad at the ready? Why did you order Garland
closed to cars shortly before the Negroes opened fire? If the shooting
were unprovoked, why was your first response to run straight toward a
house filled with homicidal colored men, without bothering to take his

gun out of its holster? With each question, the contradictions became more glaring, the inspector's answers more labored, until Darrow finally turned to the jurors, let out an audible "humph," and shrugged his shoulders in weary disbelief.[40]

Thomas Chawke subjected small, scared John Getke, the piano tuner who owned the house next to the Sweets, to the same treatment, albeit with a more combative edge. During the state's examination, Getke told Toms that Garland was deserted right before the shooting, but under Chawke's persistent questioning, he changed his mind, saying he might have seen a few people gathered on the sidewalk. "Did you surmise why a crowd was there?" demanded Chawke, and Getke said he did. "And your surmise had something to with the colored people who had moved into the neighborhood?" Again, Getke said it did. Desperate to put the witness back on track, Toms broke in to ask what Getke understood "surmise" to mean. The question seemed to remind the piano tuner of what he was supposed to be saying. "Since the last trial, I guess I kind of visualized a crowd," he explained. "I haven't a very good memory anyway." "Then you really didn't see a crowd?" said Toms. "No, I didn't," Getke replied and, that settled, stepped down from the witness box and started back to his seat. Instantly, Chawke blocked his way, towering over the man and thundering, "Will you see if you can tell us the truth? Was there or was there not a crowd?" Getke pulled himself to his full height, still far below that of Chawke, and screamed, "No!" while Toms, also on his feet, shouted his objection to the bench.

For a split second, it seemed as if a brawl were about to break out, but Murphy gaveled for order and the bailiff ushered Getke, red faced and fuming, back to the stand. Immediately, Chawke returned to the attack. "You 'surmised,' didn't you, that Mr. Toms wanted you to say no? You saw between five hundred and a thousand people there, didn't you?" "No," Getke insisted. "Do you know what a crowd is?" the attorney snarled. "Well," said the witness, "they say that one is company, two is a couple, and three is a crowd. I saw three policemen in front of the Sweet home." "At which," wrote a friend of Darrow's, "Mr. Chawke, with wrathful sardonic eyes and a look at the jury, dismissed him."[41]

To make sure that the jurors didn't miss the meaning behind all the glances their way, Darrow found a moment to make his condemnation of the witnesses perfectly plain. It was late in the first week and the defender was putting yet another Garland Avenue resident under a furious cross-examination. The witness was in the midst of making a slightly damaging admission when Lester Moll objected to his answer being admitted into evidence. Darrow exploded. "I don't believe the State has put on one witness who was present at the shooting who told the truth," he shouted, as heated as he'd been all trial. "Their own statements show they are hedging, quibbling and lying." On Toms's objection, the outburst was purged from the official record. But the jury had heard every word.[42]

Nor were the state's witnesses simply liars. With sneers so sharp they would have made H. L. Mencken proud, Darrow transformed those who took the stand from the decent men and women the prosecution claimed them to be into idiots, city cousins of the slope-browed simpletons he and his fellow sophisticates had humiliated in the backwoods of Tennessee the summer before. Patrolman Roy Schaldenbrand was trying to answer a question about the size of the crowd on Garland when he forgot what he was about to say. "I didn't think—" he hesitated. "What do you mean you didn't think?" shot Darrow. "Don't policemen think?" "No, a policeman is not supposed to think," the patrolman replied.

The people of Garland fared far worse. Time and again, Darrow mocked the witnesses' unconvincing answers, their lack of polish, their mangling of grammar and pronunciation. He knew from the first trial that the Sweets' white neighbors habitually mispronounced the cross street due north of Charlevoix, Goethe Street, calling it "Go-thee," but he hadn't made anything of it. This time he did. Marjorie Stowell, fifteen years a high school teacher, had already drawn laughs from the gallery by telling the clerk of the court her name and address not once but twice, both times in a voice so booming it rattled off the court's marble walls. Darrow began his cross-examination with a taunt. What's your name again, he asked. "You heard it the first time," she snapped. "What do you do?" Darrow drawled. "I am a teacher," she replied. "And you live near what street?" "Go-thee," she said for the third time. "You mean to tell me," Darrow scoffed, "anyone is fit to teach school in this city who pronounces 'Goethe' that way?" The next day, Stowell's humiliation made headlines in every one of Detroit's dailies.[43]

Of the various impressions the defense tried to create during cross-examination, though, one took preeminence. With almost every neighborhood witness, Darrow and Chawke circled their questioning back to the Waterworks Park Improvement Association. They never asked about the mundane activities that had filled much of the previous summer: the meeting in Harry Monet's garage at which the founding members talked of the association's rules and purposes; James Conley's consultations with other real estate agents to find the proper form for the restrictive covenants that he promised would protect the street from a Negro invasion; the association's going door to door in a fruitless search for neighbors willing to add the covenants to their deeds. Instead, Chawke and Darrow struck at individual motivation. Are you a member of the Waterworks Park Improvement Association, they'd begin. Yes, a witness would say, and the lawyers would ask the inevitable follow-up: why did you join? What did you hope to accomplish?[44]

Most of the witnesses tried to dodge the questions. "I joined because my husband did," said Della Getke, and no matter how hard Darrow pushed, she'd say no more. Edward Wettlaufer refused to remember a single thing about the association—who invited him to join, why he'd paid his dues, whether he'd ever attended a meeting. But there were breakthroughs, too. Florence Ware, who lived on the block south of the bungalow, told Darrow she joined the association "to protect my property." "Do you mean from colored people?" Darrow asked. "For the betterment of the community," she began to say, but Darrow cut her off. "Do you mean from colored people?" he asked again, his tone more insistent. Immediately, Toms objected. "Now don't interrupt the witness," he said. "You won't let her answer, and she is trying to answer your question." "She is trying not to answer," Darrow barked back, "just like the others." The objection was overruled and Murphy instructed the witness to respond. Yes, said Mrs. Ware at last, she was trying to protect her property from colored people. Edward Miller, a foreman who lived on the far end of the Sweets' block, tried a similar evasion, with even more miserable results. What was the purpose of the Waterworks Park Improvement Association, Darrow asked him. "Oh, we wanted to protect the place," he said. Against what? "Against undesirables," Miller answered. "Who do you mean by undesirables?" "Oh, people we don't want," Miller said, thinking himself cagey, but the defender demanded specifics. "Against Negroes," the witness admitted. "Anyone else?" Darrow asked, readying his knife. There was a pause while Miller thought about it. "Eye-talians," he finally said. Anyone else? Then "the witness with a Germanic name and the face of a moron," in James Weldon Johnson's scalding words, said that the people of Garland didn't want "anybody but Americans" living on their street. In went the blade. Do you know that Negroes have been in America for more than three hundred years, snarled Darrow, and that America was discovered by an "Eye-talian"?[45]

It wasn't sufficient to expose the association's discriminatory intent, though. Once a witness admitted his membership, Darrow and Chawke invariably led him back to the lawn outside Howe Elementary School in the heat of a July night, back to the moment when discrimination and the threat of violence first began to blend together. Several times, they came close to uncovering the full story of the association's mass meeting at the school yard, only to have the witness stop talking. By Saturday, May 1, they were running out of time; almost all of the prosecution's seventy-one witnesses had testified, and Toms was planning to bring his case to a close within a day or two. So when Alf Andrews took the stand, Darrow launched as vigorous a cross-examination as he could manage. Andrews wasn't any more friendly a witness than the others had been. But in the first trial, he'd been the one to say that the midsummer rally had attracted six hundred or seven hundred people. Now, under Darrow's relentless questioning, he revealed more.

The break began when Andrews said that the featured speaker that evening had been from the Tireman Avenue Improvement Association. What did the man say in his speech, Darrow asked? "He called a spade a spade when he talked," said Andrews. "Why can't you say it?" Darrow demanded. "Why can't you put it the way he did?" Andrews struggled for words. "He said that they—he offered the support of the Tireman Avenue Improvement Association to the Waterworks Improvement Association to handle the problem it was up against." "Did he say that they—the organization—made the Turners leave the[ir] house?" "Yes, he did," the witness said. "They didn't want colored people in their neighborhood and proposed to keep them out. He was very outspoken in his statements." "And you felt the same about not letting them out there?" said Darrow. Andrews admitted that he did, "if by legal means we could restrict them."

By now, the courtroom was riveted. Darrow "shoved his hands way down into his pockets," wrote a reporter who watched the exchange unfold, "let his face fill with withering scorn, hunched his shoulders. He was in full cry after his quarry."

"Did the speaker talk about 'legal means'?" he asked.

"I admitted to you that this man was radical," said Andrews.

"Answer my question. Did he talk about legal means?"

"No."

"He talked about driving them out, didn't he?"

"Yes, he was radical—I admit that."

"You say you approved of what he said and applauded it, didn't you?"

"Part of his speech," Andrews conceded.

"In what way was he radical?"

"Well I don't—I myself do not believe in violence."

"I didn't ask you what you believe in," Darrow snapped. "I said in what way was he radical? Any more you want to say about what you mean by radical, that he advocated?"

"No," said Andrews, almost pleading. "I don't want to say any more." But Darrow wasn't about to stop.

"You didn't rise at that meeting and say, 'I myself don't believe in violence,' did you?"

The thought seemed to horrify the witness. "No," he said. "I'd had a fine chance with six hundred people there!"

"What?" Darrow bellowed. "You would have caught it yourself, wouldn't you? You wouldn't have dared do it at that meeting?"

From behind him came Toms's desperate interruption. "Don't answer it!" he commanded Andrews. "I object to [the question] as very, very improper," and for once, Murphy agreed. But Darrow simply ignored the bench. "What did you mean by saying you had a fine chance?" he asked again. Toms grabbed Darrow by the arm, as if to restrain him. "Wait a minute!" he yelled. "Didn't you get the court's ruling?" Darrow shrugged him off. "What did you mean by that?" he asked again.

"You imagine I would have made myself heard with six hundred people there?" Andrews replied. "I wasn't on the platform."

Darrow shifted ground ever so slightly. "Did anybody—did *anybody* in that audience of six hundred people protest against advocating violence against colored people who moved into the neighborhood?"

"I don't know."

"You didn't hear any protest?"

"No."

"You heard only applause?"

"There was—as I stated—this meeting was in the school yard—"

Darrow broke in. "You heard nobody utter any protest, and all the manifestation you heard was applause at what he said?"

"Yes, that is all."

Again, Toms interrupted. "Did he *advocate* violence?" he asked, trying to hand the witness the answer he needed to escape Darrow's attack. But Andrews was too rattled to notice. "I said this man was radical," he told the prosecutor, seemingly annoyed that someone else was asking him questions he'd already answered. Toms tried a second time. "I know you did. Did he advocate violence?"

Andrews sat silently for a moment, then said the one word Toms didn't want to hear.

"Yes."[46]

The defense couldn't have asked for anything more than that. Ten days of dogged cross-examinations every bit as disciplined as jury selection had been, ten days of battering the prosecution's witnesses, and Darrow and Chawke had done precisely what they set out to do. By the time Toms closed his case on May 4, everyone in the courtroom knew that prejudice had a home. It lived in the cramped, crabbed houses that lined Garland Avenue.

◆

After the ferocity of its cross-examinations, the defense's presentation of its case opened in a subdued and predictable way. Darrow and Chawke brought in the requisite character witnesses—the president of Wilberforce's board of trustees, the Rev. Dr. Joshua Jones, and the college's football coach—and for an hour or so one afternoon, the director of the Detroit Urban League, John Dancy, provided an explanation of the city's racial problems so calm and judicious that even the prosecutor applauded his presentation.[47] Otherwise, the defense kept the court circling in and out of the Sweets' bungalow, just as they had in the first trial, showing the jurors snatches of two nights of terror.

Gladys's friends Edna Butler and Serena Rochelle returned with their story of seeing the mob gathered outside on the evening of September 8 and of the long night they spent huddling inside the house, too scared to go home. White reporter Philip Alder and the light-skinned colored couple, Bruce and Mary Spaulding, again told of wading through the crowd on Garland in the minutes before the shooting, their stories corroborated by the defense's one surprise witness, Thomas Chawke's cleaning lady, Theresa Hinties, who, as luck would have it, lived right across the alley from the Sweets' bungalow. Hinties set out to walk her dog on the evening of September 9, she explained in her thick German accent, but the mob in front of the Sweets was so large—at least three hundred people strong—the sidewalks were impassable, and she turned back; "I stepped me by the alley door," she said, just in time to hear the guns go off behind her. James Smith picked up the story there, describing the rampaging gangs of whites that engulfed his car as he tried to make his way down Charlevoix in the shooting's immediate aftermath.[48]

And with that the defense was complete—but for one witness. Friday morning, May 7, Darrow and Chawke brought Ossian back to the stand. By all rights, it should have been Henry, but the defense wasn't confident he could hold his own during what was sure to be a rigorous cross-examination, so the young man sat in silence—all but forgotten, thought a reporter—while his older brother took the jury on the long, bloody road from Bartow to Garland, from his hiding place in the bulrushes along the Peace River to the moment he opened his front door for Otis and Davis and saw a rabid mob across the narrow street. One man's story slotted into the nation's torturous history of race relations, an American dream darkened by nightmarish memories of rope and kerosene and a sudden, sickening confrontation with hatreds so deep they seemed bred in the bone.[49]

By early afternoon, the story was told. So Darrow returned to his seat, wearied from the day's exertions and a nagging cold, while Toms rose to begin his questioning. The rest of that day and most of the next, he kept Ossian on the stand, searching not for new information— there was none to find—but for the one misstatement, admission, contradiction that would destroy his credibility. Chawke and Darrow did what they could to protect their client, blocking Toms's most aggressive questions with objections that Murphy almost always sustained. When he had to answer, Ossian tried to be as cautious as he could; "most of the time," wrote an observer, "[the cross-examination] reminded one of a duel with swords," the prosecutor's thrusts parried by the doctor's carefully calibrated replies. At one point, Toms brandished the NAACP's tally of lynchings that Walter White had provided him. Have you read this report, he asked. Ossian said that he had. Why, then, did you fear for your life on Garland, said Toms, if you knew that there hadn't been a lynching in Michigan since 1889? "I thought that if Michigan mobs could find Negroes to lynch when there were comparatively few here," Ossian answered, "there was a good deal of danger now that there are eighty thousand of us."[50]

But there were also a few moments—the most perilous moments of the trial—when Ossian let down his guard. It wasn't that he stumbled, although after hours on the stand, he must have been exhausted. In fact, he seemed to straighten in his seat as the questions were asked. How was it that the men who were in the house on the night of the shooting all had guns? I supplied them, Ossian said, no hint of hesitation in his reply. That's not what you told the assistant prosecutor at police headquarters that evening, Toms pointed out, his chance at impeachment never better. I lied, said Ossian, "because I was scared and bewildered and denied the right of having an attorney. I thought they wanted to get me to make an incriminating statement so they could send me to prison." Now the fear was gone, replaced by unbending pride, the terrified little boy of Bartow given way to a New Negro willing to risk everything in defense of his family, his home, and his principles.[51]

"I was in Detroit last week and attended the Sweet trial," longtime activist Charles Edward Russell wrote his friend W. E. B. Du Bois after watching the scene unfold. "My dear Doctor, that was one of the great revelations—I wish you could have seen it. You would have thought better than ever of your people."[52]

◆

When the defense rested its case Saturday afternoon, Darrow left court ill and irritable, an old man feeling all of his sixty-eight years. But a day of rest and a surge of righteousness revived him, so that by the time closing statements began at half past nine Monday his blood was in full boil.[53]

The day did nothing to cool him. Assistant prosecutor Lester Moll filled the morning with an unexpectedly bitter screed against the defense, dismissing Ossian as "quasi-intelligent," scoffing at Serena Rochelle and Edna Butler as "so-called artists," and, most of all, mocking Darrow and Chawke for their misdirection of the jury. "God, how they hate to stand in front of the Dove house," he roared as his presentation reached its climax. "Breiner is dead and gone. We are interested in the right of the negro to live where he chooses. We are interested in the proposition that a jury of twelve men in this court of record will give them their due. Now let us forget about Breiner. Let us forget about that hail of lead bullets, gentlemen. Let us talk about intolerance. Take a trip down with me to the South. Take a trip back with me through the ages of history; take a trip with Doctor Ossian Sweet and stand by his side in Orlando, Florida, when he was a child seven years old. Register that remote impression of the negro instinct of which you know nothing. . . . We will put in a beautiful historical background. We will have a beautiful drop curtain. We will have a beautiful side curtain. We will have the beautiful music of Mr. Darrow's sweet lullaby, waving aside anything that bears on malice and on felonious homicide. Oh, that is beautiful. The accompaniment to this case has been beautiful. It has been soothing, and it has been pleasant until we talk of Breiner, and then the music of the voice transfers itself to the basso of the funeral march. . . ." But Moll wouldn't be seduced by the defense's performance, and neither should the jury. "Now I am carrying the brief of Leon Breiner," he said in his peroration, "and I am putting the case of Leon Breiner right on your doorstep . . . and alongside the dead body of Leon Breiner I am placing the fate of Henry Sweet. Now you can judge him, giving both their due."[54]

That afternoon, Thomas Chawke spoke in rebuttal, Moll's maudlin closing countered with a rococo condemnation. "Why deny that the greatest asset that the State has in this case is prejudice and the greatest handicap that we have on this side of the table is prejudice," he told the jurors. "I thought this case was fraught with nothing but disastrous things, and apart from the testimony, when I viewed here the sinister figure of prejudice, sitting before you twelve men in a dispensary of justice, but as I sat here this morning, and I saw an attempt made to arouse that prejudice, in order to becloud the issue here, so that you twelve men would not decide this case upon the testimony . . . I was amazed to think that a public prosecutor at this eventual hour should go to the burial place of Leon Breiner and drag his helpless body before you in order that you might send Henry Sweet to jail because Leon Breiner is dead and Henry Sweet is black instead of white."

Chawke's central goal wasn't to batter the prosecution, though, but to make the jurors see the case as part of the bitter divisions that had roiled Detroit's politics for the past two years. Darrow and Hays had tried to tap into that conflict's deep emotions during the first trial, but they'd done it with a subtlety that Chawke had no intention of repeating. "I say that this case marks an epoch in the history of the city," he said. "To those of you who have been lifelong residents of this town, as I have, the memory of your yesterdays must present a picture to you of a happy and contented citizenry, a citizenry that respected the right of the others in the town, without regard for color or creed or nationality." But the forces of hatred had been unleashed, the rights of the minority threatened by the tyranny of the mob, not just on Garland but across the city that Chawke was proud to call his home. As the afternoon wore on, the mobsters' man sounded more and more like Johnny Smith. "Now have we come to a point in the history of our city when a majority can ride roughshod and ruthlessly over the rights of a minority?" he shouted. "Is this the kind of government you prefer, or do you prefer . . . a government that would stay the hand uplifted for the injury of another? Do you prefer law and order to bloodshed and violence? Which? What will your answer be?"

It wasn't a question of principle alone but of self-preservation for all those people, like Chawke himself and at least some of the men watching him from the jury box, who didn't match the Nordic ideal.

"May the day never dawn when neighbor will be arrayed against neighbor in this city where I have spent the best part of my life and, please God, I hope to die. Here, where I have rubbed elbows with my fellow townsmen, all of these now nearly forty years; here where I have partaken of the hospitality of Jew and Gentile, colored man and white man; here, where I have grown amidst an atmosphere surcharged with liberality; that this place that I have selected as my home should ever become a place where the victims of mob fury and race hatred should be slaughtered like innocent children in the streets. Tell me, where will this lead? Today it is the colored man that is the victim of this particular kind of intolerance. Tomorrow, who will be the citizen, what portion of our citizenry will it be said to that you have rights under the law but that you dare not exercise them?"

Then, in his last few minutes before the jurors, Chawke tied the mayor directly into the case. "You have chosen as your chief executive officer a man who has denounced . . . bigotry and intolerance, and who feared that this race hatred might be a lasting stain upon the good name of the city," he said, as if it were the previous November and he were on the stump, pleading for votes. "I summon you to the side of the chief executive officer of this city. I ask you to let him lead the way, under the standard of tolerance and charity and good will toward all men that he has raised, above the strife, the turmoil, the hatred and enmity which some professional agitators would bring into this community to cause hate to run its riotous way. . . . Tell me, my fellow townsmen, what will your answer be? You have justice on the one side and injustice on the other. You have hatred and enmity, as against love, charity, and good will. These will dominate your deliberations, one or the other. We will permit you to go now, conscious of the fact that this verdict will be a righteous one; that Detroit will take its place among the fair cities of this country, as a place where government prevails under an orderly administration; where bloodshed and riot are denounced as pernicious things, things like a cancer, they eat their way into the body politic and bring about its ruin." The day was done. Almost six hours of oratory, and the Great Defender hadn't said a word.[55]

The next morning, the courtroom was as packed as it could possibly be, the gallery a jumble of black and white, the well of the court filled with spectators that Murphy had permitted to sit beyond the rail. Still there wasn't enough room, and hundreds of people remained standing in the hallway, hoping for a chance to squeeze inside. With all the noise and confusion the crowd caused, it was ten o'clock before the judge was able to get the proceedings under way. The nation's most famous agnostic ambled over to the jury box and began to preach a jeremiad for the modern age.[56]

He started in the same soft voice he'd used in his previous closing, the weight of a harsh and dangerous world resting on his slumped shoulders. "Now, gentlemen, I say you are prejudiced," he told the twelve men chosen precisely because they claimed to be open-minded. "Who are we, anyway? A child is born into this world, without any knowledge of any sort. He has a brain which is a piece of putty; he inherits nothing in the way of knowledge or ideas. If he is white, he knows nothing about color. He had no antipathy to the black. The black and the white both will live together and play together, but as soon as the baby is born we begin giving him ideas. We begin planting seeds in his mind. . . . We tell him about race and social equality and the thousands of things that men talk about until he grows up. It has been trained into us, and you, gentlemen, bring that feeling into this jury box, and that feeling which is a part of your life long training. You need not tell me you are not prejudiced. I know better."

Having exposed the sin buried in their American souls, Darrow then showed the jurors the darkness that lay at the end of the road to perdition. It was a bravura performance, sentimental, caustic, blatantly manipulative, and marvelously entertaining. "Now dropping to a whisper, now swelling until the very walls of the building seemed to vibrate in unison, his voice went on and on," wrote Josephine Gomon, "always interesting, always fascinating, always holding the attention of Judge, jurors and audience." For hours on end, he meandered through the testimony that had filled the previous few weeks, slipping in and out of the bungalow, up and down Garland, continually playing off black and white. He talked of Mary Spaulding, "modest, intelligent, beautiful; the beauty in her face doesn't come from powder or paint or any artificial means, but has to come from within; kindly, human feeling" and of her husband, Bruce, "a real gentleman" with "a good mind" and courteous manner. He spoke of Henry Sweet, "a boy, working his way through college, and he is just as good a boy as the boy of any juror in this box; just as good a boy as you people were when you were boys," and of the others who joined him in the bungalow on the fatal night, men who wanted nothing but "a chance to live; who asked for a chance to breathe the free air and make their own way, earn their own living, and get their bread by the sweat of their brows."

Most of all, he talked of Ossian, the embodiment of the American dream. "Gentlemen," he said, "a white man does pretty well when he does what Doctor Sweet did. A white boy who can start from nothing, and put himself through college, study medicine, taking postgraduate work in Europe, earning every penny of it as he goes along, shoveling snow and coal, and working as a bellhop on boats, working at every kind of employment that he can get to make his own way, is some fellow."

He spoke, too, of the people who populated "this highly cultured community near Goethe Street." Back came Marjorie Stowell, "fifteen years a school teacher and in common with all the other people in the community she calls it 'Go-thee' Street." Back came "wonderful mathematical geniuses" like John Getke who couldn't manage to count how many people gathered on the street in front of his house the night Leon Breiner died. Back came Edward Miller, "who thinks he's the only kind of American. The Negroes and the Eye-talians don't count. . . . Christopher Columbus was an Eye-talian, but he isn't good enough to associate with Miller. None of the people of brains and courage and intelligence, unless they happen to live around those four corners, are good enough, and there are no brains and intelligence to spare around those corners." Back came the "neighborly, visiting crowd" that gathered in front of the Sweets' home, "bringing them greetings and good cheer! Our people were newcomers. They might have needed their larder stocked. The crowd probably brought them ice cream and soda." Back came Alf Andrews at the school-yard rally listening to the speaker come over from Tireman Avenue—and suddenly all of Darrow's vicious wit disappeared.

"Six or seven hundred neighbors in this community listened to a speaker advocating the violation of the constitution and the laws and calling on the people to assemble with violence and force and drive these colored people from their homes," Darrow roared. "Gentlemen, in a school yard paid for by your taxes, paid for by the common people of every color, and every nationality, and every religion, that man stood there and harangued a mob and urged them to violence and crime . . . and nothing was done about it. And what else did Andrew say? He said the audience applauded this mad and criminal speech, and he applauded it, too." From that moment on, the benighted people of Garland Avenue were set on destruction. So when night fell on the eighth of September, "the mob gathered with the backing of the law. A lot of children went in front and threw the stones. They stayed for two days and two nights in front of this home and by their threats and assault were trying to drive the Negroes out. Those were the cowardly curs, and you know it. I suppose there isn't any ten of them that would come out in open daylight. . . . Oh no, gentlemen, their blood is too pure for that." And when their efforts failed—because the doctor and his friends dared to defend themselves—the Sweets' neighbors and the cops who supported them went into court and "lied and lied and lied to send these defendants to the penitentiary for life, so they will not go back to their home." Think of it, he thundered: this unconscionable cabal "violated the constitution and the law, they violated every human feeling and threw justice and mercy and humanity to the winds, and they made a murderous attack upon their neighbor because his face was black." And there was no reason for it, no cause—except for the terrifying power of racial prejudice.

There it was: a darkness so deep it made men blind. "Prejudices have burned men at the stake," Darrow told the jurors, "broken them on the rack, torn every joint apart, destroyed people by the million. Men have done this on account of some terrible prejudice which even now is reaching out to undermine this republic of ours and to destroy the freedom that has been the most cherished part of our institutions. These witnesses honestly believe that it is their duty to keep colored people out. They honestly believe that the blacks are an inferior race and yet if they look at themselves, I don't know how they can. If they had one colored family up there, some of the neighbors might learn how to pronounce 'Goethe.' It would be too bad to spread a little culture in that vicinity. They might die. They are possessed with that idea and that fanaticism, and when people are possessed with that they are terribly cruel. They don't stand alone. Others have done the same thing. Others will do the same thing as long as this weary world shall last. They may do it again, but, gentlemen, they ought not to ask you to do it for them. That is a pretty dirty job to turn over to a jury, and they ought not to expect you to do it."

By now, Darrow had been speaking for more than six hours, and those who knew him best thought him too drained to continue. "Twice he almost concluded," said a friend, "and then, as if some deep instinct warned him that he had not yet said quite all—that perhaps he had left uncovered in the minds of those men before him some tiny point upon which might hinge that kind, splendid young colored chap's whole future—he would go on." He recounted the horrors of slavery, just as he had in the first trial—ancestors trapped by slavers, the Middle Passage with its clank of chains and stench of death, generations spent in the sun-baked fields making other men rich—and as he spoke, the spirit of his beloved abolitionists seemed to surge through him. "Now that is their history," he said, every bit his father's son. "These people are the children of slavery. If the race that we belong to owes anything to any human being, or to any power in this Universe, they owe it to these black men. Above all other men, they owe an obligation and a duty to these black men which can never be repaid. I never see one of them that I do not feel I ought to pay part of the debt of my race—and if you gentlemen feel as you should feel in this case, your emotions will be like mine."

And he stretched his arms out toward the jury box, palms lifted upward in a gesture he often used, and offered redemption, thin and frail as it was. "I do not believe in the law of hate," he said. "I may not be true to my ideals always, but I believe in the law of love, and I believe you can do nothing with hatred. I would like to see a time when man loves his fellow man, and forgets his color or his creed. We will never be civilized until that time comes. I know the Negro race has a long road to go. I believe the life of a Negro has been a life full of tragedy, of injustice, of oppression. The law has made him equal—but man has not. . . . I know there is a long road ahead of him, before he can take the place which I believe he should take. I know that before him there is suffering, tribulation, and death among the blacks, and perhaps among the whites. I am sorry. I would do what I can to avert it. I would advise patience; I would advise toleration; I would advise understanding; I would advise all those things which are necessary for men who live together. . . . This is all. I ask you, gentlemen, on behalf of this defendant, on behalf of these helpless ones who turn to you, and more than that—on behalf of this great state, and this great city which must face this problem, and face it fairly—I ask you in the name of progress and the human race, to return a verdict of not guilty in this case!"[57]

For a moment, the court was silent, no one moving, no one talking as Darrow turned to take his seat. Then the crowd began to surge around him. James Weldon Johnson pushed his way through to offer his thanks. "His eyes were shining and wet," reported Johnson. "He placed his hands on my shoulders. I stammered out a few words but broke down and wept, and I was not ashamed of my tears."[58]

◆

Robert Toms led off the next morning with his closing statement, the last before Murphy handed the case to the jury. Like the defender, he talked for the better part of a day, pleading with the jury not to be fooled by all the beautiful words they'd heard from the other side.

"Back of all your sophistry, gentlemen of the defense," he said in closing, "back of all your transparent philosophy, back of your prating of the civil rights, and your psychology, and your theory of race hatred, and fear, and slavery, back of all that rises the dead body of Leon Breiner with a bullet hole in his back. . . . Leon Breiner, just a poor, insignificant American citizen, just one man in thousands, but a living human being with a right to live, without aspirations and with hopes and with ambitions, and with the God-given right to work them out, Leon Breiner, chatting with his neighbor at his doorstep, is shot through the back, from ambush, and you can't make anything out of those facts, gentlemen of the defense, or gentlemen of the jury, but cold-blooded murder." It was a solid enough performance, suitably dramatic, relentlessly aggressive, and occasionally bitter, but it was no match for the previous day's oration. One of Darrow's associates captured the tenor perfectly. "Somehow," she said, "it reminded one of the clatter of folding chairs after a symphony concert."[59]

Since the afternoon was spent by the time Toms finished, Murphy delayed instructing the jury until the following morning, Thursday, May 13. The more pedantic elements of his earlier charge had been stripped away, and the statement now read like a long discourse on the concept of justifiable homicide, capped by a warning that Darrow himself could have written: "Now gentlemen of the jury," he said, "I consider it my duty to especially caution you and warn you against prejudice or intolerance in your deliberations. . . . You will remember, gentlemen, that under the Constitution of the country, as well as the Anglo-Saxon concept of justice, all men are equal before the law. Real justice does not draw any line of color, race, or creed or class. All charged with crime, rich or poor, humble or great, white or black, are entitled to the same right and the same full measure of justice. It may be possible, human as we are, we cannot create perfect justice; but the ideal is plain, and it is our duty to strive and reach for it as sincerely as it is in our power do so."[60] So instructed, the jurors filed into the jury room to begin their deliberations.

If the previous trial were any guide, there was no point in waiting for a verdict to be reached. Someone suggested that Darrow might enjoy a quiet little speakeasy not far from the courthouse. Off they went, Clarence and Ruby, Thomas Chawke, the ever-present Josephine Gomon, and nine of their closest friends, to while away the afternoon deep in drink and conversation. They were still there three hours later—Darrow sipping port and reciting bawdy poetry to his increasingly inebriated entourage—when an officer of the court dashed in. They had to return to the court immediately, he said: the jurors were asking for a point of clarification, and before he could answer them, Judge Murphy needed to consult with counsel.[61]

It was almost four o'clock before they managed to find their way back to Murphy's chambers. Chawke and Toms prepared a reply, the two of them trading a yellow pad back and forth, wrangling over details. Just as Toms agreed to the last correction, word arrived. No need to finish; the jury was in.[62]

For the first few minutes, there was nothing but confusion. No one had seen the clerk of the court since he'd headed off with Darrow earlier in the afternoon, and while Murphy scrambled to find a replacement, the courtroom filled to suffocation—reporters, lawyers, judges, and assorted observers rushing in to hear the verdict rendered. Henry Sweet stood at the defense table, his hands clasped in front of him, his lower lip quivering ever so slightly; when Chawke leaned in to whisper a few words of encouragement, he didn't seem to notice. Darrow sat beside them, his mouth drawn in a thin line, his head leaning forward, his hands holding tight to the arm of the chair.[63]

Finally, Murphy took the bench and, with a nod, told the police officer nearest the jury room to escort the jurors into the well of the court. They came in single file, silent and somber, the foreman, young George Small, in the lead. Once they had assembled, the newfound clerk asked the required question: "Have you gentlemen in the course of your deliberations reached a verdict in the case of Henry Sweet? And if so who will answer for you?"

"We have and I will," said Small. A second's pause, an instant for the foreman to compose himself.

"Not guilty."[64]

A single clap of hands burst from the gallery, a single cheer. Then everyone seemed to move at once. Chawke and Darrow, both fighting back tears, reaching over to congratulate a stunned Henry; Toms, ashen faced, shouting for the verdict to be read again; Josephine Gomon and James Weldon Johnson joining the crowd of well-wishers rushing forward to offer their congratulations; Murphy gaveling for order that he couldn't hope to maintain.

In the midst of it all, no one seemed to notice Ossian Sweet sitting alone in the row behind his brother, his face buried in his hands.[65]

REQUIESCAM

A month after its triumph in the Sweet case, the NAACP held its annual convention on Chicago's South Side. It was a celebratory affair, as befitting a summer of hope. James Weldon Johnson spoke of the legal challenges to Jim Crow that the new Legal Defense Fund would make possible; majestic A. Philip Randolph, president of the Brotherhood of Sleeping Car Porters, made an impassioned plea for his nascent campaign to unionize the race men who worked on the Pullmans; W. E. B. Du Bois lectured on the trajectory of the Harlem Renaissance, now at the apex of its influence; and Walter White roamed through the assembly promoting his latest novel, *Flight*, just published and in need of glowing reviews. The convention didn't really begin to rock, though, until Clarence Darrow took the stage of the Auditorium Theater for a Sunday afternoon mass rally. So electric was the attraction that two thousand people had to be turned away. Those lucky enough to gain admission stood and cheered him for the brilliance of his work in Detroit, cheered again when he invoked the immortal spirit of John Brown, and again when he spoke of the course of American race relations.

Among "the new generation of white men," there were those who dared to speak of tolerance and understanding, he told the crowd, and in that generation, Darrow saw the future. Prejudice was still a mighty force, he admitted, but its decline had already begun, and in time it would be defeated.[1]

It was a remarkably upbeat message for a man who liked to dwell in darkness. But Darrow had sensed something in the Sweet trial—something in the way his words were heard, perhaps, or in the mix of people he came to know during those days or in the passionate politics that swirled around the case—that gave him hope. And he was right. In the first quarter of the twentieth century, there was no dishonor in believing that white, Anglo-Saxon Protestants stood atop an inviolate hierarchy of the races, no shame in saying that blacks, Jews, Catholics, and the immigrant masses—Italians, Irishmen, Greeks, Slavs, Poles, Turks, Russians, Mexicans, Chinese, and so many others—were by their very nature inferior beings. But, over the course of the 1930s, 1940s, and 1950s, the voices of toleration slowly pushed those ideas toward the dark corners of metropolitan America.

Not that racial and ethnic hatred disappeared. But they became disreputable, a sign of crudeness, stupidity, and moral failing, a product of the prejudice that, as Darrow had said, made men terribly cruel. As attitudes changed, the virulent racism that had swept across the urban North in the 1910s and 1920s faded away. The intelligentsia exchanged its grand theories of racial evolution for a subtle understanding of the brotherhood of man. The Ku Klux Klan shriveled to nothingness, until even the memory of its meteoric rise was lost. Shops and theaters and even some workplaces gradually abandoned the color lines they had hastily erected when the Great Migration began.

Only once, in the fevered days of World War II, were northern cities wracked by large-scale antiblack pogroms the way they'd been in Chicago, Washington, D.C., and so many other places in early days of the century. The easing of the extraordinary tensions of the 1910s and 1920s, in turn, convinced more and more northern whites that they were in fact a tolerant people, a perception reinforced by the persistence of the most blatant forms of discrimination below the Mason-Dixon Line. That's where the nation's racial problems lay, northerners concluded: in the daily humiliations of segregation, the obvious wrong of disenfranchisement, and the habitual injustice of southern courtrooms, not in the streets of New York, Chicago, and Detroit, where a black woman riding in the front of a bus was no cause for concern.[2]

In the time left him, Darrow did what he could to hurry the day when America would become a tolerant place. There were other issues he tackled in the years after Detroit: a battle against the banning of books in Boston and a defense of radicals accused of murder in the Bronx, both fought alongside Arthur Garfield Hays. But the race problem remained a passion. In 1926, Darrow joined the NAACP's executive board, and from that position became one of the most devoted of the association's white champions, contributing a portion of his considerable lecture fees to the organization, regularly consulting with James Weldon Johnson and Walter White, writing an occasional piece for the *Crisis*. And once, in the bitter winter of 1932, he and Hays tried to re-create the Sweet defense in the heart of Jim Crow, traveling at the NAACP's behest to Alabama to defend nine desperately poor black teenagers accused of raping two white girls. But the Scottsboro Boys, as they were known, already had representation provided by the American Communist Party, and they couldn't be convinced that they'd be better off with the seventy-four-year-old Great Defender. The rebuff didn't bother him much. Darrow understood that his time has passed, that the causes he'd championed now belonged in the hands of that younger generation he'd celebrated at the NAACP convention in 1926. Although he could never retire, illness eventually slowed him down, and on March 13, 1938, he passed away. To the end, said Ruby, "[Clarence] maintained that he didn't care whether he went to heaven or hell because he had so many good friends in either place."[3]

•

Not everyone involved in the Sweet case fulfilled the expectations Darrow had for the next generation. Though he talked of his role in the defense with obvious pride, Thomas Chawke showed no inclination to pursue public service. When the trial was over, he happily returned to his usual lineup of unsavory clients. That work was stimulating enough, he said—during the recess of one trial, an opponent whacked him over the head with a tire iron—and when he grew too old for its demands, he eased himself into a profitable civil practice.

Mayor Johnny Smith, meanwhile, watched his promising political career crumble beneath him. For a while after the Sweet trial, there was talk of his running for governor, but Detroit's elite were determined to see him toppled. For the next two years, they assailed Smith as a front man for Detroit's rampant vice trade, and when he stood for reelection in 1927, they found an appropriately upright candidate to oppose him. The progressive bloc again tried to rally around him, but this time there was no Klan menace to make the campaign into a crusade: Smith lost the 1927 mayoral election by eleven thousand votes. Never again did he hold an office higher than city councilman.[4]

To a remarkable degree, though, the people who circled through the Sweet case did help move America away from the brutal intolerance of the 1920s. For a quarter century after the trial, Arthur Garfield Hays continued his peripatetic campaign to secure justice for those the nation made marginal. He was in Boston pleading for clemency on the night Sacco and Vanzetti were executed; in Jersey City defending free speech when that town's brutal boss tried to silence striking union men; in Puerto Rico protesting oppression when colonial authorities sought to crush the nationalist movement with force of arms; in Harlem demanding justice when police brutality reached such obscene levels it triggered nights of rioting. And when he looked back on it all late in life, he thought of no better epitaph for his career than the words Darrow had used whenever he introduced one of his friend to Hays: "Dear Art, he's one of our kind."[5]

Reinhold Niebuhr spent a year coming to understand the depths of Detroit's racial problems on behalf of the mayor's commission. "It has been a rare experience to meet with . . . white and colored leaders and talk over our race problems," he wrote in his diary. "The situation which the colored people of the city face is really a desperate one and no one who does not spend real time can have any idea of the misery and pain which existed among these people. . . ." When it was finally presented to Johnny Smith in March 1927, the commission's report was a marvelous piece of social research, minutely detailing the depths of discrimination black Detroiters faced in health care, housing, employment, and criminal justice. As a call to action, however, it was sadly lacking, its recommendations restricted to requesting that whites be fairer in dealing with their colored neighbors. But the experience of confronting Detroit's multiple divisions had already started to move Niebuhr beyond the mild Christian liberalism the report embodied. In 1928, he left his Detroit pastorate for a teaching position at New York's prestigious Union Theological Seminary. Four years later, he published the first of a series of pathbreaking theological treatises grappling with the problem of man's duty to confront society's sins. Condemned by conservatives as dangerously radical, Niebuhr's work—at once deeply analytical and profoundly engaging—inspired two generations of politically involved students, foremost among them a young man named Martin Luther King, Jr., who read Niebuhr's books when he was twenty-one years old and forever after considered himself a disciple.[6]

Josephine Gomon and Robert Toms, meanwhile, quietly built distinguished careers. In the depth of the Great Depression, Gomon took charge of Detroit's struggling welfare system, transforming it into a national model of well-managed generosity. Like Hays, she made civil liberties her life's passion, supporting the right of working people to organize unions and women to receive equal treatment before the law, struggles that made her, in the words of one admirer, "the conscience of Detroit." No one would have expected Toms to follow a similar path, given his political commitments in the 1920s. As the Anglo-Saxon fever faded, though, the prosecutor moved in a new direction. With Darrow's endorsement to boost him, Toms was elected circuit court judge in 1929. Once he was on the bench, he proved to be a solid supporter of civil rights. In the 1930s, he joined the Detroit branch of the NAACP. And in the signal achievement of a surprisingly well-spent life, he devoted all of 1947 to confronting the greatest of racial evils, presiding over the prosecution of Nazi war criminals as a trial judge for the United States Military Tribunal at Nuremberg.[7]

It was another member of that young generation of Detroiters, though, who brought the principles espoused in the Sweet case to the highest levels of public life. When Detroit's elite defeated Johnny Smith in 1927, they undoubtedly thought they were taking their city back from the Negroes and foreigners who had put the half-deaf former pipe fitter into office in the first place. Just three years later, Frank Murphy used the same coalition of working people—black and white, Low Church Protestant, Catholic, and Jew—to make himself mayor. The election itself wasn't particularly important. But the voting bloc Murphy had assembled was of the greatest significance, for it was the same coalition that in the desperate year of 1932 elected Franklin Roosevelt president. When Roosevelt took power, he saw in "young, red-headed, idealistic" Murphy a tribune to the urban masses who anchored America's new political order.[8]

Thus began Murphy's extraordinary climb to national prominence. During the 1930s, he served as governor-general of the Philippines, governor of Michigan, and attorney general of the United States, always with the studied sympathy for the underdog he'd proclaimed when crisscrossing Detroit's east side in search of votes in 1923. His last promotion came in 1940, and it was the greatest of them all, to a seat on the United States Supreme Court. Being on the court, he said, gave him "the rarest of all opportunities to evangelize for tolerance and all things that are just." During his nine-year tenure, he did just that, defending the right of Jehovah's Witnesses not to salute the American flag, of Communist Party members to speak their minds without fear of reprisal, of protesters to picket peacefully, of accused criminals to receive fair trials. He abhorred "the ugly abyss of racism," he wrote in his searing dissent condemning the internment of Japanese Americans during World War II. And when NAACP lawyers came before the court, as they did in several critically important cases during his tenure, Murphy always gave them his vote.[9]

James Weldon Johnson was gone by then. For all his self-possession, he couldn't prevent the NAACP's incessant demands from eating away at his health, and in the summer of 1929, he opted for a calmer life as professor of literature at Fisk University. Walter White stepped into the position his mentor had vacated. He stayed for twenty-six tumultuous years, guiding the association through Depression and war with a hand so firm his critics feared he was giving the NAACP rigor mortis. There were new initiatives under his watch, of course: attacks on discrimination in government employment during the New Deal, alliances with the emerging labor movement, a long battle to desegregate the military.

Above all else, though, White's NAACP doggedly pursued the legal strategy Johnson had put in place. In his early years as secretary, White built up the Legal Defense Fund made possible by the Sweet trials until it could support a full-time staff of attorneys. Headed first by Howard law school dean Charles Houston, then by his star pupil Thurgood Marshall, the NAACP's legal department spent more than two decades using Supreme Court challenges to chip away at Jim Crow. Ever so slowly the justices flaked off pieces of the southern system: the white primary, the barring of blacks from juries, the segregation of interstate transportation, all were declared unconstitutional in the 1930s and 1940s. Then in May 1954, a year before White's death, the association's campaign reached its climax. In *Brown v. Board of Education*, the Court shattered one of Jim Crow's foundation stones, the legal segregation of schools, and by so doing fundamentally weakened the entire structure of southern apartheid. It would take another decade of struggle—and much blood—for black activists to topple the structure completely. But with the NAACP's extraordinary victory in *Brown*, Jim Crow's destruction was set in motion.[10]

◆

The North moved in a different direction. Two weeks after Henry Sweet walked out of the courthouse a free man, the Supreme Court ruled against the NAACP in the Washington, D.C., restrictive covenant case, as Moorfield Storey feared it would. With that defeat, the association lost its last hope of stopping the color line from being drawn across urban America. Over the next few decades, racism and the forces of the marketplace, which had only begun to intertwine in the 1920s, thoroughly fused together. Developers placed restrictive covenants on their deeds as a matter of course; real estate agents invariably steered colored customers away from white neighborhoods; banks and insurance companies made it ironclad policy to refuse services to blacks buying homes in white areas; and in a cruel turn of politics, the New Dealers who depended on the black vote gave these discriminatory practices government sanction by writing them into the many housing programs they created in the 1930s, so that in every one of the nation's great cities the once disconnected walls of segregation were made complete.[11]

As the walls went up, there was no outcry from even the most liberal of northern whites, no calls for an end to the obvious injustices that the marketplace inflicted. Like Darrow in Detroit, they simply shrugged their shoulders and said that they didn't know what could be done about it. Racism was a personal failing, after all, to be solved by understanding, by civility, by a softening of the human heart. When white mobs took to the streets to drive out black families that somehow managed to cross the color line, an event that happened time and again in the 1930s and 1940s, liberal whites offered swift condemnation, as they would of southern lynchings, for such heinous acts were clearly the work of prejudice. But it never occurred to them to attack the economic structures that transformed hatred into organized violence, as that wasn't where they believed the problem lay. Intolerance was wrong. But the separation of whites and blacks was to be expected, since, as Darrow said as he stood before the jury in Frank Murphy's courtroom all those years before, "the adjustment of races, the adjustment of religions, and the understandings of human beings by each other is the question of infinite time. I see no way that we can help it."[12]

Eventually, black activists forced whites to recognize the role that the marketplace played in maintaining the color line. The NAACP finally won a reversal of the Washington decision in 1948, the victory secured in a case brought to the association by a black man who had been barred from buying a home just six blocks from the house Alexander Turner had tried to make his in the summer of 1925. It took another twenty years—until the cataclysmic summer of 1968—to push through federal legislation prohibiting discrimination in the selling and financing of homes. By then, it was too late. Segregation had become so deeply entrenched in urban America it couldn't be uprooted, no matter what the law said. To this day, the nation's cities remain deeply divided, black and white neighborhoods separated by enduring discriminatory practices, racial fears and hatreds, and the casual acceptance by too many people that there is no problem to address. And of all the cities in the United States, none is more segregated than Detroit.[13]

•

When Ossian Sweet bought the house on Garland Avenue in the spring of 1925, he imagined his family living a life free of segregation's most crushing burdens. But there was no escape.

In the days after the acquittal, the accolades poured into the Sweets' apartment, just as they had after the first trial. The most welcome report, though, come from the prosecutors' office. Now that Henry was acquitted, Robert Toms let it be known that there would be no more trials; *The People v. Sweet* would never come to court again. The joy of the moment was tempered, though, by very grim news: the reason Gladys and Iva had been unable to shake their illnesses that winter was because they were afflicted with tuberculosis, contracted, they were sure, during Gladys's incarceration in Wayne County Jail. More than likely the Sweets knew of the diagnosis before the April trial. But it wasn't until Henry was safe that they sought a cure. Early that summer, Gladys took her daughter to Tucson, Arizona, where the hot, dry air was better for their damaged lungs. It didn't help. At the end of August, two months past her second birthday, Iva passed away. Gladys brought the baby home so that she might be buried beside the son she and Ossian lost in 1923. When the funeral cortege arrived at the gates of Roseland Park Cemetery, the white groundskeeper ordered them to go through the back entrance, as Negroes were expected to do. Ossian reached into his pocket, drew out a gun, and demanded that the gates be opened to him.[14]

Ossian and Gladys spent the next two years living apart, he in the apartment near Dunbar Memorial, she back in Tucson nursing her health. Finally, in the middle of 1928, he took possession of the bungalow, which had been shuttered since the shooting. A few months later, Gladys came home to die. Ossian buried her on a dark November day. She was twenty-seven.[15]

Sweet stayed in the bungalow for a quarter century. In that time, he experienced the financial success he'd dreamed of having when he was sweeping sidewalks back at Wilberforce. Shortly after the second trial, he bought Garafalo's Drugstore, the fine corner property a few streets east of his St. Aubin office. He moved his practice to the building's second floor, while on the first, he maintained a steady trade in pharmaceuticals and sundries. Although his fame assured him a permanent position on Dunbar's staff, in 1929 he left his post to run the first in what would be a series of small, rival hospitals in the heart of the ghetto. Though none of them flourished, they must have provided Ossian a healthy income, for there was money to indulge in a marvelous affirmation of his rise into the professional class. As he approached his fiftieth birthday, he began to buy tracts of land in East Bartow—enough to eclipse his father's tiny lot—and to spend part of his winters there, tending the citrus crop and enjoying the honor bestowed on a native son everyone on the colored side of town called "Big Doc."[16]

But there were losses as well, many of them bitterly hard to endure. With Gladys's death, Ossian's personal life spiraled downward. He married two more times, but both marriages ended in divorce, the second amid accusations of physical abuse. Over the years, he opened his home to several Black Bottom teenagers, at least twice offering to make the boys his sons, but those relationships also ended badly, as he demanded of them the sort of backbreaking labor he'd performed when he was young.

The public role that Ossian had adored during the trials crashed around him as well. In his insensitive way, he made an ill-advised bid for the presidency of the Detroit branch of the NAACP in 1930, running against the very men who'd rushed to his defense five years earlier; the city's Talented Tenth never forgave him for the effrontery. Twice, he ran for elective office, once for a seat in the state Senate, another time for U.S. Congress, his campaigns built on a fierce pride in his accomplishments and a touching faith in what he called "the American way of life." Twice, he was defeated.

Henry Sweet helped recoup some of the family honor. After his acquittal, he went on to Howard University—as always following his big brother's example—to earn a law degree. Upon graduation, he returned to Detroit, where he used the charm that Ossian never had to work his way up the NAACP hierarchy. By the late 1930s, he had become president of the association's Michigan conference. Then, in the summer of 1939, Henry learned that he, too, had contracted TB; six months later he was dead, another victim of the inadequate health care available to even the most accomplished of black Detroiters.[17]

At last, even Ossian's finances failed him. Not until 1950 did he pay off the land contract and assume ownership of the bungalow. Almost immediately, the property taxes fell into arrears. There's no saying what caused the problem—maybe it was the increasingly intense arthritis slowing his practice, maybe the slow decay of his tiny hospital on St. Aubin—but the debt mounted year after year, until he faced foreclosure. Rather than lose the house, Ossian sold the property in April 1958. When he left, thirty-two years after that terrible night, the neighborhood around Garland Avenue was still largely white. But Ossian passed on the bungalow to a black family, southern migrants who had come north in search of opportunity, good honest people looking for a place to raise their family in peace.[18]

With nowhere else to go, Ossian made an apartment for himself in his office above Garafalo's. It had to have been a terribly painful move, to exchange the house on Garland for the ghetto that as a young man he had sacrificed everything to leave behind. When Robert Toms saw him at a social event about that time, he was shocked by the decline; the doctor had put on weight, and the agile mind he'd displayed on the witness stand had slowed. There developed about him "a bitterness, a darkness," said another acquaintance. He never said what haunted him in those years. Maybe it was nothing more than memories: of a night dancing with Gladys at the colored Y, perhaps; of their newborn's feeble cry in a Paris apartment; of a spring evening walking through the house on Garland for the first time, seeing Gladys's face glow with happiness as she imagined it being hers; of lying on their bed, a pistol beside him, waiting for night to fall. Finally, on March 20, 1960—just as the civil rights movement was about to sweep through the South—Ossian Sweet went into his tiny bedroom, picked up a handgun, and put a bullet in his brain.[19]

NOTES

Prologue: America: 1925

1. Keith L. Bryant, Jr., "Cathedrals, Castles, and Roman Baths: Railway Station Architecture in the Urban South," *Journal of Urban History* 2 (February 1976): 195–230.

2. National Association for the Advancement of Colored People [hereafter referred to as NAACP] press release, June 4, 1925, frame 195, reel 3, part 7, NAACP Papers [microfilm edition]; "Mississippi Mob Lynches Two More Men," *Chicago Defender*, March 21, 1925, clipping in frame 722, reel 13, part 7, NAACP Papers; "Negro Burned to Death Near Scarboro, Ga.," *[Atlanta?] Journal*, March 4, 1925, frame 1172, reel 10, part 7, NAACP Papers.

3. James Grossman, *Land of Hope: Chicago, Black Southerners, and the Great Migration* (Chicago: University of Chicago Press, 1989), pp. 3–4, 11; William Tuttle, *Race Riot: Chicago in the Red Summer of 1919* (New York: Atheneum, 1970).

4. W. Hawkins Ferry, *The Buildings of Detroit: A History*, rev. ed. (Detroit: Wayne State University Press, 1980), p. 329; Sally Chappell, "As If the Lights Were Always Shining: Graham, Anderson, Probst and White's Wrigley Building at the Boulevard Link," in John Zukowsky, ed., *Chicago Architecture, 1872–1922: Birth of a Metropolis* (Munich: Prestel-Verlag, 1987), pp. 291–301; Barbara Diamonstein, *The Landmarks of New York* (New York: Harry N. Abrams, 1988), p. 308.

5. On urban America's hegemony, see Ann Douglas, *Terrible Honesty: Mongrel Manhattan in the 1920s* (New York: Farrar, Straus and Giroux, 1995). "The joy cry of wealth and power," wrote the German architect Erich Mendelsohn upon visiting 1920s New York, "the victory cry over Old Europe and the whole world. Loud beyond measure." Quoted in Robert A. M. Stern et al., *New York 1930: Architecture and Urbanism Between the Two World Wars* (New York: Rizzoli, 1987), p. 589.

6. Ellis W. Hawley, *The Great War and the Search for Modern Order: A History of the American People and Their Institutions, 1917–1933* (New York: St. Martin's Press, 1979), pp. 81–87; Alfred D. Chandler, Jr., *The Visible Hand: The Managerial Revolution in American Business* (Cambridge, Mass.: Harvard University Press, 1977), pp. 456–476; William Leach, *Land of Desire: Merchants, Power, and the Rise of a New American Culture* (New York: Alfred A. Knopf, 1993), pp. 340–341.

7. Detroit's African-American population figures from Mayor's Inter-Racial Committee, *The Negro in Detroit* (Detroit: Bureau of Governmental Research, 1926), section 2,

p. 4; New York City's population figures from Gilbert Osofsky, *Harlem: The Making of a Ghetto* (New York: Harper and Row, 1963), p. 128.

8. Jane Addams, *Twenty Years at Hull-House* (1910; repr. New York: New American Library, 1960), rep. 170; Christine Stansell, *American Moderns: Bohemian New York and the Creation of a New Century* (New York: Henry Holt, 2000), p. 334; Douglas, *Terrible Honesty*, p. 112.

9. David Levering Lewis, *When Harlem Was in Vogue* (New York: Alfred A. Knopf, 1979), p. 98.

10. "Detroit Stations," http://www.nationalmuseum.org/stations/detroit.htm, last accessed on December 13, 2001; "Jazz Age Chicago—Illinois Central Station," http://www.suba.com/~scottn/explore/sites/transport/cent_sta.htm, last accessed on December 13, 2001; Bradford Gilbert, "The Architecture of Railroad Stations," *Engineering Magazine* (1895), quoted in Ric Burns and James Sanders, *New York: An Illustrated History* (New York: Alfred A. Knopf, 1999), p. 354.

11. John Higham, *Strangers in the Land: Patterns of American Nativism, 1860–1925* (1955; repr. New York: Atheneum, 1971); Matthew Frye Jacobson, *Whiteness of a Different Color: European Immigrants and the Alchemy of Race* (Cambridge, Mass.: Harvard University Press, 1998); Iver Bernstein, *The New York City Draft Riots: Their Significance for American Society and Politics in the Age of the Civil War* (New York: Oxford University Press, 1990); Elliot Rudwick, *Race Riot in East St. Louis, July 2, 1917* (Carbondale: Southern Illinois University Press, 1964).

12. Lynn Dumenil, *The Modern Temper: American Culture and Society in the 1920s* (New York: Hill and Wang, 1995), chapters 4–6, for an excellent introduction to the tensions of the 1920s; Robert Sobel, *Coolidge: An American Enigma* (Washington, D.C.: Regnery Publishing, 1998); Calvin Coolidge, "Whose Country Is This?" *Good Housekeeping* (February 1921): 109.

13. Dumenil, *The Modern Temper*, p. 237; David M. Chalmers, *Hooded Americanism: The First Century of the Ku Klux Klan, 1865–1965* (Garden City, N.Y.: Doubleday, 1965) for an introduction to the second Klan; Detroit and Chicago Klan figures are from Kenneth Jackson, *The Ku Klux Klan in the City, 1915–1930* (New York: Oxford University Press, 1967), pp. 103, 129. A brilliant analysis of the Klan, albeit in a southern setting, is Nancy Maclean, *Behind the Mask of Chivalry: The Making of the Second Ku Klux Klan* (New York: Oxford University Press, 1994).

14. Chalmers, *Hooded Americanism*, pp. 286–288.

15. Higham, *Strangers in the Land*, chapters 10 and 11.

16. Oscar Handlin, *Al Smith and His America* (Boston: Little, Brown, 1958), p. 123.

17. Victoria W. Wolcott, *Remaking Respectability: African American Women in Interwar Detroit* (Chapel Hill: University of North Carolina Press, 2001), p. 1; Jervis Anderson, *This Was Harlem: A Cultural Portrait, 1900–1950* (New York: Farrar, Straus and Giroux, 1981), p. 142.

18. Lewis, *When Harlem Was in Vogue*, p. 165.

Chapter One: Where Death Waits

1. "The Weather," *Detroit Free Press*, September 10, 1925.

2. On the early history of Detroit, see Silas Farmer, *History of Detroit and Wayne County and Early Michigan* (Detroit: Gale Research, 1969). A brilliant analysis of Detroit's transformation is Olivier Zunz, *The Changing Face of Inequality: Urbanization, Industrialization, and Immigrants in Detroit, 1880–1920* (Chicago: University of Chicago Press, 1982), parts 1–2.

3. Allan Nevins, *Ford: The Times, the Man, the Company* (New York: Charles Scribner's Sons, 1954); Douglas Brinkley, *Wheels for the World: Henry Ford, His Company, and a Century of Progress, 1903–2003* (New York: Viking, 2003), pp. 3–160; Lindy Biggs, *The Rational Factory: Architecture, Technology, and Work in America's Age of Mass Production* (Baltimore: Johns Hopkins University Press, 1996), chapters 4 and 5.

4. Zunz, *The Changing Face of Inequality*, pp. 292–309; Robert Conot, *American Odyssey* (New York: Morrow, 1974), pp. 193–195.

5. Stephen Meyer III, *The Five Dollar Day: Labor Management and Social Control in the Ford Motor Company, 1908–1921* (Albany: SUNY Press, 1981), pp. 74–77; Steve Babson et al., *Working Detroit: The Making of a Union Town* (New York: Adama Books, 1984), pp. 22–28; "City 1,242,044 Census Shows," *Detroit Free Press*, September 27, 1925; reporter quoted in Peter Gavrilovich and Bill McGraw, eds., *The Detroit Almanac: 300 Years of Life in the Motor City* (Detroit: Detroit Free Press, 2000), p. 76.

6. Zunz, *The Changing Face of Inequality*, pp. 342–371; Richard W. Thomas, *Life for Us Is What We Make It: Building Black Community in Detroit, 1915–1945* (Bloomington: Indiana University Press, 1992), pp. 89–102; Kevin Boyle and Victoria Getis, *Muddy Boots and Ragged Aprons: Images of Working Class Detroit, 1900–1930* (Detroit: Wayne State University Press, 1997); Thomas Sugrue, *The Origins of the Urban Crisis: Race and Inequality in Postwar Detroit* (Princeton, N.J.: Princeton University Press, 1996), p. 22; Robert Dunn research notes, n.d. [c. 1926], box 1, Robert Dunn Collection, Archives of Labor and Urban Affairs, Walter P. Reuther Library, Wayne State University, Detroit, Mich.

7. Specifics on Garland Avenue are drawn from Sanborn Map Company, *Fire Insurance Map of Detroit, Michigan* (New York: Sanborn Map Company, 1929); a review of R. L. Polk and Company, *Detroit City Directory* (Detroit: R. L. Polk and Company, 1910–1920) and of Garland Avenue building permits, Detroit Building and Safety Department Index, v. 3, Burton Historical Collection, Detroit Public Library, Detroit, Mich.; and from a series of personal visits from 2001 to 2003.

8. For a snapshot of Garland Avenue, see sheets 3–10, e.d. 629, 1920 U.S. census manuscript, Detroit, Michigan, and R. L. Polk and Company, *Detroit City Directory*, 1925–1926 (Detroit: R. L. Polk and Company, 1926). On routes into the upper reaches of the working class, see Steve Babson, *Building the Union: Skilled Workers and Anglo-Gaelic Immigrants in the Rise of the UAW* (New Brunswick, N.J.: Rutgers University Press, 1991), pp. 85–94, and Dunn research notes, n.d. [1926].

9. Dunn research notes, n.d. [1926–1927]; Polk, *Detroit City Directory*, 1925–1926; 1920 U.S. census manuscript; David Montgomery, *The Fall of the House of Labor: The Workplace, the State, and American Labor Activism, 1865–1925* (Cambridge, England: Cambridge University Press, 1987), chapters 1 and 4; Nelson Lichtenstein, "'The Man in the Middle': A Social History of Automobile Industry Foremen," in Nelson Lichtenstein and Stephen Meyer, eds., *On the Line: Essays in the History of Auto Work* (Urbana: University of Illinois Press, 1989), pp. 73–99.

10. Walter Clyde, *A Million Dollar Secret* (Detroit: Walter Schulte Corp., 1927); Joyce Shaw Peterson, *American Automobile Workers, 1900–1933* (Albany: SUNY Press, 1987), pp. 72–85; Committee on Negro Housing, *Negro Housing* (1932; repr. New York: Negro Universities Press, 1969), p. 44.

11. David Alan Levine, *Internal Combustion: The Races in Detroit, 1915–1926* (Westport, Conn.: Greenwood Press, 1976), p. 158; transcript of *Detroit Free Press* story, n.d. [September 10, 1925], box 5, Clarence Darrow Collection, Library of Congress, Washington, D.C.; Marcet Haldeman-Julius, "Clarence Darrow's Defense of a Negro," *Haldeman-Julius Monthly* 4 (July 1926): 23–24; "Put Guard on Home of Negro," *Detroit Times*, September 10, 1925.

12. Transcript of Ossian Sweet statement to police, September 9, 1925, Detroit Police Department records, copy in author's possession; Gladys Sweet to Walter White, n.d. [September 1925], frames 353–360, reel 3, part 5, NAACP Papers [microfilm edition]; transcript of Norton Schuknecht testimony at the preliminary hearing, September 16, 1925, box 1, Ossian Sweet Collection, Burton Historical Collection.

13. In the course of the first trial, most witnesses from Garland Avenue demonstrated virtually no knowledge of their neighbors; most couldn't even recall their names. Time and again witnesses said they came out to the street on September 9 because of curiosity. See, for example, testimony of Edward Wettlaufer, Otto Eberhardt, Eben Draper, and Fred Benoit. Trial transcript, November 5–13, 1925 [microfilm edition], Michigan Historical Collection, Bentley Library, University of Michigan, Ann Arbor.

14. Transcript of police statements made by Ray Dove, Kathleen Dove, George Strauser, and William Arthur, September 10, 1925. On Ray Dove's profession, see transcript of his trial testimony, November 6, 1925.

15. George Suppus and Ulric Arthur trial testimony, November 10, 1925.

16. "Victim's Wife in Collapse, Is Near Death," *Detroit Free Press*, September 10, 1925; Ray Dove trial testimony. Description of the Breiners' home comes from personal observation.

17. Otto Lemhagen statement to police, September 10, 1925; Lemhagen trial testimony, November 11, 1925.

18. Norton Schuknecht to superintendent, September 9, 1925, Sweet case file, Detroit Police Department records, copy in author's possession; Eric Houghberg testimony, November 11, 1925; "Home Row Victims," *Detroit Free Press*, September 10, 1925; Houghberg statement to police, September 10, 1925.

19. "Two Principals in Riot Case," *Detroit News*, November 19, 1925, clipping at frame 66, reel 3, part 5, NAACP Papers; undated description of Ossian and Gladys Sweet, box 5, Clarence Darrow Collection, Library of Congress, Washington, D.C.; Marcet Haldeman-Julius, *Clarence Darrow's Two Great Trials* (Girard, Kan.: Haldeman-Julius Company, 1927), pp. 34–35.

20. Sweet's story is detailed in chapters 2–4.

21. On Ossian Sweet's personality, see Haldeman-Julius, *Clarence Darrow's Two Great Trials*, pp. 35–38; oral history interview with Arthur Boddie, M.D., July 13, 1998, box 2, Kellogg African-American Health Care Project, Reuther Library; oral history interview with Sherman Sweet, February 27, 2002, notes in author's possession. Particular incidents and assessments of Sweet, from which this portrait is drawn, are available throughout the notes.

22. Sanborn Map Company, *Fire Insurance Map of Detroit, Michigan;* Gladys Sweet to Walter White, n.d. [September 1925]; Haldeman-Julius, *Clarence Darrow's Two Great Trials*, pp. 29–30; Arthur Garfield Hays opening statement, November 16, 1925, frames 920–938, reel 3, part 5, NAACP Papers; 2905 Garland Avenue National Registry of Historic Places Inventory, Nomination Form, November 28, 1984, copy in author's possession; Clifford Edward Clark, Jr., *The American Family Home, 1800–1960* (Chapel Hill: University of North Carolina Press, 1986), chapter 6.

23. 2905 Garland plat book legal description, June 1, 1916, Wayne County Registrar of Deeds, Detroit, Mich.; building permit entry 587, June 16, 1916, building permits 1909–1924, Detroit Building and Safety Department Records, Burton Historical Collection; sheet 9A, e.d. 629, 1920 U.S. census manuscript, Detroit, Michigan; personal tour of 2905 Garland, October 20, 2001.

24. Gladys Sweet statement to police, September 9, 1925.

25. Gladys Sweet statement to police, September 9, 1925; Arthur Turner and Earl Moses, eds., *Colored Detroit, 1924* (Detroit: n.p. 1924), p. 121, for home addresses of African-American physicians; "The Dr. Sweet Case: A Milestone in Civil Rights," *Detroit News*, August 15, 1965.

26. "The Dr. Sweet Case"; "Race Psychology Told in Sweet's Testimony," *Detroit Free Press*, November 19, 1925; Haldeman-Julius, *Clarence Darrow's Two Great Trials*, p. 33; Robert Toms closing statement, May 10, 1926, p. 58, Bentley Library; "Police Officer, Two Negroes, and One White Killed," *Washington Post*, July 22, 1919.

27. Arthur Garfield Hays opening statement to the jury, November 16, 1925, frame 937, reel 3, part 5, NAACP Papers; Philip Dray, *At the Hands of Persons Unknown: The Lynching of Black America* (New York: Random House, 2002), pp. 240–241; Tim Madigan, *The Burning: Massacre, Destruction, and the Tulsa Race Riot of 1921* (New York: St. Martin's Press, 2001), pp. 179–182; Mark Robertson Schneider, *"We Return Fighting": The Civil Rights Movement in the Jazz Age* (Boston: Northeastern University Press, 2002), pp. 354–356.

28. "Sweet to Describe Riot Fear," *Detroit Times*, November 18, 1925; Hays opening statement November 16, 1925; Ossian Sweet statement to police, September 9, 1925. For

comparisons of housing prices in the neighborhood, see classified advertisements, *Detroit News*, September 4, 5, 8, 17, 1925.

29. Cosmopolitan League circular, n.d. [1925], frame 947, reel 2, part 5, NAACP Papers; Mayor's Inter-Racial Committee, *The Negro in Detroit* (Detroit: Detroit Bureau of Intergovernmental Research, 1926), section 9, p. 33; "Cop Kills Man Court Wanted," *Detroit Times*, August 21, 1925.

30. Kenneth Jackson, *The Ku Klux Klan in the Cities* (New York: Oxford University Press, 1967), p. 140; Levine, *Internal Combustion*, pp.157–158.

31. "Sweet to Describe Riot Fear"; Hays opening statement November 16, 1925; Gladys Sweet to White, n.d.; Turner and Moses, *Colored Detroit, 1924*, p. 24; oral history interview with Elsie Smith, June 24, 1997, box 2, Kellogg African-American Health Care Project, Archives of Labor and Urban Affairs, Wayne State University, Detroit, Mich.; Levine, *Internal Combustion*, pp.153–157.

32. "Sweet Takes Stand Today," *Detroit News*, November 18, 1925, frame 0000597, reel 4, part 5, NAACP Papers; "Sweet to Describe Riot Fear"; "Other Race Troubles Figure in Sweet Trial," *Detroit Free Press*, frames 000055–56, reel 4, part 5, NAACP Papers; oral history interview with Cecil Rowlette, August 1, 1960, Alex Baskin Collection, Michigan Historical Collection, Bentley Library, University of Michigan, Ann Arbor; oral history interview with William Osby, Sr., July 27, 1960, Baskin Collection.

33. Gladys Sweet to Walter White; sheet 4, e.d. 600, 1920 U.S. census manuscript, Detroit, Michigan, shows the racial makeup of the neighborhood where Gladys lived and the ethnic makeup of her family. On Gladys's commitment to the move, see her statement to police and Haldeman-Julius, *Clarence Darrow's Two Great Trials*, pp. 28–30.

34. "Race Psychology Told in Sweet's Testimony," frame 000059, reel 4, part 5, NAACP Papers; Osby interview, Baskin Collection.

35. Gladys Sweet to White, n.d.; trial testimony of John Hayes, November 9, 1925.

36. Wilberforce University, annual catalogue, 1911–1912, Wilberforce University Archives, Xenia, Ohio; Ossian Sweet statement to police, September 9, 1925.

37. Respondents' statements, *The People v. Sweet*, October 3, 1925, box 1, Ossian Sweet Collection, Burton Historical Collection; oral history interview with Rowlette; list of military officers, book notes, frame 931, reel 84, W. E. B. Du Bois Papers, University of Massachusetts, Amherst; "Sweet Takes Stand Today."

38. Davis's second statement to police, September 10, 1925; Ossian Sweet statement to police, September 9, 1925; Ossian Sweet statement to Frances Dent and W. Hays McKinney, September 12, 1925, frame 924, reel 2, part 5, NAACP Papers; Haldeman-Julius, *Clarence Darrow's Two Great Trials*, p. 31.

39. Haldeman-Julius, *Clarence Darrow's Two Great Trials*, p. 32; Schuknecht to superintendent; evidence list, ammunition, April 22, 1926, Detroit Police Department records, copy in author's possession; "Sweet Says He Provided Guns," *Detroit Free Press*, May 8, 1926, copy at frame 265, reel 4, part 5, NAACP Papers; Clarence Darrow, *The Story of My Life* (New York: Charles Scribner's Sons, 1934), p. 305.

40. Hays opening statement November 16, 1925; Haldeman-Julius, *Clarence Darrow's Two Great Trials*, p. 31; Bert McPherson testimony, trial transcript; Ossian Sweet statement to police.

41. Haldeman-Julius, *Clarence Darrow's Two Great Trials*, p. 32; Norris Murray statement to police, September 9, 1925; "Witness Tells of Sweet 'Mob,'" *Detroit News*, November 17, 1925, clipping at frame 49, reel 4, part 5, NAACP Papers; Hays opening statement.

42. Marriage license 240625, December 18, 1922, reel 166, Return of Marriages Recorded in Wayne County, 1922, Library of Michigan, Lansing; "Witness Tells of Sweet Mob"; Elsie Smith interview, June 24, 1997.

43. Paul Schellenberger trial testimony, November 5, 1925; Norton Schuknecht trial testimony, November 5, 1926; Hays opening statement; "Sweet Takes Stand Today."

44. Haldeman-Julius, *Clarence Darrow's Two Great Trials*, p. 32; "Defense Opens in Sweet Case," *Detroit Free Press*, May 6, 1926.

45. "Doctor Sweet Goes on Stand," *Chicago Defender*, November 28, 1925; Murray statement to police; Ossian Sweet statement to police.

46. "Other Race Troubles Figure in Sweet Trial," *Detroit Free Press*, November 18, 1925.

47. Preliminary hearing testimony, September 16, 1925, box 1, Sweet Collection; Schuknecht trial testimony, November 5, 1925; Davis statement to police, September 10, 1925; "Sweet Takes Stand Today."

48. Davis statement to police, September 10, 1925; Schellenberger preliminary hearing testimony, September 16, 1925; Gladys Sweet statement to police.

49. Gladys Sweet statement to police; Ossian Sweet statement to police; Joe Mack statement to police, September 9, 1925; Davis statement to police, September 10, 1925; Hays opening statement; Haldeman-Julius, *Clarence Darrow's Two Great Trials*, p. 33; Robert Toms closing statement, May 12, 1926, Michigan Historical Collection.

50. "Witness Tells of Sweet 'Mob'"; Haldeman-Julius, *Clarence Darrow's Two Great Trials*, p. 33; Hays opening statement.

51. Hays opening statement; Levine, *Internal Combustion*, p. 163; Harry H. Pace, "The Business of Insurance Among Negroes," *Crisis* (September 1926): 219–224; Haldeman-Julius, *Clarence Darrow's Two Great Trials*, pp. 33–34; Hewitt Watson entry, sheet 6B, e.d. 479, 1920 U.S. census manuscript, Detroit, Michigan.

52. Davis statement to police, September 10, 1926; "Dr. Sweet Wanted Home for Baby," *Chicago Defender*, December 5, 1926; Charles Washington statement to police, September 9, 1925; Hewitt Watson statement to police, September 9, 1925; Leonard Morris statement to police, September 9, 1925; Ossian Sweet statement to police; Hays opening statement; "Race Psychology Told in Sweet's Testimony."

53. Polk, *Detroit City Directory*, 1925–1926, Mack statement to police, Thomas, *Life for Us Is What We Make It*, p. 91, show the boundaries of the ghetto. I traced Sweet's likely route home on the *New National Authentic Map of Detroit and Environs* (Detroit: National Lithograph Co., 1925), available in the Map Collection, University of Michigan Graduate Library, Ann Arbor.

54. Mack statement to police; Ossian Sweet statement to police; Schuknecht trial testimony, November 5, 1925.

55. Hays opening statement; Gladys Sweet statement to police; "Race Psychology Told in Sweet's Testimony"; "Other Race Troubles Figure in Sweet Trial"; "Doctor Sweet Goes on Stand."

56. Ossian Sweet statement to police.

57. Henry Sweet statement to police, September 9, 1925; "Race Psychology Told in Sweet's Testimony."

58. Mack statement to police.

59. Ibid.; Murray statement to police.

60. Robert Toms opening statement to court, November 5, 1925; Schuknecht trial testimony, November 5, 1925; Ossian Sweet statement to police.

61. Walter White to James Weldon Johnson, September 16, 1925, frames 943–946, reel 2, part 5, NAACP Papers; Ossian Sweet statement to police; Haldeman-Julius, *Clarence Darrow's Two Great Trials*, p. 35; Ossian Sweet to Julian Perry, April 28, 1931, box 1, Ossian Sweet Collection; Sweet to Ruby Darrow, n.d., box 5, Darrow Collection; Walter White memo, December 12, 1930, box G-96, group I, NAACP Papers, Library of Congress, Washington, D.C.; Arthur Boddie interview; oral history interview with Sherman Sweet.

62. Gladys Sweet statement to police; Haldeman-Julius, *Clarence Darrow's Two Great Trials*, pp. 27–31; Gladys Sweet to White, n.d. [October 1925]; oral history interview with Otis Sweet, August 1, 1960, Baskin Collection; oral history interview with Robert Toms, November 28, 1959, Baskin Collection.

63. Oral history interview with Sherman Sweet, sheet 24A, e.d. 134, 1910 U.S. census manuscript, Bartow Town, Polk County, Florida; Haldeman-Julius, *Clarence Darrow's Two Great Trials*, pp. 27–28, 37; sixty-fourth annual report of the president, June 14, 1927, Wilberforce University Archives; Wilberforce University *Forcean* (1925), Wilberforce University Archives.

64. Norris Murray, Joe Mack, Hewitt Watson, Charles Washington, Leonard Morse statements to police.

65. Ossian Sweet, Gladys Sweet, Henry Sweet, Hewitt Watson, Joe Mack, Norris Murray, Charles Washington statements to police; Hays opening statement.

66. Haldeman-Julius, *Clarence Darrow's Two Great Trials*, p. 40; Norris Murray statement to police. There are various versions of what was said at that moment. Some accounts have Henry shouting, "The people! The people!" Others have him saying, "We'd better get up. They're coming!" Still others report him saying, "Look at that gang out there now." See "Race Psychology Told in Sweet's Testimony"; "Sweet Depicts Fear in Court."

67. Levine, *Internal Combustion*, p. 163; "Dr. Sweet Goes on Stand"; "Sweet Depicts Fear in Court"; "Race Psychology Told in Sweet Testimony."

68. "Race Psychology Told in Sweet's Testimony."

69. Ibid.; "Sweet Depicts Fear in Court"; Hays opening statement.

70. Ossian Sweet, Gladys Sweet statements to police; "Race Psychology Told in Sweet's Testimony"; "Sweet Depicts Fear in Court."

71. "Race Psychology Told in Sweet's Testimony"; "Sweet Depicts Fear in Court."

72. Ibid.

73. Ibid.; "Dr. Sweet Goes on Stand"; Otis Sweet statement to police, September 9, 1925; Davis statement to police; Otis Sweet oral history; Ossian Sweet statement to W. Hayes McKinney, September 12, 1925, frame 924, reel 2, part 5, NAACP Papers; Hays opening statement.

74. Ossian and Otis Sweet statements to police; Davis statements to police, September 9 and 10, 1925.

75. "Race Psychology Told in Sweet's Testimony"; "Sweet Depicts Fear in Court"; Ossian Sweet statement to police; Davis statement to police, September 9, 1925.

76. Eric Houghberg statement to police, September 10, 1925, copy in author's possession.

77. Houghberg statement to police; Ray and Kathleen Dove statements to police, September 10, 1925; Houghberg trial testimony, November 11, 1925.

78. Mary Henley trial testimony, November 10, 1925; William Ryan testimony at preliminary hearing, September 16, 1925; Ryan trial testimony, November 5, 1925; Houghberg statement to police; "Darrow Hints at Demand for Another Jury," *Detroit Free Press*, November 10, 1925.

79. Houghberg statement to police; Houghberg trial testimony.

80. Schuknecht statement to police; Schuknecht statement at preliminary hearing, September 16, 1925; Schuknecht trial testimony, November 5, 1925; Otto Lemhagen statement to police, September 10, 1925; "Put Guard at Home of Negroes"; "Victim's Wife in Collapse, Is Near Death."

81. Ossian Sweet statement to police; Davis statement to police, September 9, 1925.

82. Schuknecht testimony at preliminary hearing, September 16, 1925; Schuknecht trial testimony, November 5, 1925; Ossian Sweet statement to police.

83. "Sweet's Trial Will Continue," *Detroit Free Press*, April 30, 1926; Bruce Stout trial testimony, November 10, 1925.

84. Schuknecht statement to police; "Put Guard on Home of Negroes"; "Victim's Wife in Collapse, Is Near Death"; "Slaying Leads to Night Riot," *Detroit News*, September 10, 1925.

85. Schuknecht statement to police, September 10, 1925; Schuknecht testimony at preliminary hearing, September 16, 1925; Schuknecht trial testimony, November 5, 1925.

86. "Dr. Sweet Goes on Stand"; "Other Race Troubles Figure in Sweet Trial."

87. Schuknecht statement to police, September 10, 1925; "Put Guard on Home of Negroes"; "Victim's Wife in Collapse, Is Near Death"; "Slaying Leads to Night Riot."

88. Schuknecht statement to police; George Fairbairn trial testimony, November 9, 1925; Bernard Mahlmeister testimony at preliminary hearing, September 16, 1925.

89. Davis statement to police, September 9, 1925; Otis Sweet statement to police; Ossian Sweet statement to police; Mahlmeister testimony at preliminary hearing; "Dr. Sweet Goes on Stand."

90. Ossian and Otis Sweet statements to police.

91. Schuknecht trial testimony and Paul Schellenberger testimony, both on November 5, 1925; George Fairbairn trial testimony, Almarion Wolfe trial testimony, and Marvin Leach testimony, all on November 9, 1925.

92. "Dr. Sweet Goes on Stand"; Otis Sweet oral history.

93. Joe Mack statement to police; Hayes testimony at preliminary hearing, September 16, 1925; "Death Calls Troubleshooter," *Detroit News*, October 14, 1943, copy in Detroit News clipping morgue, Detroit.

94. Hays trial testimony, November 9, 1925; Otis Sweet oral history; Ossian Sweet statement to police; "Dr. Sweet Goes on Stand."

95. Otis Sweet oral history; Mahlmeister testimony at preliminary hearing; Hayes trial testimony, November 9, 1925.

96. Otis Sweet oral history.

97. Ibid.

Chapter Two: Ain't No Slavery No More

1. "Dr. Sweet Is Cross-Examined," *Detroit News*, November 19, 1925, frames 64–66, reel 3, part 5, NAACP Papers [microfilm edition], Library of Congress, Washington, D.C.; "Sweet Verdict Due This Week," *Detroit Free Press*, May 9, 1926; "Sweet's Fate to Jury Soon," *Detroit Times*, May 9, 1926.

2. "Race Psychology Told in Sweet's Testimony," *Detroit Free Press*, November 19, 1925. The DeVaughn brothers are listed in Gilla Devoud [*sic*] application, application number 737, October 2, 1869, reel 5, Freedman's Bank Records, Tallahassee Branch, National Archives, Washington, D.C.

3. For details on the Cromarties, see the family entry, p. 148, 1820 U.S. census manuscript, Bladen County, North Carolina. Most likely, young Edmond came to Alexander through Alexander's mother, Elizabeth DeVane, whose father was a slaveholder. The DeVane family entry is available at p. 282, 1820 U.S. census manuscript, Sampson County, North Carolina. The Cromartie–DeVane connection is available at http://worldconnect.rootsweb.com, searched under either "Alexander Cromartie" or "Elizabeth DeVane." Last accessed March 15, 2004. When Elizabeth's father died in 1810, his property—including slaves—was divided among his children. See George DeVane will, February 10, 1810, at http://ftp.rootsweb.com/pub/usgenweb/nc/sampson/wills/gdevane.txt, last accessed March 15, 2004.

4. Clifton Paisley, *The Red Hills of Florida, 1528–1865* (Tuscaloosa: University of Alabama Press, 1989), p. 134; Alexander Cromartie entry, p. 123, 1830 U.S. census manuscript, Leon County, Florida.

5. A. J. Hanna, *A Prince in Their Midst: The Adventurous Life of Achille Murat on the American Frontier* (Norman: University of Oklahoma Press, 1946), pp. 79, 113. Larry E. Rivers, "Slavery in Microcosm: Leon County, Florida, 1824 to 1860," *Journal of Negro History* 56 (fall 1981): 237; Julia Floyd Smith, *Slavery and Plantation Growth in Antebellum Florida, 1821–1860* (Gainesville: University Press of Florida, 1973), chapter 6.

6. Paisley, *The Red Hills of Florida*, pp. 175–180. Loveless can be traced directly to Elizabeth's father, who passed the slave to his wife in his 1810 will. Most likely, Loveless was passed on to Cornelius upon his mother's death in 1822.

7. Alexander Cromartie entry, p. 72, 1860 U.S. census manuscript, Leon County, Florida. A list of the Cromarties' slaves is available in p. 279, 1860 U.S. census, slave schedule, Leon County. Though the slaves are not listed by name, there is listed among them a pair of twelve-year-old boys the age of twins Remus and Romulus DeVaughn.

8. The ages of the DeVaughn children are taken from p. 571, 1870 U.S. census manuscript, Leon County, Florida.

9. For an introduction to the coming of the Civil War, there is no better starting point than David Potter, *The Impending Crisis, 1848–1861* (New York: Harper and Row, 1976). Also see Michael Holt, *The Political Crisis of the 1950s* (New York: Wiley, 1978) and Eric Foner's brilliant book, *Free Soil, Free Labor, Free Men: The Ideology of the Republican Party Before the Civil War* (New York: Oxford University Press, 1970).

10. Edward E. Baptist, *Creating an Old South: Middle Florida's Plantation Frontier Before the Civil War* (Chapel Hill: University of North Carolina Press, 2002), pp. 278–279.

11. George P. Rawick, ed., *The American Slave: A Composite Autobiography*, v. 17 (Westport, Conn.: Greenwood Publishing Company, 1972), pp. 246–247.

12. Edmond's death date comes from Gilla DeVaughn's application to Freedman's Bank, October 2, 1869.

13. Eric Foner, *Reconstruction: America's Unfinished Revolution, 1863–1877* (New York: Harper and Row, 1988), particularly chapter 3; Susan Brandford Eppes, *Through Some Eventful Years* (Macon, Ga.: J. W. Burke, 1926), pp. 284–285.

14. Foner, *Reconstruction*, p. 81; sub-assistant commissioner's monthly report, October 1868, frames 691–692, reel 15, RG 105, Freedman's Bureau Field Office Records, National Archives. When the DeVaughns first appear in the record after the Civil War, in 1869, they lived on a plantation close to the Cromarties'. Gilla DeVaughn Freedman's Bank application, October 2, 1869. Many freedmen did move, of course. See Leon Litwack, *Been in the Storm So Long: The Aftermath of Slavery* (New York: Random House, 1979), chapter 6.

15. The standard work on Reconstruction is Foner, *Reconstruction*. Also see W. E. B. Du Bois's path-breaking *Black Reconstruction in America* (New York: Harcourt Brace, 1935), and Steven Hahn's important new study, *A Nation Under Our Feet: Black Political Struggles in the Rural South from Slavery to the Great Migration* (Cambridge, Mass.: Harvard University Press, 2003).

16. Litwack, *Been in the Storm So Long*, pp. 450–455; James T. Campbell, *The African Methodist Episcopal Church in the United States and South Africa* (New York: Oxford University Press, 1995), pp. 53–54.

17. Rhys Isaac, *The Transformation of Virginia, 1740–1790* (Chapel Hill: University of North Carolina Press, 1982), pp. 260–264. On the connection of Methodism and the marketplace, see Charles Sellers, *The Market Revolution: Jacksonian America, 1815–1846* (New York: Oxford University Press, 1991) pp. 160–161. Wesley quoted in E. P. Thompson, *The Making of the English Working Class* (New York: Random House, 1963), p. 355. Wesley feared the effects of such success. "But as riches increase," he said, "so will pride, anger, and love of the world."

18. Sellers, *Market Revolution*, pp. 160–161; Clarence E. Walker, *A Rock in a Weary Land: The African Methodist Episcopal Church During the Civil War and Reconstruction* (Baton Rouge: Louisiana State University Press, 1982), pp. 4–11; Campbell, *The African Methodist Episcopal Church in the United States and South Africa*, chapter 1.

19. Clarence E. Walker, *A Rock in a Weary Land*, p. 13.

20. Foner, *Reconstruction*, p. 92; Litwack, *Been in the Storm So Long*, pp. 470–471; Stephen W. Angell and Anthony B. Pinn, eds., *Social Protest Thought in the African Methodist Episcopal Church, 1862–1939* (Knoxville: University of Tennessee Press, 2000), p. 5.

21. Larry Eugene Rivers and Canter Brown, Jr., *Laborers in the Vineyard of the Lord: The Beginnings of the AME Church in Florida, 1865–1895* (Gainesville: University Press of Florida, 2001), p. 46; Joe M. Richardson, *The Negro in the Reconstruction of Florida, 1865–1877* (Tallahassee: Florida State University Press, 1965), pp. 84–85. "On political subjects [the freedmen] are easily excited and the more . . . radical the address made to them the better they seemed pleased," reported a federal agent from Leon County. "In Tallahassee most of the freedmen have adapted themselves to politics as a calling." W. Martin to Allen Jackson, October 22, 1868, box 15, Freedmen's Bureau Florida Field Office Records, RG 105, National Archives, Washington, D.C. [microfilm edition].

22. Charles Sumner Long, *History of the AME Church in Florida* (Philadelphia: A.M.E. Book Concern, 1939), p. 65; Rivers and Brown, *Laborers in the Vineyard of the Lord*, p. 95; Tallahassee Branch; p. 571, 1870 U.S. census manuscript, Leon County, Florida. Edward West to Colonel Sprague, March 1867, frames 726–728, reel 9, Freedman's Bureau Field Office; teachers' monthly school report, April 1868, frame 386, reel 13, Freedman's Bureau Field Office; Gilla DeVaughn Freedman's Bank application, October 2, 1869; Romulus DeVoud [*sic*] Freedman's Bank application, application number 726, September 11, 1869, reel 5, Freedman's Bank Records; Edward West to Colonel Sprague, March 1867, frames 726–728, reel 9, RG 105, Freedman's Bureau, Field Office, National Archives.

23. DeVaughn family entry, 1870 census; sub-assistant commissioner's monthly

report, Leon County, June 1868, frame 100, reel 13, Freedman's Bureau Field Office; sub-assistant commissioner's monthly report, August 1868, frame 133, reel 13, Freedman's Bureau Field Office.

24. Paul Ortiz, "'Like Water Covered the Sea': The African American Freedom Struggle in Florida, 1877–1920," Ph.D. dissertation, Duke University, 2000, p. 25; S. I. Halliday to Jacob Ch[ ], April 19, 1869, frame 312, reel 10, Freedman's Bureau Field Office; sub-assistant commissioner's monthly report, October 1868.

25. The Joint Select Committee to Inquire into the Condition of Affairs in the Late Insurrectionary States, *Testimony* (Washington, D.C.: Government Printing Office, 1972), p. 273; Jerrell H. Shofner, *Nor Is It Over Yet: Florida in the Era of Reconstruction* (Gainesville: University of Florida Press, 1974), chapter 13.

26. Joint Select Committee, *Testimony*, p. 171; William Watson Davis, *The Civil War and Reconstruction in Florida* (1913; repr. Gainesville: University Press of Florida, 1964), pp. 526–528; Rivers and Brown, *Laborers in the Vineyard of the Lord*, p. 83.

27. Canter Brown, Jr., *Ossian Bingley Hart: Florida's Loyalist Reconstruction Governor* (Baton Rouge: Louisiana State University Press, 1997).

28. Brown, *Ossian Bingley Hart*, pp. 275–294; Canter Brown, Jr., *Florida's Black Public Officials, 1867–1924* (Tuscaloosa: University of Alabama Press, 1998), pp. 25–27.

29. Brown, *Florida's Black Public Officials*, p. 85; for Cromartie as justice of the peace, see p. 603, 1870 U.S. census manuscript, Leon County, Florida. It seems there was a good deal of dissatisfaction with Cromartie's tenure as justice of the peace among blacks in Leon County. See sub-assistant commissioner's monthly report, October 1868.

30. E.d. 483, p. 12, 1880 U.S. census manuscript, Leon County, Florida; Dora L. Sweet gravestone, Evergreen Cemetery, Bartow, Fla. The gravestone lists Dora's birthday as December 29, 1873.

31. Brown, *Ossian Bingley Hart*, pp. 293–299.

32. Foner, *Reconstruction*, pp. 575–583; Shofner, *Nor Is It Over Yet*, chapter 19.

33. Jerrell H. Shofner, "Reconstruction and Renewal, 1865–1877," in Michael Gannon, ed., *The New History of Florida* (Gainesville: University Press of Florida, 1996), pp. 263–264; Edward Ayers, *The Promise of the New South: Life After Reconstruction* (New York: Oxford University Press, 1992), p. 45; Charlton Tebeau and William Marina, *A History of Florida*, 3rd ed. (Coral Gables: University of Miami Press, 1999), chapter 18.

34. Ayers, *The Promise of the New South*, p. 52; *General Statutes of the State of Florida* (St. Augustine: Records Company, 1906), pp. 307–308; J. Morgan Kousser, *The Shaping of Southern Politics: Suffrage Restriction and the Establishment of the One-Party South* (New Haven, Conn.: Yale University Press, 1974), pp. 91–103.

35. *General Statutes of the State of Florida*, pp. 165, 213–214, 1305–1306, 1376; Ayers, *Promise of the New South*, pp. 142–146.

36. There is a vast literature on the creation of Jim Crow. Among the most influential and insightful studies are C. Vann Woodward, *Origins of the New South, 1877–1913* (Baton Rouge: Louisiana State University Press, 1951); Joel Williamson, *The Crucible of Race: Black-White Relations in the American South Since Emancipation* (New York: Oxford University Press, 1984); Ayers, *Promise of the New South;* Leon Litwack, *Trouble in Mind: Black Southerners in the Age of Jim Crow* (New York: Random House, 1998).

37. Brown, *Florida's Black Public Officials*, p. 85; Rivers, *Laborers in the Vineyard of the Lord*, p. 111; e.d. 95, p. 18, 1880 U.S. census manuscript, Liberty County, Florida, for Hubbert DeVaughn; e.d. 76, p. 36, 1880 U.S. census manuscript, Jefferson County, Florida, for Edmond DeVaughn; e.d. 88, p. 18, Leon County, Florida, for Romulus De-Vaughn; e.d. 483, p. 12, for Remus DeVaughn and his family.

38. Gavin Wright, *Old South, New South: Revolutions in the Southern Economy Since the Civil War* (New York: Basic Books, 1986), pp. 75–76, 99–106; Litwack, *Trouble in Mind*, pp. 130–138; Remus DeVaughn entry, 1880 U.S. census.

39. On Orlando and its economic context, see Benjamin D. Brotemarkle, *Beyond the Theme Parks: Exploring Central Florida* (Gainesville: University Press of Florida, 1999), pp. 12–13, and Charles W. Tabeau and William Marina, *A History of Florida* 3rd ed. (Coral Gables: University of Miami Press, 1999), chapter 18.

40. E.d. 116, p. 2; 1900 U.S. census manuscript, Orange County, Orlando, Florida; *Orlando City Directory*, 1915–1916 (no publication information), p. 134, copy available in Library of Congress, Washington, D.C.

41. Dora L. Sweet funeral program, September 1, 1957, box 2, Dovie Sweet Papers, Western Reserve Historical Society, Cleveland, Ohio; oral history interview with Sherman Sweet, February 27, 2002, Bartow, Fla.; oral history interview with Charlie McNeill, February 26, 2002, Bartow, Fla., notes of both interviews in author's possession.

42. Sherman Sweet telephone interview, January 11, 2002, notes in author's possession; Sherman Sweet interview, February 27, 2002; Henry W. Sweet gravestone, Evergreen Cemetery, Bartow, Florida; "A Special Tribute to the Sweet Family," July–August 1997, copy in author's possession; William Warren Rodgers, Robert David Ward, Leah Rawls Atkins, and Wayne Flint, *Alabama: The History of a Deep South State* (Tuscaloosa: University of Alabama Press, 1994), p. 220.

43. Henry Sweet gravestone; e.d. 132, p. 18, 1900 U.S. census manuscript, Bartow Town, Polk County, Florida; Sherman Sweet interview, February 27, 2002; Charlie McNeill interview, February 26, 2002; description of Henry Sweet is from a photograph in Sherman Sweet's possession.

44. Sherman Sweet interview, February 27, 2002; Oscar and Ossian Sweet gravestones, Evergreen Cemetery, Bartow, Fla.

45. *Sectional map of Polk County, Florida* (Buffalo, N.Y.: Associated Railway Land Department of Florida, 1890); record of transaction, May 10, 1898, Deed Record, v. 53, p. 45, Polk County, Fla., court house; for Milam family, e.d. 132, pp. 6–7, 1900 U.S. census manuscript, Bartow Town, Polk County, Florida; "City Locals," *Bartow Courier-Informant*, November 15, 1899; "Milam Closed Out," *Bartow Courier-Informant*, September 3, 1902. Indiana-born Milam, a grocer by trade, was a dabbler in real estate. For details, see grantee index, pp. 176–178, Polk County court house.

46. Canter Brown, Jr., *In the Midst of All That Makes Life Worth Living: Polk County, Florida to 1940* (Tallahassee: Sentry Press, 2001), pp. 121, 127–128, 140–146; Canter Brown, Jr., "'Bartow Is the Place for Our People to Go': Race and the Course of Life in Southern Polk County, 1865–1905" (unpublished essay in author's possession), pp. 3–8.

47. Brown, *In the Midst of All That Makes Life Worth Living*, pp. 154–159, 179–183, 194; Samuel Proctor, "Prelude to the New Florida," in Michael Gannon, ed., *The New History of Florida*, p. 277; Ayers, *Promise of the New South*, pp. 109–110.

48. Brown, *In the Midst of All That Makes Life Worth Living*, pp. 143–144, 155–156, 197–198; Sanborn Map Company, *Fire Insurance Map of Bartow, Florida* (New York: Sanborn Map Company, 1906); *Bartow: Where It Is a Pleasure to Live* (Bartow: Bartow Board of Trade, 1914).

49. "Registered and Qualified Electors, Polk County, FL, October 8, 1989," Polk County Historical Library, Bartow, Fla.; Patricia Merritt, "Fighting from Within," *Polk County Ledger*, n.d., copy available in "African American" vertical file, Polk County Historical Library; advertisement for county fair, *Bartow Courier-Informant*, March 15, 1899; "'Blind Tom' at Armory," *Bartow Courier-Informant*, April 10, 1901; minutes of town council, April 19, 1892, minute books, Bartow town hall, Bartow, Fla.; ordinance 37, Bartow Ordinance Record, v. 1, Bartow town hall; oral history interview with Claude Woodruff, February 25, 2002; "City Council," *Bartow Courier-Informant*, August 15, 1900.

50. Brown, "'Bartow Is the Place for Our People to Go,'" pp. 9–10; Brown, *In the Midst of All That Makes Life Worth Living*, pp. 199, 226–228; interview with Charlie McNeill, February 26, 2002; Charlie McNeill, "Were They Pioneers, Too?" *Polk County Historical Quarterly* 26 (September 1999): 9–11.

51. Sherman Sweet interview, February 27, 2002; Sanborn Map Company, *Fire Insurance Map of Bartow, Florida* (New York: Sanborn Map Company, 1917).

52. Sherman Sweet telephone interview, January 11, 2002; Sherman Sweet interview, February 27, 2002; Charlie McNeill interview, February 26, 2002.

53. Sherman Sweet interview, February 27, 2002; "A Tribute to the Sweet Family"; Sweet family plot, Evergreen Cemetery; 1910 U.S. census manuscript, Bartow Town, Polk County, Florida.

54. Sherman Sweet interview, February 27, 2002; *Directory of Polk County, Florida, 1913* (Bartow [?]: Polk Company Abstract Company, 1913), p. 72, copy available in Polk County Historical Library. In 1906, Henry Sweet bought three lots adjoining his land for a total of $45. See land deed November 20, 1906, deed record, v. 73, p. 90.

55. Sherman Sweet interview, February 27, 2002; "Race Psychology Told in Sweet's Testimony," *Detroit Free Press*, November 19, 1925.

56. Sherman Sweet interviews, January 11, 2002, and February 27, 2002.

57. Ibid.

58. H. K. Oliphant, "Thoughts on the Race Question," *Bartow Courier-Informant*, August 2, 1899, p. 2; Brown, " 'Bartow Is the Place for Our People to Go,' " pp. 13, 15; Brown, *In the Midst of All That Makes Life Worth Living*, p. 199; "A Historical Sketch of Union Academy," July–August 1997, copy in author's possession; minutes of the town council, January 6 and March 6, 1896.

59. "Annual Report of County Superintendent of Public Instruction," *Bartow Courier-Informant*, October 25, 1899; "List of Polk County Teachers," *Bartow Courier-Informant*, October 11, 1899; "School Term Reduced," *Bartow Courier-Informant*, July 15, 1903; Sherman Sweet interview, January 11, 2002.

60. "New School Building," *Bartow Courier-Informant*, August 20, 1902.

61. Philip Dray, *At the Hands of Persons Unknown: The Lynching of Black America* (New York: Random House, 2002), particularly chapter 2; John Dollard, *Caste and Class in a Southern Town* (1937; repr. Madison: University of Wisconsin Press, 1988), pp. 335–343; Litwack, *Trouble in Mind*, chapter 6.

62. Ayers, *Promise of the New South*, chapters 10 and 11; Williamson, *The Crucible of Race*, part 2; Glenda Gilmore, *Gender and Jim Crow: Women and the Politics of White Supremacy in North Carolina, 1896–1920* (Chapel Hill: University of North Carolina Press, 1996), chapter 4. Tillman quoted in Litwack, *Trouble in Mind*, p. 303.

63. Ayers, *Promise of the New South*, p. 110; Brown, *In the Midst of All That Makes Life Worth Living*, pp. 200–202; Zora Neale Hurston, *Mules and Men* (1935; repr. New York: Harper and Row, 1990), p. 59.

64. "The Wickedest Town in Florida," *The Illustrated American*, July 20, 1895, pp. 78–79, copy in the "African Americans" vertical file, Polk County Historical Library, Bartow, Fla.

65. "The Negro Died Last Week," *Bartow Courier-Informant*, January 11, 1899; "Bloody Scene at Kingsford," *Bartow Courier-Informant*, January 27, 1900.

66. "General Presentments," *Bartow Courier-Informant*, October 21, 1903.

67. See, for example, minutes of the town council, January 3, 1893; "Sabbath Is Violated," *Bartow Courier-Informant*, July 15, 1903.

68. The story of Fred Rochelle's lynching is recounted in "Black Brute's Heinous Crime!" *Bartow Courier-Informant*, May 29, 1901, and "Burned at the Stake," and "To the World," *Bartow Courier-Informant*, June 5, 1901. There is no census entry for Fred Rochelle. But a Henry Rochelle appears in e.d. 130, sheet 6, 1900 U.S. census manuscript, Polk County, Fla. He is a nineteen-year-old working in the phosphate pits. Serena Rochelle was recently married to Bartow's baker, a Manx immigrant.

69. "Our Sheriff Was Game," *Bartow Courier-Informant*, December 30, 1903; Brown, *In the Midst of All That Makes Life Worth Living*, pp. 225–226.

70. Marcet Haldeman-Julius, *Clarence Darrow's Two Great Trials* (Girard, Kan.: Haldeman-Julius Publishing Company, 1927), p. 33.

71. Sherman Sweet interview, February 27, 2002.

72. Charles Sumner Long to James Weldon Johnson, December 14, 1925, frame 870, reel 23, part 5, NAACP Papers.

Chapter Three: Migration

1. U.S. Bureau of the Census, *Thirteenth Census of the United States, 1910: Population by Counties and Minor Civil Divisions, 1910, 1900, 1890* (Washington, D.C.: Government

Printing Office, 1912), p. 417; Raymond Boryczka and Lorin Lee Cary, *No Strength Without Union: An Illustrated History of Ohio Workers, 1803–1980* (Columbus: Ohio Historical Society, 1982), pp. 112–113; Helen Hooven Santmyer, *Ohio Town* (Columbus: Ohio State University Press, 1962).

2. Wilberforce University catalogue, 1912–1913, Wilberforce University Archives, Xenia, Ohio; Annetta Louise Gomez-Jefferson, *In Darkness with God: The Life of Joseph Gomez, a Bishop in the African Methodist Episcopal Church* (Kent, Ohio: Kent State University Press, 1998), p. 32.

3. Edward Ayers, *The Promise of the New South: Life After Reconstruction* (New York: Oxford University Press, 1992), chapter 1; Leon Litwack, *Trouble in Mind: Black Southerners in the Age of Jim Crow* (New York: Random House, 1998), pp. 482–489; Emmett J. Scott, *Negro Migration During the War* (New York: Oxford University Press, 1920), pp. 8–12; Stewart Tolnay and E. M. Beck, "Rethinking the Role of Racial Violence in the Great Migration," in Alferdteen Harrison, ed., *Black Exodus: The Great Migration from the American South* (Jackson: University Press of Mississippi, 1991), p. 22; U.S. Bureau of the Census, *Twelfth Census of the United States*, part 2 (Washington, D.C.: Government Printing Office, 1901), p. cxi.

4. Eric Foner, *Reconstruction: America's Unfinished Revolution, 1863–1877* (New York: Harper and Row, 1988), pp. 470–472; Litwack, *Trouble in Mind*, p. 488.

5. Kevin Boyle, "Work Places: The Economy and the Changing Landscape of Labor, 1900–2000," in Harvard Sitkoff, ed., *Perspectives on Modern America: Making Sense of the Twentieth Century* (New York: Oxford University Press, 2001), pp. 102–104; Kenneth Kusmer, *A Ghetto Takes Shape: Black Cleveland, 1870–1930* (Urbana: University of Illinois Press, 1976), pp. 85–89; John Bodnar, Roger Simon, and Michael P. Weber, *Lives of Their Own: Blacks, Italians, and Poles in Pittsburgh, 1900–1960* (Urbana: University of Illinois Press, 1982), pp. 59–62; James Grossman, *Land of Hope: Chicago, Black Southerners, and the Great Migration* (Chicago: University of Chicago Press, 1989), pp. 187–189.

6. W. E. B. Du Bois, "Negro Education" (1918), reprinted in David Levering Lewis, ed., *W. E. B. Du Bois: A Reader* (New York: Henry Holt, 1995), p. 262; oral history interview with Sherman Sweet, February 27, 2002, Bartow, Fla., transcript in author's possession.

7. W. E. B. Du Bois diary entry, n.d. [1896], frame 520, reel 87, W. E. B. Du Bois Papers, W. E. B. Du Bois Library, University of Massachusetts, Amherst.

8. Wilberforce University catalogue, 1908–1909, Wilberforce University Archives; Arthur Garfield Hays opening statement to the jury, *People v. Ossian Sweet et al.*, November 16, 1925, frames 920–938, reel 3, part 5, NAACP Papers. There was a direct connection between Wilberforce and Bartow's St. James AME, the Sweets' home church. One of the church's early members also served on the university's board of trustees. See Canter Brown, Jr., "'Bartow Is the Place for Our People to Go': Race and the Course of Life in Southern Polk County" (unpublished paper in author's possession), p. 13.

9. David Levering Lewis, *W. E. B. Du Bois: Biography of a Race* (New York: Henry Holt, 1993), pp. 151–152.

10. Wilberforce University catalogue, 1909–1910, Wilberforce University Archives; Santmyer, *Ohio Town*, p. 90; forty-seventh annual report of the president, June 14, 1910, Wilberforce Archives. For views of Wilberforce, see Hallie Q. Brown, *Pen Pictures of Pioneers of Wilberforce* (New York: G. K. Hall, 1997). A standard institutional history is Frederick A. McGinnis, *A History and Interpretation of Wilberforce University* (Blanchester, Ohio: Brown Publishing Company, 1941).

11. Hays opening statement, November 16, 1925; Marcet Haldeman-Julius, *Clarence Darrow's Two Great Trials* (Girard, Kan.: Haldeman-Julius Publishing Company, 1927), p. 35.

12. Lewis, *W. E. B. Du Bois*, p. 288.

13. Foner, *Reconstruction*, pp. 144–148; Adam Fairclough, *Better Day Coming: Blacks and Equality, 1890–2000* (New York: Viking, 2001), pp. 47–48.

14. Matthew Frye Jacobson, *Whiteness of a Different Color: European Immigrants and the Alchemy of Race* (Cambridge, Mass.: Harvard University Press, 1998), chapter 2; Roosevelt quoted in Lewis, *W. E. B. Du Bois*, p. 276.

15. The standard study of Washington is Louis Harlan, *Booker T. Washington: The*

Making of a Black Leader, 1856–1901 (New York: Oxford University Press, 1972), and Louis Harlan, *Booker T. Washington: The Wizard of Tuskeegee, 1901–1915* (New York: Oxford University Press, 1983). On Wilberforce's deal with the state of Ohio, see David Gerber, *Black Ohio and the Colored Line, 1860–1915* (Urbana: University of Illinois Press, 1976), p. 331; on the role of the manual training school, see Wilberforce University bulletin, June 1925, Wilberforce University Archives; Scarborough lays out his distinction between educated and working classes in W. S. Scarborough, "The Educated Negro and Menial Pursuits," *The Forum* 26 (December 1898): 434–440.

16. Francis P. Weisenburger, "Scarborough, William Sanders," in Rayford Logan and Michael R. Winston, eds., *Dictionary of American Negro Biography* (New York: W. W. Norton, 1982), pp. 545–546; David A. Gerber, *Black Ohio and the Color Line, 1860–1915*, p. 55.

17. Wilberforce University catalogue, 1912–1913.

18. Minutes of the faculty meeting, October 21, 1913, box 17, Wilberforce University Papers, Wilberforce Archives; Wilberforce University catalogue, 1908–1909; minutes of the faculty meeting, November 2, 1909, box 16, Wilberforce University Papers; W. E. B. Du Bois notes, February 1896, frame 536, reel 87, Du Bois Papers.

19. Wilberforce University catalogues, 1908–1909 and 1912–1913; minutes of the faculty meeting, October 21, 1913, box 17, Wilberforce University Papers; Lewis, *Du Bois*, p. 176; Fifty-fourth Annual Report of the President, June 21, 1917, Wilberforce Archives; David Kennedy, *Freedom from Fear: The American People in Depression and War, 1929–1945* (New York: Oxford University Press, 1999), p. 771.

20. Gerber, *Black Ohio and the Color Line*, pp. 234–235, 257–258.

21. Gail Bederman, *Manliness and Civilization: A Cultural History of Gender and Race in the United States, 1880–1917* (Chicago: University of Chicago Press, 1995); Stephen Kantrowitz, *Ben Tillman and the Reconstruction of White Supremacy* (Chapel Hill: University of North Carolina Press, 2000), pp. 268–286.

22. Gerber, *Black Ohio and the Color Line*, pp. 65–66, 257–263; W. S. Scarborough, "The Subsidized North," *The Voice of the Negro* 4 (January–February 1907): 32.

23. Lewis, *W. E. B. Du Bois*, p. 330.

24. Fairclough, *Better Day Coming*, p. 67; Lewis, *Du Bois*, pp. 387–388.

25. Lewis, *Du Bois*, pp. 388–391; Charles Kellogg, *NAACP: A History of the National Association for the Advancement of Colored People* (Baltimore: Johns Hopkins University Press, 1967), pp. 9–19.

26. Lewis, *Du Bois*, pp. 391–407; Kellogg, *NAACP*, pp. 19–26.

27. Wilberforce University catalogue, 1909–1910; *The Tawawa Remembrancer* 1914 (no publisher available), Wilberforce University Archives; minutes of the faculty meeting, April 7, 1914, box 17, Wilberforce University Papers; minutes of the faculty meeting, February 28, 1911, box 16, Wilberforce University Papers.

28. Wilberforce University catalogue, 1912–1913; *The Tawawa Remembrancer* 1914; minutes of the faculty meeting, May 20, 1913, box 16, Wilberforce University Papers; minutes of the May 17, 1917, faculty meeting, no box number.

29. Minutes of the faculty meeting, May 12, 1914, box 17, Wilberforce University Papers.

30. Ibid.

31. Arthur Garfield Hays opening statement, November 16, 1925; Gavin Wright, *Old South, New South: Revolutions in the Southern Economy Since the Civil War* (New York: Basic Books, 1987), p. 202, for relative wage rates in Detroit and the South.

32. Olivier Zunz, *The Changing Face of Inequality: Urbanization, Industrial Development, and Immigrants in Detroit, 1880–1920* (Chicago: University of Chicago Press, 1982), pp. 219–224; Joyce Shaw Peterson, *American Automobile Workers, 1900–1933* (Albany: SUNY Press, 1987), pp. 11–14; David Katzman, *Before the Ghetto: Black Detroit in the Nineteenth Century* (Urbana: University of Illinois Press, 1973), pp. 104–123.

33. Arthur Garfield Hays opening statement, November 16, 1925; Haldeman-Julius, *Clarence Darrow's Two Great Trials*, p. 35.

34. Hays opening statement, November 16, 1925; Haldeman-Julius, *Clarence Darrow's Two Great Trials*, pp. 35–36.

35. Haldeman-Julius, *Clarence Darrow's Two Great Trials*, p. 35.

36. Paul Starr, *The Social Transformation of American Medicine* (New York: Basic Books, 1982), chapters 1, 3; Mr. Hopkins to the secretary of the interior, June 17, 1920, box 2069, RG 48, Department of Interior, Central Classified Files, 1907–1936, National Archives, Washington, D.C.

37. Starr, *Social Transformation of American Medicine*, p. 124; Martha Tracy to Hubert work, January 16, 1924, box 2064, RG 48, Department of Interior Central Classified Files, 1907–1936.

38. Arthur Link, *Woodrow Wilson and the Progressive Era, 1910–1917* (New York: Harper and Row, 1954), p. 282.

39. Lewis, *Du Bois*, pp. 529–531; Fairclough, *Better Day Coming*, pp. 92–93.

40. Fifty-fourth annual report of the president, June 21, 1917, no box number, Wilberforce University Papers; Lewis, *Du Bois*, p. 532; Hays opening statement, November 16, 1925.

41. David Kennedy, *Over Here: The First World War and American Society* (New York: Oxford University Press, 1980); Joseph McCartin, *Labor's Great War: The Struggle for Industrial Democracy and the Origins of Modern American Labor Relations, 1912–1921* (Chapel Hill: University of North Carolina Press, 1997); William Preston, Jr., *Aliens and Dissenters: Federal Suppression of Radicals, 1903–1933* (New York: Harper and Row, 1963), chapter 4.

42. Constance McLaughlin Green, *The Secret City: A History of Race Relations in the Nation's Capital* (Princeton, N.J.: Princeton University Press, 1967), pp. 171–176; Lewis, *W. E. B. Du Bois: Portrait of a Race*, pp. 532–533.

43. James Grossman, *Land of Hope: Chicago, Black Southerners, and the Great Migration* (Chicago: University of Chicago Press, 1989), pp. 13–15; Carol Marks, *Farewell—We're Good and Gone: The Great Black Migration* (Bloomington: Indiana University Press, 1989), chapter 4.

44. Elliot M. Rudwick, *Race Riot at East St. Louis, July 2, 1917* (Carbondale: Southern Illinois University Press, 1964), chapters 2–5; Eugene Levy, *James Weldon Johnson: Black Leader, Black Voice* (Chicago: University of Chicago Press, 1973), pp. 183–189; Ann Douglas, *Terrible Honesty: Mongrel Manhattan in the 1920s* (New York: Farrar, Straus and Giroux, 1995), pp. 325–326.

45. Lewis, *W. E. B. Du Bois*, pp. 539–540; Green, *The Secret City*, pp. 185, 198; Stephen Grant Meyer, *As Long as They Don't Move Next Door: Segregation and Racial Conflict in American Neighborhoods* (Lanham, Md.: Rowman and Littlefield, 2000), pp. 20–26.

46. Rayford Logan, *Howard University: The First Hundred Years, 1867–1967* (New York: New York University Press, 1969), chapters 1 and 2; James Borchert, *Alley Life in Washington: Family, Community, Religion, and Folklife in the City, 1850–1970* (Urbana: University of Illinois Press, 1980); David Levering Lewis, *District of Columbia: A Bicentennial History* (New York: W. W. Norton, 1976), pp. 152–153; William B. Gatewood, *Aristocrats of Color: The Black Elite, 1880–1920* (Bloomington: Indiana University Press, 1990), chapter 2; David Levering Lewis, *When Harlem Was in Vogue* (New York: Alfred A. Knopf, 1979), pp. 149–151; "A Service of Commemoration for Frank D. Reeves and James A. Cobb," October 19, 1976, box 2, James Cobb Papers, Moorland-Spingarn Collection, Howard University, Washington, D.C.

47. Starr, *Social Transformation of American Medicine*, pp. 117–123; Logan, *Howard University*, pp. 160–164. Gradually the AMA strengthened educational requirements so that incoming medical school students had to have some college education.

48. Howard University catalogue, 1917–1918, p. 168, copy available in Moorland-Spingarn Collection; agreement between the assistant secretary of the interior and the District of Columbia board of charities, July 1909, entry 309, box 2, Patents and Miscellaneous Division, Department of Interior, RG 48, National Archives, Washington, D.C.; AMA's report quoted in Logan, *Howard University*, p. 162.

49. Howard University catalogue, 1917–1918; Howard University *Enopron* 1920–1921, copy available in Moorland-Spingarn Collection; Howard University *Bulletin* 1, no. 4 (1921–1922): 284–285; Charles West photograph, box 1, Charles West Collection, Moorland-

Spingarn Collection; report of Freedman's Hospital, year ending June 30, 1914, box 130-13, Louis Wright Collection, Moorland-Spingarn Collection.

50. Logan, *Howard University*, p. 161; Howard University catalogue, 1917, p. 173, copy available in Moorland-Spingarn Collection; Arthur Garfield Hays opening statement, November 16, 1925.

51. Howard University *Enopron*, 1920–1921; Logan, *Howard University*, p. 160.

52. Starr, *The Social Transformation of American Medicine*, pp. 85–88; Howard University *Enopron*, 1920–1921; *Regulations of the Freedman's Hospital, 1909* (Washington, D.C.: Government Printing Office, 1909), pp. 8–17, box 3, entry 311, RG 48, Department of Interior, Patents and Misc. Division, National Archives.

53. "A Tribute to the Sweet Family," July–August 1997, copy in author's possession; Haldeman-Julius, *Clarence Darrow's Two Great Trials*, pp. 35–36.

54. Haldeman-Julius, *Clarence Darrow's Two Great Trials*, p. 36; Starr, *Social Transformation of American Medicine*, pp. 167–168.

55. Logan, *Howard University*, pp. 181–183; Arthur Garfield Hays closing statement, November 16, 1925; Kennedy, *Over Here*, pp. 191–201.

56. Madison Grant quoted in John Higham, *Strangers in the Land: Patterns of American Nativism, 1860–1925* (New York: Atheneum, 1971), p. 306.

57. Mark Robert Schneider, *"We Return Fighting": The Civil Rights Movement in the Jazz Age* (Boston: Northeastern University Press, 2002), p. 13; Stewart E. Tolnay and E. M. Beck, *A Festival of Violence: An Analysis of Southern Lynchings, 1882–1930* (Urbana: University of Illinois Press, 1995), p. 272; Lewis, *Du Bois*, p. 579; Fairclough, *Better Day Coming*, pp. 102–106.

58. Elizabeth Clark-Lewis, *Living In, Living Out: African American Domestics in Washington, D.C., 1910–1940* (Washington D.C.: Smithsonian Institution Press, 1994), p. 73; Green, *The Secret City*, pp. 190–191; "Negroes Attack Girl," *Washington Post*, July 19, 1919.

59. "Attack on Woman Leads to Race Riot," *Washington Post*, July 20, 1919; "Scores Are Injured in More Race Riots," *Washington Post*, July 21, 1919; John Shillady to A. Mitchell Palmer, July 25, 1919, frame 479, reel 5, part 12A, NAACP Papers.

60. "Police Officer, Two Negroes and One White Killed; Others Are Fatally Hurt as Races Battle in the Streets of Washington," *Washington Post*, July 22, 1919; "One Dead and Another Dying; 2000 Regular Troops Guard Capital Streets," *Washington Post*, July 23, 1919.

61. "One Riot Victim Dies; Troops Quiet Capital; Crowds Quit Streets," *Washington Post*, July 24, 1919; James Weldon Johnson, "The Washington Riots," September 1919, box 30, Clarence Darrow Collection, Library of Congress.

62. R. L. Polk and Company, *Boyd's Directory of the District of Columbia* (Washington, D.C.: R. L. Polk and Company, 1920).

63. Mark Robert Schneider, *"We Return Fighting,"* p. 301. For other personal experiences of mob attacks in Washington, see James Scott statement, August 14, 1919, frame 481, reel 5, part 12A, NAACP Papers, and Francis Thomas statement, n.d., frames 482–484, reel 5, part 12A, NAACP Papers.

64. William Tuttle, *Race Riot: Chicago in the Red Summer of 1919* (New York: Atheneum, 1970); Lewis, *Du Bois*, p. 579; Mark Robert Schneider, *"We Return Fighting,"* pp. 33–34 and chapter 5.

65. Stoddard quoted in Jacobson, *Whiteness of a Different Color*, p. 96; Higham, *Strangers in the Land*, pp. 289–296.

66. Terrell quoted in Lewis, *District of Columbia*, pp. 75–76; Allan H. Spear, *Black Chicago and the Making of a Negro Ghetto, 1890–1920* (Chicago: University of Chicago Press, 1967), pp. 219–220; Tolnay and Beck, *A Festival of Violence*, p. 272.

67. Thomas Holt, Cassandra Smith-Parker, and Rosalyn Terborg-Penn, *A Special Mission: The Story of Freedman's Hospital, 1862–1962* (Washington D.C.: Howard University Academic Affairs Division, 1975), pp. 47–48; July 1909 agreement, assistant secretary of interior and D.C. board of charities; Borchert, *Alley Life in Washington*, pp. 183–184.

68. Howard University *Bulletin* 1, no. 4 (1921–1922). Description of Ossian comes from his graduation photo, copy in author's possession.

69. Vanessa Northington Gamble, *Making a Place for Ourselves: The Black Hospital Movement, 1920–1945* (New York: Oxford University Press, 1995), pp. 30–31; Memorandum for assistant secretary, April 8, 1909, entry 311, box 32, RG 48, Department of Interior, Patents and Misc. Division.

70. W. A. Warfield to secretary of the interior, March 28, 1913; R. L. Owen to Warfield, July 21, 1921; Thomas Martin to secretary of interior, June 2, 1921; Warfield to secretary of interior, June 11, 1921; Warfield to secretary of interior, September 8, 1921, all in box 2070, RG 48, Central Classified Files.

Chapter Four: Uplift Me, Pride

1. Arthur Garfield Hays opening statement, *People v. Ossian Sweet et al.*, November 16, 1925, frames 920–938, reel 3, part 5, NAACP Papers.

2. Olivier Zunz, *The Changing Face of Inequality: Urbanization, Industrial Development, and Immigrants in Detroit, 1880–1920* (Chicago: University of Chicago Press, 1982), parts 2 and 4; Robert Conot, *American Odyssey* (Detroit: Wayne State University, 1986), pp. 241–244; "Dodge's $8,000,000 Addition Under Way," *Detroit News*, September 20, 1925; Douglas Brinkley, *Wheels for the World: Henry Ford, His Company, and a Century of Progress* (New York: Viking, 2003), pp. 275–292.

3. Zunz, *The Changing Face of Inequality*, p. 376; Reinhold Niebuhr, *Leaves from the Notebook of a Tamed Cynic* (1929; repr. New York: Harper and Row, 1980), p. 143.

4. Stephen Meyer III, *The Five Dollar Day: Labor, Management, and Social Control in the Ford Motor Company, 1908–1921* (Albany: SUNY Press, 1981), chapters 6–7; Zunz, *The Changing Face of Inequality*, pp. 313–319; David Allan Levine, *Internal Combustion: The Races in Detroit, 1915–1926* (Westport, Conn.: Greenwood Press, 1976), pp. 6–7, 24–31; Raymond Fragnoli, *The Transformation of Detroit: Progressivism in Detroit—and After, 1912–1933* (New York: Garland, 1982), particularly chapter 4; Conot, *American Odyssey*, p. 197.

5. Sunnie Wilson with John Cohassey, *Toast of the Town: The Life and Times of Sunnie Wilson* (Detroit: Wayne State University Press, 1998), p. 51; William Barlow, *"Looking Up At Down": The Emergence of a Blues Culture* (Philadelphia: Temple University Press, 1989), p. 284; Lars Bjorn with Jim Gallert, *Before Motown: A History of Jazz in Detroit, 1920–1960* (Ann Arbor: University of Michigan Press, 2001), chapters 1 and 2; "Vice Rampant, Says Holsaple," *Detroit News*, November 4, 1925.

6. Allan Nevins and Frank Ernest Hill, *Ford: Expansion and Challenge, 1915–1933* (New York: Charles Scribner's Sons, 1957), pp. 311–316.

7. Robert Dunn research notes, n.d. [1926?], box 1, Robert Dunn Collection, Archives of Labor and Urban Affairs, Walter P. Reuther Library, Wayne State University, Detroit, Mich.; Peter Gavrilovich and Bill McGraw, eds., *The Detroit Almanac* (Detroit: Detroit Free Press, 2001), p. 485; Roaldus Richmond, "Open All Night," *American Life Histories: Manuscripts from the Federal Writers' Project, 1936–1940* available at http://memory.loc.gov, last accessed December 11, 2003.

8. Record of Ossian Sweet's state medical exam, November 14, 1921, Wayne County Physicians Register, v. 10, RG 85-38, Michigan State Archives, Lansing; R. L. Polk and Company, *Detroit City Directory, 1922–1923* (Detroit: R. L. Polk and Company, 1923); Forrester Washington, "The Negro in Detroit" (Detroit: Associated Charities of Detroit, 1920), no pagination; Zunz, *The Changing Face of Inequality*, pp. 352–353.

9. R. L. Polk and Company, *Detroit City Directory, 1917* (Detroit: R. L. Polk and Company, 1917); David M. Katzman, *Before the Ghetto: Black Detroit in the Nineteenth Century* (Urbana: University of Illinois Press, 1973), p. 67; Zunz, *The Changing Face of Inequality*, pp. 137–141.

10. George Haynes, *Negro New-Comers in Detroit: A Challenge to Christian Statesmanship* (1918; repr. New York: Arno Press, 1969), pp. 8–9, 12–20; Levine, *Internal Combustion*, pp. 54–61; lyrics quoted in Lars Bjorn, "From Hastings Street to the Bluebird: The Blues and Jazz Tradition in Detroit," *Michigan Quarterly Review* 25 (spring 1986): 258.

11. Richard W. Thomas, *Life for Us Is What We Make It: Building Black Community in Detroit, 1915–1945* (Bloomington: Indiana University Press, 1992), pp. 26, 30.

12. Robert W. Adams, "Detroit's Negro Population Is Now 53,000," *The Detroiter*, July 30, 1923, p. 13, clipping in E and M Files, Negroes in Detroit, Social Surveys, Miscellaneous Materials, Burton Historical Collection, Detroit Public Library, Detroit, Mich.; Levine, *Internal Combustion*, p. 59.

13. Katzman, *Before the Ghetto*, pp. 91, 93–94; R. L. Bradby to Velma McDonald, September 25, 1926, reel 3, Second Baptist Church Collection, Michigan Historical Collection, Bentley Library, University of Michigan, Ann Arbor; minutes of the Human Resources Association of Greater Detroit, April 8, 1920, box 1, Human Resources Association of Greater Detroit Papers, Michigan Historical Collection; Sam Griggs statement, November 25, 1928, box G-95, group I, NAACP Papers, Library of Congress, Washington, D.C.

14. Joyce Shaw Peterson, *American Automobile Workers, 1900–1930* (Albany: SUNY Press, 1979), pp. 47–58; Thomas, *Life for Us Is What We Make It*, p. 107; August Meier and Elliot Rudwick, *Black Detroit and the Rise of the UAW* (New York: Oxford University Press, 1979), pp. 5–9; Robert Mansfield notes and Marcus [?] notes, n.d. [c. 1925], box 1, Robert Dunn Collection, Archives of Labor and Urban Affairs, Wayne State University, Detroit, Mich.; minutes of Human Resources Association of Greater Detroit meeting, November 11, 1920, box 1, Papers of the Human Resources Association of Greater Detroit, Michigan Historical Collections, Bentley Library, University of Michigan, Ann Arbor.

15. Washington, "The Negro in Detroit," chapter 7; Victoria W. Walcott, *Remaking Respectability: African American Women in Interwar Detroit* (Chapel Hill: University of North Carolina Press, 2001), pp. 29–30, 80–81.

16. Thomas Lee Philpot, *The Slum and the Ghetto: Immigrants, Blacks, and Reformers in Chicago, 1880–1930* (New York: Oxford University Press, 1978), chapters 6 and 8; Washington, "The Negro in Detroit," no pagination; Levine, *Internal Combustion*, pp. 130–132; Haynes, "Negro New-Comers in Detroit," p. 10.

17. Levine, *Internal Combustion*, p. 45.

18. Forrester B. Washington report, August 25, 1917, box 1, Detroit Urban League Papers, Michigan Historical Collection.

19. Polk, *Polk's City Directory*, 1922–1923, for Clinton Street; Elaine Latzman Moon, *Untold Tales, Unsung Heroes: An Oral History of Detroit's African American Community, 1918–1967* (Detroit: Wayne State University Press, 1994), p. 49; Mayor's Inter-Racial Committee, *The Negro in Detroit* (Detroit: Detroit Bureau of Governmental Research, 1926), section 2, p. 10.

20. Thomas, *Life for Us Is What We Make It*, p. 91.

21. "Conditions Among Newcomers in Detroit," spring 1918, and Detroit Urban League rental survey, October 1921, both in box 1, Detroit Urban League Papers; Washington, "The Negro in Detroit," no pagination; John Ihlder, "Booming Detroit," *The Survey* (July 29, 1916): 449; Mayor's Inter-Racial Committee, *The Negro in Detroit*, section 5; Haynes, "Negro New-Comers in Detroit," pp. 21–24.

22. Washington, "The Negro in Detroit," no pagination; Mayor's Inter-Racial Committee, *The Negro in Detroit*, section 5, p. 21.

23. Washington, "Negro in Detroit," no pagination; Mayor's Inter-Racial Committee, *The Negro in Detroit*, section 5, pp. 21–22.

24. Zunz, *The Changing Face of Inequality*, pp. 113–128, 377; Detroit Urban League Report, n.d. [spring 1918], box 1, Detroit Urban League Collection; Mayor's Inter-Racial Committee, *The Negro in Detroit*, section 5, pp. 1–2, 20–22.

25. John Dancy to James Inches, November 27, 1920; minutes of meeting, October 24, 1923, both in box 1, Detroit Urban League Collection; George E. Worthington, "Prostitution in Detroit," summer 1926, p. 6, box 14, Detroit Citizens' League, Additional Material Collection, Burton Historical Collection, Walcott, *Remaking Respectability*, pp. 106–107; F. H. Croul to Frank Doremus, December 20, 1923, Mayor's Papers, 1924, Burton Historical Collection.

26. Washington, "The Negro in Detroit," no pagination; Mayor's Inter-Racial Commit-

tee, *The Negro in Detroit*, section 6, pp. 3–6; G. Arthur Blakeslee to John Dancy, March 11, 1926, box 1, Detroit Urban League Collection.

27. Mayor's Inter-Racial Committee, *The Negro in Detroit*, section 6, pp. 8–16; Washington, "The Negro in Detroit," no pagination.

28. Washington, "The Negro in Detroit," no pagination; Mayor's Inter-Racial Committee, *The Negro in Detroit*, section 6, pp. 18–19; "Where Hygiene Is Ousting Voodooism," *Detroit Free Press*, August 26, 1923.

29. Marcet Haldeman-Julius, *Clarence Darrow's Two Great Trials* (Gerard, Kan.: Haldeman-Julius Publishing Company, 1927), p. 35; Polk, *Detroit City Directory 1922–1923*; Register of Licensed Pharmacies, v. 4, p. 398, RG 84-105, Michigan State Archives; e.d. 222, p. 2, 1920 U.S. census manuscript, Detroit, Michigan; Sanborn Map Company, *Fire Insurance Map of Detroit, Michigan* (New York: Sanborn Map Company, 1922), available at http://sanborn.umi.com.

30. Polk, *Detroit City Directory*, 1921–22, p. 1701; e.d. 223, p. 21, 1920 U.S. census manuscript, Detroit, Michigan; Arthur Garfield Hays opening statement, November 16, 1925; Farokh Erach Udwadia, *Tetanus* (Bombay: Oxford University Press, 1994), pp. 2–3, 68–71.

31. Arthur Garfield Hays opening statement, November 16, 1925; Ossian Sweet statement to police, September 9, 1925, police department file, *People v. Ossian Sweet et al.*, copy in author's possession.

32. The best source for information for the black business class is Arthur Turner and Earl Moses, eds., *Colored Detroit* (Detroit: n.p., 1924), from which the list of businessmen is drawn. On Ossian's memberships, see Walter White to Roscoe Bruce, January 20, 1926, frames 453–454, reel 9, part 2, NAACP Papers, and on his church membership, Haldeman-Julius, *Clarence Darrow's Two Great Trials*. Haldeman-Julius asserts that Ossian wasn't a religious man—that he joined his church simply for the business connections it afforded—but other evidence suggests Ossian was a devout member of the AME Church, like his parents before him. See Ossian Sweet information for Committee on Candidates, August 8, 1932, and July 12, 1950, candidate files, 1950, Civic Searchlight Collection, Burton Historical Collection.

33. Carrie Curtis, "A Tribute to Our Attorneys in the Sweet Case," *Detroit Independent*, n.d. [November 1925], clipping in Ossian Sweet biographical file, Burton Historical Collection.

34. "Doctor Edward Carter," in Joseph Boris, ed., *Who's Who in Colored America, 1928–1929* (New York: Who's Who in Colored America Corp., 1929), p. 71.

35. Information for this and the preceding paragraph comes from David Katzman, *Before the Ghetto*, chapter 5; Arthur Burns and Earl Moses, eds., *Colored Detroit*, pp. 14, 29, 121; Moon, *Untold Tales, Unsung Heroes*, pp. 37–38.

36. John Dancy to L. Mayer, June 19, 1936, box 9, Detroit Urban League Papers; http://www.cr.nps.gov/nr/travel/detroit/d28htm, last accessed March 15, 2004; Mayor's Inter-Racial Committee, *The Negro in Detroit*, section 6, pp. 16–17; Turner and Moses, *Colored Detroit*, p. 38; oral history interview of Waldo Cain, June 11, 1998, box 2, Kellogg African-American Health Care Project, Walter Reuther Library; Thomas, *Life for Us Is What We Make It*, pp. 180–184; Vanessa Northington Gamble, *Making a Place for Ourselves: The Black Hospital Movement, 1920–1945* (New York: Oxford University Press, 1995), chapters 1–2; for context.

37. Arthur Garfield Hays opening statement, November 16, 1925; Turner and Moses, *Colored Detroit*, pp. 24, 38; Katzman, *Before the Ghetto*, p. 22; H. Payton Johnson biographical sketch, Johnson Reading Room File, Burton Historical Collection.

38. David Levering Lewis, *W. E. B. Du Bois: Biography of a Race, 1868–1919* (New York: Henry Holt, 1993), p. 501; Adam Fairclough, *Better Day Coming: Blacks and Equality, 1890–2000* (New York: Viking, 2001), pp. 117–119.

39. Mark Robert Schneider, *"We Return Fighting": The Civil Rights Movement in the Jazz Age* (Boston: Northeastern University Press, 2002), pp. 12–13; "How to Stop Lynching," *The Messenger* 2 (August 1919): 8–9; David Levering Lewis, *When Harlem Was in Vogue* (New York: Oxford University Press, 1979), pp. 23–24.

40. Thomas, *Life for Us Is What We Make It*, pp. 194–201.

41. Levine, *Internal Combustion*, pp. 85, 88.

42. Ibid., pp. 65–90; Turner and Moses, *Colored Detroit*, p. 23; "Health Week Time Extended," n.d. [possibly 1925], box 1, Detroit Urban League Collection.

43. Thomas, *Life for Us Is What We Make It*, p. 230; "NAACP Secures Ending of Jim Crow Cars in Detroit," n.d. [1920], frame 705, reel 11, part 12C, NAACP Papers; Walter White to James Weldon Johnson, October 13, 1920, frames 733–734, reel 2, part 8A, NAACP Papers; Schneider, *"We Return Fighting,"* pp. 197–198.

44. Eugene Levy, James Weldon Johnson, *Black Leader, Black Voice* (Chicago: University of Chicago Press, 1973), pp. 223–226; Robert Bagnall to Walter White, December 17, 1920; clipping, *Michigan State News*, February 8, 1921, both in reel 3, part 12C, NAACP Papers.

45. Schneider, *"We Return Fighting,"* pp. 305–306.

46. M. Louise Hood to W. D. Sterns, August 3, 1925, and minutes of meeting, October 24, 1923, both in box 1, Detroit Urban League Papers; Mayor's Inter-Racial Committee, *The Negro in Detroit*, section 9, p. 22.

47. Gladys Sweet to Walter White, n.d. [October 1925], frames 353–360, reel 3, part 5, NAACP Papers; Haldeman-Julius, *Clarence Darrow's Two Great Trials*, p. 35; Robert Toms closing statement in *People v. Henry Sweet*, May 12, 1926, Michigan Historical Collection; Health Week roster of participating doctors, 1922, box 1, Detroit Urban League Papers.

48. Charles C. Alexander, *Ty Cobb* (New York: Oxford University Press, 1984), pp. 67–68; Al Stump, *Cobb: A Biography* (Chapel Hill, N.C.: Algonquin Books of Chapel Hill, 1994), pp. vii, 141, 160–161, 170.

49. Arthur Garfield Hays opening statement, November 16, 1925.

50. Lynchings figures from http://memory.loc.gov/ammem/aap/timelin3.html, last accessed March 17, 2004; Philip Dray, *At the Hands of Persons Unknown: The Lynching of Black Americans* (New York: Random House, 2002), p. 268; Tim Madigan, *The Burning: Massacre, Destruction, and the Tulsa Race Riots of 1921* (New York: St. Martin's Press, 2001), pp. 179–182; "Dr. Sweet Is Cross-Examined," *Detroit News*, November 19, 1925, frames 64–66, reel 4, part 5, NAACP Papers.

51. Schneider, *"We Return Fighting,"* pp. 354–356; Toms closing statement, May 12, 1926.

52. Arthur Garfield Hays opening statement, November 16, 1925; Haldeman-Julius, *Clarence Darrow's Two Great Trials*, p. 28.

53. Haldeman-Julius, *Clarence Darrow's Two Great Trials*, p. 28.

54. On the Mitchell family, see sheet 4, enumeration district 600, 1920 U.S. census manuscript, Detroit, Mich. There is no trace of Rosella in the Pittsburgh census. But Benjamin Mitchell appears in e.d. 138, p. 2, 1900 U.S. census manuscript, Alleghany County, Penn. Mitchell's musical career—already begun before coming to Detroit—is mentioned in Haldeman-Julius, *Clarence Darrow's Two Great Trials*, p. 28, and in Walter White handwritten notes, n.d. [September 1925], frames 374–396, reel 3, part 5, NAACP Papers; Levine, *Internal Combustion*, p. 160.

55. Mitchell entry, 1920 census; Sanborn Map Company, *Fire Insurance Map of Detroit, Michigan* (New York: Sanborn Map Company, 1915); Walter White to James Weldon Johnson, September 16, 1925, frames 943–946, reel 2, part 5, NAACP Papers.

56. Mitchell entry, 1920 census; Haldeman-Julius, *Clarence Darrow's Two Great Trials*, pp. 28, 30–31.

57. Gladys Sweet to Walter White, n.d. [October 1925]; Haldeman-Julius, *Clarence Darrow's Two Great Trials*, pp. 28–30; Mitchell entry, 1920 U.S. census manuscript.

58. Arthur Garfield Hays opening statement, November 16, 1925; Haldeman-Julius, *Clarence Darrow's Two Great Trials*, p. 28; Levine, *Internal Combustion*, p. 160.

59. Returns of marriages recorded in the County of Wayne, 1922, reel 166, Library of Michigan, Lansing; death certificate 8694, Baby Sweet, July 21, 1923, Vital Records Division, Wayne County, Mich.

60. Ossian and Gladys reported their home as Cairney Street on a variety of documents in the year after their marriage. See, for example, Baby Sweet death certificate, July 21, 1923.

61. Turner and Moses, *Colored Detroit*, p. 74; Levine, *Internal Combustion*, p. 61; Du Bois quoted in David Levering Lewis, *W. E. B. Du Bois: Biography of a Race, 1868–1919* (New York: Henry Holt, 1993), p. 566.

62. Arthur Garfield Hays opening statement, November 16, 1925.

63. John Walton, Paul Beeson, and Ronald Bodley Scott, *Oxford Companion to Medicine* v. 1 (New York: Oxford University Press, 1986), p. 332; Rosalynd Pflaum, *Grand Obsession: Madame Curie and Her World* (New York: Doubleday, 1989), p. 224.

64. Death certificate #8694, Baby Sweet.

65. Ossian Sweet passport application, August 20, 1923, reel 2353, 10Wi M-1490, RG 59, National Archives, Washington, D.C.

66. "Winter Tourists Sailing to Europe," *New York Times*, October 6, 1923; Haldeman-Julius, *Clarence Darrow's Two Great Trials*, pp. 28–29.

67. "Winter Tourists Sailing to Europe"; R. F. Foster, *Modern Ireland, 1600–1972* (London: Penguin Press, 1988), pp. 508–515; A. J. P. Taylor, *English History, 1914–1945* (New York: Oxford University Press, 1965), pp. 194–202; James Hinton, *The First Shop Stewards' Movement* (London: George Allen and Unwin, 1973); Helmut Gruber, *Red Vienna: Experiment in Working-Class Culture, 1919–1934* (New York: Oxford University Press, 1991), p. 15.

68. U.S. Department of Labor Immigration Service, List of U.S. Citizens, S.S. *Paris*, New York, June 28, 1924, p. 5, copy available at http://www.ellisisland.org.

69. Quinn, *Marie Curie*, pp. 388–389; oral history interview with Sherman Sweet, February 27, 2002, notes in author's possession; Sweet information for Committee of Candidates, July 12, 1950.

70. Brigitte Hamann, *Hitler's Vienna: A Dictator's Apprenticeship* (New York: Oxford University Press, 1999); Tyler Stovall, *Paris Noir: African Americans in the City of Light* (Boston: Houghton-Mifflin, 1996), chapter 1; Michel Fabre, *From Harlem to Paris: Black American Writers in France, 1840–1980* (Urbana: University of Illinois Press, 1993), particularly chapters 5 and 6.

71. Arthur Garfield Hays opening statement, November 16, 1925; Haldeman-Julius, *Clarence Darrow's Two Great Trials*, p. 29.

72. Ibid.

73. List of U.S. Citizens, S.S. *Paris*, New York, June 28, 1924, p. 5 lists the baby's name as Marguerite. Every other account of the family refers to her as Iva.

Chapter Five: White Houses

1. Fred Benoit testimony, *People v. Ossian Sweet et al.*, November 10, 1925, Michigan Historical Collection, Bentley Library, University of Michigan, Ann Arbor; trial testimony of Eban Draper, November 7, 1925; John Getke testimony at preliminary hearing, *People v. Ossian Sweet et al.*, September 17, 1925, box 1, Ossian Sweet Collection, Burton Historical Collection, Detroit Public Library, Detroit, Mich.

2. David Allan Levine, *Internal Combustion: The Races in Detroit, 1915–1926* (Westport, Conn.: Greenwood Press, 1976), p. 158.

3. Ray Dove Testimony, November 6, 1925; George Suppus trial testimony, November 10, 1925; Ulric Arthur trial testimony, November 10, 1925; telephone interview with Bill McGraw, November 1999.

4. "Darrow Scores Point in Sweet Murder Trial," *Detroit Free Press*, May 2, 1926; Otto Eberhardt trial testimony, November 7, 1925; articles of association, Waterworks Park Improvement Association, February 13, 1926, Michigan Department of Consumer and Industry Services, Bureau of Commercial Services, Corporation Division, Lansing, Mich.

5. Marcet Haldeman-Julius, "Clarence Darrow's Defense of a Negro," *Haldeman-Julius Monthly* 4 (July 1926): 23–24; "Stop Rioting, Smith Pleads with Citizens," *Detroit Free Press*, July 12, 1925.

6. Haldeman-Julius, "Clarence Darrow's Defense of a Negro," p. 24.

7. Marcet Haldeman-Julius, *Clarence Darrow's Two Great Trials* (Girard, Kan.: Haldeman-Julius Publishing Company, 1927), p. 32.

8. Arthur Garfield Hays opening statement, *People v. Ossian Sweet et al.*, November 16, 1925; Haldeman-Julius, *Clarence Darrow's Two Great Trials*, p. 29. Over the years, Ossian would come to claim that he'd received advanced degrees abroad, though the brief time he spent studying makes it all but impossible. See Ossian Sweet Information on Committee for Candidates, July 12, 1950, candidate files, Civic Searchlight Collection, Burton Historical Collection.

9. R. L. Polk and Company, *Detroit City Directory*, 1925–1926 (Detroit: R. L. Polk and Company, 1926).

10. Dentist registration book, 1923, p. 65, reel 1947, RG 76-2, Michigan Department of Licensing and Registration, Michigan State Archives, Lansing; R. L. Polk, *Detroit City Directory*, 1923–1924 (Detroit: R. L. Polk and Company, 1924); Arthur Turner and Earl Moses, *Colored Detroit* (Detroit: n.p., 1924), p. 55; Haldeman-Julius, *Clarence Darrow's Two Great Trials*, pp. 35–36; Lars Bjorn with Jim Gallert, *Before Motown: A History of Jazz in Detroit* (Ann Arbor: University of Michigan Press, 2001), pp. 7–10.

11. For details on Henry's college activities, see Wilberforce's yearbook, *The Forcean*, for 1925, and Wilberforce University bulletin (June 1924), both in Wilberforce University Archives, Xenia, Ohio. Also see "Doctor Sweet to Tell of Fears," *Detroit Times*, May 7, 1926; Haldeman-Julius, *Clarence Darrow's Two Great Trials*, pp. 27–28; Lester Moll closing statement, *People v. Henry Sweet*, May 10, 1926, Michigan Historical Collection.

12. "Posse Chases Man Believed to Be One of Four Who Threatened Colored Farmer," *Xenia (Ohio) Gazette*, October 13, 1924; "Martin Gets Rest While Armed Men Guard Premises," *Xenia (Ohio) Gazette*, October 15, 1924; Moll closing statement, May 10, 1926.

13. Richard W. Thomas, *Life for Us Is What We Make It: Building Black Community in Detroit, 1915–1945* (Bloomington: Indiana University Press, 1992), p. 27; "City 1,242,044 Census Shows," *Detroit Free Press*, September 27, 1924; "Cites Home Benefits of City's East Side" and "Buy Land and Hold It, Is Advice of Veteran," both in *Detroit Free Press*, October 25, 1925; Walter Clyde, *A Million Dollar Secret* (Detroit: Walter Schulte Corporation, 1927).

14. Raymond Fragnoli, *The Transformation of Detroit: Progressivism in Detroit—and After, 1912–1933* (New York: Garland, 1982), chapter 5; Sidney Fine, *Frank Murphy: The Detroit Years* (Ann Arbor: University of Michigan Press, 1957), pp. 91–102.

15. Fine, *Frank Murphy*, pp. 102–107.

16. Fine, *Frank Murphy*—the first volume in Fine's monumental biography—details Murphy's background. On Murphy's religious devotion, also see oral history interview of Robert Toms, November 28, 1959, Alex Baskin Collection, Michigan Historical Collection; oral history interview with Hilmer Gellein, n.d. [early 1970s], box 1, Ossian Sweet Collection. On Murphy's relation to women, see Josephine Gomon notes, n.d., box 9, Josephine Gomon Papers, Michigan Historical Collection. Murphy quotes from Fine, *Frank Murphy*, pp. 109, 114.

17. Fine, *Frank Murphy*, pp. 111–112; Fragnoli, *The Transformation of Reform*, pp. 263–274, quote on p. 273.

18. Fine, *Murphy*, pp. 112, 114–116, quote on p. 117. Also see Fragnoli, *The Transformation of Reform*, pp. 273–277.

19. Kenneth T. Jackson, *The Ku Klux Klan in the City, 1915–1930* (New York: Oxford University Press, 1967), pp. 118–132.

20. Jackson, *The Ku Klux Klan in the City*, p. 134.

21. "A New Al Smith—But This Time a Republican," *Literary Digest*, November 28, 1925, clipping in box 3, Mayor's Papers 1923, Burton Historical Collection; "Long Fight Is Ended for Civic Leader," *Detroit Free Press*, June 18, 1942, copy in "Smith, John W." file, Detroit Free Press Clipping Morgue, Detroit, Mich.; John Smith career summary, n.d. [c. 1930]; "John W. Smith," *Detroit Saturday Night*, September 16, 1922; "John Smith Dies, Head of Council," *Detroit News*, June 18, 1942; untitled *Detroit Times*, August 31, 1924, profile, all in "John Smith" file, Detroit News Clipping Morgue, Detroit, Mich.; Fragnoli, *The Transformation of Reform*, pp. 308–309, 313–314.

22. Jackson, *The Ku Klux Klan in the City*, pp. 133–136; Levine, *Internal Combustion*, pp. 138–141; untitled clipping, *Detroit Mirror*, December 4, 1931, clipping in "Smith, John W." file, Detroit Free Press Clipping Morgue.

23. Thomas Lloyd Jones, "Labor and Politics: The Detroit Municipal Election of 1937," (Ph.D. dissertation: University of Michigan, 1998), pp. 72, 160; Reinhold Niebuhr, *Leaves from the Notebook of a Trained Cynic* (San Francisco: Harper and Row, 1929), p. 144; Reinhold Niebuhr, "Detroit in the Twenties," unpublished typescript, n.d. [1950s], box 47, Reinhold Niebuhr Papers, Library of Congress, Washington, D.C.

24. Jackson, *The Ku Klux Klan in the City*, pp. 135–137; Levine, *Internal Combustion*, p. 140, for the vote in Black Bottom.

25. Jackson, *The Ku Klux Klan in the City*, pp. 137–139; Levine, *Internal Combustion*, p. 141.

26. Jackson, *The Ku Klux Klan in the City*, p. 141; "Klan Out to Elect Bowles," *Detroit Times*, September 23, 1925; "Bares Klan Scheming to Rule City Council," *Detroit Free Press*, October 31, 1925.

27. Haldeman-Julius, *Clarence Darrow's Two Great Trials*, pp. 29–30; Mayor's Inter-Racial Committee, *The Negro in Detroit* (Detroit: Detroit Bureau of Governmental Research, 1926), section 9, pp. 34–35.

28. Committee on Negro Housing, *Negro Housing* (1932; repr. New York: Negro Universities Press, 1969), pp. 40–42; "Restrictions for B. E. Taylor's Properties," E and M, Detroit Real Estate, Burton Historical Collection, Detroit Public Library, Detroit, Mich.; Harold Black, "Restrictive Covenants in Relation to Segregated Negro Housing in Detroit," M.A. thesis, Wayne State University, 1947, p. 6; advertisement for the Brownell Corporation, *Detroit News*, September 6, 1925; "Rigid Restrictions Urged for New Plats," *Detroit Free Press*, September 20, 1925.

29. Committee on Negro Housing, *Negro Housing*, pp. 93–104; Detroit Real Estate Board, *By-Laws* (1921), has no such prohibition. Real Estate Board, *By-Laws* (1926), part III, section 37, contains the restriction, along with a notation that the change was adopted in 1924. Both copies available in Burton Historical Collection; remarks of Ira Jayne, annual business meeting of the NAACP, January 4, 1926, frame 711, reel 13, NAACP Papers [microfilm edition].

30. "Open $150,000 Damage Suit," *Chicago Defender*, April 18, 1931; Hays opening statement, November 16, 1925.

31. Hays opening statement, November 16, 1925; "Darrow Calls Sweet to Stand," *Detroit Times*, May 6, 1925.

32. Haldeman-Julius, *Clarence Darrow's Two Great Trials*, p. 30; "Dr. Sweet Wanted Home for His Baby," *Chicago Defender*, December 5, 1925.

33. Walter White to James Weldon Johnson, September 16, 1925, frames 943–946, reel 2, part 5, NAACP Papers; White handwritten notes, n.d. [September 1925], frames 374–396, reel 3, part 5, NAACP Papers; Peter Gavrilovich and Bill McGraw, eds., *The Detroit Almanac: 300 Years of Life in the Motor City* (Detroit: Detroit Free Press, 2001), p. 485.

34. On neighborhood house prices, see classified ads, *Detroit News*, September 4, 5, 8, 17, 1925. The terms of the deal are detailed in Walter White to James Weldon Johnson, September 16, 1925; Sweet Defense Fund disbursements, n.d. [December 11, 1925], frames 811–814, reel 3, part 5, NAACP Papers; "Darrow Calls Sweet to Stand," May 6, 1926; plat book entry, 2905 Garland Avenue, Wayne County Registrar of Deeds.

35. Walter White to James Weldon Johnson, September 16, 1925.

36. "Darrow to Rest Riot Defense," *Detroit Times*, November 19, 1925; "Detroit Riot Case Trial Near Close," n.d. [November 1925], Associated Negro Press story, clipping at frame 142, reel 4, part 5, NAACP Papers.

37. Levine, *Internal Combustion*, p. 158; Ray Dove trial testimony, November 6, 1925; e.d. 629, pp. 4–9, 1920 U.S. census manuscript, Detroit, Michigan; Harry Monet trial testimony, November 10, 1925.

38. Oliver Zunz, *The Changing Face of Inequality: Urbanization, Industrial Development, and Immigrants in Detroit, 1880–1920* (Chicago: University of Chicago Press, 1982), chapter 6; Hannah Real Estate Exchange, "Real Estate Obtained Without Use of Coin or Greenbacks," 1895 pamphlet available at E and M, Detroit Real Estate, Burton Historical Collection. On sacrificing children's education in exchange for home ownership, see

Stephan Thernstrom, *Poverty and Progress: Social Mobility in a Nineteenth Century City* (Cambridge, Mass.: Harvard University Press, 1964), pp. 117–122, 155–157.

39. The development of Garland Avenue can be traced through building permit index, v. 3, Detroit Building and Safety Department Records, 1909–1924, Burton Historical Collection. Property restrictions are spelled out in deed for 2960 Garland Avenue, November 9, 1915, Wayne county Registrar of Deeds; plat books for Garland Avenue for information on Getkes' and Smiths' loans. On the transformation of the real estate market more generally, see Alexander Von Hoffman, "Weaving the Urban Fabric: Nineteenth-Century Patters of Residential Real Estate in Outer Boston," *Journal of Urban History* 22 (January 1996): 191–230.

40. E.d. 629, pp. 4–9, 1920 U.S. census manuscript, Detroit, Michigan. Polk, *Detroit City Directory*, 1925–1926; Robert Dunn research notes, n.d. [mid-1920s], box 1, Robert Dunn Collection, Archives of Labor and Urban Affairs, Wayne State University, Detroit, Mich.; e.d. 24, p. 2A, 1910 U.S. census manuscript, Mauch Shunk Township, Carbon County, Pennsylvania.

41. The President's Conference on Home Building and Home Ownership, *Tentative Report of the Committee on Finance* (Washington, D.C.: Government Printing Office, 1931), pp. 7–24; G. Walter Woodworth, *The Detroit Money Market* (Ann Arbor: University of Michigan School of Business Administration, 1932), pp. 125–130. On ubiquity of secondary mortgage market, see classified ads, *Detroit Free Press*, October 26, 1925.

42. President's Conference, *Tentative Report of the Committee on Finance*, pp. 18–21; e.d. 629, pp. 4–9, 1920 U.S. census manuscript, Detroit, Michigan; Ray Dove testimony, November 6, 1925; George Suppus testimony and Ulric Arthur testimony, November 10, 1925; Peter Gavrilovich and Bill McGraw, eds., *The Detroit Almanac: 300 Years of Life in the Motor City* (Detroit: Detroit Free Press, 2001). p. 77.

43. Mayor's Inter-Racial Committee, *The Negro in Detroit*, section 1, p. 10; R. L. Polk and Company, *City of Detroit Directory*, 1919–1920 (Detroit: R. L. Polk and Company, 1920); Levine, *Internal Combustion*, p. 155. For an intimate view of the west-side community, see The Westsiders, *Remembering Detroit's Old West Side, 1920–1950: A Pictoral History of the Westsiders* (Detroit: self-published, 1997).

44. "Beautiful Mrs. Mathies Shoots After Bricks Were Hurled," *The Detroit Independent*, April 17, 1925, clipping in box 30, Clarence Darrow Collection, Library of Congress, Washington, D.C.; case report, *People v. Fleta Mathies*, n.d. [spring 1925], box G-95, group I, NAACP Papers, Library of Congress.

45. "Beautiful Mrs. Mathies Shoots After Bricks Were Hurled," April 17, 1925.

46. Sanborn Map Company, *Fire Insurance Map of Detroit, Michigan* (New York: Sanborn Map Company, 1926); oral history interview with Cecil Rowlette, August 1, 1960, Baskin Collection.

47. "House Stoned, Negro Quits It," *Detroit News*, June 24, 1925; "Mob of 5,000 Forces Negro to Quit Home," *Detroit Free Press*, June 24, 1925; Levine, *Internal Combustion*, pp. 154–155; data regarding the Detroit cases, n.d. [October 1925?], frame 352, reel 3, part 5, NAACP Papers; oral history interview with Cecil Rowlette, August 1, 1926. Contrary to common perception, the mob was not made up exclusively of the working class. Among the leaders of the Tireman Avenue Improvement Association were the Turners' next-door neighbor, Christian Schollenberger, a building contractor, and a man who lived down the block, Ruel Caldwell, an executive in an engineering firm.

48. "Row Over Homes Brings Bullets," *Detroit News*, July 8, 1925; "Throng Wields Pistols, Guns at Negro Home," *Detroit Free Press*, July 8, 1925; "Police Rout 2,000 as Tenants' Quarrel Breaks Anew," *Detroit Free Press*, July 9, 1925; "Police Again Disburse Mob," *Detroit Free Press*, July 10, 1925; Vollington Bristol statement, November 15, 1925, box 5, Darrow Collection; Levine, *Internal Combustion*, pp. 155–157.

49. "Negroes Shoot White Youth in New Home Row," *Detroit Free Press*, July 11, 1925; John Fletcher statement, November 15, 1925, box 5, Darrow Collection; Levine, *Internal Combustion*, p. 157.

50. Gladys Sweet to Walter White, n.d. [October 1925], frames 353–360, reel 3, part 5, NAACP Papers.

51. Mark Robert Schneider, *"We Return Fighting": The Civil Rights Movement in the Jazz Age* (Boston: Northeastern University Press, 2002), pp. 305–306; R. L. Bradby to Walter White, December 14, 1925, frame 277, reel 3, part 5, NAACP Papers, for list of branch officers.

52. Lester Moll's closing statement, May 10, 1926; D. F. Moore to William Pickens, n.d. [September 1925?], frames 1106–1107, reel 2, part 5, NAACP Papers.

53. "Negroes Shoot White Youth in New Home Row," July 11, 1925; Levine, *Internal Combustion,* pp. 157–158.

54. John Smith quoted in "Argument of Clarence Darrow in the Case of Henry Sweet" (NAACP pamphlet, 1927), p. 31, box 5, Darrow Collection.

55. Oral history interview with Cecil Rowlette, August 1, 1960; Polk, *Detroit City Directory,* 1925–1926, for Sims's office; "Sweet to Describe Riot Fear," *Detroit Times,* November 18, 1925; "Darrow to Rest Riot Defense," *Detroit Times,* November 19, 1925; Walter White to James Weldon Johnson, September 15, 1925; "Darrow to Rest Riot Defense," *Detroit Times,* November 19, 1925.

56. Harry Monet trial testimony, November 10, 1925; Eban Draper trial testimony, November 7, 1925; Waterworks Park Improvement Association, articles of association, February 13, 1926; e.d. 629, p. 9, 1920 U.S. census manuscript, Detroit, Michigan.

57. E.d. 629, p. 1, 1920 U.S. census manuscript, Detroit, Michigan; Raymond Alf trial testimony, November 11, 1925; Waterworks Park Improvement Association, articles of association, February 13, 1926.

58. Association by-laws are reprinted in the trial testimony, November 10, 1925.

59. "The Weather," *Detroit Free Press,* July 14 and 15, 1925; "Free Doctor Sweet and Ten Others," *Chicago Defender,* April 25, 1931; "Darrow Scores Point in Sweet Murder Trial," May 2, 1926; Ray Dove trial testimony, November 6, 1925; John Getke trial testimony, November 9, 1925.

60. Norton Schuknecht trial testimony, November 5, 1925; R. L. Polk and Company, *Detroit City Directory,* 1910 (Detroit: R. L. Polk and Company, 1910); Polk, *Detroit City Directory,* 1925–1926; e.d. 94, p. 2, 1900 U.S. census manuscript, Detroit, Michigan, for Schuknecht's birth family; e.d. 603, p. 6, 1920 U.S. census manuscript, Detroit, Michigan, for Schuknecht's wife and children.

61. Detroit Police Department, *Sixteenth Annual Report* (Detroit: Police Press, 1925), pp. 2–3, copy available in the Library of Congress; Leslie Woodcock Tentler, *Seasons of Grace: A History of the Catholic Archdiocese of Detroit* (Detroit: Wayne State University Press, 1990), pp. 268–269; "Heart Attack Fatal," *Detroit News,* July 18, 1939; Rebecca Reed, "Regulating the Regulators: Ideology and Practice in the Policing of Detroit, 1880–1918," Ph.D. dissertation, University of Michigan, 1991, p. 152; sheet 6, e.d. 603, 1920 U.S. census manuscript, Detroit, Michigan.

62. Norton Schuknecht trial testimony, November 5, 1925; "Mayor Traces Riot to Klan" and "Letter Still in Mails, Croul Is Reserved," both in *Detroit News,* September 13, 1925, on tensions between mayor and police department.

63. Walter White to James Weldon Johnson, September 16, 1925. There were rumors that Schuknecht himself was a klansman, though there is no evidence to support the assertion. See White to Johnson, September 17, 1925, frames 1031–1032, reel 2, part 5, NAACP Papers.

64. Oral history interview with William Osby, Sr., July 27, 1960, Alex Baskin Collection; Vollington Bristol statement, November 15, 1925.

65. "Sweet Says He Provided Guns," *Detroit Free Press,* May 8, 1926; "Opens $150,000 Damage Suit," *Chicago Defender,* April 18, 1931.

66. "Other Race Troubles Figure in Sweet Trial," *Detroit Free Press,* November 18, 1925.

67. "Negroes Break Up Two Meetings of Realty Men," *Detroit Free Press,* July 17, 1925.

68. James Weldon Johnson letter to the editor, August 3, 1925, frame 964, reel 2, part 5, NAACP Papers [microfilm edition]; William Pickens to R. L. Bradby, July 31, 1925, frame 941, reel 2, part 5, NAACP Papers.

69. "Sweet Says He Provided Guns," May 8, 1926; "Opens $150,000 Damage Suit,"

April 18, 1931; "Darrow to Rest Riot Defense," November 19, 1925; Arthur Garfield Hays opening statement, November 16, 1925; Ossian Sweet, William Davis, Joe Mack, and Norris Murray statements to police, September 9, 1925, Detroit Police Department File, *People v. Ossian Sweet et al.*, copy in the author's possession.

70. Vollington Bristol statement, November 15, 1925; John Hayes trial testimony, November 9, 1925.

71. "Court Darkens KKK Sign," *Detroit Times*, October 10, 1925; Norton Schuknecht trial testimony, November 5, 1925.

72. "Free Dr. Ossian Sweet," April 25, 1931; Black, "Restrictive Covenants in Relation to Segregated Negro Housing in Detroit," p. 26.

73. "200 Police Guard Scene as 1 Is Slain and 1 Shot by Negroes," *Detroit Free Press*, September 10, 1925; "Other Race Troubles Figure in Sweet Trial," November 18, 1925.

74. Robert McPherson service record, July 12, 1929, copy in clipping morgue, *Detroit News*, Detroit, Mich.; Norton Schuknecht trial testimony, November 4, 1925; John Hayes trial testimony, November 1925.

75. "Officer Slain, Partner Kills His Assailant," *Detroit Free Press*, September 8, 1925; oral history interview with Robert Toms, November 28, 1959, Alex Baskin Collection, Michigan Historical Collection; "Fear of Riot Told at Trial," *Detroit News*, November 5, 1925; Schuknecht trial testimony, November 5, 1925.

76. Kathleen Dove statement to police, September 10, 1925; Della Getke trial testimony, November 9, 1925.

77. Clarence Darrow, *The Story of My Life* (New York: Charles Scribner's Sons, 1934), p. 305; "200 Police Guard Scene as 1 Is Slain and 1 Shot by Negroes."

78. Arthur Garfield Hays opening statement, November 16, 1925; Gladys Sweet statement to police, September 9, 1925; Kathleen Dove statement to police, September 10, 1925.

79. "Other Race Troubles Figure in Sweet Trial," November 18, 1925; Mack statement to police, September 9, 1925.

80. John Getke statement to police, September 10, 1925; Ray Dove trial testimony, November 6, 1925; Eric Houghburg statement to police, September 10, 1925; George Suppus trial testimony, Ulric Arthur trial testimony, November 10, 1925.

81. George Suppus trial testimony, Ulric Arthur trial testimony, November 10, 1925; Otis Sweet statement to police, September 9, 1925; oral history interview with Otis Sweet, August 1, 1960, Baskin Collection; "Race Psychology Told in Sweet's Testimony," *Detroit Free Press*, November 19, 1925.

Chapter Six: The Letter of Your Law

1. Norton Schuknecht to superintendent, September 9 [actually September 10], 1925, Detroit Police Department case file, copy in author's possession; "Slaying Leads to Night Riot," *Detroit News*, September 10, 1925; "Police Fear Riot Reprisals," *Detroit Times*, September 10, 1925; "200 Police Guard Scene as 1 Is Slain and 1 Shot by Negroes," *Detroit Free Press*, September 10, 1925.

2. Wayne Andrews, *Architecture, Ambition, and Americans: A Social History of American Architecture* (New York: Free Press, 1978), pp. 252–254; W. Hawkins Ferry, *The Buildings of Detroit: A History*, rev. ed. (Detroit: Wayne State University Press, 1980), pp. 214–215.

3. Fred Williams to Frank Doremus, October 4, 1923, box 3, Detroit Mayor's Papers, 1923, Burton Historical Collection, Detroit Public Library, Detroit, Mich.; minutes of meeting, October 24, 1923, box 1, Detroit Urban League Collection, Michigan Historical Collection, Bentley Library, University of Michigan, Ann Arbor; Cosmopolitan League circular, n.d. [1925], frame 947, reel 2, part 5, NAACP Papers; Mayor's Inter-Racial Committee, *The Negro in Detroit* (Detroit: Detroit Bureau of Governmental Research, 1926), section 9, pp. 5, 33–34; Sidney Fine, *Frank Murphy: The Detroit Years* (Ann Arbor: University of Michigan Press, 1975), p. 127.

4. "Sweet Verdict Due This Week," *Detroit Free Press*, May 6, 1926; Robert Toms opening

statement, *People v. Ossian Sweet et al.*, November 5, 1925, Michigan Historical Collection.

5. Transcript of William Davis statement to police, September 10, 1925, Detroit Police Department file; transcript of Ossian Sweet statement to police, September 9, 1925.

6. Oral history interview with Charles Mahoney, August 1960, Alex Baskin Collection, Michigan Historical Collection; oral history interview with Cecil Rowlette, August 1, 1960, Baskin Collection; Davis statement to police, September 10, 1925.

7. Transcript of Ossian Sweet statement to police, September 9, 1925.

8. Ibid.

9. Charles Washington, Leonard Morse, William Davis, John Latting, and Joe Mack statements to police, September 9, 1925.

10. Norris Murray, William Davis, John Latting, Charles Washington, Leonard Morse, Hewitt Watson, and Joe Mack statements to police, September 9, 1925.

11. John Latting, Hewitt Watson, and Charles Washington statements to police, September 9, 1925.

12. Joe Mack statement to police, September 9, 1925.

13. John Latting, Leonard Morse, William Davis, Joe Mack, Norris Murray, Otis Sweet, and Hewitt Watson statements to police, September 9, 1925.

14. Gladys Sweet statement to police, September 9, 1925.

15. Henry Sweet statement to police, September 9, 1925.

16. "200 Police Guard Scene as 1 Is Slain and 1 Shot by Negroes"; Ferry, *The Buildings of Detroit*, p. 230. The jailhouse was built in 1897; untitled newspaper clipping, *Detroit Free Press*, June 24, 1928, clipping in "County Jail" file, Detroit Free Press Clipping Morgue, Detroit, Mich.

17. "A Tribute to Our Attorneys in the Sweet Case," *Detroit Independent*, no date, clipping in Ossian Sweet biographical file, Burton Historical Collection, Detroit Public Library, Detroit, Mich.; "Career of Slave's Son Inspires College Drive," *Detroit Times*, May 14, 1947; "An Era Has Begun Since They Parted," *Detroit Free Press*, June 28, 1957; oral history interview with Cecil Rowlette, August 1, 1960, Alex Baskin Collection, Bentley Historical Library; Walter White to James Weldon Johnson, September 16, 1925, frames 943–946, reel 2, part 5, NAACP Papers.

18. Oral history interview with William Osby, Sr., July 27, 1960, Baskin Papers; David Alan Levine, *Internal Combustion: The Races in Detroit, 1915–1926* (Westport, Conn.: Greenwood Press, 1976), pp. 82–83; "Mahoney Scores a Double First," *Detroit Free Press*, August 1, 1954; "Charles Henry Mahoney," n.d., copy available in Detroit Free Press Clipping Morgue, Detroit, Mich.

19. William M. Beany, *The Right to Counsel in American Courts* (Ann Arbor: University of Michigan Press, 1955), p. 127; "Officer's Shot Slew Breiner, Is New Claim," *Detroit Free Press*, November 22, 1925; "Dr. Sweet Goes on Stand," *Chicago Defender*, November 28, 1925.

20. Walter White to James Weldon Johnson, September 16, 1925, frames 943–946, reel 2, part 5, NAACP Papers; W. Hays McKinney to James Weldon Johnson, frames 931–932, reel 2, part 5, NAACP Papers; "Murphy Raps Police Raiders," *Detroit Free Press*, July 14, 1925.

21. White to E. P. Lovett, October 26, 1925, frames 20–21, reel 3, part 5, NAACP Papers; oral history interview with Rowlette; White to Johnson, September 16, 1925.

22. McKinney to Johnson, September 12, 1925; Mark Robert Schneider, *"We Return Fighting": The Civil Rights Movement in the Jazz Age* (Boston: Northeastern University Press, 2002), pp. 197–199.

23. "200 Police Guard Scene as 1 Is Slain and 1 Shot by Negores"; R. L. Polk and Company, *City of Detroit Directory*, 1925–1926 (Detroit: R. L. Polk and Company, 1926).

24. Norton Schuknecht testimony, November 5, 1925, *People v. Ossian Sweet et al.*, trial transcript, Bentley Historical Library; "Police Fear Riot Reprisals"; "Slaying Leads to Night Riot"; "200 Police Guard Scene as 1 Is Slain and 1 Shot by Negroes."

25. "200 Police Guard Scene as 1 is Slain and 1 Shot by Negroes."

26. Ibid.

27. Bill McGraw, "Race, Journalism, and the Civil War: *The Detroit Free Press* and the

Riot of 1863," unpublished paper in author's possession; Frank Angelo, *On Guard: A History of the Detroit Free Press* (Detroit: Detroit Free Press, 1981), pp. 119–143; Peter Gavrilovich and Bill McGraw, eds., *The Detroit Almanac: 300 Years of Life in the Motor City* (Detroit: Detroit Free Press, 2001), p. 450; Sidney Fine, *Frank Murphy: The Detroit Years* (Ann Arbor: University of Michigan Press, 1975), pp. 96–97, 104–105, 110–113.

28. "Police Fear Riot Reprisals."

29. Josephine Gomon, draft of Frank Murphy biography, box 9, Josephine Gomon Collection, Michigan Historical Collection, "Dr. Sweet Goes on Stand"; "Officer's Shot Slew Breiner, Is New Claim."

30. Josephine Gomon book drafts; "Slaying Leads to Night Riot."

31. "Robert Morrell Toms," biographical file, Burton Historical Collection, E. A. Batchelor, "Personal and Confidential: Robert M. Toms," *Detroit Saturday Night*, January 10, 1925.

32. Toms biographical file; "Toms Named to 33rd Degree," *Detroit News*, September 27, 1945, and "Toms Denies He's Klansman," *Detroit News*, September 9, 1924, copies in Detroit News Clipping Morgue, Detroit, Mich.; Felix Holt to Walter White, March 22, 1926, frame 621, reel 9, part 2, NAACP Papers.

33. An excellent summary of the right to self-defense, both as a general principle and in Michigan law, is available in Frank Murphy's charge to the court, May 13, 1925, frames 822–854, reel 3, part 5, NAACP Papers. Also see Arthur Garfield Hays opening statement, November 16, 1925, frames 920–938, reel 3, part 5, NAACP Papers. On Toms's counterargument, see Toms opening statement, November 5, 1925, trial transcript.

34. Cover sheet for police department case file, n.d. [September 1925]; Norton Schuknecht statement to police, September 10, 1925; "Moll Demands Slayers in Riot Case Pay Penalty," *Detroit Times*, November 24, 1925.

35. Norton Schuknecht statement to police, September 10, 1925; Schuknecht to superintendent, September 9, 1925; "Put Guard at Home of Negroes"; "200 Police Guard Scene As 1 Is Slain and 1 Shot by Negroes"; "Slaying Leads to Night Riot."

36. Schuknecht statement to police, September 10, 1925.

37. Otto Lemhagen statement to police, September 10, 1926.

38. William Johnson and [?] Hoffman to Edward Fox, n.d. [September 1925?], Detroit Police Department case file, copy in author's possession; Kathleen Dove statement to police, September 10, 1925.

39. Ray and Kathleen Dove statements to police, September 10, 1925. On Ray Dove's place of birth, see the transcript of his testimony in *The People v. Ossian Sweet et al.*, November 6, 1925.

40. George Strauser, William Arthur, George Getke, and Della Getke statements to police, September 10, 1925.

41. John Getke statement to police, September 10, 1925.

42. For a sense of prison conditions, see untitled *Detroit Free Press* clipping, June 24, 1928; G. A. Thomas to Commissioner of Police, December 10, 1923, Mayor's Papers 1923, Burton Historical Collection; R. H. Ferris to Frank Murphy, April 22, 1926, reel 92, Frank Murphy Papers [microfilm edition], Bentley Library; and Detroit House of Corrections, *68th Annual Report* (Detroit: n.p., 1928), copy at Library of Congress, Washington, D.C.

43. Marcet Haldeman-Julius, *Clarence Darrow's Two Great Trials* (Girard, Kan.: Haldeman-Julius Publishing Company, 1927), p. 42; oral history interview with Otis Sweet, August 1, 1960, Baskin Collection; Otis Sweet et al. to W. E. B. Du Bois, September 29, 1925, frame 1088, reel 2, part 5, NAACP Papers.

44. William Davis statement to police, September 10, 1925.

45. Fine, *Frank Murphy*, p. 103; Gomon untitled book draft, box 9, Gomon Papers; "Ten Are Held for Murder in Race Conflict," *Detroit Free Press*, September 11, 1925; warrants against Ossian Sweet et al., September 10, 1925, box 1, Ossian Sweet Collection, Burton Historical Collection.

46. Fine, *Frank Murphy*, pp. 106, 134, 140; Sidney Fine interview with Hilmer Gellein, n.d., box 1, Sweet Collection; John Bugas to J. Edgar Hoover, January 6, 1939, Frank Murphy File, Federal Bureau of Investigation, Washington D.C.; "Warrants Issued After Death Riots," *Detroit News*, September 11, 1925.

47. R. L. Polk and Company, *Detroit City Directory*, 1923–1924 (Detroit: R. L. Polk and Company, 1924); "Property Owners Talk Plans to Sustain Values," *Detroit Free Press*, September 11, 1925; "Callahan Still Dodges Klan Questions Asked by Times," *Detroit Times*, October 30, 1925; "Mistrial Hint in Sweet Case," *Detroit News*, April 29, 1926; "Klan Answers Smith Attack," *Detroit News*, September 14, 1925.

48. "Warrants Issued After Death Riots," *Detroit Times*, September 11, 1925.

49. W. Hayes McKinney to James Weldon Johnson, September 12, 1925, frame 931, reel 2, part 4, NAACP Papers. Haldeman-Julius, *Clarence Darrow's Two Great Trials*, p. 42, says the lawyers saw their clients late Friday afternoon, not Saturday, but there is no evidence to support that claim.

50. O. H. Sweet statement, September 12, 1925, frame 924, reel 2, part 5, NAACP Papers.

51. "Citizens Back Smith on Rioting," *Detroit Times*, September 14, 1925; McKinney to James Weldon Johnson, September 12, 1925.

52. "Riot Curb Demanded by Mayor," *Detroit Times*, September 13, 1925.

Chapter Seven: Freedmen, Sons of God, Americans

1. "Seek Ten Arrests in Race War," *New York World*, September 11, 1925, clipping on frame 968, reel 2, part 5, NAACP Papers [microfilm edition], Library of Congress, Washington, D.C.

2. Robert Bagnall report, September 9, 1925, frame 992, reel 28, part 11B, NAACP Papers; James Weldon Johnson report to the NAACP board of directors, September 1925, reel 4, part 1, NAACP Papers; B. P. Young to Walter White, September 9, 1925, and copy of Norfolk, Va., city ordinance, frames 989–990, reel 28, part 11b, NAACP Papers.

3. Arthur Spingarn profile of James Weldon Johnson, n.d. [1938], box 11, Arthur Spingarn Papers, Moorland-Spingarn Collection, Howard University, Washington, D.C.

4. David Levering Lewis, *When Harlem Was in Vogue* (New York: Oxford University Press, 1979), pp. 143–144; James Weldon Johnson, *Along This Way: The Autobiography of James Weldon Johnson* (1933; repr. New York: Viking, 1968), p. 11.

5. David Levering Lewis, *W. E. B. Du Bois: Biography of a Race* (New York: Henry Holt, 1993), p. 213; Johnson, *Along This Way*, pp. 11, 65, 84–86; Eugene Levy, *James Weldon Johnson: Black Leader, Black Voice* (Chicago: University of Chicago Press, 1973), chapters 2 and 3.

6. Levy, *James Weldon Johnson*, pp. 75–98; Lewis, *When Harlem Was in Vogue*, pp. 146–149; Sondra Kathryn Wilson, *James Weldon Johnson: Complete Poems* (New York: Penguin Books, 2000), pp. 117–121; Sondra Kathryn Wilson, *The Crisis Reader: Stories, Poems, and Essays from the NAACP's* Crisis *Magazine* (New York: Modern Library, 1999), p. 33.

7. Levy, *James Weldon Johnson*, chapters 5 and 7; Mark Robert Schneider, *"We Return Fighting": The Civil Rights Movement in the Jazz Age* (Boston: Northeastern University Press, 2002), pp. 42–44; Lewis, *W. E. B. Du Bois*, pp. 25–27, 283; Ann Douglas, *Terrible Honesty: Mongrel Manhattan in the 1920s* (New York: Farrar, Straus and Giroux, 1995), pp. 326–327; Lewis, *When Harlem Was in Vogue*, pp. 143, 147–149.

8. James Weldon Johnson to Rev. R. L. Bradby, September 11, 1925, frame 929, reel 2, part 5, NAACP Papers.

9. W. Hayes McKinney to James Weldon Johnson, September 12, 1925, frame 931, reel 2, part 5, NAACP Papers; Johnson to McKinney, September 12, 1925, frame 956, reel 2, part 5, NAACP Papers; Johnson, *Along This Way*, pp. 383–384; handwritten notes, n.d. [September 12, 1925], frame 926, reel 2, part 5, NAACP Papers.

10. James Weldon Johnson, "Harlem: The Cultural Capital," in Alain Locke, ed., *The New Negro* (1925; repr. New York: Atheneum, 1974), pp. 301–311.

11. Kenneth T. Jackson, *The Ku Klux Klan in the City, 1915–1930* (1967; repr. Chicago: Ivan Dee, 1992), pp. 175–177; Walter White, "The Paradox of Color," in Locke, *The New Negro*, p. 363; "Residential Segregation," (Philadelphia) *Public Journal*, October 10, 1925,

frame 985, part 5, NAACP Papers. See also W. E. B. Du Bois, "The Shape of Fear," *North American* 23 (June 1926): p. 292.

12. Gilbert Osofsky, *Harlem: The Making of a Ghetto* (New York: Harper and Row, 1963); Johnson, "Harlem," pp. 302–308.

13. Oscar Handlin, "Introduction," in Charles Reznikoff, ed., *Louis Marshall: Champion of Liberty*, v. I (Philadelphia: Jewish Publication Society of America, 1957), pp. ix–xliii; Morton Rosenstock, "Louis Marshall," in John A. Garraty and Mark C. Carnes, eds., *American National Biography* v. 14 (New York: Oxford University Press, 1999), pp. 571–573; Stephen Grant Meyer, *As Long as They Don't Move Next Door: Segregation and Racial Conflict in American Neighborhoods* (Lanham, Md.: Rowman and Littlefield, 2000), pp. 15–28.

14. Clement E. Vose, *Caucasians Only: The Supreme Court, the NAACP, and the Restrictive Covenant Cases* (Berkeley: University of California Press, 1959), pp. 9–13, 17; Joseph Boris, ed., *Who's Who in Colored America, 1928–1929* (New York: Who's Who in Colored America Corporation, 1929), p. 94; Shelby Davidson to James Weldon Johnson, January 28, 1924, frame 9, reel 6, part 12A, NAACP Papers, Davidson to James Weldon Johnson, January 28, 1924, frames 956–961, reel 1, part 1, NAACP papers.

15. "A Service of Commemoration for Frank D. Reeves and James A. Cobb," October 10, 1975, box 2, James Cobb Papers, Moorland-Spingarn Collection, Howard University, Washington, D.C.; NAACP press release, n.d. [late 1925], frames 960–961, reel 28, part 11B, NAACP Papers; Vose, *Caucasians Only*, pp. 17–18; Schneider, *"We Return Fighting,"* p. 287.

16. NAACP press release, December 23, 1924, frame 636, reel 13, part 1, NAACP Papers; NAACP press release, September 12, 1924, frames 936–937, reel 28, part 11B, NAACP Papers; Levy, *James Weldon Johnson*, p. 229.

17. W. E. B. Du Bois, "Americanization," *Crisis* (August 1922): 154–155; Lewis, *W. E. B. Du Bois*, pp. 95–96.

18. David Levering Lewis, ed., *W. E. B. Du Bois: A Reader* (New York: Henry Holt, 1995), pp. 464, 555. The literature on racial divisions between African-American and white immigrant workers—and within the working class more generally—is growing exponentially. Particularly valuable are James R. Barrett and David Roediger, "In-between Peoples: Race, Nationality, and the New Working Class," in Rick Halpern and Jonathan Morris, eds., *American Exceptionalism? U.S. Working-Class Formation in an International Context* (New York: St. Martin's Press, 1997); Bruce Nelson, *Divided We Stand: American Workers and the Struggle for Black Equality* (Princeton, N.J.: Princeton University Press, 2001), chapters 1 and 4; and David Roediger's path-breaking, *The Wages of Whiteness: Race and the Making of the American Working Class* (London: Verso, 1991), particularly chapters 1 and 7. A thorough overview of the literature is Eric Arnesen, "Up from Exclusion: Black and White Workers, Race, and the State of Labor History," *Reviews in American History* 26 (March 1998): 146–174.

19. NAACP typescript, September 19, 1924, frame 940, reel 28, part 11B, NAACP Papers; NAACP press release, n.d. [late 1925], frames 960–961, reel 28, part 11B, NAACP Papers; NAACP press release, October 20, 1925, frames 1015–1017, reel 28, part 11B, NAACP Papers. See also NAACP press release, September 12, 1924, reel 28, part 11B, NAACP Papers, and Louis Marshall to William Borah, April 19, 1926, reprinted in Reznikoff, *Louis Marshall*, p. 464.

20. NAACP press release, September 18, 1925, frames 998–999, reel 28, part 11B, NAACP Papers; "Segregation Grows Bitter in California," *St. Louis Argus*, April 19, 1925, clipping at frame 1068, reel 28, part 11B, NAACP Papers; William Pickens to James Weldon Johnson, May 18, 1925, frame 965, reel 28, part 11B, NAACP Papers; Johnson report to the NAACP board, August 1925, reel 4, part 1, NAACP Papers; Pickens to Robert Bradby, July 31, 1925, frame 941, reel 2, part 5, NAACP Papers; Robert Bagnall to Robert Bradby, July 30, 1925, box G-95, group I, NAACP Papers, Library of Congress, Washington, D.C.

21. Gloria Garrett Sampson, *The American Fund for Public Service: Charles Garland and Radical Philanthropy, 1922–1941* (Westport, Conn.: Greenwood Press, 1996), pp. 1–3; Mark V. Tushnet, *The NAACP's Legal Strategy Against Segregated Education, 1925–1950*

(Chapel Hill: University of North Carolina Press, 1987), p. 4; James Weldon Johnson to Moorfield Storey, September 12, 1925, frames 586–587, reel 17, part 1, NAACP Papers.

22. Johnson to Storey, September 12, 1925.

23. Walter White to Claude McKay, August 28, 1925, frame 178, reel 9, part 2, NAACP Papers; White to L. M. Hussey, September 5, 1925, frame 193, reel 9, part 2, NAACP Papers; White to Julius Bledsoe, September 14, 1925, frame 213, reel 9, part 2, NAACP Papers; James Weldon Johnson to W. Hayes McKinney, September 13, 1925, frame 934, reel 2, part 5, NAACP Papers.

24. Kenneth Janken, *White: The Biography of Walter White, Mr. NAACP* (New York: New Press, 2003), pp. 3–27; Walter White, *A Man Called White: The Autobiography of Walter White* (New York: Viking, 1948), p. 3.

25. White, *A Man Called White*, pp. 5–12. White's biographer casts some doubt on the veracity of the story. Though the family was trapped inside its home, he concludes, Walter never took up arms to protect his family. See Janken, *White*, pp. 14–18.

26. Joel Spingarn to Amy Spingarn, November 22, 1926, box 15, Joel Spingarn Collection, Moorland-Spingarn Collection; Janken, *White*, pp. 190–191.

27. Janken, *White*, pp. 29–32.

28. Ibid., chapter 2; White, *A Man Called White*, pp. 50–51.

29. Levy, *James Weldon Johnson*, p. 224; Janken, *White*, pp. 64–68, 90–95.

30. Ann Douglas, *Terrible Honesty: Mongrel Manhattan in the 1920s* (New York: Farrar, Straus and Giroux, 1995), p. 354; Lewis, *When Harlem Was in Vogue*, pp. 93–94.

31. Lewis, *When Harlem Was in Vogue*, pp. 137–140; Janken, *White*, pp. 95–103.

32. Lewis, *When Harlem Was in Vogue*, p. 142; Janken, *White*, pp. 104–110; Walter White, *The Fire in the Flint* (New York: Alfred A. Knopf, 1924), pp. 140–141.

33. White, *A Man Called White*, p. 68; Edward E. Waldron, *Walter White and the Harlem Renaissance* (Port Washington, N.Y.: Kennikat Press, 1978), pp. 63–78; Lewis, *When Harlem Was in Vogue*, p. 136; Janken, *White*, pp. 108–111; *New York Tribune*, September 28, 1924; *The Nation* (October 8, 1924): 386; Lewis, *W. E. B. Du Bois: Fight for Equality*, p. 175.

34. James Weldon Johnson to W. Hayes McKinney, September 14, 1925, frame 936, reel 2, part 5, NAACP Papers; McKinney to Johnson, September 12, 1925, frame 932, reel 2, part 5, NAACP Papers.

35. Walter White to L. M. Hussey, September 14, 1925, frame 212, reel 9, part 2, NAACP Papers; White to Johnson, September 16, 1925, frames 943–946, reel 2, part 5, NAACP Papers.

36. "Jayne to Retire from Active Role," *Detroit News*, December 9, 1956.

37. Knights of the Ku Klux Klan to the Citizens of Detroit, September 12, 1925, Detroit Organizations—Ku Klux Klan File, Burton Historical Collection, Detroit Public Library, Detroit, Mich.; "Klan Attacks Mayor by Mail," *Detroit Times*, September 17, 1925; "Victim of Racial Battle Is Buried," *Detroit Free Press*, September 15, 1925; White to Johnson, September 16, 1925, frames 943–946, reel 2, part 5, NAACP Papers; Walter White handwritten notes, n.d. [September 1925], frames 374–396, reel 2, part 5, NAACP Papers.

38. White to Johnson, September 16, 1925; Sweet Defense Fund statement of cash receipts, n.d. [December 11, 1925], frames 811–814, reel 3, part 5, NAACP Papers.

39. White to Johnson, September 16, 1925.

40. "Tells of Home Row Shooting," *Detroit Free Press*, September 17, 1925. In his memoir, White says on the day of his arrival he went directly from the train station to the jail, where he met with all eleven of the accused. "One of the defendants," he wrote, "half sobbed and exclaimed, 'Thank God! We can now rest easy and get some sleep!'" White, *A Man Called White*, p. 74. White's notes from his time in Detroit indicate, however, that he didn't speak to the defendants at all and therefore only saw them at the preliminary hearing. See handwritten notes, n.d. [September 1925].

41. "Rioters Trial Is Opened," *Detroit Times*, September 17, 1925; transcript of preliminary hearing, September 16–17, 1925, box 1, Ossian Sweet Collection, Burton Historical Collection, Detroit Public Library, Detroit, Mich.; Walter White to James Weldon Johnson, September 17, 1925, frames 1031–1032, reel 2, part 5, NAACP Papers.

42. Norton Schuknecht testimony at the preliminary hearing, September 16, 1925, and Ray Dove testimony, September 17, 1925.

43. John Getke testimony at the preliminary hearing, September 17, 1925.

44. Norton Schuknecht testimony, September 16, 1925. Rowlette's handling of Schuknecht was tough enough to earn even the grudging admiration of White. See White to Johnson, September 17, 1925.

45. Ray Dove testimony, September 17, 1925.

46. John Getke testimony, September 17, 1925.

47. Walter White to James Johnson, September 18, 1925, frame 1046, reel 2, part 5, NAACP Papers. On Faust as a member of the court's liberal bloc, see Raymond Fragnoli, *The Transformation of Detroit: Progressivism in Detroit—and After* (New York: Garland, 1982), pp. 259–267.

48. White to Johnson, September 17, 1925; White handwritten notes, n.d. [September 1925]; draft agreement between NAACP and defendants, September 17, 1925, frames 1037–1038, reel 2, part 5, NAACP Papers.

49. Walter White to Ira Jayne, September 21, 1925, frames 1056–1057, reel 2, part 5, NAACP Papers; Walter White to Mose Walker, September 21, 1925, frame 1055, reel 2, part 5, NAACP Papers; Walker to White, September 22, 1926, frames 1060–1061, reel 2, part 5, NAACP Papers; White to Oscar Baker, October 5, 1925, frames 1115–1118, reel 2, part 5, NAAP Papers.

50. Walter White to R. L. Bradby, September 19, 1925, frame 1053, reel 2, part 5, NAACP Papers.

51. "[unreadable] Detroit Citizens," *Dallas Express,* September 19, 1925, clipping at frame 973, reel 2, part 5, NAACP Papers; "[unreadable] Test Up in Detroit," *St. Louis Argus,* September 18, 1925, copy at frame 972, reel 2, part 5, NAACP Papers; "Racial Clash Seems Near: Blame KKK," *Houston Informer,* September 26, 1925, copy at frame 975, reel 2, part 5, NAACP Papers; "Quell Detroit Race Clash," and "What's Wrong in Detroit?" *Chicago Defender,* September 19, 1925; James Grossman, *Land of Hope: Chicago, Black Southerners, and the Great Migration* (Chicago: University of Chicago Press, 1989), pp. 74–82.

52. NAACP press release, September 18, 1925, frames 998–999, reel 28, part 11B, NAACP Papers; NAACP press release, September 25, 1925, frame 1000, reel 28, part 11B, NAACP Papers; minutes of the NAACP board of directors, September 14, 1925, frames 42–43, reel 2, part 1, NAACP Papers; "Citizens Plan Strong Defense for Doctor," (Jacksonville) *Florida Sentinel,* September 26, 1925, clipping in frame 976, reel 2, part 5, NAACP Papers.

53. NAACP press release, September 18, 1925.

54. "Plans Completed for Sweet Defense," *Detroit Independent,* September 18, 1925, copy at frames 970–971, reel 2, part 5, NAACP Papers; "NAACP Holds Another Successful Meeting for Sweet Fund at St. John's CME Church," *Detroit Independent,* October 2, 1925, frame 981, reel 2, part 5, NAACP Papers; James Weldon Johnson report to the NAACP board, October 1925, frame 647–651, reel 4, part 1, NAACP Papers; report of the Department of Branches, October 1925, frame 652–654, reel 4, part 1, NAACP Papers; Walter White to James Weldon Johnson, September 26, 1925, frame 1002, reel 28, part 11B, NAACP Papers.

55. Sweet Defense Fund statement of receipts and disbursements, n.d. [December 11, 1925]; "Residential Segregation," (Philadelphia) *Public Journal,* October 10, 1925, copy at frame 985, reel 2, part 5, NAACP Papers.

56. Henry Strong Huntington to Charles [*sic*] Weldon Johnson, September 24, 1925, frames 1072–1073, reel 2, part 5, NAACP Papers. For Johnson's reply, see his letter to Huntington, September 29, 1925, frame 1085, reel 2, part 5, NAACP Papers.

57. Walter White to Oswald Garrison Villard, September 22, 1925, frame 1062, reel 2, part 5, NAACP Papers; typescript, "Segregation Comes North," n.d. [September 1925], frames 1047–1054, reel 28, part 11B, NAACP Papers.

58. Walter White to Ira Jayne, September 21, 1925, frames 1056–1057, reel 2, part 5, NAACP Papers; White to M. L. Walker, September 21, 1925, frame 1055, reel 2, part 5,

NAACP Papers; memorandum of telephone conversation, September 25, 1925, frame 1079, reel 2, part 5, NAACP Papers.

59. "City Wide Committee for Sweet Fund Is Organized," *Detroit Independent*, October 2, 1925, clipping at frame 980, reel 2, part 5, NAACP Papers; William Pickens to Arthur Spingarn, November 2, 1925, frame 56, reel 5, Arthur Spingarn Papers, Library of Congress; William Pickens to James Weldon Johnson and Walter White, October 25, 1925, frame 29, reel 3, part 5, NAACP Papers. Pickens claimed that Gomez defied the NAACP because, among other things, "he hates Du Bois."

60. Mose Walker to Walter White, n.d. [September 27, 1925], frame 1040, reel 2, part 5, NAACP Papers; "NAACP Holds Another Successful Meeting for Sweet Fund at St. John's CME Church."

61. Sweet defense fund, statement of receipts and disbursements, n.d. [December 11, 1925]; oral history interview with Otis Sweet, August 1, 1960, Alex Baskin Collection, Michigan Historical Collection, Bentley Library, University of Michigan, Ann Arbor.

62. I have dated Henry Sweet's visit to Detroit through "NAACP Holds Another Successful Meeting for Sweet Fund at St. John's CME Church." Sweet appeared at the September 27 mass rally, the story recounts.

63. Oral history interview with Sherman Sweet, February 27, 2002, notes in author's possession.

64. Otis Sweet, William Davis, Leonard Morse, and Charles Washington to W. Hayes McKinney, September 29, 1925; and Sweet, Davis, Morse, and Washington to W. E. B. Du Bois, September 29, 1925, frames 1086 and 1088, reel 2, part 5, NAACP Papers. The evidence indicates that Otis, Davis, Washington, and Morse asked the other defendants to sign the letter, but they refused.

65. Ibid.; Sweet, Davis, Morse, and Washington to Du Bois, October 1, 1925, frame 1108, reel 2, part 5, NAACP Papers.

66. Walter White to Ira Jayne, October 1, 1925, frame 1103, reel 2, part 5, NAACP Papers; memorandum of telephone conversation, Walter White and Arthur Spingarn, October 1, 1925, frame 1097, reel 2, part 5, NAACP Papers; White to Spingarn, October 2, 1925, frame 1111, reel 2, part 5, NAACP Papers.

67. Ira Jayne to Walter White, September 30, 1925, frame 1095, reel 2, part 5, NAACP Papers; White to Oscar Baker, October 5, 1925; "Klan Out to Elect Bowles," *Detroit Times*, September 23, 1925; "Klan Prepares for Election," *Detroit Free Press*, September 30, 1925.

68. Motion to quash, *The People of Michigan vs. Otis Sweet et al.*, September 3, 1925, box 5, Clarence Darrow Papers, Library of Congress.

69. Memorandum of telephone conversation, Walter White and Mose Walker, October 8, 1925, frames 1152–1153, reel 2, part 5, NAACP Papers; Walter White to Mr. Seligman, October 22, 1925, frames 3–4, reel 3, part 5, NAACP Papers; "Klan Sweeps Primary" and "Backers of Bowles Jubilant," *Detroit Times*, October 7 and 8, 1925.

70. N. K. McGill to Walter White, October 2, 1925, frame 1114, reel 2, part 5, NAACP Papers.

Chapter Eight: The Prodigal Son

1. James Weldon Johnson to Clarence Darrow, October 7, 1925, and Johnson to Darrow, October 8, 1925, frames 1137 and 1151, reel 2, part 5, NAACP Papers; Cora Arons to Johnson, October 7, 1925, frame 1135, reel 2, NAACP Papers; Walter White to Johnson, October 8, 1925, frame 1150, reel 2, part 5, NAACP Papers.

2. R. L. Polk and Company, *General Directory of New York City* (New York: R. L. Polk and Company, 1925), p. 1008; Irving Stone, *Clarence Darrow for the Defense* (Garden City, N.Y.: Doubleday, 1941), pp. 469–470.

3. Stone, *Clarence Darrow for the Defense*, p. 470; Clarence Darrow, *The Story of My Life* (New York: Charles Scribner's Sons, 1934), p. 302.

4. The story had had various tellings. See, for instance, Arthur Garfield Hays, *Let Freedom Ring* (New York: Liveright, 1937), pp. 196–197; Stone, *Clarence Darrow for the Defense*,

pp. 469–470, for Spingarn's account; Walter White, *A Man Called White: The Autobiography of Walter White* (New York: Viking, 1948), pp. 75–76.

5. Frank Walsh quoted in Stone, *Clarence Darrow for the Defense*, p. 171; Masters quoted in J. Anthony Lukas, *Big Trouble: A Murder in a Small Western Town Sets Off a Struggle for the Soul of America* (New York: Simon and Schuster, 1997), p. 327.

6. Christine Stansell, *American Moderns: Bohemian New York and the Creation of a New Century* (New York: Henry Holt, 2000), pp. 45–46.

7. Darrow, *The Story of My Life*, p. 14; Kevin Tierney, *Darrow: A Biography* (New York: Thomas Y. Crowell, 1934), chapters 1 and 2; Lukas, *Big Trouble*, p. 305.

8. William Cronon, *Nature's Metropolis: Chicago and the Great West* (New York: W. W. Norton, 1991), pp. 354–355; Thomas Lee Philpot, *The Slum and the Ghetto: Immigrants, Blacks, and Reformers in Chicago, 1880–1930* (1978; repr. Belmont, Calif.: Wadsworth, 1997), p. 6. On Darrow's multiple political commitments, see John Livingston, *Clarence Darrow: The Mind of a Sentimental Rebel* (New York: Garland, 1988), though Livingston's analysis of Darrow's core beliefs is very different from mine.

9. Stansell, *American Moderns*, pp. 50–55; Dale Kramer, *Chicago Renaissance: The Literary Life in the Midwest, 1900–1930* (New York: Appleton-Century, 1966), for a glimpse of Chicago's avant-garde; Gerald W. McFarland, *Inside Greenwich Village: A New York City Neighborhood, 1898–1918* (Amherst: University of Massachusetts Press, 2001); Lukas, *Big Trouble*, p. 316.

10. Clarence Darrow, *Farmington* (Chicago: A. C. McClurg, 1904); Darrow, *An Eye for an Eye* (New York: Fox Duffield, 1905); Tierney, *Darrow*, p. 144; Stone, *Clarence Darrow for the Defense*, chapter 2; Nick Salvatore, *Eugene V. Debs: Citizen and Socialist* (Urbana: University of Illinois Press, 1982), pp. 126–138; Miriam Gurko, *Clarence Darrow* (New York: Thomas Y. Crowell, 1965), p. 75.

11. For details on Darrow's labor cases, see Tierney, *Darrow*, chapters 13, 17, 20, and 22; Stone, *Clarence Darrow for the Defense;* Geoffrey Cowan, *The People v. Clarence Darrow: The Bribery Trial of America's Greatest Lawyer* (New York: Times Books, 1993). Lukas, *Big Trouble*, p. 315 for quote.

12. Darrow, "Attorney for the Defense," *Esquire*, (May 1936): 36; Lukas, *Big Trouble*, p. 314; Darrow, *The Story of My Life*, p. 76.

13. Stone, *Clarence Darrow for the Defense*, pp. 165–166; Tierney, *Darrow*, pp. 106–108, 220–226; Arthur Weinberg, ed., *Attorney for the Damned* (New York: Simon and Schuster, 1957), pp. 486–487; Lukas, *Big Trouble*, pp. 707–712, 721–723.

14. Tierney, *Darrow*, p. 182; Stone, *Clarence Darrow for the Defense*, chapters 8 and 9; Cowan, *The People v. Clarence Darrow.*

15. Tierney, *Darrow*, pp. 306–310, 317; Weinberg, *Attorney for the Damned*, p. 172; Darrow, *The Story of My Life*, pp. 226–243; Hal Higdon, *The Crime of the Century: The Leopold and Loeb Case* (New York: Putnam, 1975). Paula Fass, "Making and Remaking an Event: The Leopold and Loeb Case in American Culture," *Journal of American History* 80 (December 1993): 919–940.

16. Edward J. Larson, *Summer for the Gods: The Scopes Trial and America's Continuing Debate over Science and Religion* (Cambridge, Mass.: Harvard University Press, 1998), chapters 2–4; Arthur Garfield Hays, *City Lawyer: The Autobiography of a Law Practice* (New York: Simon and Schuster, 1942).

17. Larson, *Summer for the Gods*, pp. 140–143; Weinberg, *Attorney for the Damned*, p. 188.

18. Larson, *Summer for the Gods*, pp. 187–190; Stone, *Clarence Darrow for the Defense*, p. 458.

19. Tierney, *Darrow*, pp. 8–9; H. L. Mencken, "Aftermath," *Baltimore Evening Sun*, September 14, 1925; Darrow, *The Story of My Life*, p. 282.

20. Tierney, *Darrow*, p. 8; Darrow, *The Story of My Life*, p. 302; Clarence Darrow, "John Brown," *Crisis* (May 1926): 16; Clarence Darrow's address to the 1910 Annual Conference, Part 1, Reel 8, Part 1, NAACP Papers. I am grateful to Patricia Sullivan for providing me with the latter document.

21. Darrow, *The Story of My Life*, p. 302; Hays, *Let Freedom Ring*, p. 195.

22. Salvatore, *Eugene V. Debs*, p. 138; Tierney, *Darrow*, pp. 244–250; Stone, *Clarence Darrow for the Defense*, pp. 418–419; Larson, *Summer for the Gods*, pp. 200–201; Darrow address, 1910; "Advises Negroes to Stop Working," undated clipping [1910], box 30, Darrow Papers; David L. Lewis, *W. E. B. Du Bois: Biography of a Race* (New York: Henry Holt, 1993), p. 425; Glenda Elizabeth Gilmore, *Gender and Jim Crow: Women and the Politics of White Supremacy in North Carolina, 1896–1920* (Chapel Hill: University of North Carolina Press, 1996), chapter 4.

23. Memorandum of expenses, November 30, 1925, frames 174–175, reel 3, part 5, NAACP Papers; James Weldon Johnson to Clarence Darrow, October 14, 1925, frame 1188, reel 2, part 5, NAACP Papers; James Weldon Johnson to Walter White, October 14, 1925, frame 1182, reel 2, part 5.

24. Walter White to James Weldon Johnson, October 8, 1925, frame 1150, reel 2, part 5, NAACP Papers; Walter White to Cecil Rowlette, Julian Perry, and Charles Mahoney, October 12, 1925, frames 1155 and 1174, reel 2, part 5, NAACP Papers; Walter White to James Weldon Johnson, October 8, 1925, frame 1150, reel 2, part 5, NAACP Papers.

25. Walter White to Ira Jayne, October 22, 1925, frame 2, reel 3, part 5, NAACP Papers; White to James Weldon Johnson, October 8, 1925.

26. Louis Marshall to Moorfield Storey, September 24, 1925, in Charles Reznikoff, ed., *Louis Marshall: Champion of Liberty* (Philadelphia: Jewish Publication Society of America, 1957), p. 461; James Weldon Johnson to Walter White, October 7, 1925, frame 1006, reel 28, part 11B, NAACP Papers; minutes of the NAACP board of directors meeting, November 9, 1925, frames 52–54, reel 2, part 1, NAACP; Johnson to Moorfield Storey, October 20, 1925, frame 589, reel 17, part 1, NAACP Papers.

27. NAACP press release, October 15, 1925, frame 1189, reel 2, part 5, NAACP Papers.

28. "Darrow to Defend 11 Negroes in Detroit Mob Shooting," *New York Post*, October 14, 1925, clipping at frame 987, reel 2, part 5, NAACP Papers; "Darrow Defends Negroes," *New York World*, October 16, 1925, frame 989, reel 2, part 5, NAACP Papers; "Negro Murder Trial Inflames Detroit," *Chicago Daily News*, October 17, 1925, clipping at frame 997, reel 2, part 5, NAACP Papers; "Race Riots in Northern Cities," *Chicago Daily News*, reprinted in *Chicago Defender*, October 24, 1925; "Law for Whites and Negroes," *New York World*, reprinted in *Chicago Defender*, October 31, 1925.

29. Walter White to Wilson Midgley, October 23, 1925, frame 288, reel 9, part 2, NAACP Papers; "Darrow Delays," *Detroit Times*, October 16, 1925; "Darrow Gets Riot Case Stay," *Detroit News*, October 16, 1925; White to Mr. Seligman, October 22, 1925, frames 3–4, reel 3, part 5, NAACP Papers.

30. Leonard Mose [*sic*], William Davis, Hewitt Watson, and Charles Washington to Walter White, October 8, 1925, frame 1142, reel 2, part 5, NAACP Papers. Unlike the previous messages, this plea was not signed by Otis Sweet. Perhaps he thought better of defying his brother a second time.

31. Memorandum of telephone conversation, Mose Walker and Walter White, October 8, 1925, frames 1152–1153, reel 2, part 5, NAACP Papers; Walter White to O. H. Sweet, October 9, 1925, frame 1155, reel 2, part 5, NAACP Papers; Alex Baskin oral history interview with Otis Sweet, August 1, 1960, Alex Baskin Collection, Bentley Library.

32. Darrow, *Story of My Life*, p. 303; Walter White to James Weldon Johnson, October 14, 1925, frame 1183, reel 2, part 5, NAACP Papers. Arthur Garfield Hays vividly recalled the jailhouse visit in his memoirs. "Up two flights of steps, steel doors were unlocked to permit passage, then closed. We were ushered into a small room, dimly lighted by a dirty window, furnished with a table and a few broken chairs." See Hays, *Let Freedom Ring*, p. 198. Unfortunately, Hays wasn't there that day. See James Weldon Johnson to Arthur Garfield Hays, October 16, 1925, frame 1205, reel 2, part 5, NAACP Papers.

33. White, *A Man Called White*, pp. 76–77.

34. Walter White to Mr. Seligman, October 22, 1925, frames 3–4, reel 3, part 5, NAACP Papers; oral history interview with Otis Sweet, August 1, 1960.

35. Otis Sweet oral history, August 1, 1960.

36. James Goodman, *Stories of Scottsboro* (New York: Random House, 1994), pp. 62–64; "Clarence Darrow and American Rights, *Houston* [unreadable], November 5,

1925, frame 1126, reel 3, part 5, NAACP Papers; "Dr. Sweet," *Florida Sentinel*, November 14, 1925, frame 1126, reel 3, part 5, NAACP Papers; "Dr. Sweet," *Florida Sentinel*, November 14, 1925, frame 34, reel 4, part 5, NAACP Papers; (Little Rock) *Mosaic Guide*, November 28, 1925, frame 138, reel 4, part 5, NAACP Papers.

37. "What's Wrong in Detroit?" *Chicago Defender*, September 19, 1925.

38. "The Retention of Clarence Darrow," *Washington Daily American*, October 19, 1925, clipping at frame 1000, reel 2, part 5, NAACP Papers; "We Must Fight if We Would Survive," (New York) *Amsterdam News*, November 18, 1925, frame 57, reel 4, part 5, NAACP Papers.

39. Sweet defense fund, statement of cash receipts and disbursements, December 11, 1925, frames 811–814, reel 3, part 5, NAACP Papers; William Pickens to office, October 25, 1925, frame 19, reel 3, part 5, NAACP Papers; report of the department of branches, November 1925 and December 1925, frames 656–659, reel 4, part 1, NAACP Papers; Edward Lovett to NAACP, October 22, 1925, frame 5, reel 3, part 5, NAACP Papers; "Howard Students Rally to Support of Dr. Sweet," *Washington Daily American*, October 30, 1925; minutes of the general faculty meeting, November 3, 1925, box 17, Wilberforce University Papers, Wilberforce Archives, Xenia, Ohio.

40. Walter White to Gladys Sweet, October 27, 1925, frame 23, reel 3, part 5, NAACP Papers; R. L. Polk and Company, *Detroit City Directory*, 1925–1926 (Detroit: R. L. Polk and Company, 1926); Gladys Sweet to Walter White, October 23, 1925, frames 11–13, reel 3, part 5, NAACP Papers.

41. Gladys Sweet to Walter White, n.d. [late October 1925], frames 353–360, reel 3, part 5, NAACP Papers; W. E. B. Du Bois, "The Challenge of Detroit," *Crisis* (November 1925): 7–10; David Levering Lewis, *W. E. B. Du Bois: The Fight for Equality and the American Century* (New York: Henry Holt, 2000), pp. 154–155.

42. Marcet Haldeman-Julius, *Clarence Darrow's Two Great Trials* (Girard, Kan.: Haldeman-Julius Publishing Company, 1927), pp. 37–39; Ossian Sweet to Ruby Darrow, n.d. [1930], box 5, Darrow Papers.

43. Walter White to Wilson Midgley, October 23, 1925, frame 288, reel 9, part 2, NAACP Papers; White to Clarence Darrow, October 24, 1925, frame 18, reel 3, part 5, NAACP Papers; White to Darrow, October 20, 1925, frame 1210, reel 2, part 5, NAACP Papers; Darrow to White, October 22, 1925, frame 7, reel 3, part 5, NAACP Papers; James Cobb to Arthur Spingarn, October 24, 1925, frame 44, reel 5, Arthur Spingarn Papers, Library of Congress, Washington, D.C.; Oscar Baker to White, frames 1219–1210, reel 2, part 5, NAACP Papers; Langston Hughes to White, October 29, 1925, frame 352, reel 9, part 2 NAACP Papers.

44. Walter White to James Weldon Johnson, October 8, 1925; White to Ira Jayne, October 22, 1925; Mose Walker to White, n.d. [October 26[?], 1925], frame 26, reel 3, part 5, NAACP Papers.

45. Frank Murphy to Marguerite Murphy, November 6, 1925, box 1, Frank Murphy Papers, Bentley Historical Library, University of Michigan, Ann Arbor; Sidney Fine, *Frank Murphy: The Detroit Years* (Ann Arbor: University of Michigan Press, 1975), p. 179; Walter White to Frank Murphy, October 14, 1925, reel 3, Murphy papers.

46. "Four Throngs Acclaim Mayor," *Detroit Times*, October 13, 1925; "East Side Gives Smith Ovation," *Detroit Free Press*, October 15, 1925; "Vets Cheer Mayor at Reunion," *Detroit Times*, October 17, 1925; "Five Crowds Applaud Mayor," *Detroit Times*, October 17, 1925; "K of C Affair to Open Tonight," *Detroit Times*, October 23, 1925; "Foes Are Routed by Mayor Smith," *Detroit times*, October 24, 1925; "Where to Hear the Candidates," *Detroit News*, November 2, 1925; "Principles Scored as Disgrace," *Detroit Times*, October 15, 1925.

47. "Mayor 'Sorry' for His Foe," *Detroit News*, November 2, 1925.

48. Kerby Miller, *Emigrants and Exiles: Ireland and the Irish Exodus to North America* (New York: Oxford University Press, 1985), pp. 378–380; Charters Wynn, *Workers, Strikes, and Pogroms: The Donbass-Dnepr Bend in Late Imperial Russia, 1870–1905* (Princeton, N.J.: Princeton University Press, 1992), pp. 60–62; Jacquelyn Dowd Hall et al, *Like a Family: The Making of a Southern Cotton Mill World* (Chapel Hill: University of North Carolina Press, 1987), pp. 66–67; John Higham, *Strangers in the Land: Patterns of American Nativism*,

1860–1925 (New Brunswick, N.J.: Rutgers University Press, 1955), chapter 10; Lynn Dumeniel, *The Modern Temper: American Culture and Society in the 1920s* (New York: Hill and Wang, 1995), chapters 5–6.

49. "Attorney Raps Klan as Political Influence," *Detroit Times*, October 13, 1925; "Women Canvass Homes to Aid Mayor Smith," *Detroit Times*, October 22, 1925; "Progressives Back Mayor," *Detroit Times*, September 25, 1925; "Ku Klux Klan Assailed by Detroit Ministers," Detroit Times, November 2, 1925.

50. "Ku Klux Klan Assailed by Detroit Ministers"; Richard Wightman Fox, *Reinhold Niebuhr: A Biography* (New York: Pantheon, 1985), p. 91.

51. "Bowles No Klansman, He Says," *Detroit Times*, October 16, 1925; "Bowles Denies He's Klansman," *Detroit Free Press*, October 16, 1925; "Klan Issue Is Dodged by Bowles," *Detroit Free Press*, October 26, 1925; "Klan's Aid Disdained by Bowles," *Detroit Times*, October 27, 1925; Ku Klux Klan pamphlet, n.d. [October 1925], E and M Files—Ku Klux Klan, Burton Historical Collection, Detroit Public Library, Detroit, Mich.

52. "Pastor's Wife Would Tar All Smith Voters," *Detroit Free Press*, October 23, 1925; "Forsythe Raps 'Rome,' Smith," *Detroit Free Press*, October 26, 1925; "Bares Klan Scheming to Rule City Council," *Detroit Free Press*, October 31, 1925; "Threat Is Laid to Candidate," *Detroit Times*, November 3, 1925.

53. "Bowles Called Myth Picked Up on Crest of Crowd Movement," *Detroit Free Press*, October 26, 1925.

54. "Five Crowds Applaud Mayor," *Detroit Times*, October 17, 1925; "Mayor in District of Rival," *Detroit Times*, October 21, 1925.

55. "Detroit Police Saved Mob," *Detroit Independent*, April 17, 1925, box 30, Clarence Darrow Papers; Vollington Bristol statement, n.d., box 5, Darrow Papers; "Darrow Delays," *Detroit Times*, October 16, 1925; Walter White to Mr. Seligman, October 22, 1925.

56. Arthur Garfield Hays to NAACP, October 19, 1925, frame 1208, reel 2, part 5, NAACP Papers; Ronald Steel, *Walter Lippmann and the American Century* (New York: Random House, 1980), p. 9; theory of defense, n.d. [October 1925], and summary of precedents, n.d. [October 1925], both in box 5, Darrow Papers.

57. *Pond v. People of Michigan*, 8 Mich 150 (Mich. Supreme Crt. 1860); summary of precedents, n.d. [October 1925], motion to dismiss, n.d. [October 1925], and "Theory of the Defense," n.d. [October 1925], all in box 5, Darrow Papers.

58. Arthur Garfield Hays to NAACP, October 19, 1925, frame 1208, reel 2, part 5, NAACP Papers; "Race Question" clipping file, box 30, Darrow Papers; Walter White to Clarence Darrow, October 20, 1925, frame 1210, reel 2, part 5, NAACP Papers; White to Arthur Garfield Hays, October 21, 1925, frame 1214, reel 2, part 5, NAACP Papers; White to Darrow, October 22, 1925, frame 8, reel 3, part 5, NAACP Papers.

59. Louis Marshall to Moorfield Storey, December 12, 1924, in Reznikoff, *Louis Marshall*, pp. 460–461; Clement Vose, *Caucasians Only: The Supreme Court, the NAACP, and the Restrictive Covenants Cases* (Berkeley: University of California Press, 1959), pp. 13–19; Du Bois, "Challenge of Detroit," p. 12.

60. Darrow, *The Story of My Life*, pp. 426–428; Tierney, *Darrow*, pp. 154–155; Stone, *Clarence Darrow for the Defense*, pp. 165–166.

61. Walter White to Frank Murphy, October 28, 1925, frame 32, reel 3, part 5, NAACP Papers.

62. NAACP press release, October 30, 1925, frame 37, reel 3, part 5 NAACP Papers.

63. Josephine Gomon diary entry, October 30, 1925, box 6, Josephine Gomon Collection, Bentley Library; "Jurors Shun Sweet Trial," *Detroit Free Press*, October 31, 1925.

64. Larson, *Summer for the Gods*, pp. 147, 151–152; Marcet Haldeman-Julius, "Clarence Darrow's Defense of a Negro," *Haldeman-Julius Monthly* (July 1926): 4; "Breiner Widow and Other Principles in East Side Riot Trial," *Detroit Times*, April 28, 1926.

65. "Jurors Shun Sweet Trial." The description of Darrow as "champion of the poor" comes from his friend Judge William Holly quoted in Stone, *Clarence Darrow for the Defense*, p. 518.

66. Walter White to James Weldon Johnson, n.d. [October 31, 1925], frames 54–55, reel 3, part 5, NAACP Papers; "May Seek to Justify Slaying," *New York Herald-Tribune*, n.d. [October 31, 1925], clipping at frame 326, reel 3, part 5, NAACP Papers; "Darrow Hints Right to Shoot," *Detroit Times*, October 31, 1925; "Jurors Shun Sweet Trial"; "Darrow Wary in Riot Trial," *Detroit News*, October 31, 1925.

67. "Darrow Wary in Riot Trial"; White to Johnson, n.d. [October, 31, 1925]; e.d. 304, sheet 15A, 1920 U.S. census manuscript, Detroit, Michigan, for details on Buell; "Darrow Hints Right to Shoot."

Chapter Nine: Prejudice

1. "Jurors Shun Sweet Trial," *Detroit Free Press*, October 31, 1925; "Darrow Wary in Riot Trial" and "Court Rebukes Riot Hecklers," both in *Detroit News*, October 31, 1925 [early and late editions]; "Intimidation Charged in Sweet Case," *Detroit Free Press*, November 1, 1925; Walter White to James Weldon Johnson, n.d. [October 31, 1925], frames 54–55, reel 3, part 5, NAACP Papers [microfilm edition], Library of Congress, Washington, D.C.

2. J. Anthony Lukas, *Big Trouble: A Murder in a Small Western Town Sets Off a Struggle for the Soul of America* (New York: Simon and Schuster, 1997), pp. 525–553.

3. Clarence Darrow, *The Story of My Life* (New York: Charles Scribner's Sons, 1934), pp. 306–307; Oscar Baker to Walter White, October 21, 1925, frames 1219–1220, reel 2, part 5, NAACP Papers.

4. Clarence Darrow, "Attorney for the Defense," *Esquire*, May 1936, pp. 36, 211. Also see Darrow, *Story of My Life*, pp. 307–308.

5. Christine Stansell, *American Moderns: Bohemian New York and the Creation of a New Century* (New York: Henry Holt, 2000), pp. 23–26; Ann Douglas, *Terrible Honesty: Mongrel Manhattan in the 1920s* (New York: Farrar, Straus and Giroux, 1995), particularly chapters 2 and 7.

6. "Mayor Given Ovations at Meetings" and "Vets Rally to Aid of Smith," *Detroit Times*, October 31, 1925; "Crushing of Klan Urged," *Detroit Times*, November 2, 1925; "Negro Gatherings Hear Bowles and Smith Talk," *Detroit News*, November 2, 1925; "Mayor Smith, in Final Talk, Urges All Citizens to Vote," *Detroit Times*, November 3, 1925.

7. "Klan Settles Who's American," *Detroit Free Press*, November 3, 1925.

8. "Record Vote in Klan Fight," *Detroit Free Press*, November 3, 1925; "Pastor Pleads for Ten Judges," *Detroit News*, November 2, 1925; "Prelates of Three Faiths Urge Duty to Vote," *Detroit Times*, November 1, 1925; Leslie Tentler, *Seasons of Grace: A History of the Catholic Archdiocese of Detroit* (Detroit: Wayne State University Press, 1990), p. 301.

9. "Detroit Puts Record of Smith Up to Race," *Chicago Defender*, October 31, 1925; "Clamor Marks Bowles Meet," *Detroit Free Press*, October 27, 1925; Josephine Gomon draft biography of Frank Murphy, n.d., box 9, Josephine Gomon Papers, Michigan Historical Collections, Bentley Library, University of Michigan, Ann Arbor. For pure shock value, nothing could match the weekend's most widely publicized attack. When a reporter asked Henry Ford what he thought of the KKK, he answered with a heartfelt, if typically idiosyncratic, condemnation of an organization whose hatreds he seemed to share. "I know nothing of the Ku Klux Klan, but I will say this," he replied. "Most of these movements are ordered by Wall Street. . . . They are comprised of harebrained people who only lose the fee they pay for membership. I don't care which side of the question you're on, they have no place in America. The same goes for unions." See "Ford Endorses Mayor," *Detroit Times*, October 31, 1925.

10. "Town Talk," *Detroit News*, November 2, 1925; "Smith Re-Elected by 31,000," *Detroit Times*, November 4, 1925. In the Tireman Avenue area that had seen the worst of the summer's violence, for instance, Bowles beat Smith by a mere eight votes.

11. "Police Halt Anti-Klan Melee," *Detroit Times*, November 4, 1925.

12. Walter White to James Weldon Johnson, n.d. [October 31, 1925], frames 54–55, reel 3, part 5, NAACP Papers.

13. "Expect to Fill Riot Case Jury," *Detroit News*, November 3, 1925; "Sweet Jury Still Unfilled," *Detroit Free Press*, November 3, 1925; White to James Weldon Johnson, n.d. [October 31, 1925].

14. "3 Women Out of Riot Jury," *Detroit News*, November 4, 1925; "Call First Riot Witness Today," *Detroit News*, November 5, 1925, clipping at frame 1110, reel 3, part 5, NAACP Papers; R. L. Polk and Company, *Detroit City Directory*, 1920–1921 (Detroit: R. L. Polk and Company, 1921).

15. The jury list is available at frame 38, reel 3, part 5, NAACP Papers, and the jurors' professions are available in "Will Try to Force Tom's Hand," *Detroit Times*, November 4, 1925. To create as comprehensive a description of the jurors as possible, I reviewed their entries in either the 1920 or 1930 U.S. census manuscript for Detroit and, where possible, in both censuses. The information available there—age, marital status, children at home, race, country of origin, parents' country of origin, profession, and home ownership—was supplemented by the Detroit city directories for the mid-1920s, which provided the jurors' exact professions in the middle of the decade.

16. Irving Stone, *Clarence Darrow for the Defense* (Garden City, N.Y.: Doubleday, 1941), p. 478.

17. "Sweet Trial Presents Dramatic Court Scene," *Detroit Free Press*, November 22, 1925.

18. Detroit Police Department witness list, October 2, 1925, box 1, Ossian Sweet Collection, Burton Historical Collection, Detroit Public Library, Detroit, Mich.; "Free Doctor Sweet and Ten Others," *Chicago Defender*, April 25, 1931; Articles of Incorporation, Waterworks Park Improvement Association, May 26, 1926, Bureau of Commercial Services, Corporation Division, Michigan Department of Consumer and Industry Services, Lansing.

19. Lukas, *Big Trouble*, pp. 290–293 and chapter 14; Edward J. Larson, *Summer for the Gods: The Scopes Trial and America's Continuing Debate over Science and Religion* (Cambridge, Mass.: Harvard University Press, 1997), pp. 157–158; oral history interview with Robert Toms, November 28, 1959, Alex Baskin Collection, Bentley Historical Library.

20. Walter White to James Weldon Johnson, November 15, 1925, frame 92, reel 3, part 5, NAACP Papers; Robert Toms opening statement, November 5, 1925, trial transcript, *People v. Ossian Sweet et al.*, Michigan Historical Collection, Bentley Library, University of Michigan, Ann Arbor; testimony of Herman Craft and William D. Ryan, both on November 5, 1925, trial transcript.

21. Testimony of Norton Schuknecht, November 5, 1925, trial transcript.

22. Testimony of Bert McPherson, November 13, 1925, trial transcript.

23. Testimony of Clayton Williams, November 9, 1925; testimony of James Sprott, November 13, 1925; testimony of Paul Schellenberger, November 5, 1925, testimony of Joseph Neighbauer, November 9, 1925, testimony of Frank Lee Gill, November 6, 1925, all in trial transcript; "Sprott to Give Riot Evidence," *Detroit News*, November 12, 1925, frame 11, reel 4, part 5, NAACP Papers.

24. Testimony of George Fairbairn, Almarion Wolfe, and Marvin Leach, all November 9, 1925, trial transcript.

25. Testimony of Joseph Grohm, November 9, 1925, trial transcript; "Darrow Hints at Demand for Another Jury," *Detroit Free Press*, November 19, 1925, clipping at frame 1150, reel 3, part 5, NAACP Papers.

26. Testimony of Dwight Hubbard, November 11, 1925; testimony of Otto Lemhagen, November 11, 1925; testimony of Edward Wettlaufer, November 7, 1925; testimony of John Getke, November 9, 1925; testimony of Della Getke, November 9, 1925; testimony of Ray Dove November 6, 1925; testimony of George Suppus, November 10, 1925; testimony of Ulric Arthur, November 10, 1925; testimony of Eric Houghburg, November 11, 1925, testimony of Bruce Stout, November 10, 1925.

27. Getke testimony, November 9, 1925.

28. Hubbard testimony, November 11, 1925.

29. R. L. Polk and Company, *Detroit City Directory*, 1925–1926 (Detroit: R. L. Polk and Company, 1926); Wettlaufer testimony, November 7, 1925.

30. On the pronunciation of Goethe Street, see, for example, testimony of Otto Eber-hardt, November 7, 1925, trial transcript.

31. Testimony of Edward Belcher, November 10, 1925, trial transcirpt.

32. Testimony of Mary Henley, testimony of Fred Benoit, testimony of Harry Short, all on November 10, 1925; testimony of Eber Draper, November 7, 1925; Houghburg testimony, November 11, 1925; Eberhardt testimony, November 7, 1925.

33. Walter White to James Weldon Johnson, November 13, 1925, frames 82–84, reel 3, part 5, NAACP Papers; trial transcript, pp. 194–195, 588–601; "Sweet Plans Mistrial Plea," *Detroit News,* November 10, 1925; "Darrow Hints at Demand for Another Jury," *Detroit Free Press,* November 10, 1925; oral history interview with Otis Sweet, August 1, 1960, Alex Baskin Collection, Bentley Historical Library; "Sweet Trial Presents Dramatic Court Scene."

34. Darrow, *Story of My Life,* pp. 427–428.

35. "Sweet Trial Develops into Battle of Wits," *Detroit Free Press,* November 9, 1925, clipping at frame 1141, reel 3, part 5, NAACP Papers; Houghberg testimony, November 11, 1925.

36. "Sweet Trial Develops into Battle of Wits"; "Darrow Makes Sweet Trial Great 'Human Show,'" *Baltimore Afro-American,* November 14, 1925, frame 32, reel 4, part 5, NAACP Papers.

37. Schuknecht testimony, November 5, 1925; "Darrow, Grilling State's Witnesses, Batters Holes in Case Against Dr. Sweet," *Chicago Defender,* November 14, 1925.

38. Schuknecht testimony, November 5, 1925; "Darrow Quizzes Officer," *Detroit Times,* November 6, 1925.

39. Ray Dove testimony, November 6, 1925.

40. "Sweet Counsel Attacks Clubs," *Detroit Free Press,* November 8, 1925; testimony of Russell Burns, November 7, 1925; testimony of Raymond Alf, November 11, 1925; Della Getke testimony, November 9, 1925.

41. "'Man's House His Castle,' Argues Counsel for Sweet," *Chicago Defender,* November 21, 1925; Neighbauer testimony, November 9, 1925; testimony of Ernest Stanke, November 13, 1925; testimony of Ray Schaldernbrand, November 13, 1925; Sprott testimony, November 13, 1925.

42. Testimony of Harry Monet, November 10, 1925; Eberhardt testimony, November 7, 1925; Draper testimony, November 7, 1925; "Darrow Hits Riot Silence," *Detroit Times,* November 8, 1925; "Darrow Wins Point in Trial," *Detroit News,* November 13, 1925; "Darrow Aroused," *Detroit Times,* November 12, 1925, clipping at frames 8–9, reel 4, part 5, NAACP Papers; Darrow, *Story of My Life,* p. 308.

43. Hubbard testimony, November 11, 1925.

44. E.d. 629, sheet 9b, 1920 U.S. census manuscript, Detroit, Michigan; "Darrow Aroused"; "21 More to Be Called by State," *Detroit Times,* November 13, 1925.

45. Suppus testimony and Arthur testimony, both November 10, 1925; "Boycott Is Charged," *Detroit Times,* November 10, 1925, frames 1147–1148, reel 3, part 5, NAACP Papers; "Saw Stones Hurled at Sweet Home, Claim," *Detroit Free Press,* November 11, 1925.

46. Report of the secretary, December 1925, frames 661–664, reel 4, part 1, NAACP Papers; Walter White to James Weldon Johnson, November 15, 1925, frame 92, reel 3, part 5, NAACP Papers; Report of the Department of Branches, December 1925, frames 665–671, reel 4, part 1, NAACP Papers; White to Johnson, November 7, 1925, frames 65–66, reel 3, part 5, NAACP Papers.

47. Frank Murphy to Marguerite Murphy, November 6 and 7, 1925, box 1, Marguerite Murphy Papers, Michigan Historical Collections; "Crowd Waits in Line for Sensational Sweet Trial," *Chicago Defender,* November 14, 1925; "Another Myth Breaker," *Detroit News,* November 3, 1925; Sidney Fine, *Frank Murphy: The Detroit Years* (Ann Arbor: University of Michigan Press, 1975), pp. 86–87.

48. "Darrow Explains Evolution," *Detroit Times,* November 10, 1925; "Darrow Sees Crime Aided by Punishment," *Detroit Free Press,* November 16, 1925; report of the Department of Branches, December 1925; "1,500 Negroes Hear Darrow at Detroit," *Chicago Daily News,* November 9, 1925, clipping at frame 1135, reel 3, part 5, NAACP Papers.

49. Reinhold Niebuhr, *Leaves from the Notebook of a Tamed Cynic* (1929; repr. New York: Harper and Row, 1980), p. 88; Josephine Gomon diary entries, November 15, 1925, and undated, both in box 6, Gomon Papers.

50. Gomon diary entry, n.d. [November 1925], box 6, Gomon Papers.

51. "Darrow Tells Racial Aims," *Detroit Times*, November 9, 1925; "Darrow Says Dry Act Hasn't Killed 'Appetite,'" *Detroit Free Press*, November 9, 1925; "1,500 Negroes Hear Darrow at Detroit," *Chicago Daily News*, November 9, 1925.

52. Statement of O. H. Sweet Defense Fund, n.d. [mid-November 1925], frames 802–804, reel 3, part 5, NAACP Papers. White did send NAACP headquarters several newspaper clippings reporting Darrow's remarks, which were duly filed away.

53. Walter White to James Weldon Johnson, November 13, 1925; White to Johnson, November 15, 1925.

54. White to Johnson, November 13, 1925.

55. In fact, Darrow and Hays floated the idea in court, though the effort was half-hearted. See "Officer's Shot Killed Breiner, Is New Claim," *Detroit Free Press*, November 22, 1925. The argument certainly ran counter to Darrow's advice to criminal lawyers not to make an argument jurors would find unbelievable. See Darrow, *Story of My Life*, p. 427.

56. Walter White to James Weldon Johnson, November 15, 1925, frame 92, reel 3, part 5, NAACP Papers. Filing a motion to dismiss was standard practice for Darrow. See Lukas, *Big Trouble*, pp. 565–567. For the motion itself, see motion to dismiss, box 5, Clarence Darrow Collection, Library of Congress, Washington, D.C.

57. "Defense Asks Dismissal of Sweet Trial," *Detroit Free Press*, November 15, 1925; "'Man's Home His Castle,' Argues Counsel for Sweet"; "Defense Asks 11 Be Freed," *Detroit Times*, November 15, 1925; Arthur Garfield Hays, *Let Freedom Ring* (New York: Liveright, 1937), p. 214; Arthur Garfield Hays, *City Lawyer: The Autobiography of a Law Practice* (New York: Simon and Schuster, 1942), p. 209.

58. "Defense Asks 11 Be Freed." Also see "'Man's Home His Castle,' Argues Counsel for Sweet."

59. White to Johnson, November 15, 1925.

60. "Riot Case Plea Ruling Awaited," *Detroit News*, November 14, 1925; "Case Unproved, Declares Hays," *Detroit News*, November 14, 1925; "'Man's Home His Castle,' Argues Counsel for Sweet"; "Moll Demands Slayer in Riot Case Pay Penalty," *Detroit Times*, November 24, 1925; "Judge Murphy Denies Motion in Sweet Trial," *Pittsburgh Courier*, November 21, 1925, frame 78, reel 4, part 5, NAACP Papers.

61. Fine, *Frank Murphy*, p. 159; "New Move by Sweet Attorney," *Detroit Times*, November 17, 1925.

62. Arthur Garfield Hays opening address to the jury, November 16, 1925, frames 920–938, reel 3, part 5, NAACP Papers.

63. For this and previous paragraph, see "Other Race Troubles Figure in Sweet Trial," *Detroit Free Press*, November 18, 1925; "Dr. Sweet Goes on Stand," *Chicago Defender*, November 28, 1925; "Witness Tells of Sweet 'Mob,'" *Detroit News*, November 17, 1925.

64. The details of Sweet's testimony are recounted in Walter White to James Weldon Johnson, November 20, 1925, frames 143–145, reel 3, part 5, NAACP Papers; NAACP press release, November 20, 1925, frame 181, reel 3, part 5, NAACP Papers; "Race Psychology Told in Sweet's Testimony," *Detroit Free Press*, November 19, 1925; "Sweet Depicts Fear in Court," *Detroit Free Press*, November 20, 1925; "Darrow to Rest Riot Defense," *Detroit Times*, November 19, 1925; "Detroit Riot Case Near Close," *Arizona Times*, November 28, 1925 (Associated Negro Press story), frame 142, reel 4, part 5, NAACP Papers; "Influence of Race Wars Part of Sweet Defense," *New York Herald-Tribune*, November 18, 1925, frame 60, reel 4, part 5, NAACP Papers; "Dr. Sweet Goes on Stand," *Chicago Defender*, December 5, 1925; David Lilienthal, "Has the Negro the Right of Self-Defense?" *Nation* (December 23, 1925): 72.

65. "Dr. Sweet Is Cross-Examined," *Detroit News*, November 19, 1925; "Sweet Depicts Fear in Court"; "Witness Hurts Sweet Defense," *Detroit Free Press*, November 21, 1925; "Moll Demands Slayers in Riot Case Pay Penalty"; "Darrow Employs Sarcasm," *Detroit*

News, November 22, 1925; "Both Sides in Riot Trial to Rest Cases," *Detroit Times,* November 21, 1925.

66. Walter White to James Weldon Johnson, November 18, 1925, frame 137, reel 3, part 5, NAACP Papers; "Darrow, Hays Charge Police with Perjury," *Detroit Free Press,* November 25, 1925, clipping at frames 30–32, reel 4, part 5, NAACP Papers.

67. "Darrow, Hays Charge Police with Perjury"; "Highlights in Sweet Trial Argument," *Detroit Free Press,* November 25, 1925, frame 104, reel 4, part 5, NAACP Papers.

68. Arthur Garfield Hays closing statement, November 24–25, 1925, Bentley Library.

69. "[Unreadable] Plea Brings Tears," *Detroit Times,* November 25, 1925; Lilienthal, "Has the Negro the Right of Self-Defense?" p. 725; Clarence Darrow closing statement, November 24, 1925, Michigan Historical Collection.

70. Toms interview, November 28, 1959.

71. Darrow closing statement, November 24–25, 1925.

72. Lilienthal, "Has the Negro the Right of Self-Defense?" p. 725.

73. Ibid.; oral history interview with Charles Mahoney, August [?], 1960, Alex Baskin Collection; Josephine Gomon diary entry, n.d., box 6, Gomon collection.

74. "Tom's Closing Plea to the Jury," *Detroit News,* November 26, 1926.

75. "Sweet Jurors Still Debating," *Detroit News,* November 26, 1925.

76. Walter White to James Weldon Johnson, November 25, 1925, frame 151, reel 3, part 5, NAACP Papers; "Sweet Jurors Still Debating."

77. "Sweet Jurors Still Debating"; "Deadlock Report Is Refused," *Detroit Times,* November 26, 1925.

78. "Sweet Jurors in a Deadlock," *Detroit News,* November 27, 1925; Hays, *Let Freedom Ring,* p. 232; Walter White, *A Man Called White: The Autobiography of Walter White* (New York: Viking, 1948), p. 78.

79. "Sweet Jurors in a Deadlock"; "Darrow Asks Bail for 11 Clients in Move for New Trial," *Detroit Times,* November 27, 1925.

80. Josephine Gomon diary entry, n.d. [November 26, 1925], box 6, Gomon Papers; "Riot Jury Returns to Task," *Detroit Times,* November 27, 1925.

81. "Sweet Jurors in a Deadlock." Charles Naas's age is taken from e.d. 531, sheet 18A, the 1920 U.S. census manuscript, Detroit, Michigan.

82. "Sweet Jurors in a Deadlock."

83. NAACP press release, November 28, 1926, frame 164, reel 3, part 5, NAACP Papers; Oscar Baker to Walter White, November 30, 1925, frame 186, reel 3, part 5, NAACP Papers; White draft statement, December 8, 1925, frame 244, reel 3, part 5, NAACP Papers; "Darrow Asks Quick Retrial," *Detroit Times,* November 28, 1925.

84. "Darrow Asks Bail for 11 Clients in Move for New Trial"; "Darrow Asks Quick Retrial."

Chapter Ten: Judgment Day

1. "Darrow Asks Quick Retrial," *Detroit Times,* November 28, 1925; Arthur Garfield Hays to James Weldon Johnson, December 8, 1925, frame 251, reel 3, part 5, NAACP Papers.

2. Walter White to Roland Hayes, frame 318, reel 9, part 2, NAACP Papers; White to Russell Jelliffe, December 10, 1925, frame 333, reel 9, part 2, NAACP Papers.

3. Mose Walker to Walter White, December 16, 1925, frame 282, reel 3, part 5, NAACP Papers; Hays to Johnson, December 8, 1925; David Lilienthal, "Has the Negro the Right of Self-Defense?" *Nation,* December 23, 1925, pp. 724–725; "Noble Nordic Darrow," *Dearborn Independent,* January 9, 1926; "Detroit Sentiment Favorable to Sweets," (New York) *Amsterdam News,* December 30, 1925; Oscar Baker to White, November 30, 1925, frame 186, reel 3, part 5, NAACP Papers; Arthur Garfield Hays to gentlemen, December 31, 1925, frame 325, reel 3, part 5, NAACP Papers.

4. Walter White to Arthur Garfield Hays, December 4, 1925, and December 17, 1925, frames 356 and 357, reel 9, part 2, NAACP Papers; Ann Douglas, *Terrible Honesty: Mongrel*

Manhattan in the 1920s (New York: Farrar, Straus and Giroux, 1995), p. 125; Walter White to Frank Murphy, December 4, 1925, frames 230–231, reel 3, part 5, NAACP Papers; Frank Murphy to "Unc" [Walter White], December 31, 1925, frames 389–390, reel 9, part 2, NAACP Papers; White to Robert Toms, December 2, 1925, frame 206, reel 3, part 5, NAACP Papers.

5. Present status of the Legal Defense Fund, December 11 [1925], frame 794, reel 3, part 5, NAACP Papers; expenses to the national office, n.d. [December 1925], frame 816, reel 3, part 5, NAACP Papers; William Sears to James Weldon Johnson, November 25, 1925, frame 709, reel 22, part 1, NAACP Papers.

6. James Weldon Johnson to Henry Sachs, December 29, 1925, and Johnson to William Graves, January 23, 1926, frames 767 and 950, reel 23, part 5, NAACP Papers; David Levering Lewis, *W. E. B. Du Bois: The Fight for Equality and the American Century, 1919–1963* (New York: Henry Holt, 2000), p. 98; Walter White to Johnson, December 29, 1925, frame 321, reel 3, part 5, NAACP Papers; "Defends Negro's Right to Invade White Districts," *New York World,* December 20, 1925; "Women Make Great Progress in Aiding Defense Fund Drive," *Washington Daily American,* December 19, 1925, clipping at frame 397, reel 4, part 5, NAACP Papers; White to H. L. Mencken, December 9, 1925, frame 329, reel 9, part 2, NAACP Papers; White to Blanche Knopf, December 1, 1925, frame 321, reel 3, part 2, NAACP Papers; White to Sinclair Lewis, January 29, 1926, frame 490, reel 9, part 2, NAACP Papers.

7. Walter White to Clarence Darrow, December 8, 1925, frame 239, reel 3, part 5, NAACP Paper; Ruby Darrow to Irving Stone, n.d. [1940?], box 34, Clarence Darrow Collection, Library of Congress, Washington, D.C.; "Sing Negro Spirituals," *New York Times,* December 18, 1925; mass meeting program, December 13, 1925, frame 321, reel 13, part 11b, NAACP Papers; "Two Negro Audiences Applaud Darrow," *New York World,* December 14, 1925; "Darrow Jeers 'Noble Nordics' Before Negroes," *New York Herald-Tribune,* December 14, 1925, clipping at frame 334, reel 13, part 11b, NAACP Papers; report of field work meetings, December 1925, frames 665–671, reel 4, part 1, NAACP Papers.

8. Walter White to Gladys Sweet, November 28, 1925, frame 166, reel 3, part 5, NAACP Papers; Walter White memorandum of phone conversation, December 1, 1925, frame 194, reel 3, part 5, NAACP Papers; Walter Nelson to NAACP, December 2, 1925, frame 198, reel 3, part 5, NAACP Papers.

9. Bond postings, November–December 1925, box 1, Ossian Sweet Collection, Burton Historical Collection, Detroit Public Library, Detroit, Mich.; "Doctor Sweet Goes on Stand," *Chicago Defender,* November 28, 1925; Mose Walker to Walter White, December 9, 1925, frame 255, reel 3, part 5, NAACP Papers; R. L. Polk and Company, *Detroit City Directory,* 1925–1926 (Detroit: R. L. Polk and Company, 1926), pp. 1808, 2087. Darrow thought it would be a mistake for the Sweets to move into the bungalow until the case was settled. Clarence Darrow to White, December 26 [1925], frame 809, reel 3, part 5, NAACP Papers.

10. Alex Baskin interview with Otis Sweet, August 1, 1960, Alex Baskin Collection, Michigan Historical Collection, Bentley Library, University of Michigan, Ann Arbor; "Give Us Civil Rights," *The Arizona Times,* December 5, 1925; "Thank God for the Men and Women of New England," *The Cleveland Call,* December 5, 1925; "Dr. O. H. Sweet Thrills Big Audience," *Detroit Independent,* December 11, 1925, clipping at frame 185, reel 4, part 5, NAACP Papers; James Weldon Johnson to Ossian Sweet, December 15, 1925, frame 283, reel 3, part 5, NAACP Papers.

11. Minutes of the fifteenth annual meeting, January 4, 1926, frame 715, reel 13, part 1, NAACP Papers; advertisement, (New York) *Amsterdam News,* December 30, 1925, frame 205, reel 4, part 5, NAACP Papers; "Flay Segregation of Negroes in Cities," *New York World,* January 4, 1925; Robert Bagnall to L. F. Dyer, frame 844, reel 13, part 1, NAACP Papers; address of Arthur Garfield Hays, January 3, 1926, frames 400–407, reel 3, part 5, NAACP Papers.

12. NAACP press release, January 15, 1926, frame 415, reel 3, part 5, NAACP Papers; Robert Bagnall to James Weldon Johnson, n.d. [January 11, 1926], frames 357–358, reel

15, part 1, NAACP Papers; "Dr. Sweet Flays Detroit Police in Speech Here," *Chicago Defender*, January 16, 1926.

13. Robert Bagnall to James Weldon Johnson, n.d. [January 10, 1926], frames 356–357, reel 15, part 1, NAACP Papers; Robert Bagnall to Johnson, n.d. [January 11, 1926]; "Sweet, Wife Will Tell of Detroit Case," *Chicago Defender*, January 9, 1926.

14. Secretary's report to the board of directors, February 1926, frames 684–687, reel 4, part 1, NAACP Papers.

15. Secretary's report to the board of directors, November 9, 1925, frames 52–54, reel 2, part 1, NAACP; Stephen Grant Meyer, *As Long as They Don't Move Next Door: Segregation and Racial Conflict in American Neighborhoods* (Lanham, Md.: Rowman and Littlefield, 2000), pp. 24–31; James Cobb to Arthur Spingarn, December 16, 1925, frame 85, reel 5, Arthur Spingarn Collection, Library of Congress, Washington, D.C.

16. Moorfield Storey to James Weldon Johnson, January 12, 1926, frame 283, reel 24, part 1, NAACP Papers.

17. James Cobb to James Weldon Johnson, January 13, 1926, frames 466–467, reel 4, part 5, NAACP Papers; NAACP press release, January 1926, frames 960–961, reel 28, part 11B, NAACP Papers.

18. NAACP press release, January 1926; Clement E. Vose, *Caucasians Only: The Supreme Court, the NAACP, and the Restrictive Covenant Cases* (Berkeley: University of California Press, 1959), p. 53.

19. Louis Johnson to Moorfield Storey, May 28, 1926, reel 27, Spingarn Papers; Mark Robert Schneider, *"We Return Fighting": The Civil Rights Movement in the Jazz Age* (Boston: Northeastern University Press, 2002), p. 288; Storey to James Weldon Johnson, January 12, 1926; James Cobb to Arthur Spingarn, January 9, 1926, frame 103, reel 4, Spingarn Papers.

20. Typescript, "The Sweet Trial in Detroit," December 8, 1925, frame 244, reel 3, part 5, NAACP Papers; Clarence Darrow to Walter White, January 12, 1926, frame 414, reel 3, part 5, NAACP Papers; White to Darrow, March 9, 1926, frame 465, reel 3, part 5, NAACP Papers; Walter White report, March 21–24, 1926, frames 423–426, reel 3, part 5, NAACP Papers.

21. White report, March 21–24, 1926; license 2337, records of drugstores, v. 8, RG 87-106, Licensing and Registration, Michigan State Archives, Lansing. Sanborn Map Company, *Fire Insurance Map of Detroit, Michigan* (New York: Sanborn Map Company, 1922), provides a description of Garafalo Drugs, and e.d. 82–235, p. 19B, 1930 U.S. census manuscript, Detroit, Michigan, offers a picture of the surrounding neighborhood. For details on the Sweets' apartment building at 526 E. Hancock, see Marcet Haldeman-Julius, *Clarence Darrow's Two Great Trials* (Girard, Kan.: Haldeman-Julius Publishing Company, 1927), p. 27, and R. L. Polk and Company, *Detroit City Directory*, 1927–1928 (Detroit: R. L. Polk and Company, 1928).

22. Ossian Sweet to William Pickens, December 20, 1930, reel 26, Spingarn Papers; White report, March 21–24, 1926; Haldeman-Julius, *Clarence Darrow's Two Great Trials*, pp. 30–31, 34–40, 43–44.

23. Alex Baskin interview with Cecil Rowlette, August 1, 1960, Baskin Collection; Walter White to Clarence Darrow, December 23, 1925, and Darrow to White, January 2, 1926, frames 318 and 413, reel 3, part 5, NAACP Papers; Mose Walker to White, March 18, 1926, frame 473, reel 3, part 5, NAACP Papers.

24. Walter White memorandum of conversation, February 2, 1926, frame 439, reel 3, part 5, NAACP Papers; James Weldon Johnson to Ira Jayne, April 9, 1926, frames 519–520, reel 3, part 5, NAACP Papers; White report, March 21–24, 1926.

25. Clarence Darrow to Walter White, January 2, 1926; Herbert Friedman to White, December 4, 1925, frame 250, reel 3, part 5, NAACP Papers; William Pickens to James Weldon Johnson and Legal Committee, December 19, 1925, frame 90, reel 5, Spingarn Papers; memorandum of conversation, Clarence Darrow, Walter White, and James Weldon Johnson, February 2, 1926, frame 439, reel 3, part 5, NAACP Papers.

26. Raymond R. Fragnoli, *The Transformation of Reform: Progressivism in Detroit—*

And After, 1912–1933 (New York: Garland, 1982), pp. 321–322; Richard Fox, *Reinhold Niebuhr: A Biography* (New York: Pantheon, 1985), pp. 91–92; Mayor's Inter-Racial Committee, *The Negro in Detroit* (Detroit: Detroit Bureau of Governmental Research, 1926); William P. Lovett, "Sketches of American Mayors: John W. Smith of Detroit," *National Municipal Review* 15 (April 1926): 205–207; "Stout Ousted as Klan Dictator," "Strife-Torn Klan Showdown Due," and "Warring Kluxers to Meet Tuesday," *Detroit Times*, December 19, 20, and 22, 1925; Felix Holt to Walter White, March 22, 1926, frame 621, reel 9, part 2, NAACP Papers.

27. James Weldon Johnson to Moorfield Storey, December 30, 1925, frames 607–608, reel 17, part 1, NAACP Papers.

28. Arthur Garfield Hays, *City Lawyer: The Autobiography of a Law Practice* (New York: Simon and Schuster, 1942), pp. 203–205; Walter White to Clarence Darrow, March 13, 1926, frame 470, reel 3, part 5, NAACP Papers. Hays was also scheduled for an early April appearance on the Boston Common, where he planned to join H. L. Mencken in selling copies of the recently banned *American Mercury*. See Arthur Garfield Hays, *Let Freedom Ring* (New York: Livright, 1937), pp. 160–185.

29. White report, March 21–24, 1926. Darrow had his first contact with Chawke on Thanksgiving Day 1925, as the deliberations in the first Sweet trial dragged on. Darrow called Chawke that evening for advice on whether to accept a hung jury or insist that the deliberations continue. See Alex Baskin interview with Thomas Chawke, August 4, 1960, Baskin Collection.

30. Oscar Baker to Walter White, March 8, 1926, frames 462–464, reel 3, part 5, NAACP Papers; Walter White report, March 21–24, 1926; White to Baker, October 5, 1925, frames 1115–1118, reel 2, part 5, NAACP Papers; memorandum of telephone conversation, October 7, 1960, frames 1152–1153, reel 2, part 5, NAACP Papers; *Centennial of the Diocese of Detroit, 1833–1933* (Detroit: Michigan Catholic, 1933), p. 78; "Defense Attorney Thomas Chawke Dies," *Detroit News*, December 26, 1974, copy in "Chawke" reading room file, Burton Historical Collection.

31. White report, March 21–24, 1926; James Weldon Johnson to Ira Jayne, April 5, 1926; Thomas Chawke to Walter White, April 6, 1926; and James Weldon Johnson to Chawke, April 7, 1926, frames 503–505, reel 3, part 5, NAACP Papers.

32. "The Weather," *Detroit News*, April 19, 1926; "Darrow in Quiz for Jurors," undated clipping [*Chicago Defender*], Detroit Free Press Clipping Morgue, Detroit, Mich.; Josephine Gomon diary entry, April 20, 1926, box 6, Josephine Gomon Collection, Bentley Library; Frank Murphy to Marguerite Murphy, n.d. [April 1926], box 1, Marguerite Murphy Collection, Bentley Library; "Henry Sweet to Face Trial," *Detroit Free Press*, April 13, 1926; Clarence Darrow, *The Story of My Life* (New York: Charles Scribner's Sons, 1934), p. 311; "Jurors Are Selected for New Sweet Trial," *Detroit Free Press*, April 20, 1926.

33. "Darrow in Quiz for Jurors"; Marcet Haldeman-Julius, "Clarence Darrow's Defense of a Negro," *Haldeman-Julius Monthly* (July 1926): 12, copy in box 16, Clarence Darrow Collection, Library of Congress, Washington, D.C.; "Sweet Trial Delay Is Seen," *Detroit Free Press*, April 22, 1926; "Toms to Continue Quiz," *Detroit Times*, April 22, 1926; "Jurors Are Selected for New Sweet Trial," *Detroit Free Press*, April 20, 1926.

34. "Riot Trial Lawyers Clash," *Detroit Times*, April 21, 1926; "Sweet Trial Is Race Issue, Darrow Insists," *Detroit Free Press*, April 21, 1926.

35. Haldeman-Julius, "Clarence Darrow's Defense of a Negro," pp. 12–13; Hilmer Gellein article draft, "The Sweet Trials, 1925–26," n.d. [c. 1973], box 1, Ossian Sweet Collection, Burton Historical Collection; e.d. 221, 1930 U.S. census manuscript, Detroit, Michigan, 221 for George Small, e.d. 158 for Ralph Feulling; e.d. 723, 1920 U.S. census manuscript, Detroit, Michigan, for Edward Birnie; "Sweet Jury Slowed by Darrow," *Detroit Times*, April 20, 1926; "Sweet Trial Delay Is Seen," *Detroit Times*, April 21, 1926; "Sweet Jury Selected; Trial to Begin Monday," *Detroit Free Press*, April 25, 1926; "Court Is Surprised by Darrow," *Detroit Times*, April 25, 1926.

36. "Darrow Defends Riot Slaying," *Detroit Times*, April 26, 1926; "Police Grilled in Sweet Case," *Detroit Free Press*, April 27, 1926; transcript of Henry Sweet interrogation, September 9, 1926, copy in author's possession; Chawke interview.

37. Haldeman-Julius, "Clarence Darrow's Defense of a Negro," pp. 14–16; "Darrow Defends Riot Slaying"; Josephine Gomon draft of Frank Murphy biography, n.d., box 9, Gomon Collection; Irving Stone, *Clarence Darrow for the Defense* (New York: Doubleday, 1941), pp. 483–484. According to Chawke, Darrow had planned to delay his opening statement as he'd done in the first trial, but when he saw that Toms had brought the guns into the courtroom he decided that the impression they created had to be countered immediately.

38. Haldeman-Julius, "Clarence Darrow's Defense of a Negro," pp. 7–9; Chawke interview; "Darrow Plans Motion to Dismiss Sweet Case," *Detroit Free Press*, May 5, 1926; "Breiner Widow and Other Principals in East Side Riot Trial," *Detroit Times*, April 28, 1926.

39. "Police Hit by Darrow at Trial," *Detroit Times*, April 27, 1926; "Police Grilled in Sweet Case"; Haldeman-Julius, "Clarence Darrow's Defense of a Negro," p. 18. Emphasis is mine.

40. "Police Hit by Darrow at Trial"; Haldeman-Julius, "Clarence Darrow's Defense of a Negro," pp. 16–18.

41. "Juror May Stop Riot Hearing," *Detroit Times*, April 28, 1926; "Juror Illegal, Claim; Sweet Mistrial Seen," *Detroit Free Press*, April 29, 1926; Haldeman-Julius, "Clarence Darrow Defends a Negro," pp. 20–21.

42. "Hedging Stirs Sweet Lawyer," *Detroit News*, May 3, 1926.

43. "Darrow Plans Motion to Dismiss Sweet Case"; Kevin Tierney, *Darrow: A Biography* (New York: Thomas Y. Crowell, 1979), p. 383; "Blame Society in Sweet Trial," *Detroit Free Press*, May 4, 1926; "Darrow in Clash with Teacher," *Detroit Times*, May 4, 1926.

44. "Blame Society in Sweet Trial"; "Darrow Fights Riot Re-Trial," *Detroit Times*, April 29, 1926.

45. Haldeman-Julius, "Clarence Darrow's Defense of a Negro," pp. 21–22; "Darrow Scores Point in Sweet Murder Trial," *Detroit Free Press*, May 2, 1926; "Darrow Digs at Association," *Detroit News*, May 1, 1926; James Weldon Johnson, "Detroit," *Crisis* (July 1926): 117.

46. Haldeman-Julius, "Clarence Darrow's Defense of a Negro," pp. 22–24; "Darrow Scores Points in Sweet Murder Trial"; "Defense Ready in Sweet Trial," *Detroit News*, May 2, 1926.

47. "Surprise Given in Sweet Case," *Detroit News*, May 5, 1926; "Doctor Sweet to Tell of Fears," *Detroit Times*, May 7, 1926, clipping at frame 262, reel 4, part 5, NAACP Papers; Haldeman-Julius, "Clarence Darrow's Defense of a Negro," p. 26; John Dancy to E. K. Jones, May 12, 1926, box 1, Detroit Urban League Collection, Bentley Library. The defense opened its case on May 5.

48. "Darrow Calls Sweet to Stand," *Detroit Times*, May 6, 1926; "Defense Opens in Sweet Case," *Detroit Free Press*, May 6, 1926; "Surprise Given in Sweet Case."

49. Haldeman-Julius, "Clarence Darrow Defends a Negro," p. 28; "Sweet Verdict Due This Week," *Detroit Free Press*, May 9, 1926.

50. Haldeman-Julius, "Clarence Darrow's Defense of a Negro," p. 28; Walter White, *Rope and Faggot: A Biography of Judge Lynch* (New York: Alfred A. Knopf, 1929), p. 256; "Sweet's Fate to Jury Soon," *Detroit Times*, May 9, 1926; "Sweet Says He Provided Guns," *Detroit Free Press*, May 8, 1926, copy at frame 265, reel 4, part 5, NAACP Papers.

51. "Sweet Says He Provided Guns"; "Sweet's Fate to Jury Soon."

52. W. E. B. Du Bois, "The Sweet Trial," *Crisis* (July 1926): 114.

53. David Allan Levine, *Internal Combustion: The Races in Detroit, 1915–1926* (Westport, Conn.: Greenwood Press, 1976), p. 187.

54. Transcript of Lester Moll's closing statement, pp. 17, 54–55, 60, Michigan Historical Collection.

55. Transcript of Thomas Chawke's closing statement, pp. 4, 13, 52–55, Michigan Historical Collection.

56. "Darrow in Final Plea," *Detroit Times*, May 11, 1926; "You're All Prejudiced, Darrow Tells Jurors," *Detroit Free Press*, May 12, 1926; Johnson, "Detroit," p. 118; Haldeman-Julius, "Clarence Darrow's Defense of a Negro," p. 28.

57. Darrow's plea is reprinted in "Argument of Clarence Darrow in the Case of Henry

Sweet," NAACP pamphlet, 1927. All quotations are from the pamphlet. Details of his performance are taken from Haldeman-Julius, "Clarence Darrow's Defense of a Negro," pp. 28–32; Josephine Gomon diary entry, n.d., box 6, Gomon Papers; Johnson, "Detroit," pp. 118–119; "You're All Prejudiced, Darrow Tells Jurors," *Detroit Free Press*, May 12, 1926; "Darrow in Final Plea"; Stone, *Clarence Darrow for the Defense*, pp. 484–485. James Weldon Johnson to Walter White, May 14, 1926, frames 651–652, reel 3, part 5, NAACP Papers. Darrow later claimed that "my long sympathy for the colored people conspired to help me make one of the strongest and most satisfactory arguments that I ever delivered." Darrow, *The Story of My Life*, p. 311.

58. Johnson, "Detroit," p. 119. Others were just as moved by Darrow's plea. "As Judge Murphy left the bench I met him just inside the door of his office," Josephine Gomon recalled. "He took my hand and said, 'This is the greatest experience of my life. That was Clarence Darrow at his best. I will never hear anything like it again. He is the most Christ-like man I have ever known.'" Stone, *Clarence Darrow for the Defense*, p. 484.

59. Transcript of Robert Toms closing statement, May 12, 1926, pp. 99–100, Michigan Historical Collection; Felix Holt to Walter White, May 12, 1926, frame 34, reel 10, part 2, NAACP Papers; "Court to Rule Today in Mistrial in Riot Case," *Detroit Times*, May 13, 1926; "Sweet Denied Mistrial Move," *Detroit Free Press*, May 13, 1926; Haldeman-Julius, "Clarence Darrow's Defense of a Negro," p. 32.

60. Transcript of Frank Murphy charge of the court, May 13, 1926, pp. 30–31, Michigan Historical Collection.

61. Chawke interview; Gomon diary entry, n.d. [May 13, 1926]; Gomon draft, "The Sweet Trial," p. 43; "Henry Sweet Acquitted in Murder Trial," *Detroit Free Press*, May 14, 1926.

62. Johnson, "Detroit," pp. 119–120; "Toms May Drop Riot Cases," *Detroit Times*, May 14, 1926.

63. Haldeman-Julius, "Clarence Darrow's Defense of a Negro," p. 32; Gomon draft, "Judge of the Recorders Court," p. 43; Stone, *Clarence Darrow for the Defense*, p. 486; "Toms May Drop Riot Cases."

64. Haldeman-Julius, "Clarence Darrow's Defense of a Negro," p. 32; Johnson, "Detroit," p. 120.

65. Gomon Diary entry, n.d.; Gomon draft, p. 43; Johnson to White, May 14, 1926; "Toms May Drop Riot Case." Gomon claims that when the verdict was read Darrow slumped in his chair. A worried Toms reached out to him. "Are you all right, Mr. Darrow?" the prosecutor asked. "Oh yes," he replied. "I've heard that verdict before." Gomon draft, "The Sweet Trial," p. 44.

Epilogue: Requiescam

1. "Crowd Mass Meetings of NAACP," *Chicago Defender*, July 3, 1926; David Levering Lewis, *W. E. B. Du Bois: The Fight for Equality and the American Century, 1919–1963* (New York: Henry Holt, 2000), pp. 175–176; Kenneth Robert Janken, *White: The Biography of Walter White, Mr. NAACP* (New York: New Press, 2003), pp. 113–115; "To Fight 'Jim Crow' Laws," *New York Times*, June 28, 1926.

2. Elazar Barkan, *The Retreat of Scientific Racism: Changing Concepts of Race in Britain and the United States Between the World Wars* (Cambridge, England: Cambridge University Press, 1992); Stephan Thernstrom and Abigail Thernstrom, *America in Black and White: One Nation, Indivisible* (New York: Simon and Schuster, 1997), p. 103; Stephen Grant Meyer, *As Long as They Don't Move Next Door: Segregation and Racial Conflict in American Neighborhoods* (Lanham, Md.: Rowan and Littlefield, 2000), p. 136.

3. Kevin Tierney, *Darrow: A Biography* (New York: Thomas Y. Crowell, 1979), pp. 386–425; James Goodman, *Stories of Scottsboro* (New York: Random House, 1994), pp. 37–38; Irving Stone, *Clarence Darrow for the Defense* (Garden City, N.Y.: Doubleday, 1941), p. 518.

4. "Defense Attorney Thomas Chawke Dies," *Detroit News*, December 26, 1974;

Raymond Fragnoli, *The Transformation of Detroit: Progressivism in Detroit—and After, 1912–1933* (New York: Garland, 1982), pp. 320–328; Reinhold Niebuhr, *Leaves from the Notebook of a Tamed Cynic* (1929; repr. New York: Harper and Row, 1980), p. 144; "Long Fight Is Ended for Civil Leader," *Detroit Free Press*, June 18, 1942.

5. Arthur Garfield Hays, *City Lawyer: The Autobiography of a Law Practice* (New York: Simon and Schuster, 1942). Darrow is quoted on p. 461.

6. Niebuhr, *Leaves from the Notebook of a Tamed Cynic*, p. 143; Mayor's Inter-Racial Committee, *The Negro in Detroit* (Detroit: Detroit Bureau of Governmental Research, 1926); "Report of the Mayor's Committee on Race Relations," *Public Business* 4 (March 10, 1927), copy in box G-95, NAACP Papers, Library of Congress, Washington, D.C.; Richard Fox, *Reinhold Niebuhr: A Biography* (New York: Pantheon, 1985), chapters 5–7; Taylor Branch, *Parting the Waters: America in the King Years, 1954–63* (New York: Simon and Schuster, 1988), pp. 81–87.

7. "Ex-Judge Toms Dies at Age 73," *Detroit Free Press*, April 7, 1960; "300 Judges, Lawyers, Attend Toms' Funeral," *Detroit News*, April 10, 1960; NAACP Detroit branch membership list, June 8, 1937, frame 1090, reel 13, part 12, NAACP Papers; "Luminary of the Week," *[Detroit?] Legal Chronicle*, May 22, 1964, copy in Detroit Free Press clipping morgue, Detroit, Mich.

8. Sidney Fine, *Frank Murphy: The Detroit Years* (Ann Arbor: University of Michigan Press, 1975), pp. 215–223, 442–451.

9. Sidney Fine, *Frank Murphy: The Washington Years* (Ann Arbor: University of Michigan Press, 1984), pp. 130–131, 168–177, 381–383, 393–393, 412–424, 448, 565.

10. Eugene Levy, *James Weldon Johnson: Black Leader, Black Voice* (Chicago: University of Chicago Press, 1973), pp. 287–292; Janken, *White*, chapters 5–12; Patricia Sullivan, *Days of Hope: Race and Democracy in the New Deal Era* (Chapel Hill: University of North Carolina Press, 1996); Genna Rae McNeil, *Groundwork: Charles Hamilton Houston and the Struggle for Civil Rights* (Philadelphia: University of Pennsylvania Press, 1983); Mark V. Tushnet, *Making Civil Rights Law: Thurgood Marshall and the Supreme Court, 1936–1961* (New York: Oxford University Press, 1994); Richard Kluger, *Simple Justice: The History of* Brown v. Board of Education *and Black America's Struggle for Equality* (New York: Vintage, 1975); and, for an insider's account, Jack Greenberg, *Crusaders in the Court: How a Dedicated Band of Lawyers Fought for the Civil Rights Revolution* (New York: Basic Books, 1994).

11. James Weldon Johnson to Clarence Darrow, May 28, 1926, frame 681, reel 3, part 5, NAACP Papers; Harold Black, "Restrictive Covenants in Relation to Segregated Negro Housing in Detroit," (unpublished M.A. thesis, Wayne State University, 1947), pp. 6, 10, 24, 37–38; Kenneth Jackson, *Crabgrass Frontier: The Suburbanization of the United States* (New York: Oxford University Press, 1985); Douglas Massey and Nancy Denton, *American Apartheid: Segregation and the Making of the Underclass* (Cambridge, Mass.: Harvard University Press, 1993), chapter 2. Also see Arnold Hirsch, *Making the Second Ghetto: Race and Housing in Chicago, 1940–1960* (Cambridge, England: Cambridge University Press, 1983).

12. On white liberals and neighborhood segregation in Detroit, see Thomas Sugrue, *The Origins of the Urban Crisis: Race and Inequality in Postwar Detroit* (Princeton, N.J.: Princeton University Press, 1996), pp. 190–194, chapters 8–9; and Sidney Fine, *"Expanding the Frontiers of Civil Rights": Michigan, 1948–1968* (Detroit: Wayne State University Press, 2000), chapter 5. The beginning point for understanding mid-twentieth-century racial liberalism is Gunnar Myrdal, *An American Dilemma* (New York: Harper and Row, 1944). For an insightful recent treatment, see Gary Gerstle, *American Crucible: Race and Nation in the Twentieth Century* (Princeton, N.J.: Princeton University Press, 2001).

13. Clement Vose, *Caucasians Only: The Supreme Court, the NAACP, and the Restrictive Covenant Cases* (Berkeley: University of California Press, 1959), chapters 6–8; Hugh Davis Graham, *The Civil Rights Era: Origins and Development of a National Policy* (New York: Oxford University Press, 1990), chapter 10; Meyer, *As Long as They Don't Live Next Door*, pp. 212–221; Sugrue, *The Origins of the Urban Crisis;* Massey & Denton, *American Apartheid*, chapters 3–4; Reynolds Farley, Sheldon Danziger, and Harry Holzer, *Detroit Divided* (New York: Russell Sage Foundation, 2000), chapters 7–8; http://www.census.gov/hhes/www/housing/resseg/tab5-4.html, last accessed February 7, 2004.

14. Minutes of the NAACP board of directors' meeting, September 13, 1926, frame 98, reel 2, part 1, NAACP Papers; "Baby of Dr. Sweet Dies in Arizona," *Chicago Defender,* August 28, 1926; Elaine Latzman Moon, *Untold Tales, Unsung Heroes: An Oral History of Detroit's African American Community, 1918–1967* (Detroit: Wayne State University Press, 1994), p. 83.

15. R. L. Polk and Company, *Detroit City Directory,* 1927–1928 (Detroit: R. L. Polk and Company, 1928); NAACP press release, n.d. [June 1928], frame 169, reel 29, part 11B, NAACP Papers; death certificate 14568, November 10, 1928, Department of Health Records, Detroit, Mich.

16. "Little Is Changed Since '25 Trial," *Detroit Free Press,* November 3, 1975, copy available in Biographical Files/Negroes, "Sweet, Dr. Ossian H.," Biographical Files/ Negroes, Burton Historical Collection, Detroit Public Library, Detroit, Mich.; "Home of Mercy," *Michigan Chronicle,* June 4, 1955, clipping in box 2, Kellogg African-American Health Care Project, Archives of Labor and Urban Affairs, Wayne State University, Detroit, Mich.; Polk County, Fla., Registry of Deeds, *Index,* 1927–1956, p. 110, Polk County Building, Bartow, Fla; oral history interview with Claude Woodruff, Bartow, Fla., February 25, 2002, notes in author's possession.

17. "Wife Accuses Doctor in Suit," *Detroit Free Press,* September 30, 1947, copy available in envelope 11, "Sweet, Dr. Ossian H.," Detroit Free Press Clipping Morgue; personal correspondence with Pat Crews, February 15, 2003, copy in author's possession; "Words of Wisdom," *Detroit Free Press,* February 1, 2004; Ossian Sweet to William Pickens, December 20, 1930, reel 26, Arthur Spingarn Collection, Library of Congress, Washington, D.C.; O. H. Sweet file, July 1950, Civic Searchlight Collection, Burton Historical Collection; H. W. Sweet to Thurgood Marshall, August 27, 1937, frames 969–970, reel 13, part 12, NAACP Papers; "Negro Lawyer, Sweet, Is Dead," *Detroit Free Press,* January 21, 1940.

18. Entries for 2905 Garland, December 22, 1950–April 28, 1958, plat book, Wayne County Registrar of Deed, Detroit, Mich.; oral history interview with William Baxter, October 20, 2001, Detroit, Mich.

19. Oral history interview with Claude Woodruff; Alex Baskin interview with Robert Toms, November 28, 1959, Alex Baskin Collection, Michigan Historical Collection, Bentley Library, University of Michigan, Ann Arbor; "Bullet Is Fatal to Negro Doctor, Slay-Case Figure," *Detroit Free Press,* March 20, 1960; "Dr. Sweet's Death Recalls Infamous Housing Case Here," *Michigan Chronicle,* March 26, 1960, copy in Sweet biographical file, Burton.

ACKNOWLEDGMENTS

When I set out to tell the story of Ossian Sweet, I knew the work was going to be different than anything I'd done before. But I never guessed how far I'd travel beyond the comfort of my office or how many people would guide me along the way. Every author says his or her book wouldn't have been possible without assistance. In my case, it's true.

Like every historian, I owe an irredeemable debt to archivists and librarians. Thanks to the staffs of the Polk County (Florida) Historical Society, the Florida State Archives, the Wilberforce University Archives, the Moorland-Spingarn Center at Howard University, the Library of Congress Manuscript Reading Room, the National Archives (and its branch at Pittsfield, Massachusetts), the Western Reserve Historical Society, the Ohio Historical Society, the University of Michigan's Harlan Hatcher Library, the University of Massachusetts's W. E. B. Du Bois Library, Ohio State University's William Oxley Library, and the State Library of Michigan. As always, I relied on the patience and expertise of my friends at Wayne State University's Walter P. Reuther Library, who are too polite to say they're tired of seeing me. Imperturbable Tom Featherstone again tracked down many of the photos that appear in the book. I am particularly grateful to the librarians of the Detroit Public Library's Burton Historical Collection, who helped me wander through the collection's vast holdings, and to the extraordinary professionals at the Michigan Historical Collection at the University of Michigan's

Bentley Library, where my research began. Thanks especially to Assistant Director Bill Wallach, who not only helped me gain access to several important collections but also gave my family a place to stay for two weeks.

As important as archives were, the Sweets' story wasn't the sort that could be told straight from library shelves. I went to Bartow, Florida, not knowing a soul. Two marvelous gentlemen, Claude Woodruff and Clifton Lewis, took me under their wings, showing me through the streets of East Bartow, introducing me to its rich history and fascinating people. While in Florida, I also benefited from the kindness of Vickie Sweet, Charlie McNeill, Mike Denham, Canter Brown, and the pastor of St. James AME Church. Then there was the magical moment when Mr. Woodruff took me to meet Ossian Sweet's baby brother, Sherman Sweet, who lives in a house he built on the lot his father bought a century ago. I will never forget sitting with Mr. Sweet in his living room, listening as he talked of the past. For his time and his memories, I am forever grateful.

In Detroit, too, history opened up in unexpected ways. Daniel Baxter invited me into the bungalow on the corner of Garland and Charlevoix, which his parents, William and Ruby Baxter, bought from Ossian Sweet in 1958. To stand at the bedroom window, seeing the street as Ossian would have seen it on the night of the shooting, transformed the book, as did the opportunity to talk to the Baxters about the doctor. Brilliantly talented Arthur Beer of the University of Detroit Mercy gave me what I believe is the only existing copy of the interrogation transcripts made on the night the Sweets and their friends were arrested. Professor Alex Baskin granted me permission to use the interviews he conducted with most of the principals in the case more than forty years ago. My friend and fellow east-sider Bill McGraw made it possible for me to use the clipping morgues at both the *Detroit Free Press* and the *Detroit News*, without which it would have been impossible to trace the Sweets' story beyond 1926. Thanks as well to the *Detroit News'* editor, Tarek Hamada, and librarian Patricia Zacharias. Around the nation, Detroit has the reputation of being a tough town. But you won't find more big-hearted people no matter where you look.

Financial support for the initial research came from a University of Massachusetts Faculty Research Grant and a Bentley Library Bordin/ Gilette Research Travel Fellowship. Should they read *Arc of Justice*, I hope Fred Byron and Fran Blouin will feel their confidence in the project was well-founded. When it came time to write, I had the great luck to receive fellowships from the National Endowment for the Humanities, the American Council of Learned Societies, and the John Simon Guggenhiem Foundation. What a dream it was to have the support needed to devote myself to the book full-time. There aren't words sufficient to express my appreciation.

Arc of Justice bears the imprint of the University of Massachusetts's history department, my academic home for eight terrific years. I received great personal support from chairs Mary Wilson, Kathy Peiss, and David Glassberg. The devoted members of the AbbyandNan forum—Marla Miller, Alice Nash, Carl Nightingale, Brian Ogilvie, Max Page, and Kate Weigand—gave lots of advice, direction, and dessert. UMass also taught me to think of history as belonging not only to historians but to the public, a lesson that shaped every page of this book. My new colleagues at Ohio State University welcomed me into a stimulating atmosphere. Dean Michael Hogan and chairs Leila Rupp and Ken Andrien granted me a year's leave to work on the manuscript; Judy Wu and Steve Conn took time out from their frantic schedules to read early drafts; and Gail Summerhill provided a wonderful reading of a later version. Their comments were invaluable in helping me figure out what I was doing and how it might be made better. Jane Berger also read drafts, talked me through perplexing problems, commiserated over the challenges of transitions, and watched my daughters' impromptu performances with inspiring enthusiasm. Thank you, Jane. At the last minute, Ron McLean of Ohio State's TELR office stepped in to rescue photos from the obscurity of microfilm.

Over the years, I have leaned heavily on colleagues, friends, family, and a few folks I don't even know. Sidney Fine taught me to be a historian. With their great generosity, Patricia Sullivan and Waldo Martin made it possible for me to imagine contributing in some small way to the study of civil rights. The new generation of Detroit historians—Tom Klug, Suzanne Smith, Tom Sugrue, Heather Thompson, and Victoria Wolcott—taught me a great deal about the city, and in one short conversation, John Staudenmeier, S. J., helped me think about the complexity of Sweet's experience, much as he made me think about being an academic when I was an undergraduate. I've been fortunate to work with many extraordinarily talented students. The undergraduates at University College Dublin and the University of Massachusetts who took my civil rights courses gave me so much to think about. And the graduate students who've come my way—Grace Abarca, Babette Faehmel, Julie Gallagher, Peter Lau, Lincoln Lounsbury, Leo Maley, Marian Mollin,

Kathleen Nutter, Bob Surbrug, and so many others—taught me more than I ever taught them. To those who attended presentations at the University of Connecticut, the University of Michigan-Dearborn, Wayne State University, the University of Detroit Mercy, and Harvard University's NEH Summer Seminar on civil rights history, thank you for your suggestions and criticisms. And to three authors I never met—Taylor Branch, David Levering Lewis, and the late Anthony Lukas—I offer my deepest appreciation. Whenever I needed inspiration, which was more often that I ought to admit, I turned to their books to see how history should be written. God, how I wish I could write like that.

If I have moved a little closer to that standard, it is due to my editor, George Hodgman. Since taking on the book, George has patiently weaned me from academic prose, taught me new ways to write, made me think hard about the structure of storytelling, understood when I stumbled, and championed my work even when it didn't deserve to be championed. Scouring the Web one day, I read an article that referred to George as a "much beloved" editor. I know why. My thanks as well to Supurna Banerjee, who pushed the manuscript—and me—through the publication process, and to Henry Holt's superb production staff, which made *Arc of Justice* such a handsome book.

No one could ask for better friends than Marty Hershock, Terry and Cindy Hopman, Kevin Hurst, Bil and Katie Kerrigan, Barry Levy and Jackie Wolf, David and Camela Moskin, Mike Smith, Joe and Nancy Tolkacz, and Joe and Paula Zehetmeier, all of whom at one time or another sat and talked about the Sweets, about work, about kids, about politics, about just anything worth talking about. Our neighbors in Bexley, Ohio, have enveloped our new home in midwestern friendliness. Thanks to Terry Kemp for explaining the law to me; to Angie Mally, Tim and Lynn Johnson, and Deneece Kemp for making us feel so welcome; and to Terri Ghitman and Laura Jones for regularly asking whether I'd finished that book yet. That's really what kept me working this past year and a half.

Art and Judy Getis have made me a member of their family, a precious gift for in-laws to bestow. It's always a great pleasure to spend time with them and the rest of the Getis clan: Hilary, Jamal, Sophie, and Christina Tarazi, and Annie, Tony, Darby, Trevor, and Matty Tibbetts.

My parents, Kevin and Anne Boyle, put me up whenever I came to Detroit, read and commented on the entire manuscript, sent me bits of news, encouraged me to keep going, and sympathized with me when I needed them to. The only thing I can offer in return is my love.

Finally, there are the greatest debts.

I knew things were getting out of hand when my family went on a long-promised vacation to Disney World and instead of spending another day at the Magic Kingdom, I hustled us off for a drive through Bartow. But Abby and Nan accepted the imposition with good grace, just as they accepted all the impositions I've made in pursuit of the Sweets' story. They're the greatest kids imaginable and I am honored— absolutely honored—to be their daddy. For Vicky, thanks seem so insufficient. It was her encouragement that got me to start the book and led me to apply for the fellowships that set me to writing. Then the demands really escalated. Time and again, she talked me through trouble spots, outlined sections, read chapters, listened to doubts and complaints, cajoled, encouraged, and commiserated. As invaluable as all that has been, though, it pales in comparison to the ways in which Vicky has filled our lives with her boundless love. She has said a few times that this book is a family project, and so it is. That's why *The Arc of Justice* is dedicated to Abby, Nan, and Vicky together, my coauthors and my joys.

INDEX

ABOUT THE AUTHOR

Born and raised in Detroit, KEVIN BOYLE is an associate professor of history at Ohio State University. He is the author of *The UAW and the Heyday of American Liberalism, 1945–1968* and the coauthor (with Victoria Getis) of *Muddy Boots and Ragged Aprons: Images of Working-Class Detroit, 1900–1930*. He lives in Bexley, Ohio, with his wife, their two daughters, and an aging border collie.